1002918546

S0-BVD-819

ABORIGINAL TENURE

IN THE

CONSTITUTION OF CANADA

James (Sakej) Youngblood Henderson
Marjorie L. Benson
Isobel M. Findlay

CARSWELL

Thomson Professional Publishing

Canadian Cataloguing in Publication Data

Henderson, James Youngblood
  Aboriginal tenure in the constitution of Canada

Includes index.
ISBN 0-459-23936-8

1. Native peoples – Land tenure – Canada.* 2. Constitutional law – Canada. I. Benson, Marjorie L. (Marjorie Lynne), 1947– . II. Findlay, Isobel. III. Title.

KE7739.L3H46 2000   346.7104'32'08997   C00-930534-3
KF5660.H46 2000

The paper used in this publication meets the minimum requirements of the American National Standard for Information Sciences — Permanence of Paper for Printed Library Materials, ANSI Z39.48-1984

CARSWELL
Thomson Professional Publishing

One Corporate Plaza	**Customer Relations:**
2075 Kennedy Road	Toronto 1-416-609-3800
Scarborough, Ontario	Elsewhere in Canada/U.S. 1-800-387-5164
M1T 3V4	Fax 1-416-298-5094
	World Wide Web: http://www.carswell.com
	E-mail: orders@carswell.com

Dedicated to the land, our mother,
aki, askî, ohwetsy, askîy, oseskamikaw,
maka, awahsin, digeh, nuna
who comprehends the spirits and voices of life and humanity, and sustains
our shared life, thoughts, and values. And to making the Canadian future an
enabling environment for all.

ACKNOWLEDGEMENTS

Aboriginal hunters always speak as if the keepers of the spirits of nature are in control of the hunt. The hunters do not believe that their awareness or skills have any controlling authority in their hunt. They say the forces of nature are watching them, know everything on their minds, and what and how they behave in the hunt. The spiritual forces decide which animals will be made available and caught, thus determining the success of the hunt. The creation of this book followed this pattern, with the many spirits and forces controlling its production and contents.

In this cross-cultural and cross-disciplinary project exploring the meaning of Aboriginal and treaty rights in the constitution of Canada, our first commitment was to understand the constitutional order and how it respects and affirms the Aboriginal order. We sought to respect the knowledge, heritage, and perspectives of the Aboriginal peoples of Canada that sustain the Aboriginal order. Although the full Aboriginal world-view can only be transmitted through the Aboriginal languages in their own oral tradition, we have attempted to translate faithfully our understandings of the teachings into a written English form accessible to a wide audience. As we struggled with the time- and energy-consuming but transformative process of understanding the convergence of disciplines, concepts, and contexts in the constitutional order, we gained insights into the deep structure that is the pain of Canada's past, the hope of Canada's future. As we negotiated each word and sentence, structure and presentation, the shared understandings of each others' sounds and symbols grew into a bridge that gave us glimpses of the fresh chances and unlimited possibilities of a pluralistic Canadian future that listens to, and absorbs with humility, the knowledge accumulated over centuries by the Aboriginal peoples living with the ecology of this continent. We thank the land that held us together and the spirits of strength, justice, patience, honesty, kindness, and generosity that have made our work unfold.

Many people devoted their time, energy, spirit, knowledge, and caring to help us share our thoughts in this book. Marg Brown and Max Bilson patiently adjusted text and footnotes through constant changes as the work developed, and did so with endless good humour. Diana Kotschorek worked computer magic and gave our text style and harmony. Rick Fowler, Kathleen Makela, Ed Mazey, John Lavery, Ron Cooley, Andrew Taylor, and our editor at Carswell, Jane McDonald, all provided kindness and guidance. More generally, the teaching of the Elders and the many ideas of Leroy Little Bear, Marie Battiste, Mary Ellen Turpel-Lafond, John Borrows, Len Findlay, Don Worme, and Helen Semaganis are enfolded in our thoughts and inspired our journey. We thank our families and friends for their endurance and support during the long days and nights.

In the transforming leaf budding moon, *sâkipakâwipîsim*, under a vast blue sky, on the banks of the South Saskatchewan River, Saskatoon, Saskatchewan, May 1, 1999.

Sakej Henderson
Marj Benson
Isobel Findlay

TABLE OF CONTENTS

TABLE OF CASES

INTRODUCTION

The territory in dispute has been in Indian occupation from the date of the proclamation until 1873. ... Their possession, such as it was, can only be ascribed to the general provisions made by the royal proclamation in favour of all Indian tribes then living under the sovereignty and protection of the British Crown. It was suggested in the course of the argument for the Dominion, that inasmuch as the proclamation recites that the territories thereby reserved for Indians had never "been ceded to or purchased by" the Crown, the entire property of the land remained with them. That inference is, however, at variance with the terms of the instrument, which show that the tenure of the Indians was a personal and usufructuary right, dependent upon the good will of the Sovereign. ... There was a great deal of learned discussion at the Bar with respect to the precise quality of the Indian right, but their Lordships do not consider it necessary to express any opinion upon the point.

> Lord Watson for the Privy Council,
> *St. Catherine's Milling and Lumber Co. v. The Queen*[1]

The starting point of the Canadian jurisprudence on aboriginal title is the Privy Council's decision in *St. Catherine's Milling and Lumber Co. v. The Queen* (1888), 14 A.C. 46, which described aboriginal title as a "personal and usufructuary right" (at p. 54). The subsequent jurisprudence has attempted to grapple with this definition, and has in the process demonstrated that the Privy Council's choice of terminology is not particularly helpful to explain the various dimensions of aboriginal title. What the Privy Council sought to capture is that aboriginal title is a *sui generis* interest in land.

> Chief Justice Lamer in *Delgamuukw v. British Columbia*[2]

The written text and unwritten principles of the constitution of Canada assert a new constitutional supremacy. In 1998, the Supreme Court of Canada in the *Quebec Secession Reference*,[3] stated the principles of constitutional interpretation. The unified Court stated that the constitution of Canada is more than a written text. Although the Constitution is primarily a written one, the product of 131 years of interpretation and

---

1   (1888), 14 A.C. 46 at 54-55 (P.C.) [hereinafter *St. Catherine's*].

2   [1997] 3 S.C.R. 1010 at para. 112, 153 D.L.R. (4th) 193 (S.C.C.) [hereinafter *Delgamuukw* cited to S.C.R.].

3   *Re Reference by the Governor General in Council Concerning Certain Questions Relating to the Secession of Quebec*, [1998] 2 S.C.R. 217, 161 D.L.R. (4th) 385 (S.C.C.) [hereinafter *Quebec Secession Reference* cited to S.C.R.].

decision-making, behind the written texts are even longer historical legacies that courts need to consider to understand the underlying constitutional principles. These unstated assumptions are vital principles that inform and sustain the constitutional text.[4]

Within the lengthy history of written texts and traditions, additionally, the Constitution embraces the global framework of rules and principles governing the exercise of constitutional authority. The Court stated:

> As we confirmed in *Reference re Objection by Quebec to a Resolution to amend the Constitution*, [1982] 2 S.C.R. 793, at p. 806, "The Constitution Act, 1982 is now in force. Its legality is neither challenged nor assailable." The "Constitution of Canada" certainly includes the constitutional texts enumerated in s. 52(2) of the *Constitution Act, 1982*. Although these texts have a primary place in determining constitutional rules, they are not exhaustive. The Constitution also "embraces unwritten, as well as written rules", as we recently observed in the *Provincial Judges Reference, supra*, at para. 92. Finally, as was said in the *Patriation Reference, supra*, at p. 874, the Constitution of Canada includes "the global system of rules and principles which govern the exercise of constitutional authority in the whole and in every part of the Canadian state."

> These supporting principles and rules, which include constitutional conventions and the workings of Parliament, are a necessary part of our Constitution because problems or situations may arise which are not expressly dealt with by the text of the Constitution. In order to endure over time, a constitution must contain a comprehensive set of rules and principles which are capable of providing an exhaustive legal framework for our system of government. Such principles and rules emerge from an understanding of the constitutional text itself, the historical context, and previous judicial interpretations of constitutional meaning. In our view, there are four fundamental and organizing principles of the Constitution which are relevant to addressing the question before us (although this enumeration is by no means exhaustive): federalism; democracy; constitutionalism and the rule of law; and respect for minorities.[5]

A superficial or fragmented reading of selected provisions of the written constitutional enactment may therefore be misleading. It is necessary to make a more thorough investigation of the underlying principles animating the whole of the Constitution, including the fundamental principles identified by the Court: federalism, democracy, constitutionalism and the rule of law, and respect for minorities. These principles inform the overall appreciation of constitutional rights and obligations.

In the constitutional traditions of the United Kingdom and Canada, legality and legitimacy are linked. Canada's formation through treaties to colony to a nation-state was a gradual legal and political process within the rule of law. Like the prerogative treaties with Aboriginal nations that legitimated British settlements in North America, the *Constitution Act, 1867* was an act of nation building for the immigrants. It was the first step in the transition from British colonies in North America, each separately dependent on the imperial Parliament for its governance, to a political state in which

---

4   *Ibid.* at para. 49.

5   *Ibid.* at para. 32.

different peoples could resolve their disagreements and work toward common goals and common interests.

In the *Quebec Secession Reference*, the Court summarized the constitutional development:

> The Imperial Parliament's passage of the *Statute of Westminster, 1931* (U.K.), 22 & 23 Geo. 5, c. 4, confirmed in law what had earlier been confirmed in fact by the Balfour Declaration of 1926, namely, that Canada was an independent country. Thereafter, Canadian law alone governed in Canada, except where Canada expressly consented to the continued application of Imperial legislation. ... The proclamation of the *Constitution Act, 1982* removed the last vestige of British authority over the Canadian Constitution and reaffirmed Canada's commitment to the protection of its minority, aboriginal, equality, legal and language rights, and fundamental freedoms as set out in the *Canadian Charter of Rights and Freedoms*.
>
> Legal continuity, which requires an orderly transfer of authority, necessitated that the 1982 amendments be made by the Westminster Parliament, but the legitimacy as distinguished from the formal legality of the amendments derived from political decisions taken in Canada within a legal framework which this Court, in the *Patriation Reference*, had ruled was in accordance with our Constitution. It should be noted, parenthetically, that the 1982 amendments did not alter the basic division of powers in ss. 91 and 92 of the *Constitution Act, 1867*, which is the primary textual expression of the principle of federalism in our Constitution, agreed upon at Confederation.
>
> ...
>
> We think it apparent from even this brief historical review that the evolution of our constitutional arrangements has been characterized by adherence to the rule of law, respect for democratic institutions, the accommodation of minorities, insistence that governments adhere to constitutional conduct and a desire for continuity and stability.[6]

The imperial and constitutional history of Canada demonstrates how the structures and rights have changed to accommodate freedoms. These transformations have generally been accomplished by methods that have ensured continuity, stability, and legal order,[7] but have not necessarily created coherence or clarity of the constitutional relationship among the various parts.

To understand those relationships, it is necessary for courts and the legal profession to investigate those underlying principles that are not explicitly part of the written constitution, yet, as the Court has noted, provide the implicate architecture and lifeblood to constitutional interpretation:[8]

> Our Constitution has an internal architecture, or what the majority of this Court in *OPSEU v. Ontario (Attorney General)*, [1987] 2 S.C.R. 2, at p. 57, called a "basic constitutional structure". The individual elements of the Constitution are linked to the others, and must

---

6   *Ibid.* at paras. 46-48.

7   *Ibid.* at paras. 33 and 48.

8   *Ibid.* at para. 51.

be interpreted by reference to the structure of the Constitution as a whole. As we recently emphasized in the *Provincial Judges Reference*, certain underlying principles infuse our
Constitution and breathe life into it. Speaking of the rule of law principle in the *Manitoba Language Rights Reference, supra*, at p. 750, we held that "the principle is clearly
implicit in the very nature of a Constitution". The same may be said of the other three constitutional principles we underscore today.[9]

The Supreme Court has noted that before the constitutional reforms of 1982, the
courts ignored Aboriginal and treaty rights.[10] The constitutional reforms change this
legal context:

> the framers of the *Constitution Act, 1982* included in s. 35 explicit protection for existing
> aboriginal and treaty rights, and in s. 25, a non-derogation clause in favour of the rights
> of aboriginal peoples. The "promise" of s. 35, as it was termed in *R. v. Sparrow*, [1990] 1
> S.C.R. 1075, at p. 1083, recognized not only the ancient occupation of land by aboriginal
> peoples, but their contribution to the building of Canada, and the special commitments
> made to them by successive governments. The protection of these rights, so recently and
> arduously achieved, whether looked at in their own right or as part of the larger concern
> with minorities, reflects an important underlying constitutional value.[11]

These rights are an integral part of a unified analysis of the constitutional structure and rights. They are the unwritten legal legacy of Aboriginal law and rights, and
the unstated principles and written text of the treaty rights. Both constitutional sources
are *sui generis* (self-generating) and different from British and French law, but, as the
unanimous Court in *Sparrow* stated, the different constitutional documents must be
read together.[12]

The task of this book is to attempt to understand the place of Aboriginal tenure
or title in the Constitution of Canada. In *Delgamuukw v. British Columbia*,[13] the
Supreme Court of Canada affirmed and acknowledged a new constitutional meaning
and role for Aboriginal tenure or title in Canadian constitutional law that must be read
together with other constitutional principles and texts. The message from the modern
framers of the constitutional order and the Lamer Court is that Aboriginal tenure and
rights and treaty rights constitute a distinct legal system, with its own implicate architecture, sources, traditions, and texts that require constitutional equality with the other
parts. Both the Lamer and Dickson courts have stressed it would be a mistake to seek
answers to this *sui generis* legal system by drawing analogies to British property law.

The constitutional affirmation of Aboriginal tenure requires us to grapple with
the fluctuating stages of British land law in search of a just reconciliation for Aboriginal peoples of Canada. The doctrine of Crown tenure and derivative land holdings, the

---

9   *Ibid.* at para. 50.

10   *R. v. Sparrow*, [1990] 1 S.C.R. 1075 at 1103-1105, [1990] 3 C.N.L.R. 160 (S.C.C.) [hereinafter *Spar-
     row* cited to S.C.R.].

11   *Quebec Secession Reference, supra* note 3 at para. 82.

12   *Sparrow, supra* note 10 at 1109.

13   *Delgamuukw, supra* note 2.

basic structure of British land law, has undergone many legal transformations. The absolutist European legal principle of *nulle terre sans seigneur* (no land without a lord) informed the doctrine of tenure that asserts that all land in Britain is "held" of the Crown, but not actually "owned" by the Crown:[14]

> The [British] lawyers never adopted the premise that the King owned all the land; such a dogma is of very modern appearance. It was sufficient for them to note that the King was lord, ultimately, of all the tenants in the realm ... They treated the bundle of rights vested in mesne lords as if they were material things, and called them *seignories* or manors, and to these "things" they applied the notion of seisin just as they applied it to land itself.[15]

Ownership of land is not a distinct legal category or concept in British law, but a socio-political concept.[16] British law's conceptual heritage is of tenure, estates, and interest in land. None of these interests is absolute or total in British law; each represents fragmented, restricted, temporal, and interrelated uses of the Crown's tenure.

Many of the reformulations of tenure were legislative and judicial attempts to resolve the theoretical difficulties and paradoxes raised by the absolutist doctrine of tenure. The common law lawyers and legislators continued to acknowledge the Teutonic customary doctrines of *seisin* or physical presence and created the ideal of derivative "estates" or "titles" that allocated different interests in land among various persons. In 1905, Professor Albert Dicey commented: "[T]he paradox of modern English Land Law may be thus summed up: [T]he constitution of England has, whilst preserving monarchical forms, become a democracy, but the land law of England remains the land law appropriate to an aristocratic State."[17] In 1925, the United Kingdom Parliament minimized and reconciled these paradoxes by statutory reform.[18]

Canada has yet to confront this legal paradox. Because of this tension between absolutism and democracy in Canadian property law, contemporary professors have relegated the doctrine of tenure to a trivial historical assumption in property law, and no longer focus on the fascinating complexity of doctrines of estates or title.[19]

In the light of the constitutional affirmation of Aboriginal tenure, the fictional doctrine of Crown tenure needs to be explicated and understood. In British law, the doctrine of Crown tenure is viewed as a legal fiction; that is, an assumption created for the purposes of justice and designed not to create any injury or loss to anyone. If a legal

---

14 A.W.B. Simpson, *A History of the Land Law*, 2d ed. (Oxford: Oxford University Press, 1986) at 1; *Halsbury's Laws of England*, vol. 39, 4th ed. (London: Butterworths, 1973-86) at para. 304, "Real Property" [hereinafter *Halsbury's*]. He states that, "Technically, land is not the subject of absolute ownership but of tenure"; B. Rudden, "Notes Towards a Grammar of Property" [1980] Conv. (N.S.) 25.

15 Simpson, *ibid.* at 47-48.

16 A.D. Hargreaves, "Modern Real Property" (1956) 19 Mod. L. Rev. 14 at 17. "Ownership" is, to Hargreaves, a category of Roman law; see also J.W.C. Turner, "Some Reflections on Ownership in English Law" (1941) 19 Can. Bar Rev. 342. He states that ownership of land has no technical meaning in the common law.

17 A.V. Dicey, "The Paradox of the Land Law" (1905) 21 L.Q. Rev. 221 at 222.

18 *Ibid.* at 270-291. See *Halsbury's, supra* note 14 at para. 344-74, on "The Property Legislation of 1925."

19 *Ibid.* at para. 1.

fiction operates to create injury, it is wrongful.[20] The legal fiction of Crown tenure in British North America and Canada, however, has created loss and injury to Aboriginal peoples, even though under the Constitution of Canada colonial legal fictions or myths cannot discriminate against Aboriginal law and tenure.

The new constitutional paradox constituted by common law doctrines and Aboriginal tenures requires reconciling the diverse visions of law and land tenure. Both land tenure systems are products of a complex way of seeing land and its relationship to humanity. Reconciling these different visions of land tenure in constitutional interpretation is a task for comparative legal theory. Such a journey sharpens one's appreciation for the value of legal conceptualism. The full complexities of Aboriginal law of land tenure constitute the way of seeing Aboriginal tenure; the transplanted British common law fictions, assumptions, and categories cannot explain Aboriginal law or tenure.

In *Delgamuukw*, the Lamer Court recognized these parallel tenures. The *Delgamuukw* guidelines recognize that Aboriginal land tenure systems have always existed in North America, that both sovereigns sought to reconcile the two land tenure systems by consensual treaties in the law of nations and British prerogative law, and that unpurchased Aboriginal tenure has not been extinguished or superseded by law. The *Delgamuukw* guidelines cause a re-evaluation of past judicial decisions on Aboriginal tenure and their negative strategy of difference, which penalized Aboriginal difference. The Court ordered a new trial, rejecting the trial judge's refusal to consider the oral and symbolic histories that inform Aboriginal law and tenure as impermissible under the rules of evidence. They rejected past courts' attempts to force or integrate Aboriginal tenures into British tenure and classification of estates, making Crown tenure a totalizing, universal legal fiction that subordinates Aboriginal tenures.

The Dickson and Lamer Courts have rejected the judicial precedents and their inappropriate terminology and misleading categorization of content and proof of Aboriginal tenure. Such categorization was part of a broader colonial legacy built on false premises of the "savage" Indian and the "civilized" European, worked through inexorable plots of colonialism, patriarchy, racism, and otherness. These false differences were empowered by Hegel's master/slave dialectics as well as his concept of a governing structure of self-realization in all historical processes. Each of these processes appropriated, suppressed, and undermined Aboriginal knowledge, law, and tenure to a subordinate place in the forced unity of imported English law, rather than respecting them as distinct sources of law. These judicial decisions could not tolerate or deal with differences without integrating differences within their categories of knowledge. This book attempts to replace such thinking with constitutional principles that will allow Aboriginal peoples to share a future with Canadian people.

The *Delgamuukw* guidelines affirm and recognize that Aboriginal tenure is *sui generis* tenure: a self-generating system of land tenure protected by section 35(1) of the

---

20   *Fictio legis neminem lædit* (A fiction of law injures no one). See Sir W. Blackstone, *Commentaries on the Laws of England*, vol. III (Oxford: Clarendon Press, 1765-69) at 43.

Constitution Act, 1982. The sources, content, and meaning of a *sui generis* tenure exist in Aboriginal world-views, languages, laws, perspectives, and practices. A *sui generis* tenure does not take its source or meanings from European, British, Canadian law or practice, and exists independently of recognition of the tenure. Although both British land tenure and rights and Aboriginal land tenure and rights have some intriguing similarities at certain levels, these similarities have not been explored by the judiciary.

The Aboriginal law of land tenure and land use is ecologically orientated and generally reflects an attempt to live within changing resources. Aboriginal tenure differs among Aboriginal peoples as well as from European and British land law. Judicial attempts to identify and separate elements of Aboriginal land tenure from the Aboriginal worldview that links the community to the ecological context fail to recognize that all land tenure and use is based on the intricacy of Aboriginal worldviews.

Aboriginal tenure covers all aspects of a respectful relationship with an ecology derived from an Aboriginal knowledge system, law, and heritage.[21] The Special Rapporteur for developing the principles and guidelines to protect the heritage of Indigenous peoples in the United Nations Sub-Commission on Prevention of Discrimination and Protection of Minorities, Dr.-Mrs. Erica-Irene Daes, has articulated the appropriate framework to approach Aboriginal law and tenure:

> the heritage of an indigenous people is not merely a collection of objects, stories and ceremonies, but a complete knowledge system with its own concepts of epistemology, philosophy, and scientific and logical validity. The diverse elements of an indigenous people's heritage can only be fully learned or understood by means of the pedagogy traditionally employed by these peoples themselves, including apprenticeship, ceremonies and practice. Simply recording words or images fails to capture the whole context and meaning of songs, rituals, arts or scientific and medical wisdom. This also underscores the central role of indigenous peoples' own languages, through which each people's heritage has traditionally been recorded and transmitted from generation to generation.[22]

To reflect the ecological and Aboriginal perspective on Aboriginal law, we prefer the concept of Aboriginal tenure to that of Aboriginal title. We use Aboriginal tenure in a way cognizable to British legal and constitutional traditions: the Aboriginal order or condition under which land is sustained or held. Our emphasis on "tenure" combines the forgotten insight of the Privy Council in *St. Catherine's* about the "tenure of the Indians" with the insight of Chief Justices Dickson and Lamer that such tenure is "*sui generis*." In Canada, Aboriginal tenures are not an "interest in land" or "use and occupation" deriving from British land law; they are derived from a pre-existing system of law and its entire allocation of responsibilities in Aboriginal territory. Aboriginal law structures Aboriginal land tenure into multi-layered Aboriginal "responsibili-

---

21 See generally J. Borrows, "Living Between Water and Rocks: First Nations, Environmental Planning and Democracy" (1997) 47 U.T.L.J. 417.

22 UN Sub-Commission on Prevention of Discrimination and Protection of Minorities, Commission on Human Rights, United Nations Economic and Social Council, *Protection of the Heritage of Indigenous People: Preliminary Report of the Special Rapporteur,* UN ESC, 1994, UN Doc.E/CN.4/Sub.2/1994/31 at para. 8.

ties" ("titles") in different families or clans, defining their interrelated and cumulative "cares" ("uses" or "rights") of an ecology.

Our use of Aboriginal tenure signifies its parallel relationship with the British common law doctrine of tenure in Canadian law. Aboriginal tenure signifies its equivalency to the British tenure, and not its subordinate status. Aboriginal tenure illustrates the centrality of Aboriginal law and thought in creating a land tenure distinct from British or American land law or tenure. The term Aboriginal title is not analytically helpful since it is often confused with the British common law doctrine of "estates," "title," or "title deeds" and non-Aboriginal legal sources.[23] In British land law, "title" is generally used to describe the derivative manner in which a claim or right to land is acquired under Crown tenure, or the resulting right itself.[24] By contrast, in public international law, "title" means jurisdiction.

In Canada, Aboriginal tenure is not derived from Crown tenure; rather, Crown title is derived from Aboriginal tenure. This insight makes the reconciliation between Aboriginal tenure and Crown title more coherent, and resolves the third party interests under Crown grants as revenue sharing.

Constitutionalizing *sui generis* Aboriginal land tenures creates the conditions for authentic Canadian legal thought. *Delgamuukw* ended the legal dialectic between the familiar English system and the exoticized Aboriginal difference. In a courageous effort, the Lamer Court provided constitutional guidelines for the lower court on how to respect and reconcile Aboriginal tenure with the common law. This decision creates a new phase in reforming land law in Canada. Such reconciliation will result in a new property regime in Canada that is neither English nor Aboriginal in origin, but rather a new form of intersocietal law.[25] In other words, a respectful reconciliation will create a first generation Canadian constitutional law of property.

Such reconciliation can occur only somewhere between the spheres of operation of each tenurial system. If Aboriginal and British land tenure are to be reconciled without losing their alterity, with a respect for the other, the judiciary must create new patterns of analysis by interrogating traditional British legal analysis, specifically, colonial legal thought and analysis. A compelling metaphor for the new judicial analysis is the construction of a bridge between the two tenure systems, starting on both sides and working toward the middle. The judiciary must also come to understand Aboriginal legal thought and apply the constitutional principles of *sui generis* rights. As the Court has stated:

> The challenge of defining [A]boriginal rights stems from the fact that they are rights peculiar to the meeting of two vastly dissimilar legal cultures; consequently there will always

---

23 See generally J. Borrows, "With or Without You: First Nations Law in Canada" (1996) 41 McGill L.J. 629. See also J. Toohey's comments in *Mabo v. Queensland (No. 2)* (1992), 175 C.L.R. 1 at 178-79 (Australia H.C.).

24 K. McNeil, *Common Law Aboriginal Title* (Oxford: Clarendon Press, 1989) 10-11.

25 *R. v. Van der Peet*, [1996] 2 S.C.R. 507 at para. 42, [1996] 4 C.N.L.R. 177, reconsideration refused (January 16, 1997), Doc. 23803 (S.C.C.).

be a question about which legal culture is to provide the vantage point from which rights
are to be defined ... [26]

Such transcultural or intercultural vantage points can create a new constitutional analysis that will place "equal weight" on each perspective, thus attempting to achieve a just reconciliation among the legal cultures within Canada.

Such postcolonial judicial analysis is a bold challenge for Canadian governments, judiciary, jurisprudence, and all Canadians. Reconciling and implementing the *sui generis* constitutional rights regime will expand adjudicative neutrality in constitutional supremacy and the rule of law to deal with constitutional pluralism. In the end, a Canadian jurisprudence will emerge. It is with the hope of assisting this constitutional vision that we have prepared this book.

This work is cross-cultural and cross-disciplinary because reconciling Aboriginal tenure with Crown sovereignty means uncovering a complex history of layered understandings and multiple translations that constitute the written and unwritten record of the British common law. Rules of evidence alone are inadequate to interpret the history; knowledge of the broader cultural, political, economic, religious, and historical contexts is required. While we make every effort to be true to the documentary evidence, it is important to concede that no description is entirely innocent or neutral, that all description is at least in part a matter of interpretation for which we are accountable. Cross-disciplinary emphases complement legal with more broadly cultural forms of attention and conventions of reading. In this way, we hope to counteract some of the fragmentation of knowledge that results from different disciplinary interests among historians and lawyers and even the failure to read one another's work.

In our efforts to overcome some of the intellectual and other roadblocks in past commentary, we make choices not only in terms of the evidence we adduce but also in matters of terminology. For example, one of the difficulties in the European context is the problem of naming of disputed territory, especially in the case of the multiple invasions of the Island variously known as Pretanoi, Bretenland, England, Great Britain, and the United Kingdom. Although England and Britain have often been used synonymously in popular usage, we choose to talk of British common law in the light of a jurisdiction that extends beyond the geographical borders of England. Similarly, despite British inclination to distinguish Britain from Europe, in recognition of many practices in common, we mean Europe to include Britain.

In Part I, "The Common Law and Land," we focus on the diverse influences of Celtic, Roman, Teutonic, Norse, and Norman customs that contributed to the formation of the British common law and shaped land law in particular. Changing views of the land, from a means of continuing social cohesion to notions of property as commodity, from an agricultural society to a market economy, are traced. The difficulties in reconstructing this history derive not only from problems of translation within the early periods and from negotiating past and present perspectives, but also from contending with evidence that is contaminated and even fraudulent. The so-called false law is espe-

---

26   *Ibid.* at para. 42 [emphasis added].

cially damaging to legal history because there was no single source of case law until the 13th century and no reliable system of reporting until the 19th century, and because such authorities as Henry de Bracton, Thomas de Littleton, and Lord Coke perpetuated the frauds in their work.

In Part II, "Treaty Reconciliations," we explore treaty relations from the perspectives not only of public international law and of Aboriginal treaty orders but also of royal prerogatives in British constitutional law. In particular, we consider the framework within which the Crown acknowledged pre-existing Aboriginal sovereignty while constituting new legal orders. Even within these legal reconciliations, competing and contradictory understandings persisted on matters of authority and interpretation, especially around such quintessentially European notions as sovereignty. This part focuses on the dense network of treaty regimes that governed practices in North America: from Aboriginal compacts and federations to prerogative treaties of Great Britain to treaties marking international jurisdiction. Again we take account of the specific linguistic encoding of beliefs and practices, the myths or narratives that explain and sustain particular world-views and understandings of legal orders. It is in this area of Aboriginal epistemology and protocols that Canadian legal historians have been insufficiently attentive to the evidence—with far-reaching consequences for current efforts to rethink reconciliation of Aboriginal *sui generis* tenure with Crown sovereignty.

Part III, "Legal Protection of Aboriginal Tenure," explores the claim that British colonial law and prerogative law in particular legitimately governed the acquisition of Aboriginal tenure while determining the powers and privileges of the Crown. In the American context, despite revolutionary rejection of "undemocratic" feudal tenures and belief in American society as a guarantee of liberty, and unencumbered individual property rights as a source of individual autonomy, American law could not break completely with the principles of the British common law of property. With the 1789 constitution, the United States affirmed the allodial tenure of the Aboriginal nations and reconciled Aboriginal land tenure with the 1763 Proclamation in 1790.

Where states made land grants to individuals, the courts declared such grants void, finding for the Aboriginal nations in the absence of purchases from the nations. An 1810 Supreme Court decision concluded that, while Aboriginal tenure was a protected property right, it was a tenure system foreign to the United States tenure system. In an early version of Aboriginal tenure as *sui generis* tenure, the majority opinion was that Aboriginal tenure was an issue for conflicts of law or comparative international law. The minority view meantime characterized Aboriginal tenure as allodial within the United States tenurial system and treaties as acknowledging Aboriginal nations as independent people. In the hierarchy of United States tenures, the Aboriginal fee simple title took precedence. Nevertheless, in subsequent decisions, and without Aboriginal representation before it, the Court left a legacy of confusing *dicta* that have authorized diminishing Aboriginal tenure and property rights. Though neither party made such a claim, Chief Justice Marshall focused not on treaty purchase but on discovery and conquest, extending to universal principles European conventions that had no explicit or written authority.

Further decisions functioned to harmonize discovery and conquest principles with the *sui generis* tenure of Aboriginal tenures, granting the United States a legal monopoly to purchase Aboriginal tenure—and hence to create reserved Aboriginal tenure or Indian reservations. While the government earned millions in selling Aboriginal land as commodity, federal appropriations for Indian administration were little more than $120,000. In 1871 congress vested all treaty rights.

With the arrival in Canada of Loyalist refugees from the American Revolution, the Crown negotiated purchases of Aboriginal tenure to accommodate the colony's expanding population. Although Compacts and treaties alike provided that the courts resolve questions of Aboriginal and treaty rights, only one case in the Atlantic provinces addressed the topic even indirectly. The history of colonial actions regarding Aboriginal tenure is a history of such presumptions, neglect, competing interests, and jurisdictional ambiguity and dispute. The controlling presumption was that Aboriginal tenure was a subdivision of Crown tenure. It is also a history of the scandal of "location ticket" regimes that circumvented the Crown's powerlessness to grant clear legal title to immigrants. A series of Acts of the imperial Parliament, before and including the *Constitution [British North America] Act 1867*, attempted to remedy the situation and establish the Crown's sole authority to amend the Constitution of Canada, while maintaining the pre-existing legal orders of the provinces and transferring from the provinces to the federal Dominion exclusive administrative authority over reserved lands. The treaty relationships, however, did not allow for such delegation of authority.

In the context of statutory and case law we explore courts' efforts to comprehend prerogative protections of Aboriginal tenure and to assimilate that tenure to British common law notions of tenure without adequate understanding of Aboriginal perspectives. The record shows that even where the courts showed good will, they could not easily find means of redress. That Aboriginal signatories were never represented in proceedings or their oral understandings fully registered in the written record of treaties proved a particular impediment. The courts struggled to find terms that made the claims of Aboriginal peoples accessible and actionable without appropriating them to general property law terminology because Aboriginal title is a unique interest. The patriation of the Constitution affirmed Aboriginal and treaty rights as constitutional rights. The courts began a new interpretative regime based on *sui generis* constitutional rights. In order to act on the liberal interpretative principles the Supreme Court has recommended, we need to consider the broader historical and cultural contexts, to anticipate and counteract predispositions of the past, and to bridge what the Royal Commission on Aboriginal Peoples has called "the Cultural Divide."

To that end in Part IV, "Displacing Colonial Discourse," we confront the particular challenge of decolonizing the justice system and ensuring judicial impartiality for Aboriginal tenure. Like all other colonial legal regimes imposed upon Indigenous peoples, the British legal system has failed Aboriginal peoples. It has done so because it has assimilated as knowledge the discriminatory colonial discourse and privileged British cultural norms defined in opposition to "savagery." To counter its tenacious hold on judicial thinking, here we unpack the history and theory of the totalizing discourse. Although the Canadian Judicial Council has proscribed "personal or ideological" understandings, judicial reasoning has remained within the presumptions and protocols of colonial rationality, which it has in turn helped legitimize. Resistance to decolonization has been supported by selective attention and a culture of silence. Indeed the legacy of colonialism has been so powerful because it has been so all-pervasive as to seem natural and hence invisible. In tracing the history and theory of such thinking, we aspire to dispute and dislodge the colonial paradigms that we have inherited as knowledge, promote respect for Aboriginal legal, linguistic, and conceptual orders, and secure postcolonial justice.

The proclamation of section 35 of the *Constitution Act, 1982* challenged Canadian courts to reconcile Aboriginal tenure within the Canadian legal and constitutional order. Part V, "Judicial Reconciliation of Aboriginal Tenure," records judicial attempts to do so by decolonizing within the rule of law, while developing innovative interpretative principles within a new regime of constitutional supremacy. Interpretation is constrained by the fiduciary (and now constitutional) duty to be "generous and liberal" and by *sui generis* principles derived from Aboriginal law, knowledge, and perspectives. The *sui generis* principle affirms Aboriginal law, its vision and voice as unique forms of constitutional analysis.

It is the task of Part VI, "*Sui Generis* Aboriginal Tenure," to elaborate Aboriginal laws and knowledge as source and content of *sui generis* Aboriginal tenure. Such understanding is prerequisite to acting on the Supreme Court's ruling that laws of evidence must give due weight to Aboriginal traditions and place oral evidence "on an equal footing" with historical documents. Only when Aboriginal articulations of tenure, or the Aboriginal "langscape" of property, are accommodated will judicial reconciliation be achieved. By way of illustration, we offer a brief account of one particular Algonquian worldview of "property": that of the Mikmaq.

Part VII, "Toward Reconciliation for the Millennium," builds on judicial breakthroughs in thinking about issues of Aboriginal tenure and rights. Especially important are the implications of new constitutional understandings of Canadian sovereignty within which Aboriginal tenure and rights are foundational, and not external to the constitutional order. By incorporating Aboriginal thinking and legal orders and relinquishing interpretative privileges over Aboriginal tenure and treaties, the courts are taking important steps in decolonizing the judicial system. By resolving interpretative difficulties in the areas of treaty surrender and cession in light of their fiduciary duty to Aboriginal peoples, the courts are clarifying *sui generis* Aboriginal tenure and rights. To promote the vision of a postcolonial legal regime, this part suggests reform of Canadian institutions so that Aboriginal peoples can represent and speak for their constitutional rights in federal and provincial assemblies and all Canadians can share an inclusive democratic future.

I

THE COMMON LAW AND LAND

In [*Van der Peet*,] I held at para. 50 that the reconciliation of the prior occupation of North America by aboriginal peoples with the assertion of Crown sovereignty required that account be taken of the "aboriginal perspective while at the same time taking into account the perspective of the common law" and that "[t]rue reconciliation will, equally, place weight on each".

Chief Justice Lamer in *Delgamuukw*[1]

It has been said that the law of land in countries under the Common Law of England is a "rubbish-heap which has been accumulating for hundreds of years, and ... is ... based upon feudal doctrines which no one (except professors in law schools) understands"—and rather with the implication that even the professors do not thoroughly understand them or all understand them the same way.

Justice Ridell in *Miller v. Tipling*[2]

Introduction

To embark on a "true reconciliation" between Aboriginal tenure and the British common law, one has to understand the two different perspectives on land law. Each perspective reveals the deepest insights and presumptions that shape understanding and organize relations to the land. Before engaging with the Aboriginal perspective on land law, we will begin with the ways of seeing with which it came in contact: the British common law on land. Doctrinal and historical detail will be kept to a minimum in our efforts to trace how various people who occupied Britain viewed land use, and how they contributed to and transformed the emergent common law.[3] In particular, we

---

1   *Delgamuukw v. British Columbia*, [1997] 3 S.C.R. 1010 at para. 148, 153 D.L.R. (4th) 193 (S.C.C.); see also paras. 81, 145, 147.

2   (1918), 43 O.L.R. 88 at 97, 43 D.L.R. 469 (Ont. C.A.).

3   A more technical view of the doctrines can be found in K. McNeil, *Common Law Aboriginal Title* (Oxford: Clarendon Press, 1989) cc. 2 and 3; B. Ziff, *Principles of Property Law*, 2d ed. (Toronto: Carswell, 1996); and M. L. Benson and M. Bowden, *Understanding Property: A Guide to Canada's Property Law* (Toronto: Carswell, 1997).

explore the development of the British tenure system from seeing property as a physical presence, to aristocratic rights, to a means of creating social order, to seeing it as commodity. The patterns of change are considered in the context of British legal thought. We need to understand the historical activity of categorizing, analyzing, and explaining that informs the legal imagination, and nurtures and changes the vision of land tenure and territory. The task is a difficult one because meanings and terms transform at different times. Arising directly from irreconcilable visions of social life, these visions are simultaneously moral, political, economic, legal, and pervasive, and the resulting concepts contain more incoherence and self-contradiction than clarity.

Tracing the development of these perspectives on land law takes us beyond legal doctrine to linguistics, history, and cultural and communication theories. Since people rarely state explicitly the world-view or consciousness within which they lead their lives and formulate their visions of land, tracing conceptual development or definition is often a major problem—and particularly so in the context of British law. In British law, land tenure begins in religion and relationships, transforms into jurisprudence, a fiction of law, then into a social order and an economic theory. It arises as an explanation of the relationship between humans and things, not as an ecological vision.

Out of the various occupations of Britain and their concepts of land, the common law perspective and standards developed. British land law is derived from these diverse traditions: Celtic, Roman, Teutonic, and Norse customs; the infusion of feudal social thought; the introduction of Norman administration into a system of law; and the re-importing of Roman and Canon law to the existing order. Its legal traditions are intertwined and overlapping, subject to many perspectives, and hence the source of many intractable problems. The interrelations of these diverse concepts about land use impelled lawyers and courts to pursue the customary idea of Teutonic "*seisin*" or physical presence of people on the land against the feudal backdrop of the absolutist idea of Crown tenure. These two simultaneous and interdependent ideas prevented the absolutist idea from being fully realized in any historical period.

Although we suspect that Indigenous tenures existed in the territory now called Britain, we have no understanding about who held the land or for what purposes. Typically, the doctrine of the land tenure of the Crown denies the existence not only of Indigenous tenure but also of Indigenous peoples and identity. Thus, we can only guess the ancient inhabitants' view of the land.

A significant problem in reconstructing these legal traditions is linguistic. One cannot understand legal relationships without investigating the contexts and terms on which those relationships depend. Nor can we satisfactorily discuss the meaning of a particular word, such as "ownership," merely by giving examples of its use. Similarly, one cannot construct a dictionary that the ancient peoples never provided. Our investigation is no mere exercise in philology since the meaning of any idea is intimately tied to a world-view and to language.

An example of the challenges we face is represented by the phrase "law of England." The word "law" itself appears to be of Inuit origin. It is said to be an Old Icelandic concept that the Norse people brought back from Iceland and that was derived from the Old Icelandic word meaning "something laid or fixed." The term "law," said to have been imported as *lazu* to Teutonic thought about 1000 A.D, could be spelled many ways, including *lach, laewe, lagh, laghe, laha, lau, lauh, law*, and *laugh*.[4] Why the Teutonic people incorporated this distinct word into their language remains a mystery. It is a different concept from the touchstone of the European civil law, the Latin *lex* (a particular rule) or *ius* (fundamental rights) or Roman *res* (thing), with its forms *re* and *rem*. In addition, it is different from the French *loi* (a rule) or *droit* (body of rules). Finally, it is different from justice as in "right and wrong, and jurisprudence," as in "Goo to Oxenford or lerne lawe," or the customs of the country, as in "law of the land." The answer is elusive. Still, the fact remains the Teutonic people chose not to use any other competing term.

The term "England" is also an interpretative challenge, and it conceals choices. "Pretanoi" (4 B.C.) is the oldest known reference to the territory; the Roman occupation created the label of Britain (Brittani or Britanni).[5] The Angles and Saxons called the territory "Bretenland."[6] The description of England was derived from "the land of the Angles" (*Engla land*). *Engla* is genitive of *Engle*, the Angles, an Anglo-Saxon or Old English word based on the angular shape of the original homeland, the Anul district of Schleswig. *Ank* is the root word, the derivative of the Germanic word for "to bend." In Old English *angul* is a fishhook. Today, confusion persists with England/English often being used as synonyms for Britain/British. "England," however, does not exist constitutionally; the island territory is known as the United Kingdom of Great Britain and Northern Ireland. Although it is problematic to talk about British common law in the light of a separate Scots law, we choose to use the phrase British common law to recognize that its jurisdiction extends beyond the geographical boundaries of England.

These linguistic dilemmas are followed by evidentiary problems. Even with the best of evidence, all history and law remain a matter of selective attention on which is based an interpretation. Despite appeals to a monolithic or empirical past, historical and legal documents always require interpretation, since historical records are always tributes to what historian Hayden White has called "the fictive capability of the historian."[7] Historical events or moments are not fixed points to be "scientifically" recuperated but sites of contested meanings. Still, we need not be overcome by the temporal distance between interpreters and evidence, but we can pursue knowledge, while recognizing the constraints on the pursuit of knowledge. In obstacles to interpretation, we may also find opportunities to renew our understandings and uncover what has been obscured by interests in the past.

---

4   D. Mellinkoff, *The Language of the Law* (Boston: Little, Brown and Company, 1963) at 34, 84-85.

5   It was also called Old French *Bretaigne*, Latin *Brittania* (later *Britannia*), Old English *Breten, Bryten*; and West Germanic *Brituna* (land of Britons). Today it is known as the United Kingdom of Great Britain and Northern Ireland. Tom McArthur, ed., *The Oxford Companion to the English Language* (Oxford: Oxford University Press, 1992).

6   *Ibid.* Some of the kings were titled *Bretwalda*, which is said to echo Latin *Dux britanniarum* or leader of the Britains.

7   Hayden White, *Tropics of Discourse: Essays on Cultural Criticism* (Baltimore, MD.: John Hopkins University Press, 1978) at 89.

Even if we could resolve the problems of historical description and truth, legal history is a particularly difficult domain because historians and lawyers view the past from different perspectives. Historians tend to view legal history as a branch of social, military, or administrative history. Lawyers tend to have little interest in legal history; their interest is in judicial thinking and decisions. Often, both judges and lawyers reduce legal history to precedent or a matter of reading law backward. The history of law, however, is no mere digression.[8]

The two modes of thought and categorical scheme illustrate the problem of method or perspective in legal history. As British legal historian S.F.C. Milsom stated:

> The historian, if he is lucky, can see why a rule came into existence, what social or eco-
> nomic change left it working injustice, how it came to be evaded, how the evasion pro-
> duced a new rule, and sometimes how that new rule in its turn came to be overtaken by
> change. But he misunderstands it all if he endows the lawyers who took part with vision
> on any comparable scale, or attributes to them any intention beyond the winning of today's
> case.[9]

In this chasm between historian and lawyer, there is a failure to understand how the law is interwoven and connected to non-law: history, politics, culture, or morality. Equally difficult is our understanding of non-law sources, since the primary materials were not constructed from our modern vantage point. The difficulties are exacerbated by the problem of translation within the early periods as well as between past and present forms of conceptualizing.

What evidence exists about ancient ideas of land use and rights during the various occupations of Britain is based on works that raise deep questions about their reliability. Our problem is more than a matter of evidence, however. The evidence has been manipulated, concealed, and distorted in the standard sources. Fraudulent legal treatises compounded by modern ideological bias contaminate the available historical sources of non-narrative and narrative written records. In our survey of the development of British land law we have to negotiate such unreliable records to attempt to uncover the people's conceptualizing of their relations to the land.

1. The Legacy of Occupations

A. Celtic occupation

British oral tradition asserts that long before the birth of Christ the Celtic nomads entered the territory. They had fought their way from one end of Europe to the other. Whether these were the *Pretani*, the painted people, or an Indigenous description of the

---

8   F. Pollock and F.M. Maitland, *The History of English Law Before the Time of Edward I*, vol. 1, 2d ed. (Cambridge, U.K.: Cambridge University Press, 1899) at 87; Sir W.S. Holdsworth, *A History of English Law*, vol. 1 (London: Methuen, 1903) at 478.

9   S.F.C. Milsom, *Historical Foundations of the Common Law* (London: Butterworths, 1969) at xii.

invader is not certain.[10] The traditions say Celtic lawyers for centuries maintained a customary law in a "learnedly archaic language" that became one of the dominant languages of *Britannia*. Like ancient prayers, their law involved repetitive rituals, with any departure from the word-for-word ritual a violation of the law.

In Eire, Scotland, and Wales, the Celtic language and law survive.[11] In Scotland proper, above the Lowlands, and in Ireland, the Celtic landholding existed. So far as can be ascertained from the Brehon law,[12] land tenure was based on a customary tribal or clannish pattern. The clan structure was not uniform, but varied throughout the Highlands. We are told that this land tenure transformed into a Scots form of feudalism around the reign of David I (1124-1153).[13]

B. Roman occupation

In the first century A.D., the Romans occupied Celtic Britain bringing with them the long history of Roman law and the Latin language.[14] Classic Roman law of the *Principate*, ending in the middle of the third century, was distinct from the laws of ancient Rome. It was a system developed by technical legal craftsmen, the jurisconsults, who were steeped in Stoic philosophy and shared a commitment to the reason and order of nature: its universality and logical structure known through formal scientific methods. The jurisconsults conceived of law as abstract relations that could be made concrete in terms of any citizen or pattern of behaviour, and they organized legal knowledge, through dialectical analysis, as independent of extra-legal consideration. They gave advice on questions of law, but did not try cases in courts, and distrusted codification.[15]

Classical Roman law derived its authority from postulating a world order according to a universal rule of law. It distinguished the law of nature (*iure naturali*) from the enactments or customary law of a particular state (*iure civile*) and the law of agreements of men (*iure gentium*). The law of nature was a higher law that arose from the understanding of the cultural diversity of peoples and provoked a search for overarching principles that underlay the variety of customs.[16] These norms were viewed as

---

10   Mellinkoff, *supra* note 4 at 36.

11   *Ibid.* at 37-39.

12   William Binchy, "The Linguistic and Historical Value of the Irish Law Tracts" (1943) 29 Proceedings of the British Academy 4 at 4-11; *Foyle and Bann Fisheries Ltd. v. A-G.*, [1949] Ir. L.T.R. 29 at 41.

13   P. Hume-Brown, *History of Scotland*, vol. 1 (Cambridge, U.K.: Cambridge University Press, 1905-1911) at 70.

14   By 100 A.D. Latin already had a literary and legal history of some five hundred years. We are taking the beginning of Roman legal terminology from the ancient Roman law of the Twelve Tables of 450-400. See "The Laws of the Twelve Tables" in *The Civil Law*, ed. by trans. B.C.S.P. Scott (New York: A.M.S. Press, 1973) at 58-65 [reprint].

15   J.C. Smith and D.N. Weisstub, *The Western Idea of Law* (London: Butterworths, 1983) at 315-17. The original text of the Twelve Tables is lost.

16   R.M. Unger, *Law in Modern Society: Toward a Criticism of Social Theory* (New York: The Free Press, 1976) at 77.

common to the law of different peoples without reference to state law or agreements. In the law of nature everyone was born free and equal, and land was held and used in common.[17] The law of agreements of men lay behind the concept of wars, separate nations, the origins of kingdoms (*regna condita*), private property (*dominia distincta*), the division of land (*agris termini positi*), grouping of houses, commerce, and slavery.[18]

Roman law made a distinction between *imperium* and *dominium*, or in modern terms, sovereignty and property. *Imperium*, a concept of sovereignty, was the rule of the Emperor over families (*familia*) and citizens. *Dominium* was the concept of family property; it was rule over things by families, not by individuals. It described the relations between nearly self-sufficient or independent and equal social units of Roman society called the *familia*. Disputes between *familia* informed the civil law of Rome that dealt only with the relations or powers arising among the familial units. Since most of the civil law was concerned with the law of obligations and persons, *dominium* was conceptualized under the law of agreements rather than the law of nature.

Each *familia* was a walled-in preserve, sufficient unto itself. Title to property within a *familia*, conceived as resting in the head of the *familia*, was held absolutely.[19] A *familia* either had title or it did not. There was no difference of degree or interests. Within each preserve were relationships beyond the law. Internal use was a matter of familial custom and did not come within the jurisdiction of the civil law.

Classic Roman law assumed all men had usufructuary rights: they had natural possession of the earth and its fruits but they lacked *dominium* over it; that is, they could not have natural property rights.[20] It did not regard private property as possession (*possessio*) or a fundamental right (*ius*).[21] To possess something was to occupy it and use it (*usufruct*) but not to have individual rights in it. The law assumed that a usufructuary could have natural possession, but not civil possession since a usufructuary had no claim against other men in his society. Without civil possession, no concept of individual rights in land existed, since both these concepts were viewed as issues of the law of agreements. Similarly, the classical Roman jurists were unwilling to allow that individuals might naturally have civil possession or individual rights over other men or goods.

---

17   Theodor Mommsen and P. Krueger, eds., *The Digest of Justinian*, trans. A. Watson, vol. 1 (Philadelphia: University of Pennsylvania Press, 1985), Book 1 at 14 [reprint] [hereinafter *Digest*]. Saint Isidore of Seville, *Etymoligiarium*, vol. 4 (Strasbourg, Fr.: J. Mentelin, 1470), synthesises classical Roman law: "The *ius naturale* is common to all nations; it is what is received everywhere by natural instinct, and not by any convention. It includes the union of men and women, the bringing up of children, common possession of *everything (communis omniun possessio)* and freedom for everyone."

18   *Ibid.*, vol. 2 at I.5.

19   Today, this could be seen as a political relation. The federated families created *villae*, the *villae* expanding to become super-familial political organizations.

20   R. Tuck, *Natural Rights Theories: Their Origin and Development* (New York: Cambridge University Press, 1979) at 18. In the thirteenth century, the civil law resolved this dilemma by creating the concept of *dominium utile*, or natural property. Saint Thomas Aquinas, *Summa Theologica*, trans. Fathers of the English Dominican province, vol. 2a2ae (New York: Benziger, 1912-25) at 66.1.

21   Michel Villey, *Philosophie du droit* (Paris: Dalloz, 1982).

The jurisconsults used the term *"ius"* in the context of a mode of divine judgment to mean something objectively right and discoverable in a particular situation or the right way people should behave towards one another.[22] In modern British thought, it would be a synonym for "rights." To the jurisconsults the way rights were generated or incurred was of fundamental importance.

The Institutes of Gaius, the legal treatise by the great Roman jurist of the second century A.D., states the distinction between corporeal and incorporeal *res*. Corporeal things could be touched, and included such physical objects as soil, gold, garments or slaves. Incorporeal things could not be touched, and comprised those things that subsist in the artificial or abstract law (*iure*), such as an inheritance, a *usufruct*, or obligations (*obligatio*). Gaius stated, "It is irrelevant ... that the produce extracted from an estate is corporeal, or that what we owe as the result of an obligation may be such as an estate, a man, or money. [T]he *ius* of usufruct and the *ius* of obligation are incorporeal."[23] They were incorporeal because they arose from legal agreement. All incorporeal rights were human bonds, not relationships among objects.

In addition, *The Institutes of Gaius* made a clear distinction between having *dominion* in something and having an *ius* or right in it. In discussing the right of the *usufruct*, *The Rules of Ulpian*, a thirteenth-century treatise, commented, "the *ius* of using and taking the crop can only be attributed to the man who has the usufruct; the *dominus* of an estate does not have it, since anyone who enjoys the ownership (*quia qui habet proprietatem*) of something does not have a separate *ius* to use it and take its produce."[24]

In the later Roman Empire, the Emperor claimed bilateral relationships with all citizens, and claimed a right to intervene in their life in a variety of ways. The consequence of this relationship was that *dominium* came to be seen as a kind of civil right, distinct from the family regimes and the law of agreements. Thus, the Roman lawyers began to use *ius* to describe a property right because all right to property could be interpreted as subsisting in bilateral relationships between citizen and Emperor.[25]

The transformation of *dominium* to a kind of right arose in the context of "squatters on land" in the imperial domain of North African colonies. Emperor Hadrian resolved this problem of their pre-existing presence by giving the "squatters" the *"ius"*

---

22   Tuck, *supra* note 20 at 8-9.

23   *The Institutes of Gaius*, trans. J.A.C. Thomas (Cape Town, S.A.: Juta & Co., 1975), Book 1 at 68; see also Book 2, Title 2 "On Incorporeal Things," and Title 3 "On Servitudes" at 84-85. These writings are one of the best-preserved Roman legal treatises.

24   *Digest, supra* note 17, vol. 7 at 6.5. See also Title 19 "Concerning Owners and Their Acquisition of Property," where all property is classified as either mancipable (land situated in Italy) or not mancipable (wild beasts). Mancipable property is acquired by some people's use of certain words in the presence of a balance-holder and five witnesses (alienation), by delivery, by surrender in court, by uninterrupted possession for one or two years (usucaption), by proceeding in partition among co-heirs (adjudication), and by lapse or forfeiture under *Lex papia Poppeae*. See "The Rules of Ulpian" in *The Civil Law, supra* note 14 at 238-39.

25   E. Levy, *West Roman Vulgar Law: The Law of Property* (Philadelphia: American Philosophical Society, 1951).

to possess the land, take its crop, and transmit it to heirs.[26] It was as close as any sources in the period to making *ius* into *dominium*. Still, the Emperor considered it as *ius* only because it was a gift to the squatters. He was not transferring to them some of his own *dominium*; otherwise, the land would have been removed from imperial control.

By the time the Western provinces of the Roman Empire were amalgamated into the Germanic realm, the Roman legal concept of *dominium*—as private rights in land for a limited term or a right to transmit land or as rights tied to a particular trade—had disintegrated.[27] With the disappearance of an Emperor and his relations to other Roman citizens, the legal vocabulary was cut off from its origins and context. *Dominium* became transformed to a public right, which one possessed as a result of one's relationship with the state or public, rather than by private agreements. This transformed from a right in *personam*, available against determinate individuals, to a right in *rem*, that is to say, an indeterminate right against all the world. Nonetheless, the Roman legal categories remained in the legal tradition of Britain.

C. Teutonic occupation

Both Celtic and Roman law existed as part of the land tenure that confronted the first Germanic peoples who travelled to the territory in the middle of the fifth century.[28] With other Teutonic peoples (Saxons and Jutes), the Angles left their home in what is now Denmark and northern Germany and began a serious penetration of the territory.[29] The Teutonic peoples, especially the Angles, brought a separate language called English.[30] This language is classified by some as the Teutonic branch of the Indo-European language,[31]

---

26   T. Frank, ed., *An Economic Survey of Ancient Rome*, vol. 4 (Baltimore, MD: John Hopkins Press, 1933-40, 1959) at 94 (*isque wui occupaverint possidendi ac fruendi heredique suo relinquendi id jus datur*).

27   The concept remained but was reconceptualized as *dominium perfectum*.

28   Sir P. Vinogradoff, *The Growth of the Manor* (London: Sonnenschein, 1905) at 40-42, 120 [hereinafter Vinogradoff 1905].

29   Caesar, in *Caesar's Gallic Wars*, trans. S.A. Hanford (Markham, ON: Penguin Books, 1982), briefly describes the Germanic tribes he encountered while fighting the Gauls. Another Roman writer, Cornelius Tacitus, writing c. AD100, in *Tacitus' Germania*, trans M. Hutton, rev. E. Warmington (Cambridge, Mass.: Harvard University Press, 1970) [hereinafter *Germania*] is the principal source on these peoples' law and organization until five hundred years later when they wrote their codes.

30   The Angles and Saxons themselves called their language English as early as the ninth century. Mellinkoff, *supra* note 4 at 45.

31   L.M. Findlay, "The Future of the Subject" (1992) 18 Eng. Stud. Can. 130, reminds us that comparative grammar and linguistics comprise an imperial project of the late eighteenth and early nineteenth centuries. It created the Indo-European languages to legitimize conquest and colonization. He writes: "the move away from cultural otherness toward a common linguistic ancestry would lead to the ruthless reconstitution of difference rather than its progressive elimination. If 'we' started at the same proto-linguistic place then why have you progressed so little relative to us? If 'we' belong to the same Indo-European family, then who is to head the family household and direct its economy? If you end up as the subaltern or object and I as the sovereign subject of our erstwhile common discourse, then it is certainly no 'accident'." This imperialistic conception of Indo-European language categories can be found in Otto Schrader, *Prehistoric Antiquities of the Aryan People*, 2d ed. trans. F.B. Javons (London: C. Griffin and Co., 1890) at 110-12 where he suggests that Europeans have a right to speak of a common culture that may be traced through language rather than race.

using a runic alphabet.[32] It is often called Anglo-Saxon or Old English.[33] Taken together, the language and alphabet carried a Teutonic world-view and what Gaile McGregor calls "langscape."[34]

The basic values the Anglo-Saxons imported into the territory appear to be those common to all Germanic nations. Often the Teutonic people are characterized as invaders or conquerors,[35] but the only known tradition is that they insisted they were asked to come, given land, and stayed.[36] They settled on the soil that they had got by agreement or by force from the Celts, bringing their ancient Teutonic cultural organization and customs to the Island.

The Celts and the Teutonic people lived on the Island within their own culture and law. Both communities had existed within the concept of the "personality of the law" or the law of people. Linguistic and archaeological evidence shows that the Celts were not extirpated;[37] the Celtic language survived the Anglo-Saxon invasion of Britain, but became a secondary language. Gradually both customs blended, and dis-

---

32   Mellinkoff, *supra* note 4 at 39-41. The Indo-European language is often said to have spawned first Latin, then French as a dialect of Latin.

33   *Ibid.* at 45. The period of Old English extends from the mid-fifth-century Teutonic raids to the Norman Conquest in 1066.

34   Gaile McGregor, *The Wacousta Syndrome: Explorations in the Canadian Langscape* (Toronto: University of Toronto Press, 1985).

35   The usual account is that a local Celtic leader, Vortigern, established his authority over much of the territory in the fifth century. While engaged in fighting the Picts and Scots from the north, he arranged to settle some Saxon or Jutish chieftains in the south, in return for their assistance. Vortigern married the daughter of one of the chieftains, and offered the chieftain the whole of Kent in return for the marriage of his daughter. Then events became muddled. Vortigern temporarily lost his power to a son, who attempted to drive out the Teutonic communities. The Teutonic communities were subjected to the Viking and Danish invasions, but the Teutonic unification of possession continued until the eleventh century. King Canute (1016-1035) made England the centre of his North Sea empire, confirmed all Anglo-Saxon law, re-established efficient administration, and supported the Anglo-Saxon church. B. Lyon, *A Constitutional and Legal History of Medieval England* (New York: Harper & Row, 1960) at 19-35. The Teutonic communities consolidated their position in relation to the Celts by establishing themselves around the southern coast and rivers. The Britons temporarily halted the Teutonic expansion in the Battle of Mons Badon, thus ending the so-called first stage of the Anglo-Saxon conquest. The Teutonic expansion was said to occupy most of the Island except Wales and Scotland. In classic British history the Teutonic people came as destroyers, annihilating everything they found and substituting their own society, laws, and customs. This is inconsistent with their activities on the continent. The Teutonic or Germanic invaders there created a new ruling class, but they were absorbed into the existing Roman law and society. Yet, the question of why the Teutonic invaders in England were different from their continental relatives is never answered.

36   See *The Anglo-Saxon Chronicle, According to the Several Original Authorities*, ed. by trans. B. Thorpe (London: Longman, 1861). This is an annalistic historical narrative that records the yearly events of Britain from Caesar's invasion in 54 B.C. to the end of King Stephen's reign in A.D. 1154. It aids in reconstructing the political history of the period, and is said to derive from a set of annals composed during Alfred's reign up to 891, and then continued by church scribes.

37   Extirpation is the classical explanation of British historians. They argue that at the end of the sixth century the Celts had been as close to extirpation as a nation can be. Similar patterns of culture and organization between the Celts and the Teutons have been ascribed to "coincidences."

tinctions were merged to create a "territoriality of law," the law of a place.[38] Anglo-Saxon law comprised the customs of the community.[39] In addition, their local custom was the law of their ancient courts.[40]

Initially, no political masters existed; community leaders existed. There was a relation between the community and the leader or chief who was regarded as the fountain of honour and the giver of gifts to this community.[41] The relationships of the leader to the men of the community, based on mutual service, responsibility, and protection of life, were the principal bases of the Teutonic order on the Island. The leader was not regarded as owner of the land, nor were the men seen as vassal or tenant. Nor was this relationship seen as connected with the holding of land.[42] The people looked upon the area as the holdings of the community, rather than of any leader, individual chief, or king.[43] What the community efforts acquired, defended, or protected would be regarded as belonging to them. The personal relationship between the community and the chief was independent of land use. Although it has been supposed that this personal relationship comprised an ambiguous land holding and use regime, it was not an ideal or a system.[44] The leader was neither a territorial baron nor a feudal lord. Nor did the presence of a leader create a kingdom or a feudal order. Life was linked to the various harvests that fed the community. Because the same people protected the land and the community, it does not follow that the head or leader of a community necessarily appropriated the soil to himself or could grant it to his followers.[45]

---

38   Little evidence exists to show this sharing between the cultures. The earliest records of Celtic customs or laws are of a later date than the Teutonic *dooms* (laws).

39   Twelfth-century Britain was ruled by many different customs. There was no comprehensive or uniform notion of custom. Each shire or county had its own. The powers of the royal government were customary also; and custom at that time did not have to reach back to time immemorial to be enforced as law. A custom, it was said, was old if it had existed for ten years, very old if for twenty, and ancient if it was thirty years old.

40   Before the dispensation of common law through royal justice could exist, it had to displace the existing customary system of lay courts, where judges were unknown. Questions of law were answered on the basis of the community's knowledge of local customs. These courts were the communal courts of the shires and hundreds, the lords' seigniorial courts and the burgesses' borough courts of trade and commerce.

41   *Germania, supra* note 29, cc. 13-14. Tacitus described this Teutonic relationship as between lord and man, or *princeps* and *comes*.

42   Eventually this bond developed into that of lord and tenant, or vassalage. Originally it was a relation between the *princeps* and the *comes*, of king and his thanes, of lord and man. K. E. Digby, *An Introduction to the History of the Law of Real Property,* 1st ed. (Oxford: Clarendon Press, 1875); reprinted in Merskey and Jacobstein, eds., *Classics in Legal History,* vol. 12 (Buffalo: William S. Hein & Co., 1970-4) at 15.

43   The Old English word for king was *cyning*; the king's power was *cynindom*. See Mellinkoff, *supra* note 4 at 46.

44   Milsom, *supra* note 9 at 8.

45   Digby, *supra* note 42 at 2-3. See also C. Stephenson and F.G. Marcham, *Sources of English Constitutional History* (New York: Harper, 1937).

The *dooms* or laws of the Anglo-Saxon kings began with Ethelbert, the first Christian king of Kent.[46] They were written legal codes in Anglo-Saxon or Old English about 602-3. These laws expressed the unwritten Teutonic customs of centuries in the context of England, and are considered the original sources of the common law. These customs were similar to those governing the principal Germanic tribes on the Continent.

Another code was drawn up between 673 and 685 by two other Kentish Kings, Hlothhere and Eadric, and yet another code for Kent by King Withred in 695. Still, another collection of laws (688-694) has been preserved from the reign of Ine, the King of Wessex. Two centuries later Alfred, also King of Wessex (871-99), published more laws including Ine's code and certain laws of Ethelbert and Offa, King of the Mercians (757-796).[47]

In the tenth century, another code of law written in Anglo-Saxon was promulgated.[48] As Wessex came to control all of England in the tenth century, so too did these laws come to control all of England, although the codes never excluded customary or local law. The most noteworthy codes were those of Edward the Elder (899-925), Athelstan (925-39), Edmund (939-946), Edgar (959-75), Ethelred the Unready (979-1016), and Canute (1016-35).

Because the Teutonic leader's authority in Britain was derived from honour and respect from the community,[49] the administrative measure of the kingdom was personal[50] rather than territorial. Shire government, laws, and courts of law existed in the communities. Thus, Teutonic government was not feudal in the sense of the Continental style.[51]

The Anglo-Saxon settlements were an agricultural society, without a moneyed economy,[52] their wealth measured in cattle.[53] The customary laws of the Anglo-Sax-

---

46   Stephenson and Marcham, *ibid.* at nos. 1-9, 11-13.

47   *Offa's Laws* have disappeared except as preserved in Alfred's collections. See M.H. Turk, ed., *The Legal Code of Alfred the Great* (Halle, De.: E. Karras, 1890).

48   This is different from the codification of Germanic customs in continental Europe. These codes are written in Latin, the *Leges barbarorum*, and ed. by H.F.W.D. Fischer (Leiden, Nied.: E.J. Brill, 1948).

49   R.C. Van Caenegem, *The Birth of English Common Law* (Cambridge, U.K.: Cambridge University Press, 1973) at 8.

50   The administrative unit was the "hundred," into which the Crown merged the shires. Usually local administrative jurisdiction was limited to one hundred households. Upon this numerical idea, courts, policing, and taxes were organized.

51   Commentators often argue that their ideas were moving towards continental feudalism. We are not sure they are correct, because it seems just another justification for the *status quo*.

52   Bargain, barter, selling market, price, and merchandise were all expressed by the Old English word for cattle, *ceap* or later cheap (a good buy); Mellinkoff, *supra* note 4 at 40. Later still, the word transformed to "chattel," meaning movable personal property.

53   *Ibid.* at 40. In the runic alphabet, the letter "*F*," which made a sound *feh* or *feoh*, meant cattle, and eventually money and property. The later spelling of Old English was *fee*, which either means movable or feudal estate. This is analogous to the Hebrew alphabet, where the first letter *aleph* or *alpha* means ox, the wealth of the Hebrew.

ons were adapted to hunting, cattle-grazing, and an agricultural society.[54] Since everyone was familiar with them, no one wrote down their characteristics, and they remain an enigma to modern scholars. Anglo-Saxon law conceived of land use much differently from continental civil law and feudal traditions, and it was different from the Scandinavians' understandings and practices. Their local custom was law in their courts, and they regulated the land use.[55] The codes express little interest in possession of the land.[56] Within the customary law were the vague ideas of duration of an interest in lands in the community (including the King's), which included the freedom of transferring land interests other than inheritance to family.[57] Most British legal historians argue that the problem of reconstructing folk-land belongs to Germanic history rather than the laws of England.[58] What is clear, however, is that Anglo-Saxon customary law did not know the Roman idea of *fee* or *dominion*.[59]

Teutonic communities used the land in at least three different ways: folk-land (*folcland*), book-land (*bocland*), and lease-land (*laenland*). Folk-land was the primal use of the land; the oldest, and probably for a long time the only way to hold any parcel of land.[60] It was a customary system of landholding, in which the land was not held

---

54   For an example of the law regulating this economy, see the Laws of King Ethelbert of Kent, written into a code around 596, found in A.W.B. Simpson, "The Laws of Ethelbert" in Morris S. Arnold, *et al.*, eds., *On The Laws and Customs of England: Essays in Honour of Samuel E. Thorne* (Chapel Hill: University of North Carolina, 1981). Holdsworth, *supra* note 8, vol. 2 at 19, 20; Mellinkoff, *supra* note 4 at 46, 49.

55   When the legal profession came into existence in 1292, it had to either choose its newly emerging law from the mass of customs in existence, or else create new customs. Slowly, custom was redefined by the 1500s as that accepted by the royal courts, not by the general population. To be immemorially old the custom had to have existed on September 3, 1189, the coronation of Richard I. Other customs still ruled at local levels where royal law did not intervene and were enforced by the manor or in the county.

56   A.W.B. Simpson, *An Introduction to the History of the Land Law* (London: Oxford University Press, 1961) at 3.

57   Digby, *supra* note 42 at 21-22. The Teutonic custom was that a landholder divided his land among his sons, or, lacking sons, among his daughters. Lyon, *supra* note 35 at 96.

58   Pollock & Maitland, *supra* note 8, vol. 1 at 62.

59   The concept of "*fee*" is basic to Latin land law. The word is derived from the Latin *feodum*, meaning a *fief*, or feudal estate in land. As used in law, a *fee* is an eternal, inherited interest in the land. In the theory of essences, a *fee* is the animate force of the land. Obtaining the eternal interest in the land allowed exchanges that transferred the interest in time.

60   Folk-land is a term that occurs only in a few documents, and without any decisive explanation. The most authoritative of these documents is a law of Edward the Elder, where folk-land is contrasted with book-land and was defined as land held in common (that is, through the working of customary law) by folk right. In 1830 John Allen put forth the view that "folk-land, as the word imports, was the land of the folk or people. It was the property of the community." J. Allen, *Inquiry into the Rise and Growth of the Royal Prerogative* (New York: Burt Franklin, 1962) at 135 [reprint] [hereinafter *Royal Prerogative*]. The proposed analogy was to the Latin *ager publicus* or public land; see Sir F. Pollock, *The Land Laws*, 3d ed. (New York: Macmillan, 1896); Digby, *supra* note 42 at 3. The analogy, however, did not fit. If folk-land meant *ager publicus*, then every one who had not book-land was a mere tenant of a non-existent state. In 1893 P. Vinogradoff, "Folk-land" (1893) 8 Eng. Hist. Rev. 1 at 1-17 [hereinafter Vinogradoff 1893], rejected the analogy and reasserted the concept of land held without written title under customary law.

by any superior or lord, and was eventually categorized in feudal law as allodial land.[61] The most significant feature of folk-land was that it could not be transferred or conveyed out of the holder's family. It described a group right, the land holding of a clan or kin or family. In this sense, it was similar to the Roman concept of *familia*, but no civil law existed among families.

Each community occupied a territory or *mark* that was held in common. Each village had four areas: the towns or houses held by the heads of families, the arable or cultivated lands, the meadow-land, and the uncultivated lands.[62] The last three areas were subject to community regulation,[63] and the uses of these areas created family folk-land and responsibilities.[64]

In certain common areas of the territory, families were allowed temporary possession, without altering the community character of the land, in what was usually called "beneficial" (right of use) occupation of folk-land.[65] In Anglo-Saxon law, the allotment of the soil among the community was called "*eoel*," "*hid*," or "*alod*."[66] Evidence demonstrates that in some cases various rents, dues, or services in money or kind had to be rendered to the community, or to the King as representative of the community.[67] These renderings suggest that some areas could be permanently allotted.[68]

Within the territories, some areas, such as woods, pastures, and wasteland, were not used. Commonly, these lands would be shared by those families of the neighbouring villages; occasionally the King or his council of wise men who selected the King (*witan*)[69] had exclusive right to develop these lands.[70] Often, these lands became the

---

61 Vinogradoff argued that this concept became an allodial system of customary landholding; H.A.L. Fisher, ed., *The Collected Papers of Paul Vinogradoff*, vol. 1 (Oxford: Clarendon Press, 1928) at 91.

62 Digby, *supra* note 42 at 10-13. Although the details are not clear, the English concept of property appears to have grown from use of open land or meadow-land for cattle. It appears from this unoccupied folk-land came the concept of the King's land, or *terra regis*. Eventually, some writers suggest that such land came to be seen as originally vested in the crown, that the King is *prima facie* the owner of all unoccupied land, even of the shore below high-water-mark.

63 For example, the arable lands were divided into three fields, one of which lays fallow every third year as common pasture land.

64 J. M. Kemble, *The Saxons in England: A History of the English Commonwealth 'til the Period of the Norman Conquest*, vol. 1 (London: B. Quaritch, 1876) at 289; Vinogradoff 1893, *supra* note 60.

65 This category of land use has created some of the most confusing interpretations among the nineteenth-century scholars.

66 Kemble, *supra* note 64, vol. 1 at 90; W. Stubbs, *The Constitutional History of England in its Origin and Development*, vol. 1 (Oxford: Clarendon Press, 1875-78) at 71.

67 Digby, *supra* note 42 at 7, citing Kemble, *supra* note 64, vol. 1 at 294-98; *Royal Prerogative, supra* note 60 at 134; Stubbs, *ibid.*, vol. 1 at 76.

68 Digby, *supra* note 42 at 7.

69 This word means "to know, to be wise." It is related to modern words "witness" and "to wit." Mellinkoff, *supra* note 4 at 47.

70 Digby, *supra* note 42 at 9.

common stock from which grants and other beneficial uses were made to heads of families. Over the generations, this land became spoken of as the King's folk-land.[71]

Often in the Teutonic communities, the leader of the community shared in the cultivation of the soil and distribution of plots and harvest. At times, to protect the community and their folk-land, the leader and warriors[72] had to have an independent existence. In cycles of conquest, it was impossible for the warriors to participate in herding the cattle or the community harvest. As a result, they were given some harvest as gifts from the communities.[73]

Land held free from community or family ties was called book-land or lease-land. Book-land, a gift of land in the form of a written charter (*charta*),[74] was initially written exclusively to ecclesiastic clerks; subsequent grants to laymen retained the ecclesiastical character.[75] The lease-land was, at first, a loan of land for a life or lives.[76] Both of these land-holdings were derivative from folk-land.[77] Over the generations, when the communities granted folk-land to a certain family or church, such land uses became categorized as book-land or lease-land. These categories manifested "written uses" (or licences) of the soil. The soil remained in the community; it was merely a different relationship with the soil. In the absence of the book-land, folk-land continued to be a community resource with its seasonal cycles of collective uses or temporary uses by families.

Initially, book-land constituted recordings of former charters or grants,[78] which were artificially constructed by the Catholic Church to respond to the need of chang-

---

71   *Ibid.*, citing Professor E. Nasse, *On the Agricultural Community of the Middle Ages and Inclosures of the Sixteenth Century in England*, trans. Colonel H.A. Ouvry (London: Macmillan, 1871) at 28.

72   Tacitus, in discussing the earlier southern Teutonic communities, called these warriors the *comites* (*gesiths*). See *Germania, supra* note 29, cc. 12, 14. No detailed account exists of Teutonic communities in Britain.

73   Often this sharing process is glorified by some scholars as the beginning of royal revenue.

74   Often, book-land is now compared to what is called corporate or private property. Kemble, *supra* note 64, vol. 1 at 301. Lyon, *supra* note 35, states that during the nineteenth century scholars were convinced kings created book-land out of folk-land with the consent of the great lords. This interpretation prevailed until it was revised towards the end of the century, when most scholars agreed that folk-land became known as the royal domain, or the land belonging to the King.

75   F. W. Maitland, *Domesday Book and Beyond: Three Essays in the Early History of England* (Cambridge, U.K.: Cambridge University Press, 1897) at 243. The written form of the gift may represent a link with the ancient conveyancing ceremonies of Rome, the reciting of the *mancipato*. W. Ross, *Lectures on the History and Practice of the Law of Scotland*, vol. 2, 2d ed. (Edinburgh: Bell & Bradfute, 1822) at 65ff.

76   Holdsworth, *supra* note 8, vol. 2 at 70, 168; D.R. Denman, *Origins of Ownership: A Brief History of Land Ownership and Tenure From Earliest Times to the Modern Era* (London: Allen & Unwin, 1958) at 68-69, 82. The Celtic version of lease land in Scotland was known as *thengage* and *drengage*.

77   On the question of the relations of folk-land to book-land, see Vinogradoff 1893, *supra* note 60 at 1-17; T.F.T. Plucknett, "Bookland and Folkland" (1935-36) 6 Econ. Hist. Rev. 64; G.J. Turner, "Bookland and Folkland" in J.G. Edwards, V.H. Galbraith and E.F. Jacob, eds., *Historical Essays in Honour of James Tait* (Manchester, U.K.: Printed for the Subscribers, 1933); J.E.A. Jolliffe, "English Bookright" (1935) 50 Eng. Hist. Rev. 1 at 1-21.

78   Pollock & Maitland, *supra* note 8, vol. 1 at 60.

ing economies. These entries, categorized as gifts from the community, were registered in a book, which was called *Domesday* in 1086. The *Domesday* was a register of book-land holders before and after the Norman takeover.[79] Usually the holders of book-land were the churches[80] or large families,[81] who lacked interest in actually farming or using the land. These gifts of jurisdiction and profits, not the land itself, usually made no difference to the actual occupier of the soil; the communities and families still harvested the soil.[82]

The terms of the grants governed the rights and duties of the book-land. The gifts allowed the family to hold the land free from most burdens, although book-land holders were required to provide military service, repair roads, bridges, and fortresses.[83] However, those receiving these gifts were under no obligation to render anything in the shape of payment or services to the King and elders. Depending on the form of the gifts as expressed in the charter, the holder could regrant the soil to another.[84] Otherwise, it remained within his family.[85] Generally, some rights granted by the book were to hold court and collect taxes. In the twelfth century, book-land was merged in feudal tenures.[86]

Any head of a family, who either had beneficial occupation of folk-land or was a holder of book-land, might in turn grant beneficial enjoyment of the land to another. These grants were also written arrangements called lease-land (*laenland*) or lienland.[87] Lease-land involved loans or profitable interest in the folk-land or book-land. It

---

79   It is unclear whether entry into the book required an additional symbolic delivery or was itself sufficient. See note 109, *infra*.

80   This is the process that the great ecclesiastical corporations used to acquire their property. The Church was part of a European system of law, called Canon Law, founded in Roman Law. The Church's Canon Law was highly organized and was administered as a universal law. The jurisdiction of the Church was guarded on one side by the writ of prohibition, and on the other by the withdrawal of spiritual sanction from the lay power itself. Milsom, *supra* note 9 at 13. This tenure came to be called *frankalmoign* (free alms). It consisted of the duty to perform spiritual services. Eventually, the Church brought Roman and Latin concepts of land law into the British law.

81   These are often seen as individual grants made to the King's *thanes* or *ministri*. Hence the expression tainland or thaneland, a factual description not a partial species of tenure.

82   Digby, *supra* note 42 at 5. Book-land was coextensive with the original meaning of the terms *alod* or *alodial*; that is, that the land was not dependent upon any other community, person, or institution. In the hands of the common lawyers the concept of book-land gradually came to mean derivative tenures held by a private person or the Church.

83   *Ibid.* at 5-6. All land held under Teutonic custom had these threefold services. The duties or services toward the community were called *trinoda necessitas*. They are distinct from the feudal services of later times.

84   Pollock & Maitland, *supra* note 8, vol. 1 at 60. Some book-lands were large enough to confer powers equivalent to those of a modern tenant in fee simple.

85   Digby, *supra* note 42 at 6, citing E.A. Freeman, *The History of the Norman Conquest of England*, vol. 4 (Oxford: Clarendon Press, 1867-1879) at 732; *Royal Prerogative*, *supra* note 60 at 145d; "Laws of Alfred" in B. Griffiths, *An Introduction to Early English Law* (Norwich, U.K.: Anglo-Saxon Books, 1995) c. 41.

86   Pollock & Maitland, *supra* note 8, vol. 1 at 62-63.

87   Often this is compared with the Gallo-Frankish *precarium*.

was a lesser interest than that enjoyed by the grantor. The term of the arrangement was one to three generations, or a century. A certain quantity of the produce of the land was granted to the holder of the written document. At the expiration of the arrangement, the use returned to the book-land holder. Often, by the end of the arrangement, the family holding the interest in the produce viewed the soil as part of their family land. Thus, the arrangement was often renewed. Although the written documents of book-land and lease-land exist, whether a symbolic or actual delivery of possession was necessary or the exact method by which folk-land was transferred, if it ever was, is unknown.

The Teutonic regime was maintained by external military force, and like all forceful orders, it ended. In the late eighth century, their Scandinavian kinsmen conquered by force the Normandy and British coast. In 1016, Danish King Canute was placed on the English throne, other Norsemen (Normans) taking the Normandy throne in France. Their Norse language was similar to Anglo-Saxon.

D. Norse occupation

The Scandinavian warriors found a familiar society with a decentralized system of laws. The Scandinavians instituted changes to the existing customary order, changing the Anglo-Saxon written word *"ae "* to the Inuit-Old Iceland word *"law."*[88] In 1042, Edward the Confessor, the French-speaking son of the English Aethelred and the Norman Emma who was raised in Normandy, ascended to the English throne. During his reign (1042-1066), Edward introduced the Norman custom of sealing documents and appointed a seal keeper (*cancheler* or *chancellor*) who became the source of fairness in the emerging legal order and in relation to the land.

If it could be said that the Scandinavian kings had a land tenure law, it was the Teutonic law of possession and communal responsibility. We learn about their law only from remnants of written charters and lawsuits involving rights to possession (or *seisin*). The courts determined *seisin*, and a favourable decision only gave one use of particular land without further liability or dispute.[89] They had ideas of rights and duties among the leaders and community over the cattle and harvest, but less precise ideas of *seisin*. Yet these relationships were not regarded as consequences of a grant of land.[90]

Reading retrospectively these various descriptions of occupations, it is not difficult to see the budding of the feudal system of derivative tenures. Indeed, it is easy to link the idea of book-land to charters from the King, and the lease-land to the notion of a residuary interest in the Crown. The rent of honey, corn, or men can be viewed as dependence on a superior. These conceptual links, however, ignore the actual world-

---

88   Mellinkoff, *supra* note 4. The combined form for the Norse law in Old English was *lah*, and on this base were formed *lahmann* (lawman), *lahwita* (one who knows the law) and *byrlah* (village or local law, now bylaw).

89   Lyon, *supra* note 35 at 94-96.

90   The holder of land was said to be at liberty to commend himself or become the man, vassal, or tenant of any lord he pleased (*cum ea ire potuit quo voluit*). Digby, *supra* note 42 at 19, citing H. Hallam, *History of Europe During the Middle Ages*, vol. 2 (New York: Colonial Press, 1899) at 86.

view of the peoples regarding their land. It is an error in methodology, reasoning from the present to the past, to find a pattern that justifies an existing order. Such method ignores the dominant land holdings with no superior, as it ignores the cooperative struggles to survive through the land, and the family and community consciousness that arose in this context.

E. Norman occupation

By many accounts the descendants of the Scandinavian conquerors of western France, the Normans, conquered the Anglo-Saxon people in the Island of Britain in 1066. The Normans were led by William, the Duke of Normandy and cousin of King Edward the Confessor. The feudal law was not introduced by any decree or legislation after the so-called Conquest, although it is claimed that this military victory hurried the process of assimilation between the British and Continental landholding.[91] In the process, the Conquest created the King as lord paramount of all communities as well as the feudal doctrine of tenure. Also, the Conquest is used to justify the Crown's title to all lands in England.[92]

William, Duke of Normandy, did not profess to be a conqueror of England, however.[93] He professed to enter the domain as legitimate occupant of the throne.[94] William's cousins, Harold and his brother Tostig, likewise claimed to be the rightful successors to the throne. While Harold was fighting with his brother and the King of Norway for the Crown, William landed at Peversey to reclaim the Crown. After Harold defeated his brother, he turned to William. At the battle of Hastings, Harold died and William secured the Crown. Although the Anglo-Saxon dynasty ended, the Anglo-Saxon people, their consciousness, and order survived.

On Christmas day 1066, William was crowned "King of English" in Westminster Abbey.[95] By the verbal assent of the assembled Anglo-Saxon lords and people and the Normans, William was acknowledged lawful sovereign. It is important to note that William was not crowned King of Britain. William's mastery or authority was political

---

91 Pollock & Maitland, *supra* note 8, vol. 1 at 63; Holdsworth, *supra* note 8, vol. 2 at 78. These explanations are versions of forceful possession and military force as ordering principles. Why military victory or force should have such an exalted place in any civil or legal system is questionable. It appears to be a precarious order, a questionable means of controlling mutual antagonism and needs, even a dangerous trend in legal treaties.

92 "Title" issued in the international sense to mean political jurisdiction, not as used in British land law; see note 147, *infra*.

93 William had planned an invasion with the assent of the Holy See, but his landing was unopposed. See Freeman, *supra* note 85, vol. 1 at 3, 216-55, 677-707; and vol. 2 at 299-311.

94 Lyon, *supra* note 35 at 34. He made three claims to the kingdom: (1) That he was a cousin of Edward the Confessor by marriage; (2) that upon his visit to England in 1052 Edward had promised him the throne; and (3) that his cousin Harold, while enjoying his hospitality after being shipwrecked on the Norman coast in 1064, had promised upon his oath to support him.

95 P.V.D. Shelly, *English and French in England, 1066-1100* (Folcroft, PA: Folcroft Library Editions, 1970) at 42.

rather than territorial, since feudalism in Britain was primarily a system of control over men. The relations of men to land were undeveloped; the control by men of material objects was incidental to a human bond that unified loyalty.[96] This undeveloped relation was seen as political, but there was no idea of the state or public and private law.[97] Four centuries later, the concept of territorial sovereignty would emerge.[98]

William's claim to the English throne could not and did not displace Anglo-Saxon law with French law. This idea has been traced to the forged writing of the so-called "pseudo-Ingulphus."[99] Far from imposing immediate and drastic change, the command of William was to preserve the laws of King Edward the Confessor in lands as in other things, with the addition of those that he himself had enacted.[100] As wit-

---

96   Later writers would have difficulty conceiving of the original feudal unity. Within the feudally unified control of men they could see notions of propriety or ownership. This is the bias of preconceived notions. For example, Maine describes a *fief* as "an organically complete brotherhood of associates whose proprietary and personal rights were inextricably blended together." Sir H. Maine, *Ancient Law: Its Connection with the Early History of Society and Its Relation to Modern Ideas*, 10th ed. (London: John Murray, 1901) at 352. Pollock & Maitland also wrote, "[i]t is characteristic of the time that rights of sovereignty slide off into rights of property; the same terms and formulas cover them both." Pollock & Maitland, *supra* note 8, vol. 1 at 68; at 230 they state that *dominium*, the root word of dominion, "has to stand now for *ownership* and now for *lordship*"; that is, it covers proprietary rights and political power, ownership, lordship, sovereignty, and suzerainty. In another work, *supra* note 75 at 342-430, Maitland writes that: "At the present day no two legal ideas seem more distinct from each other than that of governmental power and that of proprietary rights ... But though this be so, we can not doubt that could we trace back these ideas to their origin, we should come to a time when they were hardly distinct from each other." Holdsworth, *supra* note 8, vol. 3 at 76, states: "the proprietary element in feudalism was so strongly developed ... that it was sometimes improperly extended to things which should never have been regarded as property." Yet still he also sees, at 462, that, "[p]olitical rights and privileges [under feudalism] were regarded as property; and the King's political rights and privileges—his prerogative—did not escape the influence of this idea."

97   Pollock & Maitland, *supra* note 8, vol. 1 at 230-31, 384. For example, on the King's personal lands, the "ancient demesne," where he was himself lord of the manor, the "customs of the manor" assumed equal authority with the law of land, since both alike were the exercise of royal jurisdiction.

98   See Part II, below.

99   An ancient, though false, tale relates that William made French the language of the English law. In a "history," since proven to be a fourteenth-century forgery, the false Ingulf wrote that the Normans of 1066 detested the English and abhorred their language; and that "the Laws of the Land" and even "the Statutes of the English Kings" were written and pleaded in French. Sir Francis Palgrave, "Review of the Pseudo-Ingulphus" (1826) 34 Quarterly Rev. 248 at 294. This false tale was promoted in the fifteenth century by Sir J. Fortescue, *De laudibus legum angliae* (New York: Garland Pub., 1979) [reprint] and in the seventeenth century in a tract by John Selden, "The Reserve or Back-Face of the English Janus" in *Tracts written by John Selden*, found in Mellinkoff, *supra* note 4 at 63-65. Yet, the written languages of the law after William were Latin and English, with Latin far in the lead. There is no evidence that an attempt was made to force French into its unaccustomed role in Britain. The first use of French in an official document is not until the thirteenth century, the year of *Magna Carta*. See Freeman, *supra* note 85, vol. 5 at 530. By 1362, French was the language of legal pleading. The best guess is that the spoken language of the law was trilingual–Anglo-Saxon, French, and Latin. See Mellinkoff, *supra* note 4 at 69.

100 A.J. Robertson, ed., *The Laws of the Kings of England from Edmund to Henry I* (Cambridge, U.K.: Cambridge University Press, 1925) at 240.

nessed by William's Charter of the City of London, he promised the French and English residents the law as it was in King Edward's day.[101] Similarly, the Saxon heir of Shirboune Castle successfully petitioned for the Castle although it had been donated to a Norman companion-in-arms of William I.[102] The Norman Conquest did not introduce a comprehensive system of feudalism into Britain.[103] What the Conquest brought to the Teutonic domain was certain administrative changes based on the only political system the Scandinavian-Normans knew—continental feudalism. While these changes did not greatly alter existing customs, they had radical historical effects, culminating in a centralized kingdom, legislative bodies, and new courts. These processes created a feudal law.

By 1085, William I had consolidated political control of Britain. Some historians have sought to assign the beginning of feudal law of tenure to this year, citing the *Anglo-Saxon Chronicle* for 1085,[104] and asserting that William I became the only real owner of the lands. Yet this myth has two problems: first, such conceptualization cannot be traced to Norman law in France;[105] and second, the concept of "ownership" can-

---

101   The Charter stated, in Anglo-Saxon: "*Will'm kyng gret ... ealle pa burhwaru binnan Londone Frencisce and Englisce freondlice; and ic kyde eow pat ic wylle pat get beon eallra paera laga weorde pe gyt waeran on Eadwerdes daege kynges.*" This is found in William Stubbs, ed., *Select Charters and Other Illustrations of English Constitutional History From the Earliest Times to the Reign of Edward the First* (Oxford: Clarendon Press, 1913) at 97. The translation into modern English is the following: "William, king, greets ... all the burghers within London, French and English, friendly; and I do you to wit that I will that ye two be worthy of all the laws that ye were worthy of in King Edward's day." This is found in Mellinkoff, *supra* note 4 at 66-67.

102   *Case of Tanistry* (1608), Dav. Ir. 28 at 41.

103   See Robert Kelham, ed., *The Laws of William the Conqueror with Notes and References* (London: Printed for Edward Brooke, successor to Messrs. Worrall and Tovey, 1779). This is a twelfth-century compilation of ten volumes, purporting to be the various legal enactments made by William during his reign. These laws supplemented and revised the Anglo-Saxon law confirmed by William in one of the enactments of the collection. The other sources are the fraudulent *Laws of Edward the Confessor.* See F. Liebermann, ed., *Leges Edwardi Confessoris,* (Halle, De.: S.M. Niemeyer, 1896) [hereinafter *Leges Edwardi*].

104   C. Plummer and J. Earl., eds., *Two of the Saxon Chronicles Parallel: With Supplementary Extracts from the Others* (Oxford: Clarendon Press, 1892-99) at 217.

105   E. Z. Tabuteau, *Transfers of Property in Eleventh-Century Norman Law* (Chapel Hill: University of North Carolina Press, 1989) at 95-108. Tabuteau states, at 97-98, that: "While certain words like *proprietas* (or *proprius*), *hereditas, alodium,* and *ius,* and *dominium* could imply full ownership, when looked at in the context of the existing Norman charters these five words do not evidence any theory of lay ownership." In Norman law, the words *proprietas* and *dominium* meant not ownership but direct exploitation. The words *hereditas* and *alodium* were virtually interchangeable. By the middle of the century, they were used for possessions that were held of lords for service (at 108). *Hereditas* described property that one's ancestors had also possessed on a permanent basis and that no ancestor had alienated permanently from the familial line of descent, regardless of whether such possession was held from a superior (at 101). *Alodium* in Normandy did not mean a possession that was owned absolutely (as it came to mean in the rest of French law), but rather "to be held of Lords," just as inheritances did (at 102). *Ius* had a wide range of meanings, but its actual use was "of my right," meaning that a person had a solid legal right, as opposed to some other claimant, but it did not define the right (at 106).

not be applied to eleventh-century law in Britain.[106] In British legal thought, the word "owner" dates from the mid-fourteenth century (1340), "ownership" from the late sixteenth century (1583), and "property," to refer to a man's valuable belongings, from the eighteenth century.[107] The place these words occupy in modern thought was occupied by the Teutonic concept of "*seisin*."[108]

Before Christmas 1085, William I held a great court at Gloucester to figure out how the land was occupied and with what sort of people. These questions were answered in the *Domesday Book*,[109] but in terms of the Anglo-Saxon hundred rather than the Norman *fiefs*.[110] In another great council in 1086 at Salisbury, William demanded oaths of fealty from royal tenants and undertenants. This process created a king to whom all free subjects owed their supreme loyalty in a form of order known as the "manorial system"[111] or feudalism.[112] William leased all the land in Britain to his tenants-in-chief on condition that they provide him with an army of five thousand knights, each of whom served for 40 days a year. The duty to furnish knights was part of the feudal land, which thus was said to be held in knight's service. The tenure, or "fee," could not be split up in such a way as to deprive the superior lord of his knight's service and other feudal dues ("incidents of tenure").[113]

The English manorial system, though short-lived, was long remembered.[114] It comprised landholding for services, involving a personal relationship of loyalty and

---

106   A.S. Diamond, *Primitive Law, Past and Present* (London: Methuen, 1971) at 260-61.

107   S. Francis, *Property* (New York: Collier and Son, 1939) at 24.

108   *Ibid.* at 36-69. Also see, J.C. Smith, "The Unique Nature of the Concept of Western Law" (1968) Can. Bar Rev. 46 at 198-202.

109   *Libre censualis, vocati Domesday-Book, additamenta ex codicantiquiss: exon domesday, inquisitio eliensis, liber Winton, Boldon book* (London: Eyre and Strahan, 1816) [hereinafter *Domesday Book*]. This book supplies a wealth of detail about the condition of the land and the people who held and worked it, and an accurate account of the incomes due the lords and king yearly. Holdsworth, *supra* note 8, vol. 2 at 183, remarks that the assumption made by the Domesday commissioners was, "that all land was held of some one" and the object of Domesday survey, "was to provide a new basis of assessment for the levy of a direct tax imposed on the land"(at 156). This was not a feudal tax; instead it was a modern one in the guise of an ancient tax like the Danegeld, an annual tax to raise funds for the protection against Danish invaders. The important point is that the political domain had begun to control an economy, rather than be based on land.

110   J.H. Round, *Feudal England: Historical Studies on the Eleventh and Twelfth Centuries* (London: Swan, Sonnenschein & Co., 1895) at 236.

111   Maitland, *supra* note 75 at 108 writes, "The term *manerium* seems to have come in with the Conqueror."

112   The terms "feudalism" and "feudal society" were invented in the eighteenth century during the Enlightenment. Prior to that time people spoke and wrote about feudal law, referring to the system of rights and obligations associated with lord-vassal relationships and dependent land tenures in the Middle Ages. H.J. Berman, *Law and Revolution: The Formation of the Western Legal Tradition* (Cambridge, Mass.: Harvard University Press, 1983) at 295-97.

113   *Ibid.* at 440.

114   "Pure feudalism had but a short life in England." Digby, *supra* note 42 at 41.

protection, a bond of union as close as that of kinship.[115] The ceremony of homage states, "I become your man of the tenement that I hold of you ... "[116] William I used the existing system of landholding to organize the fiscal feudalism, the economic structure of the kingdom.[117] He expanded the Anglo-Saxon *witan* into the Great Council (*Magna Curia*), the composition of which was not fixed. Typically, it was composed of the King and all his landed lords, other magnates, and eminent ecclesiastics. The Council advised the King on matters of state, decided cases between the disputing tenants in chief, accomplished accords between Church and state, and acted as a legislature.[118]

William I's political jurisdiction had a military component. When he sought the administration of his personal relationship between lord and men and shires government, including law and the courts of law, some barons refused to grant him loyalty. William and his Norman and Teutonic lords forced those who refused into fealty. The Norman unification was a slow and tedious conflict. Five years of scattered fighting concentrated the loose Anglo-Saxon lords under loyalty to the King. In some places, the process is said to have involved the virtual genocide of Anglo-Saxon society.[119] After 20 years, it is stated that the number of Anglo-Saxons holding book-land had been reduced from five thousand to two.[120] The resisting barons' book-land was confiscated and redistributed to the King's Court (*Curia Regis*), mostly to Norman loyalists.[121] The King's Court also decided controversies between the courtiers who held their land from the King, although these actions were considered disciplinary jurisdiction on the part of the King, not proprietary interest.

2. The Enigmatic Construction of the Common Law

How the old Teutonic codes[122] were transformed into a theory of customary or interactive laws, called the common law, remains an enigma. In Europe, these codes

---

115 Sir. W. Markby, *Elements of Law, Considered with Reference to Principles of General Jurisprudence*, 6th ed. (Oxford: Clarendon Press, 1905) at 176.

116 Pollock & Maitland, *supra* note 8, vol. 1 at 297. C.R. Noyes, *The Institution of Property* (Toronto: Longmans, Green, 1936) at 236, interpreted this ceremony to mean: "I am your subject, under your rule and jurisdiction, and in your service. I am resident of a certain tract of land which is owed to your domain, but over which I have certain rights and privileges."

117 Sir W. Blackstone, *Commentaries on the Laws of England*, vol. 2 (Oxford: Clarendon Press, 1762-69) at 48-51, thought the Anglo-Saxon had freely accepted this system. Vinogradoff 1905, *supra* note 28 at 293-96, argues that the system was imposed.

118 From this Council, the House of Lords ultimately emerged, and the House of Commons was added later in the thirteenth century.

119 F. G. Kempin, Jr., *Historical Introduction to Anglo-American Law in a Nutshell* (St. Paul, MN: West Publishing Co., 1973) at 114-15.

120 *Ibid.*

121 KG. Feiling, *A History of England: From the Coming of the English to 1918* (London: Macmillan,1950) at 82-83.

122 See notes 46-49, *supra*.

became the foundation for a civil law system, but in Britain they did not. Instead, in the century after the introduction of the Norman administration to Britain, scattered information about Anglo-Saxon customary law and codes appeared in private compilations of customs and formularies (*custumals*). These overt legal writings, beginning in the reign of Henry I (1100-1135), purport to help explain the development of the customary law of Britain, the "ubiquitous and ambiguous" concept of "common law."[123] Several attempts professed to restate the Anglo-Saxon laws in light of the Norman administrative changes. Prime among doctrinal writings by unknown authors is a volume known as *Laws of Henry (Leges Henrici)*[124] that attempts to bring the laws of Edward the Confessor (1042-1066) up to date with the new order. This book, perhaps the earliest law book after the Conquest, had little influence in the development of law. Sir Frederick Pollock and Frederic W. Maitland in *The History of English Law* wrote:

> At first sight the outcome [of the book] seems to be a mere jumble of fragments; rules brought from the most divers quarters are thrown into a confused heap. But the more closely we examine the books, the more thoroughly convinced we shall be that its author has undertaken a serious task in a serious spirit; he means to state the existing law of the land, to state it in what he thinks to be rational, and even a philosophical form. But the task is beyond his powers ... . If [parts of the book] paint English law as a wonderful confusion, they may yet be painting it correctly, and before we use hard words of him who wrote them, we should remember that he was engaged on an utterly new task, new in England, new in Europe: he was writing a legal text-book, a text-book of law that was neither Roman nor Canon law.[125]

In the same reign, another book, *Laws of Edward the Confessor,* appeared. It purported to be a collection of laws in force in Britain at the time of the Conquest derived from jury inquest. Pollock and Maitland wrote that the book "was a private work of a bad and untrustworthy kind":

> It has about it something of the political pamphlet and is adorned with pious legends ... . Unfortunately, however, the patriotic and ecclesiastical learning of his book made it the most popular of all the old lawbooks. In the thirteenth century it was venerable; even Bracton quoted from it ... . It has gone on doing its bad work down to our own time.[126]

This work guided the courts and subsequent great books of the British feudal law, especially Henry de Bracton's work, *On the Laws and Customs of England* (1256), Thomas de Littleton's *Tenures* (1481), Lord Coke's *Institutes* (1641-1644),[127] of which

---

123 A.G. Gulliver, *Cases and Materials on the Law of Future Interests* (St. Paul, Minn.: West Publishing Co., 1959) at 36.

124 L.J. Downer, ed., *Leges Henrici primi*, trans. L. J. Downer (Oxford: Clarendon Press, 1972) [hereinafter *Leges Henrici*]. See also *Leges Edwardi, supra* note 103.

125 Pollock & Maitland, *supra* note 8, vol. 1 at 99-101.

126 *Ibid.* at 103-04.

127 Sir E. Coke, *The First Part of the Institutes of the Law of England: Or a Commentary on Littleton's Tenures,* 15th ed. by Hargave and Butler (London: E. & R. Brooke, 1794).

the first volume is a *Commentary on Littleton's Tenures*.[128] Although, in the nineteenth century the *Laws of Edward the Confessor* was revealed as a forgery, this revelation came too late; the common law tradition had been built on a fraudulent foundation.[129]

Three new doctrinal writings characterized the emerging royal law and equity built upon partly forged doctrines of the customary law. The first treatise, *Treatise on the Laws and Customs of the Kingdom of England* (1187), was procedural, and was concerned with the 50 royal writs of law administered by the King's court.[130] This book recorded the beginning of the King's courts under the regime of Henry II (1154-1189). After *Magna Carta* in 1215,[131] the second book appeared: Bracton's, *On the Laws and Customs of England (1256)*.[132] It was an unfinished commentary on the more than 250 royal writs and records of King's Court of Common Pleas. The first legal treatise emerging from the Inns of Court, where lawyers and students lived and learned the traditions of the royal law, it was the only authoritative statement of British law in existence. Yet we do not know how much it reflects existing laws or customs of Britain or is the result of Bracton's studies of Roman law at Bologna. In some places in his unfinished treatise, Bracton has inserted civil-law concepts to fill the gaps of the still incomplete writ law. Rarely does he mention the Teutonic codes.

These frauds are particularly damaging to British legal history because until the reign of Edward I (1272-1307), no single place existed to look for case law on which legal research or precedents might be based. The law books referred to certain cases, traditions carried them forward, and the plea rolls of the courts contained some information, but the exact wording of the decisions was eternally lost. No reliable system of reporting cases or distinct hierarchy of courts developed until the nineteenth century.

In the middle of Edward I's reign, in the year of the enactment of the statute *Quia emptores*,[133] that prohibited the creation of new tenures by anyone except the Crown, the third doctrinal writing appeared: *The Mirror of Justices*.[134] The *Mirror of Justices*

---

128 *Littleton's Tenures* is found in T.E. Tomlins, *Lyttleton, His Treatise on Tenures*, 1841 ed. (New York: Garland Publishing, 1978) [reprint].

129 Canon law has its own history of frauds: the false decretals concocted by the Pseudo-Isidore, and the forged book of capitularies by Benedict and others. The Holy See accepted these books, which argued for the grandeur and superhuman origins of ecclesiastical power. On this false law the universal Catholic Church was founded. Pollack & Maitland, *supra* note 8, vol. 1 at 16-17. See also the *Donation of Constantine*, known in Latin as the *Constitutum Constantini*, which purported to hand temporal power over the constitution of the Christian Empire to the Papacy. A recent text is that of Horst Fuhrmann, ed., *Das Constitutum Constantini*, trans. Horst Fuhrmann (Hannover, De.: Hahn, 1968).

130 Trans. John Beames (Washington, D.C.: J. Byrne, 1900). The author is unknown, but the work has been attributed to Lord Ranulph de Glanville, a Chief Justiciar under Henry II.

131 1215 (U.K.), 17 John, c. 29; this was reconfirmed by Edward I with his seal in 1297 [hereinafter *Magna Carta*].

132 Henry de Bracton, *De Legibus et Consuetudinibus Angliae*, ed. by Sir Travers Twiss, trans. S.E. Thorne (London: Longman, 1878-83); *On the Law and Customs of England*, trans. S.E. Thorne (Cambridge, Mass.: Belknap Press for Harvard University, 1968).

133 *Quia emptores terrarum*, 1290 (U.K.), 18 Edw. I, c. 1 [hereinafter *Quia emptores*].

134 Andrew Horne, *The Mirror of Justices*, ed. by W.J. Whittaker (London: B. Quaritch, 1895).

purported to describe the current law in light of the law of King Alfred and to fill the gaps left by the customary law. Yet by the late eighteenth century, Pollock and Maitland describe it too as a fraud:

> As for the deliberate fables of later apocryphal authorities, the "Mirror of Justices" being the chief and flagrant example, they belong not to the Anglo-Saxon but to a much later period of English law. For the most part they are not even false history; they are speculation or satire.[135]

Littleton, Lord Coke, and indirectly Blackstone relied on this book. Thus in the formative stage of the legal profession and the Inns of Court, the sources of false law were all-pervasive.[136]

Also during Edward I's reign, the compilation of Year Books began a three-century practice infected with false sources of "law." The volumes of the first century were an extremely informal collection by year of notes of cases and judgments taken by lawyers and students. They were not organized according to subject matter, did not include all cases or cases in their entirety, lacked official approval, and were censored to conform to existing beliefs about the legal system.

Further, codes of false law were enacted. For example, James III's Scottish Parliament declared a set of rules known as *Leges Malcolmi* to be the authentic law of the realm. Ascribed to Malcolm II (1005-1034), these rules indicate that feudalism was established in Scotland before it reached the rest of Britain or was fully developed in France (from where feudalism was supposed to have come). Later scholars were prepared to believe the *Leges* to be genuine, but the work of Malcolm III (1058-1093).[137] More modern research, however, tends to indicate that the *Leges* were not authentic, and ascribes the rules to the reign of David I (1124-1153).[138]

British common law, including its case analysis and its professional legal education, was trapped within its fraudulent sources. Ironically, the British common lawyers were distinctly hostile to the idea that a judge could make law rather than discover it, although their own royal and common law were fabricated on such manipulated principles. Such pervasive false law contaminating the common law must be acknowledged and confronted by modern lawyers, with profound consequences for legal thought. Most lawyers and legal historians have accepted the fraudulent foundations of the common law as true legal descriptions of the past. From our perspective, it is difficult to see even partial truths in the best-supported descriptions of the past. With this caution about the manipulation of legal principles in construction of British law, let us look at the particular structure of British land law in the British feudal period.

---

135 Pollock & Maitland, *supra* note 8, vol. 1 at 28.

136 With the monopoly created by the Inns of Court from 1292, the law had to grow by drawing on its own resources (even if fraudulent), and not by borrowing from others.

137 Lord Kames, *Elucidations Respecting the Common and Statute Law of Scotland* (Edinburgh: printed for William Creech; and sold in London by T. Cadell, 1777).

138 Hume-Brown, *supra* note 13 at 70; Ross, *supra* note 75, vol. 2 at 60.

A. Teutonic *seisin*

The existing Anglo-Saxon order, based on the Teutonic concept of *seisin*,[139] retained its vitality and refractoriness.[140] In the late eleventh century and in the twelfth century, *seisin* had emerged as a distinctive legal concept throughout Europe, including Britain. Part of the feudal concept of divided interests and of the canonist concept of due process of law,[141] *seisin* characterized the situation of persons who "held" land or goods without the ability to dispose of them to others. For at least three centuries after William I, British law had only a relatively better right of *seisin,* or better right to enjoy through actual use.[142] No other word existed to describe "possession" in British law. Land transfers involved a "livery of *seisin*," which established that physical presence on the land created a person's title to land. It "seeped up from the soil and in the following two or three centuries succeeded in disintegrating and digesting feudalism for its own economic purposes."[143]

Seisin represented the connection among people and the land and things.[144] Interweaving factual and legal elements, *seisin* did not mean simply factual occupation or physical control of the land, as did the older Roman law concept of possession (*possessio*).[145] It was independent of the law of agreements, and a concept unknown to either Germanic or Roman law. While it carried a valid claim to continue the factual connection derived from actual occupation,[146] it transformed physical use into a certain procedural remedy for goods or to the land.[147] A person seised of land, goods, or rights, even a vassal, could not be removed by force by his lord.[148] As between parties, the language of reciprocal obligations was spoken. Proprietary language is inappropriate since *seisin* was not conceived of as an abstract legal right against all other people, which allowed one to enjoy one's land or things.[149] As legal historian S.F.C. Milsom

---

139 In Latin this concept was "*saisina*."

140 Hume-Brown, *supra* note 13 at 36-69.

141 Berman, *supra* note 112 at 313.

142 Pollock & Maitland, *supra* note 8, vol. 2 at 31. *Seisin* could be construed, loosely, as legal possession. Also see the "Laws of Howel Dda" in A. Kocourek and J.H. Wigmore, eds., *Evolution of Law Series: Sources of Ancient and Primitive Law*, vol. 1 (Boston: Little, Brown & Co., 1915) at 542-43. These are the "Ancient Laws" of Wales.

143 Noyes, *supra* note 116 at 231.

144 Lord Kames, *Historical Law Tracts* (Edinburgh: Printed for A. Millar, London; and A. Kincaid, and J. Bell Edinburgh, 1758), thought the same was evident in the Scottish law. He states, at 83, that, "in the original concept of property, possession was an essential circumstance, and ... when the latter was lost, the former could not longer subsist."

145 Berman, *supra* note 112 at 445. *Seisin* was split into *seisin animo* ("mental seisin") and *seisin corpore* ("physical seisin").

146 *Ibid.* at 313, 453-57.

147 McNeil, *supra* note 3 at 10-17. Within British land law, "title" is used to describe either the manner or conditions in which real property is acquired as well as the inevitable legal consequence of the acquisition.

148 Berman, *supra* note 112 at 313. This is related to the forcible ejection of the possessor in canon law called *spoliatio* ("spoliation" or "despoiling" at 240).

149 Smith, *supra* note 108.

explains, the linguistic operations were to transform British law in the thirteenth century:

> The appropriate language is that of obligation, and the terms used all involve two persons. A tenement is not a lawyer's long word for a parcel of land, but what a tenant holds of a lord for service. A tenant is not just one physically in possession but one who has been seised by a lord. The Lord seises the tenant of his tenement, and to seise is as much a transitive verb as to disseise: the subject of both was a lord and the object was a tenant. It was probably outside interference that brought about the linguistic shift, and the process may have begun before the assize. Suppose a royal command in a common passive form: cause such a tenant to be seised, or be re-seised, of such land ... . To be seised denotes a condition rather than an event, a relationship between person and land which can be discussed without necessary reference to the lord. This generates a new noun; and 'seisin' will describe the condition which is protected ... . The original active use of the verb disappears. Lords and others may disseise, but nobody seises a tenant. Indeed, the transitive came to have the land for its object: a lord will seise the tenement into his own hand. To describe the original transaction, a separate verb has to be combined with the noun. The lord puts his tenant in *seisin* or makes *seisin* to him ... . Even in such a case the point comes to be that a conveyance has not been completed rather than that a relationship has not been created ... . As between lord and tenant and within lordship, there is hardly room for any deeper proprietary concept. Seisin itself connotes not just factual possession but that signorial acceptance which is all the title there can be ... . But the question of title to a tenement would not arise during the tenure of a tenant fulfilling his obligations. It was only about the beginning and ending of the relationship that decisions had to be made: Who would be seised in the first place and has the man seised so acted as to justify his being disseised? The latter question is the subject-matter of the disciplinary jurisdiction. It is from the former that the proprietary jurisdiction and deep proprietary ideas seems to grow.[150]

The British feudal law protected *seisin* and the various "rights" that flowed from *seisin*; it did not know the distinction between *seisin* and possession, much less ownership.[151] *Seisin* was necessary for the transfer and acquisition of any right, interest, and eventual title to the land. If the actual occupation or use were lost, people lost their rights to the land and their ability to do some important acts.

The operation of *seisin* is the reason for British law's apparently illogical treatment of wrongful occupiers. British feudal law always required that the land should be in the possession of someone, and under the jurisdiction of a lord. If no possessor existed, who would be responsible for the performance of obligations to the Crown or lord? Feudal services could not be enforced against a person not in possession of the land.

---

150 S.F.C. Milsom, *The Legal Framework of English Feudalism* (Cambridge, U.K.: Cambridge University Press, 1976) at 39-41.

151 F.W. Maitland, "The Mystery of *Seisin*" in *The Collected Papers of Frederic William Maitland*, vol. 1 (Cambridge, U.K.: Cambridge University Press, 1911) at 359. However, Bracton tells us that the distinction became necessary once it was established that both the freeholder and the tenant for years had occupation of the same land. In order to keep these rights separate, "*seisin*" was reserved for freeholders, and possession for the tenant for years. See Bracton, *supra* note 132.

Consequently, to ensure the continuity of services, someone had to be in possession of the land.[152] It was the actual possessor whose heir's infancy gave the lord a military tenement and a right to wardship and marriage; it was the actual possessor's wife who received the dower of the land; it was the actual possessor who died a bastard without issue, whose land escheated to the lord.[153] Presuming that the man who was actually in possession had a right to be seised, British law did not look for book-land, or *de jure* title, tenure, or estates. This assumption was transformed into the rule that there must never be an abeyance of *seisin* in British law,[154] that there shall always be somebody effectively seised of the land.

The British doctrine of escheats was based on the principle that if at any time the lord of the manor was without a tenant, or one capable of holding land, the interest ceased to exist and the land "belonged" to the lord. The idea of an actual being on or using the land meant that for many purposes the developing royal law would treat a wrongful occupier or possessor (a disseisor) as a valid occupier or possessor. An occupier is a person who is physically on the land,[155] and the courts would affirm a possessor under the category of a "title by occupancy." However, the courts would not apply the title of occupancy to those whose possession was unexplained or known to be wrongful. Indeed, court decisions dealing with *disseisin* demonstrate the court's ability to detect wrongful *seisin*.

Seisin's significance for operation in the development of the feudal law is illustrated by the methods of transferring or conveying use of land to another, the process or livery of *seisin*.[156] It must be remembered that written documents, such as book-land and lease-land, were not the "best evidence" of a transfer of land.[157] What counted was the primitive ritual of physical transfer of tenure or use, the livery of *seisin* memorialized in feudal legal consciousness by the transfer of bits of earth and its produce from the hand of the old user to the hand of the new user, both physically present on the premises.[158] When writing came to be used for a symbolic delivery of possession, the document was laid upon the ground, and the deed was picked up instead of the bits of earth. The grantor (*feoffor*) would vacate the land, taking his goods with him; the

---

152 This notion is as strong in modern British law, under the theory of adverse possession. After illegally squatting on a piece of land for a certain time (usually 12 years) without the least excuse to be there, and without acknowledging title in someone else, the land will become theirs. There is no "positive prescription" vesting the title in the squatter, but the rights of the true owner are, in effect, destroyed. In areas where title is registered in Britain, a squatter acquires the equitable estate and on proof of occupancy may obtain rectification of the register in his favour. See the *Limitation Act*, 1939 (U.K.), 2 & 3 Geo.VI, c. 21, s. 16.

153 Maitland, *supra* note 151 at 369-72.

154 E.H. Burn, ed., *Cheshire's Modern law of real property*, 12th ed. (London: Butterworths, 1976), c. 23.

155 McNeil, *supra* note 3 at 73.

156 In law French this word designated delivery of possession.

157 Holdsworth, *supra* note 8, vol. 9 at 164.

158 Pollock & Maitland, *supra* note 8, vol. 2 at 84-86.

grantee (*feoffee*) would take physical possession.[159] The essence of the ceremony was that one could not give what one did not have. As Maitland explains:

> You cannot give what you have not got: this seems clear; but put just the right accent on the words give and got, and we have reverted to an old way of thinking. You can't give a thing if you haven't got that thing, and you haven't got that thing if some one else has got it.[160]

Paradoxically, once the judicial necessity for a public livery of *seisin* had been established, the history of land conveyances in the royal law involved creative attempts to avoid court interpretation. Other methods of conveying land such as those of the fine, common recovery, or lease and release, equally revolved around a delivery of possession, without which there could be no conveyance.[161] Often transferring the land required both a written document and a livery of *seisin* or public handing over the land to a new landholder. The written document became public evidence or title of the actual physical delivery having taken place;[162] however, the actual physical delivery up of the land, the transfer of *seisin* itself,[163] remained essential. Actual *seisin* (or its derivative concepts of occupation or possession) proved so intractable that the courts substituted the standard of "linear time."[164] In other words, an initial act or document at some point in time created a right of occupation or possession that continued until its time was terminated by some other act.

The inscrutable British rules about humans in possession of land and their legal "titles" were derived from the dominating, but untidy, concept of *seisin*. No one can be certain exactly what *seisin* was or that it ever existed to the extent it is presumed. *Seisin* is a term of old Germanic law. It seems a metaphysical concept that contemplated moral duties involving loyalty and protection between two people. Legally, it could support the inference of forcible occupation or seizing possession in a law of violence. It asserts that when one seized land, one actually sat on the land. Coke argued that it suggested peace and quiet: he who is in possession may sit down in rest and quiet.[165]

Littleton's *Tenures* (1481) introduced the Roman law term "possession" to distinguish possession of chattels from land.[166] In the thirteenth century, *seisin* had come to mean "possession." By the fifteenth century, *seisin* came to mean a freehold posses-

---

159 The common law conveyances arise in the period after William I to the *Statute of Uses* of 1535; see Gulliver, *supra* note 123.

160 Maitland, *supra* note 151 at 372.

161 Smith, *supra* note 108 at 202.

162 In Scotland, the Celtic traditions provided that livery of *seisin* had to take place on the site of the land to be transferred, and in the presence of neighbours as witnesses.

163 In the open-field system of cultivation it was very difficult to describe accurately a conveyance of a piece of land in a written document.

164 F. Pollock and R.S. Wright, *An Essay on Possession in the Common Law* (Oxford: Clarendon Press, 1888) at 1-42.

165 See generally Pollock & Maitland, *supra* note 8, vol. 2 at 29-80.

166 Smith, *supra* note 108.

sion, while "possession" itself referred to a leasehold possession. It was only in the 1830s that the term *seisin* transformed to "possession, and possession became confused with 'title.'"[167]

Kent McNeil argues that possession represents a conclusion of law and an intention. The conclusion of law arises from a sufficiently close physical relationship between a person and a parcel of land, due to one's presence on or control over it, personally or through a servant, agent, or the like. The intention is to hold the parcel of land for one's own purposes.[168] Professor McNeil distinguishes a possessor who has an unexplained, or known to be wrongful, physical presence on (or actual control of) the land. Although the possessor cannot claim title by occupancy or a specific derivative tenure, depending on the circumstances, such a person can rely on some legal "title" or evidence:

> While in possession, a mere possessor has the *title that goes with possession* [as against other trespassers and adverse claimants who cannot show a better title]. In addition, he has a *presumptive title* [under British law from competing people who have no better title or entitling conditions], provided his possession has not been shown to be wrongful by proof of a *jus tertii*. If he remains in possession long enough he will also acquire a *title by limitation* [or time against the world], due to which he will no longer be a mere possessor because his possession will then be supported by a known right. If he loses possession, he will *lose the title that goes with possession*, but retain his *presumptive title* and the *title by limitation* (if acquired). If ousted, he will also have a prima facie *title by being wrongfully dispossessed* [to recover possession, unless the ouster was lawful]. Any one of the last three titles, if unrebutted, will enable him to recover possession in ejectment or, as it has been known since 1875, an action for the recovery of land, against a defendant who cannot show a better title in himself.[169]

Even today, this concept of *seisin* resides in the possessive adjectives of the English language and world-view. English-speakers often speak of a person's house when referring to the place he or she occupies as an owner, as a tenant for years, or without legal rights at all. The English language has preserved an ancient simplicity that the analytical language of the law has obscured. To the English mind, one who occupies land is equated with having the most intimate connection with it, more than anyone else can possibly have. This, we suggest, is the ancient simplicity behind the concept of folk-land and *seisin*. It helps explain why the British common law was so favourable to the actual possessor of the land and resistant to aristocratic presumptions of tenure in feudal and manorial law and judicial procedures.

B. Feudal law

The term "feudalism" or "feudal society" was invented in the eighteenth century to define the privileged nobility and subject peasantry that became associated with the

---

167 McNeil, *supra* note 3 at 8, n. 3.

168 *Ibid.* at 6.

169 *Ibid.* at 77.

Middle Ages.[170] From the twelfth century to the Enlightenment, however, feudal law and manorial law, as distinct branches of customary law, were the conceptual categories of the European aristocracy. Feudal law referred primarily to the belief system shared by ecclesiastical and secular authorities, as well as the system of obligations and duties associated with lord-vassal relationships (fealty) and dependent land tenures (*fiefs*). Manorial law regulated the lord-peasant relations, agricultural production, and manorial life.[171] Complicating the picture, during this period mercantile, urban, and royal law overlapped.[172]

In the integrated concept of feudal law,[173] the forms of personal and economic subjection of vassal to lords transformed into reciprocal obligation and taxes. Feudal law through participatory justice ensured a lord's capacity to hold consultative assemblies to deliberate common concerns and to establish court procedures over his tenants. The combination of government and the affirmation of use and disposition of the land created lordship and affirmed the authority to hold courts and declare law.[174] The idea of feudal tenure was created though the civil procedure of the writ system in royal courts.[175] In Britain and France, unlike Germany, no separate conceptualization of land body was erected out of the customary law of the land (*landrecht* or *lex terrae*) or feudal law (*lehnrecht*).[176] The doctrine of tenures (services that tenants owed the King) never occurred to the feudal law, since neither Littleton's treatise on *Tenures* nor Lord Coke's *Commentary on Littleton* ever mentioned or alluded to the doctrines.

Customary values created the procedural rules of the writ system that defined who had *seisin* of the land through claims (*meritum*), not fundamental rights (*ius*). Courts resolved conflicting claims of *seisin* and services, gradually discovering a theory of land law that constructed duration in time as a measure for resolving competing claims.

Precipitated partially by an unexplained crisis of the land or the legal order in 1166, during the reign of Henry II (1154-1189), there began a series of petitions to the King and events that ultimately resulted in a system of royal courts and a law common to all Britain. These resulting forms of action incrementally and mystically transformed the competing visions of "rights" to land from procedural law and evidence to substantive rights.

---

170   Berman, *supra* note 112 at 295-97.

171   *Ibid.* at 295, 316-32.

172   *Ibid.* at 311, also cc. 11 "mercantile law," 12 "urban law," and 13 "royal law" at 333-519.

173   *Ibid.* at 319.

174   *Ibid.* at 312. The legal term used to express these authorities was the Latin concept of *dominium*; however, feudal *dominium* was not absolute but was usually limited, divided, and shared in a variety of ways.

175   The word "court" has been used in many senses. The early British royal councils were referred to as *curiae* or courts since the earliest justices were members of the King's Council. The word derives from the Latin word *curia* and was originally used to refer to the rectangular enclosed yard of a medieval house. It came to refer to a group of aristocrats either formally or informally gathered together.

176   Berman, *supra* note 112 at 311.

Britain was divided into local units (villages), hundreds (groups of villages), shires (counties), towns, and feudal units (manors headed by a feudal lord). Historically, the customary trial in manorial courts in conflicting *seisin* claims was judicial combat, or "pleas of the sword," the domestic law version of the international law idea of the law of war or conquest. Plaintiffs in such claims had to offer battle, or wage battle through a champion. The king could interfere only when justice was not done.

In the name of protecting the heritage of the past against new challenges, Henry II created alternatives to "pleas of the sword" by introducing the grand assize and the letter (*writ*) of right from the King.[177] These writs were designed to set forth a narrow factual test for determining which of two individuals had the claim of *seisin*; questions were submitted to a sworn inquest (jury) of neighbours. These writs established a royal jurisdiction over issuance of the writs and the proceeding of the jury.[178] Henry II enforced the rule that no freeman had to answer for his *seisin* without the King's writ.[179] No matter where the suit, a royal writ had to be purchased in order to initiate a claim for *seisin* or *disseisin*.

The writ of grand assize gave the tenant the ability to decline the trial of uncertain and dangerous combat in favour of purchasing a writ to have the dispute settled in a royal court. The parties could purchase a licence to conclude a settlement out of court or a final accord. Alternatively, four knights of the tenant's community were chosen to elect a jury of 12 knights who were required under oath to say which party had the better right to *seisin* of lands.[180]

A letter from the King, a writ of right (*breve de recto*), directed the lord to do justice between the lesser lords or tenants, and warned that if justice were not done the sheriff would settle the dispute,[181] or, alternatively, the King would hear the case. The writ of right, guaranteeing that no man would be deprived of his land without a judgment, provided a basis for what later was called "due process" of law. Later, the writ of rights was issued directly to the defendant, on the strength of the fiction that the lords had surrendered to the King their right to hold court, thus bypassing the manorial court and bringing land cases directly into the royal courts.

To remedy the defects arising from these writs dealing with *disseisin*, Henry II devised three new writs in the royal courts called the petty (later possessory) assizes.[182] The petty assize of *novel disseisin* (recent dispossession) held that no freeman could be dispossessed of his land unjustly and without judgment before a royal justice and jury

---

177 *Ibid.* at 446. A writ means a writing; it is an English translation of the Latin word *breve*, meaning "something short" and by extension, "a letter." D.M. Stenton, *English Justice Between the Norman Conquest and the Great Charter, 1066-1215* (Philadelphia: American Philosophical Society, 1964) at 53, stated that these writs "generated the English common law."

178 *Ibid.* at 448.

179 Bracton, *supra* note 132.

180 Lyon, *supra* note 35 at 293.

181 Stephenson & Marcham, *supra* note 45, No. 33e.

182 Lyon, *supra* note 35 at 290. Originally assize (*assisa*) meant the sitting of a court or of a council, but later it came to denote the enactments or decisions of the court or council.

who could restore the land.[183] This writ directed the sheriff of the county in which the land lay to gather 12 men in the neighbourhood to determine whether the person on the land had, as alleged, wrongfully taken it from the plaintiff. If the jury determined that the defendant had dispossessed the plaintiff, he was required to return the land. If he still claimed to be the true possessor, he in turn had to bring a writ of right. This procedure finally disposed of most cases.[184] The second petty assize was of *mort d'ancestor* (the death of ancestor),[185] which held that if a man died in physical possession of a heritable tenement, his heir issued the writ to secure possession of the land against the claim of any man, even if it could be established that a better claim existed in another. The jury in a royal court had to decide who possessed this land on the day when the ancestor died. The third petty assize was the *darrien presentment* (or last presentment).[186] It was devised to facilitate the settlement of disputes over the *advowson* (right to appoint to vacant position) of a church. These writs were civil procedures, which ordered a jury under oath to answer questions that settled disputes over *seisin* to a position.

Henry II also began to interfere in such disputes more arbitrarily by means of a new writ called *praecipe* (precept or command) or writ of entry. This writ was directed to the sheriff, ordering him to instruct the holder of the land to return the disputed land to the plaintiff.[187] If it were not done, the defendant would be summoned to the royal court where the case would be settled. The writ suggested that a tenant's *seisin* was flawed or resulted from a wrongful event.

Henry II's legal innovations of the assizes provided the foundations for a system of law by imposing royal jurisdiction and royal courts over matters that had previously been under local or manorial jurisdiction and law.[188] He succeeded in creating a royal judiciary operated under the control of a royal chancery, and enlisted community participation in administering justice.[189] The first treatise of British law, *Treatise on the Laws and Customs of the Kingdom of England* (1187),[190] affirmed the King's responsibility to protect the kingdom militarily, but also legitimated royal authority to enact "laws for the governance of subject and peaceful peoples."[191]

---

183 Juries of men (jury of recognition) helped to settle disputes over *seisin* since they were familiar with the facts of a certain claim.

184 Lyon, *supra* note 35 at 290-91.

185 *Ibid.* at 291.

186 *Ibid.*

187 Stephenson & Marcham, *supra* note 45, No. 30f.

188 Berman, *supra* note 112 at 442-43, writes that this was part of a general historical development in twelfth-century Europe.

189 They were organized by the *Statute of Winchester*, found in Robertson, *supra* note 100. Generally, they had the duty to keep custody of indicted prisoners until the King's justices arrived to try them. In 1344, they were given a shared power to try prisoners for felonies and breaches of the peace. Within 25 years, they were authorized to try some prisoners by themselves. It was around this time that they acquired the title of "Justice of the Peace."

190 Glanville, *supra* note 130.

191 *Ibid.* at 1.

From the writs and doctrinal writings a doctrine of *seisin* evolved to end wrongful dispossession.[192] These innovations established the principle that the royal courts could restore *seisin* to any freeman disseised without lawful judgment. Also enforced was the principle that, no matter in what court, trial by combat did not have to be accepted by the tenant in *seisin* until a writ of right had been obtained that guaranteed a judgment for land disputes. The grand assize even went so far as to encourage settlements of *seisin* disputes in royal courts. The assize guaranteed the supremacy of the royal court and of jury procedure and blazed the trail to trial by jury in other civil actions. Until the advent of the grand assize, the original writs initiating the petty assizes made the assize jury of recognition mandatory. Customary modes of trials persisted: acquittal on the oaths of witnesses (compurgation) remained until 1837 and combat until 1819; but both were reduced to insignificant proportions by the procedures of trial by jury before judges in the royal courts.

The petty assizes proved so useful that the caseload soon overwhelmed the King's Council. In 1178, five justices were appointed with a continuing commission from the King's Court to hear the civil cases involving land. These justices were the King's personal confidants who might perform many types of tasks during their careers. They constituted a Lesser Council, or Household.[193] The King chose justices from the members of this body to take care of his affairs throughout the realm, including the dispensing of justice, particularly criminal justice,[194] and saw to the punishment of those who were guilty of offences included within an expanding list of Pleas of the Crown. Initially, the justices were called the Bench, and they did not hear cases on application of the parties directly. The party first had to purchase a writ from the office of the Chancellor, who issued writs only for certain types of cases authorized by the Council, of which he was a member. The Council only authorized a limited number of these writs. The Bench's conclusions were reported to the Council, and, in theory, the Council made the actual decision. Also, the Bench supervised the shires, ensuring that the sheriffs collected the taxes.

The Great Council, the Household, and the justices of the peace became part of the King's Court, or *Curia Regis*. These institutions performed the functions of a high-

---

192 See Berman, *supra* note 112 at 453-57, who notes that the classical and post-classical Roman law that distinguished sharply between ownership and possession was inadequate to describe the fragmented feudal landholding hierarchy. See also, Lyon, *supra* note 35 at 294. Lyon writes that these petty assizes were a more fundamental question in British law of possession (*possessio*) than proprietary right or ownership. Under any of these three possessory assizes a man might be awarded possession even though he might have less right to land or presentment than his unsuccessful opponent. The writs do not settle these questions, but illustrate that behind the act of possession there was a vague and more fundamental interest in land, one that we would call proprietary right or ownership. Yet, at this time the distinction was subtle and implicate.

193 The King's advisors meeting alone constituted another distinct court.

194 Some were Justices of Gaol Delivery, who tried smaller criminal cases; others were travelling Commissioners of Oyer and Terminer (to hear and decide), who decided important criminal cases; and, until the fourteenth century, the General Eyre of the Justices in Ee, who investigated all aspects of shire administration.

er or constitutional law in Britain. This law was an amalgam of many local customs and ancient statutes called the "unwritten" or customary statutes.[195]

Slowly the royal court freed itself of subservience to the Council. In 1234, it started to keep its own records, and in 1272, it was given a chief justice. After *Magna Carta*, its location was fixed at Westminster. In the 1330s, the Bench acquired its final name, the Court of Common Pleas.[196] In addition to its jurisdiction over land cases, the Common Pleas soon acquired jurisdiction over other civil disputes, such as the enforcement of obligations. The writs were still issued by the Chancellor on the authority of the Council.

Because of the limitation of the writ system in the royal courts, both its narrow grounds of complaint and remedies, principles of equity were developed by the Chancery as an independent body of land law. This system of law developed from appeals from the royal courts to the King, as the fountain of all justice. These appeals were given to the Lord Chancellor, one of the principal secretaries of the King, and the office where writs were issued. The guiding principle of the Chancellor, and later the Court of Chancery, was the doing of justice between the parties regardless of the technical rules of the writ system. Typically, these appeals involved presenting a petition or bill to the Chancery raising a complaint, although sometimes they involved devising new writs to enable them to bring actions. The equity courts could not directly overrule the royal law courts without causing the most fundamental constitutional crises, but they could temper the ruling in individual cases. The primary method of accomplishing this task was by issuing a remedy known as an injunction, an order restraining persons from exercising or enforcing their strict legal rights.

These two systems of justice developed the nature of the feudal land holding. For centuries, both systems existed side by side: the old system of royal courts and the newer Chancery system. If the royal courts either would not act or reached results that the Chancery thought were too strict and technical and therefore unjust, the Chancellor could apply "equitable" relief. Consequently, equitable principles were applied when the royal law did not provide a suitable remedy for a particular wrong. These principles had both a substantive and procedural aspect, and led to the modern rule that one cannot obtain an equitable remedy if any adequate legal remedy is available.

Equity principles created the use, trusts, and settlements (keeping land within the family) in British land law. Typically, they recognized one person's legal tenure, but also required him in fairness to exercise his rights according to his conveyance to another person. Over time, the second party interest became equitable, creating the procedural notion of a division of tenure and estates between legal and equitable interests.

---

195 For example, the pivot of British governments is its cabinet system that is purely customary and does not depend on statutory enactment.

196 Important criminal matters, called the Pleas of the Crown, were heard in a different court. They were beyond the writ system, and the King-in-Council still heard the cases. These events, too, became more numerous and time-consuming; thus the King delegated these criminal cases to "The Justices Assigned for the holding of Pleas before the King Himself," or the King's Bench. In theory the King, but in practice the assigned justices, decided its cases. By the reign of Edward I (1272-1307), the King's Bench was sufficiently disengaged from the Council to be recognized as a separate court.

The royal courts developed the procedural idea of writs of *seisin* into "incidents" of tenure. Initially, the word "tenure," derived in British law from the Latin word *tenere* (to seize or hold), meant "a holding."[197] Tenure was the external manifestation of *seisin* used to describe the relationship between landholders in a ladder or pyramid of tenure leading from the superior lord (or king) to other lords, and between lords and tenants. Its central idea involved the human relations, the ideal of feudal lord and man, and superior and vassal relationship synonymous with feudal loyalty:

> The vassal's duty to respect his superior and to study and advance his dignity and interest before those of all others finds its counterpart in the superior's obligation to protect the vassal's person, property, possessions and good name, without regard to third parties. The observance of good faith is universally imperative in the discharge of all obligations relative to these matters in accordance with the terms and tenor of the investiture, or, if these are silent with regard to them, according to local custom.[198]

Without the bond, there is no relationship or service. To the medieval mind, the relationship was the important thing; it created life and liberties.

The bonds of fealty (*fidelitas*)[199] or homage (*homagium*)[200] to a lord were necessary before a person could become "his man" or feudal grantee. This was a simple oath to be faithful and true to the lord and acknowledged that he held a tenement from the lord;[201] but it did not involve the rituals of homage to the King. These aristocratic relationships created the basis of the honourable association of men from which flowed all the other mutual obligations. Breach of the duty of fidelity or homage in Britain was the foundation of the crime of "petit treason." It was out of trust and faith that the services were shared.

---

197 Berman, *supra* note 112 at 312. The subject of tenure, what the tenants held, was the "tenement." "Tenement" in feudal law means anything that can be held or seized, provided it be of permanent nature. It includes much beside land. "Hereditament" covers only those tenements that will descend to the person that feudal law declared the heir. E.C. Clark, *History of Roman Private Law: Part II, Jurisprudence* (New York: Biblo and Tannen, 1965) at 557.

198 Sir T. Craig, *The jus feudale*, trans. James John, Lord Clyde, vol. 2 (Edinburgh: W. Hodge, 1832) at VVII.I [reprint]. Lord Clyde's Translation, vol. 1 at 583.

199 Fealty was an oath and tie that binds the vassal to his lord; it was taken at the admittance of every tenant, to be true to the lord of whom he holds his land. *Mozley & Whiteley's Law Dictionary*, 9th ed, *s.v.* "*fidelitas.*" See Pollock & Maitland, *supra* note 8, vol. 1 at 296-307.

200 Pollock & Maitland, *ibid.* Homage was the ceremony performed by the vassal or tenant to a lord.

201 Tomlins, *supra* note 128. The ceremony is important. Littleton explains that when a person did homage to his lord he was unarmed and bareheaded. The lord was seated. The person knelt before his Lord, on both knees, and put his hands together between the lord's hands and said: "*Jeo deveigne votre home de cest jour en avant, de vie et de member, et de terrene honour, et a vours serra foial et loial, et foy a vours portera des tenements que ieo claime de tener de vous, salve le foy que ieo doy a nostre Seignior le Roy.*" (I become your man from this day forward in life and limb, and in earthly honour, and will be faithful and loyal to you, and must give you tenements which I claim to hold from you, except the duty I owe to our Lord the King). Then the lord kissed him; at §85. Similar ceremonies existed in Continental feudalism and Scotland. In French and Scottish feudalism an exception was made for those who had already become "*home de Dieu*" and had difficulties with "*jeo deveigne votre home.*" In the ritual of the salvo, they said instead "*jeo vous face homage.*"

An example of such feudal relations between the King and lords is the Sarum oath of 1086 between William I and the landholders of Britain. "[A]ll the land-owning men of any account that there were all over England, whosoever men they were" swore fealty to William. By the oath they became his men, receiving a duty to serve him faithfully, even against their own lords.[202] The oath also formulated the King's duties to his lords, including the duty to "warrant" their interest to their lands in case of challenge.[203] He also granted and confirmed certain lands to be held by him as overlord.[204]

Without a cash economy, William I and his administrators only had feudal loyalty to unite the kingdom. Fruits of the land represented the main source of wealth, since the land was not a commodity to be purchased or traded. Although it is now firmly linked with feudal relationships, Maitland pointed out that the term "tenure" had no specifically feudal significance.[205] What is characteristically feudal is not tenure of the land itself, but tenure of a manor from a feudal superior.[206] These manors were similar to the Latin *familia*: they had external relations with the King and other lords, and an internal organization under manorial law.

The dominant conceptual tool of British kings' *tenure* was the idea of fragmented land holding, in which each parcel of land was subject to overlapping claims of superiors and inferiors. The British kings applied the concept broadly, until it became the foundation theory of the royal law of land in Britain.[207] However, as they widely applied the concept to every kind of officially recognized interest in land, it became exceedingly abstract.[208] These authorities over lands were established not by way of an absolute transfer, but by leases upon certain conditions or services.[209]

Under the British system of fragmented tenures, the existing Teutonic and Norman leaders became lords under the King, while the community became tenants. The aggregate of loyalties and derivative tenures created the royal mastery or political jurisdiction of the King, and in succeeding centuries, became the source of the prerogative law. Those who held directly of the King were known as "tenants in capite" or "tenants

---

202 Simpson, *supra* note 56 at 26, citing David C. Douglas, ed., *English Historical Documents*, vol. 2, 1st ed. (London: Eyre and Spottiswoode, 1955) at 161-1, and F. M. Stenton, *The First Century of English Feudalism, 1066-1166* (Oxford: Clarendon Press, 1961) at 111.

203 Glanville, *supra* note 130, vol. 9 at 4; Tomlins, *supra* note 128 at §§143-5.

204 *Ibid.*

205 Pollock & Maitland, *supra* note 8, vol. 1 at 234, n. 1.

206 Simpson, *supra* note 56 at 47-48.

207 Holdsworth argued that the imposed system of universality of tenure had a leveling effect. Since all men were included in the system, tenure ceased to be a mark of class. The maintenance of the direct relations between the Norman King and the people, especially through the King's courts and William's requirement of direct allegiance, created the means of social and economic mobility. These factors made the feudal conception of land tenure the common law of the land, while repressing the feudal elements hostile to the state. When the economic relation to the land began to supersede the political, the choicest holdings went to the ablest and most ambitious men, who frequently held the lands in a lower form of tenure. This doctrine illustrated the essential political nature of feudalism, rather than its proprietary nature. Holdsworth, *supra* note 8.

208 Pollock & Maitland, *supra* note 8, vol. 1 at 236.

209 *Ibid.* at 94.

in chief."[210] Those who occupied the lands were called "tenants in demesne."[211] Those who stood between the King and the tenants in demesne were called mesne "lords," or "mesnes."[212] This relationship is often described by legal historians as pyramidal and represented by different horizontal strata.[213] A simplified diagram illustrates why the pyramid metaphor is so often used in this context:

King			
Tenants-(T)-in-chief (book-land)		tenants-in-chief	
mesne T	mesne T (lease-land)	mesne T	mesne T
T demesne	T demesne (folk-land)	T demesne	T demesne

This diagram shows only that part of the structure relating to occupied land. To make the analysis more complex, each tenant-in-chief could make numerous sub-grants from which even more numerous sub-sub-grants could be made. Often this pyramid of interest existed over the same piece of land.[214]

What the lords received by the King's grant was not the enjoyment of land, but jurisdictional authority over the lands and services from families who cultivated the land.[215] The holding of the land depended on personal status or conditions. The nature of the reciprocal relation was still hardly proprietary in the modern sense.[216] The land use was the condition for the performance of correlative services. Many different types of services existed that secured these interests in the land. Each set of services was divided by the royal courts into free and unfree tenures. Free tenures of chivalry

---

210 This term can be viewed as a continuation of the idea of book-land.

211 This term can be viewed as a continuation of the idea of Anglo-Saxon folk-land.

212 This term can be viewed as a continuation of the idea of Anglo-Saxon lease-land.

213 J.E. Hogg, "Effect of Tenure on Real Property Law" (1909) 25 L.Q. Rev. 178 [hereinafter "Effect of Tenure"].

214 T. Plucknett, *Concise History of the Common Law* (London: Butterworths, 1956) at 186, remarked that it is very difficult to see how this conclusion can be reached. Yet this is the Scots Law on separate flats built one above the other, and the modern law of France regarding separate ownership of different strata.

215 Simpson, *supra* note 56 at 5. He states it must not be imagined that any process of wholesale eviction took place: a system of parasitism was involved, and parasites cannot survive the destruction of their hosts (at 4). It should be noted that in the *Domesday Book, supra* note 109, there are only these three cases of tenants. There are no different species of tenure common to continental feudalism. See Digby, *supra* note 42 at 48; Maitland, *supra* note 75 at 151.

216 Noyes, *supra* note 116 at 244. It was a combination of relations with reference to the land and of personal relations. "*Tenet*" and "*servit*" were two sides of any tenure. Vinogradoff 1905, *supra* note 28 at 239.

(military),[217] socage (agricultural),[218] and ecclesiastical had *seisin*; and unfree tenures (villeinage or copyhold) had no *seisin* but had agricultural and labouring services at a manor.[219] The royal courts would protect only the tenants seized of the land; the manorial courts decided issues of unfree tenures as obligations.

In the later centuries, the tenures came to describe how the land was held from the King. Simpson notes:

> early lawyers never adopted the premise that the King owned all the land; such a dogma is of very modern appearance. It was sufficient for them to note that the King was lord, ultimately, of all the tenants in the realm, and that as lord he had many rights common to other lords (*e.g.*, rights of escheats) and some peculiar to his position as supreme lord (*e.g.*, rights to forfeitures). Naturally they catalogued these special rights, but they did not so differ in kind as to make it necessary to put the King in an entirely separate category; he was supreme lord, and that was enough. They treated the bundle of rights vested in mesne lords as if they were material things, and called them seignories or manors, and to these "things" they applied the notion of *seisin* just as they applied it to land ... . This materialistic approach to the description of tenurial hierarchy of land ownership is to be found in Bracton.[220]

If the services failed, the land "returned" to the King for redistribution. Thus, the British idea of tenure necessitated the existence of at least three separate sets of interests in the land—the interest of the King, the lord, and the tenant. As Markby noted, the holders fragmented their services, and each service was conferred upon a different person.[221] These complex pyramids of land and services were eventually changed by the resistance of the common lawyers, courts, and parliament. The concepts remained but the services owed were reduced. From the resistance to the aristocratic feudal system, a more complex hierarchical system of interests of a different kind emerged in British land law: the law of estates and interests.

Until the reign of Edward I (1272-1307), there was, of course, no single place to look for the judicial reasoning that created free and unfree tenures or to analyze the fragmentation of services. The law books referred to these decisions as "traditions" and carried them forward, while the plea rolls of the courts did not register the exact wording of the decisions. We can therefore discern only the broad outlines of the judicial resistance and interventions that created the legal categories of "estates" as time.

Once the royal courts acquired the authority to decide conflicting *seisin* claims and the capacity to restore the "*seisin*" of the land to a dispossessed person, the proce-

---

217 Kempin, *supra* note 119 at 116. The military tenant swore to the King, "to become your man for the tenement I hold of you and to bear faith to you of life and members and earthly honor against all other men." They were given confiscated land for their personal loyalty. Their services became known as knight service.

218 Services, other than military, were known as "sergeanties." They carried tenancies in land that had particular duties, called a tenant in sergeanty or servant.

219 J. Scriven, *A Treatise on the Law of Copyholds*, 7th ed. (London: Butterworths, 1896).

220 Simpson, *supra* note 56 at 47-48.

221 Markby, *supra* note 115; Noyes, *supra* note 116 at 257.

dural action was deemed "real."[222] These claims came to be categorized as the protected estates, or realty or real property.[223] If the courts would not recover the *res* and merely gave compensation for the loss, the action came to be viewed as personality or personal property.

In real action, the royal courts distinguished between possessory and proprietary actions.[224] Whereas possessory actions were limited to the right to *seisin*, proprietary actions were more comprehensive; they could involve *seisin* and the taking of fruits or profits. These writs and the courts' categorization of the actions suggest drastic changes occurring in *seisin* of the land: either ecological upheavals or perhaps a lawless wave of intruders or the pretensions of feudal lords. Something had gone wrong with the doctrine of *seisin*, a possibility reinforced by the emergence of legal treatises attempting to restate the customary laws or analyze the writ system.[225]

The courts had to resolve the relationship among coexisting and overlapping interests of the Crown, lord and tenant estates, and from their explanations that the tenant's rights in land or estates emerged in British legal thought.[226] These interests were resolved upon the plane of sequence and time,[227] rather than on any proprietary ideas. The temporal dimensions of land were known as an *estate*, a word interestingly derived from Latin *status*. Since time is divisible, the judges formulated rules that controlled the use and enjoyment of the land by assigning temporal interests to several people. Since several different people had an interest in a single piece of land in the complex pyramids of interests, the courts found it impossible to identify an estate with any material location. The royal courts' explanations focused on quantity or length of time, rather than on land itself. Thus, the concept of divisible estates and interest controlled by time became the central feature of royal law. Each claim or estate differed in time of enjoyment and carried unique possibilities.

However, the court determined that only one person at a time could be actually seised of disputed land. The courts held that there could not be two *seisins* of the same quality at the same time. They had no problem if two or more people could claim the partial estates or interests, and there could be future interests. The idea of "estate" came

---

222 Markby, *ibid.* at 578. At the beginning of a Roman legal proceeding, *res* had come to mean something between "cause of action" or "cause."

223 The notion that one could have a right *pro re* (later *ad rem*), that is, a right to the things that one has recovered, would have been incomprehensible to the Roman jurists. They only understood rights in *res*, rights in the thing.

224 Bracton, *supra* note 132, vol. 2 at 296-97. The distinction is based on the Roman unitary categories of *dominion* as applied to British estates; it fails to understand the coexisting interests in the doctrine of British estates.

225 See, *Leges Henrici, supra* note 124; Robertson, *supra* note 100; and the fraudulent treatise, the *Leges Edwardi, supra* note 103.

226 Pollock & Maitland, *supra* note 8, vol. 2 at 10; Holdsworth, *supra* note 8, vol. 3 at 351-52. Maine describes the process as a "long succession of partial ownerships, making up together one complete ownership, the *feodum* or fee." See Sir H.S. Maine, *Dissertations on Early Law and Custom: Chiefly Selected from Lectures Delivered at Oxford* (London: J. Murray, 1883) at 344.

227 Noyes, *supra* note 116 at 257.

to be used to refer to the important interests in land, while the idea of "interests" came
to refer to less important interests, such as incorporeal hereditaments or servitudes.

The courts began to categorize the tenant's *seisin*, resulting from different land-
lord and tenant relationships, as either freehold or leasehold. The essential condition of
a freehold estate was the length of time a tenant could use the land. The lord could grant
seisin to the tenant for as long as he lived (for life); or for as long as the tenant or any
of his descendants lived (in tail); or for as long as the tenant or any of his heirs, whether
descendants or not, were alive (in simple). A tenant might own one or more estates in
land; he might enjoy an estate at the present time or in the future time (reversion or
remainder); yet he never owned any of the land itself.

Under manorial law, the leasing tenant or vassal enjoyed no legal interests to the
land; he had only *seisin* of a *fief*, which was held as long as certain services were performed. Similar to Roman law, leaseholds were seen as contractual obligations,[228] and
did not come under the classification of land. The thirteenth-century courts began to
give the leasing tenant in *seisin* a possessory interest and legal interests in a moneyed
economy.[229] The condition of the leasehold were use-rights or servitudes attached to
the estate of someone else, such as right of way over a neighbour's estate, or the right
to hunt or fish on someone else's estate, or the right to an annuity charged on land. The
duration of leaseholds on successors in interest to the transfer created considerable controversy.

Courts began to distinguish between claims that could be given between people
and those that were claims on those claims. Successful claims in the courts were conceptualized as "rights," which required other men to act in some way towards the
claimant, to give him something. The courts appeared willing to extend personal claims
for *seisin* of land to existing "rights" and began moving toward claims against the entire
world, or *dominium utile* in civil law.[230]

---

228   Holdsworth, *supra* note 8, vol. 3 at 4; R. E. Megarry and H.W.R. Wade, *The Law of Real Property*, 4th
       ed. (London: Stevens & Sons Ltd., 1975), App. I.

229   A.D. Hargreaves, *Introduction to the Principles of Land Law* (London: Sweet and Maxwell, 1952,
       1963) at 48, states: "[M]aterialism is a phenomenon which pervades the whole of the mediaeval land
       law. Whenever it meets with a conception which we should not regard as a right, it tends to transform
       it into an almost concrete thing."

230   Roman law and the European civil law conceived of *dominium* as absolute, a relationship between a
       person and a thing good against the world. See Milsom, *supra* note 9 at 103. The right of *dominium*
       under British common law was always relative. It was conceived as the better *seisin* between two par-
       ties to an action. Only someone who was out of possession and wished to claim it needed to advance
       dominium. Thus it became something rather like *dominium*, abstract and ultimate. The absolute or ulti-
       mate *dominium* proved to be self-destructive: the disposition of one generation could prevent disposi-
       tions in the subsequent ones (*ibid.* at 93). The civil law court began to use *dominium utile* to describe
       a less absolute right than could be defended against all others, and could be transferred by its holder.
       This came to be known as "title."

C. Royal law

The categorization of writs and claims by the courts was opposed by Edward I and the lords and barons, who were landholders represented in parliament. In the struggle that formed between lord and tenant over estates and interests in land, the courts supported the tenants.[231] Since their tenures were affected by the judicial interpretation, the barons restricted this interpretation by legislation. Thus, Edward's legislation caused the reestablishment of many aristocratic traditions in British land law.

To untangle the courts' interpretation of estates, *Magna Carta*[232] was enacted. It declared the lords' and barons' objections to subinfeudation. It prohibited tenants from alienating so much of their services or taxes or interests that the part retained would not be sufficient to yield the services or taxes owed to their lords. This practice was designed to prevent excessive fragmentation and sub-division of the tenure that would rapidly decrease the lord's security from the services owed to him out of the land by his original tenant. *Magna Carta* also forbade the conveyance of land to corporations or religious bodies such as monasteries, since these entities could not "die" as humans die; thus the lords lost incidents such as wardship, marriage, and escheat.

Magna Carta, article 29, stated that no freeholder could be deprived (disseised) of his land, liberties or free custom except by lawful means:

> No Freeman shall be taken, or imprisoned, or be disseised of his Freehold, or Liberties, or free Customs, or be outlawed, or exiled, or any otherwise destroyed; nor will we pass upon him, nor condemn him, but by lawful Judgment of his Peers, or by the Law of the Land. We will sell to no man, we will not deny or defer to any man either Justice or Right.[233]

Also, in *Magna Carta*, the barons eliminated the writ of entry. Other parliamentary acts created the estates tail and provided that land should descend according to the conditions imposed upon it to prevent the family control over estates of land indefinitely.[234]

In 1290, the statute *Quia emptores*[235] was a more forthright attempt to meet the demands of the barons. Only the Crown could grant new freehold tenures. Only with the consent of the King could the tenants-in-chief freely transfer or subinfeudate their land holdings to others. Thus, subinfeudation to mesne or demesne tenants gradually

---

231 Lyon, *supra* note 35 at 457.

232 *Magna Carta, supra* note 131.

233 Lord Parmoor stated in *Attorney-General v. De Keyser's Royal Hotel*, [1920] A.C. 508 at 569 (H.L.), "Since Magna Carta the estate of a subject in lands or building has been protected against the prerogative of the Crown."

234 Among the Parliamentary acts were *De Viris Religiosis*, *De Mercatoribus* and *De Donis Conditionalibus* (concerning Conditional Gifts) in the *Statute of Westminster I*, 1285 (U.K.),13 Edw. I, c. 32.

235 *Quia emptores, supra* note 133.

disappeared. These statutes reveal the evolving and troubling boundaries between the barons and the courts.[236]

By the mid-thirteenth century, the complexity of feudal law in continental Europe had reached the point that all lords asserted *dominium* of some kind and the Roman law category ceased to make much sense. The great web of subinfeudation, mutual infeudation, and substitution also existed in continental Europe. The civil law courts had begun to use the term *dominium utile* to describe what the usufructuary of an estate possessed, as distinct from the *dominium directum*, to explain the estate of the superior lords. *Dominium directum* was an unrestricted right to dispose of a land or things unless prohibited by law. *Dominium utile* became a right that could be defended against all others, and that could be transferred or alienated by its possessor. This initiated the idea of vested land rights as a commodity. The process had begun whereby rights, of whatever kind, were to come to be seen as transferable.[237]

Seeking to resist the idea of land as a commodity in royal courts, Edward I and the barons created the Inns of Court to perpetuate British statutory law. Edward I introduced a more subtle and systemic strategy to control the royal courts and to strengthen aristocratic society. He created a legal monopoly in the Inns of Court to control entry into the legal profession. In 1292, he ordered that the Court of Common Pleas choose certain "attorneys and learners," thus creating the legal profession.[238] Under the Inns of Court, British lawyers taught the law students, and each generation of lawyers learned the processes of the courts and took part in the courts' business, so that the British law relied on its own traditions and resources and not on borrowing from the civil law systems. As keepers of the parliamentary statutes and customary laws, British lawyers were relatively immune from the civil and ecclesiastical law seen as threats to British aristocratic society.

Following the deliberately imposed statutes and compilations, the judges formulated explicit rules and strict definitions of the mutual duties of lord and tenant, clothing land law with highly technical legal phraseology. This bureaucratic or regulatory law blended older customs, but began to distinguish between habits and duties, or between rule-making and rule-application. The bureaucratic law system was a product of centralized rulers and their specialized staffs, not a spontaneous product of British custom or its unwritten constitution.[239]

Legal resistance to bureaucratic law emerged in subtle ways. For example,

---

236 *Ibid.* This seems to have received a wide acclaim in the royal courts. See also *De Stapulis*, 1353 (U.K.), 27 Edw. III, c. 9; *Statute of Uses*, 1535 (U.K.), 27 Hen. VIII, c. 110; *Statute of Enrollments*, 1535-36 (U.K.), 27 Hen. VIII, c. 16; *Statute of Covenants* and *Statute of Wills*, 1540 (U.K.), 32 Hen. VIII, c. 1; *Statute of Frauds*, 1677 (U.K.), 29 Car. II, c. 3; and *Thellusen Act*, 1799 (U.K.), 39 & 40 Geo. III, c. 98.

237 Tuck, *supra* note 20 at 16-17.

238 Lyon, *supra* note 35 at 457.

239 It is distinguished from the civil law system used in Continental European countries and their colonies. The civil law system can be traced back to Roman law. It consists of universal principles written in a legislative code of law, which is a comprehensive enactment of the whole of the basic law of the country. Each code of law was implemented within its territorial empire. Yet, wherever the code has been applied it has blended local customs, creating diversity within uniformity in various parts of the European Continent.

Bracton's *On the Laws and Customs of England* (1256), without attribution, included about five hundred passages of Justinian's *Digest*, asserting it as "the law" of Britain.[240] He also argued that the English customs applicable to royal courts constituted a "law" as real as that contained in ancient Roman legal text. Moreover, Bracton developed the idea of looking back to prior cases for guidance, but he also chose to reject some cases as "bad" law, while accepting others. Instead of finding law for the cases, he illustrated law by the uses of cases derived from doctrinal writings. Law, he argued, was not found in a single case nor was it the custom of the people; rather it was the total of the customs of the courts. Yet the British legal system reported only selected cases and used those as sources of authority. The system of written pleadings was intended to reduce decisions to a single point, a decided point of law that became a precedent.[241]

In the fourteenth and fifteenth centuries, the courts elaborated the parliamentary statutes, court procedure and pleadings.[242] This achievement was facilitated by the Inns of Court, which collected the judgments and rules of the British courts. The members of this guild created law for their King and country in the belief that all legal questions could be solved on the basis of history or precedent. For example, as an answer to the absolute monarchy and the idea of parliamentary supremacy, the courts and lawyers offered an implicit conception of British history as a gradual and self-contained process of development over the centuries. The future would take care of itself, they argued, so long as the traditions of the past were preserved by the law, since the law was sovereign.

D. Articulation of the common law

The perspective of the common law[243] became a self-conscious reaction to the rise of an ideology of absolutism that was developing both on the continent of Europe and in Britain.[244] It arose, in part, in response to the threat of centralized power exercised by those who proposed that law be guided by nothing but their own assessments of the demands of justice, expediency, and the common good. The royal court assumed more directive control of society and the economy, and the idea emerged that law could be used to control and direct society to serve the ends and goals of the sovereign.

---

240 See Bracton, *supra* note 132, vol. 1 at xxxvi.

241 The word is from the French for "preceding in time." It is a creature of the printed word. Its original use began in the late sixteenth century. It was not until the eighteenth century that the editors of English law dictionaries included *precedent* and its companion *stare decisis* (to stand by things decided). See Mellinkoff, *supra* note 4 at 130-41.

242 Lyon, *supra* note 35 at 613.

243 From the perspective of comparative law, Anglophone legal systems are dominated by conceptions of law and structures of legal argument typical of Anglophone rather than the Roman, or Civil, traditions. Out of British common law, however, came a body of thought about the nature of law, which began to take distinctive shape with Coke. It is to be distinguished from contemporary views of common law practice.

244 For a discussion of the history of this period, see Christopher Hill, *Intellectual Origins of the English Revolution and The Century of Revolution, 1603-1714* (Oxford: Clarendon Press, 1965); J.G.A. Pocock, *The Ancient Constitution and the Feudal Law* (Cambridge, U.K.: Cambridge University Press, 1957); and F. Hayek, *The Constitution of Liberty* (Chicago: Regnery, 1972), c. 11.

Against the spreading ideology of political absolutism, the royal courts reasserted the medieval idea that law is not something made by king, parliament, or judges, but rather is the expression of a deeper reality that is merely discovered and publicly declared by them.[245] They sought to portray legislators and judges as "not so much the creators of the law as the agents through whom it finds expression."[246] These ideas gave the medieval doctrine a distinctively historical twist, in that the deeper reality manifested in the public statutes and judicial decisions was not a set of universal rational principles, but rather historically evidenced national custom.

The common law lawyers were preoccupied with developing national law from the ancient procedures and formulae of the courts. They claimed to be unaffected by political chaos surrounding the challenge of despotism, the intellectual movements of the Renaissance and Reformation, and the rise of civil courts.[247] By shrewd litigation the legal profession wove local Anglo-Saxon law and Roman legal principles into the system of common law that protected the frailties and needs of men. The legal profession did not attempt to codify customary law or draft statutes; instead they approached litigation from three perspectives: the instrumental needs to settle a given situation, the need to express abstract reflections on the prevailing customs, and the need to draw innovative legal conclusions or public policy based on the unwritten customs of a people. The supremacy of the common law was not challenged by the kings; it established itself as a legal way of life, and it identified its perspectives with impartial law.[248] Ironically, because of the way the common law developed, it came to be viewed as the most powerful bureaucratic instrument in the sovereign's repertoire.

With the *Act of Union with Wales* (1535), the union of Crowns with Scotland in 1603, the union of parliaments with Scotland in 1707, and defining relationships with Ireland creating group pluralities, the common law sought to unify the peoples into a nation, defining social relations and power, and encompassing the conventional constitutional law of the land by defining political relations and distributing authority.[249] The judiciary nourished this perspective as the declaring voice or expounder of the common law,[250] by discovering a form of higher law related to the law of nature. All British law, according to the emerging perspective of the common law, either was, or was ground-

---

245 See Hayek, *ibid.* at 163.

246 I. Jenkins, *Social Order and the Limits of Law* (Princeton, N.J.: Princeton University Press, 1980) at 100. Sir John Davies writes in his *Irish Reports* (1612): "Neither could any one man ever vaunt, that, like *Minos, Solon,* or *Lyarogus,* he was the first Lawgiver to our Nation: for neither did the King make his own Prerogative, nor the Judges make the Rums amid Maximes of the Law, nor the common subject prescribe and limit the Liberties which he injoyeth by the Law," quoted in Pocock, *supra* note 244 at 41.

247 Lyon, *supra* note 35.

248 *Ibid.* at 639-40.

249 *Ibid.* at 46.

250 Blackstone, *supra* note 117, vol. 1 at 69, vol. 3 at 327; *Calvin's Case,* (1608) 7 Coke 1 ("the judge is the mouthpiece of a law which transcends the judiciary") [hereinafter *Calvin's Case*]; Sir M. Hale, *A History of the Common Law of England,* ed. by C.M. Gray (Chicago: University of Chicago, 1971) at 45.

ed upon, common and immemorial custom, an "ancient collection of unwritten maxims and customs,"[251] recorded in the memory of the people. It was a body of practices, attitudes, conceptions, and patterns of thought, "handed down by tradition, use, and experience."[252] The only way to show that a given rule was a part of the common law was to show how it figures regularly in standard legal argument. "[T]he only method of proving that this or that maxim is a rule of the common law, is by showing that it hath been always the custom to observe it."[253] Such rules exist in so far as they are used or relied upon. Therein lies their inherent authority:

> [T]hey are grown into use, and have acquired their binding Power and Force of Laws by a long and immemorial Usage, and by the Strength of Custom and Reception in this Kingdom. The Matters, indeed, and the Substance of those Laws, are in Writing, but the formal and obliging Force and Power of them grows by long Custom and Use.[254]

Not only were common laws practiced, but the community recognition of, and participation in, a practice over time were taken to reveal its validity, its "formal and obliging Force." Common law rested ultimately on general use and acceptance.[255] The texture of this acceptance was of great importance for the common law,[256] since the continued practice of a custom both manifested and reinforced a general sense of the reasonableness and historical appropriateness of the rules and concepts. Customary law led a double life: it constituted factual regularity of behaviour and became part of the practice by which custom or implicit norms were defined. Practice, habit, or duty became law only if it was affirmed and taken up into the practice of the community. Only time could tell whether a rule became a law, because only time—that is, the practice and use over time—validated.

However, custom as conceived by the common law was traditional and characteristically inarticulate rather than objective or expressed. Time, on this view, was not an empty placeholder for standards of conduct, or an unseen driving force. Instead, time was a rich tapestry of human conduct, words, thoughts, and sentiments of a people with whom one identified, members of a "partnership" across time. Community action, then, took on a quasi-ritualistic character: a re-enactment of patterns known and recognized through time, and continuities binding members of the social partnership without distinctions between regularity and norm, or between choice and the application of rules.

---

251 Blackstone, *ibid.*, vol. 1 at 17.

252 *Ibid.*

253 *Ibid.* at 68.

254 Hale, *supra* note 250 at 17. See also Blackstone, *ibid.*, vol. 1 at 64, 68.

255 Blackstone, *ibid.*, vol. 1 at 67, says: "in our law the goodness of a custom depends upon its having been used time out of mind; or, in the solemnity of our legal phrase, time whereof the memory of man runneth not to the contrary. This it is that gives it its weight and authority."

256 *Ibid.*

The "common law" saw that British law's development could be tacitly constructed around the immutable law of nature, human values, and social utility.[257] Writing in Latin, Selden summarized his vision of British law:

> In truth, and to speak without perverse affection, all laws in general are originally equally antient [sic]. All were grounded upon nature, and no nation was, that out of it took not their grounds; and nature being the same in all, the beginning of all laws must be the same ... . [But] although the law of nature be truly said immutable, yet it is as true, that it is limitable, and limited law of nature is the law now used in every state. All the same may be affirmed of our *British* law, or *English*, or other whatsoever ... . This rationally considered, might end that obvious question of those, who would say something against the law of *England* if they could. This their trivial demand, *When and how began your common laws?* Questionless it is fittest answered by affirming, when and in like kind as the law of other states, that is *When there was first a state in that land, which the common law now governs.* Then were natural laws limited for the conveniency of civil society here, and those limitations have been from thence, increased, altered, interpreted and brought to what now they are; although perhaps, saving the merely immutable part of nature, now, in regard of their first being, they are not otherwise than a ship, that by often mending had no piece of the first materials, or as the house that's so often repaired, *ut nihil ex pristina materia supersit*, which yet, by the civil law, is to be accounted the same still ...[258]

Selden's vision of British legal history as constant change and continuity was developed by the late sixteenth- and early seventeenth-century common law lawyers. Although Lord Coke suggested that it was essential to the authority of any given portion of the common law that it be possible to trace it back directly to Saxon (or even Roman) times,[259] the dominant view of the common law courts was articulated by Chief Justice Matthew Hale, who maintained it was impossible to trace particular portions of the present body of law to their origins.[260] Hale maintained that tracing the customs was not material, for:

> the Strength and Obligation, and the formal Nature of a Law, is not upon Account that the Danes, or the Saxons, or the Normans, brought it in with them, but [rather rests upon the fact that] they became Laws, and binding in this Kingdom by Virtue of their being received and approved here.[261]

Because the law was in a constant process of change, no plausible ground existed for claiming that the common law in any single part was identical to the ancient laws. Nevertheless, it was the same body of law. The key was not identity of components but a steady continuity with the past. The conviction of the authority of the law

---

257 Pocock, *supra* note 244, saw this view as revolutionary.

258 *Joannis Seldeni jurisconsulti: opera omnia, tam edita quam inedita*, vol. 3 (London: Printed by T. Wood for J. Walthoe, 1729).

259 See D.E.C. Yale, "Hobbes and Hale on Law, Legislation, and the Sovereign" (1972) 31 Cambridge L.J. 121 at 127, n. 33.

260 Hale, *supra* note 250.

261 *Ibid.* at 43.

was the sense that the rules and practices of the common law at present were continuous with the life and the history of the peoples whose law it was. Chief Justice Hale borrowed Selden's imagery of the Argonauts Ship to discuss the common law system:

> Use and Customs, and Judicial Decisions and Resolutions, and Acts of Parliament, tho' not now extant, might introduce some New Laws, and alter some Old, which we now take to be the very Common Law itself, tho' the Times and precise Periods of such Alternations are not explicitly or clearly known: But tho' those particular Variations and Accessions have happened in the Laws, yet they being only partial and successive, we may with just Reason say, They are the same English laws now, that they were 600 Years since in the general. As the Argonauts Ship was the same when it returned home, as it was when it went out, tho' in that Long Voyage it has successive Amendment, and scarce came back with any of its former Materials, and as Titius is the same Man he was 40 Years since, tho' Physicians tell us, That in a Tract of seven Years, the Body has scarce any of the same Material Substance it had before.[262]

New law was the result of human responses to new circumstances, not ancient customs. The traditions of false law would seem to confirm Hale's belief that it was fruitless to attempt to sort out the different sources in the history of the British law.

Justice John Vaughan developed Selden's and Hale's ideas on the British law. In 1667, he stated in the case of *Edward Thomas v. Tomas Sorrell*:

> many things are said to be *prohibited* by the *Common Law*, and indeed most things so *prohibited* were primarily *prohibited* by *Parliament*, or by a Power equivalent to it in making Laws, which is the same, but are said to be *prohibited* by the *Common Law*, because the Original of the *Constitution* or *prohibiting Law* is not to be found of Record, but is beyond memory, and the Law known onely [sic] from practical proceeding and usage in Courts of Justice, as may appear by Laws made in the time of the Saxon King, of *William the First*, and *Henry the First*, yet extant in *History*, which are now received as *Common Law*. So if by accident the Records of all Acts of Parliament now extant, none of which is older than 9 H. 3 (but new Laws were as frequent before as since) should be destroyed by fire, or other casualty, the memorials of proceeding upon them found by the Records in Judicial proceeding, would upon like reason be accounted *Common Law* by Posterity.[263]

In a 1672 case, Vaughan stated, "in truth, most of the Common Law cannot be conceived to be Law otherwise than by Acts of Parliament, or Power equivalent to them, whereof the Rolls are lost; for alwaies there was a power and practice of making new Laws."[264]

Thus, Selden, Hale, and Vaughan viewed the common law as possibly the creation of past parliaments or their equivalent. The common law was the voice of the House of Commons as well as the lawyers. The jurists saw no distinction between common and statutory law. Either form appeared arbitrary, since the various occasions for their introduction had been forgotten. It did not follow, however, that such laws

---

262 *Ibid.* at 40.

263 (1667), Vaughan 358.

264 *Edmund Sheppard v. George Gosnold* (1677), Vaughan 163.

were unjustifiable or out of date. Indeed, they assumed the method behind the emergence of a custom was rational, since the common law itself was nothing else but reason[265] or the process of reasoning habits of a people into a coherent body of rules.[266] They presumed the rational process still held good, even if no adequate historical account of it could now be given. The common law was seen to be the expression or manifestation of commonly shared values and a shared sense of its reasonableness, historical appropriateness, and the common good, which was often framed in the language of natural law.[267] Ancient customs were known and their reasonableness was determined by the people, regardless of whether they were judge or lawmaker. As Gerald Postema wrote:

> The fact that it is shared, mutually recognized, is essential. It is not enough that each member of the community believes that the rules are reasonable, good, or wise; they must also believe that others in the community believe this as well, and that fact is important for their acceptance of the law as reasonable and, in consequence, as valid. This is one reason why the sense of historical continuity is important. For it is the public demonstration of the suitability of the rules over time that qualifies them for the status as law. No demonstration of the goodness or wisdom of a rule or practice by any particular person, regardless of his intellectual power, or practical insight, or divine inspiration will suffice.[268]

The common law jurists and lawyers saw the common law as a form of legal order manifested in the practice and common life of the nation; they integrated law, morality, and culture. However, they made a distinction between the common law and its various court formulations of the rules.[269] Lord Coke distinguished the ordinary faculty of reason ("natural reason") and the special "artificial reason" of the common law processes by cases, a faculty possessed only after long study and experience.[270] Common law reasoning was viewed as analogical, arguing from particular case to particular case on the basis of similarity, rather than on deductive or inductive tracing of logical relations between abstract ideas.[271] However, Blackstone and Lord Mansfield had begun describing the common law as a "rational science" based on general, justifying principles contained with particular decisions.[272] They felt the discovery of these principles underlying the law and the "spirit of the laws" in the notion of equity[273] was especially important for the students and future practitioners of the law.

---

265 Coke, *supra* note 127, vol. 1 at §21. Also see Blackstone, *supra* note 117, vol. 1 at 77.

266 Yale, *supra* note 259 at 125-26.

267 G.J. Postema, *Bentham and the Common Law Tradition* (Oxford: Clarendon Press, 1986) at 7-8.

268 *Ibid.* at 8.

269 See Blackstone, *supra* note 117, vol. 1 at 71.

270 (1613), 12 Coke 63 at 65. See C. Fried, "The Artificial Reason of the Law or: What Lawyers Know" (1981) 60 Tex. L. Rev. 35.

271 Coke, *ibid.*

272 Blackstone, *supra* note 117, vol. 1 at 425 and 2:2. See also *Jones v. Randal* (1774), K.B. 385, Lord Mansfield.

273 Blackstone, *ibid.*, vol. 3 at 429.

Since judges made mistakes, and because novel cases empowered judges to fashion solutions or rules, no particular court decision was considered final; all decisions were corrigible.[274] Thus, the common law resisted regimentation to a logical structure flowing from first principles, in favour of a dynamic and flexible approach to cases by locating the case within the living body of law and tracing its historical development in adjudication. Confronted with a novel case, judges had to fashion new legal rules out of the materials of existing law. In the seventeenth and eighteenth century, the favoured device of common law judges for responding to new situations from within the existing laws was the use of legal fictions.[275] In each case, new needs and situations were met by incrementally reworking the old law into new legal fictions and remedies.[276]

In the seventeenth century, and especially in the eighteenth century, the common law had to find a new justification for legislation in its account of British law, for statutory law and the doctrine of the sovereignty of parliament took on a widening importance in the life of the nation.[277] The struggle between the extension of the royal prerogatives of the Crown and parliament involved the common law courts.[278] The idea of political or legislative activity of the sovereign or parliament creating new law, through exercise of their own will or temporary aggregates of arbitrary wills, was a radical departure from the common law and its legal order. This struggle overwhelmed the minds of such legal scholars as Lord Coke, Blackstone, and Fortescue. They regarded such legislation as the major cause of the confusion, incoherence, and injustice in the law of Britain.[279] They argued such exercises of power had no internal coherence, reasonableness, or justness. Blackstone's *Commentaries* reflect the inconsistency of the common law in adjusting to developing legislative and constitutional conventions of parliamentary sovereignty.[280] The common law system's preoccupation with judicial opinion rather than legislative process meant it had little to say on the legal theory of the moral or political basis of legislative authority. Most legal analysis assumes the legislative assemblies' claim to democratic credentials and accepts that once a piece of legislation has been enacted, the legal profession has a duty to make the best of it by judicial interpretation, revision, and reconstruction.[281]

Thus, in British common law jurisdiction, land law was not and is not a coherent system. It does not have a planned and implemented coherent vision. In a contradictory manner, the common law views land as the basis of the constitutional order and as a commodity to be bought and sold by individuals without restrictions. The land law is a history of "haphazard outcome of hundreds of decisions resolving individual con-

---

274 See Simpson, *supra* note 56 at 89, 94.

275 Postema, *supra* note 267 at 12.

276 See Blackstone, *supra* note 117, vol. 4 at 205-206; Sir H. S. Maine, *Lectures on the Early History of Institutions* (London: J. Murray, 1880) at 230; Pocock, *supra* note 244 at 173.

277 Postema, *supra* note 267 at 14.

278 Pocock, *supra* note 244 at 52.

279 Blackstone, *supra* note 117, vol. 1 at 10-11 and 365, vol. 4 at 443; Hale, *supra* note 250, cc. 7-8.

280 Blackstone, *ibid.*, vol. 1 at 52.

281 J. Waldron, "The Dignity of Legislation" (1995) 54 Mar. L. Rev. 633 at 641-48.

flicts over rights and obligations in a particular plot of land."[282] The legal history of common law reveals the contradictory visions, but never resolves the basic conflict. Statutory reforms and other discourses sought to resolve the paradox and contradictions of the common law perspectives on land and its uses by restructuring the land law. From the mid-seventeenth century, British common law lost its role as the language of governance and politics, its discourse of the "ancient constitution," and its idiosyncratic notions of "rights" and "liberties" of subjects; it was replaced by other discourses such as Hobbes's positivism, Harrington's classical republicanism, and Locke's contractarianism. In the Victorian era, the common law became a specialist language of analytical jurisprudence and technical complexities of procedures and remedies.

E. Restructuring land law

The *Treaty of Westphalia* (1648) ended the authority of the Holy See and created an international order on defined territorial units.[283] A number of international law theories were developed to explain the relationship between the territories and the monarchies.[284] Although no comprehensive or dominant idea of land law existed about how to organize people on the land, there were many competing ideas, all derived from a hierarchy, either ecclesiastical or aristocratic.

The interpretation of history and religion created the foundation for political and constitutional discourses. European views of land law became entangled with Reformation interpretations of Judeo-Christian Scriptures,[285] which describe God's relations to humans and the earth.[286] The written Scriptures assert that God had explicitly given humans authority over the earth, its fruits and its creatures:

> And God said, Let us make man in our image, after our likeness: and let them have dominion over the fish of the sea, and over the fowl of the air, and over the cattle, and over all the earth, and over every creeping thing that creepeth upon the earth.
>
> ...
>
> And God blessed them, and God said unto them, Be fruitful, and multiply, and replenish the earth, and subdue it: and have dominion over the fish of the sea, and over the fowl of the air, and over every living thing that moveth upon the earth.[287]

In Britain, the debate concerning land and government revolved around the opposing absolutist ideas that the Crown inherited land from God through Adam and

---

282   A.M. Sinclair and M.E. MacCallum, *Introduction to Real Property Law*, 4th ed. (Vancouver: Butterworths, 1997) at 1-2.

283   M. Shaw, *Title to Territory in Africa: International Legal Issues* (Oxford: Clarendon Press, 1986) at 1-6.

284   *Ibid.* at 13-16.

285   For the ecclesiastical ideas see M. Stogre, *That the World May Believe: The Development of Papal Social Thought on Aboriginal Rights* (Sherbrooke, Qc.: Éditions Paulines, 1992).

286   H. Grotius, *De jure belli ac pacis, libri tres, vol. 2* (Oxford: Clarendon Press, 1925) at 186 [reprint].

287   *The Bible* (King James Version) Genesis I:26, 28.

John Locke's belief that a right to possess land was a fundamental human right to be protected by the Crown. In *Patriarcha*,[288] Robert Filmer argued that God gave the world and its services not to all men but to Adam and his line by natural inheritance. It was a grant of absolute dominion and exclusive control over other humans and resources. God's grant was the beginning of absolute regal power and aristocratic society. The authority of the Stuart monarchs in Britain, Filmer suggested, could be traced back to the Adamite line, thus justifying the tenure of the Crown over both lords and tenants.[289] Locke argued that neither reason nor revelation indicates that any man had been favoured with authority from God over his fellow humans. Any person's uses or labours on the land were limitations on the authority of the Crown over the land and people.[290] His work transformed the divine right of Crown into historical entitlement of natural rights to land acquired by various individuals outside of civil society but protected by the Crown. Interestingly, neither of these authors argued the common law's version of Crown tenure.

By the seventeenth century, the complex scheme of tenures, with their variety of services and incidents, had fallen into disuse. The idea of the private raising of revenue, or the raising of revenue by the King without the sanction or control of parliament, was being questioned. The services had been commuted into money payments and the incidents were increasingly being avoided by settling the lands to *uses*. Henry VIII had tried to halt this process by enacting the *Statute of Uses, 1535*. Yet the Chancery judges and the ingenuity of British conveyancers had defeated the legislative purpose. In 1623, another Act was passed to declare that unless the Crown or its predecessor in title had been in receipt of rent or profits during the last 60 years, the Crown was prevented from claiming land by reason of any right or title.[291] In 1646, the Long Parliament passed a resolution to the effect that most forms of feudal tenure should be abolished, together with their services and incidents. Enacted as the *Tenures Abolition Act, 1660*, it abolished all the various forms of feudal tenures and their incidents to leave the tenure of

---

288   P. Laslett, ed., *Patriarcha and Other Political Works of Sir Robert Filmer* (Oxford: Blackwell, 1949) at 1-48. Filmer's "treatise," written between 1638 and 1642, was originally published in 1680. Locke is said to have read the 1680 printing. In international law it is called the patrimonial theory, based on a feudal idea of land tenure that regarded territory as a piece of private property pertaining to the ruler.

289   John Locke, *Two Treatises of Government*, ed. by P. Laslett (Cambridge, U.K.: Cambridge University Press, 1970) at 48. The Whigs attempted to exclude James, Duke of York, the brother of King Charles II, from accession to the throne of Britain in 1679-81, on the basis of popery and arbitrary government. The Tory defense was based on Filmer's treatises on Divine Right and passive obedience to hereditary succession, even if this entailed a Roman Catholic monarch.

290   *Ibid.*, Treatise 2 at §138.4: "The Supreme Power cannot take from any Man any part of his Property without his own consent. ... [I]t is a mistake to think, that the Supreme of Legislative Power of any Commonwealth, can do what it will, and dispose of the Estate of the Subject arbitrarily, or take any part of them at pleasure." His arguments were extended to Chief Justice Coke's protective rationale of existing property rights in *Calvin's Case*, *supra* note 250, to respect all existing property rights in England.

291   1625 (U.K.), 21 Jac. I, c. 2, s. 1(2); re-enacted as *Crown Suits Act, 1769* (U.K.), 9 Geo. III, c. 16, s. 1; 1861 (U.K.), 24 & 25 Vict., c. 62. It was repealed and replaced by the *Limitation Act*, *supra* note 152 at s. 30(1).

the Crown, and converted the fee and common socage into the freehold estate of the lord, and the copyhold tenure into unfree leasehold estates of the tenants. In the context of this statute, a new explanation of land law was required.

F. Commentaries on the Laws of England

Faced with these statutory changes, the practicing British lawyers of the seventeenth century and the humanist scholars realized that a new explanation was necessary. Sir Henry Spelman, a seventeenth-century historian, made it impossible to deny that feudal law was a foreign element in the British past.[292] The common law of the eighteenth century found it was possible to give an historical account of the British land law in terms of the gradual accretion of new laws and the loss of old ones.[293] Understanding this process reveals how the perspective or tradition of the common law was constructed as well as the ancient constitution.[294] The common law provided the propertied class in Britain a way to break the bonds of feudal tenure while at the same time keeping in check both the forces of absolutism and the new emerging democratic forces.[295] Confronting the changes, judges were called on to refashion the feudal law, and created legal fictions.[296]

Land law came to be seen as the bulwark that protected an interest in things. For example, Coke's interpretation of Littleton's *Treatise on Tenure* is distorted by his struggle with the Crown as well as his quest to find or invent an explanation of all legal propositions. In contrast, Blackstone's *Commentaries on the Laws of England* (1765) lacks such explanation.[297] Blackstone made the questionable and untidy developments

---

292   The original growth, propagation, and condition of *feods* and tenures See *The English Works of Sir Henry Spelman, Kt., Published in His Lifetime: Together with His Posthumous Works, Relating to the Laws and Antiquities of England*, 2d. ed. by Edmund Gibson (London: Printed for D. Browne, sen. & jun., W. Mears, F. Clay ... [etc.], 1727).

293   John Selden was the first to conceptualize the process. He remarked in *Jani anglorum facies altera* in *Tracts Written by John Selden of the Inner Temple, Esquire: The First Entitled Jani anglorum facies altera, Rendred Into English*, trans. Adam Littleton (London: Printed for R. Bassett and T. Chiswell, and are to be sold by Robert Clavell,1683) at §§ a3v-a4, that, "the times on this side of the Normans entrance, are so full of new Laws, especially such as belong to the rights of Tenancy or Vassalage; though other laws have been carefully enough kept up from the times of the Saxons, and perhaps from an earlier date ... ." Blackstone, *supra* note 117, vol. 1 at 244, referred to it as, "a mere interruption of the true course of the national life."

294   Pocock, *supra* note 244 at 173; Edmund Burke, "Speech on the Reform of Representation of the Commons in Parliament" in *The Works of Edmund Burke*, vol. 6 (Boston: C.C. Little & J. Brown, 1839) at 46; R. Ferguson, *Law and Letters in American Culture* (Cambridge, Mass.: Harvard University Press, 1984) at 14.

295   Hill, *supra* note 244 at 257-58; Christopher Hill, *Some Intellectual Consequences of the English Revolution* (Madison: University of Wisconsin Press, 1980) at 29-30.

296   Blackstone, *supra* note 117, vol. 3 at 267.

297   Even the subsequent works of Pollock & Maitland and Holdsworth in the nineteenth century accept the earlier explanations without too extensive reliance on independent research. See G.W. Thompson, *Commentaries on the Modern Law of Real Property*, vol. 1 (Indianapolis: Bobbs-Merrill, 1924) at 48-49.

of the common law appear neat and tidy. Blackstone's *Commentaries* were the first academic attempt to bring all the themes in British law together, the only systematic attempt to present a perspective on the common law system. It became the most influential source legitimizing British legal thinking in the eighteenth century.

The *Commentaries* characterized feudal law as a departure from English liberties, while ironically constructing the fiction of the ultimate tenure of the Crown over all lands. As Carol Rose commented:

> ... Blackstone launched into a quite similar pseudohistory [as Locke had] in explaining property as an institution with an origin and evolution: he, too, described human beings as beginning in a state of plenty, gradually accumulating personal and landed property, and finally creating government and law to protect property.[298]

Blackstone used the rule of natural law in defence of the institution of property,[299] but, without explanation, like Bracton, he turned to Roman law for his restructuring of the common law attributes of principles, procedures, and remedies. Also, without explanation, he attempted to "naturalize" purely social phenomena, restated as "freedom" what could be seen as servitude, and cast as rational a chaotic order. His effort began the utopian enterprise of legality. This restructuring the common law is reminiscent of the traditions of false law in the earlier centuries.[300]

Blackstone thought of "Things,"[301] not property. Blackstone's reconceptualized land law of things contained two elements: property required some "external thing" to serve as object of its rights; and the owner had "sole and despotic dominion over the thing, which one man claims and exercises over the external things of the world, in total exclusion of the rights of any other individual in the universe."[302] He seems to be thinking about absolute ownership or fiction of the Crown's tenure, but he applied the concept broadly, considering property, along with life and liberty, to be an "absolute right, inherent in every Englishman."[303] Yet his notion of absolute dominion is subject to "control and diminution ... by the laws of the land,"[304] but the law would not permit the smallest infringement of property rights, even for the good of the entire community.[305]

Blackstone's taxonomy was of things, with the nature of each thing determining its legal treatment. The basic distinctions were based on mobility: Things real and Things personal. Things real were concerned with immovable things, such as land. Blackstone divided Things real into corporeal and incorporeal hereditaments (rights to

---

298 C.M. Rose, *Property and Persuasion: Essays on the History, Theory and Rhetoric of Ownership* (Boulder, CO: Westview Press, 1994) at 26.

299 Blackstone, *supra* note 117, vol. 2 at 1-15.

300 D. Kennedy, "The Structure of Blackstone's Commentaries" (1978) 28 Buffalo L. Rev. 210.

301 K.J. Vandevelde, "The New Property of the Nineteenth Century: The Development of the Modern Concept of Property" (1979) 29 Buffalo L. Rev. 325 at 330-333.

302 Blackstone, *supra* note 117, vol. 2 at 2.

303 *Ibid.*, vol. 2 at 34.

304 *Ibid.*, vol. 1 at 134.

305 *Ibid.* at 135.

inheritances). Corporeal hereditaments were land or things that could be detected by the senses: estates in land; the freeholds of inheritance (fee simple, fee tail); and freeholds not of inheritance (for life). Incorporeal hereditaments were not things, but a "right" issuing from a thing—they became "things" only "in contemplation";[306] or "a right issuing out of a thing corporate"[307] such as advowsons, tithes, commons (*profits à prendre*), rights of way (easements), offices, dignities, franchises, annuities, and rents.[308]

Things personal were all rights in immovable things and some interests or rights in movable things. Blackstone divided Things personal into chattels real and chattels personal. Chattels real were terms for years (estates less than freehold), conditional estates (securities), and feudal relics. Chattels personal were choses in possession (corporeal) and chattels personal in action or choses in action (incorporeal). The choses in action were similar to incorporeal inheritances that existed in contemplation, as a right to hold some thing in possession at some future time,[309] a "thing rather in *potentia* than in *esse*."[310] Since no physical thing was actually possessed, the incorporeal or reifying rights fictionalized such possession.

Great confusion of land law resulted from Blackstone's categories. There is no theory unifying Roman or civil laws and the common law. Subsequent British legal commentators have called the classification and structure of land law an "ungodly jumble"[311] or a law resembling more "chaos than a system."[312] Eventually, in the 1920s, British statutes clarified the land law.[313]

The deep structural problem soon became that the protection of intangible forms of wealth created more conflicts than did tangible things, and courts began to define property as the right to value rather than the right to a thing:

> Where some tangible thing was involved, Blackstone considered any limitation in the owner's dominion to be inherent in the nature of the thing or the owner. For example, animals ferae naturae presented an example of qualified property, because their nature did not permit absolute dominion over them. Where no tangible thing was involved, as in the case of incorporeal hereditaments and choses in action, Blackstone used his reified right fiction to preserve the absolutist conception of property. Blackstone considered the incorporeal hereditament and the chose in action to be the thing which was the object of the property rights. Thus, one who had a chose in action or an incorporeal hereditament has absolute dominion over a thing. The limited property right has been reified, and the resulting thing was owned absolutely.[314]

---

306   *Ibid.* at vol. 2 at 17.

307   *Ibid.* at 19.

308   *Ibid.* at 21.

309   *Ibid.* at 389.

310   *Ibid.* at 397.

311   Pollock & Maitland, *supra* note 8.

312   Edward Jenks, *A Short History of English Law, from the Earliest Times to the Year 1938*, 6th ed. (London: Methuen, 1949) at 241.

313   *Law of Property Act*, 1922 (U.K.), 12 & 13 Geo. V, c. 16; *Land Registration Act*, 1925 (U.K.), 15 & 16 Geo. V, c. 21; *Administration of Estates Act*, 1925 (U.K.), 15 & 16 Geo. V, c. 23.

314   Vandevelde, *supra* note 301 at 333.

G. The legal fiction of Crown tenure

In the seventeenth century the courts began reconceptualizing the aristocratic idea that all lands of subjects in Britain were held by some lord, and ultimately by the Crown, lord paramount over every parcel of land in the realm.[315] Although the Crown's actual occupation was imaginary, and the lands were occupied by others, the fundamental principle of British land law became that the Crown had an "ultimate" tenure over all the lands.

Writing on the effects of the Norman Conquest on British law, Blackstone remarked in his *Commentaries:*

> ... it became a fundamental maxim and necessary principle (though in reality a mere fiction) of our English tenures, "that the king is the universal lord and original proprietor of all the lands in his kingdom: and that no man doth or can possess any part of it, but what has mediately or immediately been derived as a gift from him, and held upon feudal services." The grand and fundamental maxim of all feudal tenure is this: that all lands were originally granted out by the sovereign, and are therefore holden, either mediately or immediately, of the Crown. The grantor was called the proprietor, or *lord*: being he who retained the dominion or ultimate property of the feud or fee; and the grantee, who had only the use and possession, according to the terms of the grant, was styled the feudatory or *vassal* ... .[316]

Stripped of the now-abolished incidents of the various tenures by statutes, Blackstone's conceptualizing of remaining tenures was simple: only the Crown has allodial[317] tenure; everyone else has a delegated and derivative title, right, or interest. Blackstone continues:

> Almost all the real property of this kingdom is, by the policy of our laws, supposed to be granted by, dependent upon, and holden of, some superior lord, by and in consideration of certain services to be rendered to the lord by the tenant or the possessor of this property ... . Thus all the land in the kingdom is supposed to be holden, mediately or immediately, of the king, who is styled lord *paramount*, or above all.[318]

These two concepts are merged in modern legal thought, as Professor McNeil explains:

> As for the doctrine of tenures, its effect in this context is to give the Crown a paramount lordship over lands held by subjects. The fiction of original Crown ownership and grants was invented to explain how this feudal relationship arose. That is the fiction's purpose, and this is the extent of its application. The doctrine of tenures, though capable at common law of giving the Crown a title to land in the event an estate held of it expires, cannot be used otherwise to claim lands which subjects possess.[319]

---

315 *Grendon v. Bishop of Lincoln* (1677), 2 Plow. 493 at 498; *Taylor d. Atkyns v. Horde* (1757), 1 Burr. 60 at 109; *Halsbury's Laws of England*, vol. 8, 4th ed. (London: Butterworths, 1973-86) at para. 304 [hereinafter *Halsbury's*].

316 Blackstone, *supra* note 117, vol. 2 at 51; *Royal Prerogative*, *supra* note 60 at 125-55.

317 See notes 327ff., *infra*.

318 Blackstone, *supra* note 117.

319 McNeil, *supra* note 3 at 107.

While the Crown title came to be asserted as a fundamental maxim of British law, both landholders and legal thinkers of the day recognized it as a fiction. The legal scholars restructured the meaning of landholding to rationalize and consolidate absolutism and the idea of derivative tenures, estates, and interests. The doctrine had many conceptual problems. The King must at one time have been in *seisin* of all lands in the realm, some of which he granted out to subjects, and this theory could not be supported by historical and legal scholarship.[320] Therefore, legal writers suggested that William I acquired all the lands in Britain by conquest.[321] When this view could not be supported, the treatise writers accepted that the doctrine of tenure was mainly a fiction of law, adopted for the purpose of justifying the ultimate jurisdiction of the Crown over all lands in the realm and fictitious grants of derivative tenures or titles.[322] Professor McNeil summarizes the limitations of the fiction:

> Since the fiction encompasses royal grants as well as original Crown ownership, it generally cannot be used in England to challenge a subject's title to land. The Crown cannot, on the strength of its fictitious original title, require a person who is in possession of land to prove his right by producing a royal grant, for in most cases no grant exists. ... The Crown must prove its present title just like anyone else.[323]

Moreover, the operation of the legal fiction in the courts never acknowledged the Crown had prerogative power to abrogate or derogate from property or other legal rights.[324] Such a claim would conflict with *Magna Carta* and common law principles of protection of *seisin* (possession) and adverse possession. Both would prevent the Crown from seizing property or otherwise infringing legal rights by act of state within its own dominions.[325]

Unless the law created the fiction of possession in the Crown, the Crown title would have to be a matter of record before it could be in possession of land.[326] If the Crown asserted a right to land and had to recover the land from an intruder, but a record was lacking, the Crown could apply through an inquest of office.[327] Alternatively, where the Crown claimed possession, by record or otherwise, it could apply for a prerogative remedy of an information of intrusion.[328]

---

320 *Ibid.* at 82-83.

321 *Ibid.* at 83-84.

322 *Ibid.* at 84.

323 *Ibid.* at 84-85.

324 See Blackstone, *supra* note 117, vol. 1 at 141-45; *Halsbury's, supra* note 315 at para. 828. See *Burmah Oil Co. v. Lord Advocate*, [1965] A.C. 75 at 102 (H.L.). The Court stated: "even at the zenith of the royal prerogative, no one thought that there was any general rule that the prerogative could be exercised, even in times of war or imminent danger, by taking property required for defense without making any payment for it."

325 *Walker v. Baird*, [1892] A.C. 491 (P.C.); *Eshugbayi Eleko v. Government of Nigeria*, [1931] A.C. 662 (P.C.); *Buttes Gas v. Hammer*, [1975] 1 Q.B. 557 at 573 (C.A.).

326 McNeil, *supra* note 3 at 93.

327 *Ibid.* at 95-98.

328 *Ibid.* at 98-103.

The legal fiction of Crown tenure avoided inconsistency with the doctrine of *stare decisis*—the common law evaluative standard of law and justice was that a court of last resort could not reverse any of its own prior decisions. The doctrine of *stare decisis* (to stand by things decided) was a pillar of royal law. This doctrine states that as long as the principle derived from decisions of the highest courts in a given jurisdiction is logically essential to the instant case and is appropriate to contemporary circumstances, courts should adhere to the law as set forth. Once a rule, myth, or fiction was established by the courts, the judges and legal scholars were prevented from questioning it.

In the nineteenth century, Pollock and Maitland noted the effect of the fiction in the common law:

> Every acre of English soil and every proprietary right therein has been brought within the compass of a single formula, which may be expressed thus: *Z tenet terram illam de ... domino Rege.* The King himself holds land which is in every sense his own; no one else has any proprietary right in it; but if we leave out the account of his royal demesne, then every acre of land is "held of" the king. The person whom we may call its owner, the person who has the right of use and abuse of the land, to cultivate it or leave it uncultivated, to keep others off it, holds the land of the king either immediately or mediately.[329]

In the twentieth century, Lord Hailsham, *Halsbury's Laws of England*,[330] restates the principle as:

> No absolute ownership of land. Technically, land is not the subject of absolute ownership but of tenure. According to the doctrines of the common law there is no land in England in the hands of a subject which is not held of some lord by some service and for some estate. This tenure is either under the Sovereign directly, or under some mesne lord, or a succession of mesne lords, who, or the first of whom, holds of the Sovereign. Thus the Sovereign is lord paramount, either mediate or immediate, of all land within the realm. The tenure of land is based upon the assumption that it was originally granted as a 'feud' by the Sovereign to his immediate tenant on condition of certain services, and, where there has been subinfeudation, to the immediate tenant in turn regranted it. Although for most purposes this system, known as 'the feudal system', has lost its practical importance, it still determines the form of property in land.

D.J. Hayton, Megarry's *Manual of The Law of Real Property*,[331] restates the principle:

> The basis of English land law is that all land in England is owned by the Crown. A small part is in the actual occupation of the Crown; the rest is occupied by tenants holding either directly or indirectly from the Crown. *'Nulle terre sans seigneur'* (no land without a lord):

---

329 Pollock & Maitland, *supra* note 8, vol. 1 at 232-33.

330 *Halsbury's, supra* note 315, vol. 39 at para. 304.

331 David J. Hayton, *Megarry's Manual of the Law of Real Property*, 6th ed. (London: Stevens & Som, 1982) at 23-24.

there is no allodial land in England, i.e. no land owned by a subject and not held of some lord.

...

There are thus two basic doctrines in the law of real property. These are known as—

(i) the doctrine of tenures: all land is held of the Crown, either directly or indirectly, on one or other of the various tenures; and

(ii) the doctrine of estates: a subject cannot own land, but can merely own an estate in it, authorizing him to hold it for some period of time.

In short, the tenure answers the question "How is it held?" the estate the question "For how long?"

In English common law, the doctrine of tenure of the Crown is the given context for every subdivision of property rights. It cannot be historically justified, but exists as a fiction of the common law. Its purpose is to ensure that all estates, possessions, or interests are registered, and the resulting titles are viewed as the evidence of legitimate entitlement to use the land.

H. Allodial tenures in British land law

Allodial tenure was always a part of European land law. It was understood as an "entire" property in the land by a possessor; a territory held in "absolute ownership" without service or acknowledgement of any superior holder.[332] It was conceived of as the converse of feudal land tenure, and the tenures that feudal law replaced. Thomas Hobbes described it as "[w]hen a man holds his Land from the gift of God only, the lands Civilians call allodial."[333] Freeman noted that the King "might have his ancient allodial property."[334]

In British law, allodial tenure was analogized as the rights held by the great proprietors of British land,[335] or as the same privileges and rights as had been enjoyed by the original proprietors of Britain,[336] before feudalism.[337] Lord Coke commented that

---

332   *Oxford English Dictionary*, 1933 ed., *s.v.* "allodial."

333   J. Cropsely, ed., *A Dialogue Between a Philosopher and a Student of the Common Law* (Chicago: University of Chicago, 1971) at 1999.

334   Freeman, *supra* note 85, vol. 3 at 95; E.A. Freeman, *The Growth of the English Constitution from the Earliest Times* (New York: Macmillan, 1890) at 77.

335   A. Smith, *An Inquiry Into the Nature and Causes of the Wealth of Nations* [1776], vol. 1 (New York: Modern Library, 1937) at iii; vol. 4 at 413 [reprint].

336   T. Carte, ed., *A Collection of Original Letters and Papers: Concerning the Affairs of England, from the Year 1641 to 1660*, vol. 1 (London: James Bettenham, 1739) at 364.

337   J.F. Kirk, *History of Charles the Bold, Duke of Burgundy*, vol. 4 (London: J. Murray, 1863-68) at iii; Stubbs, *supra* note 66, vol. 1 at vii and 297.

in the *Domesday Book* the tenants in fee simple are called *alodarii*,[338] while Stubbs refers to them as "alodiars of Domesday."[339] Others equated allodial tenure with a freehold tenure or a fee simple estate. Hume called a territory "allodial" if possessed by a free title.[340] Keightley categorized it as a full propriety,[341] and Stephen characterized it as held of no one but enjoyed as free and independent.[342]

The merger of the fictitious doctrine of tenures with the idea of ultimate, paramount lordship transformed the allodial tenure into incidents of the prerogative of the Crown. It is not clear whether this transformation in legal thought was an inescapable logical deduction from the assumption of the ultimate lordship of Crown or a principle of law. The Crown could not be a tenant,[343] since it became impossible for a lord to be both lord and tenant with respect to the same land.[344] The Crown could not grant his allodial ownership to a subject.[345] Nonetheless, British law established that no person who held his land in freehold tenure or fee simple estate owned the land in Britain allodially, since ultimately everyone held under the Crown. A tenure, estate, or title became confused as measures of the ultimate interest of the Crown. Blackstone commented that there is no proper alluvium, or land, not held of the King; and no subject can have more than the usufruct or beneficial enjoyment of the land he occupies.[346]

Yet the fictions were frail. The Scottish courts have held that British subjects on the Orkney and Shetland Islands do own land allodially under Udal law.[347] When lands were owned allodially under local law, the fiction of the Crown's lordship did not apply.[348] Professor McNeil noted that "[t]he Crown's land rights would be no greater than those of the local sovereign from whom it acquired the territory, unless it proceeded to abrogate or diminish the rights of the inhabitants by act of state or legislation."[349] Crown sovereignty did apply to the British subjects in the Orkney and Shetland Islands because of personal allegiance, but the Crown's acquisition of sovereignty did not disturb the existing legal system.

---

338 Coke, *supra* note 127 at 1b.

339 Stubbs, *supra* note 66, vol. 1 at 89.

340 David Hume, *History of England from the Invasion of Julius Caesar to the Revolution in 1688*, vol. 1 (Indianapolis: Liberty Press, 1983-85) at 246, App. II.

341 T. Keightley, *History of England* (New York: Harpers & Brothers, 1860) at 77.

342 H.J. Stephen, *Commentaries on the Laws of England*, ed. by L. Crispin Warmington, vol. 1 (London: Butterworth, 1950) at 174.

343 Coke, *supra* note 127 at 1b; J.A. Chitty, *Treatise of the Law of the Prerogatives of the Crown: And the Relative Duties and Rights of Subjects* (London: Joseph Butterworths & Sons, 1820) at 378.

344 Coke, *supra* note 127 at 152b.

345 McNeil, *supra* note 3 at 92, n. 58.

346 Blackstone, *supra* note 117, vol. 2 at 51, 59 and 60; vol. 4 at 418.

347 *Smith v. Lewick Harbour Trustees*, [1903] 5 S.C. (5th) 680; *Lord Advocate v. Balfour*, [1907] S.C. 1360; C.F. Kolbert and N.A.M. MacKay, *History of Scots and English Land Law* (Berkhampstead, U.K.: Geographical Publications, 1977) at 15-17.

348 *Ibid.* See also *Amodu Tijani v. Secretary, Southern Nigeria*, [1921] 2 A.C. 399 (P.C.) at 403, 409-10, Viscount Haldane. Viscount Haldane suggested that "native title" under local law may be such as to exclude the "radical or final title of the Sovereign," or to reduce any radical right in the Sovereign to one which only extends to comparatively limited right of administrative interference." See McNeil, *supra* note 3 at 156-57, n. 117.

349 McNeil, *supra* note 3, c. 6.

The restructuring of British land law created the idea of land tenure as a necessity for creating a proprietarian order. At the same time, the rise of trade and colonization created the alternative idea of land as a commodity. Property came to be viewed as a device to create social and economic relationships and a transformation occurred from property as rights to "things" toward the idea of imaginary property.

3. Seeing Property

In European legal thought, as illustrated by perspectives of the British common law on land, seeing property became a deep study of the legal imagination; a learned, analytical conception, abstract to the senses, existing as either a fiction, or a vision, or an idea.[350] It exists only in human consciousness, and allows the believers to see the unseen, to have rights in the visualized abstractions that lie between people and things. Seeing property in modern legal thought is a web of intangible bonds that organizes modern society. Without literacy, written records, and a learned elite, the vision might have disappeared. To understand this conceptual domain of seeing property, we have traced its vision's development in British law from the first record of customs to the modern fiction.

In British legal thought, land occupation is used to denote legal relations between humans and things.[351] It forms a borderline between material scarcity and human desires, although there is no necessity to draw a conceptual wedge between humans and things. Material resources are within us as well as outside us; we are an integral part of the land. By material resources, we refer broadly to the ecology of the planet. Most studies of property have a narrower definition about the "corporeality" of the land and its resources. Typically, a piece of land is not taken to be identical with the soil and rocks at a given location.[352] Land is identified with a three-dimensional theory instead

---

350 R. McKeon, ed., *The Basic Works of Aristotle*, trans. A.W. Pickard-Cambridge (New York: Random House, 1941). Aristotle's property is a communication of a metaphysical essence that defines or indicates a transcendent identity; but is not the very heart of the identity or essence. Thus, in European thought, "property" is the dream or shadow or language of a deeper, more mysterious essence. In Aristotle's *Topica et Sophistici elenchi* he asserts that property is an absolute, which emerges into a division of identity ("what is peculiar to anything") at I.4.19, into "essences" (*topos*), then into that "which does not indicate the essence of a thing, but yet belongs to that thing alone, and is predicated convertible of it" (at I.5.17-19). Modern thought, however, rejects essences for more abstract human purposes.

351 See J. Austin, *Lectures on Jurisprudence: Or The Philosophy of Positive Law*, vol. 1 (London: J. Murray, 1904) at 357-58.

352 Often, land is defined as "the solid material of the earth." In its restrained sense it means soil, but in its typical legal sense it is a generic term comprehending every species of ground, soil or earth whatsoever, such as meadows, pastures, woods, moors, waters, marches, furze, and heath, including houses, mills, castles, and other buildings and structures. It is also said to extend indefinitely upwards and downwards to the globe's centre. See Coke, *supra* note 127 at 4a; G.W. Paton, *A Text-book of Jurisprudence*, 3d ed. (Oxford: Clarendon Press, 1964) at 508-9; P.J. Fitzgerald, ed., *Salmond on Jurisprudence*, 12th ed. (London: Sweet & Maxwell, 1966) at 416-17. For a legal method of how images construct the Canadian constitution, see W.E. Conklin, *Images of a Constitution* (Toronto: University of Toronto Press, 1989), especially "Introduction: Images of a Constitution" at 3-20.

of the sort of material objects that one might locate in the environment.[353] Others insist the cultivable soil, dazzling rocks, and solid surfaces are the primary objects of real property, thus creating land as material.[354] Thus, land is the initial manifestation of the vision of property.

As British legal philosopher H.L.A. Hart has pointed out, in law (as in philosophy) it is a mistake to think that particulars can be classified under general terms on the basis only of their possession of specified common features.[355] A watertight definition of property may not be possible in analytic jurisprudence because as many different conceptions are possible as there are linguistic traditions or societies that conceptualize and detail land use and care. Our review of the conceptual development of British land law has illustrated the dialectical path we have to travel. No comprehensive definition of "property" exists. The concept has never had any single meaning, nor can ever satisfy all of the situations and tests of the legal or lay imagination. The existing ideal types of property and their values establish the context of contradictory standards.

Typically, European property systems combine the ideal types of common property, collective property, and private property. We do not find these categories helpful because under them two major and divergent ideal types create explanatory contexts for the purpose of a property regime. Often, these ideal types are incompatible at a number of practical junctures. A modern challenge is understanding land use as a method of creating a government and legal order (proprietarian or propriety model) as against the idea of land as commodity to be exchanged (commodity or preference-satisfying model). The proprietary and commodity conceptions of property, together with their associated conceptions of individual liberty, have different visions of the purposes for which we have a property regime. Few courts of legal scholars have been consistently and exclusively committed to one or the other. The common law system in Canada, for instance, is grounded in the proprietarian model and has not fully embraced the commodity model.

A. Propriété: proprietarian order

In late seventeenth-century British thought, property became a metaphor for land.[356] This use of a French term *propriété* to describe British land law remains another legal mystery.[357] The two words had little in common. The French word "*propriété*" was never translated as "land" in Anglo-Saxon or Old English. The term *propriété* is

---

353 A. Kocoureck, *Jural Relations* (Indianapolis: Bobbs Merril Co., 1928) at 336.

354 Noyes, *supra* note 116 at 438.

355 H.L.A. Hart, "Definition and Theory in Jurisprudence" (1954) 70 L.Q. Rev. 21.

356 *Oxford English Dictionary*, 1933 ed., *s.v.* "property." The Latin word "*proprietatem,*" the quality of "*proprius*" (to own, proper), the transitional term was middle English "*proprete.*" Compare to the older concept of "land," *s.v.*

357 *Ibid.*

translated as "goods" or "movables,"[358] while land is rendered "whatsoever may be plowed" or arable land[359] The use of *propriété* in British law establishes the idea of a legal order based on property interests and marks a subtle shift away from the fictions of tenure.

British legal thought, as illustrated by the doctrine of tenure and its relationship to sovereignty, is concerned with the proper order or public good. Canadian constitutional analysis or thought is similarly concerned with constitutional order and its relations to property. Competing understandings of proprietarian order in British and Canadian legal thought share the principle that the purpose of property law is to promote preconceived notions of social and political norms. In British legal thought inherited by the Canadian federation, the public good was defined by the Crown and the fiction of the doctrine of tenures and prerogative laws. The law was whatever the sovereign established was the proper social structure, and with the creation of parliament, what the representatives thought was proper. Within this order each person and each institution had a "proper" role and position. The public good was thought to be best served if everyone fulfilled a role in the divine or social hierarchy; property was central to this plan of social stability. It anchored the subject to his (and exclusively *his*) rightful place in the proper social hierarchy. Property, of which the only important form was the freehold estate in land, was more than wealth; it was authority, or at least a source of authority. Far from being looked on as a market commodity, land meant independence from the caprices of the newly forming market system.

Furthermore, in the development of representative government in Britain and Canada, a property estate was a necessary condition for political representation and participation in government. The modern idea of a fluid society in which individuals readily move, either geographically or socially, was anathema to this mentality of the proprietarian order. The idea of Crown or state regulatory activity over property reflects the proprietarian understanding that certain activities and certain resources should not be left to regulation by the market or individuals. It reflects the core proprietarian ideas that the primary purpose of property is to maintain the proper social order and that the market cannot be relied on to create that order.

In the Canadian colonies, the incorporation of British law and property law principles was accomplished through the regulatory concept of the general reception of law.[360] In the prerogative law of colonization in the United Kingdom, the King controlled the British subjects and immigrants in the colonies.[361] British common law was considered a birthright of all subjects, making them subject to the personal jurisdiction of the Crown regardless of where they travelled.[362] Where British settlements were

---

358 *Ibid., s.v.* Compare to concepts of "chattels," *s.v.,* and "goods," *s.v.*.

359 Coke, *supra* note 127 at 4a. Lord Coke extended the definition to "comprehendeth any ground, soil or earth whatsoever."

360 See P.W. Hogg, *Constitutional Law in Canada,* 3d ed. (Toronto: Carswell, 1992) at 27-44; R.L. Barsh and J.Y. Henderson, "Aboriginal Rights, Treaty Rights, and Human Rights: Indian Tribes and Constitutional Renewal" (1982) 17 J. Can. Studies 55; McNeil, *supra* note 3 at 108-93; and B. Slattery, "Aboriginal Sovereignty and Imperial Claims" (1991) 29 Osgoode Hall L.J. 1.

361 Hogg, *ibid.* at 32.

362 R.T.E. Latham, *The Law and the Commonwealth* (Westport, Conn.: Greenwood Press, 1970) at 516-17.

authorized in territories with treaties, Aboriginal laws continued. The treaties limited the common law of colonization.[363] These treaties and the prerogative law of the King controlled the colonialists and their assemblies, which were considered by British law as inferior and dependent.[364] When representative government was granted to a colonial settlement by prerogative instruments or imperial Act, some of the King's prerogatives ended and were replaced by the unlimited authority of the imperial parliament's laws, to which all colonial law had to conform.[365]

Each colony specifically received British law as a matter of cession (maritime colonies) or conquest (Quebec and parts of Ontario) at a certain date.[366] This included the existing prerogative law, common law and existing British parliamentary acts. Until the King granted representative government to the immigrants and refugees, prerogative law was controlling and maintained the proper social structure. After receiving representative government, colonial law had to be consistent with the United Kingdom parliamentary legislation.[367]

Within the colonies, landholding was conceptualized as a proprietarian order. In terms of landholding, only the imperial Crown could purchase the land of the Aboriginal nations or people.[368] When the Crown permitted the colonialists to acquire land, they held the land of the Crown in a form of an estate; their estates were not allodial but were part of the fictitious tenurial lands.[369]

In the United States legal analysis of property, the inherited British idea of property as a foundation for legal order, is called by Carol Rose "property as propriety."[370] Gregory Alexander expands her concept in *Commodity & Propriety*.[371] According to Professors Rose and Alexander, the proprietarian conception was a well-established

---

363 See Hogg, *supra* note 360 at 27-44; Barsh & Henderson, *supra* note 360; McNeil, *supra* note 3 at 108-93; Slattery, *supra* note 360.

364 See generally K. Roberts-Wray, *Commonwealth and Colonial Law* (London: Frederick A. Prager, 1966); and C. Clark, *A Summary of Colonial Law, the Practice of the Court of Appeals from the Plantations, and of the Laws and their Administration in all The Colonies* (London: S. Sweet, 1834).

365 Hogg, *supra* note 360 at 32.

366 Benson & Bowden, *supra* note 3 at 17-20; Ziff, *supra* note 3 at 43-46.

367 "Effect of Tenure," *supra* note 213 at 32.

368 See Part II, "Treaty Reconciliations." A 1666 Royal Commission established this concept; H.P. Kraus, ed., *Sir Edmund Andros, 1637-1714, Governor of New York, Governor of the Dominion of New England, Governor of Virginia: Original Documents From His Papers, Many with the Signatures of Charles II, James II, William III, and Mary II*, vol. 1 (New York: H.P. Kraus, 1978) at 50; N.B. Shurtleff, ed., *Records of the Governor and Company of the Massachusetts Bay in New England*, vol. 1 (New York: AMS Press, 1968) at 176, 190, 198-99. This was codified in imperial law in *The Royal Proclamation of 1763*, 4 Geo. III, United Kingdom Public Record Office (PRO): c. 66/36/3693 (back of roll); RSC 1970, App. No. 1 at 123-29.

369 Ziff, *supra* note 3 at 45.

370 Rose, *supra* note 298 at 58-62.

371 G.S. Alexander, *Commodity and Propriety: Competing Visions of Property in American Legal Thought, 1776-1970* (Chicago: University of Chicago Press, 1997).

tradition in European legal-political thought and their ancient constitutions.[372] According to this tradition, property is the material foundation for creating and maintaining the proper social order, the private basis for the public good:

> This tradition, whose roots can be traced back to Aristotle, has continuously understood the individual human as an inherently social being, inevitably dependent on others not only to thrive but even just to survive. This irreducible interdependency means that individuals owe one another obligations, not by virtue of consent alone but as an inherent incident of the human condition. This view of human nature provides the basis for the political-legal principle in proprietarian thought that when individuals fail to meet their precontractual social obligations, the state may legitimately compel them to act for the good of the entire community.[373]

Professor Rose stated that property in the seventeenth through the nineteenth centuries in Europe was the mainstay of "propriety" and carried with it governing authority and a vision of good order:

> Property in this world "properly" consisted in whatever resources one needed to do one's part in keeping good order; and the normal understanding of order was indeed hierarchy— in the family, in the immediate community, in the larger society and commonwealth, in the natural world, and in the relation between the natural and the spiritual world.
>
> A person's property fixed his location in this hierarchy. Thus a monarch had his own property in the form of royal domain; in theory (though the practice was much attenuated), he should not need to tax the subjects, since the income from his domain would enable him, as the traditional phrase put it, to "live on his own." The idea was that his royal property would provide him the wherewithal to exercise his role, that of overall governance. The members of the noble estate in turn had their own land, on which they were subrulers or "co-governors"; and other subruling orders as well had the property they needed to maintain proper order as with their respective jurisdiction.[374]

The concept of trustee permeated the idea of property as propriety. Professor Rose writes, "[p]roperty endowed the haves not only with rights but also with responsibilities about the disposition of the property; their property was theirs only in trust for family, community, and commonwealth."[375] These rights were extended to public offices; all rights were seen as property, and property brought with it some measure of "proper" authority, to be exercised ideally as a trust for those to whom one was responsible for governing.[376]

---

372   *Ibid.* at 1, 44-48; Rose, *supra* note 298 at 58-59.

373   Alexander, *ibid.* at 1-2.

374   Rose, *supra* note 298 at 59-60.

375   *Ibid.* at 63.

376   *Ibid.* at 2, 60. Both socialism and communism can be viewed as alternative proprietarian models. They attempt to reveal the artificial construction of property, which creates the oppressive regimes of capitalism's landed aristocratic society.

Both Professors Rose and Alexander show the development of this proprietarian thought in the British colonies, which began as arrangements that were overtly proprietarian in character.[377] The founding charters were sources of political authority to the colonial trustees as much as they were conveyances of land, and it was expected that the founders and trustees would exercise their authority and property rights for the purpose of creating a properly ordered society.

Such a proprietarian concept of property as governance and order, Professor Alexander argues, substantiates the British concept of the commonweal that dominated early American legal thought:

> The concept of the common weal, moreover, was understood to have substantive meaning. The common law maxim *salus populi suprema est lex* (the welfare of the people is the supreme law) had real content. The public good was not understood as simply whatever the market produces, for the market was viewed as a realm in which individuals were too vulnerable to the temptation to act out of narrow self-interest rather than, as proprietarian principles required, for the purpose of maintaining the properly ordered society.
>
> Just what the proper social order is has been an enormously controversial issue throughout American history. The existence of different substantive conceptions of the proper social order means that there have been multiple versions of the proprietarian conception of property in American legal thought. Not only over time but also at any single moment, American legal writers have held sometimes radically different notions of the public good and its implications for property. All of these understandings of property share, however, a commitment to the basic idea that the core purpose of property is not to satisfy individual preferences or to increase wealth but to fulfill some prior normative vision of how society and the polity that governs it should be structured.[378]

As in a proprietarian order, the leaders of the American revolution, the British Enlightenment, and the French *siècle des lumières* affirmed the main purpose of government as protecting individual property. The notions of individual property were derived from the philosophical writing of John Locke[379] in Britain and G.W.F. Hegel[380] in Germany. Using the fictional narrative device of a "state of nature," Locke asserted

---

377 *Ibid.*, citing J.H. Plumb, *The Growth of Political Stability in England, 1675-1725* (Harmondsworth, U.K.: Penguin, 1969) at 38-39; Alexander, *supra* note 371 at 8, 26-72.

378 Alexander, *supra* note 371 at 2.

379 Locke, *supra* note 289. He states: "God the Lord and Father of all, has given no one of his Children such a Property; in his peculiar Portion of the things of this World, but that he has given his needy Brother a Right to the Surplusage of His Goods; so that it cannot justly be denyd[sic] him, when his pressing Wants call for it. And therefore no Man could ever have a just Power over the Life of another, by Right of Property in Land of Possessions." This is quoted in L.J. MacFarlane, *The Theory and Practice of Human Rights* (London: Maurice Temple Smith, 1985) at 993.

380 G.W.F. Hegel, *Philosophy of Right*, trans. T. M. Knox (Oxford: Oxford University Press, 1967).

that landholding is a natural right, hence conceptually prior to the political order, and immune to political modification and takings.[381]

In this version of the proprietarian order, the right to possess property was asserted as a fundamental human right: a basic human interest that everyone has a right to survive, and which contributes to the ethical development of the person; a human right that came to be viewed as a legal institution or concept that protected the right. These ideas were declared as fundamental premises in the United States Constitution (1789)[382] and the *Declaration des droits de l'homme et du citoyen* (1789).[383] They were incorporated into the constitution and laws of many countries. Professor Alexander argues that a revised proprietarian order persists in United States law as a discursive means of responding to the newly ascendant modern world and its culture. Meanwhile, the eighteenth-century ideology of civic republicanism reshaped the British understanding,[384] purging it of its most conspicuously hierarchical and aristocratic aspects.[385] White males stood at the top of the property-owning hierarchy, and republican ideology looked to them to create and perpetuate the proper social order and the proper polity. Married women and enslaved Africans were legally incapacitated as autonomous property owners.[386]

---

381 Locke, *supra* note 289 at 9, 18. See also, J. Tully, *A Discourse on Property: John Locke and His Adversaries* (New York: Cambridge University Press, 1980). Religious versions of this argument, to the effect that God grants human beings dominion over the Earth, are found in the classical natural rights theorists in international law. See Grotius, *supra* note 286 at 186; S. Pufendorf, *On the Duty of Man and Citizen According to Natural Law*, ed. by J. Tully, trans. M. Silverhorne (Cambridge, U.K.: Cambridge University Press, 1991) at 84. Contemporary versions of the argument take a more secular perspective. See, *e.g.*, Richard A. Epstein, *Takings: Private Property and the Power of Eminent Domain* (Cambridge, Mass.: Harvard University Press, 1985) at 11-12; Ellen F. Paul, *Property Rights and Eminent Domain* (New Brunswick, N.J.: Transaction Books, 1987) at 224-39.

382 The leaders of the American revolution asserted that life, liberty and the pursuit of happiness were fundamental human rights; hence they were incorporated into the United States Constitution. The Constitution also provides for the protection of private property. It contains provisions relating to explicit restrictions against taking property without due process and just compensation, against impairment of the obligation of contracts, against bills of attainder, and against debased currency, all backed up by the institution of judicial review. Still more important, the constitution points out that the structure of government was designed to promote economic stability and to insulate property rights from popular upheavals; M.W. MacConnell, "Contract Rights and Property Rights: A Case Study of the Relationship between Individual Liberties and Constitutional Structure" (1988) 76 Cal. L. Rev. 270.

383 Christine Fauré, ed., *Les déclarations des droits de l'homme de 1789* (Paris: Payot, 1988). The representatives of the people of France also recognized and declared that there were natural, inherent, inalienable, imprescriptible and sacred human rights. Ignorance, neglect or contempt of these rights were the sole causes of public misfortunes and corruption of government. Respect for these human rights was the end of all social institutions. Also they declared that the fundamental rights of man and citizen were liberty, property, security and resistance to oppression (Art. 3). No one ought to be deprived of the right to property, being inviolable and sacred, except in cases of evident public necessity, legally ascertained, and on conditions of previous just indemnity (Art. 17).

384 Rose, *supra* note 298 at 60.

385 Alexander, *supra* note 371 at 4-5.

386 *Ibid.* 158-211; and Rose, *supra* note 298 at 61-62.

B. Land as commodity

A modern challenge is to understand property's role in creating a constitutional order and its relationship to the idea of land as a preference satisfaction system[387] or a commodity to be exchanged.[388] Our particular challenge in Canada is to understand the tension among converging notions of property in our Aboriginal and inherited legal thought.

In British legal thought, Blackstone's *Commentaries* typified the unfolding of the dialectic of property law. He asserted the right of property in the proprietarian order of the Crown:

> There is nothing which so generally strikes the imagination, and engages the affection of mankind, as the right of property; or that sole and despotic dominion which one man claims and exercises over the external things of the world, in total exclusion of the right of any other individual in the universe.[389]

A familiar interpretation of the historical development of Anglo-American property law represents the idea of land as a commodity linked to the steady expansion of individual freedom of ownership, especially freedom of transferability. On this view, marketability of property progressively increased as courts cast off feudal British doctrine of tenure, then mercantilist restraints to acquire a fee simple empire and the "release of energy" of the market.[390]

Professor Alexander argues that this story intimately involves the relationship between modernity and property.[391] He defines "modernity" in terms of two closely linked beliefs: in the market as the dominant mechanism for structuring the social order, and in human progress through human will.[392] The key bases of proprietarian or premodern society—custom, kinship, hierarchy. and local authority—are gradually replaced by or at least subordinated to less personalized exchange transactions. In modern cultures, property is characterized by "the relationship between a person and peculiarly economic resources, a world where land itself has been largely reduced to a commodity."[393] From this perspective, individuals realize their full potential and authority through commodity-exchange relationships. Individuals are seen as more than possessors of preferences; they are also judges of values and satisfaction.

According to Professor Alexander, modernity's view of property as commodity is built on three important normative commitments: first, the moral and political prior-

---

387 Rose, *ibid.* at 52-55. This can also be seen as the morality of desire and in the idea of substantive justice concepts.

388 Alexander, *supra* note 371 at 4-7.

389 Blackstone, *supra* note 117, Book 2, "Of the Rights of Things," c. 1, "Of Property in General."

390 Alexander, *supra* note 371 at 5-6, 72-158, 243-352.

391 *Ibid.* at 10-13.

392 *Ibid.* at 11.

393 H. Hartog, *Public Property and Private Power: The Corporation of the City of New York in American Law, 1730-1870* (Chapel Hill: University of North Carolina Press, 1983).

ity of the individual over the community; second, the subjectivity of values (values as preferences); and third, the market as the primary mechanism for mediating individual preferences within society.[394] He argues that a properly ordered society may coincide with the market society, but the two are not identical. The market view of society is essentially empty, he asserts, and can and historically has yielded many different types of society. The proprietarian order, by contrast, he states, is always committed to some particular substantive view of how society should be ordered. Hence, the distinction between the proprietarian and commodity conceptions of property cannot be dissolved simply by saying that the commodity conception, too, is "proper" because it emerges from the market.[395]

The idea of land as private commodity, Professor Alexander asserts, defines property's exclusive purpose in material terms within which individuals or corporations are free to pursue their own private agendas and satisfy their own preferences, free from state coercion or other forms of external interference.[396] He argues:

> The economic expression of this preference-satisfying conception of property is *market commodity*. Property satisfies individual preferences most effectively through the process of market exchange, or what lawyers call market alienability. The exchange function of property is so important in American society that property is often thought to be synonymous with the idea of market commodity.[397]

The commodity school of property views property as a creation of artificial legislation or laws. Jeremy Bentham in *The Theory of Legislation*, speaking for the utilitarians, stated:

> The better to understand the advantages of law, let us endeavour to form a clear idea of property. We shall see that there is no such thing as natural property, and that it is entirely the work of law. Property is nothing but a basis of expectation; the expectation of deriving certain advantages from a thing which we are said to possess, in consequence of the relation in which we stand toward it. There is no image, no painting, no visible trait, which can express the relation that constitutes property. It is not material, it is metaphysical; it is a mere conception of the mind ... . But it may be asked, What is it that serves as a basis to law, upon which to begin operation, when it adopts objects which, under the name of property, it promises to protect? Have not men, in the primitive state a natural expectation to enjoy certain things,—an expectation drawn from sources anterior to law? Yes, there have been from the beginning, and there always will be, circumstances in which a man may secure himself, by his own means, in the enjoyment of certain things. But the catalogue of these cases is very limited. The savage who has killed a deer may hope to keep it for himself, so long as his cave is undiscovered; so long as he watches to defend it, and is stronger than his rival; but that is all. How miserable and precarious is such a possession! If we suppose the least agreement among savages to respect the acquisition of each other,

---

394 Alexander, *supra* note 371 at 8-13.

395 *Ibid.* at 3.

396 *Ibid.* at 1.

397 *Ibid.* [emphasis in original].

we see the introduction of a principle to which no name can be given but that of law. A feeble and monetary expectation may result from time to time from circumstances purely physical; but a strong and permanent expectation can result only from law. That which, in the natural state, was an almost invisible thread, in the social state becomes a cable. Property and law are born together and die together. Before laws were made there was no property, take away laws, and property ceases.[398]

The denial of the naturalistic law and order view for "established expectations," however, does not resolve the issue of the relationship between property and law in British thought. It merely raises the issue of how land relates to man-made law. As Bentham complained:

In almost every case in which the law does anything for a man's benefit or advantage, men are apt to speak of it, on some occasion or other, as conferring on him a sort of property ... The expedient then has been to create, as it were, on every occasion, an ideal being and to assign to a man this ideal being for the object of his property; and these sort of objects to which men of science ... came ... to give the name of "incorporeal".[399]

Bentham argued that property regimes in law had a purpose, and that purpose was to tap individual energies in order to make everyone prosperous.[400] Private property rights under this vision ought to be conceptually independent of governmental authority and not subject to political revision.

Under the influence of Bentham, John Austin, and A.V. Dicey,[401] the classic common law perspective on land transformed into analytical jurisprudence, the agent of a positivist account of law as the sovereign's command and written statute law.[402] Legal rights became based on the sovereign commands to others to act in a way that benefits a right holder, and gives the holder the capacity to bring a civil suit to vindicate that legal right, diminishing the classical common law proposition that right holders should not use rights to injure the rights of others. Analytical jurisprudence or positivism saw law as a human-created written code, independent of morality, a "set of propositions that embody the corpus of rules, principles, commands, norms, maxims, or whatever, which have, at any time been laid down."[403]

The relation of positivist law to the common law declaration of pre-existing law was never satisfactorily explained. Austin's explanation that judicial decisions codified

---

398   Jeremy Bentham, *The Theory of Legislation*, 2d ed. by Etienne Dumont and Richard Hildreth (London: Trübner, 1864), c. 8 at 111-13, "Of Property."

399   E.H. Burn and H.L.A. Hart, eds., *An Introduction to the Principles of Morals and Legislation* (London: Athlone Press, 1982) at 211.

400   The law and economics school operates under this vision of land as commodity. See R. Posner, *Economic Analysis of Law*, 3d ed. (Boston: Little, Brown, 1986) at 30.

401   Austin, *supra* note 351; A.V. Dicey, *Introduction to the Law of the Constitution*, 9th ed. (London: MacMillan, 1939).

402   M. Looban, *The Common Law and English Jurisprudence, 1760-1850* (Oxford: Clarendon Press, 1991); Postema, *supra* note 267.

403   "The Common Law and Legal Theory" in A.W.B. Simpson, ed., *Legal Theory and Legal History: Essays on the Common Law* (London: Hambledon Press, 1987) at 362.

old rules or customs, validating them as "commands," was never convincing.[404] The immemorial common law, was transformed ahistorically by positive law into "commands" to resolve contemporary problems.[405] Pre-existing legal rules, from precedents and statutes, in positivism existed for every conflict, and every case had a uniquely correct result.

Positive law, focused on public policy and premised on law as an instrument of social control, rarely mentioned politics, economics, or social theory. Rather, it was represented as interlocking sets of hierarchical distinctions, the binaries of law making and law applying, focusing judicial attention on law rather than on politics. Classical common law was transformed in the Victorian common law into Hobbes's absolute sovereign's implementing agent reluctant to acknowledge any legal diversity.[406]

In this view, property law was a private law, with its original focus on Blackstonian absolute control over things. By the 1860s, beginning with the publication of Austin's *Jurisprudence* and *Lectures* and with Maine's *Ancient Law*,[407] a consensus developed that Blackstone's absolutist concept of possession of things[408] and his intangible property and reified rights maintained by legal fictions[409] should be changed to Roman law theory:

> the law of persons and the law of things is so mixed up, that no use can be made of this classification so long as our law retains its present form ... in the case of ownership, the right to hold and enjoy the property rights is marked by the use of terms derived from Latin: the former are called rights *in rem*; the latter are called rights *in personam*.[410]

Legal analysis constructed the dichotomous distinction between rights *in rem* (rights in things or land) and rights *in personam* (personal property); the distinction was reinforced by public policy and legal affirmation of the dichotomy between the sovereign's tenure (public law) and individual will (private law).

By the beginning of the twentieth century in British legal thought, John Salmond, in the *First Principles of Jurisprudence*,[411] had conceptualized the entire common law

---

404 P.G. McHugh, "The Common-Law Status of Colonies and Aboriginal 'Rights': How Lawyers and Historians Treat the Past" (1998) 61 Sask. L. Rev. 392 at 398.

405 *Ibid.* at 400-402.

406 *Ibid.* at 398.

407 Austin, *supra* note 351; Maine, *supra* note 96.

408 Blackstone, *supra* note 117, vol. 1 at 134-35. Property was one of three, "absolute right[s], inherent in every Englishmen," that the law would not permit the smallest infringement of, even for the good of the entire community. The other inherent rights were life and liberty.

409 Where some tangible thing was involved, Blackstone considered any limitation in the owner's dominion to be inherent to the nature of the thing or owner. Where no physical thing was possessed, as with incorporeal hereditaments or a chose in action, Blackstone used his fiction of reified rights to preserve an absolutist conception of property; one had a choice of action, or an intangible right over a thing. Later courts created such fictionalized physical entities as a right to value.

410 Markby, *supra* note 115 at 63-64, §§ 134, 136; *Halsbury's*, *supra* note 315, vol. 39 at paras. 301-303.

411 Sir J.W. Salmond, *First Principles of Jurisprudence* (London: Stevens and Haynes, 1893); Fitzgerald, *supra* note 352.

into a unified scheme of property and obligations. He built his system by distinguishing between positive duties on others to act or not to act in certain ways (obligatory rights)[412] and permissive rules declaring certain conduct to be unregulated by the sovereign (optional rights);[413] property was placed in the obligatory rights category.

In his analysis of property law he rejected the distinction between rights *in rem* that were against the whole world, including the Crown, and rights *in personam* that were rights against specific individuals in favour of "real" and "personal" rights. The sovereign's tenure regulated private estates, since they arose out of grants to his subjects and their relationship to things. In the relational conception of Crown tenure, no concept of an "absolute" private property to things existed, but rather imaginary or intangible rights between the Crown and subjects, and among subjects, allocated rights to things. Within this context, Salmond defined a "real right" as a right to the maintenance of the present position of a person to a thing, a right to be left alone or not to be positively damaged; he defined a "personal right" as one to the improvement of a person in relation to a thing, a right to be positively benefited or made better off.[414] He saw property rights as a relational concept; these rights consisted of negative duties and positive rights that others had duties to acknowledge and not to invade. He also distinguished between rightful interests in possession protected by law that others have a current duty not to invade, and rightful potential interests that one has the right to receive from others. Salmond viewed obligations, such as contract and torts, as distinct from property rights and interests.[415]

In the United States, Wesley Hohfeld's "scientific" analysis of property law pointed out that property entitlements could be analyzed in a new vocabulary as a series of claims and obligations among persons, rather than among persons and their relations to land or ecology.[416] The new concept of property was defined as a set of eight legal relations among persons, rather than the Blackstonian concept of absolute dominion of things and imaginary property. Kenneth Vandevelde argued that the new twentieth-century conceptualization of property in the United States resulted in a judicial inability to use property concepts to settle controversies with far-reaching consequences for the courts' legitimacy:

---

412   This was the restatement of "other-regarding" theory of classical liberal legal thought, or the duty to look out for others and to refrain from acts that hurt others.

413   This was a restatement of the classical self-regarding theory (freedom to act in a self-interested manner) of liberalism. By 1902 Salmond had rejected the theory, and labeled these rights as "legal liberties" or interests of unrestrained activity or the permission to inflict damage on others. See J.W. Salmond, *Jurisprudence, or the Theory of Law*, 2d ed. (London: Stevens and Haynes, 1902) at 231-32.

414   *Ibid.* at 173. Compare to Lord Watson's characterization of Aboriginal tenure as "personal," in *St. Catherine's Milling and Lumber Co. v. The Queen* (1888), 14 A.C. 46 (P.C.).

415   Salmond, *ibid.* at 177-78.

416   "Some Fundamental Legal Concepts as Applied to Judicial Reasoning" (1913) 23 Yale L. J. 16. See also Bruce A. Ackerman, *Private Property and the Constitution* (New Haven, CT: Yale University Press, 1977).

Courts overcame their paralysis by deciding individual cases with overt recourse to political goals. But, in so doing, they abandoned the myth of judicial neutrality and with it their own legitimacy. This evolution illustrates the general transformation of legal reasoning. ... It demonstrated that there was nothing inevitable about the definition of property. That is, property law could not be logically deduced from the nature of things. ... [T]he broad and variable nature of the new property destroyed the fixed meaning of the concept, so that results of cases could no longer be deduced from the nature of the property rights. ... The courts avoided paralysis by deciding cases according to public policy. Property was completely positivized. The concept was defined and applied in whatever manner the courts thought expedient of public policy. But this solution to the problems of dispute resolution came at the price of the court's legitimacy. For if judges were not bound by precedent, then nothing was to prevent them from injecting their own political opinions into decisions. The "government of law, and not of men" which had seemed so clearly to exist in 1803 had been exposed as, in truth, a government of "nine old men." The creation of the new property was, in microcosm, the destruction of the rule of law.[417]

Professor Alexander argues that the public policy strengthened the view of property as a commodity and created a widely shared misconception about the historical meaning and role of property in law that must be corrected:

legal scholars, judges, historians, and political theorists have tended to accept uncritically the claim that there has been a single tradition of property throughout American history. Property, according to this mistaken view, has served one core purpose and has had a single constant meaning throughout American history to define in material terms the legal and political sphere within which individuals are free to pursue their own private agendas and satisfy their own preferences, free from governmental coercion or other forms of external interference. Property, according to this understanding, is the foundation for the categorical separation of the realms of the private and public, individual and collectivity, the market and the polity.[418]

Similarly, Jennifer Nedelsky, a University of Toronto law professor, has established in her book *Private Property and the Limits of American Constitutionalism*[419] that constitutional history of the United States from 1787 to 1937 has privileged private property over all other interests and values. Property has transformed into market property, property as commodity, property as the wall between private preference and the public weal. She sees property as having only one meaning and role throughout the legal history of the United States: "a basic individual right secure against encroachment, even by the powers of government."[420] In her view, the dominant image of the land as commodity in the constitutional hierarchy has undermined American democra-

---

417   Vandevelde, *supra* note 301 at 330, 366-67.

418   Alexander, *supra* note 371 at 1.

419   *Private Property and the Limits of American Constitutionalism: The Madisonian Framework and its Legacy* (Chicago: Chicago University Press, 1990).

420   *Ibid.* at 227.

cy, and she implies that the privileged position of private property prevents a new, more democratic political order.[421]

Professor Alexander argues that the perspective of the commodity theory of property is only half-right and must be reconciled with the lingering conception of property as order. He argues that it is difficult for modern consciousness to imagine that property is not wealth, and that it might be intended to benefit anyone other than the owner. Yet the vision of property as the basis of proper order and the common good has persisted.

In the Canadian context, Bruce Ziff comments in *Principles of Property Law*:

> Property is a social institution, affecting the pressing contemporary issues of class, race and gender. Private property is also a construct of liberalism and theories about the relationship of law and economics can provide useful insights into key property law doctrine. While I do not accept the normative basis of economic rationalism I can nevertheless appreciate the descriptive and pedagogical value of economic analysis, which I try to draw upon from time to time.[422]

We are living in an era where these two competing ideal types are changing their relationship to one another at a relatively rapid rate. In Canadian legal thought, preoccupations with Aboriginal tenure and rights, sustainable development, and environmental law and policy reassert a proprietarian order against the idea of land as commodity. New tensions are developing between environmental regulation and ecological preservation, and corporate and individual rights and autonomy. These tensions have generated a new type of constitutional and legal analysis, and fresh approaches to our understanding of Canadian property law are needed. This book is a small contribution to that large project.

---

421 Alexander, *supra* note 371 at 7, citing W.W. Fisher III's interpretation of Nedelsky, "Making Sense of Madison: Nedelsky on Private Property" (1993) 18 L. & Soc. Inquiry 547.

422 Ziff, *supra* note 3 at iii, Preface.

II

TREATY RECONCILIATIONS

[T]he doctrine of aboriginal rights exists, and is recognized and affirmed by s. 35(1), because of one simple fact: when Europeans arrived in North America, aboriginal peoples *were already here*, living in communities on the land, and participating in distinctive cultures, as they had done for centuries.

Chief Justice Lamer in *R. v. Van der Peet*[1]

Introduction

Consistent with a British land law transformed by different cultures' occupations of Britain, attempts to acquire jurisdiction and land in North America created a new concept of territory in the law of nations and the prerogative law of Great Britain. Challenged by Aboriginal law, European sovereigns created an innovative treaty order with the Aboriginal nations.[2] Both international and national legal systems shaped and determined the power the European sovereigns could exercise over Aboriginal nations and their territories.[3] Without an analysis of both legal systems and the signatories' understandings of the treaties, the British Sovereign's reliance on written treaties, agreements, and compacts makes little sense.

---

1   [1996] 2 S.C.R. 507 at para. 30, [1996] 4 C.N.L.R. 177, reconsideration refused (January 16, 1997), Doc. 23803 (S.C.C.) [hereinafter *Van der Peet* cited to S.C.R.].

2   Imperial treaties of a political nature are usually called prerogative treaties and labeled "sovereignty" treaties. See *Francis v. The Queen*, [1956] S.C.R. 618 at 625 [hereinafter *Francis*]. Prerogative treaties are documents of peace that recognize the independence of states, or establish boundaries, or establish privileges and immunities, or deal with the rights of belligerents (*Francis* at 626). It is said that the essential feature of a prerogative treaty is the "exceptional" or "extraordinary" nature of the circumstances of its formation. See A. Jacomy-Millette, *Treaty Law in Canada* (Ottawa: University of Ottawa Press, 1975) at 207-21. See also *Halsbury's Laws of England*, vol. 6, 4th ed. (London: Butterworths, 1991) at paras. 806, 981 [hereinafter *Halsbury's*]. See also *Worcester v. Georgia*, 31 U.S. (6 Pet.) 515, 8 L. Ed. 483 (U.S. 1832) [hereinafter *Worcester* cited to U.S.]; and F. S. Cohen, "The Spanish Origin of Indian Rights in the Law of the United States" (1942) 31 Geo. L.J. 1 at 17.

3   See generally I. Brownlie, *Principles of Public International Law*, 4th ed. (Oxford: Clarendon Press, 1990) at 32-35; and E.C.S. Wade and G.G. Phillips, *Constitutional and Administrative Law*, 9th ed. by A.W. Bradley (London: Longman, 1977) at 7.

Treaties provided the international and constitutional framework through which the imperial sovereign acknowledged and reconciled the foundational fact that Aboriginal nations lived on the land in distinctive, confederated nations, with their own legal order, teachings, practices, traditions, and culture. These various treaties were an attempt to reconcile pre-existing Aboriginal sovereignty with the Crown's sovereignty and to create a new shared legal order in British North America. Since the treaties were entered into for the public good of both nations, the substantive obligations and rights created within these agreements must be defined in light of this purpose.

From the British imperial viewpoint, the Sovereign and nation recognized Aboriginal national "sovereignty" by their treaties;[4] they did not convey sovereign rights. From Aboriginal nations' perspective, however, the prerogative treaties recognized the inherent dignity of Aboriginal peoples, which has always been the source of their national sovereignty. The authority of the Aboriginal nations was derived not from a monarch or from aristocratic society, but rather from the existing Aboriginal rights of the people and their consensual selection of treaty delegates. The distinction is important. Whereas the inherent authority reflected the Aboriginal concept of a kinship state and freedoms, the European term "sovereignty" emphasized secular nations or states based on absolutism or centralized governments.

The *Treaty of Westphalia* (1648) created the sovereignty of the European nations.[5] Outside Britain's realm, in the absence of an imperial inheritance to a territory or a military conquest, a consensual treaty was necessary for the King or Queen to acquire any jurisdiction or rights, hence the prerogative treaties of Great Britain with the autonomous Aboriginal nations and tribes of North America. Every treaty, European or Aboriginal, with the imperial Sovereign marks the lack of imperial or European inheritance in North America.

Two distinct treaty orders were necessary for the British Sovereign to legitimately acquire jurisdiction over foreign territory. First, the European sovereigns or nations had to acknowledge and affirm international jurisdiction in North America guaranteed by European treaties such as the *Treaty of Utrecht* (1713) and the *Treaty of Paris* (1763). Second, the sovereigns or nations had to enter treaties with the Aboriginal nations of a certain territory to create the conventional jurisdiction acquired by the European treaties. Aboriginal treaties with the Sovereign became the best expression of

---

4   Similar to the Supreme Court of Canada's rejection of British concepts to describe Aboriginal land tenure, we believe it is misleading to use European concepts to describe *sui generis* Aboriginal American Federations or Aboriginal nations' treaties with European nations. Few, if any, of the Aboriginal nations have a tradition of theological absolutism or hierocratic traditions. Indeed, the typical interpretation of sovereignty in the Cree language is "pretending to be God" (*mandohkasowin*). At the time of the signing of the first treaties with Aboriginal nations in North America, the notion of territorial sovereignty in the British-speaking world was just beginning. In the law of England, sovereign was a tripartite indenture of King, Lords, and Commons. See generally Sir W. Blackstone, *Commentaries on the Laws of England* (Oxford: Clarendon Press, 1765-69). In Canada, the foreign jurisdictions of the Crown were the last vestige of monarchical supremacy in the constitutional law of Great Britain; see *Halsbury's*, *supra* note 2, vol. 6 at paras. 806, 981 and 991.

5   M. Shaw, *Title to Territory in Africa: International Legal Issues* (Oxford: Clarendon Press, 1986) at 11-16.

the "free and voluntary choice" of the Aboriginal nations to ally themselves with alien nations. In Great Britain, these prerogative treaties brought the Aboriginal nations under the protection of the constitutional law of Great Britain and, later, the United Kingdom.

4. Public International Law

After 1648, public international law of Europe developed a number of theories to explain the relationship between territories and monarchies.[6] The *Treaty of Westphalia* ended the exclusive Christian order of the Holy Roman Empire stage of international law, in which there was a single European state, many subordinate rulers, and no recognition that diplomatic relations could exist with non-Christian societies. This world order began to disintegrate in the sixteenth century in the wake of the Reformation, expanding trade with non-Christian peoples, and the rise of independent European nation-states.

Public international law began with European scholarly debates on the legal capacity and rights of non-Christian and Aboriginal nations that took place during the century following the "discovery" of the Americas, and that developed into diplomatic practices from the sixteenth to nineteenth centuries. Public international law used treaties to demarcate the boundaries between Europe's emerging nation-states and in the subsequent expansion of European commercial interests to Asia, Africa, and the Americas.

Three historical stages define international law. The first stage involved an expanding, inclusive, and universal community of sovereign and independent secular states associated by treaties of alliance, commerce, or "protection," under a conception of natural law that recognized the equality of all peoples and states. Known as the Treaty order because its foundation was contractual, this world system achieved its zenith in the mid-1800s, when the treaty network linked more than 1,000 European states and Indigenous nations globally.

The second stage—European colonialism or imperialism—was characterized by the rapid contraction of the international community into a small club of aggressively dominant European states. During the period marked roughly by the 1885 Berlin Africa Conference and the 1945 adoption of the Charter of the United Nations, these European states arrogated oligarchic power to create and change international law, converting existing treaties of protection into instruments of domination, and denying the legal capacity of non-European peoples to govern themselves.

The third stage is still emerging in international law. The decolonization of European public international law, together with the self-determination of peoples under the Charter of the United Nations, is leading to the re-emergence of an inclusive, global, and colour-blind community of nations. These are the conditions of possibility of a postcolonial international law, such as existed under the Treaty order.

---

6   *Ibid.* at 1-6, 13-16.

For Ian Brownlie the meaning of "sovereignty" can only be understood within the historical development of international law. Studying claims of imperial sovereignty over foreign territories requires understanding how each stage conceptualized sovereignty (*imperium*) and territorial ownership (*dominium*):

> The competence of states in respect of their territory is usually described in terms of sovereignty and jurisdiction and the student is faced with a terminology which is not employed very consistently in legal sources such as works of authority or the opinions of law officers, or by statesmen, who naturally place political meanings in the foreground. The terminology as used by lawyers is also unsatisfactory in that the complexity and diversity of the rights, duties, powers, liberties, and immunities of states are obscured by the liberal use of omnibus terms like 'sovereignty' and 'jurisdiction'. At the same time, a degree of uniformity of usage does exist and may be noticed. The normal complement of state rights, the typical case of legal competence, is described commonly as 'sovereignty': particular rights, or accumulations of rights quantitatively less than the norm, are referred to as 'jurisdiction'. In brief, 'sovereignty' is legal shorthand for legal personality of a certain kind, that of statehood; 'jurisdiction' refers to particular aspects of the substance, especially rights (or claims), liberties, and powers.[7]

The ideas of state and kingship prevalent in Europe in the Middle Ages tended to place the ruler in the position of a private owner, since feudal law was the applicable "public law" that conferred "ultimate" title on the ruler. The legal doctrine of the day employed analogies from Roman private law in the sphere of property to describe the sovereign's power. The growth of absolutism in the sixteenth and seventeenth centuries confirmed the trend.[8] A treaty ceding territory had the appearance of a sale of land by a private owner, and sales of territory did occur.

In the eighteenth and nineteenth centuries, the time of most of the Aboriginal treaties, the significance of sovereignty had declined. Since sovereignty was recognized as an abstraction, the ruler was a bearer and an agent of a legal capacity that belonged to the state. The nineteenth century witnessed contradictory developments. In Europe and Latin America the principle of nationalities appeared, which, like the principle of "self-determination," has continued to gain ascendancy. At the same time, the European powers made use of the concept of *dominium* (first occupation of land), which was often political in application though legal in form. It involved the occupation of areas in America, Asia, and Africa that were often the seat of organized nations and communities. More recently, the use or threat of force by states to settle disputes or otherwise to effect a territorial gain has become illegal,[9] and the principle of *terra*

---

7   Brownlie, *supra* note 3 at 149.

8   This view is reflected in British legal scholarship by C. Wolff, *Law of Nations* [1750] (Oxford: Clarendon Press, 1934) at 144-145: "a nation which inhabits a territory has not only ownership but also sovereignty over the land and the things which are in it. In like manner, since the ownership of a nation is bound up with its sovereignty, ownership of a nation is occupied at the same time as its sovereignty."

9   S. Korman, *The Right of Conquest: The Acquisition of Territory by Force in International Law and Practice* (Oxford: Clarendon Press, 1996) pt. 2. With the rise of self-determination after World War I and the prohibition of aggressive war came the rejection of the acquisition of territory by conquest or force in public international law.

nullius has been rejected as limiting Aboriginal tenures.[10] These principles require harmonization with the pre-existing law on acquisition of territory. In the legal history of a territory, the existing sovereign falls into the hands of another sovereign, but the older sovereignty of government does not disappear in public international law.[11]

Public international law with its different ways of seeing land and jurisdiction over land creates the framework within which domestic government and laws operate. In international law, sovereignty (*imperium*) and ownership (*dominium*) are distinct legal categories.[12] *Imperium* is the legal competence of a state, including the general power of government, administration, and disposition of territory. *Dominium is* public ownership of property within the state and private ownership recognized as such by domestic law.[13]

Within public international law created by the colonizing European states, only four types of territorial regimes exist:

> ...territorial sovereignty, territory not subject to the sovereignty of any state or states and which possesses a status of its own (mandated and trust territories, for example), the *res nullius*, and the *res communis*. Territorial sovereignty extends principally over land territory, the territorial sea appurtenant to the land, and the seabed and subsoil of the territorial sea. The concept of territory includes islands, islets, rocks, and reefs. A *res nullius* consists of the same subject-matter legally susceptible to acquisition by states but not as yet placed under territorial sovereignty. The *res communis*, consisting of the high seas (which for present purposes include exclusive economic zones) and also outer space, is not capable of being placed under state sovereignty. In accordance with customary international law and the dictates of convenience, the airspace above and subsoil beneath state territory, the *res nullius*, and the *res communis* are included in each category.[14]

Despite such systematic distinctions and definitions, confusion persists in the history of international law, since both the concept of "title" to a territory and the legal competence which flows from it—"territorial sovereignty"—have been described by the concept of sovereignty. "Sovereignty" is a consequence of "title," denoting the legal

---

10   *Mabo v. Queensland [No. 2]* (1992), 107 A.L.R. 1, 175 C.L.R. 1 [hereinafter *Mabo* cited to A.L.R.].

11   Two examples of this are the occupation of Nazi Germany in the wake of World War II and the belligerent occupation of enemy territory in time of war. After the defeat of Nazi Germany in the Second World War, the four major Allied powers assumed supreme power in Germany, although the legal competence of the German state did not disappear. What occurred is akin to legal representation or agency of necessity. The German State continued to exist, and, indeed, the legal basis of the occupation depended on its continued existence. The very considerable derogation of sovereignty involved in the assumption of powers of government by foreign states, without the consent of Germany, did not constitute a transfer of sovereignty. A similar case, recognized by the customary law for a very long time, is that of the belligerent occupation of enemy territory in time of war. The important features of "sovereignty" in such cases are the continued existence of a legal personality and the attribution of territory to that legal person and not to holders for the time being.

12   Brownlie, *supra* note 3 at 108-109.

13   *Ibid.*

14   *Ibid.* at 107. There is no such notion of *res nullius* in Latin.

competence that a state enjoys in respect of its territory, but such competence is not coterminous with title.[15] "Title" to a territory or territorial sovereignty explains why the competence exists. The equivalent concept in French, "*titre*," has been defined as follows: "*Terme qui, pris dans le sens de titre juridique, designe tout fait, acte ou situation qui est la cause et le fondement d'un droit.*"[16]

In neither an unititular nor a multititular system of public international law is "title" equivalent to the concept of *dominium* or ownership.[17] A unititular system asserts there is only one "root of title" for each territory, and the present title can ultimately be traced back to that title. The first and undisputed occupation of land in a unititular system may give rise to title that is equivalent to the *dominium* of Roman law.[18] The law of nations asserts that hunting and fishing were sufficient to establish legitimate *dominium*.[19] In international law, such immemorial occupations are "owned" and, in this special sense, are "attributes of 'sovereignty,'" but should not be confused with the idea of derivative acquisition of territorial sovereignty.[20] Most Aboriginal tenure systems are unititular systems. Thus if the title to a land is in Aboriginal peoples, the British Sovereign can acquire no title to it (independently), except by a process that divests Aboriginal tenure of its original title.

The five orthodox modes of acquisition in public international law were classified as either "original" or "derivative." The various modes of acquisition of the colonization era—occupation, accretion, cession, conquest, and prescription—are consid-

---

15   *Ibid.* at 123.

16   *Ibid.* at 123-134, relying on *Dictionnaire de Basdevant, s.v.* "titre." (Term that, in the sense of juridical title, designates any fact, act, or situation that is the cause or foundation of a right.)

17   Brownlie, *ibid.*, citing T. Honoré in A.G. Guested, *Oxford Essays in Jurisprudence: A Collaborative Work* (London: Oxford University Press, 1961) at 137.

18   Brownlie, *ibid.* at 124, relying on R.Y. Jennings, *The Acquisition of Territory in International Law* (New York: Oceana Publications, 1963) at 5-6. See also G.F. Von Martens, *The Law of Nations: Being the Science of National Law, Covenants, Powers, & c., Founded on the Treaties and Customs of Modern Nations in Europe* [1760], 4th ed. (London: W. Cobbett, 1829) at 64; and *Van Savigny's Treatise on Possession: or the jus possessionis of the Civil Law,* trans. Sir Erskine Perry, 6th ed. (London: S. Sweet, 1848) at 10, 143, 149-51, for affirmation that actual possession, independent of all right, is the foundation of property in the law of nations and Roman law.

19   J. Cowell. *The Institutes of the Lawes of England: Digested Into the Method of the Civill or Imperiall Institutions: Useful for all Gentlemen Who are Studious, and Desire to Understand the Customes of this Nation* [1651] quoted by J. Gobel. *The Struggle for the Falklands* (New Haven, Conn.: Yale University Press, 1927) at 115; J.G. Heineccius, *A Methodical System of Universal Law,* vol. 1 (London: n.p. 1743) at 179: Wolff, *supra* note 8 at 140-41,157-58,160; E. de Vattel, *The Law of Nations: Or Principles of the Laws of Nature, Applied to the Conduct and Affairs of Nations* [1760], vol. 3 (Washington, D.C.: Carnegie Institute, 1917) at 85, 142-50; compare to 48 and 91.

20   Cowell, *ibid* at 150. For example, Brownlie states: "the 'sovereign rights' that a coastal state has over the resources of the continental shelf; or a prescriptive, or historic, right to fish in an area of territorial sea belonging to another state: or a prescriptive right of passage between the territorial homeland and an enclave. These rights are indefeasible except by special grant."

ered by Professor Brownlie as "unsound in principle," making "the task of understanding the true position much more difficult."[21]

As in *Delgamuukw*, modern international tribunals are concerned with proof of the exercise of sovereignty at the critical date or dates, and avoid the orthodox acquisition analysis. Since the colonization doctrines of prescription, acquiescence, and recognition as modes of acquisition have blurred the unititular system,[22] international tribunals have used a multititular system and its notions of the "better right to possess" to resolve disputes between claims of two colonizing states.[23] The multititular system is similar to the common law concept of estates.

Whereas occupation and accretion are defined as original methods of acquiring Aboriginal *dominium*, the derivative method is by a treaty cession:

> A right to possess certain territory as sovereign conferred by agreement or Treaty of cession between intending grantor and grantee, and, if the grantee takes possession in accordance with the Treaty, the Treaty provides the legal basis of sovereignty. An actual transfer is not of course possible or required if the grantee is already in occupation. The date on which title changes may be determined by the Treaty of cession. It will normally be the date on which the Treaty comes into force. Furthermore, the Treaty itself gives the intending grantee an assignable interest, and the grantee can pass his interest to a third state. Presumably, for the third state to get title, transfer is still required, and, if the sovereign refuses to give possession, the assignee can be subrogated to the Treaty right of the assignor.[24]

The maxim that no man can give another any better title than he himself has (*Nemo dat quad non habet*)[25] operates in the treaty cessions:

> The title alleged by the United States of America as constituting the immediate foundation of its claim is that of cession, brought about by the Treaty of Paris, which cession

---

21 Justice L'Heureux-Dubé's dissenting opinion in *Van der Peet, supra* note 1 at para. 108, noted "four principles upon which states have relied to justify the assertion of sovereignty over new territories. ... These are: (1) conquest, (2) cession, (3) annexation, and (4) settlement, i.e., acquisition of territory that was previously unoccupied or is not recognized as belonging to another political entity." She thought that in the "eyes of international law, the settlement thesis is the one rationale which can most plausibly justify European sovereignty over Canadian territory and the [N]ative people living on it," relying on Patrick Macklem, "Normative Dimensions of an Aboriginal Right of Self-Government" (1995) 21 Queen's L.J. 173. Whether the land occupied by Aboriginal peoples was free for English occupation is contested; relying on Brian Slattery, "Aboriginal Sovereignty and Imperial Claims" (1991) 29 Osgoode Hall L.J. 681 [hereinafter Slattery, "Aboriginal Sovereignty"]; and Michael Asch, *Home and Native Land: Aboriginal Rights and the Canadian Constitution* (Toronto: Methuen, 1984). However, in *Mabo, supra* note 10, the High Court of Australia has convincingly rejected the validity of the settlement thesis as limiting Aboriginal tenure. Also see P.G. McHugh, "The Common-Law Status of Colonies and Aboriginal 'Rights': How Lawyers and Historians Treat the Past" (1998) 61 Sask. L. Rev. 392.

22 Brownlie, *supra* note 3 at 176.

23 *Eastern Greenland Case (Norway v. Denmark)* (1933), PCIJ (Ser. A/B) no. 53 at 46; *The Las Palmas Case (U.S. v. Netherlands)* (1928), 2 R.S.A. 829 [hereinafter *Las Palmas*].

24 Brownlie, *supra* note 3 at 133.

25 Or "*nemo plus juris transferre potest quam ipse habet." Ibid.* at 176.

transferred all rights of sovereignty which Spain may have possessed in the region. ... It is evident that Spain could not transfer more rights than she herself possessed.[26]

Under certain conditions, the treaty of cession may create international servitudes or encumbrances that pass with territory ceded.[27] Also, the treaty may limit the power of disposition of a territory.

In the Treaty order stage, treaty cession was the Sovereign's preferred mode for the acquisition of jurisdiction over Aboriginal territory. However, in British law treaty reconciliations give the Sovereign derivative title good against everyone *but* the Aboriginal nations. With respect to the acquired territory, the relationships between the original tenure or title of the Aboriginal nations and the derivative title of the Sovereign are dependent on each treaty and have remained ambiguous. British and Canadian courts seldom have an opportunity to address more fundamental but controversial treaty questions such as whether the treaty nation's Aboriginal tenure to its traditional territories was continued when the Sovereign acquired its derivative title. This issue has remained beyond the limits of national legal analysis in the grey area of public international law between two legal orders entering treaty that may signify very differently to each legal order.

A. Aboriginal treaty order of North America

The American continent is the homeland and birthplace of Aboriginal nations or confederacies that co-exist by treaties and relationships.[28] Comprehending the existing Aboriginal legal orders and their visions of law, order, and diplomacy is central to understanding Aboriginal treaty order. Outside Aboriginal legal order, no body of law can define Aboriginal contexts, intentions, or motivations behind the treaties. Aboriginal law incorporates customary standards and rules, canons of behaviour, and understandings of the world. The world-view and its legal order have been discussed by non-Aboriginal scholars in terms of an ideational order of reality,[29] or cognitive orientation, or ethno-metaphysic,[30] and primitive law.

Both the Aboriginal legal and treaty orders are intimately related to Aboriginal worldviews and languages because each Aboriginal legal order and world-view is expressed in the semantic structure of its language. Recent legal historians and historians have become increasingly concerned with the interdependent roles played by language in legal, social,

---

26   *Las Palmas, supra* note 23 at 842.

27   Lord A.D.M. McNair, *The Law of Treaties* (Oxford: Clarendon Press, 1961) at 656, 665. McNair refers to, "treaties creating purely local obligations," and gives as examples territory over which the ceding state has granted to another state, "a right of transit or a right of navigation on a river, or a right of fishery in territorial or internal waters."

28   J.Y. Henderson, "Empowering Treaty Federalism" (1994) 58 Sask. L. Rev. 241 at 246-69 [hereinafter Henderson, "Empowering"].

29   W.H. Goodenough, *Cooperation in Change* (New York: Russell Sage Foundation, 1963) at 7.

30   A.I. Hallowell, *Culture and Experience* (Philadelphia: University of Pennsylvania Press, 1955) and "Ojibwa Ontology, Behavior and World View" in S. Diamond, ed., *Primitive Views of the World* (New York: Columbia University Press, 1960), reissued as *Culture in History: Essays in Honour of Paul Radin* (New York: Columbia University Press, 1969) at 49-82.

cultural, and political life, recognizing that there is no unmediated access to meaningful knowledge. Only in the contexts of language and ideas can law or history be studied, since vocabularies, metaphors, topoi of communication, and discourses encode values and frame understanding. Languages are both an architectural linguistic "prison house"[31] and a source of intelligible freedom for those who inhabit them. This is especially relevant for Aboriginal languages, many of which have never been produced in written form.

When the British arrived, the great Aboriginal federations[32] had been assembled by the Aboriginal treaty order according to their traditions and teachings. As Professor Robert Cover wrote in "*Nomos* and Narrative":

> A legal tradition ... includes not only a corpus juris, but also a language and a mythos— narratives in which the corpus juris is located by those whose wills act upon it. These myths establish the paradigms for behavior. They build relations between the normative and the material universe, between the constraints of reality and the demands of an ethic. These myths establish a repertoire of moves—a lexicon of normative action—that may be combined into meaningful patterns culled from meaningful patterns of the past.[33]

Aboriginal nations conceived of their treaty order as living agreements among kin,[34] as permanent living relationships. Central to these agreements was the sanctity of spoken sounds and promises—themselves manifestations of a holistic spiritual realm— imposing vital and living relationships, freedoms, and obligations where none existed before. As a result, the cognitive path of the Aboriginal peoples to the promises in treaties was different from, but complementary to, the path taken by the Europeans.[35]

Whereas American legal historians have written about the Aboriginal legal order,[36] few Canadian legal historians and historians have yet explored this rich

---

31   F. Jameson, *The Prison House of Language: A Critical Account of Structuralism and Russian Formalism* (Princeton, N.J.: Princeton University Press, 1972).

32   Henderson, "Empowering," *supra* note 28 at 251-63. See generally R.M. Leavitt and D.A. Francis, eds., *Wapapi Akonutomakonol: The Wampum Records. Wabanaki Traditional Law as recounted by Lewis Michell* (Fredericton, N.B.: Micmac-Maliseet Institute, 1990); I.H. Morgan, *League of the Ho-De-No Sau-nee* (New York: Burt Franklin, 1851); D.K. Richter and J.H. Merrel, eds., *Beyond the Covenant Chain: The Iroquois and Their Neighbors in Indian North America, 1600-1800* (Syracuse, N.Y.: Syracuse University Press, 1987); F. Jennings, *The Ambiguous Iroquois Empire* (New York: W.W. Norton, 1918) [hereinafter *Ambiguous Iroquois Empire*]; R. White, *The Middle Ground: Indians, Empires, and Republics in the Great Lake Regions, 1650-1815* (New York: Cambridge University Press, 1991).

33   R. M. Cover, "*Nomos* and Narrative" (1983) 97 Harv. L. Rev. 4 at 9.

34   Among the Mi'kmaq this was known as the *Nikmaq*; in Cree language *wakomagan* (family), *wakottuwin* (relationship); Fr. G. Beaudet, *Cree-English, English-Cree Dictionary* (Winnipeg: Wuertz Publishing, 1995) at 358.

35   J.Y. Henderson, "Governing the Implicate Order: Self-Government and the Linguistic Development of Aboriginal Communities" in *Linguistic Rights in Canada: Collusions or Collisions* (Ottawa: University of Ottawa Press, 1995) at 285-316.

36   See, *e.g.*, K.N. Llewellyn and E.A. Hoebel, *The Cheyenne Way: Conflict and Case Law in Primitive Jurisprudence* (Norman: University of Oklahoma Press, 1941); J.P. Reid, *A Law of Blood: The Primitive Law of the Cherokee Nation* (New York: New York University Press, 1970); R.A. Williams Jr., *Linking Arms Together: American Indian Treaty Visions of Law and Peace, 1600-1800* (Oxford: Oxford University Press, 1997).

resource.[37] If understanding Aboriginal treaty order presents difficult conceptual and translation challenges for researchers who do not speak Aboriginal languages, it is an immense but indispensable project. It entails enriched conceptual frameworks of Aboriginal legal traditions and teachings and a vast pluralistic legal order that attempted to structure just relations with other Aboriginal nations in a time of crisis and confrontation.

The Nikmanen order of these confederated Algonquian-speaking nations is illustrative of an Aboriginal treaty order. The boundaries of the Míkmaw Nation remained unchanged for centuries, despite shifting alliances among their allies.[38] They were surrounded by either their *Nikmaq* or the ocean. The *Nikmaq* (allies or friends) of the Míkmaw Nation included: the *Beothuk* (up river people) in Newfoundland; the *Wulustukw keuwiuk* (beautiful river people or *Maliseet-Passamaquoddy*) of southwestern New Brunswick and northeastern Maine; the Eastern *"Abanaki"* of Maine to Ottawa valley; various Montagnais groups north of the Saint Lawrence River; "Eskimo" or Inuit from the Strait of Belle Isle; and in the 1500s, the Saint Lawrence *Haudenosaunee*. Usually speaking a similar language and living in similar maritime and forest environments, the *Nikmaq* consensually united and disunited with the Míkmaw Nation according to their desires. A linguistic consciousness maintained unity among the allies, while each respected the others' diverse responses to common problems and experiences within their transnational order.

The Nikmanen order marks the development of a voluntary transnational law based not on the family structure, but on consensual agreements among the Aboriginal federations and European monarchies.[39] The Europeans were careful to record the Míkmaw Nikmanen or transnational confederations.[40] Confronted with a well-populated land, an organized government, and an elegant economic order, the Europeans were forced to develop new concepts of law and rights to deal with the allied people and their vast system of "friends."

---

37 J.Y. Henderson, "First Nations Legal Inheritance" (1996) 23 Man. L.J. 1; J. Borrows, "With or Without You: First Nations Law (in Canada)" (1996) 3 McGill L.J. 629; J.S. Milloy, *The Plains Cree: Trade, Diplomacy, and War, 1790-1870* (Winnipeg: University of Manitoba Press, 1988).

38 See generally, Míkmaw society in Eurocentric literature; P. Nietfeld, "Determinants of Aboriginal Micmac Political Structure" (Ph.D. Thesis, University of New Mexico, 1981) [unpublished]; B. Hoffman, "The Historical Ethnography of the Micmac of the Sixteenth and Seventeenth Centuries" (Ph.D. Thesis, University of California, Berkeley, 1955) [unpublished].

39 For a description of the Eastern confederacies, see Speck, *infra* note 79 at 492-508; W. Walker, G. Buesing and Conklin, "A Chronological Account of the Wabanaki Confederacy" in E.L. Schusky, ed., *Political Organization of Native North America* (Washington, D.C.: University Press of America, 1980) at 41-84. The Confederacy was called *lakutuwi* (or kinship) in the Passamaquoddy-Maliseet dialect of the Algonquian language, and *lakuti* in Míkmaq.

40 R.G. Thwaites, *The Jesuit Relations and Allied Documents: Travels and Explorations of the Jesuit Missionaries in New France, 1610-1791*, vol. 3 (New York: Pageant Books, 1959) at 87, 90-91 [the original French, Latin, and Italian texts, with English translations and notes]; C. Le Clercq, *Etablissement de la foy dans la Nouvelle France : contenant l'histoire des colonies françoises, et des découvertes* (Paris: A. Auroy, 1691).

From a Nikmanen perspective, relations with the Europeans or guests were part of a continuous process of trying to make peace or staying neutral in European conflicts.

Sometimes the allies cooperated in raids (called "wars" by Europeans) against common enemies, particularly against the Mohawk and the "*Armochiquois*."[41] These raids were designed not to acquire territory or wealth, but to end a conflict or enforce customary international trading laws.[42] The Nikmanen order was designed to maintain and strengthen the peace; the Nikmanen saw peace as a state of mind calling for self-discipline and forgiveness, and they understood that a crisis-based council could not implement a policy of disengagement. Presents and satisfactions for losses suffered during military raids encouraged good feelings, amity, and international harmony.

A united Confederacy emerged from these conflicts, and created the Nikmanen order. At the time of the arrival of the Europeans, the Wabanaki Confederacy comprised the Penobscot, Passamaquoddy, Malecite, and the Míkmaq.[43] It was united with the Ottawa Confederacy, comprising the Mohawk of Caughnawaga and Oka, the Têtes de Boule, and the Ottawa.[44] The extended confederacy of more than 14 nations[45] had sev-

---

41 Southern members of the Wabanaki Confederacy named by Champlain lived from the Saco River in extreme southwest Maine to Cape Cod. They were primarily an agricultural people with whom the Míkmaq traded. The northern members addressed them and their more southern allies to the Delaware Nation (*Lenape*) as *sawonehsonuk*.

42 See A. Morrison, ed., "Membertou's Raid on the Choacoet Almouchiquois: the Micmac Sack of Saco in 1607," trans. Goetz, in W. Cowan, ed., *Papers of the Sixth Algonquian Conference* (Ottawa: National Museums of Canada, 1975); Hoffman, *supra* note 38.

43 As a confederacy they were addressed as *Waponahkiyik*; Penobscot are called *Panwapskewiyik*, Passamaquoddy are *Peskotomuhkatiyik*. Malecites are *Wolastoqiyik*, and Míkmaq were *Mihkomak*.

44 See Leavitt & Francis, *supra* note 32. The Wabanakis addressed the Mohawks as *Meqiyik*, those of Caughnawauga as *Kanawkiyik*, those of Oka as *Kanasatakiyik*, the Têtes de Boule as *Epokatpacik*, and the Ottawa as *Atuwak*. *Wapapi Akonutomakonol* are "talking white beads" that comprised the records of the reason and purpose for the confederation.

45 *Ibid.* at 57-59:

Nit lahkalusonikikon olu nit nit mawe laukutuwi kisolutomuwakon. Skicinuwok newanku kehsuhkomiksuwok kenu olu kceyawi milicoposultuwok. Msi te yuktok skicinuwok 'tahcuwi oliyani-ay naks wikiniya tepahkalusioniw. ... Nit olu tan tehpu wikit tepahkalusioniw 'tahcuwi ciksotomonol tan eyikil tpaskuwakonol, or kosona osemha. Nit wikuwam tepahkalusioniw itomuwiw msi te kehsit skicin kisihtaq cuwi sankewi pomawsu. Katama apc cikawiyutultiwon. Cuwi oli pomawsuwok tahalu wesiwestulticik[,] witsehkehsulticik peskuwol te 'nikihkuwal.

The English translation is:

As for the fence implemented, that [is] that confederacy agreement. The Indians [are] fourteen tribes, but many different groups. All of the Indians had to go and live inside the fence. ... And as for whoever dwelled within the fence, he or she had to obey whatever laws were there or be whipped. That house within the fence signifies every individual Indian who made it must live peacefully. There would be no bothering one another anymore. They had to live like brothers, sisters, [with] the same parent.

eral descriptions.[46] This continental Confederacy, usually called Great Council Fire by the Wabanaki, was renewed in 1701 and in 1749; it extended the alliance to the Lakes Confederacy of the Ojibwa[47] and the Cree (*Nehiywaw*) Confederacy,[48] who were related to the Blackfoot and Lakota Confederacies.[49] This interconnectedness was continued in the treaty process with the Sovereign.

The extension of Aboriginal transnational law to include the British sovereign is reflected in the treaties, examples of which can be viewed as an extended Aboriginal system of tensions or bridges linking different world-views to a consensual order. Since the Georgian treaties typically were made within the Aboriginal protocols, the cordiality of the annual meetings and discussions were more important than the substance of the terms. Propositions were made orally at conferences and agreed to one by one with the exchange of symbolic gifts or wampum. Beyond the particular framework of obligations or rights, the agreements created a permanent, living relationship[50] consistent with an Aboriginal world-view.[51]

The prerogative treaties enabled the two world-views and different societies to make a new normative order of jurisdictions, obligations, and rights. To live in the new legal world required each culture to know not only the meaning of the alliance and its terms, but also the connections or transformations that resulted when one normative system passed through another. For example, the Wabanaki and Míkmaq applied the customary concepts of harmony and forgiveness to the British. Article 2 of the Míkmaw Compact (1752) required that "all Transactions during the Late War on both sides

---

46   The shared Wabanaki concept for joining one another in a confederacy is '*tolakutiniya*' (literally, they are related by kinship 'one other they were'). The Passamaquoddy, Malecite and Míkmaw called it the *Putusosuwakon* or the Convention Council or *kcimawe putuwosuwakon*; that is, a great joint council meeting. To meet in council is *Putuwosin*; when everybody meets in council it is *Putuwosiniya*, and their councillors were addressed as *putuwosuwinum*. In a council meeting, the alliance was addressed as *kcilakutuwakon* or Great kinship or Confederacy. However, the Penobscot as speakers for the Wabanakis often used the terms *Peskuwok* (those united into One) or *Kisakutuwok* (They are Completely United or already related). The Confederacy laws were called *tpaskuwakonol*, or measures. All these laws had to be made in wampum, and read annually or whenever asked what had happened on that occasion (*Msiw yuhtol tpaskuwakonol cuwi lihtasuwol wapapik wecihc kisokitasik tan tehpu eli kinuwi tpiyak*) See Leavitt & Francis, *ibid*. at 51-61. After King William's War (1688-1699) and King George's War (1744-1749), this Confederacy (or Great Council Fire) was extended to manage the European warfare that affected the nations. Because of unfamiliarity with the Aboriginal languages, researchers often confuse the Convention Council with the Great Council Fire. The Great Council Fire was the first confederacy in Canada. See Speck, *infra* note 79.

47   The Wabanaki addressed these Confederacies as *Sonutsekotonuk*.

48   The Wabanaki addressed this Confederacy as *Oquathu'kuk*.

49   The Wabanaki addressed these Confederacies as *Ksiyahsonuk*.

50   See H. De Puy, ed., *Bibliography of the English Colonial Treaties with the American Indians* (New York: AMS Press,1971); Borrows, *infra* note 54; Slattery, "Aboriginal Sovereignty," *supra* note 21 at 683-84, and *infra* note 54; Wildsmith, *infra* note 71.

51   R. Barsh and J.Y. Henderson, "Aboriginal Rights, Treaty Rights, and Human Rights: Indian Tribes and Constitutional Renewal" (1982) 17 J. Can. Studies at 55-81.

be buried in Oblivion with the Hatchet."[52] This fragile quest for an explicit order among the diverse federations through consensual treaties provided the foundation upon which developed the first British Empire and their colonies, and eventually the United Kingdom.[53]

B. British Treaty Order (1693-1930)

The original constitutional order of the United Kingdom was created by the consensual treaties with the Aboriginal nations in North America. After the *Treaty of Paris* (1763) and the *Royal Proclamation of 1763*, British law enshrined treaty making with Aboriginal nations and tribes as the constitutional responsibility of the imperial Sovereign in right of the United Kingdom.[54] At the time of the treaty, in the law of Great Britain the royal prerogatives were a residual monarchical power and practice created by the law of nations and affirmed in British constitutional law.[55] Originally, the royal prerogative consisted of all the powers and privileges accorded by custom to the Sovereign,[56] powers limited in England by the courts[57] and the creation of the Westmin-

---

52 In Leavitt & Francis, *supra* note 32 at 54, the idea of creating the Convention Council was expressed, "*Yuhtol pekankonikil tomkikonossisol olu naka tapihik pahqilil cuwi puskonasuwol askomiw,*" or in translation, "These bloody hatches, bows, and arrows, however, must be buried forever." Compare to the Míkmaw Compact (1752) in P.A. Cumming and N.H. Mickenberg, eds., *Native Rights in Canada* (Toronto: Indian-Inuit Association of Canada, 1972) at Art. 2 [hereinafter *Native Rights*].

53 R.L. Barsh and J.Y. Henderson, "International Context of Crown-Aboriginal Treaties in Canada" in CD-ROM: *For Seven Generations: An Information Legacy of the Royal Commission on Aboriginal Peoples* (Ottawa: Canada Communication Group, 1996); J.Y. Henderson, "The Status of Indian Treaties in International Law" in *Aboriginal Rights and International Law: Proceedings of the XXII Annual Conference, October 21-23 1993, Ottawa, Ontario* (Ottawa: Canadian Council on International Law, 1993) at 132; D.V. Jones, *License For Empire: Colonialism By Treaty In Early America* (Chicago: University of Chicago Press, 1982); see C. Alexandrowicz, *The European-African Confrontation: A Study in Treaty-Making* (Leiden: A.W. Sijthoff, 1973); C. Alexandrowicz, *An Introduction to the History of the Law of Nations in the East Indies* (Oxford: Clarendon Press,1967); *Federal Indian Law, infra* note 79; M.F. Lindley, *The Acquisition of Backward Territory* (London: Longmans, Green & Co. Ltd., 1926); A. Morris, *The Treaties of Canada with the Indians of Manitoba and the North-West Territories* [1880] (Saskatoon, Sk.: Fifth House Publishers, 1991) [reprint].

54 P.W. Hogg, *Constitutional Law of Canada*, 3d ed. (Toronto: Carswell, 1992) at 664. See also *Royal Proclamation of 1763, infra* note 298; J. Borrows, "Constitutional Law from a First Nation Perspective: Self-Government and the Royal Proclamation" (1994) 28 U.B.C. L. Rev. 1 at 15-19; and B. Slattery, *The Land Rights of Aboriginal Canadian Peoples, as Affected by the Crown's Acquisition of Their Territories* (Saskatoon, Sk.: College of Law, University of Saskatchewan, 1979) [hereinafter *Land Rights*].

55 The development of the judicial doctrines of paramountcy in United Kingdom law transferred the authority of the law of nations to constitutional law, *Halsbury's, supra* note 2 at para. 1770, n. 3.

56 Blackstone, *supra* note 4, vol. 1 at 239; H.V. Evatt, *The Royal Prerogative* (Sydney: Law Book Co., 1987); S.A. de Smith, *Constitutional and Administrative Law*, 6th ed. by Rodney Brazier (New York: Penguin, 1989), c. 6. Blackstone wrote that prerogative "assumes in its etymology (from *prae* and *rogo*) something that is required or demanded before, or in preference to, all others."

57 J.A. Chitty, *Treatise of the Law of the Prerogatives of the Crown: And the Relative Duties and Rights of the Subject* (London: Joseph Butterworths & Son, 1820) at 5.

ster Parliament.[58] By the eighteenth century the prerogative order was the residue of discretionary or arbitrary authority over foreign affairs and international law.[59] Power or privileges enjoyed equally with private persons were not considered part of the prerogative order[60] that concerned powers and privileges unique to the Crown.[61] This prerogative component of the Kingdom, one of the three major constitutional powers in Great Britain,[62] was exercised in relation to such foreign affairs as declaring war, entering into treaties, and exercising legislative powers over British colonies.[63] In 1883, Canadian Supreme Court Justice Ritchie in *R. v. McLeod* described the prerogative as follows:

> These prerogatives of the Crown must not be treated as personal to the sovereign; they are great constitutional rights, conferred on the sovereign, upon principles of public policy, for the benefit of the people, and not, as it is said, "for the private gratification of the sovereign"—they form part of and are generally speaking "as ancient as the law itself."[64]

The prerogative of the Sovereign is regarded as part of the common law because court decisions have determined its existence and extent.[65] "The treaty-making power," said Mr. Justice Duff of the Supreme Court of Canada in 1922, "is one of the preroga-

---

58 A.V. Dicey, *Introduction to the Study of the Law of the Constitution*, 10th ed. (New York: St. Martin's Press, 1965) at 424.

59 *Ibid.*

60 Hogg, *supra* note 54 at 13. Hogg gives as examples the power of a private person to acquire and dispose of property, and to enter into contracts, which are not prerogative powers because they are possessed by everyone.

61 *Ibid.*

62 B. Clark, *Native Liberty, Crown Sovereignty: The Existing Aboriginal Right of Self-Government in Canada* (Montreal and Kingston: McGill-Queen's University Press, 1990) at 37-45.

63 See Evatt, *supra* note 56; Dicey, *supra* note 58 at 460 states: "[A] treaty made by the Crown ... is valid without the authority or sanction of Parliament"; and A.B. Keith, *Responsible Government in the Dominions*, vol. 3 (Oxford: Clarendon Press, 1912) at 1102, states: "There is no real doubt that treaties made by the Crown are binding on the Colonies whether or not the Colonial Governments consent to such treaties." See also A.B. Keith, *Imperial Unity and the Dominions* (Oxford: Clarendon Press, 1916) at 35; Chitty, *supra* note 57 at 4. For a description of Crown prerogative, see generally *Halsbury's*, *supra* note 2, vol. 8 at paras. 889-1082.

64 (1883), 8 S.C.R. 1 at 26 (S.C.C.).

65 It is typical for British and Canadian domestic courts and lawyers to conceptualize the royal prerogatives as a "pre-eminence" that the sovereign enjoys over and above all other persons by virtue of the common law. The royal prerogatives were not created by the common tradition and customs of the people. The royal prerogatives were the residue of royal authority left over from a time before it was effectually controlled by the common law or statute. See *Case of Convocation* (1611), 77 E.R. 1350 (K.B.) and *Case of Proclamations* (1611), 77 E.R. 1852 (K.B.) [hereinafter *Proclamations*]. The most the British courts have said is that the King ought to be under no man, but under God and the law, because the law makes the King. See Chitty, *supra* note 57 at 5. The law of the King or Queen can best be understood as an ancient branch of the aristocratic law of nations. Although the royal prerogatives are the source for parliamentary authority, it has remained separate and inviolable from parliamentary authority, at least as a matter of constitutional law. Hogg, *supra* note 54 at 13, citing *Proclamations*.

tives of the Crown under the British constitution."[66] Until 1947, the imperial Sovereign held the exclusive right to negotiate, enter, and determine the contents of a treaty, to ratify the treaty, and to provide for implementation of its obligations in Canada.[67] Whereas the imperial Sovereign could exercise this authority directly or via the agency of a chartered company, the courts were not allowed to challenge the wisdom of the imperial Sovereign in treaty making.[68]

Three general models of prerogative treaties exist in British jurisdictions of North America: Georgian treaties in the North Atlantic territory; a number of Georgian and Victorian treaties in Upper Canada, Lower Canada, and British Columbia;[69] and Victorian treaties in the Western Indian country.[70] All treaties were founded on a permanent nation-to-nation relationship based on trust and respect,[71] and created a bilateral sovereignty in a shared territory.[72]

Thus, Aboriginal nations had a central role in forging a new society with a shared legal order. Differences in the treaties illustrate the vigorous choices of Aboriginal nations. In treaty negotiations and stipulations, these radically different societies negotiated as political equals to create a new order. No culture or social narrative occupied a privileged or dominant position in the resulting treaty order that sought to structure power and relations justly. Professor Robert Williams, Jr. characterizes the treaty process as law-creation:

> Law-creation was central to the society being constructed by Indians acting in concert with Europeans on the multicultural frontiers of Encounter era North America. For Europeans, long-held legal notions about the diminished rights of "savage" and "barbarian" peoples were forced to yield to the reality of formidable and well organized Indian tribes, with their own deeply ingrained traditions of law for governing relations between different peoples. For Indians, accommodation of the strange newcomers to their lands required adapting their long held traditions to the challenges of survival in their rapidly changing world. From this process of multicultural legal encounter emerged innumerable stories of what Robert Cover has called *jurisgenesis*—the creation of new legal meanings. Through these meanings, Indian tribes and colonial Europeans sought to define a nomos—a normative world. This world was held together by the jurisgenerative force of the common

---

66   *Re Oriental Orders in Council Validation Act, B.C.* (1922), 65 D.L.R. 577 at 599 (S.C.C.), affirmed, [1923] 4 D.L.R. 698 (B.C. P.C.).

67   Hogg, *supra* note 54 at 282-83; Letters Patent 1947, R.S.C. 1985, App. II, No. 31.

68   The treaty-making power of the Crown has been held to be non-reviewable. See *Blackburn v. Attorney General*, [1971] 1 W.L.R. 1037 (Eng. C.A.).

69   See *e.g.*, *The Missassagguas Chippewa Cessions* (1781-1849); *Six Nations* (1784-1835); *Ottawa* (1786-1836); *Vancouver Island Treaties* (1850-54); *Robinson Treaty* (1850); *Manitoulin Island Treaty* (1862); and *Williams Treaties* (1923) in R.A. Reiter, *The Law of Canadian Indian Treaties* (Edmonton: Juris Analytica, 1995), pt. 3.

70   Reiter, *ibid. Treaties No. 1, 2, 3, 4, 5, 6, 7, 8, 9, 10 and 11* (Ottawa: Queen's Printers, 1966).

71   B.H. Wildsmith, "Treaty Responsibilities: A Co-Relational Model" (1992) (Special Edition) U.B.C. L. Rev. 324 at 330-331.

72   Under prerogative treaties, the Aboriginal nations shared power with the sovereign in all ceded areas.

interpretive commitments to a law created and shared by the different peoples of Encounter era North America.[73]

The countless treaties, councils, and negotiations witness the operation of the Aboriginal order with the new guests. Aboriginal nations insisted upon the application of their traditions and principles in the conferences for ordering the new relationship and creating a multicultural society in their lands. By adapting themselves to Aboriginal legal traditions and diplomacy, European negotiators secured alliance and goodwill. The discussion at the councils and negotiations and the terms of the treaties reveal a multiplicity of Aboriginal orders interplaying with the European orders.

Typically, the prerogative treaties were made according to Aboriginal protocols emphasizing kinship: the King as "father" and the colonists as "brothers."[74] To preserve the kinship, as within a natural family, Aboriginal nations and the representatives of the King were obliged to meet again from time to time to renew the friendship, reconcile misunderstandings, and share their experiences and wealth. Thus, most of the treaties were renewal ceremonies of sustaining and adjusting the relationship. For these reasons Aboriginal nations hold the treaties as sacred.

Most treaties consist of a transcript of the proceedings and a written record of the substance of the agreement, the style illustrating both the vitality of Aboriginal protocols and world-views, and the British sovereign's acceptance of the flexible, kin-like nature of the confederation underlined by the metaphor of the chain or road. In these treaties, Aboriginal nations did not validate or accept an inferior position under the imperial Crown or under colonial governments, but instead registered their intention to create a mutual partnership and genuine dialogue about shared development.

Each written record comprises a central treaty and subsequent ratification treaties. Together these relationships with the Crown are often called treaty federalism, the original Aboriginal-prerogative federation with Great Britain in North America. By European standards the resulting written agreements drafted by the British are often unnervingly concise and vague, but this was not the result of Aboriginal naiveté or of a failure to agree. The written treaty text was a choice of the British drafters of the treaties, writing for the Crown and its servants, not for the Aboriginal nations or their people.[75]

---

73   Williams, *supra* note 36 at 28.

74   See Leavitt & Francis, *supra* note 32.

75   Canada, *Report of the Royal Commission on Aboriginal Peoples, Looking Forward, Looking Back*, vol. 1 (Ottawa: Minister of Supply and Services Canada, 1996) at 173-78 [hereinafter RCAP].

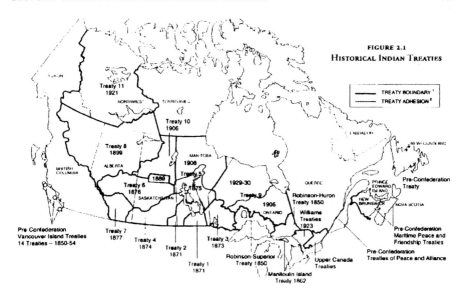

Historical Indian Treaties[76]

5. Georgian Treaties in the North Atlantic Territory

Since the claim of sovereignty over Aboriginal lands by European treaties or conquest did not extinguish Aboriginal tenure, the source of British authority in North America was created by confederations with the Aboriginal peoples around prerogative treaties. In the North Atlantic territory, the fundamental principles of the treaty order were forged in the *Treaty of Utrecht*, and realized in the Wabanaki Compact (1713-1725), and the Míkmaw Compact (1752-1789). Conforming to the holistic Aboriginal consciousness, the Wabanaki and Míkmaw Compacts were interconnected and complementary; they were not autonomous agreements. Between 1693 and 1786, more than 50 treaty conferences defined the relationship between the Aboriginal nations of the Atlantic territory and the Sovereign.[77] The Georgian treaties are often called Peace and Friendship treaties because they did not "cede" land to the

---

76 *Report of the Royal Commission on Aboriginal Peoples*, Vol. 2: *Restructuring the Relationship* at 12. This map is based on information taken from the National Atlas of Canada maps. Reproduced with the permission of the Minister of Public Works and Government Services Canada, 2000, on behalf of Privy Council Office and Natural Resources Canada.

77 Levi, *et al.*, "We Should Walk in the Tract Mr. Dummer Made" (October 1 and 2, 1992) [unpublished document distributed at New Brunswick Chiefs' Forum on Treaty Issues, St. John, New Brunswick]. See also *The Mi'Kmaq Treaty Handbook* (Native Communication Society of Nova Scotia, 1987); W.E. Daugherty, *Maritime Indian Treaties in Historical Perspectives* (Canada: Indian and Northern Affairs, 1981); *Crown Land Rights and Hunting and Fishing Rights of Micmac Indians in the Province of Nova Scotia*, rev. ed. (Union of Nova Scotia Indians, 1976).

Crown.[78] These treaties will be closely examined to amplify the context of the Aboriginal-Crown relationship and reconciliation of Aboriginal tenure.

In the southern colonies in the early seventeenth century, first the British colonists and then the Sovereign through colonial governors entered into treaties with Aboriginal nations in Virginia, Massachusetts Bay, New Hampshire, and Pennsylvania. Beginning in 1693, this evolving network of treaty commonwealth or federation with the Sovereign was extended through treaties negotiated by imperial representatives of the colony of Massachusetts to the southernmost members of the Wabanaki Confederacy. By 1730, treaties were negotiated with all members of the Confederacy—an alliance that stretched from Maine to the Maritimes, including members such as the Penobscot, Passamaquoddy, and Wuastukwiuk (Maliseet) nations.[79] The Míkmaq were allies of the Confederacy with strong political, economic, and military links to it. In the negotiation of the 1725 treaty, representatives of the Penobscot acted as spokespersons for other nations.

Representatives of the Míkmaq then ratified the treaty in several subsequent councils between 1726 and 1728. The treaty-making tradition between representatives of the British Crown and the Míkmaq continued in the middle decades of the 1700s, following a pattern in which some matters addressed in earlier treaties were reaffirmed while changing conditions gave rise to agreement on new issues. Thus, after the British established themselves in Halifax in 1749, new treaty discussions began; in 1752 a central treaty was signed by the Grand Chief and later ratified by the various district chiefs of the Míkmaw nation.

Before considering the central treaty of 1752, we need to examine the Attorney General Northey Opinion for the Crown on the status of Aboriginal nations in Crown law and the Royal Commission established to hear the Mohegan treaty claims in Connecticut. These set the framework for the *Treaty of Utrecht* and the various compacts and treaties with the Nikmanen.

---

78   In British law, a cession of territory by a treaty is a Law of nations concept. As Brownlie, *supra* note 3 at 133, n. 36, explains, "The term 'cession' is used to cover a variety of types of transaction, and it is important to seek the legal realities behind the term in each case." Neither treaties of cession nor of conquest terminate the original rights in the territory; express positive laws are required to extinguish those rights. In British law, the reserved rights doctrine is called, in the classic theory of the common law, the doctrine of continuity: *Campbell v. Hall* (1774), Lofft 655, 1 Cowp. 204 (Eng. K.B.) [hereinafter *Campbell v. Hall* cited to Lofft]; in United States law it is called the doctrine of tribal sovereignty. See F. Cohen, *Federal Indian Law* (Washington: Gov't. Printing Services, 1942) at 122 [hereinafter *Federal Indian Law*].

79   "Letter of Gyles to Dummer, 22 June 1727" in J.P. Baxter, ed., *Documentary History of the State of Maine* (Portland, Me.: Fred L. Tower Co. & Maine Historical Society, 1916) Art. 10 at 408 [hereinafter DHM]; "*La Nation Abnaquise et des sauvages ses alliez ... , 27 Juil., 1721*" in DHM at 29-63. F. Speck, "The Eastern Algonkian Wabanaki Confederacy" (1915) 17 Am. Anthro. 492 at 505-507.

A. Attorney General Northey Opinion (1703-1704)

The existing Aboriginal deeds of purchase and treaties in New England colonies affirm that Aboriginal nations, tribes, and villages were viewed by the colonizers as holding Aboriginal tenure or territorial sovereignty.[80] A 1686 deed to the town of Salem is an example:

> until the ensaling and delivery of these presents, [the Native leaders] and their ancestors were the true, sole and lawful owners of all the afore bargained premises, and were lawfully seized of and in the same and every part thereof in their own right.[81]

Other examples of Indian deeds[82] reflect the assumption or belief of the English colonizers that they could purchase the Aboriginal title, and receive a valid estate or interest in the land. At the same time, they displayed an indifference to what the Aboriginal grantors thought about the alien conveyances and written documents. Colonial historian William Cronon argued the colonists should have paid more attention to these deeds, since "what the Indians owned—or, more precisely, what their villages gave them claim to—was not the land but the things (*i.e.*, chattels) that were on the land during the various seasons of the year."[83] Discussing a 1636 Wabanaki deed, he stated:

> It is clear that the Indians conceived of this sale as applying only to very specific uses of the land. They gave up none of their most important hunting and gathering privileges, they retained rights to their cornfields, and evidently intend to keep living on the land much as they had done before.[84]

In contrast, the colonizers presumed these transactions purchased the land itself for all purposes.[85]

Historian Anthony Wallace argued that the Wabanaki southern allies, the Delaware Indians or *Lenape*, similarly distinguished use from purchase:

> To the Delaware Indian, land was an element, a medium of existence, like the air and sunlight and river. To him, 'ownership' of land meant, not exclusive personal title to the soil itself, but occupation of a certain position of responsibility in the social unit

---

80   See generally, M.D. Harris, *Origin of the Land Tenure System in the United States* (Ames: Iowa State College Press, 1953), especially c. 11; C.A. Weslager, *The English on the Delaware, 1610-1682* (New Brunswick, NJ: Rutgers University Press, 1967); G. E. Kershaw, *The Kennebeck Proprietors, 1749-1775: "Gentlemen of Large Property and Judicious Men"* (Sommersworth, NH: New Hampshire Publishing Co. for Maine Historical Society, 1975).

81   F. Jennings, "Virgin Land and Savage People" (1971) 23 Am. Q. 519; F. Jennings, *The Invasion of America: Indians, Colonialism, and the Cant of Conquest* (Chapel Hill: University of North Carolina Press, 1975) at 143.

82   J.W. Springer, "American Indians and the Law of Real Property in Colonial New England" (1968) 30 Am. J. Legal Hist. 25 at 35-44.

83   W. Cronon, *Changes in the Land: Indians, Colonists, and the Ecology of New England* (New York: Hill and Wang, 1983) at 65.

84   *Ibid.* at 67.

85   *Ibid.* at 68.

that exploited the soil. ... The "sale of land" (to use the white man's term) might, to the Delaware, be almost any mutually satisfactory change in the relationship of two groups of persons subsisting on the land. In the earlier sales, the Indians seem to have intended only to give the white a freedom to use the land in conjunction with native populations.[86]

Historian Francis Jennings elaborated on the understanding of the early land transaction:

> Under Aboriginal Delaware custom, the "sale" of land conveyed only the rights of use for residence and subsistence as long as the parties lived and were satisfied with the term of compensation. No sales were permanent. Even if all demands were met and the settlers completely satisfied, he might show up a second time for further compensation and be entirely fair and honourable according to his standards. Apparently there were complications in these customs that were better understood by Englishmen at the time than by students nowadays.[87]

These interpretations of the Aboriginal sales to colonizers were validated by a royal commission appointed in 1664 by Charles II to investigate Wabanaki complaints about colonial mistreatment in Connecticut and New England, and to inquire whether the King "had indeed a good title to that territory" by purchases from the Aboriginal nations.[88] After their investigation, the royal commission instructed colonial authorities that their confiscation of Indian hunting lands and other uncultivated areas as vacant land was illegal, because "no doubt the country is [the Indians'] till they give it or sell it, though it be not improoued [sic]."[89]

In attempting to remedy existing land titles, the Lord of Trade and the Royal Commission found that the Puritans conceded the Indians were "the true owners,"[90] and Aboriginal deeds were sufficient title to the land.[91] The magistrates of Boston asserted to the prerogative commissioners that it was far more important to hold land

---

86   A. Wallace, "Women, Land, and Society: Three Aspects of Aboriginal Delaware Life" (1947) 17 Pa. Arch. 2.

87   *Ambiguous Iroquois Empire*, *supra* note 32 at 326.

88   *Ibid.* at 17. Also see "Instruction to Colonel Nicolls &c., Commissioners to Connecticut" in Broadhead, Fernow and O'Callaghan, eds., *Documents Relative to the Colonial History of the State of New York*, vol. 3 (New York: New York State Library, 1853-87) at 55-56 [hereinafter NYCD].

89   *Ambiguous Iroquois Empire*, *ibid.* at 213.

90   P. Force, ed., *Tracts and Other Papers Relating Principally to the Origin, Settlement, and Progress of the Colonies in North America: From the Discovery of the Country to the Year 1776*, vol. 4 (New York: P. Smith, 1947) at 28.

91   C.M. Andrews, *The Colonial Period of American History*, vol. 1 (New Haven, Conn.: Yale University Press, 1934-38) at 258-260, 264, 272, 344-345, 372. Similar arguments were made by the Jesuits against Baltimore's royal charter and claims of absolute proprietorship of Maryland. The Jesuits assert the Indians owned the land: see Jesuit Provincial Knott, "Notanda or Observations, (17 November 1641)"; "Case of Conscience on Indian Lands (26 November 1641)"; and "Memorial submitted to the Holy Office or Inquisition (1642)" in T. A. Hughes. *History of the Society of Jesus in North America, Colonial and Federal* (London: Longmans, Green, 1908) pt. 1 at 170-178.

under an Indigenous treaty, or deed, or under "just conquest," than under His Majesty's authority.[92]

In the regal confirmations, which signified the Crown's approval of their estates, the Lords of Trade instructed their commissioners to confirm all title held under Indian treaties or deeds, but rejected the "just conquest" theory of title in the colonies.[93] The Royal Commission travelled into regions where "squatters" had settled on land without any title and forced them to recognize the rights of the Wabanaki tenurial system by payment of quit rents to the tribes.[94] For example, Massachusetts Bay agreed in the 1678 treaty to pay the Indians an annual quit rent "of a peck of corn" for every British family in the settlements.[95] Commissioner Andros reported that in considering Indigenous deeds more important than His Majesty's authority or English law,[96] the Puritan theocrats validated Aboriginal deeds as a source of estates of the colonizers, subject to regal sovereignty.

Under the English tenurial principles of common law, Aboriginal deeds were not viewed as an act of creation, which left the British grantee having an existence independent of the Aboriginal tenure or law. Instead, the deed created a relationship between the American Aboriginal nation and the grantee: as grantor, the American Aboriginal nation could retain a present and future interest in the granted land. In British law, this was the mischief of individual and colonial purchases of land title from the Aboriginal nations.

Aboriginal treaties created similar problems. The *Treaty of Hartford* (1638) ended the "Pequot war" in New England and declared mutual peace and friendship.[97]

---

92   H.P. Kraus, ed., *Sir Edmund Andros, 1637-1714, Governor of New York, Governor of the Dominion of New England, Governor of Virginia: Original Documents from his Papers, Many with the Signatures of Charles II, James II, William III, and Mary II*, vol. 1 (New York: H.P. Kraus, 1978) at 50; N.B. Shurtleff, ed., *Records of the Governor and Company of the Massachusetts Bay in New England*, vol. 1 (Boston: W. White, 1853 reprint. New York: AMS Press, 1968) at 176, 190, 198-99. See also P.R. Christoph and F.A. Christoph, eds., *The Andros Papers: Files of the Provincial Secretary of New York During the Administration of Governor Sir Edmund Andros, 1674-1680*, trans. Charles T. Gehring, vol. 1 (New York: Syracuse University Press, 1989) [hereinafter *Andros*].

93   Kraus, *ibid.* at 50-51.

94   C.E. Eisinger, "Puritan Justification for the Taking of Indian Land" (1948) 84 Essex Institute Hist. Coll. 131 at 141; W.C. MacLeod, *The American Indian Frontier* (New York: A.A. Knopf, 1928), c. 15, in particular at 197-200. See generally Y. Kawashima, *Puritan justice and the Indian: White Man's Law in Massachusetts, 1630-1763* (Middletown, Conn.: Wesleyan University Press, 1986).

95   K.M. Morrison, "The People of the Dawn: The Abenakis and their Relations with New England and New France 1600-1727" (Ph.D. Thesis, University of Maine, 1975) [unpublished] at 152. Also see K.M. Morrison, *The Embattled Northeast: The Elusive Ideal of Alliance in Abenaki-Euramerican Relations* (Berkeley: University of California Press, 1984).

96   *Andros, supra* note 92 at 51. This theory is confirmed in the writings of John Cotton. Another Puritan, John White, advocated the Biblical arguments but still asserted that "[t]he land affords ground enough to receive more people," and "the Natives invite us to set downe by them, and offer us what grounds wee will: so that eyther want of possession by others, or the possessors gift, and sale, may assure our right: we neede not feare a clear title to the soyle." See Eisinger, *supra* note 94 at 138.

97   "Treaty of Hartford (21 September 1638)" in A. Vaughan, ed., *Early American Indian Documents, Treaties, and Laws 1607-1789*, vol. 1 (Washington, D.C.: University Publications of America, 1979) at 6, and App. II.

The Wabanaki delegation agreed that in all future disputes or differences they would submit to English arbitration. Also, they authorized the colonialists to use force to bring to the treaty process resistant Indians, in particular the Pequot leader,[98] whose territory was distributed between the Mohegan and Narragansett nations. In the treaty of 1644, the Narragansett nation entered into an alliance with the sovereign:

> wee, the chiefe Sachems, Princes or Governours of the Nanhigansets (in that part of America, now called New England), together with the joynt and unanimous consent of all our people and subjects, inhabitants thereof, do upon serious consideration ... freely, voluntarily, and most humbly ... submit, subject, and give over ourselves, peoples, lands, right, inheritances, and possession whatsoever ... unto the protection, care and government of that worthy and royal Prince, Charles King of Great Britaine and Ireland.[99]

In 1665, King Charles II established the Narragansett Country as a royal province, separate from all other colonies and subject to rule by a prerogative commission.[100]

The Mohegan nation's relations to the King and the colonial charter became an important colonial legal dispute that turned on the interpretation of a series of treaties and agreements negotiated between 1658 and 1681. Under those treaties and agreements, certain lands had been reserved to the Mohegans under the protection of the Crown. Based on the prerogative treaties and Mohegan law, or Aboriginal *lex loci*, the Mohegans claimed to have an Aboriginal tenure to reserved lands within the boundaries of the royal colony in Connecticut.[101]

Following the Mohegan treaty, the 1662 charter stated that the greater part of the colony was "Purchased and obtained for great and valuable Consideration" and some

---

98   The English text of a 1644 treaty or covenants with the Massachusetts Bay Company illustrates the terms and conditions between the Indigenous nations and the colony:

> Wee have & by these present do voluntarily, & wthout any constraint or psuasion, but of our owne free motion, put orselues, or subjects, lands, & estates under the government and jurisdiction of the Massachusetts to bee governed & ptected by them, according to their just lawes & orders, so farr as we shall bee made capable of understanding them; & wee do pmise for orselues, & all or subjects, & all or posterity, to bee true & faithful to the said government & syding to the maintenance thereof, to or best ability, & from time to time to give speedy notice of any conspiracy, attempt, or evill intension of any which wee shall know or hear of against the same; & wee do pmise to bee willing from time to time to bee instructed in the knowledg & worship of God, ...

Springer *supra* note 82 at 33. This covenant, usually in an extended form, became the model for most subsequent agreements with the members of the Wabanaki Confederacy in New England. Similar treaties of peace and friendship were signed in Virginia after Indian wars and given statutory force by an Act of the Assembly. See W.M. Billings, ed., *The Old Dominion in the Seventeenth Century: A Documentary History of Virginia, 1606-1689* (Chapel Hill: University of North Carolina Press, for Institute of Early American History and Culture, 1975) at 226-230.

99   Springer, *supra* note 82 at 34, citing Rhode Island Archives, vol. 1 at 34.

100 Springer, *ibid.*, citing Rhode Island Archives, vol. 2 at 59-60.

101 For the best description of this case, see J.H. Smith, *Appeals to the Privy Council From the American Plantations* (New York: Octagon Books, 1965) at 418-442. See also, M.D. Walters, "Mohegan Indians v. Connecticut (1705-1773) and the Legal Status of Aboriginal Customary Laws and Government in British North America" (1995) 33(4) Osgoode Hall L.J. 786.

other parts gained by "conquest," presumably the Pequot territory, to considerably enlarge the colony.[102] In 1663, the Crown had written to Connecticut and other New England colonies stating that it had obtained a "just propriety" by grant from the "native princes from that country," and ordering the colonial authorities not to molest or disturb the colonial purchasers from planting and improving their newly acquired plantations.[103] Such interference "disturbed and obstructed the enlarging our Empire in the said New England."[104]

Chief Uncas had granted some Mohegan lands to Major John Mason, the deputy-Governor of the colony, as trustee, but had reserved other lands for the benefit of the nation. The Mohegans, through their trustee, alleged that the colonial authorities had illegally seized these lands and evicted the Mohegan residents in favour of colonists. Oweneco, the son of Mohegan Chief Uncas, petitioned the Queen-in-Council in 1703 for a Royal Commission for his Mohegan Tribe for relief from this alleged oppression by the General Court and Assembly. In petitioning the Crown for relief, Oweneco and Mason relied on the promises of 1664 royal commissioners that the Crown would examine any injuries done to them by British subjects, would do them justice, and would always protect them from any oppression.[105]

The seizure of reserved Mohegan lands had been done under the ostensible authority of a series of Acts of the General Court and General Assembly of Connecticut during the 1680-90s. In 1681, after Uncas transferred Mohegan land to colonial authorities by an agreement, the colonial authorities began parcelling out the land for settlement. The Mohegans alleged that the effect of the 1681 agreement was simply to grant the colony of Connecticut[106] a right of first purchase of the land (a pre-emptive right). The colony, by contrast, alleged the transaction had relinquished Aboriginal tenure to the lands.[107]

On receipt of the Mohegans' *ex parte* petition for relief (the colonists refused to participate), the Privy Council referred the matter to the Board of Trade, which in turn sought the advice of Sir Edward Northey, the Attorney General to Queen Anne.[108] Documents Attorney General Northey had before him were the 1662 charter, the petition and, possibly, a supporting affidavit that was consistent with the Mohegans' ver-

---

102 For the charter, see F.N. Thorpe, ed., *The Federal and State Constitutions: Colonial Charters, and Other Organic Laws of the States, Territories, and Colonies now or Heretofore Forming the United States of America*, vol. 1 (Washington, D.C.: Govt. Printing Office, 1909) at 529-530.

103 W.N. Sainsbury *et al.*, eds., *Calendar of State Papers, Colonial Series: Preserved in the State Paper Dept. of Her Majesty's Public Record Office* (Vaduz, Liech.: Kraus Reprint, 1964); *Calendar of state papers, colonial series* [supplement to v. 14]; *America and West Indies, Addenda, 1688-1696* (Vaduz, Liech.: Kraus Reprint, 1969) 1661-1668, #494 [hereinafter CSP].

104 CSP, *ibid.*

105 "Instruction," *supra* note 88.

106 The name of the colony was the Governor and Company of the Colony of Connecticut.

107 The General Court and Assembly argued that the treaties and dealings with the Mohegans since the 1640s had been merely political expedients, and created no legal liabilities to respect the lands the Indians had reserved to themselves.

108 29 February 29 1703-1704. Northey was Attorney General from 1701-1707 and from 1710-1718.

sion of events. [109] In his review, Attorney General Northey stated the background to the case:

> These Indyans and the British have ever Since [the 1658 Treaty] lived friendly with each other and the British in their Wares with the other Indyans have been always assisted by these Indyans who have quietly enjoyed the Lands they had reserved to them selves, untill about a Year or two Years agoe, the Generall Assembly of the Colony of Connecticot, made an Act that the Lands which the said Indyans had reserved to themselves, should be added or laid to the Townships of New London and Colchester, two Towns in that Colony, Since which Act the said Indians have by the Govmt of Connecticot been disseised and turned out of Possession of their reserved Lands.
>
> The said Indyans have frequently applyed themselves to the said Gennll Assembly for redress but can obtain none, So that it's fear'd these Indians having all their Lands taken from them will be under a Necessity of Joyning with the French and other Indyans now in Warr with ye British unless they be restored to their said Lands. [110]

Attorney General Northey reviewed the 1662 royal charter, which did not acknowledge the presence of Aboriginal nations by name, but recognized a greater part of the land was gained by purchases for consideration.[111] Attorney General Northey had first to deal with the jurisdictional question of whether the royal prerogative to hear the case had been ousted by the charter privileges:

> Whether this being a Controversy between the said Indians and the Govern. & Company of Connecticut Colony, Her Majesty may (notwithstanding the aforesaid Powers and Priviledges granted to the said Governor and Company) Grant a Commission to indifferent

---

109   CSP, *supra* note 103 at 1704-1705, #11.

110   See United Kingdom Colonial Office Series [hereinafter C.O.] 5/1263/70-71; CSP, *ibid.* at 1704-1705 #58; Review by Attorney General Northgate, Chalmers' Collection, New York Public Library, Connecticut, vol. 1, fols. 16b-18a [hereinafter Chalmers' Collection].

111   Thorpe, *supra* note 102, vol. 2 at 529-530:

> Whereas by the several Navigations, Discoveries, and Successful Plantations of divers of Our loving Subjects of this Our Realm of England, several Lands, Islands, Places, Colonies, and Plantations have been obtained and settled in that Part of the Continent of America called New-England, and thereby the Trade and Commerce there hath been of late Years much increased: And whereas We have been informed by the humble Petition of our Trusty and Well beloved John Winthrop [and others] ... being persons principally interested in Our Colony or Plantation of Connecticut, in New-England, that the same Colony, or the greatest part thereof, was Purchased and obtained for great and valuable Considerations, and some other Part thereof gained by Conquest, and with much difficulty, and at the only Endeavours, Expense, and Charges of them and their Associates, and under those whom they Claim, Subdued, and Improved, and thereby become a considerable Enlargement and Addition of Our Dominions and Interest there. NOW KNOW YE, That in Consideration thereof ... we have thought fit to make this grant ... .

In connection with a dispute between Connecticut and Pennsylvania, the validity of the Crown's sea-to-sea grant was denied, in part because the Dutch colony occupied the western boundary at the time of the charter. See "Legal Opinion of C. Pratt, 7 March 1761" in J.P. Bond, ed., *Susquehannah Company Papers*, vol. 2 (Ithaca, N.Y.: Cornell University Press for Wyoming Historical & Geological Society, 1962-1971) at 64-66; "Legal Opinion of C. Yorke, 30 March, 1761" in *Susquehana Company Papers*, vol. 2 at 67-69.

Persons in that or the adjacent Colonys in New England, to Enquire into, hear and determine this Matter, and also to put the Indians into Possession of their said Lands in case it shall appear they have been wrongfully disseised or dispossessed thereof.

Or what other Order or direction Her Majesty may Lawfully make or give in this behalf.[112]

He recited the portions of the charter under which the corporation was empowered to erect courts in the colony, and concluded that the Queen retained prerogative power to do justice in the case. The Mohegan treaties, he said, established prerogative jurisdiction, and the Queen could lawfully erect a court within the colony if an appeal were made to Queen-in-Council.[113]

He then considered the petition on its merits, and set out four controlling legal principles. First, when the British arrived in Connecticut, the territory was not vacant. Second, the territory was not under the King of Britain as the "sovereign ... owner," but under the sovereignty of "Onkas and some other Indians":

About 60 or 70 Years ago when ye British first went to that part of New England now called Connecticot, one Onkas & some other Indiyans were Sovereign Sachems or Princes & Owners of yt prt of the Country, who permitted the British to take up lands and settle there.[114]

In the second principle, Attorney General Northey affirmed Aboriginal sovereignty and ownership of North American lands. The Indians had the plenary title in North America so that the "Sovereign Sachems" had the right to exclude others, although they had permitted the British to use their territory.

The third principle was that the Mohegans could autonomously determine the proper use of their lands, including possible purchases by colonists, the colony, the king, or reserve the land for their exclusive use. The Mohegans had sold the greater part of their territory in Connecticut to the British settlers in the initial treaty of 1658, and Attorney General Northey stated, "before and *after* the [Charter] grant, [the Mohegans] were the owners and possessors" of these lands,[115] implying that after the grants the colonial purchasers continued to hold their lands under the authority of the Mohegan tenure. Also, they reserved "to themselves only a small tract of land":

and afterwards these Indyan Princes for a small value granted the greatest part of that Country to the Govment and Company of Connecticut Colony, the said Indyans reserving to themselves only a small Tract of Land to plant on, and to Hunt in.[116]

The fourth principle was that unless a treaty delegated authority to the King, he did not have any authority over the territory. Northey concluded that Charles II neither

---

112   See Chalmers' Collection, *supra* note 110.
113   Smith, *supra* note 101 at 425.
114   See Chalmers' Collection, *supra* note 110.
115   *Ibid.*
116   *Ibid.*

intended to dispossess the Mohegans of their reserved lands, nor did he have sufficient authority to transfer the reserved lands to the colony. Thus, the Acts of the General Court and Assembly purporting to convey reserved lands were illegal and void. They were *ultra vires* in so far as they purported to transfer land reserved for the Mohegans in the charter.

In February 1704, Attorney General Northey ruled that royal charters did not include Aboriginal lands protected by prerogative treaties.[117] The Mohegans, he concluded, had been unlawfully dispossessed:

> Upon perusal & Consideration of ye Case annexed it does not appear to me that the Lands now claimed by the Indians were intended to pass *or could pass* to the Corporation of the English Colony of Connecticut or yt *it was intended* to *Dispossess the Indians* who before and after the Grant were the Owners and possessors of the same and therefore what ye Corporation hath done by ye act mentoned in ye Case is an apparent Injury to them and Her Majty notwthstanding the powers granted to that Corporation (there not being any words in ye Grant to exclude Her Majty) may Lawfully erect a Court within that Colony to doe Justice in this matter & in ye erecting such Court may reserve an appeale to her Majty in Council & may Comand ye Governors of that Corporaton not to oppress those Indians or deprive them of their right but to doe them right notwithstanding the Act made by them to dispossess them which I am of opinion was illegal and void.[118]

Having concluded at the outset that a justiciable issue had arisen over which the Queen retained prerogative authority, he recommended to the Council of Trade and Plantations that an imperial court be erected in Connecticut to do justice in the matter. As an opinion of the Attorney General, Northey's opinion may be taken as legally authoritative under British constitutional law.[119] His analysis articulated the imperial framework for Aboriginal treaties in British law and emphasized how treaties limited rights passed under royal charters. His opinion stated to all British administrators that Aboriginal nations were autonomous territorial sovereigns, that the Aboriginal treaties with the Crown were controlling instruments under prerogative jurisdiction, and that the treaties independently determined landholding within the geographical boundaries of royal charters.

B. Royal Commission on Mohegan Indians

On the strength of the Attorney General's opinion, the Council of Trade and Plantations passed an Order-in-Council on 9 March 1704 to establish a commission to do justice in the Mohegan case. Also the King sent a letter to the Governor and Company of Connecticut advising them of the commission; ordered them to pay all due obedience to the commission; and, if the judicial inquiry found that the Mohegans had been

---

117 Smith, *supra* note 101 at 425.

118 Chalmers' Collection, *supra* note 110 [emphasis in original].

119 On the status to be ascribed to opinions of the Law Officers of the Crown, see Mansfield C.J.'s remarks in *Campbell v. Hall, supra* note 78 at 718.

deprived of their lands, ordered them immediately to put them into possession notwith-standing the Assembly Act or Order. The letter also ordered that no one molest or oppress the Indians in the future.[120]

A commission under the Great Seal ordered Dudley and ten others on 19 July 1704 to determine the complaints according to justice and equity, and to restore the Indians to their settlements if they had been unjustly dispossessed.[121] The commissioners assembled at Stonnington, Connecticut, in August 1705. The colonial authorities withdrew when they perceived that the Commission would be trying land titles, protesting the legality of the Commission. The Commission proceeded *ex parte*, and unanimously found in favour of the Indians and ordered that they be put back in possession of their lands.[122] The order was never implemented. The Colony appealed the Dudley decree. The imperial Committee of Appeals upheld the commission as being the proper method for trying Mohegan grievances, since "the Mohegan Indians are a nation with whom frequent Treatys have been made."[123] The Committee allowed the appeal on the matters of costs, but a commission of review never met.[124]

C. *Treaty of Utrecht* (1713)

The *Treaty of Utrecht* (1713) divided the boundaries of the Aboriginal nations into British and French jurisdiction.[125] The treaty was ratified by many European nations,[126] and this ratification process became a template for treaties with the Aboriginal nations. Article XIII of the *Treaty of Utrecht* formally transferred the international jurisdiction or "title" of Louis XIV the Most Christian King of France in Newfoundland to the British Crown (Anne, Queen of Great Britain) and excluded French settlement. Whereas Articles XIII and XIV recognized that this area was not previously under British sovereignty as against all European claimants, Article XIII states the French sovereign yielded and gave up the island of Newfoundland to "belong of Right wholly to Britain."[127]

The British diplomats knew that the transfer of L'Acadia was merely a symbolic concession. One British diplomat described Britain's treaty jurisdiction as "in words something, in substance little."[128] Another view was expressed by Matthew Prior, who

---

120 CSP, *supra* note 103 at 1704-1705, #171, #172, #181.

121 *Ibid.* at #200.

122 Smith, *supra* note 101 at 426.

123 NYCD, *supra* note 88, vol. 4 at 1177.

124 *Ibid.*

125 (31 March 1713). F.G. Davenport, *European Treaties Bearing on the History of the United States and Its Dependencies* (Washington, D.C.: Carnegie Institute, 1917-37).

126 *Ibid.*

127 *Ibid.* John Reeves, the legal advisor to the Committee for Trade (1787) and later Chief Justice of Newfoundland (1791), in *History of the government of Island of Newfoundland* (New York: Johnson Reprint Corp., 1967) [reprint] suggested that Newfoundland was a colony or plantation of his Majesty under the *Treaty of Utrecht*. The *Treaty of Utrecht* gave any French Crown's interest to the sovereign. Additionally, the Governor's Commission to Newfoundland in 1729 affirmatively resolved these doubts.

128 British Museum, London [hereinafter BM] Additional Manuscripts, vol. 22 at 206.

declared that the international proclamation of sovereignty over territory in North America was immaterial unless it was sustained by the industrious occupation of the settlers. Industry rather than dominion, he pointed out, would determine the ultimate control of North America.[129]

Over the next century failed attempts to define the scope of the "ancient limits of Acadia" preoccupied both British and French diplomats. A special international commission was established to determine the territorial scope of authority. The French commissioners interpreted the claim to pertain only to actual French settlements, stressing the unextinguished Aboriginal tenure of the Míkmaq. The British commissioners argued for a broader interpretation, including absentee French seigniorial grants.[130]

Article XIV further provided that French subjects had one year to remove themselves and their movable effects from the new British lands. If they remained, they would have to become British subjects, but would enjoy some religious freedoms.[131] British officials rejected the principles that the departing French residents could sell their plantation and that Articles XIII or XIV attempted to convey a right and property, which was not recognized by the general usage of the Island.[132]

In contrast to the articles dealing with the French and British, Article XV of the *Treaty of Utrecht* defined the freedoms of the Five Nations, the Haudenosaunee, and the Friends of the French Crown including the Míkmaq and Malicites:

> The Subject of France Inhabiting Canada and others, shall hereafter give no Hindrance or Molestation to the Five Nations or Cantons of Indians, Subject to the Dominion of Great Britain; nor to the other Natives of America, who are Friends to the same. In like manner, the Subjects of Great Britain, shall behave themselves Peaceably toward the Americas, who are Subjects or Friends to France; and on both Sides, they shall enjoy *full Liberty of going and coming on Account of Trade*. As also the Natives of those Countries *shall, with the same Liberty, Resort, as they please,* to the British and French Colonies, for Promoting Trade on one Side, and the other without any Molestation or Hindrance, either on the Part of the British Subjects or of the French. [133]

---

129   W.S. MacNutt , *The Atlantic Provinces: The Emergence of Colonial Society 1712-1857* (Toronto: McClelland and Stewart, 1965) at 10.

130   *Ibid.*

131   *Ibid.*

> It is expressly Provided, that in all the said Places and Colonies to be Yielded and Restor'd by the most Christian King, in pursuance of this Treaty, the Subjects of the said King may have *Liberty* to remove themselves, within a Year, to any other Place, as they shall think fit, together with all their Moveable Effects. But those who are willing to remain there, and to be Subject of the Kingdom of *Great-Britain*, are to enjoy the Free Exercise of their Religion, according to the Usage of the Church of *Rome*, as far as the Laws of *Great-Britain* do allow the same.

132   Reeves, *supra* note 127 at 55-58, citing Entries D. 406, 408.

133   Davenport, *supra* note 125 [emphasis added]. For the history of the clause, see British Demands, March 1712—United Kingdom, Public Record Office, London [hereinafter PRO], State Papers [hereinafter SP] 103/98, f. 258.; French Response to British Demands, 20 March 1712—PRO, SP 103/98, ff. 3345-6; Observations on the British Proposal, 12 August 1712—PRO, SP 103.100, f. 220; Memoir of Pontchartrain—PRO, SP 103.100, ff. 246-47; British Response—PRO, SP 103.100, f. 283; French Counter-proposal—PRO, SP 104/26 at 217.

Article XV ensured equal respect to Aboriginal nations, and made Aboriginal sovereignty, tenure, and rights a subject of the law of nations. Moreover, the article created a commission to determine the status of the Aboriginal nations: "[I]t is to be Exactly and Distinctly settled by Commissaries, who are, and who ought to be accounted the Subjects and Friends of Britain or of France."[134]

British officials interpreted Article XV of the 1713 treaty as protecting the Aboriginal nations under the laws of nations. Neither the British sovereign nor the subjects in British North America were to molest or hinder Aboriginal nations (repeating a proscription operative in British and French law). The British sovereign promised the Míkmaq would have the liberty to resort as they pleased to any colonies in North America to promote trade. The sovereign further agreed that the new boundaries created by the treaty cessions did not affect the affairs or trade with the Aboriginal nations. It granted Her Majesty an exclusive international right to negotiate with the Aboriginal inhabitants for their trade, yet ensured that no subjects of either sovereign could interfere with their migrations, liberties, trade, or place of resort. Aboriginal peoples had a treaty-protected right of mobility and immunity from European boundaries and laws.

Additionally under British prerogative law, Article XV protected Aboriginal tenure and rights as prerogative Liberties.[135] The grant of a "full Liberty," a special legal category of the law of nations, was a unique part of the prerogative order in Britain. Under the prerogative of the Crown, the use of the term "liberty" demonstrated that Her Majesty recognized exceptional rights in the Míkmaw and other Aboriginal peoples. In British law, such a liberty was an exclusive prerogative franchise vested in certain persons. In the eighteenth century, the terms "liberty" and "franchise" were interchangeable royal grants of exclusive economic rights. Sir Matthew Hale wrote in *Prerogative of the King* that "liberties or preeminences"[136] were derived from the King's *jura regalia* or realities.[137] Such liberties, he stated, included "jurisdictions, franchises, and exemptions" derived from the sovereign by express grant or charter or in the presumption of usage as well as all royal grants of exclusive rights to capture beast (*ferae naturae*).[138] Other British legal writers of the period also included exclusive rights to fisheries or game as "franchises."[139]

---

134 Davenport, *ibid.*

135 "Opinion of Attorney General Edward Northey, 5 May, 1713" in NYCD, *supra* note 88, vol. 5 at 362-63. In 1713, Attorney General Edward Northey held that land grants made by Governors of New York beyond the authority conferred in their Commissions would be void.

136 Sir M. Hale, *Prerogatives of the King* (London: Selden Society, 1976). Pre-eminences were also called sovereignty. R.H. Kersley, *Broom's Legal Maxims*, 10th ed. (London: Sweet & Maxwell Ltd., 1939).

137 Hale, *ibid.* at 201.

138 *Ibid.* at 201, 227-40.

139 Chitty, *supra* note 57 at 125; Blackstone, *supra* note 4, vol. 2 at 417; B. Murdoch, *Epitome of the Laws of Nova Scotia*, vol. 2 (Halifax: J. Howe Publishers, 1832) at 64.

By including the free liberty of trade and resort to the Aboriginal people, the British and French sovereigns formally established these Aboriginal rights by treaties as exclusive, inviolable prerogative franchises that limited the sovereign's power in regards to them in British North America.[140] On granting a liberty, the courts have held that His Majesty was powerless to revoke it.[141] As J.A. Chitty stated:

> A franchise is defined to be a royal privilege or branch of the royal prerogative subsisting in the hands of a subject, by grant from the King ... . [I]t is a clear principle that the King cannot by his mere prerogative diminish or destroy immunities once conferred and vested in a subject by royal grant. [T]he King cannot take away, abridge, or alter any liberties, or privileges granted by him or his predecessors, without the consent of the individual holding them.[142]

The prerogative treaties reserve land tenure and beneficial interest under the protection of the Crown and hence separate from the colonies.

D. Wabanaki Compact (1693-1781)

In the British version of the 1693 treaty, the Sagamores and Chief Captains of the Wabanaki Confederacy and Eastern Massachusetts Bay colony had agreed:

> That their Majesties' subjects the British shall and may peaceably and quietly enter upon, improve, and for ever enjoy all and singular their rights of lands, and former settlements and possessions with the eastern part of the said province of Massachusetts Bay, without any pretension or claims by us, or any other Indians, and be in no wise molested, interrupted or disturbed by them.[143]

The 1699 treaty safeguarded the Wabanaki lands and harvesting rights and affirmed that "use" rights and "quiet enjoyment" of His Majesty's subjects created British reservation or estates within their Aboriginal tenure.[144]

After European ratification of the *Treaty of Utrecht*, the Crown sought to consolidate its treaty authority by extending its treaty ratification process to Aboriginal nations in America. This transfer of authority between European Crowns in the *Treaty of Utrecht* was ratified by the Wabanaki Confederacy[145] in 1713 and

---

140   Chitty, *ibid.* at 119.

141   *New Brunswick Power Company v. Maritime Transit Company*, [1937] 4 D.L.R. 376 (C.A.) at 395-396.

142   Chitty, *supra* note 57 at 119, 121, 125, 132.

143   *Native Rights, supra* note 52, Art. 4 at 295.

144   MA 30: 447-48. Memorials of the Sagamnes, 8 September 1699; PRO, CO5/789, Minutes of the Massachusetts Council, 9 October 1699.

145   Wabanaki (*waponahkik*) is the sound describing the space of the dawn or land of dawn. *Uhkomiks* is their name for a related group, *kehsuhkomiksit* is many related groups or tribes. *Sakamo* is a chief, *sakamoak* is chiefs; *kcisakomak* is great chiefs. *Skicinu* is a term for the Indians; *skicin* is an Indian.

1714.[146] In the 1713 treaty, each of the member tribes expressed the "free consent of all the Indians" belonging to their "several rivers and places" to be the lawful subjects of Queen Anne, with each tribe promising its "hearty Subjection & Obedience unto the Commonwealth at Boston" as well as the Crown of Great Britain.[147] Additionally, the Aboriginal delegates agreed to "cease and forbear all acts of hostility" towards British persons and their estates and to "maintaine a firm & constant amity & friendship" with them. They agreed not to entertain any treasonable conspiracy with other nations to disturb the British inhabitants.[148]

In Article 1 of the 1713 and 1714 treaties, the Wabanaki reaffirmed their promise "not to offer the least hurt, violence or molestation" to British subjects or their "Estates."[149] In Article 3, the 1693 treaty use rights were mutually affirmed and the article saved or reserved Aboriginal territory as autonomous from the British settlements with their free liberties:

> That her Majesty's Subjects, the British, shall & may peaceably & quietly enter upon, imprive [sic], & forever enjoy, all and singular their Rights of Land & former Settlements, Properties, & possessions with the Eastern Parts of the said Province of Massachusetts Bay and New Hampshire, together with all the Islands, Isletts, Shoars, Beaches, & Fisheries within the same, without any molestation or claim by us or any other Indians. And be in no ways molested, interrupted, or disturbed therein. Saving unto the said Indians their own Grounds, & free liberty for Hunting, Fishing, Fowling and all other their Lawful Liberties & Privileges, as on the eleventh day of August in the year of our Lord God One thousand six hundred & ninety three.[150]

The British treaty commissioners were careful to explain the meaning of Article 3 of the 1713-1714 treaties to the Confederacy Delegation: "That there is care taken to

---

146　*Native Rights, supra* note 52, App. 3 at 295-309. The Wabanaki Treaties with the Crown begin with the treaty of 1676 with the Sacos, Androscoggins, Kennebecs, and Penobscots. In the treaty of 1678 the British Crown recognized Wabanaki sovereignty and dominion in New England. The Wabanaki also entered into treaties in 1690, 1693, 1699. See *The Wabanakis of Maine and the Maritimes* (Bath, Me.: Maine Indian Program, 1989) at D89-90. Manuscript copies of the treaties are in United Kingdom Public Record Office [hereinafter PRO], Colonial Office Series [hereinafter CO], organized by date. The principal colonial correspondence is contained in the Colonial Office Series. They were reorganised by the Public Record Office in England earlier this century. Prior to this Nova Scotia had organized its records in Public Archives of Nova Scotia [hereinafter PANS]. French sources are Archives nationales, Paris [hereinafter AN], Archives des Colonies [hereinafter AC], and Canada [hereinafter C11A]. Other sources are the Public Archives of Canada [hereinafter PAC], and DHM, *supra* note 79.

147　*Native Rights, ibid.* at 296-99 in Arts.1 and 7.

148　*Ibid.* at Art. 2. This is similar to the *Wapapi Akonutomakonol* agreement found in Leavitt & Francis, *supra* note 32 at 60. If any nation or group disobeyed the Confederation or Wampum laws, the others together would watch them. *(Nit ha lohkalusonihikon naka ipis nihtol nit Wapapi Tpaskuwakonol. Tan wot pelsotok, 'tahcuwi mawe skiyawal kehsuhkomiksicik).*

149　*Ibid.*

150　*Native Rights, ibid.* at 297 in Art. 3. While this article is more specific that the *Wapapi Akonutomakononol,* it is similar. It creates an "implemented fence" or boundary between the British and the Wabanaki legal jurisdictions, so that there would be no bothering one another anymore. The concept of forever is *askomiw.*

secure to you your land, as well as the British lands to them. And design is both to do Justice to you and to prevent Contention from the time to come."[151]

Despite the treaty commissioners' explanation, subsequent treaty commissioners persisted in their view that by Aboriginal deeds and the 1693 and 1713-14 treaty articles the English purchasers acquired the sole and exclusive estates of the land, thereby renouncing Wabanaki legal authority.[152] Under Nikmanen law, the Wabanaki had given the colonists a chance to enter into a particular kind of relationship with the land, and the British settlers were "guests" with a right to share the land.[153] The Wabanaki treaty conferences and subsequent treaty reconciled the meaning of the Aboriginal deeds and British purchases that were recognized and affirmed in treaties and justified good right in Wabanaki territories.[154]

The Wabanaki Compact (1725), concluded at Boston,[155] reflected a union of the terms of the *Treaty of Utrecht*, the *Wapapi Akonutomakonol*, and the previous Wabanaki treaty reconciliations. The "Severall Tribes of Eastern Indians" were represented by the Wabanaki Confederacy; His Majesty was represented by Lieutenant-Governor Dummer of Massachusetts Bay. The *Wuastukwuk* or Malecite Nation of the Saint John River (*Wulstukw*) was also part of the Confederacy. The Wabanaki Compact renewed the 1693 political and geographical status quo of the existing treaties. To clarify relations between Aboriginal tenure and British estates, Article 3 of the 1713-14 treaty was divided into two separate articles, 3 and 4, in the Wabanaki Compact.[156] Article 3 of the compact promised that the British subjects:

---

151 DHM, *supra* note 79, November 1725.

152 See "Journales of Treaty Conference on Arrowsick Island, August 9-12 1717" in DHM, *ibid.*, vol. 3 at F16-M33. For example "The Gov. [Dummer]: They must Desist from any Pretension to the Lands which the British own"; "They must not call it their Land, for the British have bought it of them and their Ancestors"; "Tell them they must be sensible and satisfied that the British own this land, and have Deeds to shew, and set forth their Purchase from their Ancestors," at 368 and 370.

153 *Ibid.* DHM, *Wiwuran*, one of the Confederacy spokesman stated, "We can't understand how our Lands have been purchased, what has been Alienated was by our Gift" at 369.

154 *Ibid.* On August 11, the Wabanaki and the Crown "agreed in the Articles of Peace, that the British should Settle, where their Predecessors had done." In the 1717 treaty they confirmed Art. 3 of the 1713 treaty and added, "And whereas, some rash and inconsiderate Persons amongst us, have molested some of our good fellow Subjects, the British, in the Possession of the Lands, and other illtreated them;—We do disapprove & condemn the same,—and freely consent that our British friends shall possess, enjoy & improve all the Lands which they have formerly possessed, and all which they have obtain a right & title unto, Hoping it will prove of mutual and reciprocal benefit and advantage to them & us, that they Cohabit with us." See *Native Rights, supra* note 52 at 299.

155 See Gov. Shute of Massachusetts Bay letter of 21 February 1718—DHM, vol. IX at 380-381; Massachusetts Bay treaty order in council of 1720—DHM, vol. XXIII at 83-84 and 87; Journal of the Treaty Conference 1720—DHM, vol. XXIII at 94-107, especially at 107-108; Gov. Shute letter to Lords Commission for Trade and Plantations, 13 March 1721 at DHM, vol. XXIII at 378-79; Lt. Gov. Dummer of New England letter to Gov. Vaudrevil of Canada—DHM, vol. I at 386-88, especially at 288; Lt. Gov. Dummer of New England letter and enclosures to Duke of Newcastle, Secretary of State—CSP vol. 35 (8 January 1726); CO 5 898 at 173-174v.

156 The Treaty Commissioners often used the distinguishing terms of "our and your Lands," as in DHM, *supra* note 79 at 196 (23 November 1725 in the House of Representatives).

Shall and may peaceably and quietly enter upon Improve and forever enjoy all the singular Rights of God and former settlements[,] properties and possessions within the Eastern parts of the said province of the Massachusetts Bay Together with all Islands, inletts[,] Shoars[sic,] Beaches and Fishery within the same without any molestation or claim by us or any other Indians and be in no way molested[,] interrupted or disturbed therein.[157]

Article 4 of the 1725 compact is patterned after existing treaties:

Saving unto the Penobscot, Naridgwalk and other Tribes within His Majesty's province aforesaid and their natural Descendants respectively all their lands, Liberties and properties not by them convey'd or sold to or possessed by any of the British subjects as aforesaid. As also the privilege of fishing, hunting, and fowling as formerly.[158]

Although the treaty acknowledged they were friends and subjects of the King, the British treaty commissioners candidly admitted they were not successful in getting the tribes to recognize King George as the sole owner and proprietor of New England and Nova Scotia.[159]

Even as successive agreements resolved some disputes, they gave rise to others occasioned by cultural and linguistic difference. After the 1726 ratification conference at Casco Bay, for example, the spokesperson for the Wabanaki Confederacy, Loron Sagourrat, wrote Lieutenant-Governor Dummer objecting to the written treaty. He wrote, "Having hear'd the Acts read which you have given me I have found the Articles entirely differing from what we have said in presence of one another, 'tis therefore to disown them that i write this letter unto you."[160] In particular, he challenged the addition of a statement that the Wabanaki acknowledge King George to be their King and had "declard themselves to the Crown of England." Identifying a crucial misconception on the part of the British, Loron wrote that during the treaty negotiations:

when you have ask'd me if I acknowledg'd Him for king i answer'd yes butt att the same time have made you take notice that I did not understand to acknowledge Him for my king butt only that I own'd that he was king [of] his kingdom as the king of France is king of His.[161]

The King's representative, William Dummer, expressed his opinion that "this will be a better and more lasting Peace than ever was made yet, and that it will last to the End

---

157 "Treaty of 1725, Article 3" in *Native Rights, supra* note 52 at 300-302.

158 *Ibid.* at 301.

159 PAC, RG 1, vol. 12 (15 December 1725).

160 DHM, *supra* note 79, vol. XXIII at 208.

161 *Ibid.* at 209. The French speakers present at the ratification confirmed that the Wabanaki "come to salute the British Governor to make peace with him and to renew the ancient friendship which has been between them before," not to submit themselves to the British King or accept responsibility for beginning the hostility with the British, or that they would live according to British law ("*Traité de paix entre les anglois et les abenakis*," 1727). This quotation is found in *Collection de manucrits*, vol. 3 (Québec: A. Côté, 1883-85) at 134-35. Compare to Art. 7 of the *Articles of Capitulation of Grenada* and judicial interpretation of that phrase in *Campbell v. Hall, supra* note 78 at 205.

of the World."[162] This reconciliation was composed of central prerogative treaties with Aboriginal peoples and subsequent ratification with various nations and tribes, affirming the existing treaty federation with the Crown.

The Confederacy's reliance on His Majesty's Government and Law as the protector of treaty and reserved land rights was an innovative and daring merger of Aboriginal and European law. It was designed to end the strictly political nature of the treaty and directly incorporate the treaties into the constitutional laws of Great Britain, beyond the will of the local colonists. It also acknowledged that British rule of law applied to protecting reserved Aboriginal property and resolving questions about Aboriginal conveyances in adjudicating property rights between British subjects and Aboriginal nations, as well as controversies among Indians and British.[163] The 1725 compact, sent to His Majesty on 8 January 1726,[164] marked a new path between the sovereign and the Indian nations.

The Confederacy speakers stated that land clarification was "the Main thing we want to come to, ... & the rest will easily come in afterward."[165] In the previous Montreal meeting, the Confederacy had claimed all the Aboriginal lands as far south as Boston. In the treaty conference the Confederacy speakers stated: "notwithstanding what we have said of Confederacy's Claiming as far as Cape Elisabeth ... [if] you can shew fair purchase of any Land, we do not Insist on having it."[166] Although the Confederacy spokesmen refused to cede any of their reserved Aboriginal tenures to the British Crown, they admitted to certain private uses.

Any British land use had to be clearly evidenced not by Crown grants but by Wabanaki treaties and deeds, which in turn had to be free from any question to be valid land transactions. Lieutenant-Governor Dummer summarized his understanding of the land reservation clause in the following words:

> That the said Indians shall Peaceably Enjoy all their Lands & Property which have not been by them Conveyed and Sold unto, or possessed by the British & be no ways Molested or Disturbed in their planting or Improvement And further that there be allowed them the free Liberty and Privilege of Hunting Fishing & Fowling, as formerly.
>
> And whereas it is the full Resolution of this Government that the Indians shall have no Injustice done them respecting their Lands.
>
> I do therefore assure them that the several Claims or Titles (or so may of them as can be had and obtained) of the English to the Lands in that part of this Province shall be produced at the Ratification of the present Treaty by a Committee to be appointed by the Court in their present Session, and Care be taken as far as possible to make out the same to the Satisfaction of the Indians and to distinguish & ascertain what Lands belong to the

---

162 Letter with Enclosures, of Lieutenant-Governor Dummer to Duke of Newcastle, 8 January 1726. CO, *supra* note 155 5/898 [hereinafter Dummer].

163 *Ibid.*

164 *Ibid.*

165 DHM, *supra* note 79, 17 November 1725.

166 *Ibid.*, 29 July 1725.

English in Order to the effectual prevention of any Contention or Misunderstanding on that Head for the Future. [167]

Loron Sagourrat, one of the treaty negotiators, stated his understanding of the treaty articles on land in a subsequent 1751 treaty conference: "Govr Dummer's treaty says we shan't loose a Foot of Ground."[168] The prevailing justification for British settlement rests on Aboriginal sale of land by written deed to British settlers. Any British settler claim to contested land would have to be proved a title deriving from lawful purchase from the Wabanaki tribes, not the imperial sovereign.

The 1725 commissioners refused any further gratuity or acknowledgement for the land purchased under "good Deeds" from their Wabanaki "Fore Fathers": Since "[y]our Ancestors have been paid for the Lands to their Satisfaction as has been proved to you," the commissioner said, "there is no reason to Expect the Lands should be paid for over again."[169] They asserted that purchased land belonged to the "King's Governor of Massachusetts"; they also used the metaphor of "Inclosures or land that are fenced in" to discuss private lands.

Whether these "estates" were under Wabanaki dominion or the British Crown remained an unresolved issue. The Wabanaki had previously acknowledged in the treaties the right of the settlers to use certain lands, while reserving all the land they used. A "sale" of land to the Wabanaki mind meant only the admission of the settlers under a Sachem's rights within the area specified.[170] Indeed, the concept of a sale was foreign not only to the Wabanaki but also to the British sovereign, since under British land law all land in the realm was owned by the Crown.

The treaties' wording did not, however, resolve all Wabanaki questions regarding British settlement. The Confederacy's predominant concern was intrusion on established territorial boundaries by the British settlers.[171] The troubling issue for the Wabanaki was how to protect their reserved land. After all, it was the failure of the New England Government's promise to protect the Aboriginal tenure that had caused the conflict. There was never any doubt as to the proper legal principles to be applied under either the pre-existing treaties or the law of Wabanaki or Great Britain, yet the proper procedure remained elusive. His Majesty's treaty commissioners suggested that some involvement by colonial authorities in any future land conveyance from the Wabanaki to British subjects would be beneficial to the tribes. The Confederacy, on the other hand, was not convinced that such involvement would ever be needed since they did not plan to convey any more lands to the British settlers.

---

167 *Ibid.* See PAC, MG 11, CO 217, Nova Scotia "A" [hereinafter NSA], vol. 17 enclosure no. 4.

168 DHM, *supra* note 79, vol. XXIII at 416 (Report of Conference at the Fort of St. George's Mass. Involving Nova Scotia's treaty commission Mascarene, 24 August, 1751).

169 DHM, *ibid.*, 27 November 1725.

170 *Ambiguous Iroquois Empire, supra* note 32 at 128-46.

171 In Leavitt & Francis, *supra* note 32 at 56-57, the idea for creating the Convention Council was expressed, "*Nit Msiw mehtewestuhtihtit[,] nit oli kisolutomuk 'tolihtuniya kci lahkahusonihikon naka tuciw 'punomoniya epahsiw kci wikuwam tepahkalusoniw,*" or, "Then when they were finished talking, all decided to make a big fence and besides they put in the middle [of it] a big house within the fence." The same approach was taken with the British Crown.

One of the Wabanaki spokesmen directly asked the treaty commissioners if the term "settlements" meant that the "British design[ed] to Build Houses further than there are any Houses now Built or Settlements made?" "When we come to settle the bounds," the treaty commissioners answered, "we shall neither Build or Settle anywhere but within our Bounds so settled [under the 1693 treaty] without your consent."[172] Later in the negotiations, the Confederacy sought to clarify the concept of "former Settlements" in Article 3:

> We desire to know the right meaning and understanding of two words. As to the Deed of Land as far as St. Georges Fort, whether Houses will be built & Settlements made as far as the British have purchased. We are free & plain in our discourse that there may be no misunderstanding afterward. As to the Lands that have not been purchased which lye Vacant in spaces between what hath been purchased, whether when the British come to Settle there shall not bear a consideration for that Land. And whether we shall not have a further gratuity or acknowledgment made to us for what has been purchased of our Fore Fathers. The reason of our Enquiring into this is, that we may be able to tell it right when we come home to the Tribes.[173]

The British commissioners, after consulting the governor, responded concerning future settlements as far as St. George's Fort, so far as the British had purchased by deed:

> Those Lands are the property of particular Persons who have the Indian right by fair purchase, as you are sensible by the Deeds which have been shown you, & you Cannot reasonably Expect that the sd. Proprietors should be hindered of making Improvemt. of what is their own however care will be taken by the Government That no Encroachmt. shall be made on you, and that they do not any wise Injure you, but treat you as Friends & good Neighbours.[174]

The commissioners assured the Confederacy leaders that they knew of "no Deeds of Lands to the Eastward" of St. George's Fort, but a "Great many to the west of it."[175]

---

172 CO, vol. 5 at 173-174v, 20 November 1725. This issue was also the topic of 1726 Treaty Conference at Falmouth in Casco-Bay. DHM, *supra* note 79, vol. 3 at F16-M33, August 1-5, 1726.

173 CO, *ibid.*

174 *Ibid.*, 26 November 1725. An example of one of these deeds is, "... Madockawando, [one of the Wabanaki treaty negotiators in 1693] deed to Sir William Phipps, Knight ... dated May 9th, 1694, Land both sides of St. Georges River bounded Eastward by Westsouwestkeeg and westward of the west of Hatches Cove Island ..." cited in Levi, *supra* note 77 at 26. This was taken from Descriptions of British Deeds in the Province of Maine drawn from Proceedings of the British "land claims" Committee established pursuant to the Peace of 1725/26. Loron, the spokesman, stated: "We can't find any Record in our Memory, nor in the Memory of Our Grand Fathers that the Penobscutt Tribe have sold any Land, as to the Deed mentioned last Winter, made by Medockewanda and Sheepscutt John they were not Penobscutt Indian, one belonging to Mechias Medockewondo, the other towards Boston, if we can find in reality that the Lands were Purchased of the right Owners, we should not have insisted upon it, nor have opened our Mouths, we would not pretend to tell a Lye about it," found in DHM, *supra* note 79, vol. 3 at F16-M33, 3 August 1726. See also Springer, *supra* note 82 at 25-58; Shurtleff, *supra* note 92, pt. II at 213 (Royal Commissioners reaffirmed Indian title to all their lands).

175 DHM, *supra* note 79, 26 November 1725.

Addressing the Confederacy's question concerning the "Lands that have not been purchased which lye Vacant in spaces between what hath been purchased," the commissioners stated that the British subjects would have to purchase it from the tribes: "[I]f the British should have a mind to purchase any of it, when they come to settle, you shall hereafter Dispose of to the British, and therefore when ever you sell any Land, it will be best for you to acquaint the Government thereof, & they will take care that you be not wrong therein."[176]

The British commissioners, as an alternative, proposed to the Confederacy that an executed instrument in the name of the Government be delivered to the Confederacy "distinguishing and securing all your Rights."[177] The treaty commissioners suggested to the Massachusetts House of Representatives the establishment of a "Committee of able Faithful and Disinterested Persons" by the Government to "receive and adjust the claims of Lands in the parts Eastward of Sagadahock & Amoroscoggin Rivers & above Merry Meeting Bay," the only valid British settlement area under the compact.[178] The House read and accepted the proposal and returned them as Instructions to the treaty Commissioners.[179]

The commissioners stated that within 12 months of the conclusion of this "Treaty of Pacification," the commissioners would "ascertain the bounds of such claims & Challenges," "with a number of Indian chiefs appointed for that purpose."[180] "Before their Just right & Title hath been duly Enquired into & made Manifest, & the Indians have had the full knowledge & understanding of such rights & Title," the commissioners stated that no British settlements were to be made beyond those lands.[181]

The Confederacy was ambivalent about the proposed claims commission concept, desiring the clarification document, but doubting the process, which was too much like a treaty conference. The Speaker informed the commissioners that they could not accept the claims commission because such action would go "beyond our Instructions" from the Confederacy.[182] The resolution of this problem was to agree to continue the 1713-14 provisions. In Article 6 of the compact, the delegation agreed with the British commissioners that disputes be settled according to His Majesty's Law:

---

176 Ibid. at 26 November 1725. In the treaty Conference held at Falmout in Casco-Bay, in July and August 1726, Lt. Gov. Dummer told the Wabanaki: "you shall have equal Justice in all Points with the Subject of His Majesty King GEORGE, either in Controversies respecting the Property of Land, or any other matters whatsoever, we don't suppose that any Gentlemen that come to produce or offer Claims of Lands there shall be their own Judges, but it shall be determined by Lawful Authority, wherein the Indians shall have the Benefit of the Law, equal with any Britishmen whatsoever, and this you may be assured of, for we don't expect a Peace to last on any other footing than that of Justice." DHM, ibid., vol. 3 at F16-M33, Treaty Conference, 4 August 1726.

177 DHM, ibid., 22 November 1725.

178 Ibid. at 196, Art. 1, 23 Nov. 1725.

179 Ibid. at 197.

180 Ibid. at Art. 2.

181 Ibid. at Art. 3.

182 Ibid. at 200, 26 November 1725.

> If any Controversy or difference at any time hereafter happen to arise between any of the British and Indian for any *reall* or supposed wrong or injury done on either side no private Revenge shall be taken for the same but proper application shall be made to His Majesty's Government upon the place for Remedy or induce thereof in a due course of Justice. We submitting ourselves to be ruled and governed by His Majesty's Laws and desiring to have the benefit of the same.[183]

The modification of the existing treaty terms remedied Dummer's official explanation for the war, namely, the Wabanaki failure to apply for proper application to the government.

During the treaty negotiations, both the Crown and the Confederacy agreed that in any dispute over land title, the British subjects—not the Wabanaki—would carry the burden of proving their title by lawful purchase. "[I]f there should be any Dispute or Controversy hereafter between the British and you respecting the Titles or Claims of Land," the treaty commission told the Wabanaki leaders, "after a fair and lawful tryal, if the British cannot make out & prove their Title to the Lands Controverted they shall disclaim them; But if the British can make out their Titles then the Indian shall Disclaim the Lands so Controverted."[184] Lieutenant-Governor Dummer summarized his understanding of the reconciliation clause in the following words:

> I do therefore assure them that the several Claims or Titles (or so many of them as can be then had and Obtained) of the British to the Lands in that part of this Province shall be produced at the Ratification of the present Treaty by a Committee to be appointed by this Court in their present Session, and Care be taken as far as possible to make out the same to the satisfaction of the Indians and to distinguish & Ascertain what Lands belong to the British in Order to effectual prevention of any Contention or Misunderstanding on that Head for the future.[185]

E. Aboriginal ratification of 1725 treaty

The initial imperial Commission to the Governors of Nova Scotia in 1717 and 1719 ordered the Governor to "send for the several heads of the said Indian Nations or clans, and promise them friendship and protection of His Majesty part."[186] Having made no existing treaties with Great Britain and wishing to remain non-

---

183   *Native Rights*, *supra* note 52 at 301.

184   DHM, *supra* note 79, NSA American and West Indies, 1724-25 (4 August 1726).

185   Dummer, *supra* note 162.

186   Instruction to Governor Philips of Nova Scotia, 19 June 1719, in L.W. Labaree, ed., *Royal Instructions to British Colonial Governors, 1670-1776*, vol. II (New York: D. Appleton, Century Co., 1935), No. 673 at 469 [hereinafter Labaree, *Royal Instructions*]. See "Statement prepared by the Council of Trade and Plantations for the King, September 8th, 1721": "It would likewise be for your Majesty's service that the sev. Governts of your Majesties Plantations should endeavor to make treaties and alliances of friendship with as many Indian nations as they can ... ." Cited Levi *et al.*, "We Should Walk in the Tract Mr. Dummer Made" (October 1 and 2, 1992) at 35 [unpublished document distributed at New Brunswick Chiefs' Forum on Treaty Issues, St. John, New Brunswick].

aligned,[187] the Míkmaw nation refused to concede wrongdoing by failing to adhere to the existing Wabanaki treaties. At the Boston treaty conference, the Míkmaq delegates rejected treaty labeled Number 239 offered by the Nova Scotia delegates.[188] After hearing the new terms, the Míkmaq stated their own understanding of the words: they were supposed to "pay all the respect & Duty to the King of Great Britain as we did to ye King of France, but we reckon our selves a free People and are not bound."[189] Faced with the Míkmaw refusal to accede to the Nova Scotia treaty of the 1725 compact, the Nova Scotia Governor and Council adopted a new strategy, agreeing on seven "Articles to be Demanded of the Indians" by Nova Scotia.[190]

On 15 December 1725, the Nova Scotia treaty commissioner, Major Paul Mascarene, in the Council Chamber in Boston, offered new terms. The Mascarene treaty promised that the "Indian shall not be molested in their persons, Hunting[,] Fishing and Planting Grounds nor in any other their lawfull Occassions by His Majesty's subject or their Dependents."[191]

On 4 June 1726, the "Chiefs and Representatives ... with full power and authority, by an unanimous consent and Desire of the said Indian Tribes, are come in Compliance with the Articles Stipulated by our Delegates as aforesaid" and do "Solemnly confirm & Ratify" the "1725 Compact."[192] The treaty was first read in English to all the officers, soldiers, and deputies. The Lieutenant-Governor of Annapolis Royal, John Doucett, administered the oath to the interpreters for the Indians, Abram Bourg and Prudane Robichau Senior, who read each paragraph of the treaty in French.[193] The

---

187 A 1630 treaty of protection existed between Sir William Alexander and the Míkmaw families in Annapolis Royal. G. Patterson, "Sir William Alexander and the Scottish Attempt to Colonize Acadia." (1893) *Proceeding and Transaction of the Royal Society of Canada* 19(2) at 82, and E. F. Slafter, ed., *Sir Wm. Alexander and American Colonization* (Boston: The Prince Society, 1873, vol. 8 & 8A, reprinted New York: Burt Franklin, 1966). See also, "Family Treaty with the British Officials at Annapolis Royal , 7 January 1723" *The New England Courant* (7 January 1723). It was signed by the members of the Grand Claude family following the imprisonment of their relatives. See also Letter of John Doucett to the Board of Trade, 29 June 1722. PAC, MG11, CO 217/4 at 118. The Lieutenant-Governor's name is spelt variously Ducett, Doucett, and Doucette in the documents. See also A.M. MacMechan, ed., *Nova Scotia Archives III. Original Minutes of His Majesty's Council at Annapolis Royal, 1720-1739* (Halifax: Public Archives of Nova Scotia, 1908) at 37-41 [hereinafter *Council Minutes*].

188 1 December 1725, PAC, MG 11, CO 217, NSA, vol. 16 at 207; PANS, CO 217, vol. 4 at 321, 348, 350.

189 PAC, NSA, MG11, CO 217, vol. 17 (2 December 1725).

190 PAC Nova Scotia "B" [hereinafter NSB], MG 11, CO 220, vol. 1 at 58-60.

191 DHM, Nova Scotia treaty commissioner, Paul Mascarene, promises to the Míkmaq (15 December 1825) enclosed in letter from Lt. Governor Armstrong of Nova Scotia to Council of Trade and Plantations [Duke of Newcastle] CSP (July 27, 1726) vol. 29 fol. 77; PANS, CO 217, vol. 4 at 321, 348, 350 (often labeled Number 239). In a 1751 treaty conference Mascarene claimed that he was at the ratification treaties at Casco-Bay, Annapolis Royal, Chibucto, see DHM, vol. XXIII at 416 (Report of Conference at the Fort of St. George's Mass. Involving Nova Scotia's treaty commissioner Mascarene, 24 August, 1751).

192 *Ibid.* Promises/Ratification of John Doucett, Lt. Gov. of Annapolis Royal to the Tribes in Nova Scotia, signed at Annapolis Royal, 4 June 1725. PAC, MG11, CO 217, NSA, vol. 5 at 3-4; *ibid.* vol. 17 at 36-41; *ibid.* vol. 38 at 108-108v, and 116-116v.; PANS, CO 217, vol. 4 at 321; PANS, CO 217, vol. 38 at 109 (the original parchment copy has not been found).

193 *Council Minutes, ibid.* at 116.

Kespokoitik (lands end) District Chief and delegates assented, signed, sealed and delivered the treaty to the Lieutenant-Governor Doucett,[194] who signed in "His Majestys Name" and delivered the treaties to the Chiefs. Doucett gave them "Entertainment and Sev.l presents as Tockens of His Majestys Protection."[195] Over one hundred Aboriginal peoples signed the agreement, some identifying themselves as chiefs of the Mikmaw Nation. Among those signing were the Chief and Delegates from "Cape Sable," the Chief of Annapolis Royal, Chignecto, Minas, Cape Breton and Newfoundland.[196] Thus, it was said that "all the Nova Scotia Tribes" entered into the compact.[197]

Many copies of the ensuing 1726 ratification treaty exist.[198] For unexplained reasons, Lieutenant-Governor Doucett told the Lords of Trade the ratification treaty promises were divided by the British drafter into two separate documents:[199] the first labeled "English to Indians,"[200] the second labeled "Indians to English."[201] The multiple iterations and fragmentation of the treaties as well as their contradictions created many interpretative problems. The Indian to the English document provides that in "case of misunderstanding between English and Indians, ... Application for Regress According to his Majesties Law.[202]

---

194 *Ibid.* Promises/Ratification of Cape Sables, Annapolis River, Pontiquet, Minis and Passamaquady Indians to Gov. of N.S., signed at Annapolis Royal, 4 June 1726. PAC, MG 11, CO 217, NSA, vol. 17 at 40; PANS, CO 217, vol. 4 at 350.

195 *Council Minutes, ibid.* at 116-117.

196 PAC, NSA , MG11 CO 217, vol. 17 at 43.

197 *Ibid.* at 40-43.

198 *Ibid.* See PAC, MG 11, CO 217, NSA, vol. 17 at 40; Promises/Ratification of Cape Sables, Annapolis River, Pontiquet, Minis and Passamaquady Indians to Governor of Nova Scotia, signed at Annapolis Royal, 4 June 1726—PANS, CO 217, vol. 4 at 350. An identical text with different signatures is found in Promises/Ratification of St. Johns, Passamaquady, Cape Sable, Chuabouacady, LaHave, Minas and Annapolis River Indians to Governor of Nova Scotia, signed at Annapolis Royal, 4 June 1726—PANS, CO 217, vol. 38, 108; PANS, CO 217, vol. 4 at 320. Promises/Ratification of St. Johns, Cape Sables, Chubenakady, Rechibutou, Jediack, Minas, Chickanecto, Annapolis River, Eastern Coast Micmacs to Governor of Nova Scotia, signed at Annapolis Royal, 4 June 1726—PANS, CO 217, vol. 38 at 116, an identical text with different signatures. To see generally the problems of tracking the treaty copies, see P. Kennedy, "Treaty texts: When Can we Trust the Written Word?" (1995) 3(1) Social Science and Humanities Aboriginal Research Exchange 1, 8, 20-25, and P. Kennedy, "Tracking the treaty text" (1989) 16(6) The Archivist 12.

199 CSP 16 August 1726, PAC, CO 217 vol. 4 at 316-21 MG11, Reel B 1023.

200 *English to Indians, Treaty,* 1726 (U.K.), 12 Geo I. No. 3 enclosure in letter of Lt. Gov. Armstrong of Nova Scotia to Council of Trade and Plantations [Duke of Newcastle] CSP, vol. 29, fol. 78; PAC , MG11, CO 217, NSA ,vol. 5 at 3-4; Promises/Ratification of John Doucett, Lt. Gov. of Annapolis Royal to the Tribes in Nova Scotia, signed at Annapolis Royal, 4 June 1725. *Ibid.* vol. 17 at 36-41 (original parchment copy has not been found); *ibid.* vol. 38 at 108-108v, and 116-116v.; PANS, CO 217, vol. 4 at 321; PANS, CO 217, vol. 38 at 109.

201 *Indians to English* Promises/Ratification of Cape Sables, Annapolis River, Pontiquet, Minis and Passaquady Indians to Gov. of N.S., signed at Annapolis Royal, 4 June 1726. PAC, MG 11, CO 217, NSA, vol. 17 at 40; PANS, CO 217, vol. 4 at 350; CO 217, vol. 4 at 82-83. Sixty-four Aboriginal signatures or totems were written on the treaties.

202 *Ibid.*

In the "English to Indians" version of the treaty,[203] "His Most Sacred Majesty, George of great Brittain" promised the Míkmaq district chiefs "all Marks of Favour, Protection & Friendship." The documents state that the Míkmaq District Chiefs and Representatives acknowledged His Majesty's "Just Title" over Nova Scotia. However, His Majesty promised the district chiefs that they "shall not be Molested in their Person's, Hunting, Fishing, and [Shooting &] Planting on their planting Grounds nor in any other Lawfull Occasions, by his Majesty's Subjects or their Dependants."[204] The sovereign promised that:

> if any Indian are Injured by any of his Majesty's Subjects or their Dependants they shall have Satisfaction and Reparation made to them According to his Majesty's Law: Where of the Indians shall have the Benefit Equally with his Majesty's other subjects.[205]

In "Indians to English" documents,[206] the "Chief and Representatives of" Míkmaq "with full Power & Authority by an Unanimous Consent and Desire of the Said Tribes" confirmed and ratified the Wabanaki Compact (1725). The written treaty states the Míkmaq District Chiefs and Representatives acknowledged His Majesty's "jurisdiction and dominion" over Nova Scotia.[207] This conflicts with previous treaties[208] and the wording of the Wabanaki Compact (1725),[209] where the Aboriginal negotiators merely acknowledged his Most Christian King and agreed to submit to "His said Majesty in as ample manner as any of our Predecessors have heretofor done."[210] This modest acknowledgement was based solely on the Míkmaq understanding that His Britannic Majesty was replacing the King of France, by the "grace of God," as Defender of the Faith. In the sacred order of Míkmáki, the King of England would be their new godfather in Acadia and Newfoundland, replacing the King of France. Even as they submitted, however, the Míkmaq reasserted their claims to freedom: they would "pay all the respect & Duty to the King of Great Britain as we did to ye King of France, but we reckon our selves a free People and are not bound."[211]

The British version of the 1726 Míkmaq ratification was substantially different from the central document of the Wabanaki Compact. Also different from Major Mas-

---

203 *Supra* note 200, CO 217, vol. 4 at 82.

204 *Ibid.* Some copies of the treaty omit this provision from the treaty text, but affirm Mascarene promise of 15 December 1725; see CSP, vol. 29, fol. 80, No. 4, CO 217, vol. 4, PAC, MG11, CO 217, NSA, vol. 17. Other copies have the phrase "Shooting & Planting," PRO, CO 217 vol. 4. The copies raise many suspicions about fraud and abuse by the British drafters and scribes.

205 *Ibid.*

206 *Supra* note 201, PAC, NSA, CO 217, vol. 4 at 83.

207 *Ibid.* However, in the negotiations they had previously refused to acknowledge the British sovereign "sole Owners & the only True & Lawfull Proprietors of the same," compare *supra* note 188 and see CSP, vol. 29, f.77 for original terms in Enclosure from Armstrong to Newcastle, 27 July 1726.

208 Compare with treaty number 239 *supra* note 188, and see CSP, vol. 29, f.77 for original terms in Enclosure from Armstrong to Newcastle, 27 July 1726.

209 PAC, NSA, CO 217, vol. 4 at 83.

210 *Ibid.* at Art. 1.

211 *Ibid.*, PAC, NSA, MG11, CO 217, vol. 17, 2 December 1725.

carene's treaty Instructions from the Nova Scotia Council, it reflected Mascarene's comments at the treaty conference that, since the circumstances of Nova Scotia were different from Massachusetts, "there will be several small Articles distinct from the Articles which they entered into with Massachusetts."[212] In July and August of 1726, a conference was held with some of the remaining Wabanaki tribes to ratify the 1725 treaty at Falmouth in the Casco Bay.[213] The 1725 treaty was also ratified with the St. Johns Indians in 1728.[214] On 16 August 1726 the "ratifycations of the Treaty of Submission" with the Eastern Indians were sent to His Majesty.[215]

The prerogative treaties, or the "great King's Talk," with the Wabanaki Confederacy displayed the four distinctive characteristics of the Aboriginal legal mind in the Nikmanen and Aboriginal order: a reliance on consensual jurisdictions rather than rule from above; a quest to share peace and friendships in the Wabanaki territory through insular, collective autonomy and boundaries; an abhorrence of warfare and quest for harmony; and an elastic respect for legal transformations of each people. Additionally, the treaties recognized and affirmed Aboriginal tenure as a distinct tenure. According to their traditional concept of sharing, they granted peaceful occupation to those British minorities who had acquired an interest in Wabanaki tenure by a fair, honest, and consensual purchase from the Wabanaki nations.

F. *Mohegan Indians v. Connecticut (1743) Royal Court of Commissioners*

The 1705 Royal Commission in *Mohegan Indians v. Connecticut* had held that protected or reserved Aboriginal lands in the treaties were not intended to pass to colonies in their royal charter, and had ordered the confiscated lands to be restored to the Mohegan Tribe.[216] The Governor and Company of Connecticut appealed, challenging the Queen's jurisdiction to establish a court within a royal colony. It argued that Connecticut had acquired absolute title to the Aboriginal tenures by conquest, that the tribe was subservient to colony authority, and that the Royal Commission was illegal because it determined title to land without a jury. The Committee of the Privy Council rejected the colony's arguments, and upheld the 1705 judgment that the Mohegans were a sovereign nation that was not subservient to the colony.[217]

---

212 PAC, NSA, CO 217 vol. 4 at 83; PAC NSA: American and West Indies, vol. 29, f. 80 at 2 December 1725. A copy of the Mascarene version of the treaty, rather than both treaty documents, was enclosed and attested to in a Letter of Lt. Gov. Armstrong to Council of Trade and Plantations, 27 July 1726. PAC, MG11, CO 217, NSA, vol. 16; C. Headlam, ed., *Calendar of State Papers, Colonial Series, America and West Indies 1726-1727*, vol. 35 (London: His Majesty's Stationery Office, 1939) at 122.

213 "Conference with the Eastern Indians at the Ratification of the Peace (1725 treaties), held at Falmouth in Casco Bay, July-August 1726," in DHM, *supra* note 79, vol. 3 at 377.

214 Ratification of 1725 Documents with St. John's Indians at Annapolis Royal, 13 May and 24 September 1728. PANS, CO 217, vol. 4 at 349; PANS, RG 1, vol. 12, doc. 4.

215 *Ibid.* Letter of Doucett to Lord of Trade, 16 August 1726—CO 217, vol. 4 at 316-321.

216 Smith, *supra* note 101 at 425.

217 *Ibid.* at 426.

When Mohegans complained that the decision was not implemented, a second commission of review was appointed in 1737. This commission, with a majority membership of Connecticut residents, refused to consider the judgments of either the 1705 commission or the appeal Committee, and it summarily dissolved the 1705 decision without permitting the Mohegans to appear.[218] The Mohegans appealed to the Privy Council, which set aside the second commission's finding because of "gross irregularities" in the proceedings,[219] and created a third and final inquiry conducted in 1743.

In 1743, the imperial Court of Commissioners, appointed by the King, affirmed the jurisdictional decisions of both Attorney General Northey and the Privy Council's Committee.[220] It was the first appellate decision to discuss the framework of Aboriginal tenure and rights in British law. It held that Indian tribes were exclusively under the exceptional and prerogative jurisdiction of His Majesty in foreign affairs, and not subordinate to either the King, parliament, or colonial government.[221] It further rejected Connecticut's assertion that the European treaties, Mohegan treaties, and their royal charter ended Aboriginal sovereignty within the colony's boundaries.

Before the imperial Court, the British subjects in possession of Mohegan lands raised the jurisdictional issue of the legality of a royal commission determining title to land without a jury under the Connecticut colonial charter and under the common law. They argued that the Mohegans were subject to Connecticut laws and governance, and that the proper jurisdiction was in the colonial courts rather than in a royal commission. The imperial Court rejected their jurisdictional claims. Commissioner Daniel Horsmanden, later Chief Justice of New York, held, over one dissent,[222] that:

> The Indians, though living amongst the king's subjects in these countries, are a separate and distinct people from them, they are treated as such, they have a polity of their own, they make peace and war with any nations of Indians when they think fit, without control from the British. It is apparent the crown looks upon them not as subjects, but as a distinct people, for they are mentioned as such throughout Queen Anne's and his present Majesty's commission by which we now sit. And it is plain, in my conception, that the soil of these countries; and that their lands are not, by his majesty's grant of particular limits of them for a colony, thereby impropriated in his subject till they have made fair and honest purchase of the natives ...[223]

The imperial Court also held that colonial controversies with the tribes of Indians protected by treaty were controlled by "a law equal to both parties, which is the law

---

218 *Ibid.* at 427-28.

219 *Ibid.* at 429-32.

220 *Ibid.* at 427-28.

221 *Ibid.* at 425.

222 Commissioner Colden was the only dissenter. He did not dispute the tenure of the Mohegans, but argued that upon issuance of the letters patent to Connecticut they had become, *"subjects* of Great Britain, enjoying the benefit and protection of the English law, and all the privileges of British subjects," and should be heard in an ordinary court.

223 Smith, *supra* note 101 at 427-28; *Certified Copy Book of Proceedings Before Commission of Review*, 1743-1769 at 118 [hereinafter *Copy Book*].

of nature and of nations" rather than by the laws of Britain, the colony Charter, or common laws.[224] The prerogative treaties with the Aboriginal nations or tribes were separate jurisdictions in British law, under the prerogative jurisdiction of foreign affairs through their treaties rather than under the local colonial officers.

The colony challenged the authority of the chief, manufactured questionable Indian deeds, and presented other spurious deeds. The Court of Commission divided 3-2 on both the precise nature of the Mohegan rights and the effect of the treaties and deeds made since 1640,[225] but affirmed some of the reserved lands for the Mohegan.[226] Commissioner Colden and two other commissioners determined that the charter had deprived the Mohegans of "legal" title; although they continued to hold an "equitable right" to remain in possession, the Mohegans had delegated this right to the colony by one or more treaties and deeds. Morris and Horsmanden dissented, arguing that the charter and treaties did not vest in the colony the "absolute Property and Right in Law of the Lands" since it was not fairly purchased from the Mohegans. The charter merely gave the colony "the sole *right to purchase* these lands" from the Mohegans, or a "Right of Preemption";[227] subsequent deeds or purchases to the colony created a "Trust" and a protective trusteeship,[228] and the Mohegans did not give up the reserved land to the colony.

The Governor of Connecticut appealed the imperial Court's decision to the Privy Council, the highest judicial authority in British law. The appeal lingered until 1773, when the Privy Council affirmed the 1743 Commission's decision;[229] the *Royal Proclamation of 1763* had already enshrined these principles of "fair and honest purchase" from the separate Indian nations in the American colonies.

---

224 Smith, *ibid.* at 434; *Copy Book, ibid.* at 118.

225 Smith, *ibid.* A 1640 grant from Uncas to the colony, 1659 conveyance in trust to Mason and his heir, 1665 and 1671 grant to Mason, and the 1681 treaty. The 1640 grant from Uncas to the colony was not recorded until 1736, and the 1665 and 1671 grants were considered questionable.

226 *Ibid.* at 434.

227 *Ibid.*; see also Horsmanden dissent in *Copy Book, supra* note 223, at 141-142, *Law Papers: Correspondence and Documents During Jonathan Law's Governorship of the Colony of Connecticut,* vol. 11 (Hartford, Conn.: Connecticut Historical Society, 1907-1914) at 156 and 165: "That the Charter of incorporation granted by King Charles the 2d to the Colony of Connecticut did not, (nor can it be construed to have been intended to) vest in the Corporation the absolute Property and Right in Law of the Lands contained with the Bounds and limits of it, which were not before the Date of it fairly purchased or obtain'd from the Indians."

228 Smith, *ibid.* Horsmanden for the dissenting commissioners stated:

But only to give the Corporation the Right of Preemption of the Lands within that Circuit which upon Purchase from Time to Time would become vested in the Corporation, and so become part of the Colony upon such Trust as mentioned in the said Charter; for I think the Crown looks upon the Natives as the Proprietors of the Soil of these Countries, as is manifested by the universal Practice of purchasing the Lands of them throughout the Colonys, and the Lands are not absolutely impropriated to his Majesty's Subjects, until they be so purchased tho' included with the Bounds and the Limits of the Royal Grant. *Copy Book, supra* note 223 at 141 and *Law Papers, supra* note 227, at 156.

229 *Ibid.* at 436-42 (15 January 1771); Order-in-Council, 15 January 1773. 3 Turnbull MSS, 89, 102b, 111a., P.C. 2/117/10.

G. *Treaty of Aix-la-Chappelle* (1748)

After the War of Austrian Succession, the French and British sovereigns mutually restored all conquests made during the war in the *Treaty of Aix-la-Chappelle* (1748). In the treaty, the French Crown reaffirmed the vague British jurisdiction over "the ancient limits of Acadia." Article III renewed and confirmed the terms of the *Treaty of Utrecht* "as if they were therein asserted, word for word." This renewal included Article XV, protecting Aboriginal sovereignty, dominion, and trading liberties as allies or "Friends" of either the British or French.[230]

H. *Penn v. Lord Baltimore*, 1750

In 1750, in *Penn v. Lord Baltimore*, the British Court of Equity declared that it did not have jurisdiction to hear boundary disputes between different charters in America or to give specific performance to agreements resolving boundary disputes;[231] charters were grants under the King's prerogative power to explore, develop, and govern foreign lands. The Court stated that its jurisdiction was limited to domestic real property cases, and did not extend to extra-territorial matters. The only remedies to such disputes were in the King's prerogative powers.

Together with the decisions of the 1743 imperial Court in *Mohegan Indians,* the holding in *Penn v. Lord Baltimore* clarified the extraordinary status of the Indian nations and tribes in royal colonies and in British law, especially prerogative law.

I. Renewing the Haudenosaunee's covenant chain

At the same time as the Wabanaki Compact, the British Crown was expanding its compact with the Haudenosaunee or Iroquois Confederation (Five Nations).[232] The treaty relationship began in 1677,[233] and in 1688 and 1701 the English documents recorded the cession of their Aboriginal territory in trust to the sovereign.[234] At the treaty conference in 1688, Governor Dongan of New York recorded that the Haudenosaunee declared themselves "just and rightful owners of all our lands" to which the French pretended to have title, and that title to these lands "were long since given and granted to the King of England, and now his Excell: who represents His Maj'sty sacred person is the owner of those land and must not suffer any encroachment upon the great King of England's territories."[235]

---

230 C. Parry, ed., *The Consolidated Treaty Series,* vol. 38 (Dobbs Ferry, N.Y.: Oceana Publications, 1969) at 297, 305-306.

231 (1750), 27 E.R. 1132 (Eng. Ch. Div.).

232 Morgan, *supra* note 32; *Ambiguous Iroquois Empire, supra* note 32.

233 Morgan, *ibid.* at 165-171.

234 For the early legal history see J.D. Hurley, *Children or Brethren: Aboriginal Rights in Colonial Iroquoia* (Saskatoon, Sk.: Native Law Centre, 1985).

235 *Ibid.* at 291; NYCD, *supra* note 88, vol. 3 at 534-35.

Legal scholar John Hurley interpreted this arrangement as the treaty cession to the King in trust: the cession gave the Crown "radical" jurisdiction over the land, but vested in the Haudenosaunee beneficial ownership of their lands, with the Crown protecting absolute Haudenosaunee possession of their lands against French or alien encroachment.[236] Subsequent treaty made explicit the trust relationship between them: the cession in trust of 1701, where the Haudenosaunee "freely and voluntarily surrendered and delivered up to our Great Lord and Master, ye King of England" their western domain.[237] Hurley interpreted these transactions through Blackstonian categories:

> if the Iroquois reserved to themselves the *dominium utile*, and ceded to the Crown the *dominium directum*, their original title must have comprised both. It must therefore have been the *plenum dominium*. In other words, the Iroquois' original title must have been in *allodium*, defined as "property in its highest degree" possessed by the owner "merely in his own right, without owing any rent or service to any superior."[238]

Between 1721 and 1733, the Crown and the Five Nations of the Haudenosaunee renewed their Covenant Chain in treaties of Friendship at Conestogoe.[239] In 1728, two other treaties were entered between the Crown and the western allies of the Haudenosaunee, the Chiefs of the Conestogoe, Delaware, Shawanese, and Cattawese Indians.[240] In 1736, a conference was convened to renew the Covenant Chain with the Haudenosaunee, with the exception of the Mohawks. Jointly, the "Six United Indian Nations," Haudenosaunee and the Shawanese, Nanticokes, and Delaware, entered into numerous treaties with the Crown concerning the provinces of Pennsylvania (1742, 1744, 1745, 1747, 1748), Virginia and Maryland (1744), Massachusetts and Connecticut (1746). Also, the Haudenosaunee and the Ohio Indian Nations (Twightees, Shawanese, Wyandots, and Delaware) participated in treaty conferences polishing the Chain in 1751 and 1753.[241]

After receiving a summary of the treaty minutes from the 1751 conference with the Haudenosaunee, Sir William Johnson wrote to General Gage:

> I have been Just looking into the Indian Records where I find in the Minutes of 1751 that those who made ye Entry Say, that Nine different Nations acknowledge themselves to be his Majesty's Subjects, altho I sat at that Conference, made entrys of all the Transactions, in which there was not a Word mentioned, which could imply Subjection.[242]

Neither the Haudenosaunee nor the Western Indian nations of the Ohio Valley, he wrote, would ever declare "themselves to be Subjects or will ever consider themselves

---

236 Hurley, *ibid.* at 291-92.

237 *Ibid.* at 293: CO 5/1046, No. 33. lx; CSP 1701, no 758. lx.

238 Hurley, *ibid.* at 298, See, Blackstone, *supra* note 4, vol. 2 at 105.

239 De Puy, *supra* note 50 at 7-9.

240 *Ibid.* at 13.

241 *Ibid.* at 17-31.

242 "Letter of Johnson to Gage, 31 Oct., 1764" in Flick, ed., *The Papers of Sir William Johnson*, vol. 4 (Albany: The State University of New York, 1925) at 395 [hereinafter Johnson Papers].

in that light whilst they have any Men, or an open Country to retire to, the very Ideal of Subjection would fill them with horror."[243]

On 18 September 1752, the Board of Trade advised the Governor of New York to ensure the inviolable observation of existing treaties with the Haudenosaunee, requested him to use all legal means to redress their complaints about being defrauded of their lands, and directed the Governor not to grant title to any person whatsoever for lands purchased individually by them from Indians. The Board reminded the Governor that when the Indians were disposed to sell any of their land, the purchase ought to be made in His Majesty's name and at public expense. The Board furthermore urged New York to meet with the Indians and forge a new general treaty with them, in cooperation with the Governors of Virginia, Pennsylvania, Maryland, New Hampshire, Massachusetts Bay and New Jersey. In so doing he was:

> to take care that all the Provinces be (if practicable) comprised in one general Treaty [with the Aboriginal nations], to be made in his Majesty's name: it appearing to us that the practice of each Province making a separate Treaty for itself in its own name is very improper, and may be attended with great inconveniences to his Majesty's service.[244]

This suggestion from the Board of Trade set the stage for the famous Albany Congress of 1754, which fuelled the southern Colonies' idea of a federated constitutional government modelled after, and designed to confront, the Haudenosaunee. It convened on 19 June with representatives from New York, New Hampshire, Massachusetts Bay, Connecticut, Rhode Island, Maryland, and Pennsylvania as well as delegates from the Haudenosaunee, Scaakticook, and Stockbridge Tribes, and the *Putuswakn* (Ottawa Confederacy or the Seven Nations that comprised the Wabanaki and Mikmaw nations).[245] The Congress recommended several improvements in the protection of tribal lands. Before the King could act, however, the Seven Years War broke out.

In 1760, Sir William Johnson secured a treaty of neutrality of the "Seven Nations of Canada," the ring of Indian villages that still protected the French settlements of Montreal and Quebec.[246] The Seven Nations (Putuswakn) renewed and strengthened the "old Covenant Chain which before this War subsisted between us, and we in the name of every Nation here present assure you that we will hold fast the Same, for ever hereafter."[247] In 1760, a separate treaty was entered into with the Huron,[248] which helped end the Seven Years War in North America, and secure British control of Quebec.

---

243 *Ibid.*

244 *Collections of the Massachusetts Historical Society,* vols. 5-6 (Boston: The Society, from 1792) at 22.

245 NYCD, *supra* note 88, vol. 6 at 850-92. The Putuswakn, the Mìkmaq-Algonquian term for the confederacy of Wabanaki Confederacy, the Mìkmaw Nation, the Christian Mohawks, and the Ottawa Confederacy. It was also called the Council of Fire, including the Ottawa Confederacy and the Seven Nations.

246 As described in *R. v. Sioui,* [1990] 1 S.C.R. 1025, [1990] 3 C.N.L.R. 127 (S.C.C.) [hereinafter *Sioui*].

247 Johnson Papers, *supra* note 242, vol. 13 at 618-619.

248 *Sioui, supra* note 246.

J. Míkmaw Compact (1752-1779)

In the reaffirmed treaty order of *Aix-la-Chappelle*, the King directly intervened in the colonial settlements of America to clarify the ancient claims to Acadia. In terms of Míkmáki, the national territory of the Míkmaq, the King-in-Council made two important decisions. For the first time in British history, the King-in-Council decided to plan a royal colony—the Nova Scotia colony—distinct in jurisdiction from the private enterprises such as Massachusetts Bay colony and New England. This decision caused much bitterness among the New Englanders, who had fought to capture Louisburg during the war, and who desired to consolidate Acadia into New England. The Míkmaq were equally disillusioned by the failure of the French sovereign to reunite Míkmáki. It is said that they realized the French were using them as pawns in an international scheme. Second, the King-in-Council applied the established legal principles deriving from *Mohegan Indians* and *Penn v. Lord Baltimore* to the new royal colony.

The initial imperial Commissions to the Governors of Nova Scotia in 1717 and 1719 ordered the Governor to "send for the several heads of the said Indian Nations or clans, and promise them friendship and protection of His Majesty's part."[249] The 1749 Commission to Cornwallis, establishing the royal colony of Nova Scotia, renewed the 1719 order and provided for the preconditions of grants of land in fee simple. The first condition was that the Governor was "directed to make grants of such land in fee simple as are not already disposed of by his Majesty to any person that shall apply to you for the same."[250] Secondly, as a condition antecedent, the Commission required that before the Governor could grant any such land to British subjects, he had:

> by & with the advice and consent of our said Council to *settle and agree with the Inhabitants* of our Province for such Lands, Tenements, & hereditaments as now are or hereafter shall be in our power to dispose of.[251]

---

249 Instruction to Governor Philips of Nova Scotia, 19 June 1719, in L.W. Labaree, *Royal Instructions, supra* note 185 No. 673 at 469. See "Statement prepared by the Council of Trade and Plantations for the King, September 8th, 1721": "It would likewise be for your Majesty's service that the sev. Governts of your Majesties Plantations should endevor to make treaties and alliances of friendship with as many Indian nations as they can ... ." Cited in Levi, *supra* note 77 at 35.

250 Labaree, *Royal Instructions, ibid.* at 581-82; See generally L.W. Labaree, *Royal Government in America: A Study of the British Colonial System Before 1783* (New Haven, Conn.: Yale University Press, 1930).

251 Labaree, *Royal Instructions, ibid.* [emphasis added]. This section applies the British principle of continuity of laws to the new royal colony. This principle is called the doctrine of Continuity in British law, and reserved rights in the United States. The principle of continuity of property rights provides that property rights, once established, continue unaffected by a change of sovereignty unless positively modified or abrogated by the new sovereign (*Campbell v. Hall, supra* note 78 at 895-96). This principle has been held to apply to Aboriginal tenure by the highest courts in the United States, Great Britain, and Canada. See *Worcester, supra* note 2 at 544 and 559; *Mitchel v. United States*, (1835), 9 U.S. (Pet.) 711 at 734 [hereinafter *Mitchel*]; *R. v. Symonds* (1847), N.Z.P.C. 387; *Nireaha Tamaki v. Baker*, [1901] A.C. 561 (New Zealand P.C.) at 579; *Southern Rhodesia, Re*, [1919] A.C. 211 at 234 (Southern Rhodesia P.C.); *Amodu Tijani v. Southern Nigeria (Secretary)*, [1921] 2 A.C. 399 (Nigeria P.C.); *Calder v. Attorney-General of British Columbia* (1970), 13 D.L.R. (3d) 64 (B.C. C.A.), affirmed, [1973] 4 W.W.R. 1 (S.C.C.) [hereinafter *Calder*]; *Guerin v. The Queen*, [1984] 2 S.C.R. 335 at 377-78, [1985] 1 C.N.L.R. 120 (S.C.C.). The Crown provided the correct procedure for settling and agreeing with the Inhabitants by public cession provisions of the *Royal Proclamation, infra* note 299.

Reading these provisions together, the original constitution of Nova Scotia confirms that the reserved Aboriginal tenure could not be granted in fee simple by the governor, that the Nova Scotia council had to settle and agree with the Míkmaw nation before any fee simple grants could be issued to colonists of their protected treaty lands.

This "settle and agree" provision, an affirmation of the treaty order established in the Wabanaki Compact, witnessed an elaboration of the requirement of "fair and honest purchase" of Aboriginal tenure by the Governor for the British sovereign. It also prevented any private purchase of Aboriginal tenure. Only if the Míkmaw nation sold their ancient tenure and the Governor bought it for the Crown through prerogative treaties could the Governor grant lands to the British settlers in fee simple.[252] In the subsequent treaties, however, the Míkmaw nation did not yield up or sell their land to the Crown; they only agreed to small British settlements within their Aboriginal tenure.

The mandatory Governor-in-Council property agreement and settlement with the Aboriginal nations or tribes under the 1749 Commission, presumably by treaties, were reinforced by other prerogative limitations on the exercise of colonial authority by the Crown. First, His Majesty made all potential legislative power subject to the "further powers" of Royal Instructions and Commands under "our signet & sign manual or by order in our privy Council." Thus, the continuing supervision of Nova Scotia was to be carried out by the King-in-Council alone, acting through the issuance of prerogative Instructions. Second, the *Commission* also included a repugnancy clause; it required all law, statutes, and ordinances to be made "agreeable to the Laws and Statutes of this our Kingdom of Great Britain." Thus, the relevant rules and principles of the United Kingdom's public law were also limitations of the colonial authorities and legislatures.[253] A crucial part of the Statutes of Great Britain was the *Statute of Frauds*,[254] which made written documents necessary in all transfer of legal estates, and applied to purchases of Aboriginal allodial tenure to the sovereign. In the subsequent treaties, however, the Míkmaw Nation did not yield up or sell their land to the Crown; they only agreed to small British settlements within their Aboriginal tenure.[255]

The Wabanaki Compact served as an archetype for the British Crown in the Míkmaw Compact (1752). On August 13-15, 1749, at a Council meeting held on board the ship, the *Beaufort Transport*, Cornwallis entered into a renewal "upon the same footing" as the 1726 treaty with the Chignecto Míkmaq.[256] In the Míkmaw Compact, the Míkmaw chiefs affirmed the 1726 and 1749 treaties and recognized the British sphere of influence in Acadia.[257] In September of 1752, the Grand Chief Cope of the Míkmaw nation arrived in Halifax with his delegation to establish the terms of peace with the

---

252 Labaree, *Royal Instructions, supra* note 186 at 469.

253 *Ibid.*

254 1677 (U.K.), 29 Car. II, c. 3

255 *Royal Instructions, supra* note 186.

256 PANS, RG 1, vol. 209; see letter Gov. Cornwallis to Duke of Bedford, PANS, CO 217. The chiefs brought a copy of the treaty with them. One of the recorded treaties in the PANS was not Mascarene promises or the 1726 treaty, but rather the rejected proposed treaty of 1 December 1725 (*Treaty No. 239), supra* note 187.

257 *Native Rights, supra* note 52 at 307-309.

British sovereign.[258] The Council stated that they were happy to have the Míkmaq come to bury the hatchet between the "British Children of His Omnipotent Majesty King George and His children the Mickmacks of This Country." They assured the Míkmaq that King George had declared that they were "his Children" and asserted that the Míkmaq "have acknowledged him for your great Chief and Father," presumably in the prior treaty ratifications of the Wabanaki Compact. The Council stated that King George "has ordered us to treat you as our brethren." Moreover, they explained, in terms recalling the *Treaty of Utrecht* and Nikmanen law,[259] that "what is past shall be buried in oblivion and for the time to come we shall be charmed to live together as Friends."[260]

The Míkmaw Compact, known to Míkmaq as *Elikawake* (in the King's House), fulfilled the previous prerogative Instruction to the British governors to enter into a treaty of protection and friendship with the Indian nations and clans.[261] His Majesty promised them that they "shall have all favor, Friendship and Protection shewn them from this His Majesty's Government."[262] The concept of "Protection" had been introduced in the 1630 treaty,[263] and to the Wabanaki in the 1713 treaty, although the 1725 compact promised only His Majesty's "Grace and favor" (Article 1).[264] The promise of

---

258   Letter of Hopson to the Board of Trade, 16 October 1752. NSA, vol. 1 at 594; PANS, MS. Documents, vol. 35, doc. 71; Nova Scotia Council Minutes on the 14th of September recorded the Grand Chief stating he was empowered by the Míkmaq to treaty with the Crown. The Council Minutes stated: "He was also asked, How he proposed to bring the other tribes of the Mickmack Nation to a Conference here [Halifax]Ðwho replyd That he would return to his own people and inform them what he had done here, and then would go to the other Chiefs, and propose to them to renew the peace, and that he thought he should be able to perform in a month, and would bring some of them with him if he could, and if not would bring their answer." This is found in T. Akins, ed., *Selections from the Public Documents of the Province of Nova Scotia* (Halifax: Annand, 1869) at 671. It was apparent that Nova Scotia's Council knew about the federated structure of the "Mickmack Nation," but little about its actual procedures.

259   See Section III(A), above.

260   CO 217/13 at 673. The Council accepted Cope's authority to carry the treaty proposal to the other Míkmaq chiefs.

   We approve of your engagement to go first and inform your people of this our answer and then the other Tribes, with the promise of your endeavors to bring them to a Renewal of the Peace. When you return here as a mark of our good Will we will give you handsome presents of such Things whereof you have the most need; and each one of us will put our Names to the Agreement that shall be made between us. And we hope to brighten the Chain in our Hearts and to confirm our Friendship every year; and for this purpose we shall expect to see here some of your Chiefs to receive annual presents whilst you behave yourselves as good and faithful children to our Great King and you shall be furnished with provision for you and your Families every year. We wish you a happy Return to your Friends and that the Sun and the Moon shall never see an End of our Friendship.

   Compare with Art. 2 of Míkmaw Compact, in *Native Rights, supra* note 52 at 307.

261   *Royal Instructions, supra* note 186.

262   *Ibid.* The Míkmaw district chiefs ratified the Wabanaki Compact in 1726 and 1749. The Crown explicitly promised them, "all Marks of Favour, Protection & Friendship." CO 217/4 at 82; PAC, NSA, MG 11. These treaties were reaffirmed as part of the Míkmaw Compact in 1752.

263   See, *supra* note 187.

264   Labaree, *Royal Instructions, ibid.* Compare to 1713 treaty and 1725 treaty (Art. 1).

"Protection" in the Wabanaki and Míkmaw Compact is one of the earliest examples of protectorates in British law.[265]

As a treaty of peace and protection, the Míkmaw Compact created boundaries for communities that respected their autonomous political and legal systems. The compact constituted an integrated legal order based on mutual obligations recognizing sharing, autonomy, and freedom of association.[266] In order to "Cherish a good Harmony" in the new relationship, the Crown promised that "so long as they shall Continue in Friendship" the Míkmaw would annually receive "Present of Blankets, Tobacco, some Powder & Shott."[267] These provisions were consideration for the British settlements and trading rights with the Míkmáki.

The Míkmaw Compact explicitly incorporated and continued the Wabanaki Compact, and reserved all Míkmaw lands, liberties, and properties to the Míkmaq that had not been conveyed or sold to the British.[268] In 1693, no British subject possessed any land in Acadia. The compact continued Míkmaw tenure and supplemented the "settle and agree" clause in the colonial charter with the fair, consensual, and honest purchase standard for land acquisition.[269] Additionally, it acknowledged and established a boundary between the reserved Míkmaw lands and the sparse British settlements affirmed by the treaties of 1726 and 1749.[270] Thus, the compact did not convey any Aboriginal tenure to the Crown or subjects.

In the 1726 and 1749 Míkmaq ratification of the Wabanaki Compact, the Míkmaq district chiefs only promised that they "shall not molest any of His Majestie's subjects or their dependents in their settlements already made or lawfully to be made, or in their carrying on their traffick and other affairs within the said Province [of Nova

---

265 Similar wording was used in the southern district of British North America, *e.g.*, Cherokee Nation treaties. See *Worcester, supra* note 2, and the 1886 treaties that set up a Protectorate among the native chiefs along the Somali Coast of Africa: "The British Government, in compliance with the wish of the undersigned Elders ... hereby undertakes to extend to them, and the territories under their authority and jurisdiction, the gracious favour and protection of Her Majesty the Queen of England." Found in *R. v. Crewe*, [1910] 2 K.B. 619 at 619, 77 S.P. 1265 (C.A.).

266 In Nikmanen law, this was the standard measure. See Leavitt & Francis, *supra* note 32.

267 Míkmaw Compact (1752), in *Native Rights, supra* note 52 at Art. 6. These terms are often called "annuities."

268 *Ibid.*, Art. 1. The date of possession had to be before 1693 according to the Wabanaki Compact. See *Native Rights, ibid.* at 295. See especially Art. 5 of the 1795 treaty between the United States and the Wyandots, Delawares, Shawanoes, Ottawa, Chipewas, Putawatimes, Miamis, Ell-River, Wees, Kickapoos, Piankashaw, and Kaskaskia for a concise summary of the status of reserved land in a treaty article. The United States and the "Friends" of the Míkmaw Nation stipulated: "The Indian tribes who have a right to those lands, are quietly to enjoy them, hunting, planting, and dwelling thereon so long as they please, without any molestation from the United States; but when those tribes, or any of them, shall be disposed to sell their lands, or any part of them, they are to be sold only to the United States; and until such sale, the United States will protect all of the said Indian tribes in the quiet enjoyment of their lands against all citizens of the United States, and against all other white persons who intrude upon the same." 7 U.S. Stat. (1795) at 49.

269 See *Mohegan Indians*, in *Copy Book, supra* note 223.

270 For actual possession in 1693 to 1760. See A.H. Clark, *Acadia: The Geography of Early Nova Scotia to 1760* (Madison: University of Wisconsin Press, 1968).

Scotia or Acadia]."[271] In the 1752 negotiations, Grand Chief Cope told the Nova Scotia authorities that the Míkmaq "should be paid for the land which the British had settled upon in this Country."[272] Compensation for the use of the settlements was provided in the Míkmaw Compact by the Crown's promise that:

> provisions, as can be procured, necessary for the Familys and proportional to the Numbers of the said Indians, shall be given the Indians half Yearly for the time to come ...[273]

Article 8 of the compact provided that the Míkmaq were to be treated as equals to the British subjects and that in any controversy the Míkmaq would be protected in their tort, contract, and property rights in "His Majesty's Courts of Civil Judicature."[274] This is a unique provision in Georgian treaties; the Míkmaw rejected political solutions and criminal law of the Wabanaki Compact in favour of civil remedies.[275] The Míkmaq leaders continued to assume responsibility for "any robbery or outrage" committed by their members against His Majesty's subjects within their settlements as in their 1726 and 1749 treaties.[276] The district chiefs remained responsible for their own communi-

---

271 This was also incorporated into the Míkmaw Compact (1752), *Native Rights, supra* note 52 at Art. 1. The promise not to molest any of His Majesty's subjects is similar to the *Wapapi Akonutomakonol* law that in united Aboriginal nations territory there would be no bothering one another anymore (*Katama apc cikawiyutultiwon*). See Leavitt & Francis, *supra* note 32 at 59.

272 Akins, *supra* note 258 at 671. This is the colonizers' version and text of the meeting. Míkmaq tradition says that the Grand Chief required payment for the British settlements.

273 Míkmaw Compact (1752), *Native Rights, supra* note 52 at Art. 5. This is the start of the Crown's notion of equalization payments and a redistributive economy.

274 *Ibid.* Article 8 clarifies Art. 6 of the 1725 compact and Art. 4 of the 1726 and 1749 Míkmaw treaties. Article 6 the Wabanaki Compact (1725) provided that, "no private Revenge shall be taken" by either the Wabanaki or the British. Instead, both sovereigns agreed to submit any controversies, wrongs, or injury between their people to His Majesty's Government for, "Remedy or induse there of in a due course of Justice." The Míkmaq affirmed Art. 6 in 1726 and in 1749 at Art. 7. Compared with the decline of feudal tenures, and corresponding development of central national legal systems, the European treaty order began to specify the effect of boundary changes on access to courts, jurisdictional clauses, and choices of law. See Art. 8 of the *Treaty of Utrecht.* The *Treaty of Paris* continued this article, but also began a reference to applying "the Law of Nations" to the disputes that might arise in the future. See Shortt & Doughty, *infra* note 280.

275 Míkmaw Compact, *ibid.* This reflects Míkmaw abhorrence of state-imposed violence—that is, both the *Putuwosuwakon's* (Convention Council) practice of whipping and British criminal law. The Nova Scotia Assembly acknowledged the sovereign's legal responsibility to protect treaty obligations and rights within its jurisdiction in *Act to Prevent Fraudulent Dealing in Trade with the Indians,* S.N.S. 1762, c. 3, see *infra* text and notes 317-323.

276 *Native Rights, supra* note 52 at 308. In these treaties, the chiefs promised to give satisfaction and restitution to the parties injured (Art. 1 confirming Art. 2, 1726 treaty). In the 1726 and 1749 Accession, the Míkmaq district chief took responsibility for "any robbery or outrage" in the British reserves. They expressly promised to make satisfaction and restitution to the "parties injured." This was an extension of the customary law of the Míkmaq to the new settlements. Thus when a Míkmaw robbed or committed an outrage against any British man, even if it happened in the settlements, British criminal law could not be applied. These terms affirmed the autonomy of the diverse legal orders. It was a positive attempt to prevent a Wabanaki or Míkmaq from asserting their law if a British man offended a Míkmaq as well as in the opposite case. Under the treaties the Aboriginal law was suspended in these cases and transferred to His Majesty's justice. In controversies between "Indians," however, the law of private revenge and family justice was and is still operative. Similarly, controversies among British settlers were settled by His Majesty's law.

ties and family conflicts in their territories.[277] The Míkmaq Compact asserted an idea of civil legal remedies as the reconciliation mechanism.[278] The political importance of the Míkmaq Compact to His Majesty is illustrated in the manner in which it was widely published in the British Empire; it was made public by a Nova Scotia Proclamation in 1752.[279]

In 1760, after the end of the Seven Years War between the British and French,[280] a Míkmaw delegation from both French and British jurisdictions met with Governor Belcher and the Legislative Assembly to renew and extend the compact.[281] Father Maillard participated in the conference, interpreting the comments of each party.[282] His official notes further reveal the legal nature of the compact as explained by Belcher, the first Chief Justice in Canada.[283]

Governor-Chief Justice Belcher began with a description of the nature of protection and allegiance under the 1752 compact. "Protection and allegiance are fastened together by links," he told the Míkmaw district chiefs.[284] Then he explained the ratification process to the Míkmaw chiefs:

> [i]f a link is broken the chain will be loose. You must preserve this chain entire on your part by fidelity and obedience to the Great King George the Third, and then you will have the security of his Royal Arm to defend you. I meet you now as His Majesty's graciously honored Servant in Government and in His Royal Name to receive at this Pillar, your public vows of obedience to build a covenant of Peace with you, as upon the immovable rock

---

277 *Native Rights, ibid.* As far back as the Great Convention Council the families retained jurisdiction over wrongs committed by their children. "*Tokec wen keq oli wapololuhket[,] cuwi semha. 'Nikihkul 'tosemhukul nit ipis*" (Now [when] someone something did wrong (*wapol*), he or she had to be whipped. His or Her parent whipped him or her [with] that whip). Leavitt & Francis, *supra* note 32 at 58.

278 *Simon v. R.*, [1985] 2 S.C.R. 387, 62 N.R. 366 (S.C.C.) [hereinafter *Simon*, cited to S.C.R.].

279 Proclamation, 24 November 1752—PANS, MS. Documents, vol. 35, doc.77; Hopson to Board of Trade, *supra* note 258 at 685-686; De Puy, *supra* note 50.

280 In Art. 40 of the French Capitulation to the British in 1760, the King promised to maintain the tribes in their Aboriginal lands. See A. Shortt and A.G. Doughty, eds., *Documents Relating to the Constitutional History of Canada 1759-1791*, vol. 1, 2d ed. (Ottawa: King's Printer, 1918), pt. 2, Sessional Papers No. 18. Article 40 continues the terms of the *Treaty of Utrecht*, *supra* note 125, and Art. 2 the *Treaty of Paris*, 1763, Shortt and Doughty at 314 also reaffirmed it. Additionally, Art. 23 of the *Treaty of Paris* confirmed Art. 40 of the Capitulation. Both the *Articles of Capitulation* and the *Treaty* ends any arguments about abrogation by hostilities or conquest. See especially, *Campbell v. Hall*, *supra* note 78 at 895-96 (articles of capitulation upon which the country is surrendered and the articles of peace by which it is ceded are sacred and inviolable according to their true intent and meaning).

281 For a list of the chiefs who had to ratify the compact, see "Col. Fry Letter to Governor Belcher, 7 March 1760" [1760] London Magazine at 377 and *Collections of the Massachusetts Historical Society, supra* note 244, vol. 10 at 115. The Wabanaki reaffirmed peace on the basis of their 1725 compact on 13 February 1760; Murdoch, *supra* note 139 at 384-85.

282 PANS, MS. Documents, vol. 37, doc. 14.

283 See "Jonathan Belcher" in *Dictionary of Canadian Biography*, vol. 4 (Toronto: University of Toronto Press, 1979) at 50.

284 Míkmaw Compact, *Native Rights, supra* note 52; NSA, vol. 1 at 699-700.

of Sincerity and Truth, to free you from the chains of Bondage, and to place you in the wide and fruitful Field of British Liberty.[285]

The "Field of British liberties," Belcher promised the assembled chiefs, would be "free from the baneful weeds of Fraud and Subtlety."[286] To ensure this, "[t]he Laws will be like a great Hedge about your Rights and properties—if any break this Hedge to hurt or injure you, the heavy weight of the Law will fall upon them and furnish their disobedience."[287]

Following customary procedures, the Governor and district chiefs buried the hatchet and washed the war paint from their bodies to forgive all past hostilities and ratify "a peace that would never be broken."[288] The Governor interpreted these symbolic acts as a guarantee of:

> British protection and Liberty, and now proceeding to conclude this memorial by these solemn instructions to be preserved and transmitted to you with charges to your Children's, never to break the Seals or Terms of this Covenant.[289]

In this way, the metaphor of the "Covenant Chain" entered into the treaty relationship.

The chief from Cape Breton Island, a French jurisdiction, speaking for the rest of the assembled chiefs, responded to Governor Belcher's commitments by promising that the Míkmaw Compact would be "kept inviolable on both Sides." He accepted His Majesty as "friend and Ally," and placed the Míkmaq into His Majesty's protection as "a safe and secure Asylum from whence we are resolved never to withdraw or depart." In the name of all Míkmaq, he stated, "As long as the Sun and Moon shall endure, as long as the Earth on which I dwell shall exist in the same State, you this day see it, so long will I be your friend and ally ... ."[290] In the subsequent ratification treaties with the "several Districts of the Michmach Nation" and the Crown,[291] the existing compact

---

285 *Ibid.*

286 *Ibid.*

287 *Ibid.* The metaphor of "the Hedge" is directly related to the Wabanaki concept of "fence (implement)" (*lahkalusonihikon*) or territorial boundaries in the *Wapapi Akonutomakonol*, and its laws (*tapaskuwakonol*). Leavitt & Francis, *supra* note 32 at 56-57.

288 The Míkmaq understanding of burying the hatchet and washing the war paint was to bar any future references to the hostilities. Yet, in courts provincial Attorney Generals have raised issue that hostilities that were supposed to be buried justify extinguishing the treaties. See *Simon, supra* note 278. The introduction of such evidence in a court of law is contrary to a strict construction of the terms of the compact and treaties as understood by the Míkmaq at the time of the treaty.

289 *Native Rights, supra* note 52.

290 *Ibid.*

291 PANS, MS. Doc., vol. 37, No. 14. Additional ratification treaties were made with the "Merimichi, Jediack, Poginouch & Cape Breton Tribes"—CO 217/8 at 276-284; and "Pictouk and Malegomich" in 1761 (*Piktukewaq aqq Epekwith*)—PANS, RG1 165 at 160-166, 187, and RG1 430 at 20-21; with the Newfoundland Míkmaq (*Ktaqtmkuk* of *Unamákik*)—CO 218/6 ff. 203-206. See also E. Chappell, *Voyage of H.M.S. Rosamound to Newfoundland and Southern Coast of Labrador* (London: J. Mawman, 1818) at 82-84 for another treaty that has not been found during the American Revolution; with "Miranichi, Restigouche, Richibucto, and Shediac Indians," "Micmac Tribes residing between Cape Tormentine and the Bay de Chaleur" at Windsor in 1779 (*Sikniktewaq & Kespékewaq*)—CO vol. 217/54 at 1252-57; and "MicMac Tribe of Restigouche" in 1786 (*Kespékewaq*)—PANS 3/4/5, June 29 and July 7, 1786. The confusion of names is part of the colonialized landscape of the treaty era.

and its obligations were continued as legal and private obligations for the Crown to defend by prerogative law and civil law.

In sum, all of the Georgian treaties with the Míkmaq retained their Aboriginal tenure for themselves and made no mention of sale of lands to the Crown. Míkmaq agreed to allow the British coastal settlements—that is, British reserves controlled by British within the Míkmaw land tenure. The peaceful enjoyment of the existing settlements cannot be equated with a purchase or cession of Míkmaw tenure.[292] The peaceful enjoyment of the settlements by colonists was derived from the treaty by the consent of the Míkmaw, and controlled by Míkmaw law.

6. Prerogative Legislation Protecting Aboriginal Tenure

Six years after the compact, on 2 October 1758, and pursuant to the authority delegated to the sovereign by the Míkmaq, a legislative Assembly was convened in Nova Scotia. British constitutional conventions establish 1758 as the date of the reception of the British law in old Nova Scotia as a settled colony[293] that included New Brunswick.[294] British law was imported, except to the extent that the law was unsuitable to the circumstances of the colony, as for example, when inconsistent with the existing compact and treaties with the Aboriginal nations.[295] Since the compacts were an existing prerogative Act made before the reception of the British common law of colonization,[296] they required no colonial legislation to be implemented. The compacts and prerogative legislation were imperial obligations and part of the existing prerogative constitution of Nova Scotia.[297]

---

292 This is the problem of Locke's theory of tacit consent in property law. See J. Y. Henderson, "The Doctrine of Aboriginal Rights in the Western Legal Tradition" in M. Boldt, J.A. Long, and L. Little Bear, eds., *Quest For Justice: Aboriginal Peoples and Aboriginal Rights* (Toronto: University of Toronto Press, 1986).

293 *Uniacke v. Dickson* (1848), 2 N.S.R. 287 (N.S. C.A.). Hogg, *supra* note 54 at 30, finds this dubious and argues that dates of reception thus derived are quite artificial and are really cut-off dates.

294 This is different from the idea that the first colonists carried British law as a birthright that filled any legal void in the new territory. This idea was also limited by the courts' determination that they be suitable to the circumstances of the territory, *e.g.*, prerogative treaties. See Hogg, *ibid.* The 1763 Proclamation "annexed" Cape Breton and Prince Edward Island to old Nova Scotia's government, while reserving the Míkmaw Hunting Grounds in all places, thus creating a different date for the reception of British law. No other documents "annexed" the reserved Hunting Grounds to any colony or to the federal government.

295 Hogg, *ibid.* at 30, 32.

296 *Ibid.* at 28.

297 Blackstone, *supra* note 4, vol. 4 at 67-68. See especially, Justice Strong in *St. Catherine's Milling and Lumber Company v. The Queen*, [1887] 11 S.C.R. 577 (P.C.) [hereinafter *St. Catherine's*, [1887]]: "[A]t the date of confederation the Indians, by constant usage and practice of the crown, were considered to possess a certain proprietary interest in the unsurrendered lands which they occupied as hunting grounds; that this usage had either ripened into a rule of the common law as applicable to the American Colonies, or that such a rule had been derived from the law of nations and had in this way been imported into the Colonial law as applied to Indian Nations ... ."

Without formal cession or purchase of Míkmaq tenure by the Crown, the effect of Article 8 of the Míkmaw Compact, the implemented 1761 Instructions,[298] and the *Royal Proclamation of 1763*[299] was to protect the Aboriginal territories or properties from British colonialists and assemblies. These prerogative laws conferred upon the Crown a *sui generis* fiduciary duty, both contractually and equitably, to protect the Míkmaw Hunting Grounds for the Crown under the law.[300]

A. 1761 Royal instructions

In 1761 Additional Instructions from the King to the Governor of Nova Scotia and the other colonies acknowledged the "inviolable" compacts and treaties that had been made with the Aboriginal nations. The Instructions stressed that the peace and security of the colonies "greatly depend upon the Amity and Alliance of the several Nations or Tribes of Indians bordering upon the said colonies." British Governors were ordered to "support and protect" the Aboriginal nations in "their just Rights and Possession and to keep a just and faithful Observance of these Treaties and Compacts which have been heretofore solemnly entered into." These Instructions, affirming the legal force of the compacts in the constitutional law of Nova Scotia, witnessed the consent of the sovereign to be bound by compacts and treaties. To ensure the treaties were respected, the sovereign ordered that the governors:

> forthwith cause this Our Instruction to you to be made Public not only within all parts of your Province inhabited by Our Subjects, but also amongst the Several Tribes of Indians living within the same to the end that Our Royal Will and Pleasure in the Premises may be known and that the Indians may be apprized of Our determin'd Resolution to support them in their just Rights, and inviolably to observe Our Engagement with them.[301]

---

298 3 Geo. III; CO 217/19:27-28; PANS micro reel B-1028 4 May 1762. See J. Singer, "Well Settled?: The Increasing Weight of History in American Indian Land Claims" (1994) 28 Ga. L. Rev. 481 at 503-508.

299 7 October 1763; Privy Council Register, Geo. III, vol. 3 at 102; PRO, c. 6613683; R.S.C. 1970, App. at 123-29 [hereinafter *Royal Proclamation* cited to R.S.C. 1970, App.]. Original text is entered on the Patent Rolls for the regnal year 4 Geo. III, and is found in the United Kingdom PRO: c. 66/3693 (back of roll); C.S. Brigham, ed., *British Royal Proclamations Relating to America*, vol. 12 (Worcester, Mass.: American Antiquarian Society, 1911) at 212-18; *Native Rights*, *supra* note 52 at 285-292; and *Land Rights*, *supra* note 54; Borrows, *supra* note 54.

300 *Native Rights*, *ibid.* at 285-286.

301 Labaree, *Royal Instructions*, *supra* note 186. PANS, RG1 30 at 58.

The 1761 Instructions were implemented in old Nova Scotia through the Nova Scotia Proclamation in 1762,[302] legally prohibiting anyone from trespassing, surveying, possessing, confiscating, or managing the reserved Míkmaw territory protected by the prerogative compacts and treaties.[303]

B. *Nova Scotia Proclamation of 1762*

"In obedience to this Royal Instruction from His Majesty,"[304] in May 1762, Governor Belcher issued the *Nova Scotia Proclamation of 1762*[305] to implement the prerogative command of the 1761 Instructions. In the 1761 ratifying treaties with the "several Districts of the Michmach Nation," Belcher had referred to the Míkmaq treaties as a compact and as a covenant of peace designed to be a protective "wall" between Míkmaq and the British subjects.[306] In the Nova Scotia Council and House of Representatives on 23 March 1762, Belcher explained the Royal Instructions:

> As it is of no inconsiderable importance to the Province and its rising Settlements, that Treaties of Peace have been concluded between this His Majesty's Government and every District of the Tribes of Indians among us, So you will readily judge with me that every reasonable Method ought to be pursued and persevering this Peace inviolate, and fixing their Affections and Attachments, from the Sense and experience of Protection, Integrity, and Friendship.[307]

Two months later, Belcher issued the *Nova Scotia Proclamation of 1762*, where he elaborated the legal concept of reserved Míkmaw tenure and its protection as affirmed by the 1761 Instructions. The 1762 Proclamation affirmed:

> [the Míkmaq] had made, and still continued to make, great Complaints that Settlements have been made, and Possessions taken, of Lands, the Property of which they have by Treaties reserved to themselves, by Persons claiming that said Lands, under Pretence of

---

302 Brigham, *supra* note 299. To make the Instructions a legally enforceable document, the sovereign commanded the Governor to make the instructions public and to issue a colonial Proclamation, in the name of the sovereign: "strictly enjoining and requiring all persons whatever who may either willfully or inadvertently have seated themselves on any Lands so reserved to or claimed by the said Indian without any lawfull Authority for so doing forthwith to remove therefrom[;] And in case you find upon strict enquiry to be made for that purpose that any person or persons do claim to hold or possess any lands within Our said Province upon pretense of purchases made of the said Indians without a proper licence first had and obtained either from us or any of Our Royal Predecessor or any person acting under Our or their Authority you are forthwith to cause a prosecution to be carried on against such person or persons who shall have made such fraudulent purchases to the end that the land may be recovered by due Course of Law."

303 *Worcester, supra* note 2; *Royal Instructions, supra* note 186; *Nova Scotia Proclamation of 1762*, in *Native Rights, supra* note 52 at 287; *Royal Proclamation, supra* note 299.

304 Letter of Belcher to Lord Commissioners of Trade, 3 July 1762—PRP, CO 217/19/22.

305 3 Geo. III; CO 217/19 at 27-28 [hereinafter the 1762 Proclamation].

306 PANS, MS. Doc., vol. 37, no. 14.

307 CO 217/19 at 31.

Deeds of Sale & Conveyance, illegally, Fraudulently, and surreptitiously obtained by said Indians.[308]

Issued in His Majesty's name, the 1762 Proclamation supported and protected the said "Indians in their just Rights and Possession and to keep inviolable the Treaties and compacts which have been entered into with them."[309] All the Míkmaw "Lands, Liberties and properties" were affirmed as reserved to themselves.[310]

Drawing from 1761 descriptions recorded by a released British captive among the Míkmaq and claims made on behalf of the Indians, the 1762 Proclamation described the protected national territory of the Míkmaq within Nova Scotia:

> strictly injoining and requiring all Persons what ever, who may either willfully or inadvertently have seated themselves on the described Land so reserved to or claimed by the said Indians, without any Lawful Authority for so doing, forthwith to remove therefrom.[311]

If they did not remove, "they will otherwise be prosecuted with the utmost Rigour of the Law."[312] For the "more special purpose of hunting, fowling and fishing, I do hereby strictly injoin and caution all persons to avoid all molestation of the said Indians in their said claims, till His Majesty's pleasure in this behalf be signified."[313] The expressions "lawful authority," "reserved" lands, the "utmost Rigour of the Law," and the special protection given to the Indian rights to hunting, fowling, and fishing linked the 1762 Proclamation to the terms and conditions of the Míkmaq Compact. The scope of the protected land was contained in many petitions to the Governor and Council describing the various jurisdictions of the district chiefs. In 1761, the released British captive stated to colonial authorities the Míkmaq conception of their lands:

> Their chief made almost a circle with his forefinger and thumb, and pointing at the end of his forefinger, said there was Quebec, the middle joint of his finger was Montreal, the joint next to the hand was Boston, the middle joint of the thumb was Halifax, the interval betwixt his finger and thumb was Pokmoosh [Pokemouche], so that the Indians would soon be surrounded [by the British] which he signified by closing his finger and thumb.[314]

Belcher's letter to the Lord Commissioners stated that he had "inquired into the nature of the Pretensions of the Indians, for any part of the Lands within this Province. A return was accordingly made by me, for a Common right to the Sea Coast from Cape Fronsac inward for Fishing without disturbance or Opposition by any of His Majesty's

---

308 *Ibid.*

309 *Ibid.*

310 *Ibid.*

311 *Ibid.*

312 *Ibid.*

313 *Ibid.* See *An Act for the Regulation of the Indian Trade,* PRO, CO 217/19/33 (NS).

314 Cited in W.D. Wallis and R.S. Wallis, *The Micmac Indians of Eastern Canada* (Minneapolis: University of Minnesota Press, 1955) at 124.

Subjects."[315] He formally described reserved or claimed Míkmaq territory under the jurisdiction of Nova Scotia in the 1762 Proclamation:

> from Fronsac Passage and thence to Nartigoneiche [Antigonish], and from Nartigonneich to Pikouk [Pictou], and from thence to Bay De Chaleurs, and the environs of Canso, and thence to Mushkoodadwet [Musquodoboit], and so along the coast, as the Claims and Possession of the said Indians.[316]

A modest claim, it makes only vague reference to the environs of Canso, referring to the Cape Breton Island and St. Johns Island. The description also did not refer to how far along the coast from Mosquodoboit the claims continued. It is questionable whether it continued to the Malicheet reserved lands around the St. Johns River toward Passamaquoddy Bay.

After Nova Scotia's initial rejection of the Míkmaq petitions, the 1761 Instructions directed colonial authorities to acknowledge these properties reserved in the treaties to the Míkmaq, without distinction among treaties, and the new territorial claims of Nova Scotia as a result of conquest of the French in Canada and the Míkmaq treaties. The 1762 Proclamation thus established a territorial distinction between Míkmáki and the British settlements in Nova Scotia, as well as affirming the individual treaty rights of hunting, fowling, and fishing without interference from Nova Scotia Government and British colonists.

C. Nova Scotia Acts

On 2 July 1762, two months after the 1762 Proclamation, the Nova Scotia Assembly passed an Act *"for Preventing Fraud in the Trade with the Indians."*[317] Belcher acknowledged and affirmed the obligation of the Law to protect against fraudulent purchases of the land reserved in the Míkmaw Compact and treaties:

> And Whereas the fraudulent purchasing of Lands from the Indians hath often times occasioned War in the Neighboring Colonies. Be it further Enacted that every Grant, Deed, Lease or any other Bargain, for any Right, title or Interest in any Lands within the Province made by any of the said Indians to any of His Majesty's Subjects shall be in law of no force or Effect, and is hereby declared null and void unless Licences shall have been First obtained from His Majesty for that purpose.[318]

This section is consistent with the settle and agree provision of the charter, the compacts and treaties, the 1761 Royal Instructions, and the 1762 Proclamation.

Noting that the Indians were "unacquainted with the law of the province and in what manner they are to protect their rights against fraud and injury,"[319] the Act imple-

---

315 PRO, CO 217/19/12.

316 PANS, micro reel B-1028 (4 May 1762).

317 S.N.S. 1762, c. 3. Compare *supra* note 274.

318 *Ibid.*

319 *Ibid.*

mented Article 8 of the treaties granting Míkmaq access to His Majesty's civil courts in Nova Scotia law and confirming the promises of the 1761 ratification treaties. The Act authorized:

> Governor, Lieutenant-Governor, or Commander in Chief, upon complaint of any Indians within this province, made to him or either of them, that they have been wronged or cheated of their furs or any other merchandise, or in any other their trade and dealing with other of His Majesty's Subjects, that the Governor, Lieutenant-Governor, or Commander in Chief, is hereby desired to direct His Majesty's Attorney General to prosecute the same, either before His Majesty's Justice, or in any of His Majesty's Courts of Record in a summary way, as the laws do direct, and such prosecution shall be deemed legal, and the judgment and execution shall issue accordingly.[320]

The new Act was approved by the Board of Trade,[321] thus formally acknowledging and ratifying the colonial obligations to protect the treaty rights within the borders of Nova Scotia. The treaty regime was a limitation on the colony and subjects, its protections constitutional and legal, and its judgment and execution required.

These Nova Scotia Acts not only defined the reserved land of the Míkmaq in Nova Scotia, but also established a clear method for having treaty rights enforced in the colonial courts. Because land speculators were attempting to sell their unlawful or fraudulent interests in Míkmaq land, on 28 August 1762, Belcher issued a second proclamation to prohibit the alienation of land by the colonialists without a Crown licence:

> Whereas many persons have alienated their Lands without licence first obtained contrary to an express condition in their Grants; and other have possessed themselves of and occupied Lands without any Authority from Government; In order therefore to prevent all such unwarrantable proceeding for the future, I have thought fit with the Advice and Consent of His Majesty's Council to Publish this Proclamation, here Declaring all persons making Alienations of Lands without License, to have incurred a forfeiture of their Grants; And all persons entering upon and occupying Land upon the Authority of the Government; liable to the Penalty of Fifty Pounds for every person offending, agreeable to a former Proclamation; And that Orders will be issued for the immediate removal of all such persons.[322]

D. *Treaty of Paris* (1763)

The *Treaty of Paris* (1763) made Great Britain the most extensive jurisdiction since Rome. The Most Christian King transferred most of His pretenses to North America under the discovery and occupation to His Britannic Majesty.[323] Article II renewed

---

320   *Ibid.*

321   PANS, MSS. Doc., vol. 31, doc.10.

322   PRO, CO 217/19/141.

323   Article 4, *Treaty of Paris*, 10 February 1763 in Shortt & Doughty, *supra* note 280.

and confirmed the *Treaty of Utrecht*, subject to the terms of the new treaty, thus including the protection of Indian allies. In addition, Article XXIII restored conquered countries or territories that were not mentioned in the *Treaty of Paris*:

> All the countries and territories which may have been conquered in whatsoever part of the world, by arms of their Britiannick and Most Faithful Majesties, as well as those of their most Christian and Catholic Majesties, which are not included in the present treaties, either under the title of cessions, or under the title of restitutions, shall be restored without difficulties and without requiring any compensation.[324]

Since the reserved territories of Aboriginal nations were not named in the *Treaty of Paris*, they were covered by this clause. Any of their territories conquered were restored in a manner consistent with the sovereign's promises to the Aboriginal allies of the French Crown as reflected in Article 40 of the Articles of Capitulation:

> The Savages or Indian allies of his most Christian Majesty, shall be maintained in the Lands they inhabit; if they chuse to remain there; they shall not be molested on any pretence whatsoever, for having carried arms, and served his most Christian Majesty. They shall have, as well as the French, liberty of religion, and shall keep their missionaries.[325]

The restoration of Míkmáki was also consistent with British law, as announced by Lord Mansfield in *Campbell v. Hall* in 1774: "the articles of capitulation upon which the country is surrendered, and the articles of peace by which it is ceded, are sacred and inviolable according to their true intent and meaning."[326] His Majesty could not "legally disregard or violate the articles in which the country is surrendered or ceded."[327] Thus, reserved territories of Aboriginal nations were protected by British law in the *Treaty of Utrecht*, Article 40 of the Articles of Capitulation, and Article XXIII of the *Treaty of Paris*. By promises of the sovereign to both Aboriginal and European sovereigns, Aboriginal tenure was considered sacred and inviolable.

E. *Royal Proclamation of 1763*

Shortly after the *Treaty of Paris*, His Majesty's Board of Trade began incorporating the international rights and obligations of the treaty into imperial law. Consistent with the other prerogative treaties and laws, in August of 1763, the Board of Trade wrote to Sir William Johnson, the northern superintendent, and declared that both the unknown tribes and nations and those in alliance or confederation with the French were

---

324 *Ibid.*

325 Shortt & Doughty, *supra* note 280, vol. 1 at 20. Article 50 of the *Act of Capitulation* made Art. 40 inviolable: "The present capitulation shall be inviolably executed in all its articles, and bona fide, on both sides, notwithstanding any infraction, and any other pretence, with regard to the preceding capitulations, and without making use of reprisals."

326 *Campbell v. Hall, supra* note 78.

327 Chitty, *supra* note 57 at 29.

"under His Majesty's immediate protection."[328] Also, the Board of Trade requested that colonial Indian Agents report on the status of the unknown tribes and nations and the allies of the French.

In October, His Britannic Majesty affirmed Aboriginal sovereignty and tenure in the American colonies in the *Royal Proclamation of 1763*.[329] The *Royal Proclamation*, implementing the new treaty obligations of the Crown in both the law of Great Britain and colonial law, affirmed and amplified: that the existing treaties and compacts with the Aboriginal nations were sacred and inviolable; that they were binding on the Crown, colonies, and subjects; that they were acts of state establishing rights; and that they were enforceable in the courts.[330]

In terms of trade, the *Royal Proclamation* centralized authority over Aboriginal trade in imperial authorities within whose regulation "Trade with the said Indians" shall be "free and open to all our Subjects."[331] All traders were required to "take out a License for carrying on such Trade" from the Governor of the Colonies as well as "give Security to observe such Regulations as We shall at any Time think fit, by ourselves or by our Commissaries to be appointed for this purpose."[332] If traders refused or neglected to follow the prerogative regulations, their licence and security were to be forfeited.

The *Royal Proclamation* clarified the status of the Indian nations under the *Treaty of Paris*. Part V expressly protected and gave effect to the existing treaty commonwealth in British North America. Similar to the intent and wording of the 1761 Instructions, centralizing Indian licences and purchases in London was designed to remedy the persistent problem of fraud, corruption, and irregularities in the colonists' purchase of Aboriginal lands, and to restore justice in the colonies. The prefatory words in the *Royal Proclamation* underline the sovereign's conclusion that the colonial authorities could not be trusted in the management of Indian lands:

> And whereas great Frauds and Abuses have been committed in purchasing Lands of the Indians, to the great Prejudice of our Interests, and to the great Dissatisfaction of the said Indians; In order, therefore, to prevent such Irregularities for the future, and to the end that the Indians may be convinced of our Justice and determined Resolution to remove all reasonable Causes of Discontent, ...[333]

In the Eastern colonies, the *Royal Proclamation* affirmatively protected the treaty and Aboriginal rights of the "several Nations or Tribes of Indians with whom we are

---

328 NYCD, *supra* note 88, vol. 7 at 535-36; J.M. Sosin, *Whitehall and the Wilderness: The Middle West in British Colonial Policy, 1760-1775* (Westport, Conn.: Greenwood Press, 1961 and 1980) at 51.

329 *Royal Proclamation*, *supra* note 299. See K.M. Harvey, "The Royal Proclamation of 7 October 1763, Common Law and Native Rights to Lands Within the Territory Granted to the Hudson Bay Company" (1973-74) Sask. L. Rev. 131; *Land Rights*, *supra* note 54.

330 See *Vajesingji Jaoravarsingji v. Secretary of State for India in Council* (1924), 51 L.R. Ind. App. 357 at 360, Lord Dunedin, citing *Cook v. Sprigg*, [1899] A.C. 572 (P.C.).

331 *Royal Proclamation*, *supra* note 299.

332 *Ibid.*

333 *Ibid.* at 128.

connected, or who live under our Protection."[334] Consistent with earlier compacts and the 1761 Instructions, the *Royal Proclamation* strictly ordered that the Indian nations within existing colonies "should not be molested or disturbed in the Possession of such Parts of our Dominions and Territories as, not having been ceded to or purchased by Us, ..."[335]

These lands were "...reserved to them, or any of them as their *Hunting Grounds*."[336] The *Royal Proclamation* thus defined the criteria for determining which Aboriginal lands in French territory were restored under both Article XXIII of the *Treaty of Paris* and Article 40 of French Capitulation. It also gave a conceptual name in British law to the lands reserved for the Indian nations or tribes in compacts or treaties.

The *Royal Proclamation* vested Aboriginal authority over lands and resources in British law as "Hunting Grounds," autonomous from the governor, assembly, and colonialists. In interpreting the Hunting Grounds section of the *Royal Proclamation*, the Supreme Court of the United States declared that the British Sovereign determined that "Indian possession or occupation was considered with reference to their habits and

---

334 *St. Catherine's, supra* note 296 at 54. Lord Watson observed that the 1763 Proclamation was made "in favour of all Indian tribes then living under the sovereignty and protection of the British Crown." This broad classification of intended beneficiaries has prevailed in recent jurisprudence. *R. v. Isaac* (1975), 13 N.S.R. (2d) 460 at 478, 497, 498 (N.S. C.A.); *Simon, supra* note 278; *The Queen v. Smith* (1980), [1981] 1 F.C. 346 at 377-380 (Fed. C.A.), reversed, [1983] 1 S.C.R. 554 without discussion on this point; *Paul v. C.P.R.* (1983), 2 D.L.R. (4th) 22 at 27-28 (N.B. C.A.), reversed, [1988] 2 S.C.R. 654 without discussion of this point. In contrast, the Judicial Committee of the Privy Council in *Re Labrador Boundary*, [1927] 2 D.L.R. 401 at 421 (J.C. P.C.) narrowly interpreted this reference in the *Royal Proclamation* to the Indians "with whom [We are] connected and who lived under his Protection" to mean, "those tribes of the Six Nations who were settled round the great lakes or beyond the sources of the rivers which fell into the River St. Lawrence from the north." The same observation was made by Judson J. in *Calder, supra* note 247 at 325. Chief Justice Davey of the British Columbia Court of Appeals in *Calder* stated that: "[u]nder the Proclamation it was desired to treat the Indian allies of the French now under British sovereignty in the same manner as the British allies, to confirm the rights of the latter and to restrain and remove encroachments upon Indian lands. It was to those Indians that the *Royal Proclamation* referred when it spoke of 'the several Nations or Tribes of Indians with whom we are connected, and who live under our Protection,'" at 68.

335 *Royal Proclamation, supra* note 299 at 127. The use of "Dominion" appears to refer to jurisdiction. In para. 60 of the *Royal Instructions*, which accompanied General Murry's commission as Governor, he is directed, with respect to the Indians, that he should "upon no account molest or distrube them in the possession of such parts of the said province as they at present occupy or possess." This Instruction also implements Art. 40 of the Articles of Capitulation, 1758. See below. Lord Watson in *St. Catherine's, ibid.*, stated that: "[t]heir possession, such as it was, can only be ascribed to the general provisions made by the royal proclamation in favour of all Indian tribes then living under the sovereignty and protection of the British Crown."

336 *Royal Proclamation, ibid.* at 127 [emphasis added]. Lord Chancellor Cave in *Re Labrador Boundary, supra* note 333 at 421, interpreted this section to mean "[t]he reservation [of Hunting Grounds] is confined to lands occupied by 'the said Indians'—that is to say, those who are referred to in the next preceding paragraph of the *Royal Proclamation* as nations or tribes of Indians with whom The King was connected and who lived under his protection." However, Chief Justice Duff felt that the Labrador Esquimaux were under the Protection of the Crown in 1763. See *Reference re Whether the Term "Indians" in s. 91(24) of the B.N.A. Act, 1867, includes Eskimo Inhabitants of Quebec.* [1939] S.C.R. 104 at 115, [1939] 2 D.L.R. 417 (S.C.C.) [hereinafter *In Re Indians* cited to S.C.R.].

modes of life; their hunting-grounds were as much in their actual possession as the cleared fields of the whites."[337]

While the compact and treaties, the Royal Instructions of 1761, and the *Nova Scotia Proclamation of 1762* had already recognized the Mi̇́kmaw territory in Nova Scotia as reserved lands, the *Royal Proclamation* affirmed all unceded and purchased lands acquired by the *Treaty of Paris* as reserved Hunting Grounds. These territories acquired from the French were Cape Breton Island, St. Johns Island, Magdalene Island, and parts of Newfoundland and Quebec. The *Royal Proclamation* annexed Cape Breton Island and St. Johns Island to Nova Scotia. In addition, the *Royal Proclamation* also prohibited governors from granting survey right or titles to lands within the boundary of "any Lands whatever, which, not having been ceded to or purchased by Us ... are reserved to the said Indians, or any of them."[338]

The sovereign asserted the sole and exclusive right to purchase the reserved land of Indian nations if they desired to sell it, establishing a special protocol requiring a public meeting under Aboriginal law to evidence the consensual purchases of the reserved land by His Majesty.[339] The *Royal Proclamation* also established strict procedures for the Crown's acquisition of vested Hunting Grounds:

> ...if at any Time any of the Said [Nations or Tribes of] Indians should be inclined to dispose of the said Lands, the same shall be Purchased only for Us [the Crown], in our Name, at some public Meeting or Assembly of the said Indians, to be held for that Purpose by the Governor or Commander in Chief of Our Colony respectively within which they shall lie, ...[340]

Even though the Hunting Grounds were considered within the colonies, this section affirmed that the Aboriginal nations retained ultimate control of the disposition of their vested lands, liberties, and properties. To reinforce the Crown pre-emptive right to purchase, the *Royal Proclamation* prohibited colonial or private acquisition of Aboriginal lands. Paragraph 3 of the *Royal Proclamation* "strictly enjoin" British subjects from making any purchase, settlements, or taking possession of any Indian lands without a special licence from the Crown.[341]

Establishing that the Hunting Grounds were not a commodity, the Royal Proclamation prohibited any individual or third party from directly acquiring any interest in

---

337 *Mitchel, supra* note 251 at 748.

338 Brigham, *supra* note 299 at 167.

339 *Royal Proclamation, supra* note 299 at 123-29. By 1739, the prohibition of the private purchase of Indian law appeared in colonial law. The preamble to South Carolina law justified the Crown monopoly: "the practice of purchasing lands from the Indians ... tend[s] to manifest prejudice of his Majesty's just right and title to the soil of this province, vested in his Majesty by the surrender of the late Lords Proprietors." See F.P. Prucha, *American Indian Policy in the Formative Years: The Indian Trade and Intercourse Acts, 1790-1834* (Lincoln: University of Nebraska Press, 1973) at 6. See also, *St. Catherine's, supra* note 296 for clarification about how the existing royal patents and instructions should be carried out.

340 *Royal Proclamation, ibid.* at 128.

341 *Ibid.* at 127.

the reserved lands from Aboriginal nations. Only the Sovereign could give individual licences to purchase, make settlements, or take possession of any land. However, no authority existed in the Crown to take possession of the Hunting Grounds with a special licence, since almost all the lands were reserved for the Aboriginal nations by treaties and compacts and had to be purchased by the Crown.

Paragraph 4 of the *Royal Proclamation* demanded the immediate removal of all colonists from the Hunting Grounds:

> And, We do further strictly enjoin and require all Persons whatever who have either wilfully or inadvertently seated themselves upon any Lands within the Countries above described, or upon any other Lands which, not having been ceded to or purchased by Us, are still reserved to the said Indians as aforesaid, forthwith to remove themselves from such Settlements.[342]

It nullified any private rights in British subjects in any settlements not ceded or purchased by the Crown. The Proclamation established special extradition procedures for all Persons found in Hunting Grounds.[343] By ordering extradition from the Hunting Grounds, this paragraph affirmed and continued the exclusive use of Aboriginal peoples within the Hunting Grounds.

The *Royal Proclamation* created the concept of "Indian country" to address the vast western lands acquired from the French in the *Treaty of Paris*. It was a concept comparable to the eastern Hunting Grounds. The Crown unilaterally reserved the Indian Country under his "Sovereignty, Protection, and Dominion," for the use of the said Indians.[344] These reserved territories were expressly distinguished from the Atlantic colonies, the new territories of the colonies of Quebec, East and West Florida acquired by the *Treaty of Paris*, and the Territory granted to the Hudson Bay Company. They included "the Lands and Territories lying to the Westward of the Sources of the Rivers which fall into the Sea from the West and North West."[345] Indian country resolved the meaning of the category of "countries" in Article XXIII of the *Treaty of Paris*. Not only did no British treaties exist in the western Indian Country, but none of the western Indian lands had been "ceded to or purchased by" France or Britain.

F. Implementation of the *Royal Proclamation*

On the evidence of the *Royal Proclamation*, the first British Empire derived from European treaties was a protectorate (*patrocinium*) of Aboriginal nations and tribes.[346] The British sovereign was not an independent or absolute authority (*imperium*); he had shared jurisdiction under Aboriginal compacts and treaties. Nor did the sovereign have

---

342 *Ibid.* at 128.

343 *Ibid.*, Pt. IV at s. 5.

344 *Ibid.* at 127. The wording "for the use of" is the classic mode of establishing a trust in British law.

345 *Ibid.* at 127.

346 See J.G.A. Pocock, ed., *The Political Works of James Harrington* (Cambridge, U.K.: Cambridge University Press, 1977) at 446.

tenure over the lands (*dominium*); most of the lands were reserved for the Aboriginal nations, with the sovereign having a derivative interest in the settlements under the compacts and treaties. Different from the older Spanish empire of conquest, the British empire in North America was an empire of treaties, both European and Aboriginal.

By uniting the antecedent prerogative laws in British North America, the *Royal Proclamation* affirmed the existing treaty reconciliations of Aboriginal tenure and rights as imperial limitations on colonial assemblies. The Proclamation affirmed the existing prerogative rights as legally enforceable obligations in the colonies. The Proclamation was not directed to the Aboriginal nations or tribes, but rather to the governors, the assemblies, and the colonists. Any act done by a colonial governor in violation of a Royal Proclamation, as public acts under the Great Seal, would be void.[347] No colonial government, officer, or subject possessed lawful authority to interfere with Aboriginal treaty order within their reserved lands or territories. Major General Gage sent the 1763 Proclamation to officers commanding the posts of Halifax, Louisburg, and Newfoundland.[348] The following year, Governor Wilmout of Nova Scotia acknowledged receipt of the *Royal Proclamation* and promised it the widest circulation.[349]

To implement the imperial administration of the protected Aboriginal nations, the Board of Trade formulated an administrative scheme. On 10 July 1764, the Board urged one general system, under the direction of "Officers appointed by the Crown, so as to set aside all local interfering of particular Provinces, which has been one great cause of the distracted state of Indian Affairs, in general,"[350] to regulate the commercial and political affairs of the Aboriginal nations throughout North America. The 1764 plan required superintendents for the northern and southern departments to control all Aboriginal trade and affairs.[351] It mandated the repeal of all colonial laws regulating Aboriginal affairs or commerce.[352] The imperial superintendents, in council with the colonial governors, would manage trade, treaty negotiations, and land purchases from Aboriginal nations.[353] The superintendents would be vested with the summary power to hear civil cases between the Indians and traders to the value of ten pounds sterling. British trading with the Indians would be limited to fixed trading posts (Truck houses), which were separate from military authority, where the superintendents or agents would have the powers of justices of peace over British subjects. Credit and trade in spirituous liquors was strictly prohibited.

---

347 *Land Rights, supra* note 54 at 284-287.

348 Gage MS., W.L.C.L.; C. E. Carter, ed., *The Correspondence of General Thomas Gage with the Secretaries of State*, vol. 2 (New York: Archon Books, 1969) at 1 (11 October 1763).

349 CO 217/21-28, 28 January 1764.

350 NYCD, *supra* note 88, vol. 7 at 634-35.

351 *Ibid.* at 635-41.

352 *Ibid.* at 637.

353 *Ibid.* Deputy Agents' Instructions were to annually visit the Tribes and hold a Congress at which all past engagements (*i.e.*, compacts and treaties) were to be repeated and ratified.

The 1764 plan did not envision any interference with the autonomous Aboriginal nations. The northern district acknowledged "the civil constitution of the Indians" and their long traditions of Aboriginal sovereignty, limiting any use of the southern district's concept of an elective "beloved man" as "Guardian for the Indian and their Rights" and advisor to the Superintendents and Agents.[354] The plan implemented the private prohibitions and restrictions of the 1763 Proclamation, proscribing private land purchase from Indians in the royal colonies:

> No private person, Society, Corporation, or Colony be capable of acquiring any property in Lands belonging to the Indians, either by purchase of or Grant, or Conveyance from the said Indians.[355]

It contemplated the establishment of "exact" boundaries between the colonies and the Indian tribes "with the consent and concurrence of the Indians."[356] General meetings of the Aboriginal nations were required at all land purchases from the Indians for the sovereign. The chiefs of each tribe claiming property in the lands had to be present; the purchased lands were to be surveyed by a sworn surveyor in their presence, and with the assistance of a person designated by the Indians.[357] The 1764 plan was never formally adopted by the King-in-Council and was eventually abandoned in 1768.[358]

G. The Treaties at Niagara, 1764

Sir William Johnson, appointed as the Superintendent of the Northern Department, found warrant in the 1763 Proclamation to re-establish peace in western Quebec, allowing him to reassure the Aboriginal Confederacies and Nations that there would be no new land frauds, and that a permanent boundary line would be made. In December 1763, General Thomas Gage wrote to Johnson, setting out his plans for "the best Manner of Making Peace with Indians." He wanted to know whether it was best to assemble the "Several Nations together" or to treaty with them separately.[359] In response Johnson chose a large meeting with all the Nations of Niagara as a "Treaty of Offensive and Defensive Alliance" that would include promises to:

> assure them of a Free Fair & open trade, at the principal Posts, & a free intercourse, & passage into our Country, That we will make no Settlements or Encroachments contrary to Treaty, or without their permission. That we will bring to justice any persons who com-

---

354 *Ibid.*

355 *Ibid.*

356 *Ibid.* "That proper Measure be [taken with] the Consent and concurrence of the Indians, to ascertain and define the precise and exact Boundaries and Limits of the Lands, which it may be proper to reserve to them, and where no Settlement whatever shall be allowed."

357 *Ibid.*

358 *Ibid.*, vol. 8 at 19-31, 55-58. However, the imperial superintendents used it to guide their management of Indian affairs and repeatedly called for its implementation. *Ibid.*, vol. 7 at 834-43 and 951-78. In 1768, the King transferred administration of Indian trade to the colonies, urging the colonial assemblies to adopt and enforce the 1764 plan.

359 Johnson Papers, *supra* note 242, vol. 4 at 279-80; Borrows, *supra* note 54 at 20-30.

mit Robberys or Murders on them & that we will protect & aid them against their & our Enemys, & duly observe our Engagements with them.[360]

Johnson further proposed on behalf of the British to draw on traditional protocols:

at this Treaty ... we should tie them down (in the Peace) according to their own forms of which they take the most notice, for example by exchanging a very large belt with some remarkable & intelligible figures thereon. Expressive of the occasion which should always be shown to remind them of their promises.[361]

Wampum laws of the Aboriginal Confederacies and Nations were to record the promises of the treaties at Niagara.

In the winter following the *Royal Proclamation*, Aboriginal leaders were invited to attend a conference at Niagara the following summer to discuss principles that would govern their relationship with the Crown.[362] Aboriginal messengers travelled with a printed copy of the *Royal Proclamation* and with various strings of wampum summoning the Aboriginal confederacies and nations to a treaty conference.[363] The treaties at Niagara were entered into in July and August 1764. The conference was, according to colonial records, "the most widely representative gathering of American Indians ever assembled,"[364] with approximately two thousand chiefs attending.[365] Over 24 nations were gathered, with "representative nations as far east as Nova Scotia, and as far west as Mississippi river, and as far north as Hudson Bay."[366] Some records indicate that the Cree and Lakota (Sioux) Nations were also present at this event.[367]

Superintendent Johnson presented to the assembled delegates the terms of what he hoped would prove a Pax Britannica for North America.[368] He read the terms of the *Royal Proclamation*, requested a promise of peace, and urged a state of mutual non-interference.[369] Presents were exchanged to certify the binding nature of the Crown's promises.[370]

When the western Aboriginal nations accepted the peace, trade was reopened and guaranteed. Prisoners were returned, and the French were barred from the villages.

---

360   *Ibid.* at 328. Letter of Johnson to Gen. Gage, 19 February 1764.

361   *Ibid.*

362   *Ibid.*; Letter of Gage to the Earl of Halifax, 13 April 1764. NYCD, *supra* note 88, vol. 7 at 617-19.

363   Johnson Papers, *ibid.* at 481; PAC, Sulpician Documents, M. 1644, #70.

364   Johnson Papers, *ibid.* at 511; see also NYCD, *supra* note 88, vol 7 at 648-50; D. Braider, *The Niagara* (New York: Holt, Rinehart and Winston, 1972) at 137; W. W. Warren, *History of the Ojibway Indians* [1885] (St. Paul, Minn.: Ross & Haines, 1957) at 219 [reprint].

365   Johnson Papers, *ibid.* See also, W.G. Godfrey, *Pursuit of Profit and Preferment in Colonial North America: John Bradstreet's Quest* (Waterloo, Ont.: Wilfred Laurier Press, 1982) at 192.

366   P. Williams, "The Chain" (L.M Thesis, York University, 1982) [unpublished] at 79 [hereinafter "The Chain"].

367   *Ibid.*

368   "Letter of Johnson to Faye, March 16 1764" in Johnson Papers, *supra* note 241 at 487.

369   Johnson Papers, *ibid.* at 309-10; Braider, *supra* note 363 at 137.

370   Johnson Papers, *ibid.*; see also "The Chain," *supra* note 365 at 82.

Johnson delivered to the Ojibway a belt of the Covenant Chain to keep on behalf of the entire "Lakes Confederacy" at Michilimackinack. He also gave them, as symbol of the King's alliance and promises, a long belt showing the 24 nations holding hands, with a ship at one end and a rock at the other. Johnson stated:

> Brothers of the Western Nations, Sachems, Chiefs and Warriors, You have now been here for several days, during which time we have frequently met to renew and Strengthen our Engagements and you have made so many Promises of your Friendship and Attachment to the English that there now remains for us only to exchange the great Belt of the Covenant Chain that we may not forget out mutual Engagements.
>
> I now therefore present you the great Belt by which I bind all your Western Nations together with the English, and I desire that you will take fast hold of the same, and never let it slip, to which end I desire that after you have strewn this Belt to all Nations you will fix one end of it with the Chipeweighs at St. Marys [Michilimackinack] whilst the other end remains at my house, and moreover I desire that you will never listen to any news which comes to any other Quarter. If you do it, it may shake the Belt.[371]

After Johnson finished speaking, the Aboriginal nations used a two-row wampum belt to reflect their understanding of the treaties of Niagara and to incorporate the promises of the *Royal Proclamation*.[372] The two-row wampum belt illustrated an autonomous relationship founded on peace, friendship, and respect; no nation would interfere with the internal affairs of any other. The belt symbolized the existing treaty order; recasting the *Royal Proclamation's* wording, "the several Nations ... with whom we are connected ... should not be molested or disturbed ... ."

In the context of commenting on another treaty in 1765, Johnson articulated his understanding of the Aboriginal intent:

> these people had subscribed to a Treaty with me at Niagara in August last, but by the present Treaty I find, they make expressions of subjection, which must either have arisen from the ignorance of the Interpreter, or from some mistake; for I am well convinced, they never mean or intend anything like it, and that they can not be brought under our laws, for some Centuries, neither have they any word which can convey the most distant idea of subjection, and should it be fully explained to them, and the nature of subordination punishment ette [sic] defined, it might produce infinite harm ... and I dread its consequences,

---

371 Johnson Papers, *ibid.* According to Ojibway teaching the two belts remained together, moving from Mackinack to Drummond Island to Manitoulin Island. They were kept at Manitowaning and Wikwemikong for over a century. In 1786 Sir John Johnson gave the Ojibway a belt that resembled the 1764 belt his father had given. The new belt also showed two men holding hands, with a chain emerging at either end of them: it was a renewal of the Covenant Chain after the American Revolution.

372 *Ibid.*; Letter of Head to Glenleg, 20 August 1836—PAC, RG 10, vol. 391; J.B. Assikinack, "Memories of the Covenant Chain." *Ibid.*, PAC, RG 10, vol. 613 21/10/1851 at 440-443.

as I recollect that some attempts towards Sovereignty not long ago, was one of the principal causes of all our troubles ... .[373]

Even in the context of a conference with unusually strong representation of the parties
to the agreement, the vagaries of translation again proved decisive. Despite the con-
certed efforts by symbolic and other means to ensure clarity and commitment to the
terms of the treaty, its meanings remained conflicted and controversial.

7. Creating the Canadian-United States Border

In September 1783, the *Treaty of Paris* ended the American Revolution and
simultaneously left a disputed boundary. When the King ceded his interests to a vast
western boundary, extending to the Mississippi River, this jurisdictional transfer created a new northern boundary between British North America and the United States,
which ran through unceded Indian country, roughly along the 45th parallel. The northern border extended to the Sainte Croix River, including what is now called Vermont.
In the House of Lords, the Earl of Carisle complained about the *Treaty of Paris*:

> Twenty-five nations of Indians made over to the United States [and in return] not even that
> solitary stipulation which our honour should have made us insist upon, ... a place of refuge
> for those miserable persons ... , some haven for those shattered barks to have been laid up
> in quiet.[374]

On both sides of the border, Aboriginal nations and tribes were deeply disturbed by the
international boundary splitting their Hunting Grounds reserved under their treaties and
the 1763 Proclamation. Further, Article XV of the *Treaty of Utrecht* had immunized the
Aboriginal nations against the British and French claims that divided their territorial
sovereignty.

The Articles of Confederation of the United States initially placed the management of Indian Affairs in the 13 states rather than in a central government. The Eastern
Superintendency of Indian Affairs was managed by the State of Massachusetts.[375]

---

373 R.A. Williams, Jr., "The Algebra of Federal Indian Law: The Hard Trail of Decolonizing and Americanizing the White Man's Indian Jurisprudence" [1986] Wis. L. Rev. 219 at 283, quoting Johnson. See
also "Letter of Johnson to Gage. 31 October 1764" in Johnson Papers, *supra* note 242 at 395, for his
reading of a 1751 treaty conference minute: "I have been Just looking into the Indian Records where
I find in the Minutes of 1751 that those who made ye Entry Say, that Nine different Nations acknowledged themselves to be his Majesty's Subjects, altho I sat at that Conference, made entrys of all the
Transaction, in which there was not a word mentioned, which could imply a Subjection."

374 J.A. Combs, *The Jay Treaty; Political Battleground of the Founding Fathers* (Berkeley: University of
California Press, 1970) at 4, citing W. Cobbett, *The Parliamentary History of England*, vol. 22 (London: R. Bagshaw, 1818) at 377.

375 F. Kidder, *Military Operations in Eastern Maine and Nova Scotia during the Revolution: Chiefly Com-
piled from the Journals and Letters of Colonel John Allan, with Notes and a Memoir of Col. John Allan*
(Albany, N.Y.: Munsell, 1867) at 313-14.

Commissioner Allan, previously the Superintendent of the Eastern District, explained the border was irrelevant to Indian Affairs:

> Indians are not subject to, or amenable to, any power; they have been always viewed as a distinct body, governed by their own customs and manners, nor will they ever tamely submit to any authority different from their own, while they remain in the present uncivilized state. Their mode of life leads them thro' the Territory of different nations, their residence uncertain and changeable, that it can not be known where they really belong except that they were born in such a district and may be called by the name of the Tribe.[376]

The *Royal Proclamation of 1763* was incorporated into the United States law in the 1790 *Trade and Intercourse Act*.[377]

The Aboriginal nations argued that His Majesty had no right to divide their reserved dominion without their consent and without compensating them for their treaty, trade, and property losses. The Mohawks, for example, told General Maclean, British commander at Niagara, that His Majesty "had no right Whatever to grant away to the States of America, their Rights or properties without a manifest breach of all justice and Equity, and they would not submit to it."[378] They thought that this issue had been resolved long ago in the controversy surrounding the 1763 Proclamation and the treaties of Niagara, where Sir William Johnson assured the Haudensaunee leader:

> You are not to believe or even think that by the line which has been described it was meant to deprive you of an extent of your country which the right of the soil which belongs to you and is in yourselves as sole proprietors.[379]

On 15 August 1791, the Governor General of North America, Lord Dorchester, told the Confederated Nations in Quebec:

> But Brothers, this line, which the King then marked out between him and the States ... could never have prejudiced your rights. Brothers, the King's right with respect to your territory were against the nations of Europe: these he resigned to the States. But the King never had any rights against you, but to such parts of the country as had been fairly ceded by yourself with your own free consent, by public convention and sale. How then can it be said that he gave away your Lands?[380]

The United States and the British Crown responded to the controversy by affirming the special status of Aboriginal nations in their international negotiations. British and American diplomats, devotees of the theories of the Scottish economist Adam

---

376   *Ibid.* at 317-18.

377   C. 33, 1 Stat. 137.

378   B. Graymont, *The Iroquois in the American Revolution* (Syracuse, N.Y.: Syracuse University Press, 1972) at 260.

379   W.H. Mohr, *Federal Indian Relations, 1774-1788* (Philadelphia: University of Pennsylvania Press, 1933) at 118.

380   S. Bemis, *Jay's Treaty: A Study in Commerce and Diplomacy* (New Haven, Conn.: Yale University Press, 1962) at 158-59.

Smith, believed that a prosperous America would make England richer. Understanding also that the United States was fiscally constrained, the diplomats strove to eliminate any obstacles to trading with the resource-wealthy Aboriginal nations.

A. *Jay Treaty* (1794)

The first commercial treaty between the British Crown and the United States was signed on 19 November 1794. *The Jay Treaty, 1794—Treaty of Amity, Commerce, and Navigation* established a joint commission to settle boundary disputes, restored United States trade with the West Indies, guaranteed British evacuation of the old Northwest, and recognized the rights of the Aboriginal nations to cross and trade along the newly created international border. Article III provided:

> It is agreed that it shall at all times be free to ... the Indians dwelling on either side of the said boundary line, freely to pass and repass by land or inland navigation, into the respective territories and countries of the two parties, on the continent of America, ... and to navigate all the lakes, rivers, and waters thereof, and freely to carry on trade and commerce with each other.
>
> ...
>
> No duty of entry shall ever be levied by either party on peltries brought by land or inland navigation into the said territories respectively, nor shall the Indians passing or repassing with their own proper goods and effects of whatever nature, pay for the same any impost or duty whatever. But goods in bales, or other large packages, unusual among Indians, shall not be considered as goods belonging bona fide to Indians.[381]

Article XXVIII provided that "...the first ten articles of this treaty shall be permanent," vesting the Indian trading liberties, free commerce, and navigation across the boundary line as permanent rights and obligations.

The nature of these treaty obligations was clarified when the United States and several Western Aboriginal nations concluded a 1795 treaty.[382] Article VIII of this treaty stipulated that all traders residing at any Indian town or hunting camp were required to hold a licence issued by the United States.[383] His Majesty considered this an infringement of Article III of the 1794 treaty, since it interfered with the British-Indian fur trade. To show that the United States was not abrogating the 1794 treaty, the United States and Great Britain entered an explanatory article in 1796 that declared:[384]

---

381 Treaty of 1794, 12 Bevans 13, (in force on 28 October 1795); 8 Stat. 116; U.S. Treaty Series No. 105 (U.S. Dept. of State) [hereinafter *Jay Treaty*].

382 Treaty with the Wyandots, and Other Indian Tribes, 3 August 1795, United States-Wyandot, Delaware and Other Indian Tribes, 7 Stat. 49.

383 *Ibid.*: "Trade shall be opened with the said Indian tribes;[...] but no person, shall be permitted to reside at any of their towns or hunting camps as a trader, who is not furnished with a license for that purpose, under the hand and seal of the superintendent of the department north-west of the Ohio ... and if any person shall intrude himself as a trader, without such license, the said Indian shall take and bring him before the superintendent or his deputy, to be dealt with according to law."(7 Stat. at 52).

384 4 May 1796, United States-Great Britain, 8 Stat. 130, (1796) U.S. Treaty Series No. 106.

...[T]hat *no stipulations in any treaty subsequently concluded by either of the contracting parties* with any other State or nation, or with any Indian tribe, can be understood to derogate in any manner from the rights of free intercourse and commerce, secured by the aforesaid third article of the [Jay Treaty] ... to the subjects of His Majesty and to the citizens of the United States, and to the Indians dwelling on either side of the boundary line aforesaid; but that all the said persons shall remain at *full liberty* freely to pass and repass, by land or inland navigation, into the respective territories and countries of the contracting parties, on either side of the boundary line, and freely to carry on trade and commerce with each other, according to the stipulations of the said [Jay Treaty].[385]

The following year, in 1796, the British Deputy Superintendent of Indian Affairs for the Northern Department, Alexander McKee, explained this provision to the head of the Putuswakn Confederacy[386] at Chenail Escarte, Upper Canada.[387] The Deputy Superintendent stated that, despite the border established by the 1763 *Treaty of Paris*, Aboriginal trade and land were protected under His Majesty's 1794 treaty with the United States:

The United States have at last fulfilled the Treaty of 1783 and the justice of the King toward all the World, would not suffer him to withhold [your] rights ... . [His Majesty] has taken the greatest care of the rights and independence of all the Indian nations who by the last Treaty with America, are to be perfectly free and unmolested in their trade and hunting grounds and to pass and repass freely undisturbed to trade with whom they please.[388]

The Putuswakn sent a messenger to the allied nations to convey this message. The *Jay Treaty* provisions were incorporated into United States law by the federal tariff acts in 1795.[389] British authority incorporated the treaties by an order of the governor-in-council (7 July 1796) in British North America:

And His Excellency the Governor by and with the advice and consent of the Said Executive Council doth hereby further order, that no Duty of Entry shall be payable or be levied or demanded by any Custom House Officer or other person or persons on any Peltries brought by land or inland Navigation into the said Province, and that Indians passing or repassing with their own proper goods and effects of whatever nature, shall not be liable to pay for such goods and effects, any impost or Duty whatever, unless the same shall be goods in Bales or other large Packages unusual among Indians, which shall not be considered as goods belonging bona fide to Indians or as goods intitled to the foregoing Exemption from Duties and imports.[390]

---

385 *Ibid.* 8 Stat. 130.

386 See *supra* note 245.

387 PAC, RG 10, to the Ojibaway, Potowatomi, Huron, and Ottawa.

388 *Ibid.* cited in Atkey, "Three Nations, Three Views" (1983) 14 *Ontario Indian* at 16-17.

389 1 Stat. 116; 8 U.S.C § 1395 (1986).

390 Cited in *R. v. Vincent*, [1993] 2 C.N.L.R. 165 (Ont. C.A.), leave to appeal refused, [1993] 3 S.C.R. ix (S.C.C.).

B. *Treaty of 1814*

At the end of the Anglo-American War of 1812, one of the key British negotiating points related to the rights of Aboriginal nations.[391] The British demanded that the United States recognize an independent Indian buffer state in the old Northwest Territory or Ohio:

> The ceded country was inhabited by numerous tribes and nations of Indians, *who were independent* of both of us and of the Americans. They were the real proprietors of the land, and we had no right to transfer to others what did not belong to ourselves. This injustice was greatly aggravated by the consideration, that those Aboriginal nations had been our faithful allies during the whole of the contest, and, yet no stipulation was made in their favour.[392]

When the United States objected, the British negotiators pointed out that the United States' treaties with the Aboriginal nations had already created such a buffer zone.[393] The United States delegation, headed by John Quincy Adams, agreed to affirm and restore the pre-war Aboriginal and treaty rights.

The *Treaty of Peace and Amity* (1814)[394] affirmed and restored the Aboriginal rights disturbed by the War of 1812. Article IX stipulated:

> The United States of America engage to put an end, ... to hostilities with all the tribes or nations of Indians ... and ... to restore to such tribes or nations, respectively, all the possessions, rights, and privileges which they may have enjoyed or been entitled to in one thousand eight hundred and eleven, previous to such hostilities. ... And his Britannic Majesty engages, ... to restore to such tribes or nations respectively all the possessions, rights, and privileges which they may have enjoyed or been entitled to in one thousand eight hundred and eleven, previous to such hostilities.[395]

In 1815, the British Deputy Superintendent General of Indian Affairs, William Claus, explained to the Putuswakn in Burlington, Upper Canada[396] the meaning of Article IX of the 1814 treaty:

> I am further instructed to inform you that in making Peace with the Government of the United States of America, your interests were not neglected nor would Peace have been made with them had they not consented to include you in the Treaty which they at first refused to listen to–I will now repeat to you one of the Articles of the Treaty of Peace which secures you the peaceable possession of all the country which you possessed before

---

391 N. Atcheson, *A Compressed View of the Points to be Discussed in Treating with the United States of America* (London: J.M. Richardson, 1814) at 5.

392 *Ibid.* [emphasis in original].

393 See Bemis, *supra* note 380 at 160; Barsh & Henderson, "Aboriginal Rights," *supra* note 51 at 39-45.

394 24 December 1814, 12 Bevans 41 (in force on 17 February 1815); 8 Stat. 218; U.S. Treaty Series 109 (U.S. Dept. of State) [often called *Treaty of Ghent*].

395 *Ibid.*

396 As well as Hurons, Delawares, Chippewas, Sauks, Creeks, Moravians, and Six Nations.

the late War, and the Road is now open and free for you to pass and repass it without interruption.[397]

Again, the "peaceable possession of all the country" and the "Road" to free trade were
guaranteed to the Aboriginal nations and tribes. This has been affirmed as an international treaty obligation continually since the *Treaty of Utrecht*.

Through the Chiefs at Caughnawaga, the Putuswakn described their understanding of the "Road" to the Passamaquoddies in a wampum belt in 1870:

> In answer also to the Wampum which you have sent to us in return therefore we send to
> you ours, specifying our Treaty that took place A.D. 1810 [sic]. Therefore, all nations and
> tribes of Indians from the East and West and from the North and South wherein our Chiefs
> from every nation and tribe were present, therefore we should bind the good-doing of our
> ancestors in its Treaty of peace. The English and American generals were present having
> freed all the Indian of Wars incurring between them, and no Boundary line should exist
> between us Indian Brethren, not any duties, taxes, or customs should be levied on us.[398]

As promised in Article IX, the United States negotiated a restoration in *Treaty of
Spring Wells* (1815) with the Aboriginal nations involved in the war.[399] It restored their
pre-war "possessions, rights, and privileges" including the "station and property"
which their chiefs had held previous to the war.[400]

C. Treaties of Upper Canada

In Upper Canada, the Indian affairs department consistently applied the principles of the *Royal Proclamation of 1763*, recognizing Aboriginal rights to land and self-
government. Out of the cooperative and protective relationship between Aboriginal
nations and the British Crown came a series of treaties that transferred land to the
Crown.[401] A 1790 document illustrates the complexity of transferring parts of Aboriginal tenure to the Crown:

> KNOW ALL MEN BY THESE PRESENTS, that we the principals Village and War Chief of the
> Ottawa, Chippawa, Pottowatony and Huron Indians Nations of Detroit for and in consid-
> eration of the Sum of Twelve Hundred Pounds Currency of the Province of Quebec at Five
> Shillings per Spanish Dollar for valuable Wares and merchandise to us delivered by the
> hand of Alexander McKee, Esquire, Deputy Agent of Indian Affairs, the receipt whereof
> we do hereby acknowledge, have by and with the consent of the whole of our said Nations,

---

397 Atkey, *supra* note 389 at 17.

398 Letter from the Chiefs at Caughwanaga to the Passamaquoddies, 27 November 1870, reprinted in *The
     Circle* (August 1977).

399 8 September 1815, United States-Wayandot, and other Tribes of Indian, 7 Stat. 131.

400 *Ibid.* at Arts. 2 and 3.

401 These provisional and confirmatory surrenders can be found in the three volumes of *Indian Treaties
     and Surrenders* (Ottawa: Queen Printers, 1891); facsimile editions reprinted by Coles Publishing Com-
     pany in Toronto, 1971, and by Fifth House Publishers (1992) [hereinafter *Surrenders*].

given, granted, enfeoffed, alienated, and confirmed, and by these presents to give, grant, enfeoff, alien and confirm unto His Majesty George the Third, King of Great Britain, France, and Ireland ... a certain Tract of Land ...

To have and to hold the said Lands and Premises hereby given and granted, mentioned or intended to be given and granted unto His said Majesty George the Third, His Heirs and Successors for the only proper use and behoof of His said Majesty George the Third, His Heirs and Successors forever.

And we the said Chiefs for ourselves and the whole of our Nations our and their Heirs, Executors and administrators do convenant, promise and grant to and with His said Majesty George the Third, His Heirs and Successors by these presents that His said Majesty His Heirs and Successors shall and lawfully may from henceforth and for ever after Peaceably and quietly have, hold, occupy, possess and enjoy the said tract of land hereby given and granted, mentioned and intended to be given and granted with all and every of the appurtenances free, clear, and discharged or well and sufficiently saved, kept harmless and indemnified of, from and against all former and other gifts, grants, bargains and sale and of, from and against all former and other Titles, troubles, charges, or incumbrances whatever, had, done or suffered, or to be had done or suffered by any of us the said Chiefs, or by anyone whatever of the said Nations our and their Heirs, Executors or administrators; And by these presents do make this our act and Deed irrevocable under any pretence whatever, and have put His said Majesty in full possession and seizen by allowing houses to be built upon the Premises.[402]

From this surrender, the treaty reserved several tracts for the Chiefs:

The reversion and reversions, remainder and remainders, rents and service of the said premises and all the estate, right, title, interest, property, claim or demand whatsoever of us the said chiefs or any other person or person whatever of our said nations, of, in, and to the said tract of land, or, of, in, and to every part and parcel thereof excepting the reserve aforesaid.[403]

When, after the treaty of 1814 and the Napoleonic wars the British home government "swept away the paupers" (its surplus people no longer needed for military campaigning)[404] to the British colonies, the settler population in eastern and central Canada grew rapidly, eventually outnumbering the Aboriginal population by ten to one.[405] From 1815 to the 1850s, there were hundreds of land transactions in Upper Canada, whereby Aboriginal tribes, many of which had existing treaties with the Crown, transferred their protected land under the *Royal Proclamation* to the imperial Crown. Recorded Aboriginal teachings in 1829 described the Aboriginal nations' intent in the agreements:

---

402 *Ibid.*, vol. 1 at 1-2.

403 *Ibid.* at 2. This treaty surrender was held as valid and binding, *R. v. Riley* (1983), [1984] 2 C.N.L.R. 154 (Ont. Prov. Offences Ct.).

404 RCAP, *supra* note 75, vol. 1 at 141, citing J.R. Miller, *Skyscrapers Hide the Heavens: A History of Indian-White Relations in Canada*, revised ed. (Toronto: University of Toronto Press, 1989) at 92.

405 RCAP, *ibid.*

Our Great Father ... said: 'The white people are getting thick around you and we are afraid they, or the yankees will cheat you out of your land, you had better put it into the hands of your very Great Father the King to keep for you till you want to settle. And he will appropriate it for your good and he will take care of it; and will take you under his wing, and keep you under his arm, & give you schools, and build houses for you when you want to settle'. Some of these words we thought were good; but we did not like to give up all our lands, as some were afraid that our great father would keep our land ... so we said 'yes', keep our land for us. Our great father then thinking it would be best for us sold all our land to some white men. This made us very sorry for we did not wish to sell it ... .[406]

The surrenders were either provisional or confirmatory. The relationship between earlier peace and friendship treaties and these later land purchase or land surrender agreements is not clear.

An example was the provisional agreement in 1819 between the Principal Men of the Chippewa nation and John Aiken, Esquire on behalf of His Majesty:

Witnesseth: that for and in consideration of the yearly sum of six hundred pounds Province currency, one-half in specie and the other in goods at the Montreal price, to be well and truly paid yearly and every year by His said majesty to the said Chippewa nation inhabiting and claiming the said tract of land which may be otherwise now as follows: ... ; and the said Adjutant, Weggishigomin, Cabibonike, Pagitaniquatoibe and Kawahkitahquebi, as well for themselves as for the Mississagua nation inhabiting and claiming the said tract of land as above described, do freely, fully and voluntarily surrender and convey the same to His Majesty without reservation or limitation in perpetuity. And the said William Claus, on behalf of His Majesty does hereby, promise and agree to pay to the said nation of Indians inhabiting as above mentioned, yearly and every year for ever the said sum of five hundred and twenty two pound ten shillings currency in goods at the Montreal price, which sum the Principal Chiefs and people, parties hereunto, acknowledge as a full consideration for the lands hereby sold and conveyed to His Majesty.[407]

These rentals remained under Aboriginal tenure, with the Crown having the use rights for annual payment of rent. Other provisional agreements with the Crown were often followed by indentures that provided additional annual compensation for "grant, bargain, sell, release, surrender and forever yielded up unto His said Majesty" other described parcels within Aboriginal tenure. The written English documents that conveyed some of the Aboriginal tenure to the Crown became standardized, although they were sometimes inaccurate or vague. After the initial purchase of land, there were invariably second or third purchases, and gradually, as the sale of their lands progressed, Aboriginal nations were confined to smaller and smaller tracts, typically in

---

406 A Statement of the Mississauga Indians Settled at Credit River, Agreed on in Their Council, 3 April 1829—NAC, RG 10, vol. 5, No. 2082-2084. The Mississauga are Ojibwa and inhabited most of south-central Ontario at the time of British settlement in the late eighteenth century.

407 *Ibid.* at 47-48. In *Henry v. The King* (1905), 9 Ex. C.R. 417, 3 C.N.L.C. 89 (Can. Ex. Ct.), it was held that a similar proceeds of the fixed yearly sum amounted to a Crown obligation. The disposition of surrendered lands by a treaty indenture of 28 October 1818 (Aietance Purchase, No. 19) applied to the maintenance of the Indians. See also *R. v. Taylor and Williams* (1981), 34 O.R. (2d) 360 (Ont. C.A.), affirming (1979), 55 C.C.C. (2d) 172 (Ont. Div. Ct.) (interpretation of *Treaty No. 20* of 1818).

areas that were least suited to European settlement, agriculture, or resource extraction. At the same time, the economies and resource-use patterns of Aboriginal nations were undermined.

8. Victorian Treaties

A. Manitoulin and Saugeen Treaties, 1836

Sir Francis Bond Head, the lieutenant-governor of Upper Canada between 1836 and 1838, sought to acquire the use of Aboriginal tenure for the immigrants. At a large gathering of Ojibwa and Odawa people at Manitoulin Island in August 1836, called for the purpose of making the annual distribution of presents, he proposed two major land transactions. These treaties were different from other treaties in that they were a recorded address from the lieutenant-governor:

> MY CHILDREN:
>
> Seventy snow seasons have now passed away since we met in Council at the crooked place (Niagara), at which time and place your Great Father, the King, and the Indians of North American tied their hands together by the wampum of friendship.
>
> Since that period various circumstances have occurred to separate from your Great Father many of his red children, and as an unavoidable increase of white population, as well as the progress of cultivation, have had the natural effect of impoverishing your hunting grounds it has become necessary that new arrangements should be entered into for the purpose of protecting you from the encroachments of the whites. ... If you would cultivate your lands it would then be considered your own property, ... but uncultivated land is like wild animals, and your Great Father, who has hitherto protected you, has now great difficulty in securing it for you from the whites, who are hunting to cultivate it.[408]

Adopting a paternal tone of concern, the address invokes a logic of inevitable encroachment on Aboriginal lands left uncultivated. The first arrangement involved relinquishing Aboriginal claims to the many islands of the Manitoulin chain and making "them the property (under your Great Father's control) of all Indians whom he shall allow to reside on them,"[409] with the promise that the region would be protected as Aboriginal territory. In particular, Bond Head proposed to provide Manitoulin Island as a protected place where they could continue their traditional pursuits in a location far removed from non-Aboriginal influences.

The second proposal involved the Lower Saugeen Peninsula, the territory of the Saugeen Ojibwa, who he proposed should move either to the Manitoulin Island region or to the northern end of what is now called the Bruce Peninsula, in the area north of Owen Sound. The Crown promised that "proper houses shall be built for you, and prop-

---

408 *Surrenders, supra* note 401, vol. 1 at 112.

409 *Ibid.* at 112-113.

er assistance given to enable you to become civilized and to cultivate land."[410] After some initial resistance, the Saugeen Ojibwa agreed to "surrender to your Great Father" over 607,000 hectares of land, and moved to the Bruce Peninsula,[411] with the assurance that "your Great Father engages for ever to protect you from encroachment of the whites."[412]

The treaties of 1836 made provision to set aside the Manitoulin Island area as a reserve, and some Indian people—perhaps some 1,000 to 1,400 persons by 1850—made the move to the island. Whereas the agents of the Crown assumed that the 1836 agreement gave the Crown title to the island, the Aboriginal nations, represented by Chief Edowishcosh, an Odawa chief from Sheshegwaning, rejected this premise:

> I have heard what you have said, and the words you have been sent to say to us. I wish to tell you what my brother Chiefs and warriors, women and children say. The Great Spirit gave our forefathers land to live upon, and our forefathers wished us to keep it. The land upon which we now are is our own, and we intend to keep it. The whites should not come and take our land from us, they ought to have stayed on the other side of the salt water to work the land there. The Great Spirit would be angry with us if we parted with our land, and we don't want to make him angry. That is all I have to say.[413]

By the early 1860s, the demand for land from non-Aboriginal interests led to a further initiative to gain control of the Manitoulin Island lands, and caused the government to proclaim the "experiment" of reserved lands a failure. In 1861-62, agents of the Crown and the government of the Province of Canada approached the Odawa and Ojibwa nations of Manitoulin, seeking to release the government from its 1836 promise to reserve the lands exclusively for Aboriginal use. The negotiations were conducted by commissioners William McDougall, the superintendent general of Indian affairs, and William Spragge. The negotiations in October 1862 were tense and difficult, with opposition particularly strong in the eastern portion of the island where the government's quest was deemed to be a betrayal of its 1836 promise. McDougall adjourned the proceedings over a weekend, "informing the Indians that those who were disposed to continue the negotiations would remain while those who had resolved to reject every proposition of the government might go home."[414] On the following Monday, he presented a revised proposal to the remaining Aboriginals excluding the territory of the eastern portion of the island. The agreement to open the western part of the island to non-Aboriginal settlement was therefore struck with a minority of the Aboriginal inhabitants on the island.[415] For seven hundred dollars and interest on the sum, the western Aboriginals:

410   *Ibid.* at 133.

411   *Ibid.* Also see O. Dickason, *Canada's First Nations: A History of Founding Peoples from Earliest Times* (Toronto: McClelland & Stewart, 1992) at 238.

412   *Surrenders, ibid.*

413   NAC, RG 10, vol. 262, pt. 1, no. 1436.

414   "Report from William McDougall to His Excellency the Governor General in Council, 3 November, 1862" in Morris, *supra* note 53 at 23.

415   *Surrenders, supra* note 401, vol. 1 at 235-36; W.R. Wightman, *Forever on the Fringe: Six Studies in the Development of Manitoulin Island* (Toronto: University of Toronto Press, 1982) at 40-46.

have, and hereby do release, surrender and give up to Her Majesty the Queen, all the right, title, interest and claims of the parties of the second part, and of the Ottawa, Chippewa and other Indians in whose behalf they act, of, in and to the Great Manitoulin Island, and also, of, in and to the islands adjacent which have been deemed or claimed by to appurtenant or belonging thereto, to have and to hold the same, and every part thereof, to her Majesty, Her heirs and successors forever.[416]

The western part of the Island would be surveyed and opened up for settlement. The Crown promised to grant by deed a certain amount of land for the benefit of each family and Ojibwa residing on the western part of the Island. The interest from the sale would be paid annually, minus the administration costs of the Superintendent. While the Ojibwa retained their fishing rights, the eastern Ojibwa remained "under the protection of the Government as formerly."[417]

B. The Lake Huron and Lake Superior Treaties of 1850

In 1841 Upper and Lower Canada joined to become the Province of Canada and subsequently leases were issued to companies to explore and mine in Ojibwa territories. Resistance by the Ojibwa to non-Aboriginal miners and surveyors had been evident for some time. From 1846 to 1849 hostilities simmered, and in 1849 Chief Shingwakonce and Chief Nebanagoching from Sault Ste. Marie addressed the Governor General in Montreal, expressing their frustration with four years of failure to address their concerns about mining incursions on their lands:

> Can you lay claim to our land? If so, by what right? Have you conquered it from us? You have not, for when you first came among us your children were few and weak, and the war cry of the Ojibway struck terror to the heart of the pale face. But you came not as an enemy, you visited us in the character of a friend. Have you purchased it from us, or have we surrendered it to you? If so when? and how? and where are the treaties?[418]

On behalf of the Crown, Commissioner William Robinson proposed that treaties be made to pursue the objectives of settlement north of the lakes, to mine valuable minerals, and to assert British jurisdiction in the face of American incursions in the area.[419] In September 1850 negotiations for the Robinson Huron and Superior treaties were concluded. The written treaties described the agreement as a purchase of Aboriginal tenure:

> THAT for, and in consideration of the sum of two thousand pounds of good and lawful money of Upper Canada, to them in hand paid, and for the further perpetual annuity of six hundred pounds of like money, the same to be paid and delivered to the said Chiefs and their Tribes at a convenient season of each year, of which due notice will be given, at such places

---

416 *Ibid.*

417 *Ibid.*

418 James Morrison, "The Robinson Treaties of 1850: A Case Study" (1993) [unpublished, research study prepared for RCAP, *supra* note 75] [hereinafter Morrison, "Robinson Treaties"].

419 *Ibid.*

as may be appointed for that purpose, they the said Chiefs and Principal men, on behalf of their respective Tribes or Bands, do hereby fully, freely, and voluntarily surrender, cede, grant, and convey unto Her Majesty, her heirs and successors for ever, all their right, title, and interest to, and in the whole of, the territory above described, save and except the reservations set forth in the schedule hereunto annexed; which reservations shall be held and occupied by the said Chiefs and their Tribes in common, for their own use and benefit.[420]

Such terminology had not been used or agreed to in negotiations. The Ojibwa understood that the treaties involved only a limited use of their land for purposes of exploiting subsurface rights where minerals were discovered;[421] they were to share in revenues from resource exploitation,[422] annuities, or cash to increase as revenues increased.[423] The treaties continued the "full and free privileges" of Aboriginal peoples to hunt in their traditional way throughout most of the surrendered territories.[424]

---

420   Also the further sum of £160 provincial currency were paid to the Indians inhabiting French River and Lake Nipissing.

421   Morrison, "Robinson Treaties," *supra* note 418.

422   And should the said Chiefs and their respective Tribes at any time desire to dispose of any part of such reservations, or of any mineral or other valuable productions thereon, the same will be sold or leased at their request by the Superintendent-General of Indian Affairs for the time being, or other officer having authority so to do, for their sole benefit, and to the best advantage; The parties of the second part further promise and agree that they will not sell, lease, or otherwise dispose of any portion of their Reservations without the consent of the Superintendent-General of Indian Affairs, or other officer of like authority, being first had and obtained. Nor will they at any time hinder or prevent persons from exploring or searching for minerals, or other valuable productions, in any part of the Territory hereby ceded to Her Majesty, as before mentioned. The parties of the second part also agree, that in case the Government of this Province should before the date of this agreement have sold, or bargained to sell, any mining locations, or other property, on the portions of the Territory hereby reserved for their use; then and in that case such sale, or promise of sale, shall be perfected by the Government, if the parties claiming it shall have fulfilled all the conditions upon which such locations were made, and the amount accruing therefore shall be paid to the Tribe to whom the Reservation belongs.

423   The said William Benjamin Robinson, on behalf of Her Majesty, who desires to   deal liberally and justly with all her subjects, further promises and agrees, that should the Territory hereby ceded by the parties of the second part at any future period produce such an amount as will enable the Government of this Province, without incurring loss, to increase the annuity hereby secured to them, then and in that case the same shall be augmented from time to time, provided that the amount paid to each individual shall not exceed the sum of one pound Provincial Currency in any one year, or such further sum as Her Majesty may be graciously pleased to order; and provided further that the number of Indians entitled to the benefit of this treaty shall amount to two-thirds of their present number, which is fourteen hundred and twenty-two, to entitle them to claim the full benefit thereof. And should they not at any future period amount to two-thirds of fourteen hundred and twenty-two, then the said annuity shall be diminished in proportion to their actual numbers.

The provision for an increase in the extremely small annuities was adjusted only once—in the 1870s. When the Ojibwa requested a further increase to reflect the real profits, the federal government's response was to rely on the English text of the treaties, which stated that such further sums were limited to what "Her Majesty may be graciously pleased to order." Morris, *supra* note 53 at 303.

424   Morris, *ibid.*: "...and further to allow the said Chiefs and their Tribes the full and free privilege to hunt over the Territory now ceded by them, and to fish in the waters thereof, as they have heretofore been in the habit of doing; saving and excepting such portions of the said Territory as may from time to time be sold or leased to individuals or companies of individuals, and occupied by them with the consent of the Provincial Government."

C. Vancouver Island Treaties 1850-1854

Between 1850 and 1854, William Douglas, governor of the Vancouver Island colony, entered into 14 treaties with the Aboriginal nations of southern Vancouver Island,[425] a Crown colony separate from British Columbia. These treaties followed a common format, of which the Teechamitsa Tribe is an early model:

> Know all men, we, the chiefs and people of the Teechamitsa Tribe, who have signed our names and made our marks to this deed on the twenty-ninth day of April, one thousand eight hundred and fifty, do consent to surrender, entirely and forever, to James Douglas, the agent of the Hudson's Bay Company in Vancouver Island, that it to say, for the Governor, Deputy Governor and Committee on the same, the whole of the lands situated and lying between Equismalt Harbour and Point Albert, including the latter, on the Straits of Juan de Fuca, and extending backward from thence to the range of mountains on the Saaanich Arm, about ten miles distant.
>
> The conditions of or understanding of this sale is this, that our village sites and enclosed fields are to be kept for our own use, for the use of our children, and for those who may follow after us; and the land shall be properly surveyed, hereafter. It is understood however, that the land itself, with these small exceptions, become the entire property of the white people forever; it is also understood that we are at liberty to hunt over the unoccupied lands, and to carry on our fisheries as formerly.
>
> We have received, as payment, Twenty seven pounds ten shillings sterling.
>
> In token whereof, we have signed our names and made our marks, at Fort Victoria, 29 April, 1850.[426]

Similar treaties were made with Kosampson Tribe, Swengwhung Tribe, Chilcowitch Tribe, Whyomilth, Cre-ko-nein Tribe, Ka-ky-aakan Tribe, Chewbaytsum Tribe, Sooke Tribe, Saanich Tribe, Queackar Tribe, Quakeolth Tribe, Saalequun Tribe, and the Isnettucet Tribe.[427]

In a recent decision, Justice McLachlin reviewed the context and tragic outcome of these treaties:

> An early governor, Governor Douglas, pronounced a policy of negotiating solemn treaties with the [A]boriginal peoples similar to that pursued elsewhere in Canada. Tragically, that policy was overtaken by the less generous views that accompanied the rapid settlement of British Columbia. The policy of negotiating treaties with the [A]boriginals was never formally abandoned. It was simply overridden, as the settlers, aided by administrations more concerned for short-term solutions than the duty of the Crown toward the first peoples of the colony settled where they wished and allocated to the [A]boriginals what they deemed appropriate. This did not prevent the [A]boriginal peoples of British Columbia from per-

---

425 See *Papers Connected with the Indian Land Question, 1850-1875* (Victoria, B.C.: R. Wolfenden, 1875) at 5-11.

426 *Ibid.*

427 *Ibid.*

sistently asserting their right to an honourable settlement of their ancestral rights—a settlement which most of them still await. Nor does it negate the fundamental proposition acknowledged generally throughout Canada's history of settlement that the [A]boriginal occupants of particular territories have the right to use and be sustained by those territories.[428]

D. Numbered treaties

In the western Indian country protected by the *Royal Proclamation*, the imperial treaty commissioners were instructed to "establish friendly relations" with the Aboriginal nations and tribes.[429] The treaties reconciled Aboriginal sovereignty and tenure in the territories. In the English text of the 11 numbered Victorian treaties the Chiefs and Headmen agreed to:

> open up for settlement and immigration, trade and such other purposes as Her Majesty may seem meet, a tract of country [described] so that there may be peace and good will between [the Chief and Headmen of the Indians] and Her Majesty and between them and Her Majesty's other subjects, and that Her Indian people may know and be assured of what allowance they are to count upon and receive from Her Majesty's bounty and benevolence.[430]

The written text also provides the Aboriginal tribes "do hereby cede, release, surrender, and yield up to the Government of the Dominion of Canada, for Her Majesty the Queen, and Her successors forever, all their rights, titles and privileges whatsoever, to the lands [described]."[431] The ratification or adhesion treaties to the central treaty is different in language and emphasis: "we transfer, surrender and relinquish" to her Majesty the Queen "for the use" of the Government of the Dominion.[432] Furthermore, these written terms were never discussed in any treaty negotiations.[433]

The Aboriginal chiefs promised to maintain "peace and good order" in the "ceded" or "transferred" land among all residents; to strictly observe the treaty; to respect, obey, and abide by the law;[434] and to aid in prosecuting certain violations by

---

428   *Van der Peet, supra* note 1 at 273.

429   Lewis H. Thomas, *The Struggle for Responsible Government in the North-West Territories, 1870-97*, 2d ed. (Toronto: University of Toronto Press, 1978).

430   *Treaty No. 4*, in Morris, *supra* note 53. The wording varies slightly in other treaties. Other purposes mentioned in the treaties are limited to travel, mining, and lumbering. Not only is there considerable doubt surrounding this technical language, but also it is often the case that the terms of the treaties are inconsistent with the oral promises made to the First Nations.

431   *Ibid.*

432   *Ibid.*

433   RCAP, *supra* note 75, vol. 1 at 175.

434   This bore a special meaning for Aboriginal leaders who undertook to make the treaties part of their own constitutional teachings. Manitoba, *Report of the Aboriginal Justice Inquiry of Manitoba*, vol. 1 (Winnipeg: Queen's Printer, 1991) at 17-46.

Indians in the ceded lands. The common article of the Victorian treaties concerning legal jurisdiction made these provisions:

> the undersigned Chiefs on their own behalf and on behalf of all other Indians inhabiting the tract within ceded, do hereby solemnly promise and engage to strictly observe this Treaty, and also to conduct and behave themselves as good and loyal subjects of Her Majesty the Queen.
>
> They promise and engage that they will in all respects obey and abide by the law, that they will maintain peace and good order between each other, and also between themselves and other tribes of Indians, and between themselves and others of Her Majesty's subjects, whether Indians or whites, now inhabiting or hereafter to inhabit any part of the said ceded tracts and that they will not molest the person or property of any inhabitant of such ceded tracts, or the property of Her Majesty the Queen, or interfere with or trouble any person passing or travelling through the said tracts, or any part thereof, and that they will aid and assist the officers of Her Majesty in bringing to justice and punishment any Indian offending against the stipulations of this Treaty, or infringing the laws in force in the country so ceded.[435]

Because the Red River territory had been occupied by the Cree, the Assiniboine, the Lakota and, more recently, the Ojibwa, the treaty discussions revolved around who had the authority to make the treaty. The *Selkirk Treaty* of 18 July 1817 was made between Lord Selkirk and three Ojibwa chiefs and the eastern branch of the Cree. The treaty secured two miles on either side of the Red River as a settlement site for one thousand Scottish families, for a consideration of one hundred pounds of tobacco and other goods in rent annually.[436] When it was proposed in the 1860s to transfer Rupert's Land to Canada, the uncertainty of the *Selkirk Treaty* necessitated the negotiation of *Treaties 1* and 2.

Ojibwa tribes in Indian country demanded treaties before they would allow the Crown to enter or use their lands and resources. They were not prepared to give up their lands, on which they depended for their livelihood, without a formal relationship that would protect and respect their jurisdiction, lands, and resources. By 1870 the Ojibwa at Portage notified the Crown that they wished to make a treaty and discuss compensation.[437] They also warned settlers not to cut wood or take possession of the lands on which they were squatting and indicated that "they were unwilling to allow the settlers the free use of the country for themselves or their cattle."[438] Until a treaty was con-

---

435 *Treaty No. 6*, in Morris, *supra* note 53 [emphasis added]. See J.Y. Henderson, "Implementing the Treaty Order" in R. Gosse, J.Y. Henderson, and R. Carter, eds., *Continuing Poundmaker & Riel's Quest: Presentations Made At a Conference on Aboriginal Peoples and Justice* (Saskatoon, Sk.: Purich Publishing, 1994) at 52. In *Treaties Nos. 8* and *10*, *supra* note 78, the Chiefs promised they would maintain peace.

436 Morris, *supra* note 53 at 13-15. For a discussion of the *Selkirk Treaty*, see Jim Gallo, "The Yellow Quill Band and The Land Question: The 1906 Expropriation and the 1908 Land Surrender of part of Swan Lake Reserve I.R. No. 7" (May 1977, revised March 1978) [unpublished, Treaties and Aboriginal Rights Research].

437 Morris, *ibid.* at 26.

438 *Ibid.*

cluded, they would allow the settlers to remain. John L. Tobias described the conditions, concerns, and initiatives that prompted these treaties:

> [I]n 1871, Canada had no plan on how to deal with the Indians and the negotiation of treaties was not at the initiative of the Canadian government, but at the insistence of the Ojibwa Indians of the North-West Angle and the Saulteaux of the tiny province of Manitoba. What is ignored by the traditional interpretation is that the Treaty process only started after Yellow Quill's band of Saulteaux turned back settlers who tried to go west of Portage la Prairie, and after other Saulteaux leaders insisted upon enforcement of the Selkirk Treaty or, more often, insisted upon making a new Treaty. Also ignored is the fact that the Ojibwa of the North-West Angle demanded rents, and created the fear of violence against prospective settlers who crossed their land or made use of their territory, if Ojibwa rights to their lands were not recognized. This pressure and fear of resulting violence is what motivated the government to begin the Treaty-making process.[439]

Following an unsuccessful attempt to negotiate a treaty in the Fort Frances region in early 1871, treaty discussions were begun with the Ojibwa tribes. The lieutenant-governor of Manitoba and the Northwest Territories, Adams G. Archibald, addressed them:

> ...till land and raise food, and store it up against a time of want. [But the Great Mother has] no idea of compelling you to do so. This she leaves to your choice, and you need not live like the white man unless you can be persuaded to do so of your own free will ... .

> Your Great Mother, therefore, will lay aside for you 'lots' of land to be used by you and your children forever. She will not allow the white man to intrude upon these lots. She will make rules to keep them for you ... as long as the sun shall shine ... .[440]

Lieutenant-Governor Archibald emphasized that they would not be compelled to settle on reserves and that they would be able to continue their traditional way of life and hunt as they always had. Negotiations respecting land, the size of reserves, and the size of annuities were long and difficult. Commissioners had trouble "in getting them to understand the views of the Government—they wishing to have two thirds of the province as a reserve." Eventually a treaty was concluded, but only after the Portage Indians withdrew from negotiations.[441]

The question of how much land would be ceded to the Crown was finally resolved by compromise when Lieutenant-Governor Archibald agreed to survey additional land around their farming communities, provide additional lands farther west as their land base became too small for their population, and provide additional lands to the plains Ojibwa. However, the written text did not include the guarantees that had been made respecting land, hunting, and fishing, and the maintenance of their way of life, nor did it contain what were termed "outside" promises respecting agricultural implements, livestock, hunting equipment, and the other promises that had been extracted. The text was similar to the Robinson Huron and Superior treaties, "surren-

---

439   J. Tobias, "Canada's Subjugation of the Plains Cree, 1879-1885" (1983) 64 Can. Hist. Rev. 520.

440   Morris, *supra* note 53 at 28, 29.

441   D.J. Hall, "'A Serene Atmosphere'? Treaty 1 Revisited" (1984) 4 Can. J. Native Studies 321.

dering" land in exchange for annuities, schools, and reserves based on a formula of 160 acres per person.[442]

In a subsequent inquiry into the matter, it was discovered that Commissioner Wemyss M. Simpson had neglected to include a record of the outside promises when he forwarded the written treaty to Ottawa. Although a subsequent memo from Commissioner Simpson rectified the error, the outside promises were ignored for some time by the federal government. Commissioner Alexander Morris acknowledged this oversight in his report to Ottawa:

> When Treaties, Numbers One and Two, were made, certain verbal promises were unfortunately made to the Indians, which were not included in the written text of the treaties, nor recognized or referred to, to when these Treaties were ratified by the Privy Council. This, naturally, led to misunderstanding with the Indians, and to widespread dissatisfaction among them.[443]

The issue of the outside promises was not settled until 1876.[444]

The Ojibwa tribes that occupied the territory from Rainy River to Lake of the Woods had an abundant and stable economy based on the commercial production of furs and trade. When traffic passed through their territory, they extracted compensation for use of the right of way through their lands. Reports to Ottawa suggested that the Ojibwa would oppose any attempt to "[open] a highway without any regard to them, through a territory of which they believe themselves to be the sole lords and masters."[445] Commissioner S.J. Dawson, who had negotiated with the Ojibwa for the right of way for the Dawson route, warned Ottawa that they were encountering people who "in their actual dealings they are shrewd and sufficiently awake to their own interests."[446] He advised they were also familiar with treaties made in the United States and that the "experience they have thus gained has rendered them expert diplomatists as compared to Indians who have never had such advantage." That the Ojibwa were aware of the negative consequences of foreign settlement was evident in their views of what it entailed:

> We see how the Indians are treated far away. The white man comes, looks at their flowers, their trees, and their rivers; others soon follow; the lands of the Indians pass from their hands, and they have nowhere a home.[447]

Because of their sense of ownership, the Ojibwa would not allow use of their lands, timber, or waterways without compensation. They were steadfast in the defence of their

---

442 RCAP, *supra* note 75, vol. 1 at 164.

443 Morris, *supra* note 53 at 126.

444 RCAP, *supra* note 75, vol. 1 at 164.

445 Canada, Department of Public Works, *S.J. Dawson's Report to the Government* (Ottawa: Queen's Printer, 1864). DPW, RG 11, vol. 265.

446 Canada, Department of Public Works, *S.J. Dawson's Report to the Government* (Ottawa: Queen's Printer, 1861). DPW, RG 11.

447 H.Y. Hind, *Narrative of the Canadian Red River Exploring Expedition of 1857 and of the Assiniboine and Saskatchewan...* (New York: Greenwood Press, 1969) at 99.

country and opposed non-Aboriginal expansion without the prerequisite treaty arrangements:

> We believe what you tell us when you say that in your land the Indians have always been treated with clemency and justice and we are not apprehensive for the future, but do not bring Settlers and Surveyors amongst us to measure and occupy our lands until a clear understanding has been arrived at as to what our relations are to be in the time to come.[448]

They approached treaty-making with knowledge that their lands were valuable and that they would direct and control change, as indicated by Chief *Mo-We-Do-Pe-Nais*:

> All this is our property where you have come. ... This is what we think, that the Great Spirit has planted us on this ground where we are, as you were where you came from. We think where we are is our property. I will tell you what he said to us when he planted us here; the rules that we should follow ... we have a rich country; it is the Great Spirit who gave us this; where we stand upon is the Indians' property, and belongs to them. ... The white man has robbed us of our riches, and we don't wish to give them up again without getting something in their place.[449]

The negotiation of *Treaty No. 3* was also long and difficult, but after two failed attempts a treaty was concluded in 1873. Throughout the negotiations the Ojibwa adhered to their terms, and Crown negotiators were forced to make concessions. The Ojibwa were concerned primarily with preserving their economic base, securing compensation or rents for the use of their lands, and ensuring that the Crown would fulfill the terms. Chief *Mo-We-Do-Pe-Nais* wanted to know how the treaty would be implemented and safeguarded, insisting that the promises made should be fulfilled by the agents of the Crown. In reply Commissioner Morris gave assurances that the "ear of the Queen's Government" would always be open, and that the Queen would "deal with her servants that do not do their duty in a proper manner."[450]

The Ojibwa retained freedom of movement throughout their territories, and negotiated free passes on the train that crossed their lands. The liquor trade in their country was prohibited, and they established that they would not be conscripted to fight in the United States should there be war between the Americans and the British. The Ojibwa would reserve lands for themselves; their spokesman said: "We do not want anyone to mark out our reserves, we have already marked them out." Provision was also made for domestic animals, farming equipment, annuities, clothing, and education. Those who were not present at treaty negotiations were asked to sign adhesions to the treaty for their traditional territories.

Treaties with the Aboriginal tribes of the plains were negotiated between 1874 and 1877. Records of negotiations and of the circumstances surrounding treaty-making

---

448   Canada, Department of Public Works, *Report to the Government* (Ottawa: Queen's Printer,1869). DPW, RG 11, vol. 265.

449   Morris, *supra* note 53 at 59-62. The words "give them up again" refer to the failure to compensate them adequately for the Dawson route.

450   *Ibid.* at 72.

show that the Aboriginal nations posed a considerable threat to the Canadian federation if they were not treated with the utmost care. During this period, Canada was also cognizant of the threat of annexation of the western territories by the United States, particularly during the Alaska boundary negotiations, which revealed that the United States contemplated expanding north to the 50th-51st boundary.

At *Treaty No. 4* negotiations, Commissioner Morris requested that the Queen's subjects be allowed to come and settle among them and farm the land. If the tribes agreed, their Great Mother the Queen would see that their needs were met, and the Queen's power and authority would protect them from encroachment by settlement. Treaty commissioners took care to emphasize the physical aspects of the "caring relationship" and treaties' safeguarding of their way of life.

Since many of their chiefs and people were not present, those that were expressed their inability to negotiate, saying they had no authority to speak for those not present.[451] Further, political differences between the Cree and the Saulteaux delayed negotiations. Aboriginal negotiators demanded that they, as owners of the land, be given the payment for Rupert's Land since compensation had been given to the Hudson's Bay Company. Morris offered the identical terms of *Treaty No. 3*, and the chiefs tentatively agreed by touching the pen.[452] However, the written text of *Treaty No. 4* is different from *Treaty No. 3*.

Commissioner Morris negotiated *Treaty No. 5* in September 1875 between the Swampy Cree and others in the vicinity of Lake Winnipeg. The Crown deemed the treaty necessary so that "settlers and traders might have undisturbed access to its waters, shores, islands, inlets and tributary streams."[453] According to Morris's report, the terms of *Treaty No. 5* were similar to Treaties 3 and 4, except that reserved land was limited to 160 acres (in place of 640 acres) for each family of five. The record of negotiations kept by commissioners had little detail about the extent of negotiations, revolving around what was being "offered" by commissioners and the lands the Swampy Cree would retain. As the Crown was intent on gaining access to and controlling the waterways, the location of reserves generated some discussion. The Cree were assured that they would be able to retain lands in their territories.

Before the negotiation of *Treaty No. 6* in August 1876, a report from W.S. Christie, chief factor of the Hudson's Bay Company in Edmonton, documented the complaint of Chief Sweetgrass, a prominent chief of the Cree country:

---

451   *Ibid.* at 86, citing a report from W.J. Christie, Indian Commissioner, and M.G. Dickieson on the *Qu'Appelle Treaty*. Piapot and the Assiniboine Chiefs were not present for negotiations in 1874. A year later commissioners were told by those absent in 1874 that they believed that a treaty had not been made: "An idea seemed prevalent among the Indians who were absent last year that no treaty had been concluded then; that all which had been done at that time was merely preliminary to the making of the treaty in reality, which they thought was to be performed this year."

452   *Ibid.* at 141-42. Morris refers to the fact that the Saulteaux (Ojibwa) were in contact with their Ojibwa brothers in *Treaties Nos. 1, 2,* and *3*.

453   *Ibid.* at 143-44.

> Great Father, – I shake hands with you, and bid you welcome. We heard our lands were sold and we did not like it; we don't want to sell our lands; it is our property, and no one has a right to sell them.[454]

Treaty No. 6 negotiations, conducted with elaborate Aboriginal (and Crown) protocols and ceremonies by both sides, were sealed with pipe ceremonies, reinforcing the spiritual context of negotiations. The major concerns of the Aboriginal negotiators focused on the loss of their food supply, the buffalo, and years of famine and disease. To reassure the Aboriginal tribes, Morris promised: "Understand me, I do not want to interfere with your hunting and fishing. I want you to pursue it through the country as you have heretofore done."[455] He assured them that they would have more land than they needed. By the end of negotiations, the terms involved annuities, education, housing, and economic assistance, relief in the event of famine, help for the indigent, grain provisions for three years, and medical aid.[456]

In September 1877, *Treaty No. 7* was made at Blackfoot Crossing between the Crown, as represented by Commissioner David Laird, and the Blood, Blackfoot, Peigan, Sarcee, and Stoney nations of the Blackfoot Confederacy. A treaty had been made between the government of the United States and the Blackfoot in 1855. From the Crown's perspective, it was essential to make a treaty with the Blackfoot to protect the existing settlements around the forts, provide for peaceful settlement, and preserve the friendly disposition of the tribes. Commissioner Laird offered inducements to make the treaty:

> The Great Mother heard that the buffalo were being killed very fast, and to prevent them from being destroyed her Councillors have made a law to protect them. ... This will save the buffalo, and provide you with food for many years yet, and it shews you that the Queen and her Councillors wish you well.

> ...Last year a Treaty was made with the Crees along the Saskatchewan, and now the Queen has sent Col. McLeod and myself to ask you to make a Treaty. But in a very few years the buffalo will probably be all destroyed, and for this reason the Queen wishes to help you to live in the future in some other way. She wishes you to allow her white children to come and live on your land and raise cattle, and should you agree to this she will assist you to raise cattle and grain ... . She will also pay you and your children money every year, which you can spend as you please. ...

> The Queen wishes us to offer you the same as was accepted by the Crees. I do not mean exactly the same terms, but equivalent terms, that will cost the Queen the same amount of money. ... The Commissioners will give you your choice, whether cattle or farming implements. ... If you sign the Treaty every man, woman and child will get twelve dollars each ... . A reserve of land will be set apart for yourselves and your cattle, upon which none others will be permitted to encroach; for every five persons one square mile will be allotted on this reserve ... .[457]

---

454 *Ibid.* at 170-171.

455 *Ibid.* at 204.

456 *Ibid.* at 218.

457 *Ibid.* at 267-69.

The Crown offered annuities, goods and benefits, and the Blackfoot agreed. They were promised that their reserved lands could not be taken without their consent and that their liberty of hunting over the open prairie would not be interfered with so long as they did not molest the settlers.[458]

In 1899, treaty commissioners negotiated with the Cree and Dene nations, whose Aboriginal tenure comprised an area from what is now northern Saskatchewan, Alberta, and British Columbia and north to the Hay River and Great Slave Lake in the North West Territories (324,900 squares miles). In *Treaty No. 8*, the Crown continued its policy of offering benefits if the Aboriginal nations would allow settlers into their territories. A pre-drafted Victorian treaty was offered for discussion. It included the usual items, as well as such things as livestock and farming equipment—items completely unsuitable to the north. Father Lacombe reported that "the Northern native population is not any too well disposed to view favourably any proposition involving the cession of their rights to their country."[459] Another report by a missionary said, "As far as I can gather they are determined to refuse either treaty or 'Scrips' and to oppose the settlement of their country by Europeans."[460]

Negotiations went on for many days at various locations and were hampered by commissioners' lack of understanding of the conditions put forward by the Cree and Dene nations. The latter refused to sign a treaty unless commissioners met their demand that:

> nothing would be allowed to interfere with their way of making a living; the old and destitute would always be taken care of; they were guaranteed protection in their way of living as hunting and trappers from white competition; they would not be prevented from hunting and fishing as they had always done, so as to enable them to earn their living and maintain their existence.[461]

It was only after the commissioners solemnly pledged their word to these provisions, in the name of Queen Victoria, that the Indians agreed to sign the treaty.[462] However, the full content of the promises or discussion was not reflected in the written treaty.

Similar promises were made in *Treaty No. 9*, the *James Bay Treaty* (1905),[463] with the Ojibwa and in *Treaty No. 10* (1906)[464] with the Chipewyan and Cree tribes in

---

458 *Ibid.* at 245-75.

459 Letter of Forget to the Secretary of Indian Affairs, 25 April 1898. NAC RG10, vol. 3848, file 75236-1.

460 Letter of G. Holmes to the Committee, 3 April 1899—NAC, Church Missionary Society, MG17 B2, microfilm A-120, doc. 68.

461 Affidavit of J.A.R. Balsillic, quoted in Réné Fumoleau, *As Long As This Land Shall Last: A History of Treaty 8 and Treaty 11* (Toronto: McClelland and Stewart, 1975) at 340, App. II.

462 *Ibid.* 74-75.

463 J. Long, *Treaty No. 9: The Negotiations 1901-1928* (Cobault, Ont.: Highway Book Shop, 1978); J. Morrison, *Treaty Research Report: Treaty Nine (1905-06), The James Bay Treaty* (Ottawa: Indian and Northern Affairs Canada, 1986).

464 K.S. Coates and W.R. Morrison, *Treaty Research Report: Treaty Ten (1906)* (Ottawa, Indian and Northern Affairs Canada, 1986).

northern Saskatchewan and Alberta. In *Treaty No. 10*, the commissioners "guaranteed that the treaty would not lead to any forced interference with their mode of life."[465]

Treaty No. 11 was to follow the same path, since the Privy Council had noted in 1891 that "a Treaty or treaties should be made with the Indians who claim these regions as their hunting grounds."[466] Commissioners were received with suspicion and mistrust, since the Dene had learned that guarantees negotiated in *Treaty No. 8* were not being respected. Throughout the negotiations, the Dene repeated their conditions for making a treaty: no reserves to restrict their movements; protection of their lands; education; medical care; and protection of wildlife and of their hunting, fishing, and trapping economies. In response, promises were made by Commissioner Conroy that "they would be guaranteed full freedom to hunt, trap, and fish in the Northwest Territories if they would sign the Treaty," since it was clear that they would not make any treaty without that guarantee.[467] Oral promises, made by Bishop Breynat as well as Commissioner Conroy (whose word alone was not enough) were made and remade at the various treaty-making sites:

> I gave my word of honour that the promises made by the Royal Commissioner, "although they were not actually included in the Treaty" would be kept by the Crown. .... They were promised that nothing would be done or allowed to interfere with their way of living ... . The old and the destitute would always be taken care of ... . They were guaranteed that they would be protected, especially in their way of living as hunters and trappers, from white competition, they would not be prevented from hunting and fishing, as they had always done, so as to enable them to earn their own living and maintain their existence.[468]

As in the outside promises of Treaties 1 and 2, Commissioner Conroy did not table the commitments and guarantees made to the Dene in the oral negotiations. The document tabled was a written text almost identical to the pre-drafted Victorian treaty that had been proposed in the *Treaty No. 8* negotiations.

A government commission was set up to examine Aboriginal native hunting rights to lands lying north of the 45th parallel. In the course of its work, the commission discovered that the description of land in an 1818 treaty was inaccurate. To correct these errors, the *Williams Treaty* (1923) was prepared and signed by seven representatives of the Hiawatha Band at Rice Lake. The province of Ontario provided the Government of Canada with the funds for consideration, and monies were paid. The terms were to "cede, release, surrender and yield up to the Government of the Dominion of Canada for His Majesty the King and His Successors forever, all their right, title, interest, claim, demand and privileges whatsoever, in, to, upon, or in respect of, the lands and premises described." The first paragraph deals with the lands north of the 45th parallel or the northern lands. The second paragraph remedies the error in the land

---

465   Canada, *Report of First Commissioner for Treaty No. 10 (J.A.J. McKenna)* (Ottawa: Queen's Printer, 1907) at 3.

466   *Ibid.* at 41.

467   *Ibid.* at 216.

468   *Ibid.* at 216.

description in the earlier treaty. The third paragraph is a broader conveying clause that most treaties called a basket clause:

> The rights of the Indians to all other lands in the province of Ontario except such reserves as have heretofore been set apart for them by His Majesty the King.[469]

9. Land Claim Agreements

Under section 35(3) of *Constitution Act, 1982*, land claims agreements can become parts of the Constitution of Canada. Section 35(3) provides that "treaty rights" include rights "that now exist by way of land claims agreements or may be so acquired." This includes the James Bay and Northern Quebec Native Claims Settlement Act and the recent Arctic land claims agreements.

Under *The Quebec Boundaries Extension Act, 1912*, the provincial government had a constitutional obligation to recognize the territorial rights of the Indian inhabitants and negotiate surrender of these rights.[470] In the negotiations, the province refused to recognize that the Crees and Inuit had any Aboriginal tenure or rights.[471] It was only after the *James Bay and Northern Quebec Agreement* (1975) and the subsequent Northeastern Quebec Agreement (1978) were entered into that Quebec stated that the Aboriginal peoples had "fundamental rights,"[472] but the government declared that they had been ceded. However, this characterization was not used in the treaty negotiation, raising important questions about the meaning of the clauses. These agreements are regarded as modern treaties with Canada.[473] They cover a vast area of northern Quebec, about 106,190 hectares (or 410 square miles) of the James Bay Crees and the Inuit of Nunavik (northern Quebec).

Section 2 of the *James Bay Agreement* contains the cession clause:

> 2.1 In consideration of the rights and benefits herein set forth in favour of the James Bay Crees and the Inuit of Quebec the James Bay Crees and the Inuit of Quebec hereby cede,

---

469 By the terms of the 1923 treaty, Justice Gonthier held that the Hiawatha Band surrendered any remaining special rights to hunt and fish in the Otonabee River area, *George Henry Howard (Appellant) v. Her Majesty the Queen*, [1994] 2 S.C.R. 299 (S.C.C.) at 305-307, Gonthier, J.

470 *An Act to extend the Boundaries of the Province of Quebec*, S.C. 1912, c. 45 at 2(c). Also see 2c of Schedule in *An Act respecting the extension of the Province of Quebec by the annexation of Ungava*, S.Q. 1912, c. 7.

471 The Supreme Court has acknowledged this negotiation stance. See *R. v. Sparrow*, [1990] 1 S.C.R. 1075 at 1103-1104: "[T]he James Bay development by Quebec Hydro was originally initiated without regard to the rights of the Indians who lived there, even though these were expressly protected by a constitutional instrument; see *The Quebec Boundary Extensions Act, 1912*, S.C. 1912, c. 45."

472 Assemblée nationale, *Journal des débats*, 4th Sess., 30th Legisl., vol. 17, no. 29 (21 June 1976) at 1597 (Quebec Minister of National Resource, Jean Cournayer).

473 *James Bay and Northern Quebec Agreement and Complementary Agreements* 1997 ed. (Québec: Les Publications du Québec, 1996); S.C. 1976-77, c. 32 [hereinafter James Bay and Northern Quebec Agreement].

release, surrender and convey all their Native claims, rights, titles and interests, whatever they may be, in and to land in the Territory and in Quebec, and Quebec and Canada accept such surrender.

2.2 Quebec and Canada, the James Bay Energy Corporation, the James Bay Development Corporation and the Quebec Hydro-electric Commission (Hydro-Quebec), to the extent of their respective obligations as set forth herein, hereby give, grant, recognize and provide to the James Bay Crees and the Inuit of Quebec the rights, privileges and benefits specified herein, the whole in consideration of the said cession, release, surrender and conveyance mentioned in paragraph 2.1 hereof.

Canada hereby approves of and consents to the Agreement and undertakes, to the extent of its obligations herein, to give, grant, recognize and provide to the James Bay Crees and the Inuit of Quebec the rights, privileges and benefits herein.

...

2.6 The federal legislation approving, giving effect to and declaring valid the Agreement shall extinguish all native claims, rights, title and interests of all Indians and all Inuit in and to the Territory and the native claims, rights, title and interests of the Inuit of Port Burwell in Canada, whatever they may be.

The Inuvialuit Final Agreement (1984), Nunavut Final Agreement (1993), and the various land claim agreements in the Arctic[474] rely on the "cede, release, and surrender" phrasing, relabelled as "certainty":

In consideration of the rights and benefits provided to Inuit by the Agreement, Inuit hereby:

(a) cede, release and surrender to Her Majesty The Queen in Right of Canada, all their aboriginal claims, rights, title and interests, if any, in and to lands and waters anywhere within Canada and adjacent offshore areas within the sovereignty or jurisdiction of Canada; and

(b) agree, on their behalf, and on behalf of their heirs, descendants and successors not to assert any cause of action, action for a declaration, claim or demand of whatever kind or nature which they ever had, now have or may hereafter have against Her Majesty The Queen in Right of Canada or any province, the government of any territory or any person based on any aboriginal claims, rights, title or interests in and to lands and waters described in Sub-section (a).

Nothing in the Agreement constitutes an admission or denial by Canada that Inuit have any aboriginal claims, rights, title or interests in and to lands and waters as described in Sub-section.

---

474 *West Arctic (Inuvialuit) Claims Settlement Act* implements the Inuvialuit Final Agreements S.C. 1984, c. 24: proclaimed in force O.I.C. 1984-2682, 25 July 1984. See also, Yukon Indian Umbrella Final Agreement (1993); Sahtue Dene and Metis Comprehensive Agreements (1993), Gwich'in Comprehensive Land Claim Agreement (1993), Champagne Agreement (1993), Nacho Nyak Dun Agreement (1993), Teslin Tlinglit Council Agreement (1993), Vuntui Gwitchin Agreement (1993), Little Salmon/Comacks Agreement (1997), and Tr'ondëk Hwë ch'in Agreement (1998).

These agreements describe Aboriginal rights within the new territory to be selected, and are intended to provide the people with land rights, national and territorial
parks, and in the future, the government easements and the northern warning system.
The Inuit-owned lands will be owned collectively and vested in designated Inuit organization; they can be transferred among the designated Inuit organizations, to Canada,
the territorial government, or to a municipal corporation. These lands can be expropriated by authorized agencies. The lands take the form of "fee simple rights" that include
surface and subsurface rights.[475] The Aboriginal peoples retained the "free and unrestricted" access to harvest the ecology.

In sum, as this part of the book evidences, more than four hundred written
treaties structured Canada out of Aboriginal tenure. Under the imperial rule of law
rather than military conquest, these treaties created treaty federalism with the British
sovereign to protect Aboriginal tenure and allow provincial federalism and settlement
to emerge. The treaties reflect a collaborative attempt by the sovereigns to discover a
way to structure a way of living together and sharing the land. After the constitutional reforms in 1982 that recognized and affirmed these treaty rights as part of the constitution of Canada, the tradition of treaty federalism was restored. Modern treaties and
agreements continued to shape and extend Canada.

Unfortunately, the rule of law failed the treaty nations and tribes. The prerogative
treaties and their guaranteed rights and obligations were not respected by the emerging
colonial legal system. In the path to nationhood, the legislatures and courts failed incrementally in the complicated attempts to protect and comprehend Aboriginal tenure in
the United States, British North America, and in Canada. These political and legal failures eroded the protected Aboriginal ways of life, dispossessed Aboriginal chiefs of
their jurisdiction in most of our reserved and ceded lands guaranteed by the treaties,
forced the peoples on to isolated reserve systems, and impoverished them. The next
part of the book will unfold this legal tragedy.

---

475 James Bay and Northern Quebec Agreement. In the Umbrella Final Agreement of the Yukon First
     Nations three different categories of land are described: Category A lands, the First Nations will have
     right "equivalent" to "fee simple title" to the surface and the land, and full fee simple title to the sub-
     surface; Category B lands they will only have fee simple surface title; and individual fee simple settle-
     ment lands.

III

LEGAL PROTECTION OF ABORIGINAL TENURE

The protection of the Aborigines should be considered as a duty peculiarly belonging and appropriate to the Executive Government, as administered either in this country or by the Governors of the respective Colonies. This is not a trust which could conveniently be confined to the local Legislature. In proportion as those bodies are qualified for the right discharge of their proper function, they will be unfit for the performance of this office. For a local Legislature, if properly constituted, should partake largely of the interest, and represent the feeling of settled opinions of the great mass of the people for whom they act. But the settlers in almost every Colony, having either disputes to adjust with the native tribes, or claims to urge against them, the representative bodies is virtually a party, and therefore ought not to be the judge in such controversies.

Report from the Select Committee on Aborigines
(British Settlements), 1837[1]

Under the present circumstance, no adequate protection can be obtained for Indian property. It would be vain to seek a verdict for any jury in this Island against the trespassers on the Reserves; nor perhaps would a member of the Bar be found willing and effectually to advocate the cause of the Indians, inasmuch as he would thereby injure his own prospects, by damaging his popularity.

Nova Scotia Indian Commissioner, 1849[2]

---

1   U.K., Select Committee on Aborigines, *Report from the Select Committee on Aborigines (British Settlements): With the Minutes of Evidence, Appendix and Index, Ordered, by the House of Commons, to be Printed, 26 June 1837* (London: [s.n.], 1837) at 77 [hereinafter Select Committee]. Found also as "Report from the Select Committee on Aborigines (British Settlements)" in *Irish University Press Series of British Parliamentary Papers, Anthropology-Aborigines*, vol. 2 (Shannon, Ireland: Irish University Press, 1968), session 11837.

2   Nova Scotia, Legislative Assembly, *Legislative Assembly of Nova Scotia Journal*, [1849] at 356 [hereinafter LANSJ].

Introduction

The legal consciousness of the British colonizers had difficulty addressing the complex issues of Aboriginal tenure and its relations to Crown tenure in the colonies. With the American Revolution, the United States forged in theory and in its courts a new concept of a fee simple empire and land as a commodity. In Canadian provinces and confederation, despite clear prerogative law to the contrary, colonizers presumed to extend the fiction of Crown tenure to Aboriginal territory and tenures. Often they argued that upon the reception of British law, the imperial Crown assumed title of all vacant lands (*terra nullius*) and the Crown had a right to grant valid estates to British subjects. At the same time that they asserted prerogative rights for their own benefit, they ignored the controlling prerogative law protecting Aboriginal nations and tenure.[3] To place these perspectives in context, this part discusses the legal attempts by colonial statutes and judicial decisions to understand and protect Aboriginal tenure in North America from the beginning of colonization to *Delgamuukw*.

10. The United States of America

The American Revolution against Britain created a different context and purpose for land law. The American leaders rejected feudal tenures to create what they saw as a proper relationship for society and property. For them, the British feudal past and its land law—specifically, feudal tenure, primogeniture, and entailment of land—were vestiges of a corrupt past against which they had revolted. For them, the very existence of the United States established liberty over tyranny: the earth belonged to the living; human society created property rights and ought to control them. Their vision of the United States was based on a "fee simple empire": cultivated land owned allodially in fee simple ownership, and individual autonomy secured by individual property rights. Hence, neither the federal nor the state governments should hold superior land tenure over any citizen, and individual citizens should own the land free of all hierarchical entanglements.[4] Since few legal concepts were as closely associated with feudal law as land tenures, the American legal reformers sought to purge the British common law of its "undemocratic" vestiges of feudal landholding and replace them with autonomous land ownership. However, despite revolutionary fervour to make a complete break with the feudal past, American law maintained an uneasy continuity with the principles of the British common law of property.

Allodial land signified "liberty" and "virtue."[5] Thomas Jefferson, for example, argued that all Virginia land, including land already held by individuals who owed

---

3   A.E. Gotlieb, *Canadian Treaty-Making* (Markham: Butterworths, 1968) at 4; N.A.M. MacKenzie, "Indians and Treaties" (1929) 7 Can. Bar Rev. 564.

4   Gregory S. Alexander, *Commodity and Propriety: Competing Versions of Property in American Legal Thought, 1776-1970* (Chicago: University of Chicago Press, 1997) at 26.

5   *Ibid.* at 54.

tenurial obligations to the state, should be allodial in character. Additionally, he proposed that all governments sell lands within their jurisdiction in fee simple. Federal land law implemented this policy in *The Northwest Ordinance of 1787* and in western lands.[6]

To purge the common law of elements considered incompatible with individual freedom, to increase individual wealth, and to limit courts' authority over land conveyances, American legal reformers sought to replace the common law with new legislative codes. They viewed legislative codes as the democratic voice that demystified the law, made it accessible to ordinary citizens, and enhanced the marketability of land.[7] Between 1820 and 1860 the British common law of property was therefore reformed by legislative enactments. The revised statutes of New York articulated the legal reformers' conception of property:

> All lands within this state are declared to be allodial, so that, subject only to the liability to escheat, the entire and absolute property is vested in the owners, according to the nature of the respective estates; and all feudal tenures, of every description, with all their incidents are abolished.[8]

These reforms affirmed the purpose of what Chancellor Kent's *Commentaries* called "property law": to fulfill private intentions and increase the marketability of land.[9] The attendant "triumph of imaginary property" meant the shift from landholding "to a form of property that was represented by pieces of paper, but rested on nothing more real than imagination."[10] With this shift came new types of intangible and speculative interests in land, including promissory notes, banknotes, certificates of public debt, highly fluid paper titles, paper money, credit, and the creation of banks.

These legal reforms enabled negotiable paper to succeed over the common law restrictions against assigning personal interests in land or "choses in action."[11] Professor Alexander claims the triumph of imaginary property "was based on nothing more than promises, hopes and expectations."[12] British common law prohibited such expectation interests as the basis of property rights because lawyers viewed them as both unnatural and politically dangerous: only future interests in landed estates by an expectant heir were considered legitimate expectation-based property interests.[13]

After the establishment of the Constitution in 1789, the United States affirmed the allodial tenure of the Aboriginal nations to their territories, and sought to reconcile

---

6   *Ibid.* at 51-52.

7   *Ibid.* at 97.

8   See c. 1, § 3, 1829 N.Y. Rev. Stat., art. 1; also see the earlier statute that abolished the British concept of land tenure, the *Act of February 20, 1787.*

9   The intent-frustrating rules of the common law of things were the Rule in *Shelley's Case*, the Rule against Perpetuities, and the Doctrine of Worthier Title. See Alexander, *supra* note 4 at 115.

10   Alexander, *ibid.* at 69-71.

11   *Ibid.* at 70.

12   *Ibid.*

13   *Ibid.* at 70-71.

the Aboriginal tenure through treaties. According to Felix Cohen, British practices and pre-Revolutionary precedents demonstrate three central principles: (1) that both parties to the treaty are sovereign powers; (2) that the Indian nations or tribes had a transferable title to the land; and (3) that the acquisition of Indian lands could not be left to individual colonists but was to be controlled as a government monopoly.[14] The federal government reconciled Aboriginal land tenure with the principles of the *Royal Proclamation of 1763*[15] through section 4 of the *Indian Trade and Intercourse Act* (1790):

> [n]o sale of lands made by and from Indians, or any nation or tribe of Indians within the United States, shall be valid to any person or person, or to any state, whether having the right of pre-emption to such land or not, unless the same shall be made and duly executed at some public treaty, held under the authority of the United States.[16]

The triumph of imaginary property extended to Aboriginal territories. It existed as the state right to make derivative grants to individuals of unpurchased Aboriginal tenure. This was a relic of Crown tenure and federal law that survived to the fee simple empire. In addressing problems of state grants to individuals in Aboriginal territory, the state courts found that the Aboriginal nations held the land but imaginary contingent future interests could be conveyed by the state to land speculators. For example, in 1791, the Supreme Court of Kentucky stated:

> [t]he old claim of the Crown, by the treaty of 1763 [Paris], extended to, and was limited by the river Mississippi, ... the dormant title of the Indian tribes remained to be extinguished by government, either by purchase or conquest, and when that was done it inured to the benefit of the citizen who had previously acquired a title from the crown and did not authorize a new grant of the lands as waste or unappropriated ... the Indian title did not impede ... the power of the legislature to grant the land ... .[17]

If there was a state grant to an individual, in the absence of a treaty purchase of Aboriginal title, the courts held that the state granted a "bare legal estate" to the grantee (the first purchaser); a second grant was prohibited and invalid, since the state had nothing to transfer to the second purchaser.[18]

In the 1790s, the Supreme Court of Pennsylvania concluded that some of its settlements were illegal,[19] since "the soil belonged to the aborigines, and the lands had not been purchased from the Indians."[20] The court acknowledged that "it was the European usage, for the sovereign to bestow charters on their subjects of such territory... . But the more solid and equitable title must rest on the foundation of fair pur-

---

14   Felix S. Cohen, *Handbook of Federal Indian Law* (Washington, D.C.: United States Government Printing Office, 1942) at 47.

15   R.S.C. 1970, App. II, No. 1 at 123-29 [hereinafter 1763 Proclamation].

16   25 U.S.C. § 177 (1790).

17   *Marshall v. Clark.* 1 Ky. 77 at 80 (1791).

18   *Ibid.* at 80-81.

19   *Hughes v. Dougherty*, 1 Yea. 497 at 498 (S.C. Penn. 1791).

20   *Sherer v. McFarland*, 2 Yea. 224 at 225 (S.C. Penn. 1797).

chases from the original tenants of the soil."[21] Where the colonial government "bought lands from the natives, and gave them valuable considerations" subsequent "settlements" were valid.[22] Later court decisions affirmed the earlier decisions. If the state made a grant to a person with full knowledge the land was not purchased from the Aboriginal nations, the grant passed only bare title, but the state had nothing left to grant the same land to a second purchaser. If the state mistakenly thought the land had been purchased from Aboriginal nations, the first grant would be void as induced by deception or mistake.[23] If the grantees (first purchasers) in turn passed grant of land to others, unaware that the land was not purchased of the Indians, no right was passed.[24]

By an 1803 treaty known as the Louisiana Purchase, the United States purchased from France the Louisiana Territory, land extending from the Mississippi River to the Rocky Mountains. Although the Constitution did not specifically authorize the federal government to acquire new territory by treaty, the Senate concurred with the treaty.[25] After the Louisiana territory purchase, President Jefferson proposed a constitutional amendment to clarify the relationship between the federal government and Aboriginal nations in the territory:

> The province of Louisiana is incorporated with the U.S. and made part thereof. The right of occupancy in the soil, and of self-government, are confirmed to the Indian inhabitants, as they now exist. Preemption only of the portions rightfully occupied by them, and a succession to the occupancy of such as they may abandon, with the full rights of possession as well as of property and sovereignty in whatever is not or shall cease to be so rightfully occupied by them shall belong to the U.S.[26]

Under the proposed amendment, Congress would have authority "to exchange the right of occupancy in portions where the U.S. have full rights for lands possessed by Indians within the U.S. on the East side of the Mississippi"; to police all persons therein, not being Indian inhabitants; and to regulate trade and intercourse between the Indian inhabitants and all other persons. The Congress would have no authority to dispose of the lands of the Louisiana province otherwise, however, until a new amendment should give that authority. Although the proposed amendment was a declarative statement of the existing law and character of Aboriginal tenure and sovereignty,[27] Congress did not act on the proposal. This set the stage for judicial interpretation of expectation interests of land speculators in Aboriginal territory.

---

21 *Weiser v. Moody*, 2 Yea. 127 (S.C. Penn. 1796).

22 *Ibid.*

23 *Ibid.* at 127-28.

24 *Thompson v. Johnson*, 6 Bin. 68 (S.C. Penn. 1813).

25 A.P. Whitaker, *The Mississippi Question, 1795-1803: A Study in Trade Politics, and Diplomacy* (New York: Appleton-Century, 1934).

26 American Indian Policy Review Commission, *Report on Trust Responsibilities and the Federal-Indian Relationships: Including Treaty Relationships* (Washington, D.C.: U.S. Government Printing Office, 1976) at 107-108 [hereinafter *Report on Trust Responsibilities*].

27 Ernest C. Downs, "How the East Was Lost" (1975) 1 Am. Indian J.

In 1807, the Supreme Court of North Carolina confronted the situation of treaty reserved land and treaty cessions of Aboriginal tenure. A 1783 state legislature affirmed treaty reserved land to the Cherokee nation in the treaties and prevented any other person from entering the reserved land, and made all entries and grants of the reserved lands "utterly void."[28] Nonetheless, in 1787 the state made a grant to an individual of reserved Aboriginal tenure. The Supreme Court held in an unreported case[29] that this grant was void and conveyed no title; in the 1783 statute the state had divested itself of "all title" to the reserved lands and the officers of the state were not authorized to issue grants.[30] In the *Treaty of Holston, 1791*, the Cherokee nation ceded their tenure to the United States. In 1803 North Carolina made a grant of the same land to another.[31] Justice Stone interpreted that in the 1791 treaty the Cherokee nation ceded their "right of exclusive possession" to the federal government:

> It may be observed that neither the European governments, nor the governments of the United States, nor that of North Carolina, have considered the Indian title other than a mere possessory right ... The treaty of 1791, with the Cherokees, cannot be considered, therefore, as conveying a title to the soil of the land to the United States. It can only be received as a relinquishment of that possessory right which alone had been yielded to the Indians.[32]

Before the treaty cession the state held a bare title that was not a legal interest, subject to the Indian right; any state deeds were null. After the treaty cession the state acquired the possessory interest in the land. They had both "title" and possessory interests and thus could make grants. What was lost to the courts was that all their title and interests were derived from the Cherokee nation by treaty conveyance to the federal government.

In 1810, the Supreme Court of the United States had to confront false titles and imaginary property schemes that reached indirectly into the issue of unpurchased territories of the Aboriginal nations in Yazoo land speculation case, *Fletcher v. Peck*.[33] The Georgia legislature in 1795 statutorily authorized the governor to convey 35 million acres of land to four land-speculating companies for $500,000. These companies were given exclusive privileges to sell and settle the land. The statute claimed the Yazoo land was in the vague western portion of Georgia, now constituting the states of Alabama and Mississippi.[34] Professor Alexander argues:

> [t]ypical of most land speculation at the time, the sale was corrupted by bribes, mostly of cash and shares in the companies. A year later, after public scandal over the bribes had

---

28   *Den on Demise of Strother v. Cathey*, 1 N.C. 162 at 164 (S.C. N.C. 1807).

29   *Ibid.* at 164 called *Strother v. Avery*.

30   *Ibid.*

31   *Ibid.*, n. 25.

32   *Ibid.* at 168. See *Worcester v. Georgia*, 31 U.S. (6 Pet.) 515, 8 L. Ed. 483 (U.S. 1832) [hereinafter *Worcester* cited to U.S.], for description of the *Treaty of Holston, 1791*.

33   10 U.S. (6 Cranch) 87 (U.S. 1810) [hereinafter *Fletcher v. Peck*].

34   Alexander, *supra* note 4 at 188.

broken out and a new legislature elected, the deal was rescinded. In the meantime, the four original land companies had already sold millions of acres of the Yazoo land to other out-of-state land speculators and individual settlers, mostly from New England. The sale earned enormous profits for the original Yazoo companies.[35]

The scandal was exposed, the legislature was defeated, and the newly elected legislature repealed the act.

After the legislative rescission, the land speculators attempted to protect their interest. Some New England buyers acquired a legal opinion regarding the validity of the original sale to third persons who were "innocent" of the alleged fraud or corruption.[36] Based on this legal opinion, one John Peck sold his holding to one Robert Fletcher, and by prearrangement, Fletcher sued Peck to try title, arguing that the sale breached the contract's covenant of good title, thus challenging the validity of the legislative appeal.[37] This "feigned" case posed the conflict between the security of land titles created by the legislature, and the power of the legislature to correct its prior acts that were the direct result of corruption. The lands were subject to a variety of conflicting claims: the grantee and purchaser under the Georgia statute, the United States government,[38] Spain,[39] and at least four Aboriginal nations who were in possession. The Aboriginal nations were not represented in any phase of the litigation.

The majority decision of the Court, authored by Chief Justice Marshall, held that a legislature was competent to repeal any act that a former legislature was competent to pass, but it was not valid to repeal land titles being transferred to individuals who relied on a legislative act. The contract clause of the federal Constitution protected vested rights of the innocent purchaser of the title. Thus the Court saw vested property rights as an integral part of the fee simple empire and constitutional order.[40]

The Court also had to determine whether the disputed territory was within the boundaries of Aboriginal nations, the United States, or the state of Georgia. Although this was the controlling jurisdictional conflict in the factual context, the Court's decision minimized the issue.[41] Joseph Story and John Quincy Adams[42] for the land companies argued that the Aboriginal nations' claim to the land "depends upon the law of nations, not upon municipal rights."[43] They submitted that Indian tribes were independent nations, but they "had no idea of property in the soil," and had a "mere occupan-

---

35   *Ibid.* at 189.

36   *Ibid.* Alexander Hamilton wrote the opinion.

37   *Ibid.*

38   President Washington had forbidden Georgia's first attempt to sell the Yazoo land. See C.G. Haines, *The Role of the Supreme Court in American Government and Politics, 1789-1835* (New York: DaCapo Press, 1944) at 109.

39   Alexander, *supra* note 4 at 190.

40   *Ibid.* at 188.

41   Haines, *supra* note 38 at 314-28.

42   Perhaps the two most influential lawyers in America at the time.

43   *Fletcher v. Peck, supra* note 33 at 142.

cy for the purpose of hunting."[44] Such occupancy "was not like our tenures," but rather "a right regulated by treaties, not by deeds of conveyances."[45] The treaties, they argued, were the "effects of conquest."[46]

The Court was united in the opinion that Aboriginal tenure existed as a recognizable and protectable property right, but diverged in characterizing the nature and source of Aboriginal tenure and its relation to the claims of Georgia. Chief Justice Marshall for the majority held that the land was within Georgia's jurisdiction. The existing doctrine of the bare legal estate of the state had transformed into a fee simple estate:

> It was doubted, whether the state can be seised in fee of lands, subject to Indian title, and whether such a decision that they were seised in fee might not be construed to amount to a decision that their grantee might maintain an ejectment for them, notwithstanding that title. The majority of the court is of the opinion, that the nature of Indian title, which is certainly to be respected by all courts, until it be legitimately extinguished is not such as to be absolutely repugnant to seisin in fee on the part of the state.[47]

Chief Justice Marshall's conclusion can be interpreted as viewing unpurchased Aboriginal tenure as a tenure system distinct from the fee simple tenurial system; thus no conflict existed between them. The majority view implied that Aboriginal tenure was neither dependent upon nor operated within the land tenure of the United States. As a distinct land tenure system of independent nations, until purchased by treaty, Aboriginal tenure was an issue of conflicts of law or comparative international law. Thus the majority opinion did not attempt to incorporate unpurchased Aboriginal tenure into the land tenure system of the federal or state governments. In suggesting the dual tenure systems were compatible with each other, this decision was an early version of Aboriginal tenure as a *sui generis* tenure.

Justice Johnson for the minority did not see two independent land tenure systems; he saw Aboriginal tenure as "fee-simple absolute title" or allodial tenure within the United States tenurial system.[48] He concluded that Aboriginal nations had "the absolute proprietorship of their soil";[49] the treaties had acknowledged the Indian nations as an independent people.[50] Johnson rejected the idea of any "bare legal estate"

---

44   *Ibid.* at 121-23.

45   *Ibid.*

46   *Ibid.* at 121.

47   *Ibid.* at 142-43. By 1839, the Supreme Court of the United States in *Clark v. Smith*, 339 U.S. 195 (U.S. 1839) characterized the relations between Aboriginal tenure and the Crown and the United States thus: "The ultimate fee (encumbered with the Indian right of occupancy) was in the crown previous to the Revolution, and in the states of the Union afterwards, and subject to grants" (at 201). The Court noted that these grants of the ultimate fee of Indian hunting grounds had financed the revolutionary war, allowing North Carolina and Virginia to raise money to pay their officers and soldiers, and should not be rejected. However, the grantees of the "ultimate fee" had to be perfected by a treaty extinguishment of Indian interests.

48   *Fletcher v. Peck, ibid.* at 147.

49   *Ibid.*

50   *Ibid.*

of the states of imaginary property being transformed into a fee simple estate: "Can, then, one nation be said to be seized in lands, the rights of soil of which is in another nation?"[51] Applying the common law prohibition of dual seisin or possession to systems of tenure, Johnson could not comprehend how a "seisin in fee" of Georgia was not absolutely repugnant to the existing Aboriginal tenure. "[O]f an estate in fee simple in the lands in question, subject to another estate [in the Aboriginal nations]," Johnson noted, "we know not what nor whether it may not swallow up the whole estate decided to exist in Georgia."[52] "The question is," Johnson said, "whether it can be correctly predicated of the interest or estate which the State of Georgia had in these lands, 'that the state was seized, thereof, in fee simple'."[53]

In the view of Justice Johnson, the interest of the state of Georgia in the Aboriginal territory was a "mere possibility" or "preemption"; the federal government had a future interest in acquiring the Aboriginal tenure.[54] The only method of acquiring Aboriginal tenure by the federal government under the *Indian Trade and Intercourse Act* was by purchasing their lands:[55] "All the restriction upon the right of soil in the Indian amounts only to an exclusion of all competitors from their market."[56]

"[I]f the interest of Georgia was nothing more than a pre-emptive right, how could that [right] be called a fee simple?"[57] pleaded Justice Johnson, "when the interest in the State of Georgia was nothing more than a power to acquire a fee-simple by purchase, when the tribal proprietor should be pleased to sell?"[58] A fee simple estate may be held in reversion, Johnson noted, "but our law will not admit the idea of its being limited after a fee-simple."[59] A fee simple estate under the federal and state land tenure systems had no restrictions nor could it be qualified nor made subject to any contingency, but rather might last forever, since it constituted the absolute ownership or allodial tenure.[60] A pre-emptive ownership in American tenurial law, in contrast to a fee simple estate,[61] was merely a right of first acceptance or refusal if the owner of a fee simple land chose to place it on the market. It was, in other words, a contingent future interest, subject to a fee simple owner's motivation and desires.

As Justice Johnson had established that the land was under the possession and

---

51   *Ibid.* at 146-47.

52   *Ibid.* at 146.

53   *Ibid.*

54   *Ibid.*

55   *Ibid.* In 1740, the charter grantee of all of Georgia had purchased the Aboriginal tenure of some Indian nations by a treaty. In *Georgia v. Canatoo* (1843) repr. *in Washington National Intelligencer* 8/24, the Supreme Court of Georgia asked: "if he [the charter grantee, Mr. Oglethorpe] could not divest the Indians of their rights to dig gold on their lands not ceded to him, how can [the government of] Georgia do it now with no higher right, indeed with precisely a similar right," at 8/24.

56   *Fletcher v. Peck, ibid.* at 147.

57   *Ibid.*

58   *Ibid.* at 147.

59   *Ibid.*

60   A.J. Casner and W.B. Leach, *Cases and Texts on Property* (Boston: Little, Brown, 1969) at 1008.

61   *Ibid.*; *Fletcher v. Peck, supra* note 33 at 146.

control of sovereign Aboriginal nations and had never been extinguished,[62] the Aboriginal interest was that of fee simple absolute proprietors. In the hierarchy of United States tenures, he reasoned the Aboriginal nations had a higher title than either the state or the federal government.[63] The interest of the state of Georgia was a pre-emptive interest that had already been transferred to the federal government.[64] Johnson's analysis confirmed the conceptual problems of applying British common law principles to Aboriginal tenure. His analysis would end the state grants to land speculators and lead to creating the idea of land as a commodity.

In 1821, the Attorney General of the United States in the *Seneca Lands* opinion clarified the conflicting visions of Aboriginal tenure emerging from *Fletcher v. Peck*:

> So long as a tribe exists and remains in possession of its lands, its title and possession are sovereign and exclusive ... . Although the Indian title continues only during their possession, yet that possession has been always held sacred, and can never be disturbed but by their consent. They do not hold under the States, nor under the United States; their title is original, sovereign, and exclusive.[65]

In this view, Aboriginal tenures were distinct and separate, neither held under nor emanating from the land tenure systems of state or federal governments. Aboriginal tenures were allodial tenures.

A second "feigned" case, *Johnson and Graham's Lessees v. M'Intosh*, created by the Illinois-Wabash Company syndicalists, sought a new context for resolving conflicting claims for Aboriginal tenure.[66] Decided at the height of an emerging instrumental conception[67] of land as a commodity in United States law, the case leaves a legacy of confusing *dicta* that have been interpreted as authority for diminishing Aboriginal tenure and property rights.

The case involved a dispute between two non-Aboriginal purchasers of the same piece of western lands. Without any Aboriginal representation before the court, both parties advanced why they should be declared the valid purchasers. The Lessees, who were never in possession of the land, claimed an earlier title to tracts of land for which they had 1773 and 1775 deed poll conveyances[68] purportedly from the Illinois and

---

62   *Fletcher v. Peck, ibid.*

63   *Ibid.* at 147.

64   *Ibid.*

65   1 Op. Atty Gen. 465 (1821).

66   21 U.S. (8 Wheat.) 543, 5 L .Ed. 68 (U.S. 1823) [hereinafter *M'Intosh*].

67   M.J. Horwitz, "The Emergence of an Instrumental Conception of American Law, 1780-1820" (1971) 5 Perspectives In Am. Hist. 285 at 309-13.

68   A deed poll (*charta de una parte*, so called because the paper is polled or cut even, not indented) is a one-party deed. Usually the grantor makes and executes the document. Such a written form is a manifesto or declaration to all the world of the grantor's act and intentions. See *Jowitt's Dictionary of English Law*, s.v. "deed poll"; R. Megarry and H.W.R. Wade, *The Law of Real Property*, 5th ed. (London: Stevens, 1984) at cxxiv; Sir Edward Coke, *An Abridgement of the Lord Coke's Commentary on Littleton*, by Sir Humphrey Davenport, vol. 9a (New York: Garland Publishing, 1979) at 229; T.E. Tomlins, ed., *Lyttleton, His Treatise of Tenures* (New York: Garland Publishing, 1978) at 259; and *The New Shorter Oxford English Dictionary*, s.v. "deed poll." See also *Evans v. Patterson*, 71 U.S. 224 at 230 (U.S. 1868).

Piankashaw Nations.[69] William M'Intosh, the possessor, claimed the same tracts by an 1818 purchase from the United States,[70] who had obtained the land by 1785 treaty cession from the Piankashaw nation.[71] The Lessees brought an action for ejectment in the Illinois courts; the lower court affirmed for the federal patent to M'Intosh.[72] When the Lessees appealed to the Supreme Court, a unanimous Court affirmed the federal patent to M'Intosh was valid.

The stipulated facts of both parties asserted that since the "discovery" of the North American continent by Europeans:

---

69   *M'Intosh, supra* note 66 at 543-44. The stipulated facts claimed that the value of the 1773 deed was, "$24,000 dollars, current money of the United States, and upwards," paid and delivered to the Illinois nation at Kaskaskias, "who freely accepted it, and divided it among themselves," at para. 14. They also claimed that the 1775 deed was valued at $31,000 and upwards for land on both sides of the Ouabache or Wabash river, and paid to the Tabac and the chiefs of the Piankashaw Nation at Vincennes (Post St. Vincent), at paras. 15-16. The conveyances were held at British military posts and one public council. Prerogative law prohibited this deed poll, for the terms of the *Royal Proclamation of 1763, supra* note 15, prohibited Aboriginal land purchases by individuals. At paras. 12, 15, the deed stated that, "for a good and valuable consideration in the said deed stated, grant, bargain, sell, alien, lease, enfeoff, and confirm, to the said [grantees] and their heirs and assigns forever, in severalty, or to George the Third, the king of Great Britain and Ireland, his heirs and successors, for the use, benefit, and behoof of the grantees, their heirs and assigns, in severalty, by whichever of those tenures they might most legally hold [the land]." None of the grantees or any proxy ever obtained, or had actual possession of, any part of the lands: see para. 24. They repeatedly petitioned Congress unsuccessfully from 1781 to 1816 to acknowledge and confirm their title under the deeds. Thomas Johnson was one of the grantees of the 1775 conveyance; he died in 1819 and by his written will and testament devised his undivided share of the two tracts of land to his son, Joshua Johnson, and his heirs, and his grandson, Thomas J. Graham, at para. 22. These grantees and the devisee were all inhabitants of Maryland, at para. 23. The devisees entered the tracts of land under the will, and become thereof seized as the law required, at para. 23. See generally, the Illinois-Wabash Company syndicalists, suffering traders, and Vandalia colonialists in R.A. Williams Jr., *The American Indian In Western Legal Thought: The Discourse of Conquest* (New York: Oxford University Press, 1990) at 256-65, 289-300, 309-310.

70   The patent conveyance of 20 July 1818 was for 11,560 acres situated within the State of Illinois and contained within the 1775 deed poll from the Piankashaw Indians. He claimed that he entered these lands under the patent, and became possessor before the institution of the suit. For M'Intosh's argument, see Williams, *ibid.* at 310-12.

71   *Treaty of 3 August 1795* (Piankashaw, Wyandots, Delawares, Shawanoes, Ottawas, Chipewas, Putawatimes, Miamies, Eel-rivers, Weea's, Kickappos, and Kashaskias), Art. 3 in C.J. Kappler, *Indian Affairs: Laws and Treaties* (New York: AMS Press, 1971). Originally the Piankashaw were a member of the Miami Nation (*Oumamik*), who separated to become their own nation, hence their name, "those who separate." They were Algonquian speakers. Their ancient village was on the Wabash River at the Vermilion junction. Later, they created the settlement at Chippekawkay on the Wabash river (the present site of Vincennes, Ind.). See F.W. Hodge, *Handbook of American Indians North of Mexico*, vol. 2 (Washington, D.C.: Government Printing Office, 1907-10) at 240-241. The parties omitted the Treaty conditions from the stipulated facts. They relied on the 1783 *Act of Virginia* authorizing their Congressional delegates to, "convey, transfer, assign and make over to the United States, in Congress assembled, for the benefit of the said States, all right, title and claim, as well of soil as jurisdiction, which Virginia had to the territory" (defined by 1609 letters patent in the northwest of the Ohio) "with the reservations, limitations, and conditions of the 1783 Act." In 1784 the Virginia delegates conveyed by deed poll such land to the United States, at para. 19.

72   This court decision has not been found.

[the continent] was held, occupied and possessed, in full sovereignty, by various independent tribes of nations of Indians, who were the sovereigns of their respective portions of the territory, and the absolute owners and proprietors of the soil; and who neither acknowledged nor owed any allegiance of obedience to any European sovereign or state whatever; and that in making settlements within this territory, and in all the other parts of North America, where settlements were made, under the authority of the English government, or by its subjects, the right of soil was previously obtained by purchase or conquest, from the particular Indian tribes or nation by which the soil was claimed and held; or the consent of such tribe or nation was secured.[73]

Though neither party claimed by discovery or conquest, but rather through purchase and conveyance,[74] Chief Justice Marshall commented extensively on the United States title based on the international fictions of discovery and conquest, never discussing the relevant 1795 treaty purchase of the lands by the United States. The doctrine of discovery, he said, gave a title against all other European nations to the European nation discovering a continent.[75] It gave a right to acquire Aboriginal lands in America,[76] which the European nations asserted should be regulated as among themselves.[77] The Court took the European convention, despite having no explicit or written authority, to create a "universal recognition of these principles."[78]

What the Court did not say was that neither the British Crown nor the United States had discovered the lands in question. France had "discovered" the lands, from whom Britain, and in turn the United States, had acquired them.[79] The Court acknowl-

---

73   *M'Intosh, supra* note 66 at para. 3.

74   See generally N. Newton, "At the Whim of the Sovereign: Aboriginal Title Reconsidered" (1980) 31 Hastings L.J. 1215; J.Y. Henderson, "Unraveling the Riddle of Aboriginal Title" (1977) 5 Am. Indian L. Rev. 75.

75   The Court used the term "governments" at 573. Marshall's discussion of discovery seems to be drawn from E. de Vattel, *The Law of Nations: Or, Principles of the Law of Nature, Applied to the Conduct and Affairs of Nations and Sovereigns* (Philadelphia: T & J.W. Johnson, 1883) at §§ 207-209. See generally Williams, *supra* note 69 at 317.

76   *M'Intosh, supra* note 66 at 573.

77   *Ibid.* The Court subsequently rephrased the issue, saying at 584: "Thus, all the nations of Europe, who have acquired territory on this continent [by European treaties], have asserted in themselves, and have recognized in others, the exclusive right of the discoverer to appropriate the lands occupied by the Indians." Later the Court stated, at 587, that the United States maintained that discovery gave, "an exclusive right to extinguish the Indian title of occupancy, either by purchase of by conquest." Appropriation may be a different concept from acquisition.

78   *Ibid.* at 574.

79   *Ibid.* at 583-85. Their interests were acquired through Art. 2 of the *Treaty of Paris* by which the United States acquired from Great Britain its "properiety [sic] and territorial rights"; Great Britain acquired its jurisdictional interest from France. The same principles apply to the *Treaty of Ghent* (1814), which fixed the boundaries of the United States after the War of 1812 with Great Britain. Found in A. Toynbee, *Major Peace Treaties of Modern History, 1648-1967,* ed. by F.L. Israel (New York: McGraw Hill, 1967).

edged that any European nation's title was subject to the "Indian right of occupancy."[80] Thus the United States title was not an absolute title.[81] The discovering nation's "ultimate dominion, a power to grant the soil,"[82] was subject to what the Court concluded was Aboriginal tenure of the Indians as "the rightful occupants of the soil, with a legal as well as just claim to retain possession of it,"[83] which the Court called the "Indian title"[84] or "Indian right of occupancy."[85] This title, Mr. Justice Marshall said, was beyond the power of the courts to deny.

Alternatively, reminiscent of British feudal narratives, Chief Justice Marshall discussed European "title by conquest."[86] This was title "acquired and maintained by force."[87] "Conquest," he said, "gives a title which the Courts of the conqueror cannot deny, whatever the private and speculative opinions of individuals may be, respecting the original justice of the claim which has been successfully asserted."[88] Again, the factual context is that British claims were not derived by conquest against the Aboriginal nations, but rather against European nations, in particular Spain and France, and as far west as the Mississippi River.[89] European treaties to Great Britain had transferred these claims, and it was through the treaties that Britain had an international title to the lands.[90]

The Court asserted unnamed and inconclusive "frequent and bloody wars" between Europeans and Aboriginal nations, which caused the Indians to leave the land

---

80   *The Definitive Treaty of Peace and Friendship Between His Britannick Majesty, the Most Christian King, and the King of Spain: Concluded at Paris, the 10th day of February 1763, to Which the King of Portugal Acceded on the same Day* (London: E. Owen and T. Harrison, 1763); *M'Intosh, ibid.* at 584-85: "It has never been doubted, that either the United States, or the several states, had a clear title to all the lands within the boundary lines described in the treaty, subject only to the Indian right of occupancy."

81   *M'Intosh, ibid.* at 588. The Court stated: "An absolute title to land cannot exist, at the same time, in different persons, or in different governments. An absolute, must be an exclusive title, or at least a title which excludes all other not compatible with it. All our institutions recognized the absolute title of the crown, subject only to the Indian right of occupancy; and recognize that absolute title of the crown to extinguish that right. This is incompatible with an absolute and complete title in the Indians." This must also mean that the Crown title is not absolute and complete either—a strange proposition, since the institutions of the United States do not recognize the absolute title of the Crown. Nor did the *Treaty of Paris* pass more than claims to the territory.

82   *Ibid.* at 574.

83   *Ibid.*

84   *Ibid.* at 587. This was the concept used in *Fletcher v. Peck, supra* note 33.

85   *M'Intosh, ibid.* at 574, 585, 588.

86   *Ibid.* at 588-91.

87   *Ibid.* at 589.

88   *Fletcher v. Peck, supra* note 33 at 588. This conquest appears to be the American Revolution against Great Britain. No conquest was involved in the facts as presented. This issue was raised in the context of the Court's rejection of the issue in terms of the rights of agriculturalists, merchants and manufacturers (on abstract principles) to expel hunters from the territory they possess, or to contract their limits. See Vattel, *supra* note 75 at § 81.

89   *Fletcher v. Peck, ibid.* at 588.

90   *Ibid.* at 588-89.

to follow the game, [91] and allowed the Crown to parcel out the land to its subjects. These subjects' claims to the land were either immediately from the Crown, or mediately, through its grantee or deputies. Such claims were not a title of conquest, however, but of abandonment. [92]

The Marshall Court did not rely on either discovery or conquest in reaching its decisions. Neither was in question in the case, since both parties had stipulated the sovereign tribes or nations of Indians were the "absolute owners and proprietors of the soil." [93] The Lessees' interest under the deed poll had been conveyed to the Federal government in 1784, and federal title was perfected by the 1795 treaty purchase. The Court relied on a "new and different rule" created in *Fletcher v. Peck*, that unextinguished "Indian title, which is certainly to be respected by all courts, until it be legally extinguished, is not such as to be absolutely repugnant to seisin in fee on the part of the state." [94] The Court affirmed the principle of *sui generis* Aboriginal tenure distinct from federal or state land tenure system. [95]

The Court's discussion of the law of nations for discovery and conquest as the source of federal title was technically unnecessary. If the Piankashaw nation had been involved in the litigation, they would have been able to place in evidence the 1795 treaty with the United States, where they had sold the involved lands to the United States, acknowledged their nation to be under the protection of the United States, and had reserved some of their Aboriginal tenure for themselves. [96] This treaty was never introduced to the Court or mentioned in the pleadings; instead the attorneys argued legal principles derived from European international custom of the law of nations rather than from the controlling treaties and constitutional law.

---

91   *Ibid.* at 590.

92   *Ibid.* at 590-591.

93   *Ibid.* at 544-45 at para. 3. In British law, this category is allodial tenure. Allodial tenure is land not held of any lord or superior, in which, therefore, the owner has an absolute property and not a mere estate under another tenure. No subject in England can hold land allodially. See *Jowitt's Dictionary of English Law, s.v.* See also, J.Y. Henderson, "M'kmaq Tenure in Atlantic Canada" (1995) 18 Dal. L.J. 196 at 267-91.

94   *Fletcher v. Peck, ibid.* at 592.

95   *Oneida Indian Nations v. County of Oneida*, 414 U.S. 661 at 667 (U.S. 1974); *United States v. Alcae Band of Tillamooks*, 329 U.S. 40 at 46 (U.S. 1946); *United States ex rel. Haupai Indians v. Santa Fe Pacific Railroad*, 314 U.S. 339 (U.S. 1941) [hereinafter *Santa Fe*].

96   Kappler, *supra* note 71 at Arts. 3 and 5, *Treaty of Aug. 3, 1795* (Piankashaw, Wyandots, Delawares, Shawanoes, Ottawas, Chipewas, Putawatimes, Miamies, Eel-rivers, Weea's, Kickappos, and Kashaskias). All lands adjacent to the post of St. Vincennes were purchased by the United States for a quantity of goods to the value of $20,000 that the United States delivered to the tribes, and the promise of an annual delivery of goods valued at $9,500 to the tribes, $500 of which went to the Piankashaw: 1795 7 U.S. Stat. 49. Article 1 of the *Treaty of June 7, 1803* (Piankashaws, Delawares, Shawanoes, Putawatimies, Miamies, Eel Rovers, Weeas, Kickapoos, Kashasias nation of Indians) clarifies the 1795 treaty cession along the Wabash river, because the United States found it difficult to determine the precise limits of the land where Indian title has been extinguished, and gives up all claims to land adjoining to or in the neighborhood of the extinguished land: 1795 7 U.S. Stat. 74.

Without the treaties' purchase in evidence, the Court unanimously agreed that Piankashaw law exclusively governed the grantees' rights under the deed poll. The federal courts had no jurisdiction over these issues of Piankashaw land tenure and law. The Court hinted that if the deed poll had been protected in a subsequent treaty cession, it would have been a vested property right:

> The person who purchases lands from the Indians, within their territory incorporates himself with them, so far as respects the property purchased; holds their title under their protection, and subject to their laws. If they annul the grant, we know of no tribunal [of the United States] which can revise and set aside the proceedings.[97]

In a subsequent case, the Court held that a Spanish land grant derived from the Aboriginal nation's deed poll explicitly protected in an Indian treaty had continuing legal validity,[98] even though Congress had continually rejected their deed poll.

The Supreme Court of the United States in *M'Intosh* affirmed the distinct theory of Aboriginal tenure as allodial property, and as a different proprietarian order[99] deriving solely from Aboriginal authority, and autonomous from either the state or federal land tenure systems. The conflicting claims to Aboriginal land were to be adjusted by Aboriginal laws and federal treaties and laws. In the case of *Jackson v. Porter* in 1825, Justice Smith Thompson (Circuit Court, New York) restated the holding in *M'Intosh*, as follows:

> A purchaser, from the natives, at all events, could acquire only the Indian title, and must hold under them and according to their laws. The grant must derive its efficacy from their will, and if they choose to resume it and make a different disposition of it, courts cannot protect the right before granted. The purchaser incorporates himself with the Indians, and the purchase is to be considered in the same light as if the grant had been made to an Indian; and might be resumed by the tribe, and granted over again at their pleasure.[100]

In 1830 in *Cherokee Nation v. Georgia*,[101] Chief Justice Marshall articulated the relationship between Georgia jurisdiction and Aboriginal tenure reserved for the Cherokee nation under a treaty with the United States:

> [t]he Indians are acknowledged to have an unquestionable, and, heretofore, unquestioned right to the lands they occupy, and that right shall be extinguished by a voluntary cession to our government.[102]

---

97   *Fletcher v. Peck, supra* note 33 at 593-94. See also *New Jersey v. Wilson*, 11 U.S. (7 Cranch) 164 (U.S. 1812).

98   See especially *Mitchel v. United States*, 34 U.S. (9 Pet.) 711 (U.S. 1835) [hereinafter *Mitchel*]. Many examples of such provisions for non-Indian lands appear in the treaty. *E.g.*, Kappler, *supra* note 71 at 433, 572; R.L. Barsh and J.Y. Henderson, *The Road: Indian Tribes and Political Liberty* (Berkeley: University of California Press, 1980) at 46, n. 63.

99   *M'Intosh, supra* note 66 at 593-94.

100 1 Paine. 475, 13 Cas. (No.7143) 1 (Cir. Ct. N.Y. 1825).

101 30 U.S. (5 Pet.) 1 (U.S. 1830) [hereinafter *Cherokee Nation*].

102 *Ibid.* at 17. Compare to the opinion in *Holland v. Peck*, 8 Mart. & Y.119 at 120 (Tenn. S.C. 1823) that held: "The Cherokees, though living within the limits of Tennessee, and upon lands the dominion of which belongs to this state, and having themselves only the usufruct thereof."

Justice Baldwin analogized that "Indians have rights of occupancy to their lands as sacred as the fee simple, absolute of the whites."[103] Justices Story and Thompson, dissenting on jurisdictional issues, characterized the reserved land in a *sui generis* manner:

> notwithstanding we do not recognize the right of the Indians to transfer the absolute title of their lands other than to ourselves, ... the principle is universally admitted, that this occupancy belongs to them as a matter of right, and not by mere indulgence. They cannot be disturbed in the enjoyment of it, or deprived of it, without their free consent; or unless a just and necessary war should sanction their dispossession. In this view of their situation, there is as full and complete recognition of their sovereignty, as if they were the absolute owners of the soil.[104]

In 1832, in *Worcester v. Georgia*, Supreme Court Chief Justice Marshall explicitly harmonized the discovery and conquest principles with the concept of the *sui generis* tenure of Aboriginal nations:

> America, separated from Europe by a wide ocean, was inhabited by a distinct people, divided into separate nations, independent of each other and the rest of the world, having institutions of their own, and governing themselves by their own laws. It is difficult to comprehend the proposition, that the Inhabitants of either quarter of the globe could have rightful original claims of dominion over the inhabitants of the other, or over the lands they occupied; or that the discovery of either by the other should give the discoverer rights in the country discovered, which annulled the pre-existing right of its ancient possessors.[105]

The Court stated that title by discovery allocated the "exclusive right to purchase, but did not found that right on a denial of the rights of the [Aboriginal] possessor to sell."[106] Crown charters and other European and United States grants to third parties were "blank paper" so far as the rights of the Aboriginal nations were concerned.[107] In the absence of Aboriginal consent by treaty, discovery had no effect on Aboriginal nations.

---

103   *Cherokee Nation, ibid.* at 48.

104   *Ibid.* at 55.

105   *Worcester, supra* note 32 at 541, 544. Vattel, *supra* note 75 at § 208 writes that, "it is not difficult to determine" that extravagant claims and pretensions based upon the doctrine of "discovery" would be, "an absolute infringement of the natural rights of men, and repugnant to the views of nature."

106   *Worcester, ibid.* at 544.

107   *Ibid.* at 546, 544. See *Arnold v. Mundy*, 6 N.J.L. 1 at 84 (N.J. C.A. 1821). The Court stated that: "The soil is none of his [referring to Charles IIs grant of a Charter to the Duke of York]; it is the natives' by the *jus gentium*, the law of nations"; *Odgen v. Lee*, 6 Hill 546 at 548 (N.Y. S.C. 1844) [hereinafter *Odgen*]. The Court said: "But these grants [Crown charters and patents] were not intended to convey, and the grantees never pretended that they had acquired an absolute fee in the land. They neither took nor claimed any thing more than the ultimate fee, or the right of dominion after the Indian title should be extinguished."

The Court stated the Cherokee nations had never been conquered by the United States or voluntarily relinquished their inherent sovereignty to the United States.[108] Rather, they had entered into treaties that were part of the supreme law of the land under Article VI of the United States Constitution: "The Indian nations had always been considered as distinct, independent political communities, retaining their original natural rights, as the undisputed possessors of the soil from time immemorial."[109]

United States Supreme Court Justice Baldwin in *Mitchel v. United States*[110] (1835) held that friendly Aboriginal nations in Florida "were considered as owning them [their lands] by a perpetual right of possession"[111] that "could not be taken without their consent."[112] Indian occupation or possession was equal to the fee simple of British law:

> [it] was considered with reference to their habits and modes of life; their hunting grounds were as much in their actual possession as the cleared fields of the whites; and their rights to its exclusive enjoyment in their own way and for their own purposes were as much respected, until they abandoned them, made a cession to the government, or an authorized sale to individuals.[113]

In 1844, the Mississippi High Court of Errors and Appeals stated: "Before the treaty, the land belonged to the Choctaws as a nation ... . Theirs was a right to retain possession, and to use it according to their own discretion, though not to dispose of the soil except to the government."[114] The Supreme Court of New York commented: "The title by occupancy has been uniformly acknowledged, both by the colonial and state governments, from the first settlement of this country down to the present day, and it cannot now be successfully questioned in the judicial tribunal."[115] The New York Court of Errors clarified these decisions:

> [that] the Indian title to land is an absolute fee, and that the pre-emption right conceded to Massachusetts, was simply a right to acquire by purchase from the Indians their ownership of the soil, whenever they should choose to sell it.[116]

By 1873, the Supreme Court of the United States interpreted *Johnson v. M'Intosh*:

---

108 *Worcester, ibid.* at 542-46.

109 *Ibid.* at 559, 560.

110 *Supra,* note 98 at 749. Under the *Royal Proclamation of 1763, supra* note 15, Baldwin noted that in Florida, like Québec: "the king waived all rights accruing by conquest or cession, and thus most solemnly acknowledged that the Indians had rights of property they would cede or reserve, and that the boundaries of his territorial and proprietary rights should be such, and such only as were stipulated by these treaties."

111 *Mitchel, ibid.* at 746.

112 *Ibid.* at 749.

113 *Ibid.* at 746.

114 *Coleman v. Tish-Mo-Mah,* 4 S. & M 440-48 (1844), Calyton J.

115 *Odgen, supra* note 107 at 549.

116 *Fellows v. Lee,* 59 U.S. (5 Den.) 628 (U.S. 1846).

[t]he authority of that case has never been doubted. The right of the Indians to their occupancy is as sacred as that of the United States to the fee. ... This right of use and occupancy by the Indians is unlimited. They may exercise it at their own discretion.[117]

The Court held that what the United States had by discovery was a legal monopoly to purchase Aboriginal title by treaties.[118] The legal monopoly operated less as a denial of Indian title and right than it did as a bar to any private purchaser who might disdain existing governments, cast off allegiance, and stand upon independent lands and territory as one "who would be king" in a fee simple empire.

In the United States, 366 treaties were enacted to purchase Aboriginal tenure and create reserved Aboriginal tenure called Indian reservations. These treaty land purchases fuelled the American economy; the federal government relied on the sale of ceded land for revenue. Because of the abhorrence of taxation, until 1845 these sales comprised at least 10 per cent of the federal reserve.[119] By 1850, the resale of Indian lands to third parties provided the federal government with $2,299,272.65 to satisfy financial obligations and services of the treaties, including direct payments to the Indians. While government sales of land provided $5,273,100 in loans to the federal government, Kentucky, Alabama, Tennessee, Maryland, Michigan, Missouri, Indiana, and Arkansas from the Aboriginal trust accounts, total federal appropriations for national Indian administration amounted to only $121,500.[120]

In 1871, the Congress ended the treaty land reconciliation with the Aboriginal nations, but vested all existing treaty rights and obligations:

---

117 *U.S. v. Cook*, 86 U.S. (19 Wall.) 591 at 592-93, 22 L. Ed. 210 (U.S. 1873) [hereinafter *U.S. v. Cook*]; see also *Leavenworth, Lawrence, and Galveston Railroad Company v. United States*, U.S. 92 (2 Otto) 733 at 754, 23 L. Ed. 634 (U.S. 1875); *Beecher v. Wetherby*, 95 U.S. 517 at 526, 24 L. Ed. 440 (U.S. 1877). The Court stated: "the right of the Indians to their occupancy is as sacred as that of the United States to the fee, but it is only a right of occupancy"; *Buttz v. Northern Pacific Railroad*, 119 U.S. 55 at 67-68, 30 L. Ed. 330 (U.S. 1886). The Court declared: "This right of occupancy was protected by the political power and respected by the courts until extinguished when the patentee took the unencumbered fee."

118 *U.S. v. Cook, ibid.* See *United States v. Kagama*, 118 U.S. 375, 30 L. Ed. 228 (U.S. 1886). Federal law acknowledged this fact, *e.g., Proclamation of Continental Congress, September 22, 1783* in *Journals of the Continental Congress, Edited From the Original Records in the Library of Congress*, vol. 25 (Washington, D.C.: U.S. Government's Printing Office, 1904-1937) at 602.; Art. 3 of the *Northwest Ordinance*, July 13, 1787, *ibid.*, vol. 32 at 340-341. Beginning in 1790 and stretching to 1834, Congress enacted a series of Trade and Intercourse Acts designed to regulate Indian trade; one provision declared any Indian land cession other than those made under the authority of the United States null and void. This included any cession made to a State. *Trade and Intercourse Act*, c. 33, § 1, 1 Stat 137 (1790); *Trade and Intercourse Act*, c. 161, § 12, 4 Stat. 729 at 730-731 (1834) (codified at 25 U.S.C. § 177 (1988 & Supp. II 1990)). *Joint Tribal Council of the Passamaquoddy Tribe v. Morton*, 388 F. Supp. 649 (D. Me.), affirmed, 528 F. 2d 370 (1st Cir. 1975); *Maine Indian Claims Settlement Act*, 25 U.S.C. §§ 1721-1735 (1988). These provisions were derived from the *Royal Instructions* (1761) and *Royal Proclamation of 1763, supra* note 15.

119 U.S. Census, *Statistical History of the United States from Colonial Times to the Present* (Stamford, Conn.: Fairfield Publishers, 1960) at 712-13.

120 *Report of Trust Responsibilities, supra* note 26.

> No Indian nation or tribe within the territory of the United States, shall be acknowledged or recognized as an independent nation, tribe or power with whom the United States may contract by treaty; nor obligation of any treaty law fully made and ratified with any such Indian nations or tribe prior to March 3, 1871, shall be hereby invalidated or impaired.[121]

This Act did not prevent future cession of western Aboriginal lands, but it changed the mechanism to executive agreements. In subsequent enactments creating western territories, the Congress acknowledged the sanctity of Aboriginal tenure and sovereignty. In 1872, the United States Supreme Court in *Holden v. Joy* held Aboriginal tenure "as absolute, subject only to the preemptive right of purchase acquired by the United States as successors of Great Britain."[122]

The Revised Statutes codified these decisions in the title of Territories incorporated into the western Statehood Enabling Acts:

> Nothing in this title shall be construed to Impair the rights of person or property pertaining to the Indians in our Territory, so long as such rights remain unextinguished by treaty between the United States and such Indians, or to include any territory which, by treaty with any Indian tribe, is not, without the consent of such tribe, embraced within the territorial limits or jurisdiction of any state or Territory, but all such territory shall be excepted out of the boundaries and constitute no part of any Territory now or hereafter organized until such tribe constitute its assent to the President to be embraced within a particular Territory.[123]

In *United States ex rel. Haupai Indians v. Santa Fe Pacific Railroad Co.*,[124] the Court held that the railroad was liable for trespass damages for illegal use of the Aboriginal tenure, rejecting the argument that Aboriginal tenure had to be based upon a treaty, statute, or formal governmental action. A series of executive[125] and congressional actions[126] that had mistakenly treated Aboriginal tenure as public land did not divest them of their tenure, since Aboriginal tenure continues as a perpetual right of use and occupancy virtually equivalent to fee simple interests against all but the United States. The United States Supreme Court stated Aboriginal tenure is a question of fact rather than a question of law, and affirmed that Aboriginal occupancy finding no recognition in any statute or other formal governmental action is not conclusive.[127]

---

121 25 U.S.C. § 17. The treaty is the "Supreme Law of the Land" under Art. 6 of the United States Constitution. When exceptional circumstances require existing treaty rights to be abrogated by Congressional act, an obligation arises to pay just compensation: *United States v. Creek Nation*, 295 U.S. 103 (U.S. 1935).

122 84 U.S. 211 at 244, 21 L. Ed. 523 (U.S. 1872).

123 R.S.U.S., § 1839.

124 *Supra* note 95.

125 *Ibid.* at 351 (report of the Surveyor General); at 354-56 (Indian Department moving Indians to a congressionally created reservation).

126 *Santa Fe, ibid.* at 347 (congressional railroad grant); *ibid.* at 348-49 (grant of certain parcel to citizens); *ibid.* at 353 (statute setting up separate reservations for Hualapai Indians).

127 *Ibid.* at 347, citing *Cramer v. United States*, 261 U.S. at 229 (U.S. 1923).

11. British North America

In British North America, the judicial and political structure of the British colonies prevented judicial reconciliation of Aboriginal tenure and Crown tenure. British colonial law viewed Aboriginal lands as a part of the Crown tenure, not as a distinct or *sui generis* land tenure system as the United States courts had decided. Because the imperial Crown in the treaties, the royal instructions, proclamations, and laws prohibited royal governors from surveying or passing patent to the reserved Aboriginal lands, requiring all persons to be removed from unceded or unpurchased Aboriginal lands and prohibiting any private purchases of Aboriginal tenure, the colonial legal system viewed Aboriginal land as part of the Crown's tenure.

Within a year of the American Revolution, the imperial order in the Atlantic provinces and Upper and Lower Canada was upset by Loyalist refugees from the southern colonies who tripled the colony's population to 42,000.[128] These refugees brought the idea of a proprietarian order, a "fee simple empire," to Canadian law. Because the Crown had to purchase Aboriginal tenure from the Aboriginal nations to accommodate the new refugees, it issued prerogative Instructions that forbade any free grants of land in North America.[129] In Upper and Lower Canada, the governors negotiated many new treaties for land surrenders, but the Maritime provinces did not. After ignoring the problem, the Maritimes attempted to correct it by proclamations and colonial law, which resulted in the imperial Crown's intervening to establish its authority over Aboriginal nations and treaties.

Since Aboriginal tenure was viewed as Crown tenure, the colonial courts did not play an active role in reconciling Aboriginal nations' tenure with Crown sovereignty or in asserting and defending their treaty rights or land tenure. The courts rarely noted the prerogative treaties or the 1763 Proclamation; they focused on colonial legislation. Although the Mikmaw Compact and treaties provided for the civil courts to resolve controversies, between 1763 and 1869, for example, in the Atlantic provinces there is only one recorded case that deals, even indirectly, with Aboriginal issues: *The King v. Watson*.[130] The imperial colonial office and legislative record illustrated a clashing of interests in the reserved lands, yet the courts were silent. Because of the way the courts were established, the courts even under colonial legislature were ineffective in dealing with these issues.

---

128 L.F.S. Upton, *Micmacs and Colonists: Indian-White Relations in the Maritimes, 1713-1867* (Vancouver: U.B.C. Press, 1979) at 78.

129 Board of Trade 6/20; Public Record Office, Royal Instructions, 1768, 1775, 1786; Public Archives of Canada, Manuscript Group 40 B7, at 90-102 (Arts. 48, 60 and 61), 116-160 (Art. 38), 231-237 (Arts. 31 and 39); Public Record Office, Colonial Office Series, MG 42/316, fo.65. The full list of archival sources, with abbreviations used throughout: United Kingdom Colonial Office Series [CO], United Kingdom Public Record Office [PRO], Privy Council [PC], Public Archives of Canada [PAC], Manuscript Group [MG], Record Group [RG], Public Archives of Nova Scotia [PANS], Public Archives of New Brunswick [PANB], Journal of the Legislative Assembly of New Brunswick [JLANB]. Also see note 2, above, for another abbreviation, LANSJ.

130 (1828), 1 N.B.R. 188 (N.B. S.C.) [hereinafter *Watson*].

In Upper Canada, the case of *Church v. Fenton* illustrated the common law perspectives toward "Indian title" and "Indian lands" in Crown tenure.[131] The case involved lands surrendered for sale to the imperial Crown by a 1854 treaty from the "Chiefs, Sachems and Principal men of the Indian tribes resident at Saugeen and Owen Sound" of the "Peninsula known as the Saugeen and Owen Sound Indian Reserve."[132] The surrendered lands were retained under the control and management of the Indian Department, and in 1857 sold by a contract to a private purchaser for payment in ten annual installments. The purchaser assigned to another, who assigned to the patentee and plaintiff. After acquiring the patent in 1869, however, in 1872 the Grey county sold by tax deed the same land to another purchaser for taxes due between 1863 and 1869; in the following year the purchaser sold the land by deed to the defendant. The patentee argued that the lands remained "Indian lands" under Crown jurisdiction and were not subject to provincial taxes until he acquired the patent.

In determining that the purchased Indian lands by a contract of sale were subject to provincial taxation by the provincial Assessment Acts as "ordinary unpatented land," Judge Gwynne of the Ontario Court of Common Pleas articulated his understanding of Indian lands' relationship to Crown land. He stated that the British Crown waived its right to conquest over all the lands in the province until a treaty of surrender extinguished "Indian title":

> Prior to the execution of this treaty of surrender, Her Majesty was seised of the lands therein mentioned in right of her Crown, but ... the Crown had imposed upon itself this restriction, that it never would exercise its right to sell or lease those lands, or any part of them, until released or surrendered by the Indians, for the purpose thereby of extinguishing what was called Indian title...[133]

When reserved and protected Aboriginal lands were surrendered, the consideration paid was an Indian "annuity" derived from the "interest accruing from the proceeds of the sale" to a purchaser. Under provincial statutes, the surrendered Indian title under the control and management of the Indian Department was designated "Indian lands" to distinguish them from other Crown lands designated "Public lands." The sale of public lands was "provincial revenue" and could be applied for public uses of the province.[134] Indian titles surrendered for sale by treaty before confederation and sold by contract to a purchaser were not transferred to federal jurisdiction "lands reserved for the Indians" within section 91(24) of the *Constitution [British North America] Act, 1867*, even if the patent was issued after confederation.[135]

Crown officials understood the reserved territories of the Aboriginal nations (Indian title), which had not been ceded or purchased, within the British colonies to be

---

131 (1878), 28 U.C.C.P. 384 (Ont. C.P.), affirmed (1879), 4 O.A.R. 159 (Ont. C.A.), affirmed (1880), 5 S.C.R. 239 (S.C.C.) [hereinafter *Fenton*].

132 *Ibid.* at 385-86.

133 *Ibid.* at 388.

134 *Ibid.*

135 *Ibid.* at 398-400.

part of Crown tenure in North America. They viewed Aboriginal tenure as an "inferior" Crown interest under British common law. Specifically, the colonialists interpreted the phrases "Crown lands" or "King's Domaine"[136] and "waste land," as in British law, as lands that were within the Crown tenure and not directly or indirectly granted to a tenant. For the prerogative governments in the colonies, "Crown land" had a different meaning: specifically, protective jurisdiction over unceded and unpurchased Aboriginal tenure. Under prerogative laws, the Crown had an unperfected ultimate or future title, for example, the exclusive right to purchase Aboriginal tenure when the nations were willing to sell their lands. Crown grants to colonizers of reserved lands were not considered appropriate; they were not expectation interests to be perfected by Crown purchases.

A. Colonial legislative protection

In the Atlantic royal colonies, the loyalists believed a landed aristocracy was the proper order by which the Crown could preserve its authority in the colonies. The imperial parliament, however, refused to make large, free grants of land to the loyalists to establish such an aristocratic order out of the lands acquired from the Maliseet nation by treaties.[137] Under this land cession, the prerogative Instructions allowed the Governor of Nova Scotia only to grant a hundred acres to each head and family plus fifty acres for each member.[138] In 1784, the Crown created New Brunswick and Cape Breton separate from Nova Scotia, with each colony being granted the Nova Scotia framework.

Instead of negotiating land surrender treaties with the Aboriginal nations as in Upper Canada, the Atlantic colonies established a licence of occupation and "location ticket" regime[139] to urge new immigrants to till newly turned land at the edges of the reserved lands. In British and colonial law, a licence was merely permission given to the occupier of land, which, without creating any interest in the land, allowed the licensee to do some act that would otherwise be trespass.[140] In unceded Aboriginal ter-

---

136   See Opinion of Suckling, Attorney General of Québec, 1 August 1766. PAC, RG 1, E1, vol. 3 at 264-65; "Letter of Governor Murray to Lords of Trade, 26 May 1767" in Canada, *Labrador Boundary Case: Documents Accompanying Canada's Case*, vol. 6 (Ottawa: Department of Justice, 1927) at 2799.

137   See W.S. MacNutt, *The Atlantic Provinces: The Emergence of Colonial Society, 1712-1877* (Toronto: McClelland & Stewart, 1965) at 1. These lands were at the mouth of the St. John River and the shores of Passamaquoddy Bay.

138   *Ibid.* at 95.

139   *Ibid.* at 149-50. There is no existing definition for location ticket or licence of occupation in British land law. In civil law in Quebec, a location ticket exists in colonization land; see *Marcoux v. L'Heureux* (1921), 63 S.C.R. 263a (S.C.C.) (The deputy minister had express power to adjudicate or cancel a "license of occupation"); *Howard v. Stewart* (1914), 50 S.C.R. 311(S.C.C.) (the holder of a location ticket had an interest in the land capable of being sold); *Green v. Blackburn* (1908), 40 S.C.R. 647 (S.C.C.) (The expression "proprietor of the soil" is not intended to designate the holder of a location ticket, and, consequently, persons holding Crown lands, merely as locatees, have no vested preferential rights to grants from the Crown of the mining rights).

140   *Thomas v. Sorrel* (1673), Vaughan 330 at 351.

ritory, these Crown officials wrongly granted land to colonials; after ten years' occupation of the granted land, the grantees were to pay quit rents. Because the families refused to pay these quit rents, however, they never acquired any legal title.[141]

In 1793, the Superintendent of Indian Affairs described to the Lieutenant-Governor of Nova Scotia the legal "scandal" of the location tickets system within lands reserved for the Aboriginal nations, arguing that petitions against the trespassers were legitimate.[142] Lord Selkirk's diary noted that the Nova Scotia immigrants were nevertheless satisfied with the licenses of occupation, which were generally accepted as security in lieu of clear legal title that the government was powerless to grant.[143] By 1815, reports affirmed there were thousands of unlicenced squatters clearing the forest in the backwoods of Nova Scotia and especially New Brunswick.[144]

The imperial Parliament took a negative view of fraudulent and imaginary land regimes in the Atlantic provinces and colonialists' failures to pay quit rent. In 1829, the Undersecretary for the Colonies determined that land grants to families in British North America were hopelessly inefficient because of local mismanagement, the jobbing of speculators, and official favouritism.[145] In the 1830s, the Select Committee on Aborigines of the British Settlements of United Kingdom Parliament began an extensive investigation of the problem, most of its evidence coming from colonial civil servants' testimony about the widespread abuse of Aboriginal tenure and treaty rights. In its compendious 1836 Report, the Select Committee established a global policy that a just order required imperial authority over Aboriginal nations and tribes, not colonial control or trust administration:[146]

> The protection of the Aborigines ... is not a trust which could conveniently be confined to the local Legislature, ... they will be unfit for the performance of this office. For a local Legislature, if properly constituted, should partake largely of the interest, and represent the feeling of settled opinions of the great mass of the people for whom they act. But the settlers in almost every Colony, having either disputes to adjust with the native tribes, or claims to urge against them, the representative bodies is virtually a party, and therefore ought not to be the judge in such controversies. [147]

In 1843, the imperial Parliament acknowledged and affirmed the continuing prerogative treaty jurisdiction over foreign lands acquired by treaties as separate from the parliamentary or colonial administration regimes.[148]

---

141 *Ibid.* at 149-50, 157.

142 PAC, Monk Papers, MG 23, G 11-19 at 1051-55.

143 PC, 7 White 1958 at 54-55.

144 MacNutt, *supra* note 137 at 149-50.

145 PRO, CO at 217/146.

146 Select Committee, *supra* note 1.

147 *Ibid.* at 77, 26 June 1837.

148 *Foreign Jurisdiction Act,* 1843 (U.K.), 6 & 7 Vict., c. 94; *Foreign Jurisdiction Act,* 1890 (U.K.), 45 Vict., c. 37; *Foreign Jurisdiction Act,* 1913 (U.K.), 3 & 4 Geo. V, c. 16.

In 1838, the Nova Scotia legislative assembly convened a special committee to attempt to restore the prerogative order. Its report concluded that "the whole reserve originally made for the use and benefit of the Indians, ... should be faithfully continued, ... placing reliance upon the promises of Government; to prevent the Indians from believing that" any British subject can trespass upon their reserves "with impunity" or all trespassers can be "treated with as much lenity and forbearance" as persons who have taken "unauthorized possession of the waste lands of the Crown in various parts of the Province."[149] The Colonial Office, unimpressed with the report, noted that the Aboriginal claims for fair treatment were not based on any debt of gratitude but rather "resolved themselves into an equitable right to be compensated for the loss of land."[150]

In 1842, the Nova Scotia Assembly enacted *An Act to provide for the Instruction and Permanent Settlement of the Indians*,[151] creating a Commissioner of Indian Affairs with these responsibilities:

> supervision and management of all lands that are, or may hereafter be, set apart as Indian Reservations; or for the use of the Indians—to ascertain and define their boundaries—to discover and report to the Governor all cases of intrusion—and of the transfer or sale of the said lands—or for their use and possession by the Indian; and generally, to protect the said Indians from encroachment and alienation and preserve them for the use of the Indians.[152]

Where the Commissioner found "any intrusion, encroachment, or unauthorized settlement or improvement upon any such lands," the Assembly authorized the Commissioner to proceed by information to courts, "notwithstanding the legal title by Grant or otherwise, may not be vested in Her Majesty." [153] After two years, in 1845, the Indian Act Commissioner acknowledged: "it will not be easy for any Commissioner holding a seat in the Provincial Assembly to do justice to the Indian, and to retain the goodwill of his constituents."[154]

In New Brunswick, the Lieutenant-Governor instructed that a report on the tribes in the province be prepared, which in turn advised that "Their Great Mother the Queen should retain the Title in Trust" of reserved lands, and the management of Indian Affairs should be placed under the immediate superintendence of the Executive.[155] In

---

149 PANS, MSS documents, vol. 430, doc.187.

150 CO 217/178, ff. 78-88.

151 S.N.S. 1842, c. 16 [hereinafter *Instruction and Permanent Settlement Act*]. *Watson, supra* note 130, dealt with the effects of a Crown purchase in 1807 on two tracts of land that had been claimed by the Indians for over one hundred years. The Crown, out of possession for 20 years, and Watson entered the lands and took possession. Watson pleaded that since the Crown had not been in possession for 20 years, he could not be ousted of his adverse possession. The court did not think it was necessary to call the defence, and directed the jury to find for Watson.

152 *Instruction and Permanent Settlement Act, ibid.* at s. 3.

153 *Ibid.* at s. 5.

154 LANSJ, [1845] at 170. At 188 the Committee for Indian Affairs of the Assembly recognized, "the propriety of legal steps being taken to punish and remove the intruders."

155 W.D. Hamilton and W.A. Spray, *Source Material Relating to the New Brunswick Indians* (Fredericton, N.B.: Hamray Books, 1977) at 83-110. In private trust law in Britain and Nova Scotia, the Crown could not assume the position of trustee because equity could not issue orders that were enforceable against the Sovereign: *Casebeard v. A.G.* (1819), (EX) 6 Price 411, E.R. 856.

1841, the Lieutenant-Governor issued two Proclamations requiring those who had illegally occupied "Lands reserved by the Crown for the benefit of the Indian Tribes within this Province" to leave immediately and desist from cutting the timber or be prosecuted under action for information by the Crown before the Supreme Court.[156]

These recommendations or proclamations were never implemented. A select committee of the New Brunswick Assembly opposed both measures,[157] following which the provincial Attorney General and Solicitor General issued an opinion that the Executive Council could lease reserved Indian lands on its own authority to trespassers; that instructions from London were only required before Indian lands could be sold.[158] In 1844, the Legislative Council enacted *An Act to Regulate The Management and Disposal of the Indian Reserves in This Province*,[159] designed to break up "the extensive tracks of valuable Land reserved for the Indians." The Act authorized the executive council to lease or sell parts of these lands at Public Auction to the highest bidder, and to "lay off" the Indian reserves into "villages or Town Plots, for the exclusive benefit of the Indians," and make free grants and location tickets to the Indians. The money raised, less a 5-per cent commission, which was applied to the local Commissioner and placed in the Provincial Treasurer, was to be applied to the exclusive benefit of the Indians, especially for the relief of the aged and infirm.

New Brunswick's 1844 Act and the land sale policy proved to be a failure. The New Brunswick squatters refused to lease or purchase the reserved lands. Since no trespasser was to be ejected, there was no reason to purchase or lease the land.[160] What lands were sold were purchased on the installment system. Very little money found its way into the Indian Fund. Timber licenses were issued that allowed timber operators to cut on the reserved lands, but the government neglected to collect the stumpage fees.[161]

Meantime, in 1837, the Upper Canada legislative assembly established an act for disposing of public lands,[162] or lands that were "open for location" and not "otherwise specially reserved."[163] Lands reserved to Indians were distinct from public lands and wasteland. Justice Gwynne, for example, held that the act "did not affect the lands vested in Her Majesty in which the Indians were interested."[164] Public lands were defined as those lands proceeds from the sale of which constituted public revenue of the province rather than the imperial Indian Department.[165] In 1850, an Act to protect the

---

156 PANB, RG 2, RS 7, vol. 40 at 226, 229.

157 JLANB, [1843] at 206-208, 235-36.

158 Report of the Attorney-General and Solicitor-General, 22 February, 1842. PANB, RG 2, RS 6, vol. 4 at 325, 328-29.

159 S.N.B. 1844, c. 47. Assented to by Her Majesty in Council 3rd September.

160 PANS, RG 2, RS 7, vol. 40 at 214-22; RS 8, Indians.

161 Hamilton & Spray, *supra* note 155 at 128-29.

162 *An Act to Provide for the Disposal of the Public Lands in This Province, and for Other Purposes Therein Mentioned*, S.P.U.C 1837, c. 118.

163 *Ibid.* at s. (e).

164 *Fenton, supra* note 131.

165 *Ibid.*

Indians in Upper Canada from imposition and the property occupied or enjoyed by them from trespass and injury[166] established that the treaty commissioner was the agent for the imperial Crown and affirmed the necessity of purchase for Aboriginal tenure:

> That no purchase or contract for the sale of land in Upper Canada, which may be made of or with the Indians or any of them, shall be valid unless made under the authority and with the consent of Her Majesty, her heirs and successors, attesting, by an instrument under the Great Seal of the Province, or under the Privy Seal of the Governor thereof for the time being.[167]

In 1853, *An Act respecting the sale and management of the Public Lands* provided for orders-in-council to apply to "Indian lands under the management of the Chief Superintendent of Indian Affairs"; in these lands the superintendent would "exercise the same powers" that the Crown land Commissioner exercised in Crown lands.[168]

B. Responsible government

The Crown introduced responsible government in the provinces of Canada, Nova Scotia, and New Brunswick in 1848, in Prince Edward Island in 1851, and in Newfoundland in 1855.[169] In 1849 in prerogative Instructions, the Crown accorded governmental authorities to Nova Scotia, securing administrative authority of the Crown lands and mineral resources to the Assembly, although the beneficial interest in the lands was not transferred. Similar Instructions were given in New Brunswick. These prerogative grants of responsible government distinguished Nova Scotia and New Brunswick from Upper and Lower Canada, which created the province of Canada by the imperial Parliament's *Union Act* (1840).[170] No similar imperial Acts were passed for Nova Scotia or New Brunswick.

The 1848 vesting of government authorities established colonial or local control over Aboriginal tenure in Nova Scotia and New Brunswick. By 1849, the Nova Scotia Indian Commissioner and the Míkmaw leaders were equally convinced that the Nova Scotia courts could not protect or enforce the vested Aboriginal tenure and rights. The Commissioner identified in the Assembly the consequences of competing interests for Aboriginal rights:

> Under the present circumstance, no adequate protection can be obtained for Indian property. It would be vain to seek a verdict for any jury in this Island against the trespassers on the Reserves; nor perhaps would a member of the Bar be found willing and effectual-

---

166 S.P.C. 1850, c. 74.

167 *Ibid.* at s. 1. See also *An Act to Encourage the Gradual Civilization of the Indian Tribes in this Province, and to Amend the Laws Respecting Indians*, S.P.C. 1857, c. 26, s. 1.

168 S.P.C. 1860, c. 2, s. 9.

169 A. Todd, *Parliamentary Government in the British Colonies*, 2d ed. (London: Longman, 1894).

170 (U.K.), 2 & 3 Vict., c. 35.

ly to advocate the cause of the Indians, inasmuch as he would thereby injure his own prospects, by damaging his popularity.[171]

To remedy the failure of the judicial system, especially the consequences of self-interested juries, the Commissioner advised the Assembly to confer upon "the heads of Indian families the right to vote at the election of the Members of Assembly" based on their possession and occupation of the reserved lands.[172] The Assembly rejected this suggestion. By 1851, the Commissioner concluded that the *Indian Act* remedies were a failure, and nothing short "of destroying the houses and barns of the trespassers now existing" would solve the problem.[173]

In response, the Assembly sought to strengthen the statutory protections for the reserved Aboriginal tenure under an *Act Relative To Crown Land Department* (*Crown Land Act*, 1851),[174] and *An Act Concerning Indian Reserve Act* (*Indian Reserve Act*, 1859).[175] The reserved lands protected by prerogative treaties and by the royal instructions and proclamations were concealed by these statutes, and lands reserved for Indians became equated with these statutory reserves. By conflating Míkmaw tenure with Crown law, the acts viewed Míkmaw tenure as a subdivision of Crown tenure. The *Crown Land Act* delegated the administrative duty of protecting the reserved lands to the Governor-in-Council rather than to the Assembly,[176] gave authority to divide existing reservations to the Commissioner of Crown Land rather than to the Commissioner of Indian Affairs, and vested all Indian Lands in the Commissioner of Crown Lands for the purpose of protecting the Aboriginal rights of those who settled there.[177]

The continuing breakdowns of the judicial system caused the reserved lands issue to be brought before the entire Assembly.[178] The *Indian Reserve Act* supplemented the existing statutory protections. Since the lands reserved for the Aboriginal nations were never surveyed, the Assembly directed the Governor-in-Council to have "surveys, plans, and reports to be made of lands reserved for the benefit of Indians" and distinguished from the "improved lands."[179] The Act also decentralized the administrative regime, appointing local commissioners[180] with managerial and remedial duties: (a) to "protect" the lands reserved for the benefit of Indians; (b) to "superintend the survey, leasing, and sale thereof when ordered"; (c) to "take charge of the interest of the Indians"; (d) to "promote the settlement of the Indians"; and (e) to "prevent tres-

---

171 LANSJ, [1849] at 356.

172 *Ibid.* at 356.

173 LANSJ, [1851] at 233.

174 R.S.N.S. 1851, c. 28.

175 S.N.S. 1859, c. 44. Assented to 30 May 1859 [hereinafter *Indian Reserve Act*].

176 *Ibid.* at s. 5. It provided that, "the Governor-in Council may reserve for the use of the Indians of this Province such portions of lands as may be deemed advisable, and make a free grant thereof for the purposes for which they were so reserved."

177 *Ibid.* at s. 12.

178 LANSJ, [1859] at 424-25.

179 *Indian Reserve Act, supra* note 175 at s. 1.

180 *Ibid.* at s. 2.

passing on the reserves."[181] These duties overlapped with the Chief Commissioner and his deputy commissioners under the *Indian Act* and the Commissioner of Crown lands under the *Crown Land Act.*

In protecting the reserved lands and preventing trespassing, the *Indian Reserve Act* provided that if the intruders were in "possession of and made improvements" within the reserved lands, the commissioner had the duty to "take prompt measures for the removal of the intruders and occupants, and for applying the lands for the benefit of the Indians."[182] Should any persons make an entry upon reserved lands after 1859 "with a view of acquiring possession or occupancy," any commissioner by the warrant of any two Justices of the Peace could "summarily remove" them.[183] To supplement the *Indian Act* information pleading, a legal warrant procedure was added.

In 1864, when the Legislative Assembly enacted *An Act to facilitate the perfecting of Titles in the Island of Cape Breton*[184] to resolve conflicting claims involving Crown lands, the Míkmaq nation protested and renewed its request for formal legal title to all its reserved Lands:

> That petitioners, aborigines of that part of the Western Continent now called Nova Scotia, have by means of treaties made in former days with their British subjects, and which as such, they acknowledge due allegiance to Her Majesty Queen Victoria; they would respectfully, yet firmly, claim the rights, the privileges and the protection given to British subjects.
>
> That as a part of these, and now to Petitioners a matter of the deepest importance, being one on which their very existence depends, is their right as British subjects to hold lands in their own names, or in trust for them, in the names of others; subject to such terms and regulations as under every circumstance connected with these lands may be just and lawful.[185]

The petition acknowledged the failure of the rule of law to protect their tenure as reason for their request to hold their lands in their own names. The Crown's "inefficient and nominal protection" of their property rights that had denied them any "redress of the injuries" required a new remedy:

> [I]nstead of enforcing the supremacy of the law and vindicating the authority of the Government by promptly removing and punishing these lawless invaders of the Indians' rights, Petitioners have learned with surprise, that a Provincial Act has recently been passed, unconstitutional and unprecedented in the annals of modern British Legislation, not for the purpose of punishing these contemptuous men and reducing them to obedience, but for the purpose of giving them those land they have forcibly wrested from the Indians ... . That this extraordinary proposal of this Protector of the Indian's Rights, to

---

181 *Ibid.*

182 *Ibid.* at s. 10.

183 *Ibid.*

184 S.N.S. 1859, c. 66.

185 24 September 1749. Original in Míkmaq and French reprinted (1988) 1 Le Canada Francais 17.

deprive them of these rights by entering into a compromise with the violators of them ... shows a most unaccountable attempt to deprive the Indian of those very rights that he was entrusted to defend.[186]

The Governor-in-Council, however, never authorized the commissioners to sell the reserved lands on the Island or elsewhere.

In 1859, the province of Canada enacted *An Act to prevent trespasses on Public and Indian Lands*;[187] and in 1860 enacted the *Act Respecting the Management of Indian Lands and Property*.[188] The Act made the Crown land commissioner the chief superintendent of Indian Affairs, further confusing the issue between Indian lands and public lands:

all lands reserved for the Indians or for any tribe or band of Indians, or held in trust for their benefit shall be deemed to be reserved and held for the same purpose as before the passing of this Act but subject to the provisions.[189]

Section 4 affirmed and clarified the 1763 Proclamation provision regarding Aboriginal land purchase,[190] exempting Indian territory from the public lands provisions until a treaty purchase.[191] The courts held that until Indian territory "was acquired by purchase from the aboriginal tribe to which it had belonged," the land was not available for disposition, since it was not public land.[192]

To address anomalies in different jurisdictions and re-establish order in all the colonies, the imperial Parliament in 1865 enacted the *Imperial Colonial Laws Validity Act*, which affirmed that prerogative Acts and imperial statutes could not be abrogated or amended in any way by self-governing colonies.[193] Any colonial law repugnant to any imperial Act was void and inoperative to the extent of such repugnancy, but a colonial law was not void if it was repugnant to a received statute or rule of the common law.

C. *Constitution Act, 1867*

The enactment of the *Constitution [British North America] Act, 1867* by the imperial Parliament and Crown continued the separate treaty jurisdiction and tenure of the Aboriginal nations, establishing a new federal government by a compact with the separate provinces in British North America.[194] The 1867 Act was a statutory consti-

---

186 *Ibid.*

187 C.S.C. 1859, c. 81.

188 S.P.C. 1860, c. 151.

189 *Ibid.* at s. 2.

190 *Ibid.* at s. 4.

191 *Ibid.* at s. 4.

192 *R. v. McCormick* (1859), 18 U.C.Q.B. 131 at 133 (U.C. Q.B.).

193 (U.K.), 28 & 29 Vict., c. 63. As A.V. Dicey, *The Law of the Constitution* (London: MacMillan, 1960) at 147, n. 1, said about federal constitutions: "[t]he truth is that a federal constitution partakes of the nature of a treaty, and it is quite conceivable that the authors of the constitution may intend to provide no constitutional means of changing its terms except the assent of all the parties to the treaty."

194 (U.K.), 30 & 31 Vict., c. 3, reprinted in R.S.C. 1985, App. II, No. 5 [hereinafter *Constitution Act, 1867*].

tution, enacted by the United Kingdom Parliament, proclaimed by the imperial Crown, allocating the distribution of jurisdictional authorities. Neither of the orders of governments had the right to modify the *British North America Act* by themselves or together; only the Crown in imperial Parliament could amend the Constitution of Canada.

The Preamble of the Act clearly stated the purposes of the Union:

> Whereas, the Provinces of Canada, Nova Scotia, and New Brunswick, have expressed their Desire to be federally united into One Dominion under the Crown of the United Kingdom of Great Britain and Ireland with a Constitution similar in Principle to that of the United Kingdom ...[195]

The Act's terms specifically continued the existing authority of Her Majesty over the confederating provinces. Article 7 continued the pre-existing distribution of jurisdiction of Nova Scotia and New Brunswick, but not the province of Canada;[196] section 88 continued the pre-existing constitution of Nova Scotia and New Brunswick;[197] and section 129 continued most of the pre-existing legal order of the United Kingdom in the three provinces.[198] The courts have interpreted the Act as neither expanding nor curtailing in any respect the rights and privileges of Her Majesty or any existing relations with the sovereign; the existing prerogative rights continued to exist in the interstitial portions of the Act.[199]

In the new division of political authority, the imperial Parliament conferred on the federal dominion exclusive administrative authority over "Indians and Lands reserved for Indians."[200] This section terminated the existing authority of the three unit-

---

195 *Ibid.*, Preamble.

196 It states, "The Provinces of Nova Scotia and New Brunswick shall have the same Limits as at the passing of the Act."

197 It states: "The Constitution of the Legislature of each of the Provinces of Nova Scotia and New Brunswick shall, subject to the Provision of this Act, continue as it exists at the Union until altered under the Authority of the Act."

198 "Except as otherwise provided by this Act, all Laws in force in Canada, Nova Scotia, or New Brunswick at the Union, and all Courts of Civil and Criminal Jurisdiction, and all legal Commissions, Powers, and Authorities, and all Officers, Judicial, Administrative, and Ministerial, existing therein at the Union, shall continue in Ontario, Quebec, Nova Scotia, and New Brunswick respectively, as if the Union had not been made; subject nevertheless (except with respect to such as are enacted by or exist under Acts of Parliament of Great Britain or the Parliament of the United Kingdom of Great Britain and Ireland) to be repealed, abolished, or altered by the Parliament of Canada, or by the Legislature of the respective Province, according to the Authority of the respective Province, according to the Authority of the Parliament or of that Legislature under this Act."

199 *Liquidators of Maritime Band v. Receiver General of N.B.*, [1892] A.C. 375.

200 Section 91 reads: "It shall be lawful for the Queen, by and with the Advice and Consent of the Senate and House of Commons, to make Laws for the Peace, Order, and good Government of Canada, in relation to all Matters not coming within the Classes of Subjects by this Act assigned exclusively to the Legislatures of the Provinces; and for greater Certainty, but not so as to restrict the Generality of the forgoing Terms of this Section, it is hereby declared that (notwithstanding any in this Act) the exclusive Legislative Authority of the Parliament of Canada extends to all Matters coming within the Classes of Subjects next hereinafter enumerated; ... (24) Indians and Lands reserved for the Indians....And any Matter coming within any of the Classes of Subject enumerated in this Section shall not be deemed to come within the Class of Matters of a local or private Nature comprised in the Enumeration of the Classes of Subjects by this Act assigned exclusively to the Legislature of the Provinces."

ing provinces under section 129, and effectively transferred the pre-existing Aboriginal tenure and prerogative treaty obligations from provincial authorities in three provinces to the federal Crown. Thus, Canada assumed the obligations for implementing the existing Aboriginal and treaty rights. These matters were no longer constitutionally deemed local or private matters or assigned exclusively to the provincial legislatures.

Nevertheless, the federal government had no authority to change or modify these Aboriginal and prerogative obligations. As Judge Read, the author of the *Statute of Westminster,* later acknowledged, "[n]o colonial legislation could amend its own constitution."[201] Indeed, even if the Queen in imperial Parliament had so desired, it is questionable under the United Kingdom laws whether the Crown could have delegated such an authority over the Míkmaq nation to Canada since the treaties did not delegate authority to the imperial Crown to modify its treaty relationship. After Confederation, the colonial legislators and judges borrowed the fictional doctrine of parliamentary supremacy and a positivist philosophy of the law, as a result of which their focus was less on whether legislative measures were "just" than on whether they were "legal" in the narrower sense.

12. Canadian Judicial Interpretation

After Confederation in 1867, the early provincial courts and the judicial committee of the Privy Council in Britain tried to comprehend the imperial law protecting Aboriginal tenure from colonial authority and subjects, and its relationship to prerogative treaties with the Indian nations. Their efforts were flawed, however, because the courts did not attempt to analyze the nature or source of Aboriginal tenure or the meaning of the Aboriginal grantors in the treaties of cession. Instead the courts looked for imperial recognition of Aboriginal tenure, focused on policy and legislative issues, and sought to resolve the issue of proprietary and administrative rights under the *Constitution Act, 1867.*

In *R. v. The St. Catharines Milling and Lumber Company,*[202] the Ontario Chancery Court and Court of Appeals, the Supreme Court of Canada, and the judicial

---

201 [1948] C.B.R. 621 at 625.

202 This case was first heard as *R. v. The St. Catharines Milling and Lumber Company* (1885), 10 O.R. 196 (Ont. H.C.); then by the Ontario Court of Appeal, *R. v. The St. Catharines Milling and Lumber Company* (1886), 13 O.A.R. 148 (Ont. C.A.); then by the Supreme Court of Canada, *The St. Catharines Milling and Lumber Company v. The Queen* (1887), 13 S.C.R. 577 (S.C.C.); and finally by the Privy Council, *St. Catherine's Milling and Lumber Company v. The Queen* (1888), 14 A.C. 46 [hereinafter *St. Catherine's* cited to court]. See generally, S. Barry Cottam, "Indian Title as a 'Celestial Institution': David Mills and the St. Catherine's Milling Case" and A.J. Hall, "The *St. Catherine's Milling and Lumber Company* versus *The Queen*: Indian Land Rights as a Factor in Federal-Provincial Relations in Nineteenth Century Canada" in K. Abel and J. Friesen, eds., *Aboriginal Resource Use in Canada: Historical and Legal Aspects* (Winnipeg: University of Manitoba Press, 1991) at 47-267; S.L. Harring, *White Man's Law: Native People in Nineteenth-Century Canadian Jurisprudence* (Toronto: University of Toronto Press for Osgoode Society of Canadian Legal History, 1998), especially c. 6, "A More than Usually Degraded Indian Type: *St. Catherine's Milling* and Indian Title Case" at 125-47.

committee of the Privy Council addressed the consequences of a treaty cession of Aboriginal territory under the *Constitution Act, 1867,* which was silent on the topic, although the terms of the treaty were not. In the ten judicial opinions, in their diversity and inconsistency, the courts failed to justify the major and controversial constitutional innovation that they created. Like the parties, the Canadian and British courts manipulated the imperial law protecting Aboriginal tenure and avoided the actual terms of the treaty to attempt to justify their proprietary right over the resources.

Notwithstanding these limitations, the judicial interpretations on Aboriginal tenure and treaty land cession came to be viewed by subsequent Canadian courts as leading cases and binding precedents. Because in the common law tradition holding a case cannot be separated from its facts, the judicial comments on Aboriginal tenure and treaty cessions were not controlling precedents. Most opinions avoided applying the imperial law in a disciplined conception respecting royal prerogatives and laws protecting Aboriginal tenure, the common law traditions of possession, and giving careful, candid judicial reasoning to the issues of treaty cessions in Canadian federalism. The judicial interpretations of treaty cession and Aboriginal tenure became tools of provincial federalism and advancing colonization rather than specific intentions of either party to the treaties. The opinions became examples of instrumental legal reasoning, with the British rules of law becoming eerily irrelevant in the context of Aboriginal tenure and rights under a treaty with the imperial Crown. Instead of holding the imperial Crown to the terms of its treaty, explaining the meaning of treaty cessions between Aboriginal tenure and the Crown, the decision treated the conflict as a matter of the constitutional allocation of legislative power between the federal and provincial governments.

A. *St. Catherine's Milling and Lumber Company v. The Queen*

As in the tradition of contrived cases in the United States that created the legal doctrine of Aboriginal tenure, in *St. Catharine's Milling and Lumber Company,*[203] the province of Ontario[204] sought to enjoin the Company from cutting timber under a dominion (federal) license, bringing to the Chancery court a constitutional dispute about which level of government had jurisdiction to benefit from revenue and resources acquired by a treaty cession of Aboriginal territory by the Ojibwa tribe. This was not a case that involved the land itself, but the beneficial use to lease the land and to obtain revenue from these leases. The Ojibwa signatories of the 1873 Treaty (*Treaty No. 3*) were unrepresented in these equitable proceedings and never had an opportunity to present their understanding of the treaty cession or their continuing relationship to the ceded lands.

As had the parties in *Fletcher v. Peck* and *Johnson v. M'Intosh,* the parties in *St. Catherine's* framed their conflicting claims to resources and revenues by stipulating

---

203   *St. Catherine's, ibid.,* Ont. H.C.

204   The name of the province is an Iroquorian word describing "beautiful water."

that the involved land was within state or provincial jurisdiction, in this case Ontario.[205] They did not, however, stipulate that at Confederation the Ojibwa lands were part of the province. By 1883, the time of the dominion timber lease to the Company,[206] the constitutional location of the involved forest was contested and uncertain: it could have been within the jurisdiction of "lands reserved for the Indians" under section 91(24) of the *Constitution Act, 1867*, federal jurisdiction in the province of Manitoba, or within the lands granted to the Hudson's Bay Company. In 1870, the federal government purchased the Hudson's Bay Company entitlements.[207]

The stipulation of the parties prevented any judicial determination of the constitutional location of the Ojibwa land at Confederation, after the 1873 Treaty, or the time of the dominion timber lease. At Confederation, Chancellor Boyd suggested the forests were located within unceded and unpurchased Ojibwa tenure, protected by the 1763 Proclamation, and not part of any confederating province.[208] In 1870, when the province of Manitoba was created out of the Northwest Territory,[209] the dominion retained jurisdiction over the lands and natural resources that included the Ojibwa lands.[210] After the 1873 Treaty, the uncertain boundary between eastern Manitoba and western Ontario was referred to arbitration; most of the treaty lands were held to be part of Ontario.[211] The dominion did not accept the decision,[212] and in 1881 the federal Parliament enlarged the boundaries of Manitoba to include the treaty territories.[213] In 1883, the dominion issued a licence to the Company to cut timber, aware that Ontario claimed jurisdiction and was contesting the enlarged boundaries. In 1884, a year before the action to enjoin the Company, the judicial committee of the Privy Council ruled the 1878 arbitration decision was correct.[214] The imperial Parliament, however, did not pass the *Ontario Boundary Act* (1889)[215] confirming that decision until after the privy council had ruled on the *St. Catherine's* case. Additionally, the timber lease was most likely in the drainage basin of the Hudson's Bay Company, thus in its jurisdiction until the 1873 Treaty, [216] but this issue was never raised.

---

205 *Supra* note 202, Ont. H.C. at 204.

206 *Ibid.* at 196, 197-98, 203.

207 R.S.C. 1970, App. 9.

208 *St.Catherine's, supra* note 202, Ont. H.C. at 204, 206-207, and 226. In the Supreme Court of Canada Strong J. adopted the same view; Lord Watson in the judicial committee did not discuss this issue.

209 *The Manitoba Act, 1870*, R.S.C. 1970, App. 8, s. 30. The jurisdiction over lands and natural resources was granted to Manitoba in the *Constitution Act, 1867, supra* note 194.

210 *Ibid.* App. 11.

211 *St. Catherine's, supra* note 202, Ont. H.C. at 230-231. See generally, Ontario Legislative Assembly, *Correspondence, Papers and Documents, of Dates from 1856 to 1882 Inclusive: Relating to the Northerly and Westerly Boundaries of the Province of Ontario, Printed by Order of the Legislative Assembly* (Toronto : C. Blackett Robinson, 1882).

212 *Ibid.,* Dom. Sess. Papers 1883, vol. 16, No. 12, Paper 95, at 3.

213 *Ibid.*

214 *Ibid.* at 204.

215 *Canada (Ontario Boundary) Act*, 1889 (U.K.), 52-53 Vict., c. 28, reprinted in R.S.C. 1985, App. II, No. 16.

216 Brian Slattery, *The Land Rights of Indigenous Canadian Peoples, as Affected by the Crown's Acquisition of Their Territories* (Saskatoon, Sk.: Native Law Centre, 1979) at 226.

The province contested the right of the dominion government to grant a timber license on grounds that the treaty surrender of the land by the Ojibwa conveyed their "whole rights and title" in surrendered lands to the jurisdiction of the Crown in right of the province.[217] Alternatively, the province argued that Aboriginal peoples had no concept of property recognizable in British law, and since no Aboriginal territorial interest or tenure existed in French law, no interest survived the *Treaty of Paris* (1763) to be protected by the 1763 Proclamation.

The Company argued the Aboriginal nations and tribes had owned the land and resources at Confederation, and had passed their proprietary rights to the forest to the dominion by the explicit wording of the 1873 Treaty: that the Saulteaux Tribe "cede, release, surrender, and yield up to the Government of the Dominion of Canada, for Her Majesty the Queen and Her successors forever, all their rights, titles, and privileges whatsoever, to the lands."[218] Under the treaty, they argued, the dominion had a right to lease the land to the Company, and the province had no interest in the ceded land.

Chancellor Boyd accepted the provincial arguments. He held that the Crown's "title" was derived from its conquest of France.[219] His judgment articulates the colonialist's racial perspective derived from Darwinian thought on Aboriginal life and tenure:

> Indian peoples were found scattered wide-cast over the continent, having, as a characteristic, no fixed abodes, but moving as the exigencies of living demanded. As heathens and barbarians it was not thought that they had any proprietary title to the soil, nor any such claim thereto as to interfere with the plantations, and the general prosecution of colonization. They were treated "justly and graciously," as Lord Bacon advised, but no legal ownership of the land was ever attributed to them.[220]

Relying in part on the policies and practices of British Columbia and the old province of Canada,[221] Boyd stated the claims of the Indians by "virtue of their original occupation is not such as to give any title to the land itself":

> but only serves to commend them to the consideration and liberality of the Government upon their displacement; that the surrender to the Crown by the Indians of any territory adds nothing in law to the strength of the title paramount, ...[222]

---

217 *Ibid.* at 199-201, 203.

218 *Treaty No. 3 Between Her Majesty the Queen and the Saulteaux Tribe of the Ojibbeway Indians at the North West Angle of the Lake of the Woods, with Adheisions* (Ottawa: Queen's Printer, 1966) at 2.

219 *St. Catherine's*, *supra* note 202, Ont C.A. at 204. Hagarty C.J. and Osler J. of the Ontario Court of Appeal rejected Boyd's analysis and held that the 1873 Treaty transferred the title to the land to the sovereign.

220 *St.Catherine's*, *supra* note 202, Ont. H.C. at 206. He considered the "Saulteaux (i.e. Falls en) tribe of the Ojibbeway" that signed *Treaty No. 3* as "more than usually degraded," *ibid.* at 227. For the Darwinian legacy in Victorian colonial thought see Hall, *supra* note 202 at 267-68. Also see Part IV, below.

221 *St. Catherine's, ibid.* at 232-35.

222 *Ibid.* at 234.

After the 1763 Proclamation had created reserved hunting grounds, Boyd declared that certain imperial Acts—the *Quebec Act, 1791*[223] and the 1803 imperial statute[224]— "superseded" certain parts of the 1763 Proclamation by bringing the "Indian territories"[225] within colonial limits rather than imperial control, thus subjecting them to the "control and jurisdiction" of the governor of the provinces. These Acts did not interfere with the existing tenure of the land as defined by the laws of England or by the King's prerogatives, but gave them legislative authority over Indian lands. The 1763 Proclamation remained operative as a "declaration of sound principles" guiding executive action in disposing claims to Aboriginal tenure, but was "obsolete" under existing provincial legislative authority concerning Indian lands or reserves.[226]

Boyd relied on the "classical judgment" of Chief Justice Marshall in *Johnson v. M'Intosh* to reconcile Aboriginal tenure with Crown tenure: "[a]ll our [English] institutions recognize the absolute title of the Crown, subject only to the Indian right of occupation, and recognize the absolute title of the Crown to extinguish that right."[227] Boyd declared:

> This right of occupancy attached to the Indians in their tribal character. They were incapacitated from transferring [title] to any stranger, though it was susceptible of being extinguished. The exclusive power to procure its extinguishment was vested in the Crown, a power which as a rule was exercised only on just and equitable terms. If this title was sought to be acquired by others than the Crown, the attempted transfer passed nothing, and could operate only as an extinguishment of the Indian right for the benefit of the title paramount.[228]

Before Confederation, he stated, "ungranted" Aboriginal lands within any province were part of public lands of the Province; after Confederation, these Aboriginal lands were "an interest other than that of the province" that burden any provincial interest in the land under section 109 of the *Constitution Act, 1867*.[229] When these protected Aboriginal title or rights were purchased or paid compensation and new reserves allocated to them, the ceded land fell under the provincial jurisdiction and the new reserves were under the dominion jurisdiction.[230]

---

223 *Constitution Act, 1791*, 31 Geo. III, c. 31 (U.K.); R.S.C. 1970, App. II, No. 3 at s. 42.

224 *An Act for extending the Jurisdiction of the Courts of Justice in the Provinces of Lower and Upper Canada, to the Trial and Punishment of Persons guilty of Crimes and Offences within certain parts of North America adjoining to the said Provinces* (U.K.) 43 Geo. III, c. 138.

225 "Indian territory" in the Dorchester Regulations or Instruction of 1794 referred to Aboriginal lands not purchased and not ceded, PAC, RG 10, vol. 789 at 6768-6770, Art. 2.

226 *Supra*, note 202, Ont. H.C. at 227.

227 *Ibid.* at 209. See also Patterson J. of the Ontario Court of Appeals, relied on in the interpretation of *M'Intosh, supra* note 66, in Joseph Story, *Commentaries on the Constitution of the United States*, 5th ed. by M.M. Bigelow (Buffalo, N.Y.: W.S. Hein, 1994), that Indian nations and tribes had some sovereignty over the land, which included the right to sell or transfer it to the British sovereign, at 169; see also Ritchie C.J.'s majority opinion in the Supreme Court of Canada. Lord Watson substituted a British law analysis of this classical interpretation in the judicial committee of the Privy Council.

228 *St. Catherine's, ibid.*, citing *Doe d. Sheldon v. Ramsay*, 9 U.C.R. at 133.

229 *St. Catherine's, ibid.* at 230.

230 *Ibid.*

Chancellor Boyd narrowly read and interpreted the constitutional clause "land reserved for the Indians" in section 91(24) of the *Constitution Act, 1867* as distinct from the reserved Aboriginal lands under the 1763 Proclamation:

> There is an essential difference in meaning between the "reservations" spoken of in the Royal Proclamation, and the like term in the B.N.A. Act. The proclamation views the Indians in their wild state, and leaves them there in undisturbed and unlimited possession of all their hunting ranges, whereas the Act, though giving jurisdiction to the Dominion over all Indians, wild or settled, does not transfer to that government all public or waste lands of the Provinces on which they may be found at large. [231]

To Boyd, the territorial jurisdiction of the dominion extends only to specific lands reserved for them by the *Indian Act* for the purpose of civilizing the inferior Indians:

> Now it is evident from the history of "the reserves," that the Indians there are regarded no longer as in a wild and primitive state, but as in a condition of transition from barbarism to civilization. The object of the system is to segregate the red from the white population, in order that the former may be trained up to a level with the latter. ... The distinctive feature of the system in Canada was the grouping of the separate tribes for the purposes of exclusive and permanent residence within circumscribed limits. ... Here they are furnished with appliances and opportunities to make themselves independent of the precarious subsistence procured from the chase; they are encouraged to advance from a nomadic to an agricultural or pastoral life, and thus to acquire ideas of separate property, and of the value of individual rights to which, in their erratic tribal condition, they are utter strangers, so that, ultimately, they may be led to settle down into the industrious and peaceful habits of a civilized people.[232]

According to Chancellor Boyd, in the treaty-recognized "land reserves," the Ojibwa became "in a special sense, wards of the State, ... surrounded by [the Crown's] protection while under pupilage," and have their rights "assured in perpetuity" in the lands set part as reserves under dominion jurisdiction. On the "legally recognized tenure" of the "land reserves," the Indians have all the "advantages and safeguards of private resident proprietors"; they have a claim "upon the bounty and benevolence of the Crown"; they "have a present right as to the exclusive and absolute usufruct";[233] and "a potential right of becoming individual owners in fee after enfranchisement."[234] Boyd held it was unreasonable that the dominion government should be burdened with large annual payments to the tribe without having sufficient land to generate such

---

231 *Ibid.* at 228. This view was a romantic version of colonization and imposed public apartheid. It was based on the assumption of European superiority and Aboriginal inferiority. See Part IV, below.

232 *Ibid.* at 228-29.

233 *Ibid.* at 230. An exclusive and absolute usufruct is not known in British law. *The Shorter Oxford English Dictionary on Historical Principles, s.v.* "Usufruct": "1. Law. The right of temporary possession, use, or enjoyment of the advantages of property belonging to another, so far as may be had without causing damage or prejudice to it. 2. Use, enjoyment, or profitable possession (of something) at 1811." Usufructuary is defined as "1. Law. One who enjoys the usufruct of a property." See *Mr. Justice Smith v. The Queen*, [1983] 1 S.C.R. 554 (S.C.C.) at 568-69.

234 *St. Catherine's, ibid.*

funds.[235] When the civilizing purposes were ended in those reserves created by the dominion, the legal and equitable title to the reserves reverts from the dominion trusteeship to the province wherein the lands are territorially situated.[236]

Without explanation, Chancellor Boyd held "Indian title" under the 1763 Proclamation was extinguished by the terms of the 1873 Treaty. The treaty cession of Aboriginal title freed the land from the trust relationship of the 1763 Proclamation, and it reverted or inured to the benefit of the province.[237] The province was the "proper constitutional owners" or "constitutional proprietor by title paramount."[238] The Ontario Court of Appeals, the Supreme Court of Canada, and the judicial committee of the Privy Council upheld the province's claim to the treaty land cession, but they did so based on distinct interpretations of the *Constitution Act, 1867*, rather than judicial interpretation of the 1873 Treaty.

In 1888, the judicial committee of the Privy Council, the final court of appeal in the British empire,[239] held that by prior imperial Acts before Confederation, the province acquired a potential jurisdictional interest but not constitutional ownership over the Aboriginal territory ceded by 1873 Treaty. The judicial committee characterized the issue as "beneficial interests":

> ...with respect to that area, a controversy has arisen between the Dominion and Ontario, each of them maintaining that the legal effect of extinguishing the Indian title has been to transmit to itself the entire beneficial interest of the lands, as now vested in the Crown, freed from incumbrance of any kind, save the qualified privilege of hunting and fishing mentioned in the treaty. ... Although the present case relates exclusively to the right of the Government of Canada to dispose of the timber in question to the appellant company, yet its decision necessarily involves the determination of the larger question between that government and the province of Ontario with respect to the legal consequences of the treaty of 1873.[240]

Lord Watson traced the Crown's relations to the Ojibwa tenure. Before the treaty, he reasoned that Ojibwa tenure was a present proprietary tenure anchored under the general provision of the 1763 Proclamation, making it clear that the imperial Crown did not have a present proprietary tenure derived from any symbolic act of possession or discovery convention.[241] The Crown acquired its potential rights to purchase the Abo-

---

235 *Ibid.* at 235.

236 *Ibid.* at 234.

237 *Ibid.*

238 *Ibid.* This characterization was rejected by the Lord Watson of the judicial committee of the Privy Council for "beneficial use."

239 Until 1952, the judicial committee was the final court to which decisions of the Supreme Court of Canada could be appealed: P. Hogg, *Constitutional Law of Canada*, looseleaf ed. (Toronto: Carswell, 1997), pt. 8-4.

240 *St.Catherine's, supra* note 202, P.C. at 52-53.

241 *Ibid.,* Ont. C.A. at 159-161, Burton J.A.; *ibid.* at 168, 172, Patterson J.A.; *ibid.,* S.C.C. at 599-600, Ritchie C.J. with Fournier J. concurring.

riginal lands by international conquest or force from the French sovereign[242] through French cession in the *Treaty of Paris* (1763).[243]

The Ojibwa tenure survived the French cession. Lord Watson affirmed that the forest tract had been in Ojibwa occupation from the date of the 1763 Proclamation until the 1873 Treaty. He affirmed that under the 1763 Proclamation the lands were reserved for the Ojibwa and administered for the imperial Crown by the provincial government until Confederation, when the dominion had been assigned these protective and administrative obligations or services:[244]

> The policy of these administrations has been all along the same in this respect, that the Indian inhabitants have been precluded from entering into any transaction with a subject for the sale or transfer of their interest in the land, and have only been permitted to surrender their rights to the Crown by a formal contract, duly ratified in a meeting of their chiefs or head men convened for the purpose.[245]

Their Lordships noted that "[w]hilst there have been changes in the administrative authority, there has been no change since the year 1763 in the character of the interest which its Indian inhabitants had in the lands surrendered by the treaty."[246]

Their Lordships rejected the dominion's and provincial argument that proprietary rights necessarily followed legislative power and relied on the concept of a "beneficial interest" in the ceded tract:

> There can be no *à priori* probability that the British Legislature, in a branch of the statute which professes to deal only with the distribution of legislative power, intended to deprive the Provinces of rights which are expressly given them in that branch of it which relates to the distribution of revenues and assets. The fact that the power of legislating for Indians, and for lands which are reserved to their use, has been entrusted to the Parliament of the Dominion is not in the least degree inconsistent with the right of the Provinces [of Ontario and Quebec] to a beneficial interest in these lands, available to them as a source of revenue whenever the estate of the Crown is disencumbered of the Indian title.[247]

Their Lordships noted that the imperial Acts before Confederation created the provincial administrative interest in reserved Aboriginal tenure, but these Acts did not trans-

---

242 *Ibid.*, Ont. H.C. at 204, Boyd Ch.; *ibid.*, Ont. C.A. at 173; *ibid.*, S.C.C. at 601, Ritchie C.J. with Fournier J. concurring; *ibid.* at 639, Henry J.; *ibid.* at 645, Taschereau J.

243 *Ibid.*, P.C. at 53: "The capture of Quebec in 1759, and the capitulation of Montreal in 1760, were followed in 1763 by the cession to Great Britain of Canada and all its dependencies, with the sovereignty, property, and possession, and all other rights which had at any previous time been held or acquired by the Crown of France. A royal proclamation was issued on the 7th of October, 1763, shortly after the date of the Treaty of Paris ... ."

244 *Ibid.* at 55.

245 *Ibid.* at 54.

246 *Ibid.*

247 *Ibid.* at 59.

fer to the province "any legal estate in the Crown lands, which continued to be vested in the Sovereign."[248]

In interpreting the wording of *Constitution Act, 1867*, their Lordships declared that whenever public land is described as "the property of" or as "belonging to" the dominion or the province, Canadian courts must remember that the "land itself" is vested in the sovereign.[249] Such expressions in the *Constitution Act, 1867* "merely import that the right to its beneficial use, or to its proceeds, has been appropriated to the dominion or the province," not proprietary ownership.[250] Such expressions illustrate the division of use and interest between the provinces and the dominion, not the undivided sovereign estate in Aboriginal tenure itself.

Their Lordships stressed that section 109 of the *Constitution Act, 1867* reserved to the provinces their existing beneficial interest in Crown lands, mines, minerals, and royalties within the confederated provinces, which had been transferred in the prior imperial acts:

> All Lands, Mines, Minerals, and Royalties belonging to the several Provinces of Canada, Nova Scotia, and New Brunswick at the Union, and all Sums then due or payable for such Lands, Mines, Minerals, or Royalties, shall belong to the several Provinces of Ontario, Quebec, Nova Scotia, and New Brunswick in which the same are situate, or arise, subject to any Trusts existing in respect thereof, and to any Interest other than that of the Province in the same.[251]

At Confederation, their Lordships held that the Ojibwa tenure was lands reserved for the Indians, which had not been purchased by the Crown and had not been assigned to lands belonging to Ontario, and was an interest other than the provinces' under section 109.[252] They noted that if the Indians had "released their interest" to the province between 1840 and Confederation, the revenues derived would have been the property of the province, even though the "title" to the released lands would remain in the sovereign.[253]

Additionally, their Lordships were uncomfortable with the dominion's characterization of unpurchased Aboriginal tenure under the 1763 Proclamation as the "entire" property of the land in unceded lands:

---

248 *Ibid.* at 55.

249 *Ibid.* at 56.

250 *Ibid.*

251 *Constitution Act, 1867, supra* note 194 at s. 109.

252 *St.Catherine's, supra* note 202, P.C. at 58-59; see also S.C.C. at 608-616, Strong J. However, Lord Watson asserted Aboriginal tenure had its origins in British law in the 1763 Proclamation. Recent decisions of the Supreme Court of Canada have argued it was recognized in the prerogative legislation; see *Guerin v. The Queen*, [1984] 2 S.C.R. 335, [1985] 1 C.N.L.R. 120 (S.C.C.) [hereinafter *Guerin* cited to S.C.R.]; *Calder v. Attorney-General of British Columbia*, [1973] S.C.R. 313, [1973] 4 W.W.R. 1 (S.C.C.) [hereinafter *Calder* cited to S.C.R.].

253 *St. Catherine's, ibid.* at 55.

...It was suggested in the course of the argument for the Dominion, that inasmuch as the proclamation recites that the territories thereby reserved for Indians had never "been ceded to or purchased by" the Crown, the entire property of the land remained with them. That inference is, however, at variance with the terms of the instrument, which shew that the tenure of the Indians was a personal and usufructuary right, dependent upon the good will of the Sovereign. [254]

Many legal factors created this judicial attitude: the reserved Aboriginal tenure in the 1763 Proclamation in the western lands were unilaterally declared by the sovereign to be reserved for the use of the Indians as part of the sovereign's protection and dominion. The controlling factor, however, was that tenure had been ceded to the sovereign in the 1873 Treaty; thus their Lordships stated:

> There was a great deal of learned discussion at the Bar with respect to the precise quality of the Indian right, but their Lordships do not consider it necessary to express any opinion upon the point. [255]

Instead, their Lordships described the relations between reserved Aboriginal tenure and the sovereign in terms of classical common law categories:

> It appears to them to be sufficient for the purposes of this case that there has been all along vested in the Crown a substantial and paramount estate, underlying the Indian title, which became a plenum dominium whenever that title was surrendered or otherwise extinguished. [256]

The key to their Lordships' category is the common law distinction between tenure or title and estates. The Aboriginal nations and peoples held the "tenure" or "title" to the land itself, and according to the 1763 Proclamation the sovereign had a paramount "estate" in purchasing the Aboriginal tenure.

Prior to a treaty purchase under the 1763 Proclamation, the sovereign's "estate" is a future expectation interest in purchasing the Aboriginal tenure. The United States courts called this interest a "pre-emptive right". The sovereign "estate" protected Ojibwa tenure, as Aboriginal nations had title and possession good against every one. Their Lordships' characterization of the sovereign relationship with the reserved Aboriginal

---

254 *Ibid.* at 54. See also Justices Gwynne and Strong in the Supreme Court of Canada who characterized the unceded Aboriginal tenure as including the absolute property.

255 *Ibid.* at 55. Justice Strong of the Supreme Court of Canada in *St. Catharines Milling,* searching for a metaphor for the relations between the Crown and the Aboriginal nations in the prerogative law, described it as similar to the feudal relations of lord and tenant in British common law or the Roman and civil law division of property between the proprietor and a usufructuary. He summarized Aboriginal tenure under prerogative law: "the recognition by the Crown of a usufructuary title in the Indians to all unsurrendered lands. This title, though not perhaps susceptible to any accurate [British] legal definition in exact legal terms, was one which nevertheless sufficed to protect the Indians in the absolute use and enjoyment of their land, whilst at the same time they were incapacitated from making any valid alienation otherwise than to the Crown itself, in whom the ultimate title was, in accordance with the English law of real property, considered as vested." (13 S.C.R. 577 at 608).

256 *Ibid.* at 55.

tenure was similar to the relationship and purposes between the sovereign and the tenants in chief in the doctrine of tenure in British law: the Crown protected existing estates and only had an ultimate title of escheats, that ultimate title not substantial or paramount to any other interest. The tenants in chief estate or a freehold estate have never been minimized in British land law because they were personal and usufructuary rights.

When the Aboriginal tenure is purchased by the sovereign, their Lordships stated, the sovereign may acquire a *plenum dominium,* a Roman law category of a "full ownership; the property in a thing united with the usufruct."[257] By the wording of the 1873 Treaty, the legal consequence of the cession of the reserved Aboriginal tenure by the Ojibwa was interpreted by their Lordships as a cession to the sovereign, rather than a dominion:

> By the treaty of 1873 the Indian inhabitants ceded and released the territory in dispute, in order that it might be opened up for settlement, immigration, and such other purpose as to Her Majesty might seem fit, "to the Government of the Dominion of Canada" ... It was argued [by the Dominion] that a cession in these terms was in effect a conveyance to the Dominion Government of the whole rights of the Indians, with consent of the Crown. That is not the natural import of the language of the treaty, which purports to be from beginning to end a transaction between the Indians and the Crown; and the surrender is in substance made to the Crown. [258]

The judicial committee referred to the 1873 Treaty as "a formal treaty or contract,"[259] rejecting the Canadian courts' characterization of the treaty as a diplomatic act[260] and their interpretation that the treaty did not recognize any existing legal title in the Aboriginal nations.[261]

Their Lordships interpreted the language of the treaty cession as "fully vested in the Crown" with all revenue derivable from the "sale" being the interest of the province because of existing imperial statutes before confederation:

> ...[I]t is abundantly clear that the commissioners who represented Her Majesty, whilst they had full authority to accept a surrender to the Crown, had neither authority nor power to take away from Ontario the interest which had been assigned to that province by the Imperial Statute of 1867.[262]

However, this interest had not vested at Confederation, since the sovereign retained a paramount estate to the Aboriginal tenure:

---

257 *Black's Law Dictionary, s.v.* "usufruct."

258 *St.Catherine's, supra* note 202, P.C. at 60.

259 *Ibid.* at 51.

260 *Ibid.*

261 *Ibid.* at 64, rejected by Taschereau J. of the Supreme Court.

262 *Ibid.* at 60. This is a questionable conclusion, because imperial authority could always change existing laws of the colonies or foreign territories, especially rights that had not vested.

...all beneficial interest in such lands within the provincial boundaries belonging to the Queen, and either producing or capable of producing revenue, passed to the Province, the title still remaining in the Crown.[263]

Imperial law, under the 1763 Proclamation, the 1775 and 1789 Instructions, forbade settlements in, or surveys of, reserved Aboriginal tenure. Although the governors had the authority to settle and agree with the Aboriginal nations, they could not make any grants in these lands since the Crown had no right to dispose of them.[264] These instructions prevented any grant of lands not purchased or ceded from the Aboriginal nations and tribes. Following the creation of the royal province of Upper Canada by the *Constitution Act, 1791*,[265] and the *Union Act* (1840),[266] the "Indian Territory" continued as distinct from public lands (or lands purchased from the Aboriginal nations) and waste land.[267] The imperial Acts transferred the King's prerogatives touching the "waste land" to the provincial government,[268] which permitted the province to collect annual payments of territorial revenues and realize moneys from the sale of land. It had also assigned to the provinces the management and sale of the public lands in section 92(5) of the *Constitution Act, 1867*.[269]

Throughout these imperial Acts, the sovereign estate in the Ojibwa tenure was no more than a present protective interest, with a future expectation interest of purchasing Ojibwa tenure. Their Lordships admitted that if the Ojibwa had been "the owners of fee simple of the territory" which they surrendered in the 1873 Treaty, the province might not have derived any benefit from the cession, since the land was not vested in the sovereign at Confederation.[270] Their Lordships' refusal to analyze the nature of Ojibwa tenure protected by the 1763 Proclamation denied the dominion its asserted authority. Their Lordships declared that the sovereign had a "present proprietary estate in the land," that the "Indian title" was a burden, thus viewing the Ojibwa tenure as vested in the sovereign at Confederation, but as an interest other than the province.[271]

---

263   *Ibid.*, P.C. at 55.

264   The instructions stated: "To give unto the Governors and Councils of our said Three new Colonies, upon the Continent full Power and Authority to settle and agree with the Inhabitants of our said new Colonies or with any other Person who shall resort thereto, for such Lands, Lands, Tenements and hereditaments, as now are, or shall hereafter be in Our Power to dispose of; and then to grant to any such Persons or Person upon such Terms, and under such moderate Quit-Rents, Services and Acknowledgments," R.S.C. 1970, App. I at 126 (similar to Nova Scotia Commission); 1775 Royal Instructions, Art. 38. PAC, MH 440 B7, 116-60; 1786 Instruction, Art. 30 combined the Proclamation and 1775 Instructions by adding, "You are not to allow any Settlements to be made beyond the Boundaries ascertained to the different posts among the Indian Nations within the Limits of Our Province of Quebec."

265   *Ibid.*, App. 3 at s. 42.

266   *Ibid.*, App. 4 at s. 42.

267   B. Clark, *Indian Title in Canada* (Toronto: Carswell, 1987) at 47-51; citing instructions to Superintendent General of Indians, and Dorchester Regulations 1794.

268   1837 (U.K.), 7 Will. IV, c. 118.

269   See also *St. Catherine's, supra* note 202, Ont. C.A. at 156, Haggarty J.; *ibid.*, S.C.C. at 613-17, Strong J.

270   *Ibid.*, P.C. at 58.

271   *Ibid.*

The treaty cession was interpreted as ending the reserved but unanalyzed Ojibwa tenure, and the lands accruing to the province were an interest in revenues rather than an interest in the land itself. The province had to relieve the sovereign and the dominion of all the treaty obligations undertaken by Her Majesty and partially fulfilled by the dominion:

> Seeing that the benefit of the surrender accrues to her, Ontario must, of course, relieve the Crown, and the Dominion, of all obligations involving the payment of money which were undertaken by Her Majesty, and which are said to have been in part fulfilled by the Dominion Government. [272]

Their Lordships broadly interpreted the constitutional phrase "lands reserved for the Indians" in section 91(24) of *Constitution Act, 1867,* and rejected the narrow reading of the phrase by Chancellor Boyd and other judges:

> counsel for Ontario referred us to a series of provincial statutes prior in date to the Act of 1867, for the purpose of shewing that the expression "Indian reserves" was used in legislative language to designate certain lands in which the Indians had, after the royal proclamation of 1763, acquired a special interest, by treaty or otherwise, and did not apply to land occupied by them in virtue of the proclamation. The argument might have deserved consideration if the expression had been adopted by the British Parliament in 1867, but it does not occur in sect. 91(24), and the words actually used are, according to their natural meaning, sufficient to include all lands reserved, upon any terms or conditions, for Indian occupation. It appears to be the plain policy of the Act that, in order to ensure uniformity of administration, all such lands, and Indian affairs generally, shall be under the legislative control of one central authority.[273]

They declared that the phrase was directly convertible to lands that had "never been ceded to or purchased by," as in the 1763 Proclamation, even if the Indian nations or tribes never signed a treaty of protection with the imperial Crown.

The Saulteaux Tribes of the 1873 Treaty were not represented in these proceedings and therefore never had a chance to present their understanding of the treaty to the courts. Without evidence of the grantor's intent, motivation, or understanding of the "Treaty of the Lake of the Woods," as they called it, the courts were limited in their capacity to interpret the legal consequences of the treaty. To give a just account of the treaty and its intent and meaning, the judiciary needed the Saulteaux grantors' perspective, as prescribed by Lord Mansfield's decision in *Campbell v. Hall* (1774):

---

272   *Ibid.* at 60. In *A.G. Canada v. A.G. Ontario,* [1897] A.C. 199 (P.C.) the judicial committee remarked, in *obiter,* that, as a matter of fair play, the federal and provincial governments should share the cost for fulfilling the treaty promises, but did find legal liability in the federal government, rather than the province. Federal-provincial agreements resolve some of these issues.

273   *St. Catherine's, ibid.* at 59.

the articles of capitulation upon which the country is surrendered, and the articles of peace by which it is ceded, are sacred and inviolable according to their true intent and meaning.[274]

The Saulteaux grantors had many independent issues about the treaty cession that were ignored by the parties. They could have affirmed an absolute property in the land or allodial lands by the 1763 Proclamation and the *Treaty of Niagara*. They could have introduced the evidence of the treaty conferences that confirmed their relations to the land as what Chief *Mo-We-Do-Pe-Nais* stated to the treaty commissioners: the Great Spirit had "planted them [Ojibwa] in the lands" and gave them the "rules" (laws) for respecting the land, and they considered it their property.[275] The chiefs could have shown that they had never agreed to have the treaty extinguish their Aboriginal tenure. They could have asserted that no extinguishment of their Aboriginal tenure to the Crown could be accomplished by a treaty of cession, that by the sovereign's rules in the 1763 Proclamation a "purchase" was the only valid conveyance of Aboriginal tenure, and that a cession or surrender of land is not a purchase of land.

They could have documented the treaty commissioners' failure to discuss the extinguishment of their land or jurisdiction over their lands,[276] even though the Crown may have intended to acquire their land and even though the legal language of the written treaty texts characterized it as a cession or transfer rather than as an extinguishment. They could have argued that the terms of the treaty were not an extinguishment because extinguishment was contingent on various future treaty obligations or services and affirmation of continuing Aboriginal rights. This would have challenged the courts' view of the vesting of the title in the sovereign at Confederation and the provincial interest in the lands.

They could have explained that the entire treaty must be read to grasp the mutual intent of the sovereign and the Saulteaux chiefs. Specifically, the cession clause must be read with the peace and good order clause. In the peace and good order clause, the Crown and the chiefs agreed that the chiefs would continue to have jurisdiction over the ceded lands and, particularly, control of the property rights within the surrendered lands:

---

274 (1774), 1 Cowp. 204 at 208 [hereinafter *Campbell v. Hall*]; affirmed in *R. v. Secretary of State* (1981), [1982] 2 All E.R. 118 (Eng. C.A.) at 124. Joseph Chitty, *Treatise on the Law of the Prerogatives of the Crown and the Relative Duties and Rights of the Subject* (London: J. Butterworth, 1820) at 29: "Nor can the King legally disregard or violate the articles in which the country is surrendered or ceded; but such articles are sacred and inviolable, according to their true intent and meaning."

275 Alexander Morris, *The Treaties of Canada with the Indians of Manitoba and the Northwest Territories: Including the Negotiations on Which They Were Based, and Other Materials Relating Thereto* (Toronto: Belfords, Clarke, 1880) at 59-62.

276 Canada, *Report of the Royal Commission on Aboriginal Peoples*, vol. 2 (Ottawa: Queen's Printer, 1996) at 75. After an intensive study of the treaties, The Report of the Royal Commission stated: "in many instances the historical treaties did not result in the voluntary cession of Aboriginal title; that title may well continue to exist over the large portion of the Canadian land mass dealt with in the numbered treaties. This result, already contemplated by the trial decision in *Paulette*, would place the land regime in the parts of Canada covered by the treaties of cession in the same position as most of British Columbia, the Atlantic provinces, certain parts of the Northwest Territories and Quebec, as well as other areas where the Crown never attempted to obtain a cession of Aboriginal title."

the undersigned Chiefs on their own behalf and on behalf of all other Indians inhabiting the tract within ceded, do hereby solemnly promise and engage to strictly observe this treaty, and also to conduct and behave themselves as good and loyal subjects of Her Majesty the Queen. They promise and engage that they will in all respects obey and abide by the law, that they will maintain peace and good order between each other, and also between themselves and other tribes of Indians, and between themselves and others of Her Majesty's subjects, whether Indians or whites, now inhabiting or hereafter to inhabit any part of the said ceded tracts and that they will not molest the person or property of any inhabitant of such ceded tracts, or the property of Her Majesty the Queen, or interfere with or trouble any person passing or travelling through the said tracts, or any part thereof, and that they will aid and assist the officers of Her Majesty in bringing to justice and punishment any Indian offending against the stipulations of this treaty, or infringing the laws in force in the country so ceded.[277]

In other treaty clauses, the chiefs promised "to become responsible to Her Majesty for the faithful performance, by their respective band of such obligations as shall be assumed by them."[278]

Under the terms of the treaty, the sovereign vested in the chiefs—and not the dominion or the province—jurisdiction over the surrendered land. The sovereign could not unilaterally abrogate the Ojibwa jurisdiction in the treaty and grant it either to the dominion or a province. The chiefs could have explained that in the treaty negotiation they did not agree to transfer their lands to be administered by the province; the terms of the treaty made the imperial Crown a treaty fiduciary, with the dominion of Canada the named fiduciary agent for the sovereign:

> The Saulteaux Tribe of the Ojibbeway Indians and all other the Indians inhabiting the district thereinafter described and defined, do hereby cede, release, surrender, and yield up to the Government of the Dominion of Canada, for Her Majesty the Queen and Her successors forever, all their rights, titles, and privileges whatsoever, to the lands included with the following limits.[279]

The chiefs' intent, as grantor, should be controlling. The courts would have to explain why the province of Ontario was not mentioned as the fiduciary agent of the sovereign if the existing imperial Acts required such results.

Moreover, the chiefs could have argued that, since timber was not an enumerated purpose of the treaties, the sovereign would need the chiefs' consent and compensation for this use. They could have shown that their avocation of hunting was related to the timber cutting within the surrendered land:

277 *Treaty No. 4 Between Her Majesty the Queen and the Cree and Saulteaux Tribes of Indians at Qu'Appelle and Fort Elice* (Ottawa: Queen's Printer, 1966) at 4. See J.Y. Henderson, "Implementing the Treaty Order" in R. Gosse, J.Y. Henderson, and R. Carter, eds., *Continuing Poundmaker & Riel's Quest: Presentations Made At a Conference on Aboriginal Peoples and Justice* (Saskatoon, Sk.: Purich Publishing, 1994) at 52; See J.Y. Henderson, "Empowering Treaty Federalism" (1994) 58 Sask. L. Rev. 241 at 258-59.

278 *Treaty No. 4, ibid.* at 1.

279 *Treaty No. 3, supra* note 218 at 2.

such tracts as may be required or taken up from time to time for settlement, mining, lumbering by her said Government of the Dominion of Canada, or by any of the subjects thereof duly authorized therefor by the said Government.[280]

In the treaty, the dominion had an exclusive role in negotiating and acquiring lumbering rights from the chiefs. Under the doctrine of continuity, transferring land to another sovereign by treaty has never been presumed to disturb private rights, and in Ojibwa law rights to harvest timber was considered a private right. This would have challenged their Lordships' view:

> [that] the treaty leaves the Indians no right whatever to the timber growing upon the lands which they gave up, which is now fully vested in the Crown, all revenues derivable from the sale of such portions of it as are situate within the boundaries of Ontario being the property of that Province.[281]

The chiefs could have pointed out that the specific forest tracts might have been designated for the reserved land of one of the Saulteaux families by the treaty.[282] After the judicial committee decision, in 1889 Justice Ferguson of the High Court Bench stated that provincial timber license in reserved land created by the 1850 treaties were void, since the estate of the Crown was not freed from the Indian title.[283]

Since the treaty's terms and obligations were meant to be sacred and enduring, the chiefs could have shown that the written treaty was not a complete record, emphasizing important discrepancies between the record of the negotiations, Ojibwa language and symbolic records, and the wording of various written documents.[284] The published provisions of the treaty significantly conflict with Treaty Commissioner Morris's notes presented to Chief Powassan at the time the treaty was signed, known as the "Paypom Treaty." In ways similar to the "outside promises" of *Treaty 1* and *Treaty 2*, the written record and text of 1873 Treaty remained incomplete and misleading. If the treaty text was inconsistent with the actual treaty negotiations, the emerging common law of contracts had already recognized that certain categories such as duress or mistake invalidated such interpretations.

The relationship between the terms of the 1873 Treaty and the *Constitution Act, 1867* was never addressed from these perspectives. The colonial courts and system of law allowed racial bias and social engineering to prevail over vested treaty rights under

---

280   *Ibid.* at 3.

281   *St.Catherine's, supra* note 202, P.C. at 60.

282   *Ibid.*

283   *Attorney General of Canada v. Francis*, [1889] 2 C.N.L.C. 6.

284   The Treaty and Aboriginal Rights Research Centre, "We have kept our Part of the Treaty" (1995) [unpublished, research paper archived at the Centre] at 3: "The actual and binding terms of the Agreement known as Treaty # 3 are not identical with Treaty # 3 as published by Canada. No single document completely covers all terms of the Agreement know as Treaty #3. All records of negotiations, and recollections of the participants, must be considered to develop a full understanding of the terms that are part of Treaty #3. True knowledge of the Agreement known as Treaty # 3 was held by the chiefs and repeated when Canada later breached its promises."

the rule of law. The tragic result was to remove from the imperial Crown and dominion the revenue to fulfill the existing treaty obligations, and to devise the conditions for the poverty of the Aboriginal peoples under new taxing powers created by the federal government.

B. Developing Aboriginal tenure

After *St. Catherine's*, the federal-provincial conflict continued over natural resources. In *Ontario Mining Company v. Seybold et al.*,[285] Chancellor Boyd held that when the Saulteaux surrendered an Indian reserve (365,225 acres) created under the 1873 Treaty to the dominion, the dominion could not sell the land to a mining company even if it was to be sold for Indians' "benefit" and the money held in trust. If the reserve land was not being used or occupied by Indians, the reserve was freed from the special treaty privilege, and the lands reverted to the province because at confederation the "territorial and proprietary ownership of the soil was vested in the Crown" for the benefit of the province of Ontario. The Ontario Divisional Court,[286] the Supreme Court of Canada,[287] and the judicial committee of the Privy Council[288] affirmed this opinion. Their Lordships reasserted the distinction between proprietary rights and legislative jurisdiction against the dominion but not against the province:

> By s. 91 of the British North America Act, 1867, the Parliament of Canada has exclusive legislative authority over "Indians and lands reserved for the Indians." But this did not vest in the Government of the Dominion any proprietary rights in such lands [reserved for Indians], or any power by legislation to appropriate lands which by the surrender of the Indian title had become the free public lands of the province as an Indian reserve, in infringement of the proprietary rights of the province.[289]

The dominion government had no ability to sell or lease Indian lands for the benefit of the tribe or to meet its treaty obligations. Under these decisions, the dominion was forced to negotiate political and jurisdictional agreements with the provinces, rather than rely on judicial determination. Thus, the critical issues of Aboriginal and treaty rights were not brought before the courts, and were treated as policy issues rather than legal issues.

---

285 *Ontario Mining Co. v. Seybold (The Star Chrome case)*, [1903] A.C. 73 (P.C.), affirming (1901), 32 S.C.R. 1 (S.C.C.), affirming (1900), 32 O.R. 301 (Ont. Div. Ct.), affirming (1899), 31 O.R. 386 (Ont. Ch.) [hereinafter *Star Chrome* cited to reporter].

286 *Ibid.*, O.R.

287 *Ibid.*, S.C.R.

288 *Ibid.*, A.C.

289 *Ibid.* at 82. Legislative jurisdiction over property was distinguished from tenure or ownership of property under the *Constitution Act, 1867*; *R. v. Robertson* (1882), 6 S.C.R. 52 (S.C.C.) at 122; *A.G. Ontario v. Mercer* (1883), 8 A.C. 767 (P.C.) at 776; *A.G. Canada v. A.G. Ontario*, [1898] A.C. 700 (P.C.) at 709; *A.G. Quebec v. Nipissing Central Railway Co.*, [1926] A.C. 715 (P.C.), affirming (1925), [1926] S.C.R. 163 (S.C.C.); and *St. Eugene de Guigues (Municipality) v. C.P.R.*, [1937] S.C.R. 451 (S.C.C.).

In *Sparrow*, the Supreme Court of Canada summarized the judicial avoidance of Aboriginal tenure and rights:

> It is worth recalling that while British policy towards the native population was based on respect for their right to occupy their traditional lands, a proposition to which the Royal Proclamation of 1763 bears witness, there was from the outset never any doubt that sovereignty and legislative power, and indeed the underlying title, to such lands vested in the Crown. ... And there can be no doubt that over the years the rights of the Indians were often honoured in the breach ... As MacDonald J. stated in *Pasco v. Canadian National Railway Co.* ...: "We cannot recount with much pride the treatment accorded to the native people of this country."

> For many years, the rights of the Indians to their aboriginal lands—certainly as legal rights—were virtually ignored. The leading cases defining Indian rights in the early part of the century were directed at claims supported by the Royal Proclamation or other legal instruments, and even these cases were essentially concerned with settling legislative jurisdiction or the rights of commercial enterprises. For fifty years after the publication of Clement's *The Law of the Canadian Constitution* (3rd ed. 1916), there was a virtual absence of discussion of any kind of Indian rights to land even in academic literature. By the late 1960s, aboriginal claims were not even recognized by the federal government as having any legal status. Thus the *Statement of the Government of Canada on Indian Policy* (1969), although well meaning, contained the assertion (at p. 11) that "aboriginal claims to land ... are so general and undefined that it is not realistic to think of them as specific claims capable of remedy except through a policy and program that will end injustice to the Indians as members of the Canadian community". In the same general period, the James Bay development by Quebec Hydro was originally initiated without regard to the rights of the Indians who lived there, even though these were expressly protected by a constitutional instrument ... .[290]

The modern judicial framework for the articulation of Aboriginal tenure and rights began with *Calder v. A.-G. of B.C.*[291] The *St. Catherine's Milling* decision was still considered controlling law: Aboriginal tenure existed by virtue of the 1763 Proclamation, not on the basis of Aboriginal use and occupation of land or Aboriginal laws from time immemorial. The Nisga'a lawyer admitted that the Crown had title to the land in question; the action was for a declaration that Nisga'a tenure to their ancient homelands, now in northwestern British Columbia, had not been extinguished.[292] Justice Hall, speaking for three members of the Supreme Court of Canada, held that the Nisga'a had an existing Aboriginal title based on their own legal "concepts of ownership"[293] and original use and occupancy, similar to the British common law rule of possession as proof of ownership.[294] He said the continuity of Nisga'a tenure was consis-

---

290   *R. v. Sparrow*, [1990] 1 S.C.R. 1075 at 1103-1104, [1990] 3 C.N.L.R. 160 (S.C.C.), affirming (1986), [1987] 1 C.N.L.R. 145 (B.C. C.A.) [hereinafter *Sparrow* cited to S.C.R.].

291   *Supra* note 252.

292   *Ibid.* at 352-53, 410.

293   *Ibid.* at 354-55, 368-75, esp. 372, 375, 387-89. The comments view the Nisga'a tenure as a separate system of legal tenure.

294   *Ibid.* at 368, 375, 401-404.

tent with the colonial assertion that all lands in British Columbia "belong to the Crown in fee."[295] Speaking for the other three members of the court, Justice Judson held that whatever title the Nisga'a may have once had, it had since been extinguished. He agreed with Justice Hall that Nisga'a tenure in British Columbia was an Aboriginal legal system and occupancy-based; their tenure was not derived from either 1763 Proclamation or treaties:

> Although I think that it is clear that Indian title in British Columbia cannot owe its origin to the Proclamation of 1763, the fact is that when the settlers came, the Indians were there, organized in societies and occupying the land as their forefathers had done for centuries. This is what Indian title means and it does not help one in the solution of this problem to call it a "personal or usufructuary right". What they are asserting in this action is that they had a right to continue to live on their [own] lands as their forefathers had lived and that this right has never been lawfully extinguished. There can be no question that this right was "dependent on the goodwill of the Sovereign".[296]

By recognizing that the 1763 Proclamation was not the sole source of Aboriginal tenure, the Court effectively overturned the judicial committee's grant theory in *St. Catherine's Milling* on the nature and source of Aboriginal tenure.

Some months later, the Quebec Superior Court ordered a halt to the James Bay hydroelectric project on similar grounds: the Cree and Inuit Aboriginal title had not been extinguished by the Crown in right of Quebec.[297] The Quebec Court of Appeal later lifted the injunction,[298] and the Supreme Court of Canada refused leave to appeal the matter further. By then, however, all sides had determined that a negotiated solution was better than continued litigation. The result was *the James Bay and Northern Quebec Agreement* (1975).[299]

In the *Baker Lake*[300] case, Justice Mahoney of the Federal Court of Canada, Trial Division, held that in the Northwest Territories the Inuit had an occupancy-based Aboriginal tenure to the Baker Lake area. Following *Calder*, the court held the common law recognized Inuit tenure although it could be abridged. Justice Mahoney set out the elements to be established: the claimants and their ancestors were members of an organized society that occupied the territory over which they asserted Aboriginal title; the occupation was to the exclusion of other organized societies; and the occupation was

---

295 *Ibid.* at 410-11. Although the Crown cannot, under the doctrine of tenure, own an estate in fee, Justice Hall stated the admission that one should "merely state what was the actual situation under the common law and add nothing new or additional to the Crown's paramount title."

296 *Ibid.* at 328. All estates in British law are dependent either directly or indirectly on the will of the sovereign, so it is difficult to understand the Court's continued stress on it in Aboriginal tenure.

297 *Société de la Baie James v. Kanatewat* (1974), [1975] C.A. 166.

298 *Gros-Louis v. Société de la Baie James*, [1974] R.P. 39 (C.A.).

299 *James Bay and Northern Quebec Agreement*, incorporated in the *James Bay and Northern Quebec Native Claims Settlement Act*, S.C. 1976-77, c. 32.

300 *Hamlet of Baker Lake v. Minister of Indian Affairs and Northern Development*, [1979] 3 C.N.L.R. 17, [1980] 1 F.C. 518 (Fed. T.D.), additional reasons at (1979), [1981] 1 F.C. 266, [1982] C.N.L.R. 139 (Fed. T.D.).

an established fact at the time sovereignty was asserted by Britain. Justice Mahoney found that the Inuit of Baker Lake met all these requirements. The only remaining question, therefore, was whether Inuit tenure had been extinguished, either by the transfer of the lands to the Hudson's Bay Company or by the subsequent admission of Rupert's Land into Canada. He found that neither had the effect of extinguishing the Inuit tenure, since the Crown had shown no clear and plain intention to extinguish it. The court's reasoning, as in *Calder*, established that Aboriginal tenure could co-exist and continue with Canadian settlement or development, but did not explain why both could exist.

In the *Guerin* case in 1984,[301] the Supreme Court found that the federal government was in a fiduciary relationship with Indian bands and was therefore responsible for properly managing the surrendered reserve lands. Because of federal mismanagement of lands that were surrendered for a Vancouver golf course, the band in question was awarded $10 million in damages. The Court, speaking through Justice Dickson,[302] characterized the fiduciary relationship between the Crown and Aboriginal people as being *sui generis* and as having the capacity to evolve.[303] Justice Dickson found the fiduciary relationship arose out of the "concept of Aboriginal, native or Indian title,"[304] defined by *Calder* as "a legal right derived from the Indians' historic occupation and possession of their tribal lands."[305]

Aboriginal tenure, Justice Dickson said, is an independent legal right that, although recognized by the 1763 Proclamation, predates it; the Proclamation was a declaratory act, not a grant.[306] He went on to discuss the nature of Aboriginal tenure, examining the language used to describe it, rejecting the view that Aboriginal tenure or title was a personal or usufructuary right.[307] Instead, he stated that Aboriginal tenure was *sui generis*, a unique interest in the land that could not be described adequately in terms of English land law:[308]

---

301 *Guerin, supra* note 252.

302 *Ibid.* at 376-82, Beetz, Chouinard and Lamer JJ. concurring. Mr. Justice Estey found that the Crown acted as the statutory agent of the Indian Band (tribal or community interest) in arranging a lease of their reserved land with a non-Indian (at 394). Madam Justice Wilson, on behalf of three other members of the court, described the Crown's liability in terms of breach of a trust. She felt that the surrender document in the case created an express trust in the Crown (at 355). Madame Justice Wilson noted that the *Indian Act* provisions did not create a fiduciary obligation towards Aboriginals on reserves, but the Act, "recognized the existence of such an obligation" (at 356). Her Ladyship saw Indian title as a proprietary or beneficial interest sufficient to constitute a trust *res* or *corpus*.

303 *Ibid.* at 356. The nature of the relationship involved gave rise to the fiduciary duty. The categories of fiduciary obligations, like those of negligence, should not be considered closed.

304 *Ibid.* at 376.

305 *Ibid.*, C.N.L.R. at 132; *R. v. Van der Peet*, [1996] 2 S.C.R. 507 at para. 34, [1996] 4 C.N.L.R. 177 (S.C.C.), reconsideration refused (January 16, 1997), Doc. 23803 (S.C.C.) [hereinafter *Van der Peet* cited to S.C.R.].

306 *Guerin, ibid.* at 335, 377-79.

307 *Ibid.* at 379-80. He discussed *St. Catherine's, supra* note 202; *Star Chrome, supra* note 285, A.C.; *Amodu Tijani v. Southern Nigeria (Secretary)*, [1921] 2 A.C. 399 (P.C.) at 404; and *Calder, supra* note 252.

308 *Guerin, ibid.* at 382.

It appears to me that there is no real conflict between the cases which characterize Indian title as a beneficial interest of some sort, and those which characterize it a personal, usufructuary right. Any apparent inconsistency derives from the fact that in describing what constitutes a unique interest in land the courts have almost inevitably found themselves applying a somewhat inappropriate terminology drawn from general property law. There is a core of truth in the way that each of the two lines of authority has described native title, but an appearance of conflict has nonetheless arisen because in neither case is the categorization quite accurate.[309]

Justice Dickson's insight that Aboriginal tenure cannot be described in British tenure categories began to explain why Aboriginal tenure could co-exist with Canadian settlement and development. Dickson stated the Indians' interest in land is an independent legal interest in Canadian law, but distinct from Anglo-Canadian general property law.[310] Dickson stated that since this enforceable legal interest was not created by either the legislative or executive branches of government, it is not a derivative title or estate under the Crown or made by law of any government under its derived powers.[311] Describing the legal right as derived from the Indians' historic occupation and possession of their tribal lands,[312] Dickson further asserted that the Crown had a legal and fiduciary duty to protect Aboriginal nations' land.[313]

C. Reserved Aboriginal tenure in treaties

The first review of the reserve tenure under the Míkmaw treaties and the prerogative Instruments and Proclamation in the Atlantic provinces in the Nova Scotia Supreme Court Appeal Division was conducted by Chief Justice MacKeigan in 1975 in *Isaac v. The Queen*.[314] He concluded that "original Indian rights" as defined in

---

309 *Ibid.* This characterization does not take one much further than the *Royal Proclamation of 1763, supra* note 15. See Slattery, *supra* note 216.

310 *Guerin, ibid.* at 378, 385. See B. Slattery, "The Legal Basis of Aboriginal Title" in F. Cassidy, ed., *Aboriginal Title in British Columbia: Delgamuukw v. the Queen* (Lantzville, B.C.: Oolichan Books, 1992) at 117-21. He argues for an intersocietal law of aboriginal rights as the keystone of our common Constitution.

311 *Guerin, ibid.* at 377, 379.

312 *Ibid.* at 335.

313 *Ibid.* at 376. A *sui generis* or unique fiduciary obligation arose in this case from the Crown's duty to protect and preserve a collective Aboriginal interest in land. The Band made this possible through a surrender for lease to the federal government under s. 18(1) of the *Indian Act*. The Band retained the governance of the Crown's dealings with third parties in relations to the Band's interest in the reserved Indian land. The obligation has its roots in the *sui generis* nature of Aboriginal or Indian title, and the historic powers and responsibilities assumed by the Crown.

314 (1975), 13 N.S.R. (2d) 460 (N.S. C.A) [hereinafter *Isaac*].

Worcester existed among the Míkmaq.[315] He further held that these original rights arose in English customary or common law and were confirmed by the 1763 Proclamation and other authoritative declarations.[316] In his analysis of the 1763 Proclamation he stated, "[t]he 'lands reserved' apparently included all lands in Nova Scotia which the Indians had not ceded or sold to the Crown."[317] He further declared that subsequent treaty, agreement, or competent legislation had not altered the 1763 Royal Proclamation.[318] In conclusion, MacKeigan C.J. stated:

> No Nova Scotia treaty has been found whereby Indians ceded land to the Crown, whereby their rights on any land were specifically extinguished, or whereby they agreed to accept and retire to specified reserves, although thorough archival research might well disclose record of informal agreements especially in the early 1800's when reserves were

315 *Ibid.* at 475. Because of *R. v. Syliboy* (1928), [1929] 1 D.L.R. 307, 50 C.C.C. 389 (N.S. Co. Ct.) [hereinafter *Syliboy* cited to D.L.R.], denying the 1752 Treaty was valid. The Chief Justice did not consider the rights of hunting within the context of the treaty. Ironically, however, the Chief Justice did reverse the *Syliboy* ruling that the *Royal Proclamation of 1763, supra* note 15 did not apply to Nova Scotia (at 481). In 1982, the Chief Justice affirmed the *Syliboy* decision in *R. v. Cope* (1981), 49 N.S.R. 555 (2d) at 564 (N.S. C.A.), leave to appeal refused (1982), 51 N.S.R. (2d) 370 (note) (S.C.C.); as did Hart and MacDonald A.J.J., in *R. v. Simon* (1982), 49 N.S.R. (2d) 566 at 572-77 (N.S. C.A.). In 1985, the Supreme Court of Canada reversed these decisions, in *Simon v. R.*, [1985] 2 S.C.R. 387, 62 N.R. 366 (S.C.C.) [hereinafter *Simon* cited to S.C.R. unless otherwise stated].

316 *Isaac, ibid.* at 478. The Chief Justice stated that: "The Proclamation was clearly not the exclusive source of Indian right ... but rather was 'declaratory of the aboriginal rights' ... . I am of the opinion that the Proclamation in its broad declaration as to Indian rights applied to Nova Scotia including Cape Breton. Its recital (p.127) acknowledged that in all colonies, including Nova Scotia, all land which had not been 'ceded to or purchased by' the Crown was reserved to the Indians as 'their Hunting Grounds'. Any trespass upon any lands thus reserved to the Indians were forbidden." This passage was cited with approval by the Nova Scotia Appeal Division in *Denny v. The Queen*, 94 N.S.R. (2d) 253 at 26, [1990] 2 C.N.L.R. 115 (N.S. C.A.) [hereinafter *Denny* cited to N.S.R.]. This case dealt with the Aboriginal right to fish beyond the strict perimeter of Indian Reserves.

317 *Isaac, ibid.* at 479. MacKeigan J. offered an unconvincing explanation of "ceded" lands. Rather than a treaty cession he speculated that: "'Ceded' land presumably included lands then occupied with the assumed or forced acquiescence of the Indians, such as those at Halifax, Lunenburg, Liverpool and Yarmouth, and the former Acadian lands taken over by New England 'planters'. Later the 'lands reserved' as 'Hunting Grounds' were, of course, gradually restricted by occupation by the white man under Crown grant which extinguished the Indian right on the land so granted. Indeed, the land where that right exists may have in time become restricted in Nova Scotia to the reserved lands which we now know as 'Indian reserves'." This belief in implied extinguishment by Crown grants, and hence white occupation, is inconsistent with the terms of the treaties, prerogative law and English law, since Nova Scotia has a prerogative constitution that prohibits anyone from trespassing on lands not purchased from Indians. MacKeigan does not attempt to resolve the inconsistency between the *Royal Proclamation of 1763, supra* note 15, or the *Statute of Frauds* (1677, 29 Cha. II, c. 3), and the lack of written cessions or purchases. His interpretation of extinguishment by occupation under Crown grants or leases was raised before the Supreme Court of Canada in *Simon, supra* note 315, and in *R. v. Sioui*, [1990] 1 S.C.R. 1025, [1990] 3 C.N.L.R. 127 (S.C.C.) [hereinafter *Sioui* cited to S.C.R.]. They rejected implied extinguishment for lack of clear proof, stating that extinguishment cannot be lightly implied.

318 *Isaac, ibid.* at 478. See especially s. 25 of the *Canadian Charter of Rights and Freedoms*, Part I of the *Constitution Act, 1982*, being Schedule B to the *Canada Act 1982*, (U.K.), 1982, c.11 [hereinafter *Charter*]. It states that the rights arising from the *Royal Proclamation of 1763, supra* note 15, continue to be valid.

established by executive order. ... I have been unable to find any record of any treaty, agreement or arrangement after 1780 extinguishing, modifying or confirming the Indian right to hunt and fish, or any other record of any cession or release of rights or lands by the Indians. ... The review has confirmed that Indians have a special relationship with the lands they occupy, not merely a quaint tradition, but rather a right recognized in law.[319]

In *Guerin*, the Supreme Court of Canada further defined the *sui generis* fiduciary duty of the Crown toward reserved lands in the context of the 1763 Proclamation and the *Indian Act*.[320] In *Simon*,[321] the Court held the 1752 Treaty was valid against contemporary provincial hunting regulations, rejecting the province's argument that the treaty was not valid because it did not cede land to the Crown.[322] Also, it overruled an earlier case holding the same 1752 Treaty to be legally meaningless, because the Mík-maq were "uncivilized people or savages":

> But the Indians were never regarded as an independent power. A civilized nation first discovering a country of uncivilized people or savages held such country as its own until such time as by treaty it was transferred to some other civilized nation. The savages' rights of sovereignty even of ownership were never recognized.[323]

The Supreme Court rejected this concept:

> It should be noted that the language used ... reflects the biases and prejudices of another era in our history. Such language is no longer acceptable in Canadian law and indeed is inconsistent with a growing sensitivity to native rights in Canada.[324]

The Supreme Court rejected the concept of "civilized nation" discovery being relevant in a treaty context, and established that the 1752 Treaty was *sui generis*, an independent source of law in Canada that did not depend on international law or British law. It established special interpretative rules for these treaties: they were to be interpreted as Aboriginal treaty negotiators would have understood them; ambiguous terms were to be construed in their favour;[325] reviewing courts were to apply a fair, large, and

---

319   *Isaac, ibid.* at 479, 483, 485. At 483-84, Chief Justice MacKeigan concluded that: "The history of the next eighty-seven years discloses little concern for the Indians. The incoming settlers pushed them back to poorer land in the interior of the province. The government gradually herded them into reserves and made sporadic and unsuccessful attempts to convert them into agricultural people."

320   *Guerin, supra* note 252.

321   *Simon, supra* note 315 at 404.

322   *Ibid.* In the Supreme Court of Canada in *Simon* the Province of Nova Scotia argued that the 1752 Treaty was not a valid treaty, because it did not cede land to the Crown or delineate boundaries. They further argued that occupancy by the white man under Crown grant or lease had extinguished the treaty reservation and gave absolute title in the land covered by the 1752 Treaty to the Crown (*ibid.* at 408-10). The Court found it unnecessary to come to a final decision on extinguishment by occupation of Crown grant or lease (*ibid.* at 405-406).

323   *Ibid.* at 399.

324   *Ibid.* at 399.

325   *Ibid.* at 402.

liberal construction of treaties in favour of the Indians;[326] and strict proof was required to extinguish a treaty-protected right.[327] The Court affirmed that the 1752 Treaty created mutually binding legal obligations;[328] provided a civil mechanism for dispute resolution;[329] and that its obligations have continuing legal validity and force since it has not been terminated.[330]

Justice Dickson accepted "that under certain circumstances a treaty could be terminated by the breach of one of its fundamental provisions,"[331] but rejected the idea of conquest or subsequent hostilities as doing so:[332]

> Once it has been established that a valid treaty has been entered into, the party arguing for its termination bears the burden of proving the circumstances and events justifying termination. The inconclusive and conflicting evidence presented by the parties makes it impossible for this Court to say with any certainty what happened on the eastern coast of Nova Scotia 233 years ago. As a result, the Court is unable to resolve this historical question. The Crown has failed to prove that the Treaty of 1752 was terminated by subsequent hostilities.

> I would note that there is nothing in the British conduct subsequent to the conclusion of the Treaty of 1752 and the alleged hostilities to indicate that the Crown considered the terms of the Treaty at an end. Indeed, His Majesty's Royal Instructions of December 9, 1761, addressed inter alia to the Governor of Nova Scotia, declared that the Crown "was determined upon all occasions to support and protect the ... Indians in their just rights and possessions and to keep inviolable the treaties and compacts which have been entered into with them ..." These Royal Instructions formed the basis of the Proclamation issued by Jonathan Belcher, Lieutenant Governor of Nova Scotia on May 4, 1762 which also repeated the above words.[333]

---

326 *Ibid.* at 402-403.

327 *Ibid.*

328 *Ibid.* at 398-401.

329 *Ibid.* at 401, referring to Art. 8.

330 *Ibid.* at 403-407.

331 *Ibid.*

332 At 403-404, Dickson J. stated:

> In accordance with the finding of the Nova Scotia Court of Appeal, the Crown argued that the Treaty of 1752 was terminated and rendered unenforceable when hostilities broke out between the Micmac and the British in 1753. The appellant maintained that the alleged hostilities were sporadic and minor in nature and did not, therefore, nullify or terminate the Treaty. It was further argued by the appellant, relying on L.F.S. Upton, *Micmac and Colonists: Indian-White Relations in the Maritimes 1713-1867* (1979) [*supra* note 128], that the English initiated the hostilities and that, therefore, the Crown should not be permitted to rely on them to support the termination of the Treaty. Finally, the appellant submitted that, even if the Court finds that there were sufficient hostilities to affect the Treaty, at most it was merely suspended and not terminated.

> In considering the impact of subsequent hostilities on the peace Treaty of 1752, the parties looked to international law on treaty termination. While it may be helpful in some instances to analogize the principles of international treaty law to Indian treaties, these principles are not determinative. An Indian treaty is unique; it is an agreement *sui generis* which is neither created nor terminated according to the rules of international law.

333 *Simon, supra* note 315 at 404-405.

In 1990, the Supreme Court indirectly addressed unceded or unpurchased Aboriginal tenure in the 1760 Treaty in the *Sioui* case.[334] At issue was a document that the federal government argued was a mere safe conduct pass issued by British authorities to members of the Wendat (Huron) nation. This case, expanding the definition of what is considered a treaty in Canadian law, emphasized "[t]he *sui generis* situation in which the Indians were placed" in the context of their relations with the competing European powers.[335] Justice Lamer cited *Worcester v. Georgia* to the effect that treaties between European nations and Aboriginal nations were similar to international agreements,[336] concluding that it was "good policy to maintain relations with them very close to those maintained between sovereign nations" and that "the Indian nations were regarded in their relations with the European nations which occupied North America as independent nations."[337]

Justice Lamer stated treaty interpretation always involves territorial questions of Aboriginal tenure, rejecting the idea that silence in treaty implies that land issues can be ignored:

> ...the treaty essentially has to be interpreted by determining the intention of the parties on the territorial question at the time it was concluded. It is not sufficient to note that the treaty is silent on this point. We must also undertake the task of interpreting the treaty on the territorial question with the same generous approach toward the Indians that applied in considering earlier questions. Now as then, we must do our utmost to act in the spirit of Simon.[338]

---

334 *Sioui, supra* note 317 at 1044.

335 *Ibid.* at 1056.

336 *Ibid.* at 1054.

337 *Ibid.* at 1053. At 1052-53, Lamer J. stated:

> [W]e can conclude from the historical documents that both Great Britain and France felt that the Indian nations had sufficient independence and played a large enough role in North America for it to be good policy to maintain relations with them very close to those maintained between sovereign nations.
>
> The mother countries did everything in their power to secure the alliance of each Indian nation and to encourage nations allied with the enemy to change sides. When these efforts met with success, they were incorporated in treaties of alliance or neutrality. This clearly indicates that the Indian nations were regarded in their relations with the European nations which occupied North America as independent nations. The papers of Sir William Johnson ... who was in charge of Indian affairs in British North America, demonstrate the recognition by Great Britain that nation-to-nation relations had to be conducted with the North American Indians.

338 *Ibid.* at 1068. This decision protects Aboriginal and treaty rights and insulates them from past encroachment due to non-use, subsequent colonial acts, and modern statutes. Additionally, the confirming prerogative legislation renders the implicated extinguishment theory unconstitutional. This decision is consistent with the International Court of Justice decision in the *Case Concerning Right of Passage over Indian Territory (Portugal v. India)*, [1960] I.C.J. Rep. 6. In interpreting an old indigenous treaty, the court ruled: "that the validity of a treaty concluded as long ago as the last quarter of the eighteenth century, in the conditions then prevailing on the Indian Peninsula, should not be judged on the basis of practices and procedures which have since developed only gradually."

In the treaty context, Lamer rejected implied or third party extinguishment of reserved Aboriginal tenure and rights, adding the requirement that Indians who are party to a treaty must consent to its extinguishment.[339]

The immediate issue in *Sioui* was whether the Wendat were entitled by the 1760 Treaty to practice certain ancestral religious rites in Jacques Cartier Park. These rites involved cutting down trees and making fires, contrary to regulations under the *Quebec Parks Act*. The 1760 Treaty protected the free exercise of the Wendat customs and religion, and the evidence acknowledged that long before the treaty the Wendat made regular use of the territory covered by the park. The Crown argued the rights of the Wendat had to be exercised in accordance with the province's legislation and regulations designed to protect the park and other users of it. Lamer rejected that argument, finding the treaty reconciliation showed mutual intentions to preserve Wendat customs. Confronted with the conflicting interests of the Crown and the Wendat, the Court preferred to balance their modern interests: "Protecting the exercise of the customs in all parts of the territory frequented when it is not incompatible with its occupancy is in my opinion the most reasonable way of reconciling the competing interests."[340] The Court found that exercising the Aboriginal rights of the Wendat protected by the treaty was compatible with the rights of the Crown.[341]

In contrast, the courts in *Bear Island*[342] rejected the *Teme-Augama Anishinabai* (Deep Water People, in Ojibwa) claim of Aboriginal tenure to some 4,000 square miles of land in the Temagami area in northeastern Ontario. No evidence was presented that the Crown ever entered a treaty cession of the territory, or purchased it. The trial court judgment in 1984 found that there were no Aboriginal title or rights. The Ontario Court of Appeal concluded that the *Robinson-Huron Treaty* (1850) had the effect of unilaterally extinguishing the Ojibwa tenure: the Crown had formed an implied, unilateral intention to extinguish that tenure; and the *Teme-Augama Anishinabai* had implicitly ratified the 1850 Treaty that unilaterally extinguished their tenure.[343] The court stated they had exchanged their Aboriginal rights for two main rights: the right to annuities and the right to a reserve.

In 1991, the Supreme Court concluded that the trial judge was wrong and added that, on the basis of the facts as the trial judge found them, there had been "an aboriginal right" but that some "arrangements" made sometime after the treaty amounted to an adhesion to the treaty that ceded their Aboriginal tenure.[344] This implied adhesion to the 1850 Treaty had extinguished the *Teme-Augama Anishinabai* tenure and rights.

---

339 *Simon, supra* note 315 at 1061-66.

340 *Sioui, supra* note 317 at 1071.

341 *Simon, supra* note 315 at 405-406. This reaffirmed *Sioui, ibid.*

342 *Ontario (A.G.) v. Bear Island Foundation,* [1991] 2 S.C.R. 570, 3 C.N.L.R. 79 (S.C.C.), affirming (1989), 68 O.R. (2d) 394 (Ont. C.A.), affirming (1984), 15 D.L.R. (4th) 321 (Ont. H.C.).

343 *Ibid.* O.R. at 419.

344 *Ibid.* S.C.R. at 575. The problem is that the 1850 Treaty had a specific purchase price and annuity, which the Court never addressed in its brief opinion.

The Supreme Court remarked that, since the adhesion was unfulfilled, the Crown might have violated its fiduciary obligations.

D. Constitutional guidelines for Aboriginal tenure

In 1997, the Supreme Court gave constitutional guidelines for Aboriginal tenure, rejecting the trial court decision on Aboriginal tenure in *Delgamuukw v. British Columbia*,[345] and ordering a new trial. Understanding the background to the case is important to understanding the guidelines. In 1991, Chief Justice McEachern of the Supreme Court of British Columbia rejected outright the claim of the Gitksan[346] and Wet'-suwet'en to Aboriginal tenure and sovereignty over their traditional lands in northern British Columbia. Their hereditary chiefs had brought an action against the province alleging that from time immemorial they and their ancestors had occupied and possessed approximately 22,000 square miles of northwestern British Columbia They claimed unextinguished Aboriginal tenure to their own territory and the right to govern it by Aboriginal laws, claiming damages for the loss of all lands and resources in the area transferred to third parties since the establishment of the colony.

Chief Justice McEachern described Gitksan and Wet'suwet'en life and social organization before contact in terminology reminiscent of the language rejected by the Supreme Court of Canada in the *Simon* case.[347] Chief Justice McEachern concluded that in *St. Catherine's Milling* the judicial committee "got it right when it described the aboriginal interest as a personal right rather than a proprietary one."[348] He also found that whatever rights the Aboriginal people had before British Columbia's colonization were extinguished by the 1858 imperial Parliament act authorizing the Queen to appoint a governor of the new colony and make provision for its laws and administration. He reasoned that in 1871, when the colony was united with Canada, all legislative jurisdiction was divided between Canada and the province, leaving no room for any Aboriginal jurisdiction or sovereignty. The Aboriginal peoples' only surviving right was to use unoccupied Crown land for their traditional pursuits of hunting and fishing for sustenance purposes, subject to the colonial laws and until such time as the land was acquired for a purpose incompatible with the existence of such a right.

The Gitksan and Wet'suwet'en appealed; the British Columbia Court of Appeal split on the various issues raised at trial, with a majority of three judges generally upholding the trial decision and dismissing the appeal.[349] Two judges dissented on a

---

345 *Delgamuukw v. British Columbia,* [1997] 3 S.C.R. 1010 (S.C.C.), reversing in part (1993), 104 D.L.R. (4th) 470 (B.C. C.A.), affirming in part (1991), 79 D.L.R. (4th) 185 (B.C. S.C.) [hereinafter *Delgamuukw* cited to S.C.R. or to the Court].

346 Gitxsan is the proper spelling. *The Canadian Oxford Dictionary,* ed. Katherine Barber (Toronto: Oxford University Press, 1998) gives *kitxsan,* meaning literally people of the Skeena River.

347 *Simon, supra* note 315.

348 *Delgamuukw, supra* note 345, McEachern J. (B.C. S.C.).

349 *Ibid.,* B.C. C.A.

number of grounds and would have allowed the appeal.[350] In all, the Court of Appeal issued four separate judgments.

Chief Justice Lamer for a unified Supreme Court held that Aboriginal tenure is part of the Constitution of Canada:

> Aboriginal title at common law is protected in its full form by s. 35(1). This conclusion flows from the express language of s. 35(1) itself, which states in full: "[t]he *existing* aboriginal and treaty rights of the aboriginal peoples of Canada are hereby recognized and affirmed" (emphasis added). On a plain reading of the provision, s. 35(1) did not create aboriginal rights; rather, it accorded constitutional status to those rights which were "existing" in 1982. The provision, at the very least, constitutionalized those rights which aboriginal peoples possessed at common law, since those rights existed at the time s. 35(1) came into force. Since aboriginal title was a common law right whose existence was recognized well before 1982 (e.g., *Calder, supra*), s. 35(1) has constitutionalized it in its full form.[351]

The Supreme Court held that Aboriginal tenure and rights are constitutional rights independent of British traditions and are protected by constitutional supremacy and the rule of law. The source of Aboriginal tenure is both Aboriginal law and prior occupation of the continent.[352]

The Supreme Court declared that as long as Aboriginal nations, tribes, and peoples maintain their relationship to their land, Aboriginal tenure continues. Aboriginal tenure endures for as long as the connection with the land is honoured and respected by Aboriginal peoples. It is a real property right held collectively by all members of an Aboriginal nation according to Aboriginal order and law. Within the Aboriginal nation, tribe, or peoples, Aboriginal law and community decisions will determine the proprietary titles, rights, and interests of the family or members.[353]

The Supreme Court has established that Aboriginal tenure is comparable and equal tenure to the British doctrine of Crown tenure.[354] The *sui generis* nature of Aboriginal tenure emphasizes that the Aboriginal legal order allocates uses of an ecology among the communities and families and precludes the application of "traditional real property rules" to explain the content of that title.[355] As La Forest J. stated in his con-

---

350   *Ibid.*

351   *Ibid.*, S.C.C. at para. 133.

352   *Ibid.* at paras. 114, 126. Compare *Mabo v. Queensland [No. 2]* (1992), 175 C.L.R. 1, 107 A.L.R. 1 (H.C.) [hereinafter *Mabo* cited to A.L.R.], in which Brennan J., writing the principal majority judgment, said: "Native title has its origin in and is given its content by the traditional laws acknowledged by and the traditional customs observed by the indigenous inhabitants of a territory. The nature and incidents of native title must be ascertained as a matter of fact by reference to those laws and customs," at 42; see also Deane and Gaudron JJ. at 65-66, 83; compare to Toohey J. at 146-50.

353   *Mabo, ibid.* at 107-108.

354   *Delgamuukw, supra* note 345 at paras. 114-15; see *Mabo, ibid.* at 35-36 (Brennan J.); 59-60, 64-65 (Deane and Gaudron JJ.) and Toohey J. at 140-42.

355   *Delgamuukw, ibid.* at para. 130; *St. Mary's Indian Band v. Cranbrook (City)*, [1997] 2 S.C.R. 657 (S.C.C.) at para. 14, additional reasons at, [1997] 2 S.C.R. 678 (S.C.C.).

curring opinion: "This *sui generis* interest is not equated with fee simple ownership; nor can it be described with reference to traditional property law concepts."[356] Aboriginal tenure may nevertheless operate in a manner consistent with the British doctrine of tenure. In both systems, for example, it is impossible for land not to be used or not to be owned. If the land is unowned, it will be deemed to be owned by the collective Aboriginal nation in Aboriginal law or the Crown in British law.

Aboriginal tenure is an ecological order; it has diverse visions of a shared order and processes behind its allocation of resources to family or kinship entitlement and responsibilities. Reviewing courts must respect not only the Aboriginal legal order, but also enforce its decisions against non-Aboriginals, since both processes are protected by section 35(1). Chief Justice Lamer in *Van der Peet* stressed that reviewing courts must define constitutional rights of Aboriginal peoples "in a manner which recognizes that Aboriginal rights are *rights* but which does so without losing sight of the fact that they are rights held by Aboriginal peoples because they are *Aboriginal*."[357]

13. Interpretation of Section 35

In 1982, the *Canada Act*[358] provided for the protection of the Aboriginal order in section 35 of the *Constitution Act, 1982*,[359] and in section 25 of the *Charter*.[360] Section 35 provides:

(1) The existing aboriginal and treaty rights of the aboriginal peoples of Canada are hereby recognized and affirmed.

(2) In this Act, "aboriginal peoples of Canada" includes the Indian, Inuit and Métis peoples of Canada.

(3) For greater certainty, in subsection (1) "treaty rights" includes rights that now exist by way of land claims agreements or may be so acquired.

(4) Notwithstanding any other provision of this Act, the aboriginal and treaty rights referred to in subsection (1) are guaranteed equally to male and female persons.

These Aboriginal and treaty rights are part of the "supreme law of Canada,"[361] and are

---

356 *Delgamuukw, ibid.* at para. 190.

357 *Van der Peet, supra* note 305 at para. 20.

358 *Canada Act 1982* (U.K.), 1982, c. 11.

359 *Constitution Act, 1982*, being Schedule B to the *Canada Act 1982* (U.K.), 1982, c. 11 [hereinafter *Constitution Act, 1982*]. In the *Constitution Amendment Act*, Proclamation, 11th July 1983, S.I./84-102, C.Gaz. 1983.117.2984, these constitutional rights were explicitly "guaranteed equally to male and female persons." For its counterpart in the *Charter*, see *supra* note 318 at s. 28. Sometimes, the treaties affirm the freedom of religion: see Treaty of 1726 with the Mı́kmaq.

360 *Charter, supra* note 318.

361 *Constitution Act, 1982, supra* note 359 at s. 52(1). It states that: "The Constitution of Canada is the supreme law of Canada, and any law that is inconsistent with the provisions of the Constitution is, to the extent of the inconsistency, of no force or effect."

sequestered from control by reasonable limits prescribed by democratic law in the *Charter*.

Section 25 of the *Charter* provides special protection for Aboriginal and treaty rights against the new individual rights located in the *Charter*:

> The guarantee in this Charter of certain rights and freedoms shall not be construed so as to abrogate or derogate from any aboriginal, treaty or other rights or freedoms that pertain to the aboriginal peoples of Canada including
>
> (a) any rights or freedoms that have been recognized by the Royal Proclamation of October 7, 1763; and
>
> (b) any rights or freedoms that now exist by way of land claims agreements or may be so acquired.[362]

Reviewing courts are precluded from interpreting any individual freedoms in the *Charter* to limit Aboriginal and treaty rights or other rights.

Section 25 maintains the constitutional integrity of section 35.[363] These two sections are complementary, locating a legitimate constitutional source for Aboriginal and treaty rights in the conscience of the nation. While section 35 protects Aboriginal and treaty rights from other constitutional authority, section 25 protects these rights from individuals, their groups, and their chosen governments.[364]

A. Aboriginal rights

In *Sparrow*[365]—the first appeal that required the Supreme Court of Canada to explore the scope of section 35(1) of the *Constitution Act, 1982*—the context involved a member of the Musqueam Band in British Columbia charged under the federal *Fisheries Act* with fishing with a drift net longer than that permitted by the terms of his band's food fishing licence.[366] He was fishing in a part of the Fraser River where his ancestors had fished from time immemorial. The Supreme Court of Canada declared

---

362   *Charter, supra* note 318.

363   *Constitution Act, 1982, supra* note 359. It is broader than the rights defined in s. 35. Some are defined rights, such as the *Royal Proclamation of 1763, supra* note 15, and modern land claim settlements, while others are undeclared rights; see *Charter, supra* note 318 at s. 26.

364   Also, s. 24(1) of the *Charter, ibid.*, provides for judicial intervention to protect Aboriginal and treaty rights that have been infringed or denied by either the federal government or provinces.

365   *Sparrow, supra* note 290.

366   *Ibid.* Sparrow was convicted at trial on the basis that an Aboriginal right could not be claimed unless it was supported by a special treaty, and that s. 35(1) of the *Constitution Act, 1982, supra* note 359, accordingly had no application. An appeal to the County Court was dismissed for similar reasons. The Court of Appeal held that the conviction was based on an erroneous view of the law, and set aside the conviction, directing a new trial. That decision was appealed and cross-appealed. The issues before the Supreme Court were whether Parliament's power to regulate fishing is now limited by s. 35(1) of the *Constitution Act, 1982*, and, more specifically, whether the net length restriction in the licence is inconsistent with that provision.

that existing Aboriginal rights protected under section 35 of the *Constitution Act, 1982* are *sui generis,* and that the federal government has a constitutional responsibility to act in a fiduciary capacity with respect to these constitutional rights. The Court described the relationship between the government and Aboriginal peoples as "trust-like, rather than adversarial, and contemporary recognition and affirmation of aboriginal rights must be defined in light of this historic relationship."[367]

The Supreme Court of Canada reflected on the strength of the constitutional promise to Aboriginal peoples:

> ...s. 35(1) of the *Constitution Act, 1982,* represents the culmination of a long and difficult struggle in both the political forum and the courts for the constitutional recognition of aboriginal rights. ... Section 35(1), at the least, provides a solid constitutional base upon which subsequent negotiations can take place. It also affords aboriginal peoples constitutional protection against provincial legislative power. We are, of course, aware that this would, in any event, flow from the *Guerin* case, *supra,* but for a proper understanding of the situation, it is essential to remember that the Guerin case was decided after the commencement of the *Constitution Act, 1982.* ... [368]

The Supreme Court relied on Professor Lyon's interpretation of section 35(1):[369]

> ...the context of 1982 is surely enough to tell us that this is not just a codification of the case law on aboriginal rights that had accumulated by 1982. Section 35 calls for a just settlement for aboriginal peoples. It renounces the old rules of the game under which the Crown established courts of law and denied those courts the authority to question sovereign claims made by the Crown.[370]

Accordingly, the Court stated federal powers under section 91(24) of the *Constitution Act, 1867* have to be read together with section 35(1) of the *Constitution Act, 1982.* The federal power must be reconciled with the federal duty, and the best way to achieve that reconciliation is to require that government justify any regulations that infringe Aboriginal rights.[371] The Court reminded reviewing courts that "the honour of the Crown" is at stake in dealings with Aboriginal peoples.[372]

In the result, the Supreme Court held that an existing Aboriginal right cannot be limited by historical governmental regulations, stating "an existing aboriginal right cannot be read so as to incorporate the specific manner in which it was regulated before 1982."[373] Past federal fisheries legislation and provincial regulations were not sufficient to extinguish the constitutional rights of the Musqueam people; their fishing rights continued, subject only to justified conservation regulations.

---

367   *Ibid.* at 1108.

368   *Ibid.* at 1105.

369   Noel Lyon, "An Essay on Constitutional Interpretation" (1988) 26 Osgoode Hall L.J. 95 at 100.

370   *Sparrow, supra* note 290 at 1106.

371   *Ibid.* at 1109.

372   *Ibid.* at 1107, relying on Blair J.A. in *R. v. Agawa.*

373   *Ibid.* at 1091, 1093-1101.

The Supreme Court emphasized the principles of constitutional interpretation of *sui generis* rights under section 35(1).[374] Existing Aboriginal rights must be proven to exist in 1982 (*i.e.*, unextinguished), and are to be interpreted with flexibility to permit their evolution over time.[375] The sovereign's clear and plain intentions or words must prove any assertion of extinguished rights.[376] After 1982, the Court rejected the claim that Aboriginal rights can be extinguished by federal acts or regulations, even if they are regulated in "great detail."[377]

B. Interpreting treaty rights

The Supreme Court of Canada has affirmed that Aboriginal treaties with the imperial Crown are "sacred" agreements.[378] The Court has established important interpretative principles for these *sui generis* treaties,[379] which created a new framework for analysis of treaty land cessions and related rights.[380] The Supreme Court in *Badger* distinguished Aboriginal rights from treaty rights in section 35 of the *Constitution Act, 1982*:

> ...[A]boriginal and treaty rights differ in both origin and structure. Aboriginal rights flow from the customs and traditions of the [N]ative peoples. To paraphrase the words of Judson J. in *Calder, supra*, at p. 328, they embody the right of Native people to continue living as their forefathers lived. Treaty rights, on the other hand, are those contained in official agreements between the Crown and the [N]ative peoples. Treaties are analogous to

---

374 *Ibid.* at 1101-1109. In this case the Court stated that s. 35(1) must be interpreted in a purposive and liberal way so as to entrench the existing Aboriginal rights. These rights must not be viewed in a vacuum. Aboriginal history and traditions must be examined to determine the purposes of these rights. The s. 35(1) rights are relative to other constitutional rights, in ss. 91 and 92 of the *Constitution Act, 1867, supra* note 194. Aboriginal claimants must show that they are a holder of a right, and demonstrate *prima facie* interference with that right. Any conflicting legislation, to be valid, must be constitutionally justified.

375 *Sparrow, ibid.* at 1091-93. The Court refused to equate "existing" with the concept of being in actuality or exercisable, overruling *R. v. Eninew* (1984), 10 D.L.R. (4th) 137, 32 Sask. R. 237 (Sask. C.A.). This approach answers the problem of how law can persist as order in a world of pervasive change and progression.

376 *Sparrow, ibid.* at 1098-99; *R. v. Alphonse*, [1993] 5 W.W.R. 401, [1993] 4 C.N.L.R. 19 (B.C. C.A.).

377 *Sparrow, ibid.* at 1095-1101, 1111-19. In *Denny, supra* note 316 at 263, the Nova Scotia Appeal Division affirmed the Aboriginal right to fish for food strictly on a constitutional interpretation of s. 35(1) of the *Constitution Act, 1982, supra* note 359, and independent from the force and effect of the terms of the Mi'kmaq treaties. The court stated that: "based upon the decision in *Isaac*, this [Aboriginal] right has not been extinguished through treaty, other agreements or competent legislation. Given the conclusion that the appellants possess an aboriginal right to fish for food in the relevant waters, it is not necessary to determine whether the appellants have a right to fish protected by treaty."

378 See *R. v. Badger*, [1996] 1 S.C.R. 771 at para. 41 (S.C.C.) [hereinafter *Badger*]; *Sioui, supra* note 317 at 1063; *Simon, supra* note 315 at 401. This interpretive principle is derived from the leading British case, *Campbell v. Hall, supra* note 274.

379 *Simon, ibid.* at 404.

380 J.Y. Henderson, "Interpreting *Sui Generis* Treaties" (1997) 36 Alta. L. Rev. 46.

contracts, albeit of a very solemn and special, public nature. They create enforceable obligations based on the mutual consent of the parties. It follows that the scope of treaty rights will be determined by their wording, which must be interpreted in accordance with the principles enunciated by this Court.[381]

In *Nowegijick*,[382] Justice Dickson held the written treaties and their terms must be liberally construed, with doubtful expressions resolved in favour of the Indians.[383] In *Simon*, he affirmed that "Indian treaties should be given a fair, large and liberal construction in favour of the Indians."[384] The Court's justification of these principles is the context of the treaty negotiation, in which the Crown enjoyed a superior bargaining position over the diverse Aboriginal languages and cultures. From the perspective of the Aboriginal nations, the treaties were negotiated in translated languages, and written in a foreign text that incorporated references to technical British legal concepts unfamiliar to Aboriginal knowledge:

> The treaties, as written documents, recorded an agreement that had already been reached orally and they did not always record the full extent of the oral agreement: [citation omitted] The treaties were drafted in English by representatives of the Canadian government who, it should be assumed, were familiar with common law doctrines. Yet, the treaties were not translated in written form into the languages (here Cree and Dene) of the various Indian nations who were signatories. Even if they had been, it is unlikely that the Indians, who had a history of communicating only orally, would have understood them any differently. As a result, it is well settled that the words in the treaty must not be interpreted in their strict technical sense nor subjected to rigid modern rules of construction. Rather, they must be interpreted in the sense that they would naturally have been understood by the Indians at the time of the signing. This applies, as well, to those words in a treaty which impose a limitation on the right which has been granted. See *Nowegijick*, *supra*, at p. 36; *Sioui*, *supra*, at pp. 1035–36 and 1044; *Sparrow*, *supra*, at p. 1107; and *Mitchell*, *supra*, where La Forest J. noted the significant difference that exists between the interpretation of treaties and statutes which pertain to Indians.[385]

The Court requires judges to analyze the broader historical and legal context of each treaty to correct past injustices:

> [Treaties] must be understood in the context of this Court's sensitivity to the historical and continuing status of aboriginal peoples in Canadian society. The above-quoted statement [of the *Nowegijick-Simon* principles] is clearly concerned with interpreting a statute or

---

381 *Badger, supra* note 378 at para. 76.

382 *Nowegijick v. The Queen*, [1983] 1 S.C.R. 29, [1983] 2 C.N.L.R. 89 (S.C.C.).

383 *Ibid.* at 36; in *Jones v. Meehan*, 175 U.S. 1 (U.S. 1899), it was held that Indian treaties, "must ... be construed, not according to the technical meaning of [their] words ... but in the sense in which they would naturally be understood by the Indians." *Badger, supra* note 378 at para. 52: "Treaties and statutes relating to Indians should be liberally construed and any uncertainties, ambiguities or doubtful expressions should be resolved in favour of the Indians."

384 *Simon, supra* note 315 at 402.

385 *Badger, supra* note 378 at para. 52. In addition, when considering a treaty, a court must take into account the context in which the treaties were negotiated, concluded, and committed to writing.

treaty with respect to the persons who are its subjects—Indians—not with interpreting a statute in favour of Indians simply because it is the State that is the other interested party. It is Canadian society at large which bears the historical burden of the current situation of native peoples and, as a result, the liberal interpretative approach applies to any statute relating to Indians, even if the relationship thereby affected is a private one. Underlying *Nowegijick* is an appreciation of societal responsibility, and a concern with remedying disadvantage, if only in the somewhat marginal context of treaty and statutory interpretation.[386]

In the interpretation of the text, the Court has held that reviewing courts must reach a proper understanding of the meaning that particular treaties held for their signatories at the time; construing various textual provisions as the Aboriginal negotiators may be taken to have understood them.[387] Courts must recognize that contemporary oral evidence of the meaning of provisions of a treaty may not necessarily capture the understanding of the treaty that the Indians had at the time a treaty were entered, but it is relevant to explain the Aboriginal understanding.[388]

Even if the written treaties do not comply with modern formal requirements, courts must give effect to the intent that signatories had at the time they were entered into:[389]

> ...it is necessary to point out that on numerous occasions in modern days, rights under what were entered into with Indians as solemn engagements, although completed with what would now be considered informality, have been whittled away on the excuse that they do not comply with present day formal requirements and with rules of interpretation applicable to transactions between people who must be taken in the light of advanced civilization to be of equal status.[390]

In other words, treaties should not be undermined by the application of the interpretive rules we apply today to contracts entered into by parties of equal bargaining power.[391]

In *Mitchell*, Chief Justice Dickson explained the two related interpretative principles, and how they interacted:

> ...(1) ambiguities in the interpretation of treaties and statutes relating to Indians are to be resolved in favour of the Indians, and (2) aboriginal understandings of words and corresponding legal concepts in Indian treaties are to be preferred over more legalistic and tech-

---

386 *Mitchell v. Peguis Indian Band*, [1990] 2 S.C.R. 85 at 99, [1990] 3 C.N.L.R. 46 (S.C.C.) [hereinafter *Mitchell* cited to S.C.R.].

387 *R. v. Horseman*, [1990] 1 S.C.R. 901 at 911, [1990] 3 C.N.L.R. 95 (S.C.C.), Wilson J., dissenting (Dickson C.J. and L'Heureux-Dubé J. concurring) [hereinafter *Horseman* cited to S.C.R.].

388 *Ibid.* at 908, Wilson J. dissenting on other points.

389 See *Delgamuukw, supra* note 345 at paras. 84-87; *Horseman, ibid.*, Cory J. (Lamer, La Forest and Gonthier JJ., concurring), Wilson J. dissenting on other points (Dickson C.J. and L'Heureux-Dubé J. concurring).

390 Wilson J., dissenting in *Horseman, ibid.* at 907; *R. v. White and Bob*, [1965] S.C.R. vi, affirming (1964), 50 D.L.R. (2d) 613 at 649 [hereinafter *White and Bob*].

391 *White and Bob, ibid.* at 651-52.

nical constructions. In some cases, the two elements are indistinguishable, but in other cases the interpreter will only be able to perceive that there is an ambiguity by first invoking the second element.[392]

In terms of treaty cession of land, in *Horsemen* and *Badger*, Justice Cory regarded them as conditional agreements, with their validity dependent upon the fulfillment of the other treaty rights:[393]

> In exchange for [jurisdiction over] the land [and a right to authorize settlements on the land in Victorian treaties], the Crown made a number of commitments, for example, to provide the bands with reserves, education, annuities, farm equipment, ammunition, and relief in times of famine or pestilence.[394]

Justice La Forest in *Mitchell* expanded the shared interpretation of conditional treaty rights:

> Simply put, if treaty promises are to be interpreted in the sense in which one may assume them to have been naturally understood by the Indians, one is led to conclude that the Indian signatories to the treaties will have taken it for granted that property given to them by treaty would be protected regardless of *situs*. ... Similarly, when the Crown acquits treaty and ancillary obligations through the payment of moneys relating to assistance in spheres such as education, housing, and health and welfare, it cannot be accepted that Indians ever supposed that their treaty right to these entitlements could be compromised on the strength of subtle legal arguments that the property concerned, though undoubtedly property to which the Indians were entitled pursuant to an agreement engaging the honour of the Crown, was notionally situated off the reserve and therefore subject to the imposition of taxes or to attachment. It would be highly incongruous if the Crown, given the tenor of its treaty commitments, were permitted, through the imposition of taxes, to diminish in significant measure the ostensible value of the benefits conferred.[395]

---

392   *Mitchell, supra* note 386 at 98.

393   *Horseman, supra* note 387 at 928: "It can be seen that the Indians ceded title to the Treaty 8 lands on the condition that they could reserve exclusively to themselves 'their usual vocations of hunting, trapping and fishing throughout the tracts surrendered ...'."

394   *Badger, supra* note 378 at para. 39.

395   *Mitchell, supra* note 386 at 135. La Forest J. supported his view that Indians assumed their treaty benefits were given unconditionally:

> I would point to the following extract from the report of the Treaty Commissioners in respect of Treaty No. 8. The passage is eloquent testimony to the fact that native peoples feared that the imposition of taxes would seriously interfere with their ability to maintain a traditional way of life on the lands reserved for their use, and, additionally, leaves no doubt that Indians were promised that their entitlements would be exempt from taxation: 'There was expressed at every point the fear that the making of the Treaty would be followed by the curtailment of the hunting and fishing privileges, and many were impressed with the notion that the Treaty would lead to taxation and enforced military service.

> We assured them that the Treaty would not lead to any forced interference with their mode of life, that it did not open the way to the imposition of any tax, and that there was no fear of enforced military service'.

In treaty implementation, the Court directed reviewing courts not to assume the federal government intended to renege on the treaty obligations or commitments;[396] instead they should assume that Parliament intended to live up to its obligations under treaties.[397] Consequently, courts should interpret treaty rights, if the language sustains it, so as to implement and be fully consistent with solemn commitments embodied in the treaties.[398] These interpretative principles under section 35 limit the court's previous position that it could not question an unambiguous decision on the part of the federal government to modify its treaty obligations.[399]

In order to act on these liberal interpretative principles, courts are faced with considering the broader historical and cultural contexts from which the signatories' understandings of the treaties derive. With such knowledge the courts can anticipate and counteract past misconceptions and help forge a justice system respectful of Aboriginal knowledge, law, and heritage. The next part takes up the court's challenge to decolonize judicial thinking by tracing the history and theory of colonial discourse.

---

396 *Horseman, supra* note 387 at 908.

397 *Sparrow, supra* note 290 at 1107-1108; *R. v. Taylor and Williams*, 34 O.R. (2d) 360 at 367, [1981] 3 C.N.L.R. 114 (Ont. C.A.); *R. v. Smith*, [1935] 3 D.L.R. 703 at 705-706, [1935] 2 W.W.R. 433 (Sask. C.A.); *R. v. Strongquill*, [1953] 2 D.L.R. 264 (Sask. C.A.); *Prince and Myron v. The Queen* (1963), [1964] S.C.R. 81 (S.C.C.); and *R. v. Wesley*, [1932] 2 W.W.R. 337 (Alta. C.A.), Hall J.

398 *Horseman, supra* note 387 at 907-908. In *Mitchell, supra* note 386 at 134 for example, La Forest J. interpreted the terms "presents" and "annuities" of the Indians in the deeming section of s. 90(1)(b) of the *Indian Act* as a reference to moneys the Crown committed itself to giving Indians pursuant to the treaty cession of jurisdiction over their lands.

399 *Sikyea v. The Queen*, [1964] S.C.R. 642, 49 W.W.R. 306 (S.C.C.); *R. v. George*, [1966] S.C.R. 267 (S.C.C.); and *Moosehunter v. The Queen*, [1981] 1 S.C.R. 282 at 293, [1981] 1 C.N.L.R. 61 (S.C.C.).

IV

DISPLACING COLONIAL DISCOURSE

There is no human being who is not the product of every social experience, every process of education, and every human contact with those with whom we share the planet. Indeed, even if it were possible, a judge free of this heritage of past experience would probably lack the very qualities of humanity required of a judge. Rather, the wisdom required of a judge is to recognize, consciously allow for, and perhaps to question, all the baggage of past attitudes and sympathies that fellow citizens are free to carry, untested, to the grave.

Canadian Judicial Council's *Commentaries on Judicial Conduct* (1991)[1]

But the mystery of the colonial is this: while he remains alive, his instinct, always and forever creative, must choose a way to change the meaning and perspective of this ancient tyranny.

George Lamming, *The Pleasures of Exile*[2]

Introduction

More than two decades of commissions, inquiries, reports, special initiatives, conferences, and books have established the totalizing effects of colonization on Aboriginal peoples in Canada.[3] The common conclusion is that decolonization is a neces-

---

1   *R.D.S. v. The Queen*, [1997] 3 S.C.R. 484 (S.C.C.) at para. 119 [hereinafter *R.D.S.*].

2   Cited in S. Slemon and H. Tiffin, *After Europe: Critical Theory and Post-Colonial Writing* (Sydney, N.S.W.: Kangaroo Press, 1989).

3   Canada, Indian and Northern Affairs, *Indians and the Law* (Ottawa: Canadian Corrections Association and the Department of Indian and Northern Affairs, 1967); Law Reform Commission of Canada, *Report No. 34, Aboriginal Peoples and Criminal Justice: Equality, Respect and the Search for Justice* (Ottawa: The Law Reform Commission of Canada, 1991); Nova Scotia, *Royal Commission on the Donald Marshall Jr. Prosecution* (Halifax: The Commission, 1989); Ontario, *Report of the Osnaburgh/Windigo Tribal Council Justice Review Committee* (Ontario: The Committee, 1990); Manitoba, *Report of the Aboriginal Justice Inquiry of Manitoba* (Winnipeg: Queen's Printer, 1991); Alberta, *Justice on Trial: Report of the Task Force on the Criminal Justice System and Its Impacts on the Indian And Métis People of Alberta* (Edmonton: the Task Force, 1991); Saskatchewan, *Report of the Saskatchewan Indian Justice Review Committee* (Saskatoon: The Committee,1992); British Columbia, *Report on the Cariboo-Chilcotin Aboriginal Justice Inquiry* (Victoria: The Inquiry, 1993); Québec, *Jus-*

sary and urgent reform. Specifically, in *Gladue v. The Queen*,[4] the Lamer Court affirmed:

> Statements regarding the extent and severity of this problem are disturbingly common. In *Bridging the Cultural Divide*, supra, at p. 309, the Royal Commission on Aboriginal Peoples listed as its first "Major Findings and Conclusions" the following striking yet representative statement:
>
> > The Canadian criminal justice system has failed the Aboriginal peoples of Canada— First Nations, Inuit and Métis people, on-reserve and off-reserve, urban and rural—in all territorial and governmental jurisdictions. The principal reason for this crushing failure is the fundamentally different world views of Aboriginal and non-Aboriginal people with respect to such elemental issues as the substantive content of justice and the process of achieving justice.

In 1994, at the federal and provincial justice ministers' conference, Canada's justice ministers collectively reached the same conclusions. Ministers agreed that the Canadian justice system has failed and is failing Aboriginal peoples and that a holistic approach including the "healing process" is essential in Aboriginal justice reform. They agreed that the reforms must make the general system "equitable in every sense" for Aboriginal peoples; that reforms must make the system "work" with Aboriginal communities; and that they must reflect the "values" of Aboriginal peoples. Also they agreed that they must build "bridges" between the general system and Aboriginal practices, traditions, and approaches.[5] Finally, they pledged to work together with Aboriginal leaders on these priorities, and in future meetings to analyze the implications for Aboriginal people of all issues on the agenda. The Attorney General's conclusions were a definitive statement of the issues facing Aboriginal peoples in the Canadian legal system, a systemic statement beyond individual case analysis.

In 1996, the Royal Commission on Aboriginal Peoples issued a report entitled *Bridging the Cultural Divide* on Aboriginal peoples and the criminal justice system in Canada. Summarizing a large number of other commissions, inquiries, reports, and conferences on Aboriginal justice, the report affirmed the failure of the criminal justice system. It drew two conclusions: that a remarkable consensus exists on how the structural problems of Canadian colonialism have allowed the justice system to fail Aboriginal peoples; and that despite the hundreds of recommendations from commissions, task forces, and inquiries, the justice system continues to fail in relating to Aboriginal peoples. The report found that colonization has systematically undermined the tradi-

---

tice for and by the Aboriginals: Report and Recommendations of the Advisory Committee on the Administration of Justice in Aboriginal Communities, submitted to the Minister of Justice and the Minister of Public Security (Québec: Advisory Committee on the Administration of Justice in Aboriginal Communities, 1995); Canada, *Bridging the Cultural Divide: A Report on Aboriginal People and Criminal Justice in Canada* (Ottawa: Minister of Supply and Services Canada, 1996).

4   *Gladue v. The Queen*, [1999] 2 C.N.L.R. 252 (S.C.C.) at para. 62; online: University of Montreal <http://www.droit.umontreal.ca/doc/csc-scc/en/rec/html/gladue.en.html>.

5   "Final Statement of the Canadian Ministers of Justice" (Justice Ministers' Conference, Ottawa, 24 March 1994) [unpublished].

tional Aboriginal world-view and justice system and created racism as the fundamental lens for viewing Aboriginal peoples. The result of the "disorderly symptoms" of the colonial mentality has been an over-representation of Aboriginal peoples in the criminal justice system. This legal failure derives from the different views of Aboriginal and non-Aboriginal peoples in Canada on the content of justice and the means of achieving justice.

Far from being a Canadian anomaly, these conclusions are global. The failure of imposed foreign legal jurisdiction over Indigenous nations has haunted each British colony's legal system. In recent decades, each commonwealth country that has studied the problem has reached a similar conclusion: that the British legal system is not succeeding with Aboriginal peoples. The failure is a function of relationships of force rather than justice.[6]

Faced with such overwhelming evidence, one must analyze the totalizing discourse of colonization theory and consider how it has been assimilated to a discriminatory and unjust legal regime. Law was (and continues to be) a central process in legitimating colonization and its institutional and social arrangement. The political empire and legal framework of colonization are bound at the level of simple utility (as propaganda, for instance). They are also bound together at a purposive and unconscious level, where they lead to the naturalizing of artificially constructed values based on the dualism of Aboriginal "savagery" and British or French "civilization." This rational dualism empowered the privileged norms of British cultural values that became deeply embedded in Canadian political and legal consciousness.

In the process of constitutional reform, the Canadian courts have increasingly confronted the totalizing discourse of colonization. Courts are faced with the particular manifestations of its interpretative monopoly; we must now face its theory and history. In this part, we consider the idea of judicial impartiality to create a framework for understanding the totalizing discourse of colonization. We briefly examine the nature of the resistance to decolonizing the law before turning to efforts of the common law courts to decolonize or neutralize existing colonial law in relation to Aboriginal tenure and rights.

14. Judicial Impartiality

Under the rule of law, since adjudication is interpretation,[7] judges are held to the highest standards of impartiality. Though a well-established principle, this idea has remained ambiguous in application. In *R.D.S. v. The Queen*, Justice Cory states:

---

6   See Jeremy Webber, "Relations of Force and Relations of Justice: The Emergence of Normative Community Between Colonists and Aboriginal Peoples" (1995) 33 Osgoode Hall L.J. 623.

7   O.M. Fiss, "Objectivity and Interpretation" (1982) 14 Stan. L. Rev. 738.

> A system of justice, if it is to have the respect and confidence of its society, must ensure that trials are fair and that they appear to be fair to the informed and reasonable observer. This is a fundamental goal of the justice system in any free and democratic society.[8]

Sections 7 and 11(d) of the *Canadian Charter of Rights and Freedoms* have expressly anchored in the constitution of Canada the right to trial by an impartial tribunal.[9] All adjudicators owe a duty of fairness to the parties who must appear before them.[10] To fulfill this duty, they must simultaneously be and appear to be unbiased.[11] Fairness and impartiality must be both subjectively present and objectively displayed to the informed and reasonable observer. If the words or actions of a presiding judge give rise to a reasonable apprehension of bias to the informed and reasonable observer, this will render the trial unfair.[12]

Reviewing courts have contrasted judicial impartiality with "bias." Judicial impartiality is "a state of mind or attitude of the tribunal in relation to the issue and the parties in a particular case."[13] The state of mind of a fair and impartial adjudicator is defined as disinterest in the outcome, meaning that she or he is open to persuasion by the evidence and submission.[14] Bias has an attitudinal and behavioural component.[15] A biased or partial adjudicator is one who is in some way predisposed to a particular result, or who is closed with regard to particular issue.[16] This state of mind has been considered a "leaning inclination, bent or predisposition towards one side or another or a particular result" or "preconceived biases" that affect the decision, or a closed judicial mind.[17]

The Supreme Court views allegations of a reasonable apprehension of bias as "entirely fact-specific."[18] A judicial finding of apprehension of bias in an adjudicator has a "high threshold." Reviewing courts can displace a presumption of judicial integrity with "cogent evidence" that demonstrates something the judge has done giving rise to a reasonable apprehension of bias.[19] The presumption and high threshold are applied equally to all judges, regardless of their background, gender, race, ethnic origins, or other characteristics.[20] The requirement that justice should be seen to be done means

---

8   *R.D.S., supra* note 1 at para. 91.

9   *Ibid.* at para. 93.

10   *Ibid.* at para. 92.

11   *Ibid.*

12   *Ibid.*

13   *Ibid.*

14   *Ibid.* at para. 104, citing *Valente v. The Queen*, [1985] 2 S.C.R. 673 (S.C.C.) at 685.

15   *R.D.S., ibid.* at para. 107.

16   *Ibid. at* para. 105, citing *Liteky v. U.S.*, 114 S.Ct. 1147 at 1155 (U.S. 1994). L'Heureux-Dubé and McLachlin JJ. endorsed Cory J.'s comments on judging in a multicultural society, the importance of perspective and social context in judicial decision-making, and the presumption of judicial integrity.

17   *R.D.S., ibid.* at para. 106.

18   *Ibid.* at para. 136.

19   *Ibid.* at para. 117.

20   *Ibid.* at para. 115.

that the person alleging bias does not have to prove actual bias, only a reasonable apprehension of bias—a substantial, or real likelihood, or probability of bias. Inappropriate words,[21] unfortunate and unnecessary comments,[22] or a mere suspicion of bias are not enough.[23]

The requirement of impartiality is a high standard for any adjudicator. All judges owe a fundamental duty to the community to render impartial decisions and to appear impartial.[24] Judges must then strive to ensure that no word or action during trial or in delivering judgment might leave the reasonable, informed person with the impression that an issue was predetermined or that a judge decided a question based on stereotypical assumption or generalization. The Canadian Judicial Council, in *Commentaries on Judicial Conduct* (1991), has observed that the duty to be impartial:

> does not mean that a judge does not, or cannot bring to the bench many existing sympathies, antipathies or attitudes. ... Rather, the wisdom required of a judge is to recognize, consciously allow for, and perhaps to question, all the baggage of past attitudes and sympathies that fellow citizens are free to carry, untested, to the grave.

> True impartiality does not require that the judge have no sympathies or opinions; it requires that the judge nevertheless be free to entertain and act upon different points of view with an open mind.[25]

Good judges should have a wealth of personal and professional experience that they will apply with sensitivity and compassion to the cases that they hear. The sound belief behind encouraging greater diversity in judicial appointments was that women and visible minorities would bring an important perspective to the difficult task of judging.[26] Justices L'Heureux-Dubé and McLachlin,[27] for example, differed from their colleagues in construing positively judges' experiences and their implications for decision-making:[28]

> In our view, the test for reasonable apprehension of bias established in the jurisprudence is reflective of the reality that while judges can never be neutral, in the sense of purely objective, they can and must strive for impartiality. It therefore recognizes as inevitable and appropriate that the differing experiences of judges assist them in their decision-making process and will be reflected in their judgments, so long as those experiences are relevant to the cases, are not based on inappropriate stereotypes, and do not prevent a fair and just determination of the cases based on the facts in evidence.[29]

---

21 *Ibid.* at para. 153.

22 *Ibid.* at para. 158.

23 *Ibid.* at para. 112.

24 *Ibid.* at para. 120.

25 *Ibid.* at para. 119.

26 *Ibid.*

27 *Ibid.* at para. 27.

28 *Ibid.* at para. 28.

29 *Ibid.* at para. 29.

To apply the reasonable apprehension test, they found it necessary to distinguish between the impartiality required of all judges, and the idea of judicial neutrality. They drew on Justice Cardozo's affirmation of impartiality, while recognizing the fallacy of judicial neutrality:[30]

> There is in each of us a stream of tendency, whether you choose to call it philosophy or not, which gives coherence and direction to thought and action. Judges cannot escape that current any more than other mortals. All their lives, forces which they do not recognize and cannot name, have been tugging at them—inherited instincts, traditional beliefs, acquired convictions; and the resultant is an outlook on life, a conception of social needs ... . In this mental background every problem finds its setting. We may try to see things as objectively as we please. None the less, we can never see them with any eyes except our own. ... Deep below consciousness are other forces, the likes and the dislikes, the predilections and the prejudices, the complex of instincts and emotions and habits and convictions, which make the [person], whether he [or she] be litigant or judge.[31]

In their judgment, the Canadian Judicial Council's *Commentaries on Judicial Conduct* (1991) meant that "[t]rue impartiality does not require that the judge have no sympathies or opinions; it requires that the judge nevertheless be free to entertain and act upon different points of view with an open mind."[32]

Judicial inquiry into the factual, social, and psychological context within which litigation arises is typical. A conscious, contextual inquiry has become an accepted step toward judicial impartiality.[33] Judges may gain an understanding of the context or background from expert witnesses,[34] or academic studies properly placed before the court,[35] and from the judge's personal understanding and experience of society where judges live and work. Impartial judges may take notice of actual racism known to exist in a particular society.[36] Judges, acting as fact-finders, must inquire into those forces, and be aware of the context in which the alleged crime occurred.[37] This process of "enlargement of the mind" is consistent with, and an essential precondition of, judicial impartiality. Any reasonable person would see such enlargement as an important aid to judicial impartiality.[38]

---

30   Benjamin N. Cardozo, *The Nature of the Judicial Process* (New Haven, Conn.: Yale University Press, 1921).

31   *R.D.S., supra* note 1 at para. 34, citing Cardozo, *ibid.* at 12-13, 167.

32   *R.D.S., ibid.* at para. 35.

33   *Ibid.* at para. 42, citing Professor Jennifer Nedelsky, "Embodied Diversity and the Challenges to Law" (1997) 42 McGill L.J. 91 at 107, who offers the following comment: "What makes it possible for us to genuinely judge, to move beyond our private idiosyncrasies and preferences, is our capacity to achieve an 'enlargement of mind.' We do this by taking different perspectives into account. This is the path out of the blindness of our subjective private conditions. The more views we are able to take into account, the less likely we are to be locked into one perspective É . It is the capacity for 'enlargement of mind' that makes autonomous, impartial judgment possible."

34   *R.D.S., ibid.* at para. 44.

35   *Ibid.*

36   *Ibid.* at para. 47.

37   *Ibid.* at para. 41.

38   *Ibid.* at para. 45.

The fact-specific onus of demonstrating bias[39] is to be heard by an "informed reasonable person."[40] Justices L'Heureux-Dubé and McLachlin conclude that such a person understands the impossibility of judicial neutrality, but demands judicial impartiality. The reasonable person is cognizant of the racial dynamics in the local community, including the existence of widespread and systemic discrimination against others,[41] and, as a member of the Canadian community, is supportive of the principles of equality.[42] They stated:

> Before concluding that there exists a reasonable apprehension of bias in the conduct of a judge, the reasonable person would require some clear evidence that the judge in question had improperly used his or her perspective in the decision-making process; this flows from the presumption of impartiality of the judiciary. There must be some indication that the judge was not approaching the case with an open mind fair to all parties. Awareness of the context within which a case occurred would not constitute such evidence; on the contrary, such awareness is consistent with the highest tradition of judicial impartiality.[43]

In their view, allegations of perceived judicial bias will succeed if the impugned conduct, taken in context, truly demonstrates that a judge has decided an issue based on prejudice or generalizations. An overriding principle arising from these cases is that reviewing judges must consider bias in the context of the circumstances, and in light of the whole proceeding.[44]

According to the Canadian Judicial Council, the Canadian judiciary cannot infer knowledge from its general view of society or the "prevalent attitude of the day," because such understandings are "personal or ideological."[45] Such ideological judicial reasoning is considered an error of law, and cause for a new trial.[46] This rule frames the problems that Aboriginal peoples face in Canadian courts, particularly respecting the totalizing ideology of colonialism, its strategies and manifestations. Despite such explicit caveats on the "personal and ideological," Canadian judicial reasoning has never secured independence from other forms of reasoning and views of society. To the extent that judicial reasoning remains part of the historically located inquiry and discourse of colonization, with similar visions of society, methods and prejudices, it requires cleansing for the sake of Aboriginal and non-Aboriginal people committed to justice.

Colonization has animated Canadian legal consciousness, uniting the historical events and superimposing various methods of legal analysis. Colonial law sought to make understandable the hidden but predetermined legal content of an imposed politi-

---

39   *Ibid.* at para. 114.

40   *Ibid.* at para. 111.

41   *Ibid.* at para. 47.

42   *Ibid.* at para. 48.

43   *Ibid.* at para. 49.

44   *Ibid.* at para. 141.

45   *Ibid.* at para. 10.

46   *Ibid.* at paras. 10, 25.

cal and economic order of the Hobbesian "artificial man-state" within the context of Aboriginal territory or the "state of nature." Its overlapping methodological processes, embodying the deductive prejudice about language and interpretation, were transformed into analytical jurisprudence or positivism that saw law as commands; formalism that inferred lower-order propositions from higher-order ones; conceptualism that explored the rules and doctrines that organized the categories of the rights system; to the present form of policy-oriented and principle-based style of purposive legal analysis. Contemporary judicial reasoning combines all these processes together, often without adequate reflection.

Out of the history of colonization ideologies and rationalities, modern judicial reasoning or analysis has derived a fragmented method as well as new constitutional reforms to discover a connected set of social and political policies and principles. Its present purposive mode of analysis, interpretation, and discourse is based on the idea that it is recognizing and affirming the purpose or intent of constitutional provisions that already exist in the law, waiting to be made explicit by the courts. At the same time modern judicial reasoning seeks to make sense of different coexisting political ideas, social life, and cultural pluralities to improve the law in its tactical application to specific conflicts.

In conflicts between the government and the marginalized and powerless Aboriginal peoples and their constitutional rights, judicial reasoning or interpretation undermines itself, like every imaginative practice, when it refuses to confront the colonial origins, assumptions, principles informing government statutes, regulations, and policy. Only recently have constitutional reforms allowed a post-colonial order to emerge, permitting courts to decolonize the law to ensure that Aboriginal peoples effectively enjoy their constitutional rights. To enact a post-colonial jurisprudence, judicial reasoning must understand the nature of colonization, and free the rule of law from this unjust legacy of colonial societies made for the benefit of the Crown and its colonizers. That colonial legal system was organized as a dual system of law: formal justice regimes for the colonizers and substantive justice regimes for Aboriginal peoples.

Approaching colonization or an empire as an organic or natural evolution has impeded change by concealing the law's role as architecture and sustainer of colonialism. The legacy of colonialism is that Canadian legal reasoning has often been inclined to put the best face on colonization ideology, treating it not as an artificial and accidental set of compromises, but as a rational framework to be perfected in the language of impersonal policy and principle. Appealing to general and neutral laws was not only propaganda or myth, but also the authority that legitimated and sustained colonial laws and institutions over Aboriginal peoples. Fragmented modern thought hides the relationship between colonialism and law by representing law primarily as legislative, administrative, and judicial rules, procedures, and techniques in any given nation state, as a technical device for getting things done. That the law is typically presented as not having a history or as having a limited view of the recent past obscures the connection between religious thought, secular theory, nationalism, and modern law.

The legal complicity with colonialism is all too often unappreciated or strategically avoided in law schools and practices. As Albert Memmi explains:

> The laws establishing his exorbitant rights [as a colonialist] and obligation of the colonized are conceived by him. ... A foreigner, having come to a land by the accidents of history, he has succeeded not merely in creating a place for himself but also in taking away that of the inhabitant, granting himself astounding privileges to the detriment of those rightfully entitled to them. And this not by virtue of local laws, which in a certain way legitimizes this inequality by tradition, but by upsetting the established rules and substituting his own. He thus appears doubly unjust. He is a privileged being and an illegitimately privileged one; that is, a usurper.[47]

For example, the idea of individualism arose as a manifestation of the colonizers' liberties in the colonial situation, and as a way of maintaining these liberties. What may be an emancipatory idea for the British colonizer required the oppression and domination of Aboriginal peoples. The relationships among individualism, personal rights regimes, and colonialism have not been sufficiently explored. In the context of the discipline of law, known for its commitment to unmask injustice and oppression, such neglect and avoidance of the jurispathic traditions of law in supporting colonialism are remarkable. To explore this neglected area is a necessary corrective to a prevailing amnesia in the legal profession and the common outlook that it has stood apart, or acted as neutral agent in the oppression of Aboriginal peoples.

The need for dismantling colonial thought, its strategy of hierarchical differentiation, and its legal traditions has been highlighted in recent case law, as well as in the intersections of postmodernism, critical race theory, feminist criticism, and post-structuralist theory. Although contemporary jurists and lawyers continue to peel away the layers of colonial law and expose its biases and prejudices originating in the English or French languages and world-views, the colonial legacy persists.

The decolonization of Canadian law is best understood as a struggle to limit reliance on foreign sources of law. The repatriation of the Constitution from the imperial parliament, creating constitutional supremacy, was part of the decolonization process and a search for an equitable constitutional order. The judiciary has attempted to end the legal fictions of colonial law, and limit the governmental ability to annex, determine, and verify partial truths as total truths.[48]

In the legal process, colonial power is built not only on control over law, life, and property, but also on control over language and the means of communication. The function of the English and French languages in Canada as vehicles of colonial law requires that post-colonial law redefine itself by including Aboriginal laws and languages and creating *sui generis* legal categories and standards. Because the colonial ideas were presented to courts and lawyers as "universal," moreover, contemporary legislatures,

---

47 A. Memmi, *The Colonizer and the Colonized*, trans. Howard Greenfield (New York: Orion Press, 1965) at 9.

48 M. Foucault, "The Political Function of the Intellectual" (1977) 17 Radical Philosophy 12; Foucault, "Afterword: The Subject and Power" in H.L. Dreyfus and P. Rabinow, *Michel Foucault: Beyond Structuralism and Hermeneutics* (Chicago: Chicago University Press, 1982).

courts, and lawyers have had particular difficulty in understanding these implicit cognitive contexts and frameworks.

The legal legacy of colonization's "universals" is more than genocide[49] and legal tyranny; it is systemic colonialism, sexism, and racism. The philosopher Iris Young provides definitions of prevailing domination and oppression that are especially applicable to the decolonization project. She defines "domination" as the various conditions that inhibit or prevent people from participating in political life, law- and decision-making; she defines "oppression" as the systemic processes in society that inhibit or prevent the dominated from communicating in contexts where others can listen, and prevent them from developing their human skills to resolve material deprivations.[50] According to Young's analysis, domination and oppression are established by intolerance[51] embedded in the unquestioned norms, habits, symbols, and everyday practices that inform law.[52] Intolerance advances from unconscious assumptions that underlie institutional rules and collective reactions; it is a consequence of following these givens or rules and accepting these reactions in everyday life.[53]

The modern manifestations of oppression and domination cannot be reduced to one essential definition or unified phenomenon or assigned causal or moral primacy; they operate pervasively as a collective consciousness or assumptive context of modern thought. Only a plural explanation of this consciousness can comprehend its magnitude. Young asserts there are at least five faces of oppression: exploitation, marginalization, powerlessness, cultural imperialism, and violence.[54] Historian Lise Noël argues that such pervasiveness in Canada makes the oppressor invisible:

> The oppressor has no apparent existence. Not only does he not identify himself as such, but he is not even supposed to have his own reality. His presence is so immediate and dense, and his universe coincides so totally with the Universe, that he becomes invisible. Rarely seen, rarely named, he is unique, nonetheless, in having a full existence; as the keeper of the word, he is the supreme programmer who confers various degrees of existence on those who are different from himself ... . As the embodiment of the universal, the dominator is also the only Subject, the Individual who, never being considered to belong to a particular group, can study those impersonal categories of the population who pose a "problem," represent a "question," constitute a "case," or simply have a "condition."[55]

Thus, in a variety of contexts—history, theory, statutory and case law—this part attempts to make visible colonization and its adjudicative legacy in contemporary legal

---

49   L. Noël, *Intolerance: A General Survey*, trans. A. Bennett (Montreal and Kingston: McGill-Queen's University Press, 1994) at 100.

50   I. Young, *Justice and the Politics of Difference* (Princeton, N.J.: Princeton University Press, 1990) at 33-38.

51   Noël, *supra* note 49 at 5. Noël states that, "[i]ntolerance is the theory; domination and oppression are the practices."

52   H.L.A. Hart, *The Concept of Law* (New York: Oxford University Press, 1961) at 56.

53   Young, *supra* note 50 at 41.

54   *Ibid.* at 42-65.

55   Noël, *supra* note 49 at 11.

analysis. Only then can constitutional supremacy eliminate the colonial legal legacy[56] to transform legal analysis to respect Aboriginal constitutional rights, so that Canadian law may fulfill its primary avocation of creating, sustaining, and protecting an enlightened and democratic society.

15. A History of Colonial Reasoning: Dualism, Diffusion, and Difference

Canada was not created in the smooth, flowing seasons of Aboriginal thought; it was created in the jagged path of colonialism and empire. Colonialism is an artificial construct of European elites using political ideology and human-made legal rules. It presumes the anarchy of the state of nature, the need for an artificial man-state, and law as command. Attempting to immunize the colonial consciousness and order from criticism or reconstruction by threatening nihilism as the only alternative, colonial ideology justifies brute force to maintain itself, and law justifies the process. To understand colonialism, we need to re-examine the political and legal thought of seventeenth- and eighteenth-century Europe, the period that originated the modern state. The British political theorist and scientist Thomas Hobbes, in arguing that there is no such thing as natural order or any justice in nature, created the modern, artificial state. After experiencing the ruinous English Civil War of 1642-1648, Hobbes wrote his famous work on political absolutism, *Leviathan; or the Matter, Form, and Power of a Commonwealth, Ecclesiastical and Civil,* published in 1651.[57]

Hobbes considered philosophy to be a practical study of two kinds of "bodies": natural and civil. He declared that natural bodies included everything for which there is rational knowledge of causal processes. He did not believe there was a universal reality that corresponded to universal ideas and words, but considered all reality to be subjective and all groupings created by artificial agreements. The "state of nature" was a non-political and anti-political condition. The constitutive elements of the natural state are primarily and fundamentally individuals who are free and equal. They live in natural associations such as families or households. Hobbes asserted that the state of nature and civil society are opposed to one another. Civil society arose to correct or eliminate the shortcomings of natural associations. The transformation from individual or family freedom and equality to civil society does not occur because of nature, but rather takes place through one or more conventions made by individuals who are interested in leaving the state of

---

56   J.M. Blaut, *The Colonizer's Model of The World: Geographical Diffusionism And Eurocentric History* (New York: Guilford Press, 1993). We have relied heavily on Blaut's analysis.

57   See Thomas Hobbes, *Leviathan* [1651] (Chicago: Encyclopaedia Britannica, 1952); R. Tuck, *Hobbes* (Oxford: Oxford University Press, 1989). In his political treatise, Hobbes compares the state, with its innumerable competing members, to the largest of natural organisms—the whale, or leviathan. By this analogy, Hobbes argues that the state, like the whale, requires a single controlling intelligence to direct its motion.

nature. Civil society "made by the wills and agreement of men" Hobbes called "the Commonwealth."

Hobbes argues that only through a primal covenant between "men":

> is created that great LEVIATHAN called a COMMON-WEALTH, or STATE (in Latine CIVITAS), which is but an *Artificiall man*, though of greater stature and strength than the natural ... and in which, the *Soveraignty* is an Artificiall Soal. The pacts and covenants, by which the parts of this body politic were at first made, set together, and united, resemble that *Fiat*, or the *Let us make man*, pronounced by God in the Creation.[58]

According to Hobbes, the force that impels the transfer of power to an artificial state is negative necessity. He believed the "natural passions" of Europeans were incompatible with existing political society and that left to their own devices, people would oppose each other in "a war as is of every man against every man."[59] Given the rough equality of physical and mental ability among men, Hobbes argued, they needed a superordinate power to make and sustain a political covenant.[60] Consequently, the origin and foundation of the state, or artificial man, is a voluntary and deliberate act. The principle of legitimation of artificial civil society is consent rather than a natural society of families or households.

Hobbes did not find any direct evidence of men at war against one another in their natural state in Europe. He used the North American Indian to provide evidence of this natural state of warfare:[61]

> It may peradventure be thought there was never such a time or condition of war as this; and I believe it was never generally so, over all the world: but there are many places of America, except the government of small families, the concord whereof dependeth on natural lust, have no government at all, and live at this day in that brutish manner.[62]

Thus, Hobbes used North America to illustrate the universal negative standards of primal chaos.[63] From this idea of warfare in the natural state, Hobbes derived his necessary artificial man-state and the positive content of the law of the land in its unconditional and unlimited validity.[64]

---

58   *Ibid.* at 47 [original emphasis]. Ironically, this is the Roman legal idea of *status civilis* or "the civil condition"; at the greatest level of generality, "state" does indeed mean "condition" or "way of being" ("the state of one's health").

59   *Ibid.* at 85.

60   *Ibid.* at 100-103. At 100, the terms on which a person enters the covenant are stated thus: "I authorise and give up my right of governing myself to this [artificial] man, or to this assembly of men, on this condition; that thou give up thy right to him, and authorise all his actions in like manner."

61   *Ibid.* at 99.

62   *Ibid.* at 87-88.

63   *Ibid.* Hobbes also invokes, at 86, the similar antagonistic condition existing between "king and persons of sovereign authority," but he does not develop the comparison.

64   E. Cassirer, *The Philosophy of the Enlightenment*, trans. F.C.A. Koelln and J. Pettegrove (Boston: Beacon Press, 1955) at 19.

The savage state envisioned by Hobbes provided more than the force creating and sustaining law and political society. It also created a terrifying repository of negative values attributed to Aboriginal peoples:

> Whatsoever therefore is consequent to a time of war, where every man is enemy to every man, the same is consequent to the time wherein men live without other security than what their own strength and their own invention shall furnish them withal. In such condition there is no place for industry, because the fruit thereof is uncertain: and consequently no culture of the earth; no navigation, nor use of the commodities that may be imported by sea; no commodious building; no instruments of moving and removing such things as require much force; no knowledge of the face of the earth; no account of time; no arts; no letters; no society; and which is worst of all, continual fear, and danger of violent death; and the life of man, solitary, poor, nasty, brutish, and short.[65]

For Hobbes, only the artificial man-state can end the savage state of nature and create civil society, and he secures this pact and its artificial creations—the commonwealth and the sovereign—against any change or possibility of legitimate disturbance. The artificial man-state is total and eternal.[66] Hobbes concluded that rebellion against the man-state breaks society's basic contract and is punishable by whatever penalty the sovereign may exact to protect his subjects from a return to the original state of nature. The sovereign subject who creates the compact becomes comprehensively committed to all actions of the sovereign "as if they were his own."[67]

Hobbes also created positive law. His purpose was not to show what is law here and there, but what is law in general.[68] In the man-state, laws are the "command" of the sovereign to the sovereign subjects,[69] and only the sovereign can make valid laws.[70]

---

65   Hobbes, *supra* note 57 at 87. The lack of logic is apparent. For example, a person cannot live a solitary life in a community so small that everyone knows everyone else. The security of a close community is policed by the tight social controls typical of such groups. This passage has served colonizers as a catalogue for assigning negative values to the differences perceived in Aboriginal society, particularly the evils of the absence of property—in the savage state there can be no security of possession and expectation: "there be no propriety, no dominion, no *mine* and *thine* distinct; but only that to be every man's that he can get, and for so long as he can keep it" (*ibid.* at 86, [original emphasis]); and the beneficial effects of positive law, *ibid.* at 88, where he states that, "where there is no common power, there is no law," and a law cannot, "be made till they have agreed upon the person that shall make it."

66   *Ibid.* at 101.

67   *Ibid.* The rise of state sovereignty had far-reaching effects on European political thought. It slowly limited the older contexts of ecclesiastical and private law and prerogative. This process was reflected in Immanuel Kant's declaration in 1797 that the only natural political relation was that between single individuals and states. By this time, the medieval notion of a society made up of smaller societies had been generally discredited. Hegel argued that the modern state was the "mind on earth." The Hegelian state, however, was not a Hobbesian state. It was a monarchy moderated by the law-drafting functions of disinterested civil servants. It was moderated above all by the Hegelian notion that individuals must be able to find subjective satisfaction in being willing members of a rational, free institution that secures the pursuit of absolute values inherent in philosophy, art, and religion. See generally *The Philosophy of Right*, trans. T.M. Knox (Oxford: Clarendon Press, 1942).

68   Hobbes, *supra* note 57 at 130.

69   *Ibid.*

70   *Ibid.* at 131.

The "laws of nature" cannot be "properly law" until they take form as a sovereign command.[71] This command theory went on to become the predominant notion in British jurisprudence.[72]

After Hobbes distinguished the state of nature from civil society, the state of nature became the starting point of Eurocentric discussions of government and politics. The state of nature was the conditionality or given in the context of the modern state or civil society. Those who attempted to construct a rational theory of the state began from the dichotomy of the Aboriginal peoples in a state of nature and an antithetical civilized society.

The reports that flowed from the Americas in the sixteenth and seventeenth centuries supported the philosophers' theory of the state of nature. Indians were seen as "without subordination, law, or form of government," and there were increasing efforts "to civilize this barbarism, to render it susceptible of laws."[73] The evidence used in constructing the theory of the state of nature was limited, and knowledge that would undermine the strategy was ignored. Indeed, copious evidence existed that Aboriginal peoples of North America were not savage.[74] Anthropologist M. T. Hodgen puzzles over:

> why identifications of contemporary savagery with classical antiquity, or with old phases of other historical cultures, should ever have been made at all. So much is certain: it was not because of the validity of the correspondences cited ... . The number of plausible likenesses elicited ... were at best relatively few and usually trivial ... [and] they were offset, and the conclusions derived from them were neutralized, by an overwhelming body of divergences which were seldom mentioned, much less assembled for comparison of relative proportions.[75]

Challenging evidence was not simply disregarded. Political and legal philosophers changed such evidence to conform to their theories. For example, they identified Aboriginal cultures with lack of progress despite powerful evidence to the contrary. When

---

71   *Ibid.*

72   Hart, *supra* note 52. However, it did involve an immediate problem in that people have to know of commands in order to obey them. Hence, the command of the Commonwealth is law only to those who have the means to take notice of it: "Over natural fools, children or madman there is no law, no more than over brute beasts." See J. Austin, *The Province of Jurisprudence Determined*, 2d ed. (London: Murray, 1832), and J. Austin, *Lectures on Jurisprudence, or, the Philosophy of Positive Law* (London: John Murray, 1861-63) [hereinafter Austin, *Lectures on Jurisprudence*]. Nevertheless, if law were to be dependent on popular knowledge, this could undermine the whole edifice of authority. With uncharacteristic equivocation, Hobbes opts largely for the maxim that ignorance of the law is no excuse. Hobbes, *supra* note 57 at 119.

73   J. Axtell, *The Invasion Within: The Conquest of Cultures in Colonial North America* (New York: Oxford University Press, 1985) at 50.

74   *Ibid.*, c. 13.

75   M.T. Hodgen, *Early Anthropology in the Sixteenth and Seventeenth Centuries* (Philadelphia: University of Pennsylvania Press, 1964) at 354-35.

they did recognize the ability of these cultures to change, they attributed this to Aboriginal imitation of European culture.[76]

By the early eighteenth century, the usual explanation of the origin of the state, or "civil society," began by postulating an original state of nature in which primitive humans lived on their own and were subject to neither government nor law.[77] As the first systematic theorist of the philosophy of liberalism and Hobbes's greatest immediate English successor, John Locke took up the state of nature idea where Hobbes left off.

In 1690, Locke published *Two Treatises of Government*.[78] While he opposed Hobbes's view that the original state of nature was "solitary, poor, nasty, brutish, and short," and maintained that the state of nature was a happy and tolerant one, he argued that humans in the state of nature are free and equal, yet insecure and dangerous in their freedom. Like Hobbes, Locke had no proof of his theory. The state of nature was an intellectual idea, since no historical or social evidence validated its assumptions.[79] There was nothing to disprove the idea either, and Locke simply stated: "[I]t is not at all to be wonder'd that *History* gives us but a very little account of Men, *that lived together in the State of Nature*."[80]

Locke rejected Hobbes's idea that, for the sake of self-preservation, individuals surrendered their rights to a supreme sovereign through a social contract, and that this sovereign was the source of all morality and law. Locke argued that the social contract preserved the pre-existing natural rights of the individual to life, liberty, and property, and that the enjoyment of individual rights led, in civil society, to the common good:

> When natural men entered civil society, they surrendered only such rights as are necessary for their security and for the common good. ... Those who are united into one Body, and have a common establish'd Law and Judicature to appeal to, with Authority to decide Controversies between them, and punish Offenders, *are in Civil Society* one with another; but those who have no such common Appeal, I mean on Earth, are still in the state of Nature, each being, where there is no other, Judge for himself, and Executioner; which is, as I have before shew'd it, the perfect *state of Nature*.[81]

---

76 B.G. Trigger, *Native and Newcomers: Canada's "Heroic Age" Reconsidered* (Kingston and Montreal: McGill-Queen's University Press, 1985) at 51, 65. This transforms into the idea that Aboriginals need European law, but when they accommodate to the immigrants' legal system the Aboriginals lose all their Aboriginal rights. See *R. v. Van der Peet*, [1996] 2 S.C.R. 507, [1996] 4 C.N.L.R. 177 (S.C.C.), affirming, [1993] 4 C.N.L.R. 221 (B.C. C.A.), reversed, 58 B.C.L.R. (2d) 392, [1991] 3 C.N.L.R. 161 (B.C. S.C.), affirming (1990), [1991] 3 C.N.L.R. 155 (B.C. Prov. Ct.) [hereinafter *Van der Peet* cited to S.C.R. or to the Court].

77 P. Stein, *Legal Evolution: The Story of an Idea* (Cambridge, U.K.: Cambridge University Press, 1980) at 1.

78 J. Locke, *Two Treatises of Government* [1689], ed. by P. Laslett (Cambridge, U.K.: Cambridge University Press, 1970).

79 In their historical political evolution, European states have gone from feudal states to the society of orders (*Standestaat*), to absolute monarchy, to constitutional monarchy, and so forth. There has not been any reciprocal consent of free and equal individuals in the creation of the state.

80 Locke, *supra* note 78 at 378, para. 101 [original emphasis].

81 *Ibid.* at 36, para. 87 [original emphasis].

In short, each individual who joins society retains fundamental rights drawn from natural law that relates to the integrity of person and property.

In Locke's theory, a sovereign with limited powers is the source of governmental authority. "The *Supream Power*," Locke wrote, "*cannot take* from any Man any part of his *Property* without his own consent. ...[I]t is a mistake to think, that the Supream *Legislative Power* of any Commonwealth, can do what it will, and dispose of the Estates of the Subject *arbitrarily*, or take any part of them at pleasure."[82] The reason for this limitation on any government was that people bring property rights into political society, which is set up specifically to protect these rights:

> For the preservation of Property being the end of Government, and that for which Men enter into Society, it necessarily supposes and requires, that the People should *have Property*, without which they must be suppos'd to lose that by entring into Society, which was the end for which they entered into it, too gross an absurdity for any Man to own.[83]

Locke saw property rights as "natural rights" independent of political society or any civil framework, established before the origin of political society, and constraining the Crown and popular will. Therefore, it is not open for governments to abrogate, derogate, or reorder them based on what governments think society ought to do.

Locke did not apply his theory of property to the Aboriginal nations of America:

> There cannot be a clearer demonstration of any thing, than several Nations of the *Americans* are of this, who are rich in Land, and poor in all the Comforts of Life; who Nature having furnished as liberally as any other people, with the materials of Plenty, *i.e.* a fruitful Soil, apt to produce in abundance, what might serve for food, rayment, and delight; yet for want of improving it by labour, have not one hundreth part of the Conveniencies we enjoy; And a King of a large and fruitful Territory there feeds, lodges, and is clad worse than a day Labourer in *England*.[84]

Locke ties entry into political society under a central, sovereign command with the need to secure property: "The great and *chief end* therefore, of Mens uniting into Commonwealths, and putting themselves under Government, is *the Preservation of their Property*."[85] He delineates law as a response to "many things wanting ... in the state of Nature." The "Civiliz'd part of Mankind" is characterized by "positive Laws"[86] that are absent in the natural state. These positive laws are a response to the natural chaos of individual assertions of passion and self-interest:

> *First*, [in the state of nature] There wants an *establish'd*, settled, known *Law*, received and allowed by common consent to be the Standard of Right and Wrong, and the common measure to decide all Controversies between them. ... *Secondly*, In the State of Nature there wants *a known and indifferent Judge*, with Authority to determine all differences

---

82   *Ibid.*, vol. 2 at 138 [original emphasis].

83   *Ibid.*

84   *Ibid.* at para. 41 [original emphasis].

85   *Ibid.* at 395, para. 124 [original emphasis].

86   *Ibid.* at 331, para. 30.

according to the established Law. ... *Thirdly*, In the state of Nature there often wants *Power* to back and support the Sentence when right, and to *give it* due *Execution*.[87]

The theory that Aboriginal nations lacked positive law had self-serving implications for European aristocracy and colonizers. If they had nothing resembling European law, then they had no government until they allied themselves with a European Crown. The implication was that Aboriginal nations needed a relationship with a European Crown. With some false pride, the British looked upon their laws as the most rational, efficacious, and perfect in the whole world; hence the Crown was initially uncritical of any proposals to impose English legal traditions on Indigenous societies. These attempts failed as the "lawless" Indigenous nations rejected the imposition of British (and French) law and the leadership imposed by Europeans.[88]

Generally, British settlers on the northern Atlantic coast followed Thomas Hobbes's view of Aboriginal peoples;[89] they made little effort to discover the nature and substance of Aboriginal legal systems or laws. Young Henry Spelman, perhaps the first Englishman to live among the Aboriginal nations of the Virginia colony, apologized in his memoirs that "concerning ther lawes my years and understandinge made me the less to looke after bycause I thought that Infidels were lawless."[90] Spelman's preconception of the lawless Aboriginal was shared by most of the commentators of his age. Believing that the Aboriginal people had no laws, most immigrants did not look for them. John Smith wrote of Powhatan in the Virginia colony that neither "[h]e nor any of his people vnderstand any letters wherby to write or read; the only lawes wherby he ruleth is custome."[91] Colonial legal theorists asserted that law was a particular kind of legal system—the European legal systems[92]—and they rejected the idea that law was common to all society.[93]

Nearly a century later these views had created an English dogma of lawlessness among the Aboriginal peoples. Robert Beverley, Edmund Burke and Dr. Douglass illustrate this tradition. Beverley explained that "having no sort of Letters ... they can have no written Laws; nor did the Constitution in which we found them, seem to need many. Nature and their own convenience has taught them to obey one Chief, who is

---

87   *Ibid.* at 396, paras. 124-26 [original emphasis]. Also see Adam Smith, *An Inquiry Into the Nature and Causes of the Wealth of Nations* [1776] (New York: A.M. Kelley, 1966) c. 1, pt. 2 [reprint]; W. Blackstone, *Commentaries on the Law of England,* 14th ed. (Oxford: Clarendon Press, 1765Ð69) at 5.

88   Robert A. Williams, Jr., *The American Indian in Western Legal Thought* (Oxford: Oxford University Press, 1990) at 151-226.

89   Hobbes, *supra* note 57.

90   Sir H. Spelman, "Relation of Virginea" in A.G. Bradley, ed., *[E.] Arber, Travels And Works Of Captaine John Smith, President Of Virginia, And Admiral Of New Englands* (Edinburgh: J. Grant, 1965) at ci, cx-c.

91   Smith, "A Map of Virginia, With a Description of the Country, the Commodities, People, Government and Religion" in Bradley, *ibid.* at 41, 81.

92   See A.R. Radcliffe-Brown, "Primitive Law" in *Encyclopedia of the Social Sciences,* vol. 9 (New York, Macmillan, 1933) at 202.

93   See B. Malinowski, *Crime and Customs in Savage Society* (London, Routledge, 1947) at 68-69.

arbiter of all things among them."[94] Both Edmund Burke and Dr. Douglass criticized the lack of any "absolute compelling power" among the Aboriginal peoples of North America.[95] The Aboriginal peoples came to be seen as either governed by pure arbitrary will, as Smith and Beverley conceived it, or living in a rude democratic chaos as Douglass and Edmund Burke argued. These theories were constantly contradicted by the abundant evidence from their own writings of the existence of routine, orderly, customary process, especially in the area known to British law as family law.[96]

In *The Spirit of Laws*, Montesquieu presented a study of legal change from "primitive origins" to "civilization"; his "four stages" theory,[97] derived from the state of nature concept, was viewed as "scientific" and influenced the eighteenth-century Scottish[98] and British social theorists more generally.[99] He suggested that all groups pass through four stages or cycles: from the "lowest and rudest" stage of hunting, to pastoral, and agricultural stages, to "polished" commerce.[100] This theory replaced the feudal-allodial distinction in the proprietarian order with a theory of "neutral" cycles of production favouring property as commodity, and suggesting that time and history favoured individual private estates.[101] In the nineteenth century, his ideal transformed into "progress" or an "evolutionary" theory of social and human development.[102]

In 1832, John Austin reinterpreted Hobbes within British jurisprudence and colonialism.[103] A professor of jurisprudence at the University of London, Austin defined law as the command of a political superior to a political inferior.[104] In Austin's system,

---

94   R. Beverley, *The History And Present State Of Virginia*, ed. by L. Wright (Chapel Hill: Pub'd for the Institute of Early American History and Culture at Williamsburg, Va., by the University of North Carolina Press, 1947) at 225-226.

95   E. Burke, *An account of the European settlements in America* (London: Printed for R. and J. Dodsley, 1760) at 176; W. Douglass, *A Summary, Historical And Political, Of The First Planting, Progressive Improvements, And The Present State Of The British Settlements In North America* (London: R. and J. Dodsley, 1760) at 160.

96   R. Beverley, *supra* note 94 at 170-171; W. Byrd, *The Westover Manuscripts: Containing the History of the Dividing Line Betwixt Virginia and North Carolina, A Journey to the Land of Eden* (Petersburg, Va.: E. and J. C. Ruffin, 1841) at 166; Spelman, *supra* note 90 at cviii; Spelman, "An account of the Indians in Virginia" (1959) 16 Wm. & Mary Q. at 233-34, 288.

97   R. Meeks, *Social Science and the Ignoble Savage* (Cambridge, U.K.: Cambridge University Press, 1976).

98   Including the civil republican thinkers of the Scottish Enlightenment: David Hume, Adam Smith, John Millar, Adam Ferguson, William Robertson, and Lord Kames, a lawyer. See G. Bryson, *Man and Society: The Scottish Inquiry of the Eighteenth Century* (Princeton, N.J.: Princeton University Press, 1945).

99   J.G.A. Pocock, ed., *The Political Work of James Harrington* (Cambridge, U.K.: Cambridge University Press, 1977); Sir. H. Maine, *Ancient Law: Its Connection with the Early History of Society and Its Relation to Modern Ideas* [1861] (New York: E.P. Dutton, 1917) [reprint].

100   According to Adam Smith, *supra* note 87.

101   G.A. Alexander, *Commodity & Propriety: Competing Visions of Property in American Legal Thought, 1776-1970* (Chicago: University of Chicago Press, 1997) at 64-65.

102   Stein, *supra* note 77; P. Stein, "The General Notions of Contract and Property in Eighteenth-Century Scottish Thought" (1963) 63 Jurid. Rev. 1 at 1-13.

103   Austin *Lectures on Jurisprudence, supra* note 72.

104   *Ibid.*, vol. 1 at 1, 5.

an exclusive and independent sovereign was accorded general and habitual obedience by its subjects. This subjection was a necessary precondition for "political society" and law.[105] Thus, positive law depended on the existence of a sovereign.[106]

The exclusive foundation for Austin's positive law is "savagery" in nature. He distinguished a general state of savagery that he called "natural society" as opposed to "political society":

> A natural society, a society in a state of nature, or a society independent but natural, is composed of persons who are connected by mutual intercourse, but are not members, sovereign or subject, of any society political. None of the persons who compose it lives in the positive state which is styled a state of subjection: or all the persons who compose it live in the negative state which is styled a state of independence.[107]

Following in the tradition of Hobbes and Locke, Austin illustrates natural society by "the savage ... societies which live by hunting or fishing in the woods or on the coasts of New Holland," and by those "which range in the forests and plains of the North American continent."[108]

Austin characterizes the state of nature as completely wild and lawless.[109] Moreover, even if natural society were not wild and lawless, he asserts:

> Some ... of the positive laws obtaining in a political community, would probably be useless to a natural society which had not ascended from the savage state. And others which might be useful even to such a society, it probably would not observe; inasmuch as the ignorance and stupidity which had prevented its submission to political government, would probably prevent it from observing every rule of conduct that had not been forced upon it by the coarsest and most imperious necessity.[110]

---

105 *Ibid.* at 17-23, 170.

106 *Ibid.*, vol. 2 at 313.

107 *Ibid.*, vol. 1 at 176.

108 *Ibid.* at 184. Austin also draws on both a general and existent state of savagery, and the "imaginary case" of a solitary savage child abandoned in the wilderness, which he takes "the liberty of borrowing from . . . Dr. Paley," vol. 1 at 82. The borrowing could be from W. Paley, *The principles of moral and political philosophy* (Dublin: [s.n.], 1785) at 5. This solitary savage was, "a child abandoned in the wilderness immediately after its birth, and growing to the age of manhood in estrangement from human society." As such, it could not be a "social man," would not appreciate the necessity of property, would be in total conflict with "his" fellows, and hence, "the ends of government and law would be defeated," vol. 1 at 85. The savage "mind" is "unfurnished" with certain notions essential for society. These, "involve the notions of political society; of supreme government; of positive law; of legal right; of legal duty; of legal injury," vol. 1 at 85.

109 Austin, *Lectures on Jurisprudence. ibid.*, vol. 2 at 9.

110 *Ibid.* at 258. Additionally, Austin does take into account the domestic challenge of the "poor and ignorant" to British order, vol. 1 at 62. This affliction is attributed to their ignorance of "the imperative good of property and capital." Its cure lies in a full appreciation of the principles of utilitarian ethics, particularly of the Malthusian variety: "if they adjusted their numbers to the demand for their labour, they would share abundantly, with their employers, in the blessings of property." Distinguishing them from the "stupid" savage who can only respond to the imperatives of the inexorable, vol. 2 at 258, "the multitude ... can and will," come to, "understand these principles," vol. 1 at 60.

Thus, the irredeemable savage in natural society is the ultimate case against which Austin's theory of law is constituted.

European philosophers and lawyers have noted that the elaboration, transmission, and refinement of the theory of the state of nature and the rise of the artificial state accompanied the rise and development of bourgeois society in Europe. Few have noted that the rise of the artificial state accompanied colonialism. The meaning of the artificial state spanning artificial colonies in various states of nature has been largely ignored.

John Locke and his disciples reasoned that since property was a creature of written law, societies lacking written law had no property.[111] Locke envisaged law as wholly the instrument of social policy and arising only when resources became so scarce that men must agree upon some scheme for allocating them. The absence of law therefore implied an absence of scarcity. The "fact" that Indians had no law conveniently proved they would not mind giving up a modest portion of their surplus lands to the English.

Bentham and analytical jurisprudence transformed the state of nature into natural liberties as a vast field of human activity and under a rationally governed legal system to be unregulated by the sovereign command:

> every efficient law whatever may be considered as a limitation or exception, grafted on a pre-established universal law of liberty. The non-commanding and permissive phases of the law placed side by side and turned toward the universal system of human actions are expressed by the before-mentioned universal law of liberty: a boundless expanse in which the several efficient laws appear as so many spots; like islands and continents projecting out of the ocean.[112]

In Bentham's vision of the legal system, laws were coercive because they confer "rights" by imposing duties on others not to interfere with individual liberty or security, and must be justified by the standard of utility. Laws imposing duties on others were presumptively invalid because they encroached on liberties. "Legal liberties" were viewed as permissions to do self-regarding acts that had no effect on the interest of others; "legal rights" provided security from being harmed by others or having interests adversely affected by their acts, which were justified by standards of utility; "legal powers" were the liberty to hurt others or to affect their interests adversely to maximize social utility, and limited exemptions from the imposed duty not to harm others or to

---

111 Locke, *supra* note 78, c. 5. A similar argument is found in C. Molloy, *De jure maritimo et navali: Or, A Treatise Of Affaires Maritime And Of Commerce*, 4th ed. (London: Printed and are to be sold by A. Swalle, 1690) c. 5; A leading figure in Connecticut land speculation, John Bulkey popularized Locke in North America. J. Bulkey, "An Inquiry Into The Rights Of The Aboriginal Natives To The Lands In America, And The Titles Derived From Them" in Roger Wolcott, *Poetical Meditations, Being the Improvement of Some Vacant Hours* (New London, Conn.: Printed and Sold by T. Green, 1725).

112 J. Bentham, *On Law in General*, ed. by H.L.A. Hart (London: University of London, Athlone Press, 1970) at 119-20. Some of the great unrecognized islands of the sovereign's command in North America were the Aboriginal treaties and the *Royal Proclamation of 1763* (U.K.), 2 & 3 Geo. 3, reprinted in R.S.C. 1985, App. II. that limited the colonizer's freedoms.

affect their interest. Legal powers worked by "contrection" to interfere physically with "things" or bodies; and "imperation" to control the mental faculties of a person to conform to a command.[113]

In British colonies, the structure and origins of legal categories were mediated through colonization theory. The colonizers' dominant conceptual tool has been a broadly defined "liberalism," the idea of sovereign or state power and individual rights and freedom.[114] Liberalism was a mystical invitation to European colonizers to act in a self-interested manner, without impediments from the sovereign or state, as long as their actions did not harm other Europeans or the sovereign.[115] This belief system affirmed their freedom to engage in the pursuit of happiness, wealth, power, and prestige at the expense of others. The security from harm that allowed such freedom of action was applied by the sovereign's governmental powers and the rule of law.

Property and its counterpart, sovereignty, have played a critical role in colonial liberal thought: property was understood as the collection of freedoms held by "private" individuals or corporations in the colonies; sovereignty was the protection of the powers of the homeland state. Legal rights and liberties of colonizers to land were "necessarily" accompanied by the duties on Aboriginal peoples not to interfere with their acts. This self-regarding theory had no account of competing laws when Aboriginal life was viewed as resembling the "state of nature"; or when the colonizer government intentionally inflicted damage on Aboriginal peoples who had no legal recourse; or when colonizers inflicted extensive harms on Aboriginal peoples against the sovereign commands embodied in treaties and prerogative acts. When these conceptual failures required solutions, their defect proved fatal: these major problems undid analytical jurisprudence or positivism and converted it into legal conceptions that defined legal liberties as freedom to harm others.[116] This concept retained the subtlety of the positivist method and vocabulary, creating simultaneously the law of colonization for Aboriginal peoples and liberalism for the colonizers.

The European ethnocentric theory of diffusionism was derived from the state of nature theory and is the academic source of the false polarity between civilized and savage peoples, postulating the superiority of Europeans and their descendants over Aboriginal peoples. The modern understanding of this theory is labelled "Eurocentrism" or Eurocentric thought.[117] Eurocentrism is an "ultra" theory of modern thought and the context for many smaller theories—historical, geographical, psychological,

---

113   *Ibid.* at 137-38.

114   See R. M. Unger, *Knowledge and Politics* (New York: The Free Press, 1975) [hereinafter *Knowledge and Politics*].

115   See generally J.W. Singer, "The Legal Rights Debate in Analytical Jurisprudence from Bentham to Hohfeld]" [1982] Wis. L. Rev. 978.

116   J. Salmond, *Jurisprudence, or the Theory of Law*, 6th ed. (London: Sweet and Maxwell, 1920); W. Hohfeld, "Some Fundamental Legal Conceptions as Applied in Judicial Reasons" (1913) 23 Yale L. J. 16. These theories incorporate the concept of damage without legal wrong (*damnun absque injuria*) into analytical jurisprudence. See E.P. Weeks, *The Doctrine of Damnum Absque Injuria Considered in Relation to the Law of Torts* (San Francisco: S. Whitney, 1879).

117   Samir Amin, *Eurocentrism* (New York: Monthly Review Press, 1989).

sociological, and philosophical—which can be labelled Eurocentric diffusionism. Eurocentrism is a systemic phenomenon more than a matter of individual attitudes in the sense of biases and prejudices. As the Supreme Court has recognized in *Calder* and *Simon*, rejecting the Eurocentric caricature of Aboriginal peoples and their knowledge is vital to decolonizing Canadian law and explaining the *sui generis* context of Aboriginal law, tenure and rights.

Historical and political geographer, James Blaut, describes in *The Colonizer's Model of the World*[118] the effect of Eurocentrism as a dominant intellectual theory in Western thought during the past five centuries. It remains the foundation to all dominant scholarship, opinion, and law, constructing the imaginative and institutional context of modern thought, framing what educated and usually unprejudiced Europeans and Canadians accept as true propositions supported by "the facts." Eurocentric diffusionism depicts the world as divided into zones, similar to the "four-stage" theory, each representing a level of modernity, civilization, or development. The classical division was one with three great bands: "civilization,"[119] "barbarism," and "savagery." Although the division has been modified through time, its basic framework has remained unchanged. It is based on two assumptions: that most human communities are uninventive; and that only a few human communities (or places, or cultures) are inventive and thus remain the permanent centres of cultural change or progress. On a global scale, this creates a model of a world with a single European centre that is creative and progressive and a surrounding, stagnant Aboriginal periphery.

This polarity of a European inside and the Aboriginal outside is central or integral to the diffusionist theory. From this dualism, diffusionism asserts the strategy of totalizing difference between the two peoples based on some intellectual or spiritual factor: something characteristic of the "European mind," the "European spirit," "Western Man"; something that leads to creativity, imagination, invention, innovation, rationality, and a sense of honour or ethics—"European values." Aboriginal failure to progress is, in this view, due to a lack of this intellectual or spiritual factor.

Classical Eurocentric diffusionism exists as many variations of this dualism, two of which have particular significance for Aboriginal people. First, the diffusionist myth of an emptiness (*terra nullius*) of basic cultural institutions, a lack of cities, and a lack of law justified settler colonialism and the actual physical movement of Europeans into non-European regions, such as Canada, displacing or eliminating the Aboriginal peoples. This proposition of emptiness made possible a series of claims about an empti-

---

118 *Supra* note 56. See also J. Derrida, *Of Grammatology*, trans. G.C. Spivak (Baltimore, Md.: Johns Hopkins University Press, 1976). Derrida deconstructs the binary polarities of the centre and the margin that comprise Eurocentrism. As in Eurocentric diffusionism, he asserts that the dialectic operates geographically and conceptually; it articulates the power relations between Europe and the colonies, deconstructing the idea, the authority, and the assumed superiority of Eurocentric thought.

119 In modern thought the civilization distinction is often divided into "high" and "low" culture.

ness of intellectual creativity and spiritual values, sometimes described by Europeans as an absence of "rationality."[120]

Secondly, diffusionism asserts that non-Europeans "progress," modernize, and develop by imitating European innovative, progressive ideas, which flow into the emptiness as air flows into a vacuum. This diffusion may be spread by European bearers of European ideas of commerce or new products. The diffusion of civilizing ideas from Europe to Aboriginal peoples is viewed as adequate compensation for the confiscation of material wealth by Europeans from Aboriginal ecologies. However, the European colonizers believed nothing could fully compensate them for their "gift" of civilization to the Aboriginal peoples because of the danger or possibility that Aboriginal traits could counter diffusion, corrupting the civilized core, making them victims. These ancient, atavistic traits were viewed as evil things, such as black magic, vampires, plagues, and "the bogeymen." Since Europe was "advanced" and non-Europe was backward, any ideas that diffused into Europe from elsewhere must inevitably be uncivilized.[121]

The antidiffusionists (often called "evolutionists" or "independent-inventionists") hold that the classical diffusionists had too sour a view of human ingenuity; they were believers in spatial (European) elitism. However, they accepted the idea that humanity has a European core and an Aboriginal periphery, believing that Europe is the centre of cultural evolution and that Europeans are more inventive and innovative than everyone else, especially when discussing the missionizing or modernizing effects of Europeans. Aboriginal peoples were the lowest stages of human development, but had the potential to assimilate.[122]

A strong critique of Eurocentrism is underway in all fields of social thought. These critiques, such as post-colonial and post-structural thought, reveal that the assumptions and beliefs that constructed Eurocentrism are not universal but rather are derived from local and artificial knowledge. Moreover, critical scholars have exposed the assumptions and empirical, factual beliefs of Eurocentric law, history, geography, and social science as false necessity[123] that has very often gained acceptance for prejudicial reasons. These critiques raise anguished discourse about knowledge and truth that quickly slips into paradigm maintenance by its advocates. As a result, Eurocentrism has proven resistant to change, retaining a persuasive intellectual power in academic, political, and legal realms.

---

120   Nevertheless, classical diffusionism arbitrarily asserts that some non-European regions were "rational" in some ways and to some degree. Thus, for example, the Middle East during biblical times was rational; China was somewhat rational for a certain period in its history; and other regions like North America and Africa were absolutely lacking in the faculty of reason.

121   Blaut, *supra* note 56 at 21-26.

122   *Ibid.* at 24-26.

123   R. Rosaldo, *Culture and Truth: the Remaking of Social Analysis* (Boston: Beacon Press, 1989); R.J. Coombe, "Object of Property and Subject of Politics: Intellectual Property Laws and Democratic Dialogue" (1991) 69 Tex. L. Rev. 18 at 18-53; Edward Said, *Culture and Imperialism* (Cambridge, Mass.: Harvard University Press, 1992); Blaut, *supra* note 56; No'l, *supra* note 49; R. M. Unger, *False Necessity: Anti-Necessitarian Social Theory in the Service of Radical Democracy. Part I of Politics, a Work in Constructive Social Theory* (Cambridge, U.K.: Cambridge University Press, 1987).

Eurocentric thought does not claim to be a privileged norm, since this would also imply cultural relativism, which asserts that values are specific to each cultural context.[124] Rather, Eurocentric thought claims to be universal and general.[125] Indeed, Eurocentrism has two premises that forbid Europeans from resting content with developing their own society or part of the world. The first premise involves the search for knowledge. This quest was an outgrowth of Aristotle's "wonder" that he found at the beginning of all thought and of Socrates' dialogues by which he engaged with each person capable and willing to listen. Every wonder and dialogue was examined for its universality, and life was to be tested by questioning its "universal good." This quest for truth, universal values, and virtue informs the idea of the universal civilization, and partially explains why Europeans left their lands and went to such efforts to see and control the world.

The second motivation for Europeans was the messianic prophecy of monotheistic religions. Europeans had a belief in, and a commitment to, a messianic dream: a new heaven, a new earth, and a transformed people. The Judaic vision of linear time moved toward a predetermined end; Christianity supplemented this vision with divine commands to the disciples to proselytize.[126]

What Socrates and the prophets of the Bible shared was the notion of a universal mission inviting the attention of all humans. National laws of the time attempted to end the idea of this new knowledge and the transformation to a universal civilization. The executions of Socrates and of Christ were both legally sanctioned and have made subsequent generations suspicious of legal institutions and aware of the contradictions in preserving legal order and doing justice. With these deaths came questions about the limits and nature of politics and law, out of which came the idea of a civil republic, and the search for universal knowledge, truth, and a just order.

Diffusionism's claim to universality often means domination.[127] Universality creates cultural and cognitive imperialism, which establishes a dominant group's knowledge, experience, culture, and language as the universal norm. Noël summarizes the function of universalism in colonialism:

---

124 See R. Benedict, *Patterns of Culture* (Boston: Houghton Mifflin, 1934). Cultural relativists sought to demonstrate that standards of morality and normalcy are culture-bound and called into question the ethnocentric assumption of European superiority. A.D. Renteln, *International Human Rights: Universalism Versus Relativism* (Newbury Park]: Sage Publications, 1990) at 66.

125 Relativists claim that such universality is a cloak for projecting culturally specific beliefs onto other cultures that possess different world views or "inner logic." Renteln, *ibid.* at 67-72.

126 There are many examples of this search. For example, in the Hebrew Bible or Old Testament, when the Lord asked whom He should send on the journey, Isaiah replied, "Here I am: send me," Isaiah 6. In the New Testament, the disciples of Christ are told to go forth to baptize all nations and to teach the things that have been commanded to them, Matthew 28:19. Christ said to Peter, "[F]eed my sheep," John 21:17. Some time later, as the Acts of the Apostles narrated, those disciples who witnessed the Ascension were told immediately that they were wasting their time standing there, "looking up into the sky," John 21:17.

127 Noël, *supra* note 49 at 12.

> To present himself as the ideal human type, the dominator often invoked irreducible laws sanctioned by Nature, God, or History. In his view, the power he exercised over the oppressed was not so much the result of undue reliance on force as the effect of uncontrollable imperatives, if not a Higher Will. In relation to the universal model that the oppressor seemed to represent, the dominated always appeared to be afflicted with some defect or intrinsic failing.[128]

Universal norms mandate, by definition, bringing all others under their laws, expectations, and norms. The assumed normality of the dominators' values and identity constructs the differences of the dominated as inferior and negative.[129] Thus arises the consciousness of the immigrant-colonizer and the civilized-savage, which the colonized have to accept if they are to survive. This binary consciousness has justified separating Aboriginal peoples from their ancient land tenure and its resources, and transferring wealth and productivity to the colonialists and the mother country.[130]

Often when the colonized become aware of the colonizers' vision of them and reject it, they experience what W.E.B. Du Bois called "double consciousness":

> This sense of always looking at one's self through the eyes of others, of measuring one's soul by the tape of a world that looks on in amused contempt and pity.[131]

Double consciousness occurs when the colonized assert they are human, but the dominators reject this assertion and impose their standards as universal and normal. Noël writes:

> After long endorsing the logic of a discourse taught to them as the only one that was valid, the dominated began to feel doubts. At first vague and fleeting, these doubts were aroused by the oppressor's own failure to live up to his idealized model of humanity. As the oppressed became more actively aware of their own worth, their doubts grew more insistent. Gradually, the dominated ceased to see the oppressor's defense of his special interests as the inevitable tribute owed to a superior being. Divine, natural, or historical laws that espoused such narrow designs became suspect. It eventually came to mind that these laws were pure creations of a group wishing to legitimize its privileges.[132]

---

128 *Ibid.* at 147.

129 Young, *supra* note 50 at 58-61.

130 Memmi, *supra* note 47 at 126: "When all is said and done the colonizer must be recognized by the colonized. The bond between the colonizer and the colonized is thus both destructive and creative. It destroys and recreates the two partners in the colonization process as colonizer and colonized: the former is disfigured into an oppressor, an uncouth, fragmented human being, a cheat solely preoccupied with his privileges, the latter into a victim of oppression, broken in his development and accepting his own degradation." In his introduction to the 1967 Beacon Press edition at xxiv-xxv, Jean-Paul Sartre stated that the immigrant-colonizer is "one for whom privilege and humanity are one, who becomes a human being through exercising his rights; and the other [Aboriginal-colonized], for whom a denial of rights sanctions misery, chronic hunger, ignorance, or, in general, subhumanity." See Sartre, "Colonialisme et Néocolonialisme" in *Situations* (Paris: Gallimard, 1964) c. 5.

131 W.E.B. Du Bois, *The Souls of Black Folk: Essays and Sketches* (New York: New American Library, 1969) at 45.

132 Noël, *supra* note 49 at 149.

The colonialists or oppressors are immune from double consciousness because they are the embodiment of the universal; they have the privilege of not being considered as a member of any specific group. European learning has established them as the universal model of civilization to be imitated by all groups and individuals. The anomalous ability of Eurocentric academics and lawyers to energize and legitimize the rhetoric of universalism remains vast and powerful:

> The opinions of the theorists and functionaries of Religion, Law, and Science thus had the effect of legitimizing the relationship of domination by accrediting the thesis of the dominator as the ideal model for humanity. Taking their cue from the very inferiority that they have attributed to the oppressed, theologians and ministers of religion, legislators and magistrates, researchers and scholars believe they may claim the exclusive right to determine the fate of the oppressed.[133]

Because they considered themselves the ideal and universal model for humanity and carriers of superior culture and intelligence, colonizers believed they had the power to interpret differences. Such belief shaped the institutional and imaginative assumptions of colonization and modernism. Using the strategy of differences, colonialists felt privileged to define human competencies and deviances such as sin, offense, and mental illness. They also believed they had the authority to impose their tutelage on the colonized and to remove from them the right to speak for themselves. [134]

French philosopher Michel Foucault locates at the outset of the colonizing period a shift in the fundamental mode whereby knowledge is acquired:

> The activity of the mind ... will ... no longer consist in *drawing things together*, in setting out on a quest for everything that might reveal some sort of kinship, attraction or secretly shared nature within them, but, on the contrary, in *discriminating*, that is, in establishing their identities. ... In this sense, discrimination imposes upon comparison the primary and fundamental investigation of difference.[135]

The strategy of difference is not simply abstract or analytical, but directly affects secular Eurocentric identity and order. Despite its pretension, colonial thought was less interested in the constitution of universal human nature than in a quest for understanding the different forms of human awareness of other people, of nature, and of themselves in each historical social life.[136] Through this strategy of difference, Eurocentric thinkers spread artificial contexts of racism, ethnicity, and gender around the world.

---

133 *Ibid.* at 48.

134 D. Kennedy, "A New Stream of International Law Scholarship" (1988) 7 Wis. Int'l L.J. 1 at 3. Kennedy criticizes twentieth-century scholarly output in international law as bound in, "European doctrinal formalism."

135 M. Foucault, *The Order of Things: An Archeology of the Human Sciences* (London: Tavistock, 1970) at 55.

136 R. M. Unger, *Law in Modern Society* (New York: The Free Press, 1976) at 5.

The strategy of racism allowed colonialists to assert Eurocentric privileges while exploiting Aboriginal peoples in an inhuman way.[137] As Memmi explains: "Racism is the generalized and final assigning of values to real or imaginary differences, to the accuser's benefit and at his victim's expense, in order to justify the former's own privileges or aggression."[138] Colonizers had a better claim to subjugate Aboriginal peoples to Eurocentric thought if they defined them as "the other" in simple and reductive ways.[139] The strategy of stressing differences between European "civilization" and New World savages became a dominant theme of European, British, and Canadian legal and literary texts.

Difference is an extension of the dualistic impetus of Eurocentric thought. With the rejection of the noun-God's commandments and the unitary, suprahistorical intelligible human essence of classical thought,[140] Eurocentric thought perceived categories and made inferences[141] through logical analysis and causal explanation. Each provided an interpretation of what it means to account for something both in the sense of telling what it is like (description) and in the sense of establishing why it had to follow from something else (explanation in the strict sense).

The global terror that resulted from colonial ideology created the legal idea of the right to inflict damage without legal wrong, conceptualized as "all harms are allowed unless expressly prohibited."[142] The consequent damage inflicted on Aboriginal peoples is well documented. The infamy of slavery, the carnage of the "Middle Passage," and the conquest of Aboriginal nations in South America are a part of that legacy. The Atlantic slave trade represents the largest and most callous forced migration imposed upon any peoples anywhere in the world. Conservative estimates of Indigenous Africans forced to be a commodity range from 15 to 20 million; recent writers estimate that a better estimate is 60 to 150 million.[143] For example, in 1650, Africa's population was 21.2 per cent of the known world population; by 1920 it was 7.7 per cent. In contrast, from 1650 to 1750, Europe's population grew by only 3 per cent, but at the height of colonialism (1750-1900) the population rose by 400 per cent. By then, Europe's population spilled over to the rest of the world, with 1 million emigrants a year going to other continents. By 1914, Britain boasted of an empire 140 times its size; Belgium,

---

137 "Everyone has felt the contempt implicit in the term 'native', used to designate the inhabitants of a colonized country. The banker, the manufacturer, even the professor in the home country, are not natives of any country: they are not natives at all. The oppressed person, on the other hand, feels himself to be a native; each single event in his life repeats to him that he has not the right to exist." Jean-Paul Sartre, "Materialism and Revolution" in *Literary and Philosophical Essays*, trans. A. Michelson (London: Hutchinson, 1968) at 215.

138 A. Memmi, "Attempt at a Definition" in Memmi, *Dominated Man: Notes Toward a Portrait* (Boston: Beacon Press, 1969) at 185.

139 Noël, *supra* note 49 at 109.

140 *Ibid.*

141 See generally *Knowledge and Politics, supra* note 114.

142 Sir. J. W. Solomon, *The Law of Torts: A Treatise on the English Law of Liability for Civil Injuries*, 4th ed. (London: Stevens and Haynes, 1916) at 8-9.

143 H.A. Bulhan, *Frantz Fanon and the Psychology of Oppression* (New York: Plenum Press, 1985) at 43.

80 times; Holland, 60 times; France and Germany, 20 times.[144] These European nations were on the verge of colonizing the entire Aboriginal peoples of the earth.

Around the world the colonists created new hierarchies, governments, and legal systems that believed in the absolute superiority of Europeans over the colonized, the masculine over the feminine, the adult over the child, the historical over the ahistorical, and the modern or "progressive" over the traditional or "savage." These artificial political orders reflected ways of thinking defined by binary polarities: modern and primitive, secular and non-secular, scientific and unscientific, expert and layman, normal and abnormal, developed and underdeveloped, vanguard and led, liberated and savable.[145] Through a curious transposition, the colonizers called upon the colonized to justify themselves:[146] primitive people would one day, the colonizers said, learn to see themselves as masters of nature and, thus, masters of their own fate and a brave new world.[147] The psychological consequence of this strategy is currently being unfolded. Despite the political and economic analysis, the psychological impact of colonization on the British and their descendants and Aboriginal peoples has yet to be adequately analyzed.

The extension of colonial strategies to Europe led in part to two world wars that began unravelling Eurocentric thought, its rational duality, and its interpretative monopolies over the "other." The carnage illustrated the limitations of Enlightenment vision of reason to structure artificial societies, and Eurocentrism's inherent categorical quandaries and annihilating dialectical structure.

Eurocentric rational dualities created a knowledge system in which a subject perceives an object in terms of negation or difference. In this world-view, the subject always centres the dialectic on the self as an observer, although it is outward looking. Within this perspective, little space, if any, exists for a dialogue or conversation between the self and other. There is little tolerance of otherness; it remains outside dominant narratives. Alternatively, Eurocentric thought has appropriated the other as a form of knowledge; yet the other is the unknowable. If the other is knowable, it is appropriated by incorporation into existing categories: the "equal" or "same" category of the self, or the mystical other outside the existing categories, or *sui generis*. Both tactics stimulate Eurocentric diffusionism, colonialism, racism, and other strategies of difference.

Eurocentrism relies heavily on noun-centred structures of Indo-European languages, whose dialectical structure emphasizes subject-verb-object relations within sentences. French philosopher Jacques Derrida has argued that linguistic operations are instrumental in producing both self and other and mediating access to external reality.[148] He argues that language is a partial instrument of social stratification, which car-

---

144 *Ibid.*

145 A. Nandy, *The Intimate Enemy: Loss and Recovery of Self Under Colonization* (New Delhi: Oxford University Press, 1983) at x.

146 *Ibid.* at ix, citing Albert Camus.

147 *Ibid.*

148 Derrida, *supra* note 118.

ries within it an oppressive view of the self and other. The linguistic structure reinforced and justified Eurocentrism and the political idea of empire, which were centred on the inherent superiority of the Indo-European people over all others, the dialectic of their self and unknowable others, and the mystery of how its knowledge system (and therefore theory, history, or law) can comprehend and incorporate the "other."

French philosopher Emmanuel Levinas noted that Eurocentric philosophy has been struck with the horror of the other that remains the other.[149] He noticed that the other was an insurmountable "allergy" to the Eurocentric quest for totality, the desire for unity and universal monotheism. Through its vision of totality, he argued, Eurocentrism sacrificed the present to the future: the future will bring forth an "ultimate," objective meaning of oneness.

Since the First World War, European twentieth-century thought is a continuous attempt to extract itself from the rational dualities or binary categories, but no alternative has been found. Negation or contradiction does not resolve the problem because the dialectic already includes negation and opposition as the working of resistance. Nor does ignoring, excluding, or extirpating the dialectic's processes resolve the problem, as Eurocentric thought, history, and law have revealed. If displacement can never be complete, however, thinkers have remained committed to the project of dismantling Enlightenment rationality.

To understand the horror of the Second World War, both German and French scholars re-examined the Enlightenment traditions. Fascism seemed to have stopped the progress of reason, and ended the Enlightenment artificial construction of society (of which many Eurocentric scholars thought Marxism was the fullest political development).[150] In Germany, Max Horkheimer and Theodor Adorno's *Dialectic of Enlightenment* (1944)[151] consolidated this insight as it built on the Frankfurt School of critical thinkers. They attempted to explain how reason had developed into fascism, human genocide, and human rights violations. Their answer was that Enlightenment's dialectic of reason had always contained a measure of irrationality, and the negative part of reason had led to tyranny and domination. The very capabilities of rationality that enabled Europeans to "free" themselves from nature and control had become an instrumental device to dominate them. Europeans had rationalized nature into productive commodities, while fascism rationalized their humanity into empty and passive consumers.

The task for critical scholars was to eliminate the irrationality that had produced fascism. They had to redefine reason and the forms of identity thinking that had defined existence as an indistinguishable element of the collective. In this way the autonomy and spontaneity of the individual might retrieve the original goal of Enlightenment.

---

149 Emmanuel Levinas, "The Trace of the Other" in M.C. Taylor, ed., *Deconstruction in Context* (Chicago: Chicago University Press, 1986) at 346-47.

150 See generally R. Young, *White Mythologies: Writing History and the West* (London: Routledge, 1990) c. 1.

151 Max Horkheimer and Theodor Adorno, *Dialectic of Enlightenment*, trans. John Cumming (New York: Herder and Herder, 1972); Theodor Adorno, *Negative Dialectics*, trans. E. B. Ashton (New York: Seabury Press, 1973).

Jurgen Habermas has continued their efforts to unpack the ideological interests of knowledge and locate "praxis" and a theory of social conflict that accounts for emancipation or the negation of domination.[152]

In contrast, French thinkers Amié Césaire, Frantz Fanon, and Michel Foucault saw fascism as European colonialism brought home to Europe:[153] after the First World War, a country deprived of an overseas empire (Germany) sought to colonize the colonizers and acquire a world empire. The French thinkers did not try to purge the irrationality out of rational thought; instead, they analyzed reason itself. They saw irrationality as simply reason's negative other, an excluded but necessary feature of dialectic. Despotic Enlightenment was based on reason, its grand political and legal projects and universal truth-claims were all intimately related to European colonialism. Their project promoted the relentless critique of the collusive forms of European knowledge that created colonization and a direct analysis of its effects. For Foucault this comprised a vigorous critique of historicism and its relation to the operations of knowledge and power (or historicist forms of knowledge).[154]

The French thinkers focused on ways to undo reason's own tendency to domination, dogmatism, and despotism. Specifically, they challenged rationality's claims to universality. Reason had to be liberated from itself. From this perspective, it becomes possible to understand the distrust of totalizing systems of knowledge that depend upon theory and ideas. Foucault and Jean François Lyotard sought to isolate the singularity or contingent event in reason as opposed to universality. The search for the singularity that refused all conceptualization constructed a new form of knowledge, respecting the other without trying to absorb or assimilate it into the self. Denaturalizing the given disciplinary and other boundaries, re-valuing the different, the other, and respecting the local over the universal have been crucial to post-structuralists' and postmodernists' challenges to modernity.

The deconstruction of Eurocentric knowledge or self illustrates the extent to which Europe's others, such as Aboriginal peoples, have been its narcissistic self-image through which it artificially constructed and compared itself. Deconstruction involves decentring and decolonizing European thought or *episteme*—a process of reconceptualizing the familiar placement of phenomena into categorizes, including legal categories.

---

152 J. Habermas, *The Theory of Communicative Action*, trans. T. McCarthy (Boston: Beacon Press, 1984).

153 A. Césaire, *Discourse on Colonialism*, trans. J. Pinkham (New York: Modern Reader, 1972). Frantz Fanon, *The Wretched of the Earth*, trans. C. Farrington (New York: Grove Press, 1963); Frantz Fanon, *A Dying Colonialism*, trans. H. Chevalier (New York: Grove Press, 1965); Frantz Fanon, *Black Skin, White Mask*, trans. C.L. Markman (London: MacGibbons & Kee, 1968); Foucault, *supra* notes 48, 135.

154 Foucault, *supra* notes 48 and 135; also see Michel Foucault, *The Archaeology of Knowledge and the Discourse on Language*, trans. A.M. Sheridan Smith (New York: Pantheon Books, 1972); Foucault, *Madness and Civilization; A History of Insanity in the Age of Reason*, trans. R. Howard (London: Tavistock Publications, 1971).

Levinas' *Totality and Infinity* is an example of the deconstruction of Eurocentrism.[155] He defined politics as the art of foreseeing war and of winning it; war is a political form of the appropriation of the others, and underpins all ontological thinking with its violence. The violence involved in politics is more than just physical force, injuring or annihilating persons. It is also "ontological imperialism," a process of "interrupting their continuity, making them play roles in which they no longer recognize themselves, making them betray not only commitments but their own substance."[156] Such destructive activities to Levinas should not be immune from ethical or moral consideration, since war is the philosophical concept of being (ontology) itself. He argued that politics should not be placed before morality, since being has always been defined by comparison with the others and by appropriation of others to forge an identity. Once defined as identities, they are appropriated into larger orders or categories (such as knowledge, history, or state).

His objection to Eurocentric totalization was its inherently violent and negative reaction toward the other. Eurocentric knowledge always views the other as a threat; its only response is to appropriate the other into sameness or formal equality. Eurocentrism is unable to let the other remain outside its theories; such separate singularity destroys its vision of totality. Its ontological imperialism forces the alterity of the other to vanish into sameness; forcing the other to be neutralized as a means of integration or assimilation to maintain the totalizing discourse. Any difference will be treated in the same way, since Eurocentric knowledge must appropriate the other, in an act of violence and reduction, to sustain its superiority.

Because of these tendencies, Eurocentric ontology becomes a philosophy of power and control rather than a philosophy of existence. For example, an Eurocentric historiographer assimilates all particular existences and events into the structure of universal history, a chronological order or grand narrative. This narrative becomes analogous to nature itself,[157] ignoring the alterity of the others, their interpretation of time and events, their heritage or culture. Levinas proposed that instead of violence toward the other, European thought should learn to respect the other and accept an infinite separation of the other from sameness. The idea of infinity is the antidote to totality that marks a relationship always exterior to Eurocentrism.[158]

Although large explanatory projects such as Marxism have lost credibility in the wake of political disappointment, Eurocentric scholarship clings to the vocabulary of theoretical singularity systems it claims to have renounced; for example, in viewing capitalism as a single, economic and legal regime with an institutional logic of its own, or in distinguishing between reformist humanization and revolutionary replacement of the established order. Positive social sciences treat basic colonial arrangements and

---

155 E. Levinas, *Totality and Infinity: An Essay on Exteriority*, trans. A. Lingis. (Pittsburgh, Pa.: Duquesne University Press, 1969) [hereinafter Levinas, *Totality and Infinity*]; see also A. Peperzak, *To the Other: An Introduction to the Philosophy of Emmanuel Levinas* (West Lafayette, Ind.: Purdue University Press, 1993).

156 Levinas, *Totality and Infinity, ibid.* at 21.

157 *Ibid.* at 55.

158 *Ibid.* at 22

preconceptions as the cumulative residue of countless past episodes of problem solving or compromise, or as the outcome of trial-and-error convergence toward the best available practices. In such an intellectual climate, transforming and inventing the formative structures of a post-colonial society become almost literally unimaginable, and Aboriginal peoples are driven back to an understanding of politics as colonial discourses.[159]

Eurocentric rational dualities are nevertheless unravelling in modern legal thought.[160] Professor Duncan Kennedy provided a jurisprudential framework to analyze and describe how judicial reasoning responds to failing dualities:

> The history of legal thought since the turn of the century is the history of the decline of a particular set of distinctions—those that, taken together, constitute the liberal way of thinking about the social world. Those distinctions are state/society, public/private, individual/group, right/power, property/sovereignty, contract/tort, law/policy, legislature/judiciary, objective/subjective, reason/fiat, freedom/coercion ... . Although these distinctions are not synonymous, they are all in a sense "the same." By this I mean that it is hard to define any one of them without reference to all, or at least many of the others, and that if one understands the common usage of one of them, one understands ... all the others.[161]

He suggests that there is a sequence of six stages in a rational duality's passage from "robust good health to utter decrepitude."

One of the main vehicles of colonial oppression was control over Aboriginal language and communications systems and colonial dialects of English. In the British colonizer model, the received standard English (RS–English) asserted the speech of southeast England as a universal norm in civilization, education and law, thus marginalizing all colonial "variants" as impurities or deviants. RS–English became the medium through which a hierarchical structure of knowledge and power was perpetuated in the distant colonies. Colonial subservience and marginality to RS-English became a source of conflicted energy as Aboriginal languages were viewed as primitive and unacceptable.

Robert Phillipson demonstrates[162] that many of the basic terms used in English and French analyses of Aboriginal peoples and their knowledge are ideologically loaded with diffusionist tenets. Present language continues to reflect a European way of conceptualizing the rational dualities of the self and others and tends to reinforce colonial myths, racism, and stereotypes. Many English concepts establish a pattern of Eurocentric self-exaltation that creates an idealistic image of itself and a devaluation of Aboriginal knowledge. For example, European nations have languages, while "tribes" have dialects; European nations have knowledge, while tribes have culture. Similar perspectives have shaped a broad understanding of Aboriginal knowledge systems.

---

159 R.M. Unger, *What Should Legal Analysis Become?* (New York: Verso, 1996).

160 D. Kennedy, "The Stages Of The Decline Of The Public/Private Distinction" (1982) 130 U. Pa. L. Rev. 1349.

161 *Ibid.* at 1349.

162 Robert Phillipson, *Linguistic Imperialism* (Oxford: Oxford University Press, 1992).

British linguistic hegemony created an identity crisis among the colonial immigrants and among some of the Aboriginal peoples as the infinite others. A valid and active sense of self for immigrants may have been eroded by dislocation resulting from migration, the experience of enslavement, transportation, or voluntary removal for indentured labour. For Aboriginals, a sense of self may have been destroyed by cultural denigration of the other, the conscious and unconscious oppression of personality and culture by a supposedly superior racial or cultural model. The alienation of vision and the crisis of self-image can be seen in the shared attempt to construct a "place" and in conceptions of Aboriginal territory, tenure, and rights.

16. Property Law as Colonial Category

Like modern thought more generally, legal thought is a process of categorizing phenomena. At the core of legal thought, categorizing determines how the courts will treat a topic, regardless of whether the process is seen as mechanical, as by the formalists, or as politically motivated, as by the instrumentalists.[163] The categories in Canada and other colonies constitute another legacy of colonization.

Colonial categories and conceptualization of place inflect literature and law. Language's relationship to place has been a complex problem for Canadian immigrants, as much for farmers as for writers, scholars, and jurists. This dilemma has remained a major feature of colonial consciousness. The concept of land is a cultural construct shaped and reshaped by various forces. The earth is "landscape"; it becomes "langscape," as Gaile McGregor calls it,[164] when it reveals human attitudes and perceptions in languages or in *paysage intérieur* (the landscape of the mind).

As colonial literature and art illustrate, immigrants to Canada are haunted by their dislocation from their homeland and their relations to the new place. Until recently, nature has been ignored, and denied, romanticized or exploited; colonial writers and arts have often viewed the landscape as negative in the wilderness/civilization dualism. Canadian society has incorporated this predominantly negative view into moral and legal co-ordinates. This gothic vision of the landscape as an unconscious realm, chaos, or a cruel and meaningless other created a terror of the soul.[165] Also it created a pervasive anxiety to recover an effective identifying relationship between self and place and cognitive authenticity; in short, this anxiety created a national as well as a personal crisis of identity. Those who are unaffected by dislocation and place either view the new land as an object to be exploited or have had their valid and active sense of self

---

163 K. J. Vandevelde, "The New Property of the Nineteenth Century: The Development of the Modern Concept of Property" (1980) 29 Buffalo L. Rev. 324.

164 Gaile McGregor, *The Wacousta Syndrome: Explorations in the Canadian Landscape* (Toronto: University of Toronto Press, 1985).

165 N. Frye, *The Bush Garden: Essays on the Canadian Imagination* (Toronto: Anansi, 1971) at 141-42; Margaret Atwood, *Survival: A Thematic Guide to Canadian Literature* (Toronto: Anansi, 1972); Marcia B. Kline, *Beyond the Land Itself: Views of Nature in Canada and the United States* (Cambridge, Mass.: Harvard University Press, 1970).

eroded by dislocation or destroyed by cultural denigration. An emerging environmental consciousness offers a hope of renewal and reconciliation among immigrants, the landscape, and Aboriginal peoples.

Why the immigrants, formally unconstrained and theoretically free to continue in possession and practice of "Englishness" or "Europeaness", created a crisis of self-image and alienation of vision, or why they manifested a tendency to seek an alternative, differentiated identity, are questions that remain unanswered, trapped in the mystery of rational dualities. They await a process of self-apprehension in Canadian consciousness.

In 1965, D.E.S. Maxwell discussed these problems in literature in British colonies such as Canada. These colonies dispossessed the Aboriginal peoples, occupied the land, established transplanted British societies, and retained the English language. Yet, having no ancestral contact with the territory, the colonists' writings exhibited a characteristic discontinuity between language and place. Common themes of this discontinuity were problems of exile, finding and defining "home, physical and emotional confrontations with the new land and its ancient and established meaning, and the involvement of racial politics. Their sense of displacement, cultural fragmentation, and colonial domination are found in their unquestioningly clinging to a belief in the adequacy of the imported language."[166] Professor Maxwell asserts that descriptions of land, climate, and seasons, were linguistic areas where mistranslation could not be overlooked. This linguistic dilemma created a "double vision" where identity was constituted by unsettling differences. These differences are illustrated in colonial literature by the thematic use of allegory, irony, magic realism, discontinuous narratives, and recurrent structural and formal patterns of exile. The pattern of exile, for example, is a manifestation of the ubiquitous concern with place and displacement and the complex material circumstances implicit in the transportation of language (largely unmodified) and its imposed and imposing relation on and with the new environment.

These themes emphasize the importance of the disjunction between language and place.[167] These themes and patterns are not accidental. They inform a psychic and historical condition. Despite exploiting the landscape and regarding the Aboriginal peoples as disposable, colonialists did not feel at home in the place colonized. Out of this sense of displacement emerged the discourse of place, the *Unheimlichkeit* or "not at homeness"[168] or living in the "other." Such experiences eventually caused writers to

---

166   D.E.S. Maxwell, "Landscape and Theme" in J. Press. ed., *Commonwealth Literature: Unity and Diversity in a Common Culture* (London: Heineman, 1965) at 82-99. Maxwell identified two groups: the settler colonies and the invaded colonies. The settler colonies other than Canada were New Zealand, Australia, and the United States. In invaded colonies, such as India or Nigeria, the colonial powers colonized the Indigenous peoples on their own territories. In those colonies, writers were not required to adapt to a different landscape and climate, but had their own ancient and sophisticated response to their marginalization by English in its cultural and imperial totality. Where English actually supplanted the writer's Aboriginal languages, or simply offered an alternative, its use caused a disjunction between the apprehension of, and communication about, the world.

167   W.H. New, *Among Worlds: An Introduction to Modern Commonwealth and South African Fiction* (Erin, Ont.: La Presse Porcepic, 1975).

168   Martin Heidegger, *Being and Time*, trans. J. Macquarrie and E. Robinson (New York: Harper & Row, 1962).

question the appropriateness of imported language to place. The rational dualities became haunting distinctions between an authentic experience of the real world and an inauthentic experience of the ideological contexts, order and disorder, reality and imaginality, power and impotence, even being and nothingness.

These literary and cultural themes and patterns are also inscribed in political and legal life. The material forces of politics, economics, and law in the imperial framework carry the imprint of the same psychic, historical, and linguistic conditions, reflected, for example, in the quest for a nourishing national identity, the problems surrounding bilingualism, the explosion of academic and legal languages, and the quest for a new constitution.

The most widely shared manifestation of this alienation in Canadian consciousness is the construction of place. The alienating discontinuity between the experience of place and the language to describe it occurs for those whose languages seem inadequate to describe a new place, for those whose languages have been and continue to be systematically destroyed by colonization, and for those whose languages have been and remain deprivileged by the imposition of the language of colonizing power(s). Some mixture of these can describe the situation in colonized and post-colonial society.

Those who speak English in North America share this alienation once they realize that its vocabulary, categories, and legal codes are inadequate or inappropriate to describe the fauna, the physical and geographical conditions, or the cultural practices they have developed in a new land. Ngugi wa Thiong'o seeks to escape from the implicit body of assumptions to which the English language is firmly attached, its aesthetic and social values, the formal and historically limited constraints on genre, and the oppressive political and cultural assertion of metropolitan dominance over the colonies and Aboriginal peoples.[169]

Historically, the English language had some capacity to account for the ecology of colonial experience through, for example, assimilating Latin and other languages. Colonizers struggled to develop a conscious and appropriate linguistic code based on the experience of a new place, identifiably different in its ecology. Dennis Lee, a Canadian writer, theorized these problems:

> The colonial writer does not have words of his own. Is it not possible that he projects his own condition of voicelessness into whatever he creates? [t]hat he articulates his own powerlessness, in the face of alien words, by seeking out fresh tales of victims? [T]he language was drenched with non-belonging ... words had become our enemy.[170]

The problem of an imported language and the "alien" Aboriginal landscape has been taken up as a conflict in Canadian writing. Dennis Lee and Robert Kroetsch identify the problem as a mismatch between language and landscape. The landscape has been and is the wrong historical, cultural, and physical environment for great English literature. The Eurocentric mind searched for a comforting reality to fill the gap

---

169 Ngugi wa Thiong'o, *Decolonizing the Mind: The Politics of Language in African Literature* (London: Currey, 1986).

170 Dennis Lee, "Cadence, Country, Silence: Writing in Colonial Space" (1974) 3 Boundary 2 162 at 163.

between its world-view and the land. While immigrants walked on the land, the Euro-centric mind recoiled at the actual landscape. The hope was that progressive familiari-ty with the land and the adaptation of the language to it could bridge the gap. It has not.

That gap between language and landscape, Robert Kroetsch wrote, was the per-ceived "inauthenticity" of the spoken European language to a colonial and Aboriginal space:

> At one time I considered it to be that task of the Canadian writer to give names to his expe-rience, to be the namer. I now suspect, that, on the contrary, it is his task to un-name ... the Canadian writer's particular predicament is that he works with a language within a litera-ture, that appears to be his own ... . But ... there is in the Canadian word a concealed other experience, sometimes British, sometimes American.[171]

The failure to appropriate an authentic means of communication creates silence. Understanding the silence, Lee suggests, should be the basis for a Canadian literature:

> Beneath the words our absentee masters have given us, there is an undermining silence. It saps our nerve. And beneath that silence, there is a raw welter of cadence that tumbles and strains toward words and that makes the silence a blessing because it shushes easy speech. That cadence is home ... . The impasse of writing that is problematic to itself is tran-scended only when the impasse becomes its own subject, when writing accepts and enters and names its own conditions as it is naming the world.[172]

Lee describes this experience of being "gagged" for want of authentic words, while other writers unreflectively used inauthentic words. Writing for him had become a problem in itself: "[I]t had grown into a search for authenticity, but all it could manage to be was a symptom of inauthenticity." He decided that if he could establish the par-ticular inauthenticity of words he used, he could write.[173] Behind the problem of writ-ing itself lay the central and unavoidable questions of the relationship between the imported European and the Aboriginal, between ancestry and destiny, man-made and natural, and language and place. These questions remain at the heart of post-colonial writing and theory; D.H. Lawrence captured this dilemma:

> America hurts, because the land has a powerful disintegrative influence upon the white psy-che. It is full of grinning unappeased Aboriginal demons, too, ghosts, and it persecutes the white men ... . America is tense with latent violence and resistance ... . Yet one day the demons of America must be placated, the ghosts must be appeased, the Spirit of Place atoned for.[174]

Similarly, Carlos Williams in *In the American Grain* wrote:

> that the Indians were natural to the land, the "right" expression of them, whereas the immigrants were always crucially divorced from the land they called theirs. Still, he

---

171 Robert Kroetsch, "Unhiding the Hidden: Recent Canadian Fiction" (1974) 3 J. of Can. Fiction 43.

172 Lee, *supra* note 170 at 165, 166.

173 Ibid. at 156, 158.

174 Quoted by James Anaya, "Native Land Claims in the United States: The Unatoned-For Spirit of Place" (1994) 18 Cultural Survival Q. 52.

wrote, The land! Don't you feel it? Doesn't it make you want to go out and lift dead Indians tenderly from their graves, to steal from them–as if it must be clinging even to their corpses–some authenticity ... ."[175]

In the American lands, he said the "Indian spirit is master. It enters us, it defeats us, it imposes itself."[176]

The problems of inauthenticity and its ultimate insolubility, Lee concluded, generate the Canadian obsession with victimization.[177] The Canadian "victim position" is informed by the political domination by the United States or by Britain and France and by the problems of language born in other landscapes. Canadians, in Lee's terms, do not have their own language but are forced to use the languages of others. The colonial imagination drives Canadians continually to recreate the experience of writing with their non-belonging to the land. The first necessity of the colonial writer, Lee argues, is for the imagination to come home, yet the "words of home are silent":

> Try to speak the words of your home and you will discover–if you are a colonial–that you do not know them ... . To speak unreflectingly in a colony, then, is to use words that speak only alien space. To reflect is to fall silent, discovering that your authentic space does not have words. And to reflect further is to recognize that you and your people do not in fact have a privileged authentic space just waiting for words; you are, among other things, the people who have made an alien inarticulacy of a native space which may not exist ... . But perhaps—and here was the breakthrough—perhaps our job was not to fake a space of our own and write it up, but rather to find words for our space-lessness. Instead of pushing against the grain of an external, uncharged language, perhaps we should finally come to writing with the grain.[178]

While avoiding the untenable nationalist or ideological position, Lee partially answers the problems of the transplanted and transported post-colonial landscape. Thus, in the typical alien consciousness, people dreamed up the land to fill the crisis of emptiness. They created an architectonic "langscape" or word world as an artifact, a syncretic vision of European language and Aboriginal landscape.[179]

Scott Momaday, a Kiowa author, suggests:

> Once in his life a man ought to concentrate his mind upon remembered earth, I believe. He ought to give himself up to a particular landscape in his experience, to look at it from as many angles as he can, to wonder about it, to dwell upon it. He ought to imagine that he touches it with his hands at every season and listens to the sounds that are made upon

---

175 William Carlos Williams, "Champlain" in *In the American Grain* (New York: New Directions Books, 1956).

176 *Ibid.*, "Ponce de Leon."

177 An example is novelist M. Atwood's account of Canadian literature, *supra* note 165.

178 Lee, *supra* note 170 at 163.

179 See generally McGregor, *supra* note 164; Krim Benterrak, *et al.*, *Reading the Country: Introduction to Nomadology*, Rev.ed. (Fremantle, W.A.: Fremantle Arts Centre Press, 1996); L. Ricou, *Vertical Man/Horizontal World: Man and Landscape in Canadian Prairie Fiction* (Vancouver: U.B.C. Press, 1973).

it. He ought to imagine the creatures there and all the faintest motions of the wind. He ought to recollect the glare of noon and all the colors of dawn and dusk.[180]

The post-colonial legal context witnesses an analogous process. English land law emerged from particular cultural myths and traditions of another time and place alien to Aboriginal America. Behind the legal authority of Eurocentric langscape of the "fee this or that" are hidden assumptions about the universal features of language, epistemologies, and value systems.

The imperial expansion of a Eurocentric theory of land beyond England and Europe has had a radically destabilizing effect on the concept of legal universality and neutrality. In pushing the Aboriginal peoples to the margins of experiences, the colonists pushed their own inherited philosophical assumptions and traditions to their limits. This alienating process initially served to dominate and regulate the Aboriginal world-views. However, in recent efforts to decolonize the law in the British colonies, it has turned upon itself and pushed theory and language through a mental barrier.

17. Judicial Orders to Decolonize Existing Law

The term "decolonization," which arose after the Second World War as a public international law remedy for colonization, refers to the process of liberating those peoples formerly colonized by European powers. Although some parts of the world were decolonized in the 1960s, more than three-quarters of the people living in the world today have had their lives negatively shaped by the experience of the totalizing discourse of colonization. As one of humanity's shared tragedies and shared legacies, its pervasive influence on the perceptual and conceptual frameworks remains insufficiently unfolded. Decolonization, a new and fragile legal transformation in European legal traditions, is still in its infancy. Because the colonial legacy is slowly ending and is no longer a seamless web, however, we are now able to discern its legal path.

Decolonization is more than a movement away from colonial political control. It is a movement away from the totalizing discourse of European values and systems, including the language that communicates these values. The most important part of decolonization requires decolonizing the mind. This is the task facing all thinkers; Aboriginal thinkers face the task of articulating "indigeneity" and distinguishing it from colonial intellectual traditions.

The decolonization era seeks remedies to make a more extraordinary and equitable world, a future post-colonial world built on respecting ecological and human diversity. The struggle to decolonize the legal order is reflected in the conflict between people and nation states. There are 171 states around the earth within which live some 5,000 peoples or cultures. Many of the states are creations of European empires not of the peoples' choosing. Those people are considered "ethnic" peoples or "minorities"

---

180 Scott Momaday, *The Way To Rainy Mountain* (Albuquerque: University of New Mexico Press, 1969) at 83.

who share a language, culture, history and territory, but are not viewed as having the right of self-determination or a right to control or even to participate in the affairs of the state or its legislative assembly.

The magnitude of the problem is illustrated by United Nations statistics: if the population of the world were condensed into a global village of 1,000 people, the village would have 730 Aboriginal people (564 Asians, 86 Africans, and 80 Aboriginal Americans) and 270 Euro-Americans (210 Europeans, 60 Americans-Canadians).[181] Yet almost two-thirds of the earth's people are not in control of a global agenda or national public policy, politics, or economic institutions. The "global village" remains dominated by the colonial and Eurocentric trained experts, and the colonized are still chained to Eurocentric world-views: cognitively here, physically and socially there, and psychologically everywhere.

In Australia, Canada, and New Zealand, the highest courts have ordered judiciaries to decolonize existing imperial and colonial law. They have directed reviewing courts to confront and reassess past injustices found in statutes and the common law toward Aboriginal tenure and Aboriginal and treaty rights. On grounds of either international human rights standards or constitutional supremacy, they have directed lower courts to create a just context for respecting Aboriginal tenure and rights on an equal basis to Crown tenure and "settler" rights. In decolonizing the law, these courts have attempted to understand Aboriginal law as distinct from Victorian common law of colonization, often called by the colonized Aboriginal peoples "predatory" justice.[182]

In the past, British courts under the doctrine of parliamentary sovereignty did not evaluate the positive law of colonial governments. This judicial limitation allowed colonizers to achieve political and economic ascendancy by disregarding prerogative laws involving Aboriginal and treaty rights.[183] Judicial reasoning justified taking Aboriginal tenure under a prejudicial assumption of the inevitability of assimilation and progress, and allowed colonial governments to diminish the opportunities for self-expression and authentic participation by Aboriginal peoples in Canadian institutions.

Questions of Aboriginal tenure and rights and colonial law are different in many ways from the issues British or Canadian courts normally decide. Many Aboriginal peoples have expressed concern about the role of the courts in adjudicating Aboriginal issues. The courts are seen as a product of the British legal and political system and as such are perceived as biased in addressing Aboriginal issues. Many judges have likewise wondered whether these issues are inherently unsuitable for disposition by the courts ('non-justiciable'), or pondered how to overcome their legal bias toward British and Canadian law. The Supreme Court of Canada and the High Court in Australia have affirmed that these issues are justiciable and that judges can overcome the colonial biases. In decolonizing the colonial order, courts can describe rights to governments

---

181 United Nations, *Innovations and Network for Development* (New York: World Development Forum, 1990) at 1.

182 See generally W. Churchill, *Since Predator Came: Notes from the Struggle for American Indian Liberation* (Littleton, Colo.: Aigis Pub., 1995).

183 *Sparrow v. The Queen*, [1990] 1 S.C.R. 1075, [1990] 3 C.N.L.R. 160 (S.C.C.) [hereinafter *Sparrow* cited to S.C.R.].

and peoples, but they cannot make a relationship based on those rights work.

In *Taylor and Williams*, Justice MacKinnon of the Ontario Court of Appeal began articulating a decolonizing approach to Aboriginal and treaty rights:

> Cases on Indian or aboriginal rights can never be determined in a vacuum. It is of importance to consider the history and oral traditions of the tribes concerned, and the surrounding circumstances ... relied on by both parties ... . Although it is not possible to remedy all of what we now perceive as past wrongs in view of the passage of time, nevertheless it is essential and in keeping with established and accepted principles that the courts not create, by a remote, isolated current view of past events, new grievances.[184]

The Supreme Court of Canada has decolonized Canadian law by small increments. In *Calder*[185] the Supreme Court of Canada recognized that, even in the absence of prerogative treaties and the 1763 Proclamation, Aboriginal tenure and rights existed within and were protected by British common law.[186] Without constitutional status, the courts held that under the parliamentary supremacy doctrine the federal Parliament could, at any time, extinguish or regulate those rights.[187] In *Guerin*[188] Justice Dickson created statutory fiduciary obligations on the "concept of [A]boriginal, native or Indian title,"[189] and held that "Aboriginal title as a legal right *derived from the Indians' historic occupation and possession of their tribal lands*."[190] In *Van der Peet*, the Supreme Court noted that although the constitutional structure of the United States is different from that of Canada, the relevancy of the general principles of early decisions of Chief Justice Marshall of the United States Supreme Court provides Canadian courts with a "structure and coherence to an untidy and diffuse body of customary law based on offi-

---

184 *R. v. Taylor and Williams*, 34 O.R. (2d) 360 at 364, [1981] 3 C.N.L.R. 114 (Ont. C.A.).

185 *Calder v. Attorney-General of British Columbia*, [1973] S.C.R. 313, [1973] 4 W.W.R. 1 (S.C.C.), affirming (1970), 13 D.L.R. (3d) 64 at 66 (B.C. C.A.), affirming (1969), 8 D.L.R. (3d) 59 at 66 (B.C. S.C.) [hereinafter *Calder* cited to S.C.R. unless otherwise stated].

186 *Van der Peet, supra* note 76 at para. 28. Justice L'Heureux-Dubé's dissenting opinion, on other grounds, stated that these common law "principles define the terms upon which the Crown acquired sovereignty over Native people and their territories," at para. 114.

187 *Kruger v. The Queen* (1977), [1978] 1 S.C.R. 104 at 112 (S.C.C.); *R. v. Derriksan* (1975), 60 D.L.R. (3d) 140 (B.C. C.A.), affirmed (1975), 71 D.L.R. (3d) 159 (S.C.C.). Justice L'Heureux-Dubé's opinion in *Van der Peet, supra* note 76 at para. 125, restates the limitation: "Prior to 1982, the doctrine of Aboriginal rights was founded only on the common law and Aboriginal rights could be extinguished by treaty, conquest and legislation," as they were, "dependent upon the good will of the Sovereign." See *St. Catherine's Milling and Lumber Co. v. The Queen* (1887), 13 S.C.R. 577 (S.C.C.) [hereinafter *St. Catherine's*]; also *R. v. George*, [1966] S.C.R. 267 (S.C.C.) [hereinafter *George*]; *Sikyea v. The Queen*, [1964] S.C.R. 642, 49 W.W.R. 306 (S.C.C.) [hereinafter *Sikyea*]; and *Calder, supra* note 185; see also, regarding the mode of extinguishing Aboriginal rights, Kenneth Lysyk, "The Indian Title Question in Canada: An Appraisal in the Light of Calder" (1973) 51 Can. Bar Rev. 450.

188 *Guerin v. The Queen*, [1984] 2 S.C.R. 335, [1985] 1 C.N.L.R. 120 (S.C.C.) [hereinafter *Guerin* cited to S.C.R. unless otherwise stated].

189 *Ibid.* at 376.

190 *Ibid.* at 132 C.N.L.R.; *Van der Peet supra* note 76 at para. 34

cial practice."[191] In addition, the Court considered the judicial analysis of native title and rights by the High Court of Australia in *Mabo v. Queensland [No. 2]*[192] as "persuasive" authority in Canadian courts[193] and similar to its *Van der Peet* decision.[194]

As the judicial decolonization process has gathered momentum, the courts have had to confront the misconceptions of the past, particularly the stereotypes of Aboriginal people as "savages" and the histories of Aboriginal peoples. The courts have had to correct the colonial fictions and privileges, such as *terra nullius*, settled colonies, and the universal and absolute Crown ownership. The courts have acknowledged and recognized that profound differences in culture, world-view, and communication styles exist between Aboriginal law and the perspectives of the common law. In particular, they have found that due respect must be accorded to the legitimacy and authority of the oral traditions of Aboriginal people to shed light on the past and mark the way to a better future.[195]

Achieving a post-colonial balance between Aboriginal and non-Aboriginal perspectives on Canadian law will require substantial and sustained effort to understand Aboriginal legal systems that operate within Aboriginal and treaty rights. The constitutional reforms and the Supreme Court of Canada have given the judiciary an early start on the project and emphasized its urgency. However, many courts perceive they have already arrived at the limits of constitutional analysis and the law as legitimate tools for determining rights, and recommend a negotiated political settlement based on such rights as they have found to exist. An eloquent plea to this effect is found in the judgment of Justice Lambert of the British Columbia Court of Appeal in *Delgamuukw*:

> So, in the end, the legal rights of the Indian people will have to be accommodated within our total society by political compromises and accommodations based in the first instance on negotiation and agreement and ultimately in accordance with the sovereign will of the community as a whole. The legal rights of the Gitksan and Wet'suwet'en peoples, to which this law suit is confined, and which allow no room for any approach other than the application of the law itself, and the legal rights of all [A]boriginal peoples throughout British Columbia, form only one factor in the ultimate determination of what kind of community we are going to have in British Columbia and throughout Canada in the years ahead. In my view, the failure to recognize the true legal scope of [A]boriginal rights at common law, and under the Constitution, will only perpetuate the problems connected

---

191 *Van der Peet, ibid.* at para. 35, citing B. Slattery, "Understanding Aboriginal Rights" (1987) 66 Can. Bar Rev. 727 at 759 [hereinafter Slattery, "Understanding Aboriginal Rights"].

192 *Van der Peet, ibid.* at paras. 38-40.

193 *Ibid.* at para. 38.

194 *Ibid.* at para. 40.

195 *Delgamuukw v. British Columbia,* [1997] 3 S.C.R. 1010 at paras. 80-107, [1998] 1 C.N.L.R. 14 (S.C.C.), reversing, [1993] 5 W.W.R. 97 (B.C. C.A.), affirming (1991), 79 D.L.R. (4th) 185 (B.C. S.C.) [hereinafter *Delgamuukw* cited to S.C.R. unless otherwise stated]; Letter from Chief Justice H.M. Howell, Manitoba Court of Appeal, to the Governor General in Council, 2 December 1907. NAC, TG10, vol. 3617, file 4646-1; this is also quoted in Richard C. Daniel, *A History of Native Claims Processes in Canada, 1867-1979* (Ottawa: Department of Indian Affairs and Northern Development, 1980) at 113.

with finding the honourable place for the Indian peoples within the British Columbian and Canadian communities to which their legal rights and their ancient cultures entitle them.[196]

However, this approach must be critically reconsidered. Constitutional supremacy requires courts to find a fair and just reconciliation of constitutional principles, just as under the constitutional division of powers the government's laws and policies must be consistent with the constitutional principles. Canadian history has taught us that representative governments often reflect a majority view that disregards the constitutional rights of minorities, and that principled decisions of the courts are required to protect minority rights.

In *Sparrow*, the Supreme Court affirmed that constitutional reforms required the decolonization of accumulated precedents: "Section 35 calls for just settlement for aboriginal peoples. It renounces the old rules of the game under which the Crown established courts of law and denied those courts the authority to question sovereign claims made by the Crown."[197] Constitutional law scholars Peter Hogg and Mary Ellen Turpel-Lafond described such a decolonization process:

> [i]t is an important task of constitutional lawyers and elected officials to review those [constitutional] doctrines that reflect the Eurocentric bias of Canadian constitutional law and government ... and embark on the reordering of institutions and doctrine that is required to give full expression to the longstanding Aboriginal presence in Canada.[198]

The following section details judicial attempts to decolonize the common law and offers long judicial quotations to capture something of the spirit and reasoning of the justices.

A. *Terra Nullius* in public international law

When courts applied Victorian common law assumptions about Aboriginal peoples without laws or concepts of property, the Aboriginal tenures or rights vanished and these *sui generis* rights did not have to be reconciled "with the institutions or the legal ideas of civilized society." In 1851, for example, the Court of Queen's Bench in Upper Canada rejected the idea that the Haudenosaunee or the Six Nations could have legal rights to their reserved lands: "We cannot recognize any peculiar law of real property applying to the Indians—the common law is not part savage and part civilized."[199] Jus-

---

196 *Delgamuukw, ibid.,* W.W.R. at 379-80.

197 *Sparrow, supra* note 183 at 1106. The Supreme Court of Canada concluded that: "For many years, the rights of the Indians to their aboriginal lands—certainly as legal rights—were virtually ignored ... For fifty years after the publication of Clement's the Law of the Canadian Constitution (3rd ed. 1916) there was a virtual absence of discussion of any kind of Indian rights ... ."

198 P.W. Hogg and M.E. Turpel-Lafond, "Implementing Aboriginal Self-Government: Constitutional and Jurisdictional Issues" (1995) 74 Can. Bar Rev. 187 at 192.

199 *Sheldon v. Ramsay* (1851), 9 U.C.Q.B. 195 at 123.

tice Hall in *Calder* contested such thinking.[200] In the trial court's judgment and Court of Appeal's decision, the justices wrote that the Nisga'a were "undoubtedly at the time of settlement a very primitive people with few of the institutions of civilized society, and none at all of our notions of private property."[201] Writing for the three justices who found that Aboriginal tenure was not a creation of British or Canadian statutory law or common law[202] and had not been extinguished by statutory law,[203] Justice Hall condemned the judicial reliance on the ancient savage-civilization dualism in the assessment of notions of private property:

> The assessment and interpretation of the historical documents and enactments tendered in evidence must be approached in the light of present-day research and knowledge disregarding ancient concepts formulated when understanding of the customs and culture of our original people was rudimentary and incomplete and when they were thought to be wholly without cohesion, laws or culture, in effect a subhuman species. This concept of the original inhabitants of America led Chief Justice Marshall in his otherwise enlightened judgment in *Johnson v. McIntosh*, which is the outstanding judicial pronouncement on the subject of Indian rights to say, "But the tribes of Indians inhabiting this country were fierce savages whose occupation was war ..." We now know that that assessment was ill-founded. The Indians did in fact at times engage in some tribal wars but war was not their vocation and it can be said that their preoccupation with war pales into insignificance when compared to the religious and dynastic wars of "civilized" Europe of the 16th and 17th centuries. Marshall was, of course, speaking with the knowledge available to him in 1823. Chief Justice Davey in the judgment under appeal, with all the historical research and material available since 1823 and notwithstanding the evidence in the record which Gould J. found was given "with total integrity" said of the Indians of the mainland of British Columbia: "...They were undoubtedly at the time of settlement a very primitive people with few of the institutions of civilized society, and none at all of our notions of private property." In so saying this in 1970, he was assessing the Indian culture of 1858 by the same standards that the Europeans applied to the Indians of North America two or more centuries before.[204]

Justice Hall ordered Canadian courts to re-examine their notions of Aboriginal society, law, and peoples and begin the adjudicative search to create equality between Aboriginal law and British law.

The Supreme Court of Canada in *Simon* continued to decolonize the colonial notions of savage people without sovereignty or "ownership," rejecting the precedent based on these concepts.[205] Speaking for a unified Court, Chief Justice Dickson over-

---

200 *Calder, supra* note 185.

201 *Ibid.* See also the lower court decisions in *Calder*.

202 *Ibid.* All the justices, at 385, agreed that Nisga'a title existed in the common law and was an "original and previous possession" of the land.

203 *Ibid.* Three other justices, in an opinion written by Justice Judson, found that the Nisga'a title had been extinguished by statutory law. This arose from their understanding of the relations between parliamentary sovereignty and common law.

204 *Ibid.* at 346-47.

205 *R. v. Simon*, [1985] 2 S.C.R. 387 at 399, 62 N.R. 366 (S.C.C.) [hereinafter *Simon* cited to S.C.R.]; *R. v. Syliboy* (1928), [1929] 1 D.L.R. 307 at 313, 50 C.C.C. 389 (N.S. Co. Ct.) [hereinafter *Syliboy*].

ruled the existing precedent that established "[t]he savages' right of sovereignty even if ownership were never recognized" by the British sovereign or international law.[206] He held the 1929 holding was "substantively unconvincing" and "a bias and prejudice of another era in Canadian law."[207] Additionally, he found the holding inconsistent with a growing constitutional sensitivity to Aboriginal rights.[208]

The judicial characterization that British law did not recognize the "savages' right of sovereignty" or "ownership" of a territory, and that it maintained the legal fiction of *terra nullius* and its related manifestation in the common law category of a "settled" colony, was rejected by the Australian High Court in *Mabo* in 1992:

> The facts as we know them today do not fit the "absence of law" or "barbarian" theory underpinning the colonial reception of the common law of England. That being so, there is no warrant for applying in these times rules of the English common law which were the product of that theory.[209]

The High Court was addressing a dispute between the Meriam people and the Crown regarding who had title to the Murray Islands. Six of the seven High Court justices condemned the application of *terra nullius* and "settled colonies" as unjust discrimination based on prejudicial and false assumptions. The Court affirmed that Aboriginal tenure or "native title" existed in Australian common law; that its source was in the Aboriginal law and traditions that connected them with the land; that it was a right to possess, occupy, use and enjoy the land good against the whole world;[210] and that it reduced and qualified the doctrine of the underlying title of the Crown in the colonies.[211] Chief Justice Lamer in *Van der Peet* acknowledged the High Court of Australia decision in *Mabo*[212] on the nature and basis of Aboriginal tenure as persuasive[213] and similar to the Canadian decisions.[214]

In reaching its conclusion, the High Court unpacked the biased and prejudicial fictions of *terra nullius* and the "settled colony" category, which the Australian courts

---

206 *Simon, ibid.* In *Syliboy, ibid.* at 313-14, acting Judge Patterson stated:

> [T]he Indians were never regarded as an independent power. A civilized nation first discovering a country of uncivilized people or savages held such country as its own until such time as by treaty it was transferred to some other civilized nation. The savages' rights of sovereignty even of ownership were never recognized. Nova Scotia had passed to Great Britain not by gift or purchase from or even by conquest of the Indians but by treaty with France, which had acquired it by priority of discovery and ancient possession; and the Indians passed with it.

207 *Simon, ibid.*

208 *Ibid.*

209 *Mabo and Others v. State of Queensland [No. 2]* (1992), 107 A.L.R. 1 (H.C.) at 26, 175 C.L.R. 1 (H.C.), Mason, CJ., Brennan, Deane, Toohey, Gaudron and McHugh JJ., (Dawson J. dissenting) [hereinafter *Mabo* cited to A.L.R.].

210 *Ibid.* at 27-28.

211 *Ibid.* at 26-42.

212 *Van der Peet, supra* note 76 at paras. 38-40.

213 *Ibid.* at para. 38.

214 *Ibid.* at para. 40.

had used to dispossess the Aboriginal peoples. It relied on the International Court of Justice's analysis of *terra nullius* in its *Advisory Opinion on Western Sahara:*[215]

> "Occupation" being legally an original means of peaceably acquiring sovereignty over ter-ritory otherwise than by cession or succession, it was a cardinal condition of a valid "occu-pation" that the territory should be terra nullius—a territory belonging to no-one—at the time of the act alleged to constitute the "occupation" (cf. *Legal Status of Eastern Green-land, P.C.I.J., Series A/B, No.53,* pp.44 f. and 63 f.). In the view of the court, therefore, a determination that Western Sahara was a "terra nullius" at the time of the colonisation by Spain would be possible only if it were established that at that time the territory belonged to no-one in the sense that it was then open to acquisition through the legal process of "occupation". ... Whatever differences of opinion there may have been among jurists, the State practice of the relevant period indicates that territories inhabited by tribes or peoples having a social and political organization were not regarded as terrae nullius. It shows that in the case of such territories the acquisition of sovereignty was not generally considered as effected unilaterally through "occupation" of terra nullius by original title but through agreements concluded with local rulers. On occasion, it is true, the word "occupation" was used in a non-technical sense denoting simply acquisition of sovereignty; but that did not signify that the acquisition of sovereignty through such agreements with authorities of the country was regarded as an "occupation" or a "terra nullius" in the proper sense of these terms. On the contrary, such agreements with local rulers, whether or not considered as an actual "cession" of the territory, were regarded as derivative roots of title, and not original titles obtained by occupation of terrae nullius.[216]

The High Court noted Judge Ammoun's separate opinion on the spiritual notion of ancestral relations as the basis of the ownership of the soil:

> Mr. Bayona-Ba-Meya [Zaire representative] goes on to dismiss the materialistic concept of terra nullius, which led to this dismemberment of Africa following the Berlin Confer-ence of 1885. Mr. Bayona-Ba-Meya substitutes for this a spiritual notion: the ancestral tie between the land, or "mother nature", and the man who was born therefrom, remains attached thereto, and must one day return thither to be united with his ancestors. This link is the basis of the ownership of the soil, or better, of sovereignty. This amounts to a denial of the very concept of terra nullius in the sense of a land which is capable of being appro-priated by someone who is not born therefrom. It is a condemnation of the modern con-cept, as defined by Pasquale Fiore, which regards as terrae nullius territories inhabited by populations whose civilization, in the sense of the public law of Europe, is backward, and whose political organisation is not conceived according to Western norms.[217]

Judge Ammoun concluded that "the concept of *terra nullius* ... stands condemned."[218] The International Court of Justice held that Western Sahara at the time of colonization by Spain in 1884 was not a territory belonging to no-one (*terra nullius*).

---

215 *The Western Sahara Case* (*Morocco v. Western Sahara; Mauretania v. Western Sahara*), Advisory Opin-ion, [1975] I.C.J.R. 16 at 39 [hereinafter *Western Sahara*].

216 *Mabo, supra* note 209 at 27-28.

217 *Ibid.* at 28.

218 *Ibid.* at 28.

Since *terra nullius* had been recognized as a fundamental principle in Australian common law, the High Court addressed *terra nullius* in relation to the doctrine of precedent and the so-called weight of legal history argument:

> If this were any ordinary case, the court would not be justified in re-opening the validity of fundamental propositions which have been endorsed by long-established authority and which have been accepted as a basis of the real property law of the country for more than one hundred and fifty years ... . Far from being ordinary, however, the circumstances of the present make it unique. As has been seen, the two propositions in question provided the legal basis for dispossession of the Aboriginal peoples of most of their traditional lands. The acts and events by which that dispossession in legal theory was carried into practical effect constitute the darkest aspect of the history of this nation. The nation as a whole must remain diminished unless and until there is an acknowledgment of, and retreat from those past injustices. ... For the reasons which we have explained, that re-examination compels their rejection. The lands of this continent were not terra nullius and "practically unoccupied" in 1788.[219]

The High Court rejected the continuing application of the fiction of *terra nullius* to territory inhabited by Aboriginal people within Australia:

> Inevitably, one is compelled to acknowledge the role played, in the dispossession and oppression of the Aboriginals, by the two propositions that the territory of New South Wales was, in 1788 terra nullius in the sense of unoccupied or uninhabited for legal purposes and that full legal and beneficial ownership of all the lands of the Colony vested in the Crown, unaffected by any claims of Aboriginal inhabitants. Those propositions provided a legal basis for and justification of the dispossession. They constituted the legal context of the acts done to enforce it and, while accepted, rendered unlawful acts done by Aboriginal inhabitants to protect traditional occupation or use. The official endorsement, by administrative practice and in judgments of the courts, of those two propositions provided the environment in which the Aboriginal peoples of the continent came to be treated as a different and lower form of life whose very existence could be ignored for the purposes of determining the legal right to occupy and use their traditional homelands.[220]

Justice Brennan acknowledged that to state the common law in this way involves overruling cases that have held the contrary, but justified the Court's rejection of *terra nullius* on the grounds of racial discrimination:

> If it were permissible in past centuries to keep the common law in step with international law, it is imperative in today's world that the common law should neither be nor be seen to be frozen in an age of racial discrimination. ... Whatever the justification advanced in earlier days for refusing to recognize the rights and interests in land of the indigenous inhabitants of settled colonies, an unjust and discriminatory doctrine of that kind can no

---

219 *Ibid.* at 82-83. Compare to *Vermont v. Elliott*, 161 A.2d 210 (1992), which holds that at some point the weight of history overtakes, crushes, and obliterates Aboriginal claims; *Delgamuukw, supra* note 195, B.C. C.A. at 370, Lambert J., who maintained that extinguishing or eliminating Aboriginal title and rights by passage of time or weight of history is not part of the law of British Columbia and should be resolutely rejected.

220 *Mabo, ibid.* at 82.

longer be accepted. The expectations of the international community accord in this respect with the contemporary values of the Australian people. ... To maintain the authority of those cases would destroy the equality of all Australian citizens before the law. The common law of this country would perpetuate injustice if it were to continue to embrace the enlarged notion of terra nullius and to persist in characterising the indigenous inhabitants of the Australian colonies as people too low in the scale of social organization to be acknowledged as possessing rights and interests in land.[221]

In place of *terra nullius*, Justice Brennan asserted universal human rights of the International Covenant on Civil and Political Rights as controlling Australian law:[222]

> The opening up of international remedies to individuals pursuant to Australia's accession to the Optional Protocol to the International Covenant on Civil and Political Rights brings to bear on the common law the powerful influence of the Covenant and the international standards it imports. The common law does not necessarily conform with international law, but international law is a legitimate and important influence on the development of the common law, especially when international law declares the existence of universal human rights. A common law doctrine founded on unjust discrimination in the enjoyment of civil and political rights demands reconsideration. It is contrary both to international standards and to the fundamental values of our common law to entrench a discriminatory rule which, because of the supposed position on the scale of social organisation of the indigenous inhabitants of a settled colony, denies them a right to occupy their traditional lands.[223]

B. The "settled colony" in common law

In decolonizing the law, Australasian and Canadian scholarship has also rejected the legal fiction of settled colonies in the common law. British common law recognized only two types of sovereign title in England and territorial acquisition: descent and conquest.[224] As the classic common law transformed into the Victorian common law of

---

221   *Ibid.* at 28-29, 41, Brennan J.

222   *Ibid.* at 29. See United Nations, Human Rights Committee, *Selected Decisions of the Human Rights Committee under the Optional Protocol*, UNHRC, 1980, Communication No. 78, vol. 2 at 23 [hereinafter *Selected Decisions*]. Canada has acceded to the Optional Protocol. H. Kindred, *et al., International Law Chiefly as Interpreted and Applied in Canada*, 4th ed. (Toronto: Emond Montgomery, 1987) at 635-82. See generally *Lovelace v. Canada*, (1985), in *Selected Decisions, ibid.*, vol. 1 at 83; *Lubicon Lake Band [Ominiyak] v. Canada (1990)*, Human Rights Committee, *Annual Report*, UN GAOR, 45th Sess., Supp. No. 40, UN Doc. A/45/40., vol. 2, para. 32.1 at 27; *M'kmaq People v. Canada (1992)*, Human Rights Committee, *Annual Report*, UN GAOR, 47th Sess., Supp. No. 40, UN Doc. A/47/40. at 213; *R. L. et al. v. Canada (1992)*, Human Rights Committee, *Annual Report*, UN GAOR, 47th Sess., Supp. No. 40, UN Doc. A/47/40 at 366-74; see M. Turpel, "Indigenous Peoples' Right of Political Participation and Self-Determination: Recent International Legal Developments and the Continuing Struggle for Recognition" (1992) 25 Cornell Int'l L.J. 579.

223   *Mabo, ibid.*

224   *Calvin's Case* (1608), 7 Coke 1a, 77 E.R. 377 [hereinafter *Calvin's Case*]. For example, the issue in England was whether James I took his sovereign title by descent from Edward the Confessor or by the right of the conquest of William I. See J.Y. Henderson, "M'kmaw Tenure in Atlantic Canada" (1995) 18 Dal. L.J. 196 at 287-91; P.G. McHugh, "The Common Law Status of Colonies and 'Aboriginal rights': How Lawyers and Historians Treat the Past" (1998) 61 Sask. L. Rev. 287 at 393.

colonization,[225] these categories transformed into two distinct types of colonies: the "conquered or ceded" colonies and the "settled" colonies.[226] In a conquered colony, a legal presumption continued the pre-existing laws and property rights until the Crown altered them;[227] the same rule applied to ceded colonies, though the prerogative may have been limited by the treaty of cession.[228] A "settled" colony was regarded as desert, uninhabited land where English law applied automatically as a "birthright" of the Eng-

---

225   See Richard West, "Legal Opinion" in G. Chalmers, *Opinions of Eminent Lawyers, on various Points of English Jurisprudence, chiefly concerning the colonies, fisheries, and commerce of Great Britain*, vol. 2 (London: Reed & Hunter, 1814) at 200.

226   Blackstone, *supra* note 86, vol. 1, c. 4 at 106-108. He states that:

>   Plantations or colonies, in distant countries, are either such where the lands are claimed by right of occupancy only, by finding them desert and uncultivated, and peopling them from the mother-country; or where, when already cultivated, they have been either gained by conquest, or ceded to us by treaties. And both these rights are founded upon the law of nature, or at least upon that of nations. ... Our American plantations are principally of this latter sort, being obtained in the last century either by right of conquest and driving out the natives (with what natural justice I shall not at present inquire) or by treaties. And therefore the common law of England, as such, has no allowance or authority there; they being no part of the mother-country, but distinct (though dependent) dominions. They are subject, however, to the control of the parliament.

>   *Forbes v. Cochrane* (1824), 2 B. & C. 448 at 463, 107 E.R. 450 at 456.

227   *Blankard v. Galdy* (1693), Holt 341, 90 E.R. 1089 [hereinafter *Blankard*]; *Campbell v. Hall* (1774), 98 E.R. 848 at 895-96 [hereinafter *Campbell v. Hall*]; *Beaumont v. Barrett* (1836), 1 Moo. P.C. 59,12 E.R. 733. The Crown had a prerogative power to make new laws for a conquered country although that power was subject to laws enacted by the Imperial Parliament, *Campbell v. Hall, ibid.* at 895, 896. Lord Sumner, in *Re Southern Rhodesia*, [1919] A.C. 211 at 233 (P.C.) [hereinafter *Re Southern Rhodesia*], understood "the survival of private proprietary rights on conquest to be that, ... it is to be presumed, in the absence of express confiscation or of subsequent expropriatory legislation, that the conqueror has respected them and forborne to diminish or modify them." This view accords with the old authorities, such as *The Case of Tanistry* (1608), Davis 28, 80 E.R. 516; *Witrong and Blany* (1973), 130 C.L.R. at 397 [hereinafter *Witrong*]; see also the Indian title in Ontario under the *Royal Proclamation of 1763, supra* note 112; *St. Catherine's, supra* note 187.

228   See the discussion in Sir K. Roberts-Wray, *Commonwealth and Colonial Law* (New York: Frederick A. Praeger, 1966) at 214; *Sammut v. Strickland*, [1938] A.C. 678 (P.C.) [hereinafter *Sammut*]; *Blankard, ibid.* Viscount Haldane, in *Amodu Tijani v. Southern Nigeria (Secretary)*, [1921] 2 A.C. 399 (P.C.) at 407 [hereinafter *Amodu Tijani*]: "A mere change in sovereignty is not to be presumed as meant to disturb rights of private owners; and the general terms of a cession are prima facie to be construed accordingly." Contrary to his judgment in *Vajesingji Joravarsingji*, Viscount Dunedin subsequently accepted in *Sakariyawo Oshodi v. Moriamo Dakolo*, [1930] A.C. 667 [hereinafter *Oshodi*], that the decision in *Amodu Tijani* laid down that the cession of Lagos in 1861, "did not affect the character of the private native rights," at 668. Lord Denning, speaking for the Privy Council in *Adeyinka Oyekan v. Musendiku Adele*, [1957] 2 All E.R. 785 (P.C.) at 788 [hereinafter *Adele*]:

>   In inquiring ... what rights are recognized, there is one guiding principle. It is this: The courts will assume that the British Crown intends that the rights of property of the inhabitants are to be fully respected. Whilst, therefore, the British Crown, as Sovereign, can make laws enabling it compulsorily to acquire land for public purposes, it will see that proper compensation is awarded to every one of the inhabitants who has by native law an interest in it: and the courts will declare the inhabitants entitled to compensation according to their interests, even though those interests are of a kind unknown to English law.

lish colonizers.[229] If the local law in the foreign territories was unsuitable for Christian Europeans, the Victorian common law held that British colonizers were regarded as living under the law of England,[230] and that the law was not amenable to alteration by exercise of the prerogative[231] but only by the imperial Parliament or by the local legislature.[232]

Once a colonizer acknowledged that a foreign territory was inhabited by Aboriginal peoples, the idea of a settled colony was not applicable and courts had to establish the nature and incidents of Aboriginal tenure and rights. To acquire their common law birthrights in inhabited colonies, the colonizers began to argue to the colonial office that for a territory inhabited by "savages" their savage laws were unsuitable. Also to receive the benefits of British law, the colonizers associated Aboriginal peoples on the land with uninhabited or practically unoccupied lands.[233] Lawyers argued that such designations had legal consequences for tenure, law, and rights of the Aboriginal peoples.

Justice Brennan outlined the relationship between the savage-civilization dualism, *terra nullius,* and the common law in the courts:

> When British colonists went out to other inhabited parts of the world, including New South Wales, and settled there under the protection of the forces of the Crown, so that the Crown acquired sovereignty recognised by the European family of nations under the enlarged notion of terra nullius, it was necessary for the common law to prescribe a doctrine relating to the law to be applied in such colonies, for sovereignty imports supreme internal legal authority. The view was taken that, when sovereignty of a territory could be acquired under the enlarged notion of terra nullius, for the purposes of the municipal law that territory (though inhabited) could be treated as a "desert uninhabited" country. The hypothesis being that there was no local law already in existence in the territory, the law of England became the law of the territory (and not merely the personal law of the colonists). Colonies of this kind were called "settled colonies". Ex hypothesi, the indigenous inhabitants of a settled colony had no recognised sovereign, else the territory could

---

229 Blackstone, *supra* note 86, vol. 1, c. 4 at 107. For an evolution of the distinction see McHugh, *supra* note 224 at 402-429; Roberts-Wray, *ibid.* at 625-36; K. McNeil, *Common Law Aboriginal Title* (Oxford: Clarendon Press, 1989) at 108-192.

230 *Ruding v. Smith* (1821), 2 Hag. Con. 371, 161 E.R. 774; *Freeman v. Fairlie* (1828), 1 Moo. Ind. App. 306 at 323-25, affirming 18 E.R. 117 at 127-28, 137 [hereinafter *Freeman*]; cf. *Campbell v. Hall, supra* note 227 at 895-96. See also *Yeap Cheah Neo v. Ong Cheng Neo* (1875), 6 L.R. 381 at 393; *R. v. Willans* (1858), 3 Kyshe 16 at 20-25; *Re Loh Toh Met* (1961), 27 M.L.J. 234 at 237-43; and *Khoo Hooi Leong v. Khoo Chong Yeok,* [1930] A.C. 346 at 355. This rule was applied even to English residents in Oriental countries not under British sovereignty: *The "Indian Chief"* (1801), 165 E.R. 367 at 373-74.

231 *Sammut, supra* note 228.

232 *Ibid.*; Sir. W.S. Holdsworth, *A History of English Law,* vol. 9, 3d ed. (London: Methuen, 1944) at 84; *Kielley v. Carson* (1843), 4 Moo. P.C. at 84-85, 13 E.R. 233; *Falkland Islands Co. v. The Queen* (1863), 2 Moo. P.C. (N.S.) 266 at 273, 15 E.R. 902; *Sabally and N'Jie v. H.M. Attorney-General,* [1965] 1 Q.B. 294.

233 "The Resolution of 1722 (October 25)" in St. G.I. Sioussat, ed., *The English Statutes in Maryland* (Baltimore: Johns Hopkins Press, 1903), App. 1 at 73 and 744; *Freeman, supra* note 230 at 324-25, Stephen J.; *Cooper v. Stuart* (1889), 14 A.C. 286 at 291, Lord Watson. He held that British law must apply to British colonizers in the Colony of New South Wales.

have been acquired only by conquest or cession. The indigenous people of a settled colony were thus taken to be without laws, without a sovereign and primitive in their social organisation.[234]

In 1919, the judicial committee in *Re Southern Rhodesia*[235] had articulated these premises into the Victorian common law of colonization. It held that before the arrival of the British colonizers no law or no sovereign law-maker existed in the territory.[236] Speaking for the judicial committee, Lord Sumner expressed the problems of reconciling the savage-civilization dualism:

> The estimation of the rights of aboriginal tribes is always inherently difficult. Some tribes are so low in the scale of social organization that their usages and conceptions of rights and duties are not to be reconciled with the institutions or the legal ideas of civilized society. Such a gulf cannot be bridged. It would be idle to impute to such people some shadow of the rights known to our law and then to transmute it into the substance of transferable rights of property as we know them.[237]

Their Lordships articulated the "fatal inconsistency" between recognizing Aboriginal tenure and rights and the purposes of colonization:

> the maintenance of their rights was fatally inconsistent with white settlement of the country, and yet white settlement was the object of the whole forward movement, pioneered by the Company and controlled by the Crown, and that object was successfully accomplished, with the result that the aboriginal system gave place to another prescribed by the Order in Council.[238]

This decision articulated the premise of "white supremacy" and "progress" as legal principles in Victorian colonization.

In *Mabo*, the Solicitor-General of Queensland argued the "general" principle that the Murray Islands were acquired as a "settled" colony by British colonizers because territory was not acquired by the sovereign from the Meriam people by conquest or cession. When the territory of a settled colony became part of the Crown's dominions, the law of England so far as applicable to colonial conditions became the law of the colony. The Solicitor-General argued that the law of England became not merely the personal law of the English colonizers; it also became the law of the land, protecting and binding colonizers and Indigenous inhabitants alike. The common law was the common law of all "subjects" within the Colony, who were equally entitled to the law's protection as subjects of the Crown.

---

234 *Mabo, supra* note 209 at 24, Brennan J.

235 *Re Southern Rhodesia, supra* note 227 at 233. Compare to *Amodu Tijani, supra* note 228, in which the judicial committee admitted the possibility of recognition not only of usufructuary rights, but also of interests in land vested in a community rather than an individual or set of individuals.

236 The judicial committee rejected an argument that the Aboriginal people: "were the owners of the unalienated lands long before either the Company or the Crown became concerned with them and from time immemorial ... and that the unalienated lands belonged to them still."

237 *Re Southern Rhodesia, supra* note 227 at 233-34.

238 *Ibid.* at 234.

The High Court in *Mabo* reconciled Crown sovereignty with Aboriginal tenure. It asserted that bringing the common law to Australia did not deprive Aboriginal peoples of their pre-existing tenures. Sovereignty is a concept of public international law that may give an ultimate or radical title to the Crown over a territory, but it is subject to the pre-existing Aboriginal tenure and its uses and occupations. The right to possess and use the land in a colony is governed by British common law, and it is also subject to the existing Aboriginal tenure and its possession and uses.

Similar to Justice Hall and Chief Justice Dickson, Justice Brennan rejected the "barbarian" theory supporting the fiction of a settled colony:

> It would be a curious doctrine to propound today that, when the benefit of the common law was first extended to Her Majesty's indigenous subjects in the Antipodes, its first fruits were to strip them of their right to occupy their ancestral lands. Yet the supposedly barbarian nature of the indigenous people provided the common law of England with the justification for denying them their traditional rights and interests in land ... . As the Indigenous inhabitants of the settled colony were regarded as "low in the scale of social organisation", they and their occupancy of colonial land were ignored in considering the title to land in a settled colony. Ignoring those rights and interests, the Crown's sovereignty over a territory which had been acquired under the enlarged notion of terra nullius was equated with Crown ownership of the lands therein, because, as Stephen C.J. said, there was "no other proprietor of such lands". Thus, a Select Committee on Aborigines reported in 1837 to the House of Commons that the state of Australian Aborigines was "barbarous" and "so entirely destitute ... of the rudest forms of civil polity, that their claims, whether as sovereigns or proprietors of the soil, have been utterly disregarded." The theory that the indigenous inhabitants of a "settled" colony had no proprietary interest in the land thus depended on a discriminatory denigration of Indigenous inhabitants, their social organisation and customs.[239]

Justice Brennan revealed the modern judicial choices required by the false theories of the past:

> As the basis of the theory is false in fact and unacceptable in our society, there is a choice of legal principle to be made in the present case. This Court can either apply the existing authorities and proceed to inquire whether the Meriam people are higher "in the scale of social organisation" than the Australian Aboriginals whose claims were "utterly disregarded" by the existing authorities or the Court can overrule the existing authorities, discarding the distinction between inhabited colonies that were terra nullius and those which were not. ... If the international law notion that inhabited land may be classified as terra nullius no longer commands general support, the doctrines of the common law which depend on the notion that Native peoples may be "so low in the scale of social organisation" that it is "idle to impute to such people some shadow of the rights known to our law" can hardly be retained.[240]

In choosing to decolonize the existing precedents and eliminate racial discrimination from the common law, Justice Brennan concluded: "The fiction by which the rights and

---

239   *Mabo, supra* note 209 at 26-27.

240   *Ibid.* at 27-28.

interests of Indigenous inhabitants in land were treated as non-existent was justified by
a policy which has no place in the contemporary law of this country."[241] He addressed
the High Court's judicial responsibility and its ability to modify the peace and order of
Australian society to make it a more just order and to enforce human rights:

> In discharging its duty to declare the common law of Australia, this Court is not free to
> adopt rules that accord with contemporary notions of justice and human rights if their
> adoption would fracture the skeleton of principle which gives the body of our law its shape
> and internal consistency. Australian law is not only the historical successor of, but is an
> organic development from, the law of England. Although our law is the prisoner of its his-
> tory, it is not now bound by decisions of courts in the hierarchy of an Empire then con-
> cerned with the development of its colonies. ... [S]ince the *Australia Act* 1986 (Cth) came
> into operation, the law of this country is entirely free of Imperial control. The law which
> governs Australia is Australian law. The Privy Council itself held that the common law of
> this country might legitimately develop independently of English precedent. Increasingly
> since 1968, the common law of Australia has been substantially in the hands of this court.
> Here rests the ultimate responsibility of declaring the law of the nation. Although this
> court is free to depart from English precedent which was earlier followed as stating the
> common law of this country, it cannot do so where the departure would fracture what I
> have called the skeleton of principle. The court is even more reluctant to depart from ear-
> lier decisions of its own. The peace and order of Australian society is built on the legal
> system. It can be modified to bring it into conformity with contemporary notions of jus-
> tice and human rights, but it cannot be destroyed. It is not possible, a priori, to distinguish
> between cases that express a skeletal principle and those which do not, but no case can
> command unquestioning adherence if the rule it expresses seriously offends the values of
> justice and human rights (especially equality before the law) which are aspirations of the
> contemporary Australian legal system. If a postulated rule of the common law expressed
> in earlier cases seriously offends those contemporary values, the question arises whether
> the rule should be maintained and applied. Whenever such a question arises, it is neces-
> sary to assess whether the particular rule is an essential doctrine of our legal system and
> whether, if the rule were to be overturned, the disturbance to be apprehended would be
> disproportionate to the benefit flowing from the overturning.[242]

As had Justice Hall, Justice Brennan rejected the application of the legal fiction
of the settled colony over present knowledge and appreciation of Aboriginal law and
life.[243] He rejected an earlier holding that it was beyond judicial authority to set aside
the legal fictions by characterizing them as a question of law, rather than questions of
fact.[244] The settled colony category was valid only between the relations of the Crown

---

241 *Ibid.* at 28.

242 *Ibid.* at 18-19.

243 *Ibid.*

244 *Ibid.* at 145, reversing *Milirrpum v. Nabalco Pty. Ltd.* (1971), 17 F.L.R. 141, Blackburn J. The earlier
     holding specifically rejected the assumptions of the judicial committee on the questions of law about
     the settled colony of New South Wales and the factual evidence that "shows a subtle and elaborate sys-
     tem highly adapted to the country in which the [Aboriginal] people led their lives, which provided a
     stable order of society and was remarkably free from the vagaries of personal whim or influence. If ever
     a system could be called, 'a government of laws, and not of men'," at 267.

to the British colonizers, and Justice Brennan rejected the validity of the settler colony category as extinguishing Aboriginal law and tenure.

C. Aboriginal tenure and rights in civil law or common law

Related to the settled colony fiction is the assumption that all valid titles or interests in foreign territories must be evidenced by Crown grants. In *Mabo*, the High Court confronted the submission that while the classical common law recognized the Aboriginal possession in British colonies, the Victorian common law governing colonization abolished pre-existing customary rights and interests in land except as expressly recognized by the new sovereign.[245] The High Court found the treaty cession cases of colonized India were not controlling, and were not in accord with the weight of authority.[246] In terms of conquest, pre-existing rights are "presumed, in the absence of express confiscation or of subsequent expropriatory legislation, that the conqueror has respected them and forborne to diminish or modify them."[247] In terms of a treaty cession, any "change in sovereignty is not to be presumed as meant to disturb rights of private owners; and the general terms of a cession are prima facie to be construed accordingly."[248] Lord Denning, speaking for the judicial committee in *Adeyinka Oyekan v. Musendiku Adele*,[249] summarized the controlling principle:

> The courts will assume that the British Crown intends that the rights of property of the inhabitants are to be fully respected. Whilst, therefore, the British Crown, as Sovereign, can make laws enabling it compulsorily to acquire land for public purposes, it will see that proper compensation is awarded to every one of the inhabitants who has by native law an interest in it; and the courts will declare the inhabitants entitled to compensation according to their interests, even though those interests are of a kind unknown to English law...[250]

Justice Brennan acknowledged that to state the common law principles in this way involved overruling cases that held the contrary, but asserted it was necessary to sus-

---

245 These questions arise in the context of a treaty cession where the recognition by the sovereign of pre-existing rights and interests possessed under the old regime was a condition of their recognition by the common law. If not, the pre-existing rights are lost. See *Secretary of State for India v. Bai Rajbai*, [1915] L.R. 42, Ind. App. 229 at 237, 238-39; *Vajesingji Joravarsingji v. Secretary of State for India*, [1924] L.R. 51, Ind. App. 357 at 360-361; *Secretary of State for India v. Sardar Rustam Khan*, [1941] A.C. 356 at 370-372; *Amodu Tijani, supra* note 228 at 407; *Oshodi, supra* note 228 at 668. This principle explains why the Victorian treaties expressly recognized the Chiefs' authority over all ceded territories in the peace and good order provisions.

246 *Mabo, supra* note 209 at 38-40.

247 *Ibid.* at 40, citing Lord Sumner in *Re Southern Rhodesia*. This view accords with the old authorities of *The Case of Tanistry, supra* note 227; *Witrong, supra* note 227; *Re Southern Rhodesia, supra* note 227.

248 *Mabo, ibid.* See also *Amodu Tijani, supra* note 228 at 407; *Sobhuza II. v. Miller*, [1926] A.C. at 525, in which the usufructuary title of an Indigenous community, which their Lordships thought to be generally usufructuary, was held to survive as a burden on the radical or ultimate title of sovereign; *Calder, supra* note 185 at 416, and Judson J. in dissent on this point at 156, 157.

249 *Supra* note 228.

250 *Ibid.* at 788; *Mabo, supra* note 209 at 40.

tain the equality of all Australian citizens before the law.[251] He declared the preferable rule was that a mere change in sovereignty does not extinguish Aboriginal tenure; accepting that "the antecedent rights and interests in land possessed by the Indigenous inhabitants of the territory survived the change in sovereignty. Those antecedent rights and interests thus constitute a burden on the radical title of the Crown."[252]

Justice Brennan explained that if the Crown by prerogative law in a foreign territory confiscated private property as an act of State[253] or if it extinguished private property,[254] no judicial recognition of the pre-existing rights and interests would be possible; but in these situations, the loss of the pre-existing rights or interests was attributable to the clear and plain wording of the sovereign, not to an absence of an act of recognition of those pre-existing rights or interests.[255] Neither the acquisition of sovereignty nor the transfer of beneficial ownership to the Crown nor the reception and operations of the common law dispossessed the Indigenous inhabitants of their title.[256]

In *Adams*[257] and in *Côté*[258] the Supreme Court of Canada held that Aboriginal tenure needs no recognition in civil law or British common or positive law, since it was a manifestation of a pre-existing Aboriginal legal order. Because Aboriginal tenure is a land tenure system distinct from British tenure, it needs no external recognition of its existence or its exercise. The Supreme Court of Canada relied on Professor Slattery's understanding of the doctrine of Aboriginal rights:

> The doctrine of aboriginal rights, like other doctrines of colonial law, applied automatically to a new colony when the colony was acquired. In the same way that colonial law determined whether a colony was deemed to be "settled" or "conquered", and whether English law was automatically introduced or local laws retained, it also supplied the presumptive legal structure governing the position of native peoples. The doctrine of aboriginal rights applied, then, to every British colony that now forms part of Canada, from Newfoundland to British Columbia. Although the doctrine was a species of unwritten British law, it was not part of English common law in the narrow sense, and its application to a colony did not depend on whether or not English common law was introduced there. Rather the doctrine was part of a body of fundamental constitutional law that was logically prior to the introduction of English common law and governed its application in the colony.[259]

---

251 *Mabo, ibid.* at 41.

252 *Ibid.*

253 *Ibid.* See also *Secretary of State in Council of India v. Kamachee Boye Sahaba* (1859), 7 Moo. Ind. App. 476, 19 E.R. 388; but *Attorney-General v. Nissan*, [1970] A.C. 179 (U.K. H.L.) at 227, and *Burma Oil Co. Ltd. v. Lord Advocate* (1964), [1965] A.C. 75 (U.K. H.L.) disagree.

254 *Mabo, ibid.* See also *Winfat Ltd. v. Attorney-General*, [1985] A.C. 733.

255 *Mabo, ibid.* at 50.

256 *Ibid* at 42, 50.

257 *R. v. Adams*, [1996] 3 S.C.R. 101 (S.C.C.) [hereinafter *Adams*].

258 *R. v. Côté*, [1996] 3 S.C.R. 139 [hereinafter *Côté*].

259 *Ibid.* at para. 49, citing Slattery, "Understanding Aboriginal Rights," *supra* note 191 at 737-38.

In *Roberts v. Canada*,[260] the Court held that the law of Aboriginal tenure represents a distinct legal source in the federal common law rather than a subset of the common or civil law of property law.

In *Delgamuukw*, Chief Justice Lamer held that Aboriginal tenure and rights are independent sources of constitutional law and are both constitutional and legal rights. Section 35(1) constitutionalized "existing" common law rights: "Since aboriginal title was a common law right whose existence was recognized well before 1982 (e.g., *Calder, supra*), s. 35(1) has constitutionalized it in its full form."[261] The source of Aboriginal title is both Aboriginal law and prior occupation of the continent by Aboriginal nations, tribes, and peoples. Chief Justice Lamer in *Delgamuukw* declared that prior occupation is relevant in two different ways: first, because of the physical fact of occupation, and second, because aboriginal title originates in part from pre-existing systems of aboriginal law.[262]

D. French colonial law and Aboriginal tenure and rights

In *Côté* and in *Adams*, the Supreme Court of Canada was faced with decolonizing French colonization and its law in relation to British colonization and Aboriginal tenure and rights. In *Côté*, the members of the Algonquin nation, who were on an expedition to teach traditional fishing methods located within the appellants' traditional hunting and fishing grounds, were convicted under Quebec's *Regulation respecting controlled zones* of entering a controlled harvest zone (Z.E.C.) without paying the required fee for motor vehicle access. Franck Côté was also convicted under the *Quebec Fishery Regulations* of fishing within the zone without a valid licence. The Superior Court and the Court of Appeal upheld the convictions. The Algonquins challenged their convictions on the basis that they were exercising an Aboriginal right and a concurrent treaty right to fish on their ancestral lands under the 1769 Treaty at Swegatchy as recognized and protected by section 35(1) of the *Constitution Act, 1982*. The Court of Appeal had held that the appellants enjoyed a treaty right to fish under the 1769 Treaty.

The Supreme Court addressed three questions: (1) whether an Aboriginal fishing or other right must be necessarily incident to a claim of Aboriginal tenure, or whether Aboriginal rights exist independently of a claim of Aboriginal title; (2) whether the constitutional protection of section 35(1) extends to Aboriginal practices, customs, and traditions that may not have achieved legal recognition under the colonial regime of

---

260 [1989] 1 S.C.R. 322 (S.C.C.) at 340. See the views of the common law in Canada, *Partners in Confederation: Aboriginal Peoples, Self-Government and the Constitution* (Ottawa: Minister of Supply and Services, 1993) at 20.

261 *Delgamuukw, supra* note 195 at para. 133.

262 *Ibid.* at paras. 114, 126. Compare to *Mabo, supra* note 209 at 58, in which Brennan J., writing the principal majority judgment, said: "Native title has its origin in and is given its content by the traditional laws acknowledged by and the traditional customs observed by the indigenous inhabitants of a territory. The nature and incidents of native title must be ascertained as a matter of fact by reference to those laws and customs"; see also Deane and Gaudron JJ. at 87-88, 110; compare to Toohey J. at 187-92.

New France prior to the commencement of British sovereignty in 1763; and (3) whether a provincial regulation was of no force or effect because it infringed a treaty right to fish.

In *Adams*, a Mohawk was similarly charged with fishing without a licence in Lake St. Francis in the St. Régis region of Quebec contrary to *Quebec Fishery Regulations*. George Adams was convicted at trial; the Quebec Superior Court and Quebec Court of Appeal upheld the conviction. He asserted *Quebec Fishery Regulations* were of no force and effect to his Aboriginal rights by virtue of sections 52 and 35(1) of the *Constitution Act, 1982*. Similar to *Côté*, the Court of Appeal held the regulations infringed the appellant's Aboriginal right to fish for food.

Chief Justice Lamer speaking for a unified Court in both decisions dismissed their convictions,[263] holding the Aboriginal peoples involved were not obliged to prove Aboriginal tenure or title over the Z.E.C. as a precondition to demonstrating the existence of an ancestral right to fish. Aboriginal rights exist independent of Aboriginal tenure, Aboriginal tenure being a manifestation of Aboriginal rights. The Court held that the constitutional entrenchment and recognition of those Aboriginal rights—those practices, customs, and traditions central to the distinctive culture of pre-existing Aboriginal societies—were not limited to continuous and historical occupation of a specific tract of land, and may have an important link to the land. However, the Court declared Aboriginal rights were site-specific: depending on activity prior to contact, they can be limited to a specific territory or site; and they can be exercised on a specific tract of land. The substantive claims in these cases were characterized as a "site-specific right to fish for food" and that that right included the incidental right to teach Aboriginal customs and traditions to a younger generation to ensure the cultural continuity. The Court held that *Quebec Fishery Regulations* unjustifiably infringed on the Aboriginal right to fish.

Also in both cases, Chief Justice Lamer rejected the Quebec Attorney General's claim that the Algonquin or Mohawk nations could not assert the existence of Aboriginal tenure within the former boundaries of New France because of French colonial law and the legal transition to British sovereignty following military conquest. In rejecting the claim, Chief Justice Lamer relied on the purposes of section 35(1) of the *Constitution Act, 1982*.

The Attorney General of Quebec asserted that the French Crown in its "*Ancien Regime*" and colonial law did not legally recognize any pre-existing Aboriginal inter-

---

263 *Delgamuukw, ibid.* Chief Justice Lamer spoke for Sopinka, Gonthier, Cory, McLachlin, Iacobucci and Major JJ. La Forest J. agreed that even though the Aboriginals have no Aboriginal tenure, these traditional rights to fish by natives were Aboriginal rights, characterizing the Aboriginal fishing rights as a constitutional "servitude." L'Heureux-Dubé J. agreed with the reasons of Lamer C.J., subject to her concurring comments made in *Adams, supra* note 257. In *Adams*, Lamer spoke for La Forest, Sopinka, Gonthier, Cory, McLachlin, Iacobucci and Major JJ., with L'Heureux-Dubé J. concurring that Aboriginal rights can be incidental to Aboriginal title but need not be; they are severable from and can exist independently of Aboriginal title. She stated that the strict conditions for recognizing Aboriginal title at common law are not applicable when an appellant seeks not the broadest right to occupy and use a tract of land, but only the limited right to fish upon it.

est in land upon discovery; instead the French Crown assumed full ownership of all discovered lands by symbolic possession and conquest. Accordingly, French colonizers
never engaged in the consistent practice of the British Crown of negotiating treaty cessions or formal territorial surrenders with the Aboriginal peoples.[264] Within France's
former colonial possessions in Canada, the Attorney General argued that the colonial
law did not recognize the existence of an Aboriginal tenure or *sui generis* interest in
land:

> The effects of French sovereignty and of the legal system specific thereto are therefore
> clear: *no aboriginal right could have survived the assertion of French sovereignty over the
> territory of New France.*[265]

He argued that the toleration of the French Crown toward Aboriginal activities, such as
hunting and fishing, represented a "general liberty" accorded to all of the King's subjects, rather than the recognition of a special right enjoyed by Aboriginal peoples.[266]
Furthermore, the Attorney General argued that following capitulation to the British
Crown, pre-existing French colonial law was fully received under the terms of *The
Quebec Act*,[267] and under the general principles of the British law of conquest according to *Campbell v. Hall.*[268] In the absence of a formal renunciation of the French colonial system, the British common law "incorporated the non-existence of aboriginal
rights within New France in its doctrine of aboriginal title."[269]

In rejecting these arguments, the Court noted that in public international law, the
French Crown in its diplomatic relations and practices following the 1713 *Treaty of
Utrecht* maintained that Aboriginal peoples were sovereign nations rather than mere

---

264 G.F.G. Stanley, "The First Indian 'Reserves' in Canada" (1958) 4 Revue de L'Histoire de l'Amérique
     Française 179 at 209-10, initially summarized this perspective. He states:

> [a]t no time was there any recognition on the part of the French crown of any aboriginal proprietary
> rights in the soil. The French settler occupied his lands in Canada without any thought of compen-
> sating the native. There were no formal surrenders from the Indians, no negotiations, and no treaties
> such as marked the Indian policy of the British period. The lands which were set aside for the Indi-
> ans were granted not of right but of grace, ... whatever rights the Indians acquired flowed not from
> a theoretical aboriginal title but from the clemency of the Crown or the charity of individuals.

     Henri Brun, "Les droits des Indiens sur le territoire du Québec" (1969) 10 C. de D. 415 at 428-30,
     affirmed this construction; Henri Brun, *Le territoire du Québec: six études juridiques* (Québec: Les
     Presses de L'Université de Laval, 1974) at 64; reaffirmed by L. C. Green, *The Law of Nations and the
     New World* (Edmonton: University of Alberta Press, 1989) at 223.

265 *Côté, supra* note 258 at para. 42.

266 *Ibid.* at para. 44.

267 *Quebec Act, 1774*, R.S.C. 1985, App. II, No. 2.

268 See *Campbell v. Hall, supra* note 227 at 1047-48; *Sammut, supra* note 228; compare with *The Queen
     v. Secretary of State for Foreign and Commonwealth Affairs, ex rel. Indian Association of Alberta,
     Union of New Brunswick Indians, Union of Nova Scotia Indians*, [1982] 2 All E.R. 118, [1981] 4
     C.N.L.R. 86 (Eng. C.A.), Lord Denning M.R. [hereinafter *Secretary of State* cited to C.N.L.R.].

269 *Côté, supra* note 258 at para. 45.

subjects of the monarch,[270] and maintained that they could not cede title to lands occupied by Aboriginal peoples in the Maritimes as such peoples were independent nations allied with the French Crown, rather than mere royal subjects.

The Court was not persuaded that the status of Aboriginal peoples in French colonial law or the scope of colonial law was as clear as the Attorney General submitted,[271] since modern legal historians and historians have argued that the French Crown only assumed "ownership" of the lands lining the St. Lawrence River that it actually occupied and organized under its seigneurial land tenure system.[272] Furthermore, even if the Attorney General's characterization of French colonial system was accurate, the Court determined it was doubtful that French colonial law governing relations with Aboriginal peoples was mechanically received by the common law upon the commencement of British sovereignty:

> It is true that under *The Quebec Act, 1774*, and under the legal principles of British conquest, the pre-existing laws governing the acquired territory of New France were received and continued in the absence of subsequent legislative modification. It is by these legal means that the distinct civilian system of private law continues to operate and thrive within the modern boundaries of the province of Quebec. But while the new British regime received and continued the former system of colonial law governing the proprietary relations between private individuals, it is less clear that the advent of British sovereignty continued the French system of law governing the relations between the British Crown and indigenous societies. In short, the common law recognizing aboriginal title was arguably a necessary incident of British sovereignty which displaced the pre-existing colonial law governing New France.[273]

Chief Justice Lamer noted that the Attorney General's view, if adopted, "would create an awkward patchwork of constitutional protection for aboriginal rights across the nation, depending upon the historical idiosyncrasies of colonialization over particular regions of the country."[274] Relying on Justice Brennan's reasoning in *Mabo* that colo-

---

270 *Ibid.* at para. 48. See P.A. Cumming and N.H. Mickenberg, *Native Rights in Canada*, 2d ed. (Toronto: General Publishing Ltd., 1972) at 81-83, 96-98. The French Crown disavowed responsibility for Indian attacks on the British, on the grounds that Aboriginal nations were independent allies of the French monarch rather than his royal subjects. See R.O. MacFarlane, "British Indian Policy in Nova Scotia to 1760" (1938) 19 Can. Hist. Rev. 154 at 160-161; W.S. MacNutt, *The Atlantic Provinces: 1712-1857* (Toronto: McClelland & Stewart, 1965) at 29-30; G.F.G. Stanley, *New France: The Last Phase, 1744-1760* (Toronto: McClelland & Stewart, 1965) at 80-85.

271 *Côté, ibid.* at para. 46.

272 *Ibid.* at para. 47 See generally Slattery, "Understanding Aboriginal Rights," *supra* note 191 at 768-69; B. Slattery, "Did France Claim Canada upon Discovery?" in J. M. Bumsted, ed., *Interpreting Canada's Past*, vol. 1 (Toronto: Oxford University Press, 1986) at 2-26; Cumming & Mickenberg, *supra* note 270 at 83-84; and Richard Boivin, "Le droit des autochtones sur le territoire québécois et les effets du régime français" (1995) 55 R. du B. 135 at 156-60. Also, for the historian's interpretation, see W.J. Eccles, "Sovereignty-Association, 1500-1783" (1984) 65 Can. Hist. Rev. 475 at 480-487; C.J. Jaenen, "French Sovereignty and Native Nationhood during the French Regime" in J. R. Miller, ed., *Sweet Promises: A Reader on Indian-White Relations in Canada* (Toronto: University of Toronto Press, 1991) at 20.

273 *Côté, ibid.* at para. 49.

274 *Ibid.* at para. 53.

nial law's justification for refusing to recognize the Aboriginal tenure, rights, and interests was unjust and discriminatory, the Court rejected the Quebec submission.[275]

Rather than affirming French colonial law as British colonial law, Chief Justice Lamer's decision relied on the terms and purpose of the constitutional enactment of section 35(1):

> I do not believe that the intervention of French sovereignty negated the potential existence of aboriginal rights within the former boundaries of New France under s. 35(1) [of the *Constitution Act, 1982*]. The entrenchment of aboriginal ancestral and treaty rights in s. 35(1) has changed the landscape of aboriginal rights in Canada. As explained in the *Van der Peet* trilogy, the purpose of s. 35(1) was to extend constitutional protection to the practices, customs and traditions central to the distinctive culture of aboriginal societies prior to contact with Europeans. If such practices, customs and traditions continued following contact in the absence of specific extinguishment, such practices, customs and traditions are entitled to constitutional recognition subject to the infringement and justification tests outlined in *Sparrow, supra* and *Gladstone, supra*.
>
> As such, the fact that a particular practice, custom or tradition continued, in an unextinguished manner, following the arrival of Europeans *but* in the absence of the formal gloss of legal recognition from French colonial law should not undermine the constitutional protection accorded to aboriginal peoples. Section 35(1) would fail to achieve its noble purpose of preserving the integral and defining features of distinctive aboriginal societies if it only protected those defining features which were fortunate enough to have received the legal recognition and approval of European colonizers. I should stress that the French Regime's failure to recognize legally a specific aboriginal practice, custom or tradition (and indeed the French Regime's tacit toleration of a specific practice, custom or tradition) clearly cannot be equated with a "clear and plain" intention to extinguish such practices under the extinguishment test of s. 35(1).[276]

Chief Justice Lamer declared the Quebec perspective of Aboriginal rights "cannot be reconciled with the noble and prospective purpose of the constitutional entrenchment of aboriginal and treaty rights in the *Constitution Act, 1982*."[277] He held that the Attorney General's argument:

> risks undermining the very purpose of s. 35(1) by perpetuating the historical injustice suffered by aboriginal peoples at the hands of colonizers who failed to respect the distinctive cultures of pre-existing aboriginal societies ... Therefore, even on the assumption that the French Crown did not legally recognize the right of the Algonquins to fish within the Z.E.C. prior to the commencement of British sovereignty, it remains open to the appellants to establish that they enjoyed an aboriginal right to fish within the Z.E.C. under the principles of *Van der Peet, Gladstone*, and *N.T.C. Smokehouse Ltd.*[278]

---

275 *Ibid.* See also *Mabo, supra* note 209 at 42.

276 *Côté, ibid.* at paras. 51-52.

277 *Ibid.* at para. 53.

278 *Ibid.* at para. 54.

E. Statutory acts or regulations and Aboriginal tenure and right

In another decolonizing strategy, the Supreme Court in *Sparrow* rejected the Crown's arguments that Aboriginal rights can be extinguished by federal Acts or regulations; instead it stated that historical statutory or regulatory control of an Aboriginal right does not mean that the right is extinguished, even if the control is exercised in "great detail."[279] As in *Mabo*, the Court stated that the sovereign's intention is controlling and extinguishment of Aboriginal rights could only be proven if the sovereign's written command is clear and plain.[280] This analysis underscored the necessity of constitutional principles of interpretation regarding existing Aboriginal rights under section 35(1).[281] It interpreted "existing" Aboriginal rights as unextinguished, and interpreted them with flexibility to permit their evolution over time.[282]

F. The theory of universal and absolute Crown ownership

In *Mabo*, the Meriam people accepted the idea that the Crown assumed a "radical or ultimate" title to the Murray Islands by the 1878 annexation by prerogative laws, but challenged the conclusion that the Crown acquired "absolute beneficial ownership" of the land in the Murray Islands when it acquired sovereignty. The Solicitor-General of Queensland argued that in a settled colony the Crown assumed the absolute beneficial ownership of all land in the territory so that the colony became the Crown's demesne and no right or interest in any land in the territory could thereafter be possessed by any other person unless granted by the Crown.[283] The Solicitor-General argued that these general principles of colonization law were controlling of the case,

---

279 *Sparrow, supra* note 183 at 1095-1101, 1111-19. *Denny v. The Queen*, 94 N.S.R. (2d) 253 at 263, [1990] 2 C.N.L.R. 115 (N.S. C.A.), affirmed the Aboriginal right to fish for food strictly on a constitutional interpretation of s. 35(1) of the *Constitution Act, 1982*, and independent of the force and effect of the terms of the M'kmaq treaties; *Constitution Act, 1982*, being Schedule B to the *Canada Act 1982* (U.K.), 1982, c. 11, s. 35(1). They stated: "based upon the decision in *Isaac*, this [Aboriginal] right has not been extinguished through treaty, other agreements or competent legislation. Given the conclusion that the appellants possess an aboriginal right to fish for food in the relevant waters, it is not necessary to determine whether the appellants have a right to fish protected by treaty" (at 263).

280 *Sparrow, ibid.* at 1098-99; *R. v. Alphonse*, [1993] 5 W.W.R. 401, [1993] 4 C.N.L.R. 19 (B.C. C.A.).

281 *Sparrow, ibid.* at 1101-1109. In this case the Court stated that s. 35(1) must be interpreted in a purposive and liberal way so as to entrench the existing Aboriginal rights. These rights must not be viewed in a vacuum. Aboriginal history and traditions must be examined to determine the purposes of these rights. The s. 35(1) rights are relative to other constitutional rights, in ss. 91 and 92 of the *Constitution Act, 1867, infra* note 303. Aboriginal claimants must show they are holders of a right and *prima facie* interference with the right, then any conflicting legislation, to be valid, must be constitutionally justified.

282 *Ibid.* at 1091-93. The Court refused to equate "existing" with the concept of being in actuality or exercisable. See *R. v. Eninew* (1984), 10 D.L.R. (4th) 137, 32 Sask. R. 237 (Sask. C.A.). This approach answers the problems of how law can persist as order in a world of pervasive change and progression.

283 *Mabo, supra* note 209 at 15-16.

and could not be rebutted by any facts or contexts of a particular territory. Justice Brennan rejected this argument: "[S]uch a ground of distinction discriminates on the basis of race or ethnic origin for it denies the capacity of some categories of indigenous inhabitants to have any rights or interests in land."[284]

Justice Brennan relied on the distinction between the Crown's holding land and its feudal tenure to refute the assumption of the Crown's "universal and absolute" beneficial ownership of all land. Citing Roberts-Wray,[285] Sir John Salmond,[286] Professor D.P. O'Connell,[287] A.W.B. Simpson, [288] and Blackstone,[289] he declared:

> The acquisition of territory is chiefly the province of international law; the acquisition of property is chiefly the province of the common law. The distinction between the Crown's title to territory and the Crown's ownership of land within a territory is made as well by the common law as by international law. ... It was only by fastening on the notion that a settled colony was terra nullius that it was possible to predicate of the Crown the acquisition of ownership of land in a colony already occupied by Indigenous inhabitants. It was

284   *Ibid.* at 15-16.

285   *Ibid.* at 30. Roberts-Way, *supra* note 228 at 625, states:

> If a country is part of Her Majesty's dominions, the sovereignty vested in her is of two kinds. The first is the power of government. The second is title to the country ... This ownership of the country is radically different from ownership of the land: the former can belong only to a sovereign, the latter to anyone. Title to land is not, *per se*, relevant to the constitutional status of a country; land may have become vested in the Queen, equally in a Protectorate or in a Colony, by conveyance or under statute ... The distinction between these two conceptions has, however, become blurred by the doctrine [of] the acquisition of sovereignty over a Colony ... .

The acquisition over Aboriginal lands has been reversed by *Mabo*.

286   *Mabo, ibid.* Salmond, *supra* note 116 at 554, states that:

> The first conception pertains to the domain of public law, the second to that of private law. Territory is the subject-matter of the right of sovereignty or *imperium* while property is the subject-matter of the right of ownership or *dominium*. These two rights may or may not co-exist in the Crown in respect of the same area. Land may be held by the Crown as territory but not as property, or as property but not as territory, or in both rights at the same time. As property, though not as territory, land may be held by one state within the dominions of another.

287   *Mabo, ibid.* at 31. D.P. O'Connell, *International Law,* 2d ed. (London: Stevens, 1970) at 378: "This doctrine [of act of state], which was affirmed in several cases arising out of the acquisition of territory in Africa and India, has been misinterpreted, so that the substantive rights themselves have not survived the change." This was cited by Hall J. in *Calder, supra* note 185, S.C.R. at 404-405.

288   *Mabo, ibid.* A.W.B. Simpson, *A History of the Land Law,* 2d ed. (New York: Oxford University Press, 1986) at 47:

> This attitude of mind also encouraged the rejection of any theory which would say that the lord 'owned' the land, and that the rights of tenants in the land were *iura in re aliena*. Such a theory would have led inevitably to saying that the King, who was ultimately lord of all land, was the 'owner' of all land. The lawyers never adopted the premise that the King owned all the land; such a dogma is of very modern appearance. It was sufficient for them to note that the King was lord, ultimately, of all the tenants in the realm, and that as lord he had many rights common to other lords (*e.g.* rights to escheats) some peculiar to his position as supreme lord (*e.g.* rights to forfeitures).

289   *Mabo, ibid.* Blackstone, *supra* note 86, vol. 2, c. 1 at 8: "Occupancy is the event at which the title was in fact originally gained; every man seizing such spots of ground as he found most agreeable to his own convenience, provided he found them unoccupied by any one else."

only on the hypothesis that there was nobody in occupation that it could be said that the Crown was the owner because there was no other. If that hypothesis be rejected, the notion that sovereignty carried ownership in its wake must be rejected too. Though the rejection of the notion of terra nullius clears away the fictional impediment to the recognition of Indigenous rights and interests in colonial land, it would be impossible for the common law to recognise such rights and interests if the basic doctrines of the common law are inconsistent with their recognition.[290]

Justice Brennan rejected the argument that when the Crown assumed sovereignty over the Murray Islands, it became the "universal and absolute beneficial owner," declaring that the argument rested on the false idea that no other proprietor exists.[291] This assumption was "buttressed by three positive bases" in the common law: the feudal doctrine of tenure; patrimony of the nation and raising revenue by land grants; and the prerogative of the Crown to own vacant lands in a new colony. The High Court found "none of the grounds advanced for attributing to the Crown an universal and absolute ownership of colonial land is acceptable":[292]

> ...it is not a corollary of the Crown's acquisition of a radical title to land in an occupied territory that the Crown acquired absolute beneficial ownership of that land to the exclusion of the Indigenous inhabitants. If the land were desert and uninhabited, truly a *terra nullius*, the Crown would take an absolute beneficial title (an allodial title) to the land for the reason given by Stephen C.J. in *Attorney-General v. Brown*. ... there would be no *other* proprietor. But if the land were occupied by the indigenous inhabitants and their rights and interests in the land are recognised by the common law, the radical title which is acquired with the acquisition of sovereignty cannot itself be taken to confer an absolute beneficial title to the occupied land. Nor is it necessary to the structure of our legal system to refuse recognition to the rights and interests in land of the Indigenous inhabitants. The doctrine of tenure applies to every Crown grant of an interest in land, but not to rights and interests which do not owe their existence to a Crown grant. The English legal system accommodated the recognition of rights and interests derived from occupation of land in a territory over which sovereignty was acquired by conquest without the necessity of a Crown grant.[293]

Justice Brennan argued that the ultimate title of the Crown was "a logical postulate" required to support the fictional doctrine of Crown tenure in foreign territories, its purpose to allow the sovereign the capacity to purchase Aboriginal tenure and to grant an interest to subjects in purchased land. However, he affirmed that the recognition of the ultimate title of the Crown was "quite consistent" with recognition of Aboriginal tenure:

> there is no reason why land within the Crown's territory should not continue to be subject to Native title. It is only the fallacy of equating sovereignty and beneficial ownership of land that gives rise to the notion that Native title is extinguished by the acquisition of sov-

---

290   *Mabo, ibid.* at 31.
291   *Ibid.* at 19-20.
292   *Ibid.* at 38.
293   *Ibid.* at 34.

ereignty. ... Once it is accepted that Indigenous inhabitants in occupation of a territory when sovereignty is acquired by the Crown are capable of enjoying—whether in community, as a group or as individuals—proprietary interests in land, the rights and interests in the land which they had theretofore enjoyed under the customs of their community are seen to be a burden on the radical title which the Crown acquires. The notion that feudal principle dictates that the land in a settled colony be taken to be a royal demesne upon the Crown's acquisition of sovereignty is mistaken.[294]

Additionally, Justice Brennan rejected that the "settled colony" category could confiscate Aboriginal rights and interest in the land without compensation, and force Aboriginal people into poverty:

If the conclusion at which Stephen CJ arrived in *Attorney-General v. Brown* be right, the interests of indigenous inhabitants in colonial land were extinguished so soon as British subjects settled in a colony, though the indigenous inhabitants had neither ceded their lands to the Crown nor suffered them to be taken as the spoils of conquest. According to the cases, the common law itself took from indigenous inhabitants any right to occupy their traditional land, exposed them to deprivation of the religious, cultural and economic sustenance which the land provides, vested the land effectively in the control of the Imperial authorities without any right to compensation and made the indigenous inhabitants intruders in their own homes and mendicants for a place to live. Judged by any civilised standard, such a law is unjust and its claim to be part of the common law to be applied in contemporary Australia must be questioned.[295]

By rejecting the theory that the Crown acquired absolute beneficial ownership of land in a settled colony, the Court brought the common law into conformity with Australian history and affirmed the idea of equality of all Australian citizens before the law.[296] Justice Brennan declared:

the common law of Australia rejects the notion that, when the Crown acquired sovereignty over territory which is now part of Australia it thereby acquired the absolute beneficial ownership of the land therein, and accepts that the antecedent rights and interest in land possessed by the indigenous inhabitants of the territory survived the change in sovereignty. Those antecedent rights and interest thus constitute a burden on the radical title of the Crown.[297]

Consistent with Justice Brennan's rejections of the absolute and beneficial ownership of land and the acceptance of the antecedent rights and interest of the Indigenous inhabitants as a burden on the ultimate title of the Crown in *Mabo*,[298] Justice McLachlin, in *Van der Peet*, stated that the first principle of British law in Canada was "that the Crown took subject to existing Aboriginal interests in the lands they traditionally occupied and their adjacent waters, even though those interests might not be of a type recognized by British law."[299] According to Justice McLachlin, the second principle deriving from the first was the right to continue to use the land:

---

294   *Ibid.* at 36-37.

295   *Ibid.* at 18.

296   *Ibid.* at 41.

297   *Ibid.*

298   *Ibid.*

299   *Supra* note 76 at para. 275.

the interests which Aboriginal peoples had in using the land and adjacent waters for their sustenance were to be removed only by solemn treaty with due compensation to the people and its descendants. This right to use the land and adjacent waters as the people had traditionally done for its sustenance may be seen as a fundamental Aboriginal right. It is supported by the common law and by the history of this country. It may safely be said to be enshrined in s. 35(1) of the *Constitution Act, 1982.*[300]

G. British land law categories and Aboriginal tenure

In *Amodu Tijani v. Southern Nigeria*[301] the judicial committee began to appreciate the unconscious judicial bias in Aboriginal tenure cases: "There is a tendency, operating at times, unconsciously, to render that [native] title conceptually in terms which are appropriate only to systems which have grown up under English law. But this tendency has to be held in check closely."[302] In *Guerin*, the Supreme Court of Canada abandoned the Victorian colonial characterization of Indian title as "a personal and usufructuary right" as unhelpful.[303] Justice Dickson declared that Aboriginal tenure remained unaffected by the assertion of Crown sovereignty;[304] it was a pre-existing legal right independent of the 1763 Proclamation or any statutory or executive act;[305] it remained *sui generis* tenure *distinct* from British land law concepts; and it included

---

300   *Ibid.*

301   *Amodu Tijani, supra* note 228 at 399.

302   *Ibid.* at 403, dissenting on other points.

303   *Ibid.* at 381. In *Mabo, supra* note 209 at 156-57, the trial court Justice Toohey observed that, "an inquiry as to whether it is 'personal' or 'proprietary' ultimately is fruitless and certainly is unnecessarily complex." As applied to Aboriginal tenure or title, "personal" is not used in opposition to a "real" right in land; in *A.G. Quebec v. A.G. Canada* (1920), [1921] 1 A.C. 401 (P.C.) at 410-11, the Privy Council interpreted "personal" to mean that Indian title was inalienable except to the Crown. This is a restatement of the prerogative doctrine of the imperial Crown's pre-emption of Indian title explicitly stated in the *Royal Proclamation of 1763, supra* note 112, and s. 91(24) of the *Constitution Act, 1867* (U.K.), 30 & 31 Vict., c. 3, reprinted in R.S.C. 1985, App. II. No. 5 [hereinafter *Constitution Act, 1867*], and implicitly in s. 109 of the *Constitution Act, 1867*; see also *Guerin, supra* note 188 at 380. See also *Smith v. The Queen*, [1983] 1 S.C.R. 554 (S.C.C.) at 569. The Court held that Indian title is inalienable to anyone, whether to an individual or to the Crown.

304   *Guerin, supra* note 188 at 378.

305   *Ibid.* at 379. Justice Wilson stated that Indian title has an existence apart altogether from s. 18(1) of the *Indian Act* (*Ibid.* at 352). The Supreme Court in *Calder, supra* note 185 had already conceded that Aboriginal title derives from sources independent of the Crown. As a legal right, the ultimate source of Aboriginal title is derived from historical occupation and use of the land, independent of treaty, executive orders, or legislative enactments. See *Johnson v. M'Intosh*, 21 U.S. (Wheat. 8) 543, 5 L.Ed. 681 (U.S. 1823) [hereinafter *M'Intosh*]; *Worcester v. Georgia*, 31 U.S. (Pet.6) 515, 8 L.Ed. 483 (U.S. 1832). In *Mitchell v. Peguis Indian Band*, [1990] 2 S.C.R. 85 at 382, [1990] 3 C.N.L.R. 46 (S.C.C.) [hereinafter *Mitchell*], Dickson C.J. restated this position:

   ...that aboriginal understanding of words and corresponding legal concepts in Indian treaties are to be preferred over more legalistic and technical constructions. This concern with aboriginal perspective, albeit in a different context, led a majority of this Court in *Guerin* to speak of the Indian interest in land as a *sui generis* interest, the nature of which cannot be totally captured by a lexicon derived from European legal systems.

the right to use the land according to Aboriginal discretion.[306] The Court stated that federally reserved Indian lands were part of Aboriginal tenure, with the same Aboriginal interests.[307]

In *Canadian Pacific Ltd. v. Paul*,[308] the Supreme Court reaffirmed this idea:

> The inescapable conclusion from the Court's analysis of Indian title up to this point is that the Indian interest in land is truly *sui generis*. It is more than the right to enjoyment and occupancy although, as Dickson J. pointed out in *Guerin*, it is difficult to describe what more in traditional [English] property law terminology.[309]

Similarly, in *Delgamuukw*, Associate Justice Macfarlane of the British Columbia Court of Appeals explained: "[t]he courts have identified aboriginal rights as *sui generis*. Their unique nature has made them difficult, if not impossible, to describe in traditional property law terminology."[310] Chief Justice Lamer in *Delgamuukw* characterized the existing precedents:

> The subsequent jurisprudence has attempted to grapple with this definition, and has in the process demonstrated that the Privy Council's choice of terminology is not particularly helpful to explain the various dimensions of aboriginal title. What the Privy Council sought to capture is that aboriginal title is a *sui generis* interest in land. Aboriginal title has been described as *sui generis* in order to distinguish it from "normal" proprietary interests, such as fee simple. ... [I]t is also *sui generis* in the sense that its characteristics cannot be completely explained by reference either to the common law rules of real property or to the rules of property found in aboriginal legal systems. As with other aboriginal rights, it must be understood by reference to both common law and aboriginal perspectives.[311]

Because the Crown took jurisdiction over Aboriginal territories subject to existing Aboriginal law, the Court directed reviewing courts to undertake an Aboriginal analysis for Aboriginal tenure, rights, and interests.[312] Dickson C.J. restated this position in the context of treaty and statutory interpretation:

> that aboriginal understanding of words and corresponding legal concepts in Indian treaties are to be preferred over more legalistic and technical constructions. This concern with

---

306   *Guerin, ibid.* at 378.

307   *Ibid.* at 379, 382.

308   *Canadian Pacific Ltd. v. Paul*, [1988] 2 S.C.R. 654 at 677-78, [1989] 1 C.N.L.R. 47 (S.C.C.) [hereinafter *Paul*]; *Uukw v. R.*, [1987] 6 W.W.R. 155 (B.C. S.C.).

309   *Ibid.* at 678.

310   *Delgamuukw, supra* note 195, B.C. S.C. at 23 and Hutcheon J.A. at 262-64: "The Aboriginal rights to land are of such a nature as to compete on an equal footing with proprietary interests." Similarly, in the Australian case *Mabo, supra* note 209 at 156-57, Deane and Guadron JJ. observed that: "The preferable approach is that adopted in *Amodu Tijani* [*supra* note 228] and by Dickson J. in the Supreme Court of Canada in *Guerin* [*supra* note 188], namely, to recognize the inappropriateness of forcing the Native title to conform to traditional common law concepts and to accept it as *sui generis* or unique."

311   *Ibid.* S.C.C. at para. 112.

312   *Ibid.*

> aboriginal perspective, albeit in a different context, led a majority of this Court in *Guerin supra*, ... to speak of the Indian interest in land as a *sui generis* interest, the nature of which cannot be totally captured by a lexicon derived from European legal systems" [313]

Discerning an Aboriginal analysis requires drawing on Aboriginal languages that reveal the structure and content of their laws and traditions.[314] Courts considering a claim to the existence of an Aboriginal tenure or right must focus specifically on the traditions, customs, and practices of the particular Aboriginal group claiming the right.[315] These Aboriginal languages and their modes of analysis will be problematic for reviewing courts, since existing case law has not demonstrated or evaluated Aboriginal legal analysis or perspectives in affirming Aboriginal tenure, rights, and interests.

18. Colonial Biases in Canadian Law

Common law judges and lawyers have difficulty grasping constitutional or legal transformation,[316] since their arguments typically emphasize the doctrinal continuity of law despite changes in legal thought, rules, and their judicial justifications.[317] Some Eurocentric thinkers and their legislative assemblies remain adamant and are in no mood for reconciliation; they have no wish for atonement, as if colonial legacies of violence never existed or do not matter. A culture of silence or a convenient amnesia surrounds much of colonialism and its violence to the human soul.

In Canada, by virtue of the adjudicative process in a multicultural society struggling to overcome its colonial legacy, an ideological conflict over colonization appears in most Aboriginal lawsuits. Constitutional interpretation plays a crucial role in such lawsuits, as when a legislative power is contested by an Aboriginal person asserting an Aboriginal or treaty right. When the Crown charges an Aboriginal defendant for violation of federal or provincial law, even if the Aboriginal defendant has no desire to become a virtual representative for Aboriginal peoples and their constitutional rights, the lawsuits invoke these constitutional rights to evaluate their behaviour and existing social conflicts over resources.

Decolonization requires understanding and confronting colonial discourse in each lawsuit and in our legal consciousness, recognizing that most Canadian law is built upon the Victorian common law of colonization rather than the long established

---

313 *Mitchell, supra* note 305 at 108.

314 *Ibid.* See generally, J.Y. Henderson, "Governing the Implicate Order: Self-Development and the Linguistic Development of Aboriginal Communities" in S. Léger, ed., *Linguistic Rights in Canada: Collusions or Collisions?* (Ottawa: University of Ottawa, 1995) at 285.

315 *Van der Peet, supra* note 76 at para. 69.

316 H.J. Berman, *Law and Revolution: The Formation of the Western Legal Tradition* (Cambridge, Mass.: Harvard University Press, 1983).

317 "Tortious interference with Contractual Relations in the Nineteenth Century: The Transformation of Property, Contract and Tort" (1980) 93 Harv. L. Rev. 1511.

patterns, customs, or habits of Aboriginal law or the classical common law of English society. Courts need to resist the resilient structures of colonialism and its self-interest, and perform their new task in the constitutional order by accommodating Aboriginal legal analysis and expanding legal consciousness.

Aboriginal peoples have been virtually shut out of the Canadian courts and legislative assemblies for over a century; much of the jurisprudence that affects their claims, commencing in Canada with the *St. Catherine's Milling* case, was determined without their participation. These decisions enshrined the ideology of colonialism and its manifestation in the common law regarding Aboriginal and treaty rights. Additionally, from 1927 until 1951 the *Indian Act* prohibited, by statutory law, anyone from raising money for financing Indian claims and threatened to disbar any attorney who litigated an Aboriginal tenure or rights case.[318] In most funding agreements to Indians bands by Indian and Northern Affairs Canada, similar principles prevent using the funds for litigation without the minister's permission. Out of these conditions came a jurisprudential and constitutional foundation about Aboriginal peoples' rights that denied Aboriginal peoples the opportunity to defend and advocate their legal position before the courts.

The British Columbia Court of Appeal in *Delgamuukw*[319] rejected the notion that judicial declarations should affect the rights of parties without those parties being present in the proceedings. These judicial insights create a new model for reviewing courts to overrule colonial prejudices in Canadian decision-making. Existing judicial decisions should be overruled if they substantially fail to satisfy the standards of systemic consistency and social congruence with constitutional rights of Aboriginal people; if they are based on colonial ideology, bias, and prejudices and its manifestations, such as racism or sexism; and if the values that underlie the standards of doctrinal stability and the principle of *stare decisis* are contaminated with colonial ideology.[320] Under the *R.D.S.*[321] decision, the biases and prejudices of judges of the colonization era should be rejected, since they could prevent a fair trial and a decision of an impartial tribunal. Colonial assumptions, ideologies, or rules applied as "universal" or "objective" values obstruct impartiality, equity, parity or fundamental fairness in adjudication. In adjudicating Aboriginal tenure and rights, the judicial analysis must refocus on the existing constitutional law, its interpretative principles for reconciling constitutional rights, the transcultural pluralism of a multicultural society, and the new human rights discourses of public and private international law decolonization.

The strength of the ideology of colonialism in judicial thought should not be underestimated. Even after constitutional reform, for example, in 1991, Chief Justice McEachern of the British Columbia Supreme Court in the trial court of *Delgamuukw*

---

318 *Indian Act*, R.S.C. 1927, c. 98, s. 141, repealed by the *Indian Act*, R.S.C. 1951, c. 29.

319 *Delgamuukw, supra* note 195, B.C. S.C.

320 M.A. Eisenberg, *The Nature of the Common Law* (Cambridge, Mass.: Harvard University Press, 1988) at 104-105 (*e.g.*, the judicial values of even-handedness, protecting justified reliance, preventing unfair surprise, replicability, and support).

321 *Supra* note 1.

characterized the Aboriginal plaintiffs' ancestors as lacking the "badges of civiliza-tion"[322] and as "primitive people."[323] Moreover, he concluded that "Aboriginal life in the territory was, at best, 'nasty, brutish and short'."[324] In McEachern's judgment, Abo-riginal society was devoid of law and there was a legal and jurisdictional vacuum before British sovereignty—a restatement of the settled colony doctrine rejected in *Mabo*.[325] Aboriginal people "governed themselves in their villages and immediately surrounding areas to the extent necessary for communal living, but it cannot be said that they owned or governed such vast and almost inaccessible tracts of land in any sense that would be recognized by [British] law."[326]

Such characterizations reflect the persistence of the basic terms of colonization and the difficulties of securing a fair and just post-colonial constitutional order. As in the international decolonization movement, the current task for courts in Canadian law is to revise, stretch, and supplement legislative and judicial categories inherited from the past in the interests of a new legal order. This includes respect for Aboriginal knowledge, perspectives, and understanding. When confronted with colonial ideology, decolonization requires finding an appropriate healing process by reassessing and changing legal doctrine and justification.

Decolonization requires that the Attorneys General of Canada and the provinces no longer rely on the ideology, preconceptions, and unchallenged assumptions of the colonizer: "ordering" Canada by rule from above rather than "inherent" rights; choos-ing arguments and precedents about the "public interest" that hinder constitutional reforms in favour of Aboriginal peoples; and glorifying, even if inadvertently, colo-nization, its birth, its institutional structure and underlying myths.

In its judgment in *Sparrow*,[327] the Supreme Court directed Canadian govern-ments to embrace a fiduciary relation with Aboriginal people:

> [T]he Government has the responsibility to act in a fiduciary capacity with respect to abo-riginal peoples. The relationship between the Government and aboriginals is trust-like, rather than adversarial, and contemporary recognition and affirmation of aboriginal rights must be defined in light of this historic relationship.[328]

---

322   *Delgamuukw, supra* note 195, B.C. S.C. at 229.

323   *Ibid.* at 222. For the organization of the racist assumptions, see R. Ridington, "Fieldwork in Courtroom 55: A Witness to Delgamuukw" in F. Cassidy, ed., *Aboriginal Title in British Columbia: Delgamuukw v. The Queen* (Montreal: Institute for Research on Public Policy, and Oolichan Books, 1992) 206 at 212-17.

324   *Ibid.* at 208, quoting a construction of Aboriginal life from Thomas Hobbes, who never visited Amer-ica and who most believe was speaking of the English civil war in *Leviathan, supra* note 58 at 87.

325   *Ibid.* at 223.

326   *Ibid.* at 221-22. The idea that Aboriginal law did not exist prior to British settlement is a dominant or controlling theme in most of the British Columbia fishing cases, which wrongfully relied on Depart-ment of Fishery regulations to examine Aboriginal fishing.

327   *Sparrow, supra* note 183.

328   *Ibid.* at 1108.

The constitutional fiduciary obligation marks the border between the constitutional rights of Aboriginal peoples and governmental power. Typically, private fiduciary law is concerned with the duty of loyalty, and usually does not require the beneficiary to suffer any harmful infringement to allege a breach of obligation.[329] This constitutional fiduciary obligation requires the Crown to exercise its power with respect to Aboriginal peoples with utmost loyalty. Protecting and enhancing the neglected rights of the Aboriginal peoples requires the Crown to act as an impartial constitutional fiduciary for Aboriginal peoples. The Court recognized that entrusting the special fiduciary obligations to the existing governments would be difficult to reconcile with colonial visions of the public interest: "[t]he constitutional recognition and affirmation of aboriginal rights may give rise to conflict with the interest of others given the limited nature of the resource."[330] In practice the federal and provincial Attorneys General and their departments have not embraced the trust-like characterization of their duty to Aboriginal peoples.

In litigation, the Crown's arguments against the constitutional rights of Aboriginal peoples have drawn criticism from the courts. In *Guerin*, Justice Wilson analyzed the Crown's invoking the "political trust" defence that asserted Aboriginal rights were only "politically enforceable" and legally meaningless, stating that "it was quite apparent that ... the Crown renounced the defence both at trial and through ministerial statements made out of court."[331] She went on to say "that the Crown's tactics in this regard left a lot to be desired" and that the Crown's behaviour did not "exemplify the high standard of professionalism we have come to expect in the conduct of litigation."[332] Such trial advocacy is the visible legacy of the deep structure of colonial ideology and values.[333] Old legal colonial and racial distinctions that should have collapsed with the constitutional reaffirmation of Aboriginal and treaty rights survive in incoherence and gray areas under the authority of equality of the laws.

Three questions emerge from the Crown's instrumental use of legal concepts derived from the colonial era. First, has the Crown violated the Supreme Court's requirement for judicial "sensitivity" to constitutional rights of Aboriginal people in Canada? Second, is the Crown violating the Court's requirement to act in a "fiduciary capacity" in a trust-like context with respect to Aboriginal peoples? Third, is the Crown

---

329   *Lac Minerals Ltd. v. International Corona Resources Ltd.*, [1989] 2 S.C.R. 574 (S.C.C.) at 657, La Forest J.

330   *Sparrow, supra* note 183 at 1115.

331   *Guerin, supra* note 188 at 353.

332   *Ibid.*

333   A noted Aboriginal law professor and past President of the American Bar Association, Rennard Strickland (Cherokee), suggests that United States history is more about genocidal extermination; See R. Strickland, "Genocide-At-Law: An Historical and Contemporary View of the Native American Experience" (1986) 34 U. Kan. L. Rev. 713.

acting in a "conspiracy" to maintain the old colonial rules rather than apply the new constitutional rights of Aboriginal peoples?

Aboriginal peoples have always insisted upon a fair trial and an impartial tribunal. They insist on having the federal or provincial laws re-examined by the courts in the light of their constitutional rights and in the face of more sophisticated legal research on colonization and racism. To continue to invoke precedents of a biased colonial legal order in the context of Aboriginal and treaty rights is rather like suggesting that earlier debates over whether women were persons are still relevant in litigation respecting gender equality, and debates on slavery as human commodities are relevant in interpreting human rights statutes. Mr. Justice Brennan's approach in *Mabo* is more helpful: "[I]t is imperative in today's world that common law should neither be nor be seen to be frozen in an age of racial discrimination."[334]

The colonial ideological legacy and its legal vocabularies have always been ambiguous about Aboriginal status, right, and tenure. Aboriginal assertions of equal protection of the law, viewed by judges as claims by the exotic "other," define the deep structure of modern adjudication. The Canadian judiciary did not consider Aboriginal tenure as the protected "other" property system in the founding constitution of Canada in section 91(24) of the *Constitution Act, 1867*, the "Lands reserved for Indians." Instead, judicial decisions creatively established the doctrines of discovery[335] and conquest,[336] civilization,[337] and governmental guardianship and public trusteeship of Aboriginal peoples[338] as justification for acquiring and "extinguishing" Aboriginal tenure.[339] Consequently, courts denied Aboriginal tenure as the source of all Crown title or estates. Colonizers argued either that the land was "vacant" or that the land was not part of an Aboriginal legal order and should be turned into a commodity to the social and economic benefit of immigrants. Thus courts permitted the development of a landholding system that was associated with colonial values, created and sustained by racial hierarchies or castes, transferring interests from the protected to the powerful. Courts perpetuated this result, even

---

334   *Mabo, supra* note 209 at 28.

335   *M'Intosh, supra* note 305; *St. Catherine's, supra* note 187; *Van der Peet, supra* note 76.

336   *M'Intosh, ibid.; Tee-Hit-Ton Indians v. United States*, 348 U.S. 272 (U.S. 1955) [hereinafter *Tee-Hit-Ton*].

337   Also known as manifest destiny. This includes the doctrine of superiority of agriculture over hunting.

338   *Cherokee Nation v. Georgia*, 30 U.S. (5 Pet) 1 at 16 (U.S. 1831); *United States v. Kagama*, 118 U.S. 375 at 383-85 (U.S. 1886). The guardianship and trust doctrine are derived from European cultural superiority. See "Rethinking the Trust Doctrine in Federal Indian Law" Note (1985) 98 Harv. L. Rev. 422 at 426-29.

339   *Tee-Hit-Ton, supra* note 336; see Williams, *supra* note 88 and S. Korman, *The Right Of Conquest: The Acquisition Of Territory By Force In International Law And Practices* (Oxford: Clarendon Press, 1996).

though it was antithetical to the constitutional wording of section 91(24) and the rule of law designed to protect legal interests in land, including those of Aboriginal nations and tribes.

To sustain colonization, the United States, New Zealand, and Canada abrogated the treaty order and its rights as well as Aboriginal rights; these rulings have now been overruled.[340] Although Aboriginal peoples were excluded from the vote and legislatures, colonizers constructed and justified by judicial activism the unlimited plenary Congressional legislative power[341] or Parliamentary sovereignty[342] over Aboriginal nations and peoples; yet when faced with legislative power that sought to assimilate, civilize, and modify the constitutional or treaty status of Aboriginal nations and tribes,[343] colonial judges rejected such judicial activism. When faced with protecting Aboriginal or treaty rights from federal, state or provincial authority, the deep structure of the colonial legacy affirms "superior" legislative powers through ambiguous tests such as the justified infringement test,[344] which operates through judicial discretion and interpretation, rather than the text of sections 35(1) and 52(1). The Supreme Court has rejected the idea that section 35(1) only protects those Aboriginal and treaty rights recognized in regulated form in 1982, and has affirmed that these rights are not determined by reference to governmental action, but by Aboriginal laws, traditions, and perspectives.[345]

Under section 35(1) interpretative principles, courts are required to step outside the existing legal regimes and enter the Aboriginal legal regimes. But judicial opinions demonstrate that courts have difficulty disentangling themselves from the existing precedents and legislative schemes,[346] as in courts' continued reliance on the federal regulatory category of the "right to fish for food purposes" as controlling Aboriginal

---

340 *Lone Wolf v. Hitchcock*, 187 U.S. 553, compared to *Sioux Nation of Indians v. United States*, 601 F.2d 1157 at 1173 (Ct. Cl. 1979), Nichols J. concurring, affirmed 448 U.S. 371. *Lone Wolf* "appeared to say that Indian tribes had acquired no rights by treaty which the Congress was bound to respect"; *Wi Parata v. Bishop of Wellington* (1877), 3 N.Z. Jur. (NS) S.C. 72 at 78. *Treaty of Waitangi (1840)* is a "simple nullity"; compare to *New Zealand Maori Council v. Attorney-General*, [1987] 1 A.N.L.R. 641 (*State-Owned Enterpises Act* must be interpreted consistent with principles of *Treaty of Waitangi*); *Syliboy, supra* note 205, compared to *Simon, supra* note 205.

341 *United States v. Wheeler*, 435 U.S. 313 at 322-23 (U.S. 1978); see generally, R.A. Williams Jr., "The Algebra of Federal Indian Law: The Hard Trail of Decolonizing and Americanizing the White Man's Indian Jurisprudence" [1986] Wis. L. Rev 219.

342 *Re Eskimos*, [1939] S.C.R. 104 (S.C.C.); *Sikyea, supra* note 187 at 155-62; *George, supra* note 187; *A.-G. Canada v. Lavell* (1993), [1974] S.C.R. 1349 (S.C.C.); P.W. Hogg, *Constitutional Law of Canada*, 3d ed. (Toronto: Carswell, 1992) at 301-314.

343 *Menominee Tribe of Indians v. United States*, 607 F.2d 1335 at 1338-39 (Ct. Cl. 1979) cert. denied 445 U.S. 950 (1980).

344 *William v. Lee*, 358 U.S. 217 (U.S. 1958); *Sparrow, supra* note 183.

345 *Sparrow, ibid.* at 1106-1107.

346 See A. Bowker, "*Sparrow's* Promise: Aboriginal Rights in the B.C. Court of Appeal" (1995) 53 U.T. Fac. L. Rev. 1.

rights to fish. Empowered by the judiciary, legislatures have resisted changes in federal or provincial laws that remain based on colonial values of assimilation or elimination of Aboriginal law, heritage, culture and values.

In recent constitutional analysis of Aboriginal rights, the Supreme Court of Canada has confronted colonial bias and its contradictions, as in treating British law and Aboriginal law as both different and part of the same constitutional order. In 1973 in *Calder*, Hall J. condemned the practice of invoking "ancient concepts formulated when understanding of the customs and culture of our original people was rudimentary and incomplete."[347] In 1984 in *Simon v. The Queen*, Chief Justice Dickson rejected existing precedent that reflected the "biases and prejudices" of the colonial era in legal history, and that is "no longer in Canadian law."[348] In *Sparrow*, the Supreme Court rejected the existing precedents as controlling the context of constitutional rights of the Aboriginal peoples, and renounced "the old rules of the game under which the Crown established courts of law and denied those courts the authority to question sovereign claims made by the Crown."[349]

In the multi-layered context of Aboriginal and treaty rights of Aboriginal peoples, few Canadian courts have explored the definition of judicial impartiality or bias or ideological partiality of colonization. The unified Supreme Court in *Williams* addressed this issue in the context of potential jurors and held the prosecution and the defence are entitled to challenge potential jurors for cause on the grounds that "a juror is not indifferent between the Queen and the accused."[350] Lack of "indifference," which may be translated as "partiality,"[351] refers to the possibility that a juror's knowledge or beliefs may affect the way he or she discharges the jury function in ways improper or unfair to an accused Aboriginal person. The "predisposed" state of mind caught by the term "partial" may arise from a variety of sources; four classes of potential juror prejudice have been identified—interest, specific, generic, and conformity.[352] Generic prejudice is a prejudice against Aboriginal people that arises from stereotypical attitudes or the nature of the crime itself.

Adjudication involving the generic bias or prejudice usually grounded in colonization ideology raises complex and subtle issues for judge and jurors:

> To suggest that all persons who possess racial prejudices will erase those prejudices from the mind when serving as jurors is to underestimate the insidious nature of racial preju-

---

347 *Calder, supra* note 185 at 346.

348 *Simon, supra* note 205 at 399.

349 *Sparrow, supra* note 183 at 1106.

350 *R. v. Williams*, [1998] 1 S.C.R. 1128 [hereinafter *Williams*].

351 *Ibid.* at para. 9. The synonyms for "partial" *in Burton's Legal Thesaurus*, 2d ed. (New York: MacMillan, 1992) at 374, illustrates the attitudes that may serve to disqualify a juror: "...bigoted, ... discriminatory, favorably disposed, inclined, influenced, ... interested, jaundiced, narrow-minded, one-sided, partisan, predisposed, prejudiced, prepossessed, prone, restricted, ... subjective, swayed, unbalanced, unequal, uneven, unfair, unjust, unjustified, unreasonable."

352 See Neil Vidmar, "Pretrial Prejudice in Canada: A Comparative Perspective on the Criminal Jury" (1996) 79 Jud. 249 at 252.

dice and the stereotyping that underlies it. As Vidmar, *supra*, points out, racial prejudice interfering with jurors' impartiality is a form of discrimination. It involves making distinctions on the basis of class or category without regard to individual merit. It rests on preconceptions and unchallenged assumptions that unconsciously shape the daily behaviour of individuals. Buried deep in the human psyche, these preconceptions cannot be easily and effectively identified and set aside, even if one wishes to do so. For this reason, it cannot be assumed that judicial directions to act impartially will always effectively counter racial prejudice.[353]

Section 27 of the *Charter* has constitutionalized this requirement by acknowledging that judges must interpret the right to a fair trial and individual rights in a manner that is consistent with the preservation and enhancement of the multicultural heritage of Canadians.[354] *R.D.S.* holds that judges must be particularly sensitive to the need to be fair to all heritages, races, religions, nationality, and ethnic origins.[355] Justice McLachlin stressed in *Williams* that these assumptions:

> shape the daily behaviour of individuals, often without any conscious reference to them. In my opinion, attitudes which are engrained in an individual's subconscious, and reflected in both individual and institutional conduct within the community, will prove more resistant to judicial cleansing than will opinions based on yesterday's news and referable to a specific person or event.[356]

Additionally, because of the force of subconscious prejudices and the need for judicial cleansing of colonization, section 25 of the *Charter* mandates that courts may not interpret the individual *Charter* rights as derogating or abrogating any constitutional rights or "other rights" of Aboriginal peoples. Section 35(1) prevents legislative powers from unjustifiably infringing on Aboriginal rights.

If an Aboriginal party has a reasonable apprehension that the judicial conduct or decision is based on colonization or its ideologies, these values colour and taint the entire trial proceedings.[357] Such judicial conduct resists judicial cleansing:

> Racial prejudice and its effects are as invasive and elusive as they are corrosive. We should not assume that instructions from the judge or other safeguards will eliminate biases that may be deeply ingrained in the subconscious psyches of jurors. Rather, we should acknowledge the destructive potential of subconscious racial prejudice by recognizing that the post-jury selection safeguards may not suffice. Where doubts are raised, the better policy is to err on the side of caution and permit prejudices to be examined. Only then can we know with any certainty whether they exist and whether they can be set aside or not.[358]

---

353 *Williams, supra* note 350 at para. 21.

354 *R.D.S., supra* note 1 at para. 95.

355 *Ibid.* at para. 95.

356 *Ibid.* at para. 21.

357 *Ibid.* at para. 100.

358 *Williams, supra* note 350 at para. 21.

Reviewing justices will give the judge's factual findings and credibility some judicial deference, but they cannot cure the taint of bias, actual or perceived.[359] Correct results cannot alleviate the effects of a reasonable apprehension of bias arising from other words or conduct of the judge.[360] The taint of bias makes the court without jurisdiction.[361]

These subconscious biases and prejudices exist in many forms in the Canadian legal system, and have caused a systemic failure of the legal system for Aboriginal peoples. Such failure can be illustrated by the Supreme Court's struggle to "define" Aboriginal rights from either an Aboriginal perspective or British law perspective or through both perspectives. In *Delgamuukw*, Justice Macfarlane of the British Columbia Court of Appeal noted that judicial power to define contains the "danger" that old, inappropriate legal concepts could be "unconsciously" applied to Aboriginal rights cases in a way that would fail to uphold the purposes of section 35(1).[362] This judicial danger has been affirmed in most of the fishing cases.

In *Van der Peet*, Dorothy Van der Peet, a member of the Sto:lo nation, was prosecuted for selling ten salmon to a friend. The British Columbia Provincial Court exercised the court's power of definition and found that Sto:lo trade in salmon was originally "incidental and occasional only," and not a part of a "market system," although a commercial market did develop by 1846 in connection with Hudson's Bay Company posts. Mrs. Van der Peet's sale of ten fish to a friend is part of the "incidental and occasional" traditions of Aboriginal peoples, but the court held it was insufficient to constitute an Aboriginal right. The Court of Appeal and the Supreme Court held that Mrs. Van der Peet's sale was not an Aboriginal right, because sales were "created" by British settlers.[363]

Writing for a majority of the Supreme Court, Chief Justice Lamer embraced what he characterized as a "purposive approach" to the task of defining "Aboriginal rights" under section 35(1). The purpose of enshrining a reference to "Aboriginal rights" in the constitution, he asserted, was to achieve a "reconciliation of the pre-existence of Aboriginal societies with the sovereignty of the Crown."[364] Without any recourse to learned treatises or *travaux préparatoires*, the Chief Justice's interpretation of the purposes of section 35(1) included neither the purposes of the Aboriginal peoples nor the purposes identified in courts in *Secretary of State*[365] or *Sparrow*.[366] Despite the "historic powers and responsibilities assumed by the Crown" over Aboriginal peoples that inform the

---

359 *R.D.S.*, *supra* note 1 at paras. 98-102.

360 *Ibid.* at para. 100.

361 *Ibid.* at para. 101.

362 *Delgamuukw*, *supra* note 195, B.C. C.A. at 127, Macfarlane J.A. quotes from *Amodu Tijani*, *supra* note 228 at 403: "There is a tendency, operating at times unconsciously, to render that title conceptually in terms which are appropriate only to systems which have grown up under English law. But this tendency has to be held in check closely."

363 *Van der Peet*, *supra* note 76.

364 *Ibid.* at 539.

365 *Secretary of State*, *supra* note 268 at 98-99.

366 *Sparrow*, *supra* note 183 at 1101-1111.

honour of the Crown and the constitutional fiduciary duties, the colonial legal regimes failed to recognize Aboriginal claims to land and Aboriginal and treaty rights. This purposive neglect led the Aboriginal peoples to request and to succeed in acquiring constitutional protection for their pre-existing rights.[367] If it were not for the interference of the colonial legal regimes that breached the regimes' fiduciary obligation to the imperial Crown, Aboriginal peoples would have continued to exercise Aboriginal rights under their laws or their treaties and would not have needed constitutional protection. This was the Aboriginal purpose for section 35(1) as affirmed by the Court in *Sparrow*.

In *Van der Peet*, Chief Justice Lamer recognized that Enlightenment philosophy's strategy of differences and theory of colonization cannot define Aboriginal rights. They are created by Aboriginal philosophical precepts and law, and they are equal to the personal rights in the *Charter* in the constitutional order:

> *Aboriginal* rights cannot, however, be defined on the basis of the philosophical precepts of the liberal enlightenment. Although equal in importance and significance to the rights enshrined in the *Charter*, [A]boriginal rights must be viewed differently from *Charter* rights because they are rights held only by [A]boriginal members of Canadian society.[368]

If the courts must view them differently, how will they avoid the negative totalizing discourse of the past? How will they avoid viewing Aboriginal rights from the perspective of the colonizer, a majoritarian attitude toward rights that denies the equality of peoples, overlooking that Aboriginal rights are *lex loci* that give Aboriginal people their own inherent legal dignity and legal respect in Canadian society? Is the needed judicial interpretation an exercise in comparative legal thought rather than different legal thought? How do the equality clauses of the *Charter* and the supremacy clause of the *Constitution Act* mandate the courts to act? How is this interpretation different from section 25 of the *Charter*, which prevents courts from using personal rights of the *Charter* to abrogate or derogate from Aboriginal and treaty rights?

Justice Lamer noted the task of the courts in defining or interpreting Aboriginal rights:

> The task of this Court is to define aboriginal rights in a manner which recognizes that aboriginal rights are *rights* but which does so without losing sight of the fact that they are rights held by [A]boriginal people because they are *[A]boriginal*. The Court must neither lose sight of the generalized constitutional status of what s. 35(1) protects, nor can it ignore the necessary specificity which comes from granting special constitutional protection to one part of Canadian society. The Court must define the scope of s. 35(1) in a way which captures *both* the [A]boriginal and the rights in [A]boriginal rights.[369]

"Aboriginal," the Chief Justice reasoned, necessarily refers to what existed on this continent before the Crown arrived.[370] It is therefore the courts' task to ascertain

---

367   See *Calder*, *supra* note 185, and *Delgamuukw*, *supra* note 195.

368   *Van der Peet*, *supra* note 76 at para. 19.

369   *Ibid.* at para. 20. The constitution did not "grant" special constitutional protections to Aboriginal peoples; it affirmed and recognized those existing rights.

370   *Ibid.*

"the crucial elements of those pre-existing distinctive societies," those elements that are "integral" to the "identity" of each Aboriginal nation.[371] The significance of a challenged practice to an Aboriginal nation itself is a necessary but insufficient factor;[372] to qualify for section 35(1) protection, the practice must be "a central and significant part of the society's distinctive culture,"[373] as interpreted by the court, and must not have existed in the past "simply as an incident" to other cultural elements[374] or as a response to European influences.[375] A challenged practice, however, need not distinguish an Aboriginal nation from all other human societies.[376]

"Reconciliation" implies a judicial balancing process that "takes into account the Aboriginal perspective while at the same time taking into account the perspective of the common law," the Chief Justice explained, adding that "[t]rue reconciliation will, equally, place weight on each."[377] Still, the Chief Justice explained that Aboriginal perspectives must be rendered "cognizable to the non-Aboriginal legal system"[378] through this process of judicial adjustment or accommodation, while remaining silent on common law perspectives being cognizable to Aboriginal law. The majority of the Supreme Court proposed a two-stage decision-making process. In the first stage, judges must examine the historical roots of the challenged practice to determine its centrality to the precolonial Aboriginal culture. If it passes this test, the challenged practice must then be adjusted to make it "cognizable" to the imported legal system. Only then can the practice enjoy the status of an "existing right" under section 35(1).

This decision-making process adds two problematic and inconsistent hurdles to the Supreme Court's analysis of "existing aboriginal rights." According to *Sparrow*,[379] a practice "existed," and became constitutionally entrenched in 1982, if it had existed before the accession of Crown sovereignty, and had not clearly and properly been extinguished by the Crown before 1982. *Van der Peet* now requires, in addition, that the pre-colonial practice be shown to have been "central" to the Aboriginal nation's culture (which arguably could result in a smaller set of eligible practices).

---

371 *Ibid.* at 548-49. This is the contemporary judicial reflection of the inside (core) and outside (periphery) model of nineteenth-century Eurocentric diffusionist thought applied to Aboriginal order. See Blaut, *supra* note 56 at 13-17.

372 *Van der Peet, ibid.* at 552.

373 *Ibid.* at 553, 564 [emphasis added].

374 *Ibid.* at 560.

375 Defenders of a practice must demonstrate "continuity" with pre-contact conditions (*ibid.* at 554), although this does not disqualify practices that have evolved or changed as a result of contact with European cultures (*ibid.* at 558-59, 561-62).

376 *Ibid.* at 560-566. See the Chief Justice's discussion of "distinctness" as opposed to "distinctiveness." The Chief Justice explained the challenged practice must simply be one of the elements that, "made the society what it was."

377 *Ibid.* at 551.

378 *Ibid.* Compare *Adele, supra* note 228 at 788 (interests in land under Indigenous legal systems should not be expropriated without compensation, "even though those interests are of a kind unknown to English law").

379 *Sparrow, supra* note 183.

Both *Sparrow* and *Van der Peet* reasoning continues to value the "pure" over the composite, mixed, or mosaic.[380] Such distinctions have historically not only created the racial masks, identities, and politics of Indians, Métis, and Inuit, but have also attempted to perpetuate the idea of the "pure" or integral Aboriginal law and rights before European colonization. The result is to reject the Aboriginal compromises with the colonizers and their resulting inter- and intraculturality, cross-culturality, or syncretic visions as ineligible for constitutional protection.

Inconsistent with the requirement of an integral or central place of a pure Aboriginal culture, the decisions required that these Aboriginal customs or practices be publicly reconciled with British law. Why this judicial reconciliation receives constitutional protection while the past private Aboriginal compromises with British practices and law do not is difficult to explain or justify. The Court's judicial reconciliation test permits Aboriginal rights to be circumscribed or extinguished prior to 1982 by the existence of British settlement and Aboriginal accommodation to their presence. This is similar to the fictions of a settled colony and barbarous peoples rejected in *Mabo*.[381] It does not imply an equal and different source of rights in Canadian law.

In the *Van der Peet* trilogy, the Aboriginal right involved was the right to sell fish, rather than the right to fish. In *Van der Peet*, the right of an Aboriginal woman to sell fish was rejected as not being a pure Aboriginal right. In *N.T.C. Smokehouse Ltd.*,[382] a divided Court held that Sheshaht and Opetchesaht fishers did not have an Aboriginal right to sell some 119,000 pounds of salmon to a non-Aboriginal commercial processor, since it was "incidental" (not central) to their "culture." The Court did not require that these practices be reconciled with British law. By contrast, in *Gladstone*,[383] a divided Court held that two Heiltsuk fishers who tried to sell 4,200 pounds of herring spawn on kelp to a Vancouver-area retailer was held to be "central" to their Aboriginal rights. What is most disturbing about this conclusion is that the Sheshaht and Heiltsuk are neighbours, traditionally living and fishing on the Queen Charlotte Strait within roughly 250 kilometres of one another, and were members of the same traditional trading network. It appears that Aboriginal trade is not a multi-party enterprise: the party that sells has an Aboriginal right; the party that purchases does not. The decisions appear unaware of the illogic of these conclusions.

---

380 See the works of the Aboriginal legal scholars who have often been labeled the "post-colonialists" in Canadian law, such as John Borrows, Harold Cardinal, Mary Ellen Turpel-Lafond, Leroy Little Bear, Sakej Henderson, Patricia Monture-Okanee, June McCue. Of special importance is Mary Ellen Turpel, "Aboriginal Peoples and the Canadian Charter: Interpretive Monopolies, Cultural Differences" [1989-1990] Can. Hum. Rts. Y.B. 3; J.S. Anaya, *Indigenous Peoples in International Law* (New York: Oxford University Press, 1996); Williams, *supra* note 88; R. Barsh and J.Y. Henderson, *The Road: Indian Tribes and Political Liberty* (Berkeley: University of California Press, 1980).

381 *Van der Peet*, *supra* note 76 at 548-49, and 552, 553, 564.

382 *R. v. N.T.C. Smokehouse Ltd.*, [1996] 2 S.C.R. 672, [1996] 9 W.W.R. 114 (S.C.C.) [hereinafter *Smokehouse*]. *Smokehouse* responds to the quandary of Chief Justice Lamer in *Van der Peet* that Aboriginal rights are a special species of law that only applies to Aboriginal people; in this case a provincial corporation, a non-Aboriginal entity, asserted Aboriginal rights as a defence. Many difficult issues surround the company's standing to use Aboriginal rights.

383 *R. v. Gladstone*, [1996] 2 S.C.R. 723, 137 D.L.R. (4th) 648 (S.C.C.) [hereinafter *Gladstone* cited to S.C.R.].

If the Heiltsuk were a mercantile people who lived by trading fish before the European settlers, should it not follow that they retain an Aboriginal right to harvest fish commercially without external interference? According to *Gladstone*, the constitutional right of the Heiltsuk to fish commercially entitles them to a "priority" in year-to-year allocations of fish stocks; the government of the day may continue to manage and divide the resource as long as it is properly "respectful" of the Heiltsuk Aboriginal right. The Chief Justice acknowledged that this "respectful" standard was inherently "vague."[384] Hence the discretion of the constitutional "fiduciary," elected by mostly non-Aboriginal peoples, remains paramount over self-defined constitutional rights, interests, and needs of Aboriginal beneficiaries. Is this not colonialism in another guise?

Under the original *Sparrow* test, reaffirmed by the majority in *Van der Peet*,[385] the Crown is permitted to encroach upon the exercise of an "existing aboriginal right" if it can show an acceptable environmental "justification." *Gladstone* extended this justification by affording the government another opportunity to interfere and prevent Aboriginal peoples from using their constitutional rights for "commercial" purposes: absent sufficient environmental "justification" for restricting the right, the court permits the constitutional fiduciary to allocate the resource concerned between Aboriginal right-holders and other Canadians.

The fiduciary's freedom to share Aboriginal nations' traditional resources with immigrants flows from the Court's principle in *Van der Peet* that all "pure" or central Aboriginal rights must be "reconciled" with the imported legal system by the courts. This leaves all peripheral Aboriginal rights by judicial interpretation the exclusive rights of other Canadians. In neither decision has the court awarded any compensation to Aboriginal peoples for the "reconciliation," which sustains the economic monopoly that other Canadians have derived from colonialism. Justice Macfarlane characterized Mrs. Van der Peet's sale of fish to a friend as:

> an asserted Indian right to sell fish allocated for food purposes on a commercial basis. The result would be to give Indian fishers a preference or priority over other Canadians who seek a livelihood from commercial fishing.[386]

Does this not repeat the colonial myth that Europeans have an economy, and Aboriginal peoples did not?[387]

Also such reasoning ensures a non-competitive place for Aboriginal peoples in the market economy. The effect of the Court's principle of reconciliation in the definition and justification processes is not to merge Aboriginal and British legal systems, but rather to protect non-Aboriginal commercial privileges to the fishery from harm by

---

384 *Ibid.* at 766-67. The United States Supreme Court original ruling on Aboriginal tenure in *Fletcher v. Peck*, 10 U.S. (6 Cranch) 87 (U.S. 1810) held that the courts must "respect" it.

385 *Van der Peet, supra* note 76 at 526.

386 *Ibid.*, [1993] 4 C.N.L.R. 221 (B.C. C.A.) at para. 30.

387 See Blaut, *supra* note 56, c. 2, "The Myth of the European Miracle," at 50-151.

eliminating Aboriginal rights to compete.[388] This is another manifestation of the colonial legacy, as is the concern in *Gladstone* with granting exclusive rights to Aboriginal peoples and with the lack of "internal limits" to the right to fish, permitting the government to impose external limits.[389] Such reasons reflect the invisible political power and interest-group pluralism against which Aboriginal rights are defined, as Justice Cory noted in *Nikal*:

> It has frequently been said that rights do not exist in a vacuum, and that the rights of one individual or group is necessarily limited by the rights of another ... The government must ultimately be able to determine and direct the way in which these rights should interact.[390]

The decisions do not mention who controls those governments, or that Aboriginal peoples and their constitutional rights are seldom directly represented in them.

Beyond creating economic monopolies in other Canadians, the reconciliation of pure Aboriginal rights found inconsistent with imported British law is a distortion of the Dickson Court's use of the term "reconciliation" and "regulation" in *Sparrow*:

> Rights that are recognized and affirmed are not absolute. Federal legislative powers continue, including, of course, the right to legislate with respect to Indians pursuant to s. 91(24) of the *Constitution Act, 1867*. These powers must, however, now be read together with s. 35(1). In other words, federal power must be reconciled with federal duty and the best way to achieve that reconciliation is to demand the justification of any government regulation that infringes upon or denies aboriginal rights.[391]

In other words, the Dickson Court decisions use "reconciliation" to refer to a limitation on federal power, while the Lamer Court decisions use the same term to suggest a limit on the scope of Aboriginal rights.[392] This logic does not address the issue that the reception of British law in the colony was subject to Aboriginal law.

"Reconciliation" was drawn from contemporary Canadian constitutional jurisprudence on the division of powers[393] and applied to the constitutional rights of Aboriginal peoples. The Dickson Court decisions held that two conflicting powers must be read together. Not a matter of extinguishment, reconciliation is required only where it is impossible for Aboriginal rights to coexist with other constitutional rights. The concept of reconciliation in the Lamer Court decisions is broader and more con-

---

388   Similar rejection of the treaty right to hunt commercially is found in *R. v. Horseman*, [1990] 1 S.C.R. 901, [1990] 3 C.N.L.R. 95 (S.C.C.) and *R. v. Badger*, [1996] 1 S.C.R. 771 (S.C.C.).

389   *Gladstone, supra* note 383 at 761, 764 and 766-67.

390   *R. v. Nikal*, [1996] 1 S.C.R. 1013 (S.C.C.) at para. 92.

391   *Sparrow, supra* note 183 at 1109.

392   The result is reminiscent of the United States Supreme Court's reasoning and conclusion in *Oliphant v. Suquamish Indian Tribe*, 435 U.S. 191 at 208 (U.S. 1978) that the accession of American sovereignty "implicitly" divested Indian tribes of those powers of self-government that American courts decide today had been, "inconsistent with their status" as Indians a century ago. See R.L. Barsh and J.Y. Henderson, "The Betrayal: *Oliphant v. Suquamish Indian Tribe* and the Hunting of the Snark" (1979) 63 Minn. L. Rev. 609.

393   *Harvey v. New Brunswick (A.-G.)*, [1996] 2 S.C.R. 876 (S.C.C.) at paras. 56, 69, 70.

fusing. Taken to its extreme, the "reconciliation" test may have the effect of extinguishing everything that had not already been judicially recognized before 1982, which does not reflect accurately the purposes of constitutional negotiators.[394]

Locating the "centrality," "integrality," or "purity" of the Lamer Court test is philosophically impossible. It cannot be objectified by reviewing courts, as the test is inescapably subjective and not static; the test wrongly presumes that fragmented, rather than holistic, Aboriginal cultures exist. The test is built on the fictions of settled colony, the reception of the common law, and the social-Darwinist conception of "primitivity" rejected in *Mabo*.[395] Moreover, the test is inconsistent with the Court's rejection of the "crazy patchwork" of colonial regulations approach (the frozen rights position);[396] its rejection of the "historical idiosyncrasies of colonialization";[397] its recognition of Aboriginal rights' capacity to "evolve,"[398] and to be exercised in a "contemporary manner."[399] While the Dickson Court provides that government regulation and policy cannot determine the content and scope of Aboriginal rights,[400] the Lamer Court's definitional processes freeze the evolution of these rights at the appearance of an English man in the Aboriginal territory or at the abstract assertion of a foreign sovereign.

The *Van der Peet* test encodes colonial paternalism because the courts and laws of the colonizer are assumed superior and not equal to Aboriginal laws in regulating Aboriginal cultures and in authoritatively defining and reconciling the nature and meaning of Aboriginal cultures. These philosophical problems have already produced confusion and back-tracking in the Supreme Court's efforts to apply *Van der Peet* to other facts.[401] Subsequent fishing-rights decisions, *Adams*[402] and *Côté*,[403] hold that centrality was not an essential issue, concluding that fishing had been an "important and significant source of subsistence" and ruling for the Aboriginal parties. In *Delgamuukw*, the Supreme Court created a different test for Aboriginal tenure.

---

394 In the words of one of them, now the Saskatchewan Premier, Roy Romanow, "[o]ne can argue that the purpose of inserting 'existing' might be to freeze aboriginal rights as defined on 17 April 1982," but "that view, which is offered by many credible constitutional lawyers, is one that I do not share." R. Romanow, "Aboriginal Rights in the Constitutional Process" in M. Boldt and J.A. Long, eds., *The Quest For Justice: Aboriginal Peoples and Aboriginal Rights* (Toronto: University of Toronto Press, 1985) 73 at 81. See a review and analysis of positions taken by Aboriginal negotiators, R.L. Barsh and J.Y. Henderson, "Aboriginal Rights, Treaty Rights, and Human Rights: Indian Tribes and 'Constitutional Renewal'" (1982) 17 J. Can. Stud. 55.

395 See R.L. Barsh and J.Y. Henderson, "The Supreme Court's *Van der Peet* Trilogy: Naive Imperialism and Ropes of Sand" (1997) 42 McGill L.J. 993.

396 *Sparrow, supra* note 183 at 1091,1093.

397 *Côté, supra* note 258 at para. 53.

398 *Sparrow, supra* note 183 at 1093.

399 *Ibid.* at 1090.

400 *Ibid.* at 1101.

401 *Smokehouse, supra* note 382 and *Gladstone, supra* note 383, announced the same day as *Van der Peet*, involved more overtly profit-oriented fisheries, also in British Columbia.

402 *Supra* note 257 at 128.

403 *Supra* note 258 at 180-181.

The cumulative hurdles announced by the Court to prove an Aboriginal right now form a formidable threshold: the Aboriginal practice at issue must be shown to be pre-existing and central; it must be shown never to have been extinguished by the Crown prior to 1982; it must have been infringed by government action after 1982; the government action must be shown to have lacked adequate justification; and it must be shown to go beyond the reasonable discretion, enjoyed by the Crown as a "fiduciary" to determine whether the Aboriginal community concerned has been given an adequate "priority" to enjoy the resources it has traditionally utilized. These judicial tests illustrate the incoherence of case-by-case determination of Aboriginal rights in terms of constitutional principles and the broad scope of the Court's structural and episodic discretion over the constitutional rights of Aboriginal peoples.

The deepening reach of the Court authority in constitutional interpretation could overwhelm its legitimacy. These tests translate into a heavier evidentiary burden at trial on Aboriginal peoples, who lack resources to pursue their claims and who derive no income from their constitutional rights, as well as greater risk of an adverse ruling, amounting to a present-day judicial extinguishment of constitutional rights rather than judicial reconciliation. Under the constitutional phrase "recognizing and affirming" Aboriginal rights, the courts have no explicit authority to change, modify, or extinguish Aboriginal rights; rather they should describe the unfamiliar rights and attempt to define them. To do more is to transform rights from the Aboriginal peoples' heritage and values into products of the Canadian judicial imagination and legal categories, which risk unconsciously affirming the colonial ideologies as principles of constitutional interpretation of Aboriginal rights, failing to understand the meaning of these *sui generis* rights from an Aboriginal rightholders' perspective. Aboriginal people experience these tests as affirming the ancient Aboriginal wisdom that you cannot be the doctor if you are the disease.

An alternative, decolonizing basis upon which *Van der Peet* could have been decided is suggested by Chief Justice Lamer's interpretation of Aboriginal tenure in *Delgamuukw*[404] and by both dissenting Justices in *Van der Peet*.[405] This basis would affirm Aboriginal law and the "doctrine of continuity," by which the common law absorbs (or "receives") the Aboriginal law or *lex loci* of a territory at the moment of the assertion of jurisdiction by the Crown.[406] Aboriginal or local law remains intact unless and until it is clearly and plainly altered by the Crown in the exercise of its prerogative jurisdiction or, today, by Parliament. The doctrine of continuity was first expressed by Lord Coke in the classical common law in a case involving the fate of land rights in Scotland following its union with England,[407] and was subsequently applied generally to overseas territories acquired by the Empire.[408]

---

404 *Delgamuukw, supra* note 195 at paras. 126-43.

405 *Van der Peet, supra* note 76 at 599-600, L'Heureux-Dubé J., 642-44 McLachlin J.

406 See *Re Southern Rhodesia, supra* note 227 at 233, affirmed and interpreted in *Amodu Tijani, supra* note 228 at 407, and *Adele, supra* note 228 at 788. A similar principle is found in Articles 4, 5 and 8 of the *Convention on Indigenous and Tribal Peoples*, 27 June 1989, 28 I.L.M. 1382 (ratified thus far by seven states; Canada is not among them).

407 *Calvin's Case, supra* note 224 at 17b.

408 *Campbell v. Hall, supra* note 227 at 1047-48.

The failure to adopt this approach in *Van der Peet* is particularly troubling in light of the fact that the Dickson Court had already relied upon it as grounds for concluding that the 1763 Proclamation[409] had confirmed Native title, rather than creating or conferring Aboriginal rights to unsurrendered lands.[410] Moreover, this was precisely the paradigm adopted by the High Court of Australia in *Mabo* in which Justice Brennan observed that: "[n]ative title has its origin in and is given its content by the traditional laws acknowledged by and the traditional customs observed by the indigenous inhabitants of a territory."[411] The *Van der Peet* decision quotes the foregoing passage from *Mabo* with approval but misconstrues its significance.[412] It is advanced as support for the proposition that rights should be regarded as "Aboriginal" only if they are rooted in antiquity, emphasizing the use of the adjective "traditional" by the High Court while disregarding the concept—"laws"—to which that adjective was attached.

According to the decolonization model, as Chief Justice Lamer noted in *Delgamuukw*, however, what section 35(1) entrenched was the Aboriginal law and legal system, the *sui generis lex loci*, of Aboriginal nations, to the extent that their own laws had not clearly been extinguished prior to 1982. To state the proposition somewhat differently, section 35(1) is a choice-of-law rule. Under section 52 of the *Constitution Act, 1982*, this choice-of-law rule has become part of "the supreme law of Canada" and overrides any ordinary legislation inconsistent with it.[413]

The Dickson Court appears to be asserting this interpretation of section 35(1), as were many legal commentators. In *Guerin*, Chief Justice Dickson observed that past efforts to characterize "Indian title" had been confounded by a failure to appreciate its *sui generis* nature, which is to say that its source rests outside general British or Canadian law and its categories.[414] The Dickson Court extended this analysis to "Aboriginal rights" as a whole,[415] as well as to treaty rights.[416] If the source of Aboriginal tenure and rights is not to be found in the legal system imported from the British Isles, what source could they have other than the Aboriginal legal systems that are indige-

---

409 *Royal Proclamation of 1763, supra* note 112.

410 *Guerin, supra* note 188 at 378. Also, as noted below, Chief Justice Lamer referred with approval to *Mabo, supra* note 209, which in turn relied on the continuity doctrine.

411 *Mabo supra* note 209 at 58. We take it that Brennan J. referred to Indigenous law as a "question of fact" in the same sense that any issue of the content of foreign law is ordinarily regarded as a question of fact to be adduced through the testimony of legal scholars who qualify as experts within those legal systems.

412 *Van der Peet, supra* note 76 at 545-46. To its credit, the British Columbia Supreme Court concluded that "aboriginal rights" must be determined in accordance with First Nations' own legal systems. Hence Dorothy Van der Peet was entitled to do whatever lay within her rights in Sto:lo law .

413 Sections 35(1) through 52 overrides any inconsistent provisions of the *Charter* itself, in accordance with s. 25 of the *Charter*.

414 *Supra* note 188 at 380. See also *Paul, supra* note 308 at 678; B. Slattery, "The Legal Basis of Aboriginal Title" in Cassidy, *supra* note 321 at 117.

415 *Sparrow, supra* note 183 at 1111-12.

416 *Simon, supra* note 205 at 404; *Badger, supra* note 388 at 78.

nous to North America?[417] The logical conclusion of this line of reasoning would be adopting a principle of deference to the *sui generis lex loci*, absent unambiguous evidence of a surrender of the right by treaty.

Rather than deferring to Aboriginal laws, however, the *Van der Peet* decision has the Court assuming authority to determine from extrinsic evidence—and centuries after the fact —what made each Aboriginal society what it was.[418] The Court thereby discards the traditional British Commonwealth framework, whereby Aboriginal peoples retained the rights defined by their own laws, and replaces it with *ex post facto* judicial extinguishment. Such judicial interpretation conflicts with the spirit and purposes of the constitution: section 25 of the *Charter* prevents courts from using *Charter* rights to abrogate or derogate from Aboriginal and treaty rights or their elected representatives from extinguishing Aboriginal rights by legislation. To modify a constitutional right of the Aboriginal peoples requires a constitutional amendment.

A central function of judicial thought is the reconciliation of what appears to be conflicts among legal ideas, ideologies, rights, interests, and institutions. Adjudication not only permits judges to deal in a cognitively effective way with the chaotic mass of rules and agencies, but also to reveal that what many perceive as confusion, insecurity, rivalry, or danger are part of a latent constitutional order that has a legitimate claim to our respect and represents a goal for constructive striving.

A constitution entrenches the most sacred principles upon which a country is founded, and upon which its elected representatives dare not trespass. In 1982, Canadian leaders negotiated a *Charter of Rights and Freedoms* for the express purpose of clarifying what it means to be Canadian, and section 35 to clarify the rights and meaning of Aboriginal peoples of Canada. A core of shared rights and values was intended to bind Canadians together and inoculate them against the centrifugal forces of language and against the legacy of colonialism. It is difficult to see how the Court concluded that the strongest rights provision in the *Constitution Act, 1982* (strong enough to override the *Charter*) should be given the weakest and least consistent application. The *Van der Peet* trilogy shows that unconscious bias and dangers still exist in judicial thought about Aboriginal rights, and is a reminder of the colonial legacy. Aboriginal law and legal traditions are the constitutional measure of Aboriginal order and attempts at consensual reconciliation with the colonists. Section 35(1) was intended to be a constitutional shield, not another strand of a colonial web of domination and oppression.

---

417   See J. Borrows, "Constitutional Law from a First Nations' Perspective: Self-Government and the Royal Proclamation" (1994) 28 U.B.C. L. Rev. 1; and J.Y. Henderson, "Empowering Treaty Federalism" (1994) 58 Sask. L. Rev. 241. Note the distinction between the scope of "Aboriginal rights" as defined by the Supreme Court and what we refer to here as Aboriginal law, meaning what is defined and preserved as part of *sui generis* Aboriginal legal systems. Compare P. Monture-Angus, *Thunder in My Soul: A Mohawk Woman Speaks* (Halifax, N.S.: Fernwood, 1995) at 131-68, on the inadequacy of the term "aboriginal rights" from an Aboriginal perspective.

418   *Supra* note 76 at 561.

V

JUDICIAL RECONCILIATION
OF ABORIGINAL TENURE

Where apparent conflicts between different constitutional principles arise, the proper approach is not to resolve the conflict by subordinating one principle to the other, but rather to attempt to reconcile them.

Justice McLachlin in *Harvey v. New Brunswick (A.-G.)*[1]

...[A]boriginal rights are truly *sui generis*, and demand a unique approach to the treatment of evidence which accords due weight to the perspective of aboriginal peoples. However, that accommodation must be done in a manner which does not strain "the Canadian legal and constitutional structure" ([*Van der Peet*] at para. 49).

Chief Justice Lamer in *Delgamuukw*[2]

Introduction

In *Secretary of State*,[3] Lord Denning held that in "patriating" the constitution, section 35 does all that can be done to protect the rights and freedoms of the Aboriginal peoples of Canada. It specifically guarantees Aboriginal and treaty rights and freedoms and entrenches them as part of the constitution, not to be diminished or reduced except by the prescribed constitutional amendments. No longer, Lord Denning held, will the United Kingdom Parliament have power to pass any law extending to Canada, but the "Dominion" parliament will have power to do so in accord with a new constitution for Canada:

> I think that the obligations under the proclamation and the treaties are obligations of the Crown in respect of Canada. They are not obligations of the Crown in respect of the Unit-

---

1   [1996] 2 S.C.R. 876 at 917, 137 D.L.R. (4th) 142 at 170-171 (S.C.C.) [hereinafter *Harvey*].

2   *Delgamuukw v. British Columbia*, [1997] 3 S.C.R. 1010 at para. 82 (S.C.C.) [hereinafter *Delgamuukw* cited to S.C.R. unless otherwise stated]; (1993) 104 D.L.R. (4th) 470 (B.C. C.A.).

3   *R. v. Secretary of State for Foreign and Commonwealth Affairs* (1981), [1982] 2 All E.R. 118 (Eng. C.A.) [hereinafter *Secretary of State*].

ed Kingdom. It is, therefore, not permissible for the Indian peoples to bring an action in this country to enforce these obligations. Their only recourse is in the courts of Canada. ... They will be able to say that their rights and freedoms have been guaranteed to them by the Crown, originally by the Crown in respect of the United Kingdom, now by the Crown in respect of Canada, but, in any case, by the Crown. No parliament should do anything to lessen the worth of these guarantees. They should be honoured by the Crown in respect of Canada 'so long as the sun rises and river flows'. That promise must never be broken.[4]

The proclamation of section 35 of the *Constitution Act, 1982*, Professor Brian Slattery argued, "posed an unusually difficult task" for Canadian courts; they would have to resolve disputes of "daunting historical" dimensions.[5]

The constitutionalizing of Aboriginal tenure changes the structure of property law in Canada. Its effect on Aboriginal peoples is similar to the due process clause of the fourteenth amendment of the United States constitution (1868), which protected citizens against deprivation of life, liberty, and property by the state. In determining the meaning of the due process clause, the United States Supreme Court decisions reflected a shared conception that its task was one of correcting an imbalance of power in the constitutional democracy.[6] Seeking to reconcile the future of democracy to an increased and active governmental regulation of corporate accumulations in a changing market, the Court sought to enhance a balance of power by creating a fixed and inviolable separation between public and private life.[7] Its decisions balanced the dialectical concepts of proprietarian order with property as commodity by explicitly acknowledging at times that a public role for property could control private property interests. Similarly, in Canada, ancient and new forms of property rights could be protected against infringement, if the courts could be persuaded they fell under the category of Aboriginal tenure.

In *Delgamuukw*, the Court said that *sui generis* Aboriginal tenure must be accommodated in Canadian constitutional analysis in a manner that does not strain "the Canadian legal and constitutional structure." To the extent that the constitutional structure itself strains the legal structure, this will be a difficult reconciliation.

In the legal history of property as commodity, the common law courts found unwanted indeterminacy and irremediable conflicts. The animating idea of nineteenth-century legal positivism was to manifest the hidden legal content of a free political and economic order. Its content consists in a system of property and contract rights and of public-law arrangements and entitlements safeguarding the private order. Attempts to move from abstraction to concreteness in the definitions of rules and concepts revealed unimagined diversity and layers of conflict.

---

4   *Ibid.* at 129-30.

5   B. Slattery, "The Constitutional Guarantee of Aboriginal and Treaty Rights" (1982/83) 8 Queen's L.J. at 232-33.

6   Gregory S. Alexander, *Commodity and Propriety: Competing Visions of Property in American Legal Thought, 1776-1970* (Chicago: University of Chicago Press, 1997) c. 9, especially at 250, "The Dilemma of Property in Public Law during the Age of Enterprise: Power and Democracy."

7   *Ibid.*

The Austinian version of the doctrine that one should use one's rights so as not to injure the rights of others (*sic utere tuo ut alienum non laedas*)[8] attempted to establish a private property regime where each rightholder could enjoy absolute discretion within the citadel of the right. So long as the rightholder did not invade anyone else's zone of right and property, he could indulge his desires, treating the estate or interest as an alternative not only to personal dependence but also to social interdependence.

Practical lawyers, however, discovered that the conflict among rights was both pervasive and unavoidable. Hohfeldian perspectives showed the doctrine was either wrong or circular: wrong because one can interfere with the rights of others by economic competition and the free actions of other rightholders; and circular because the doctrine gives no legitimacy to the existence of others' rights that interfere with a rightholder. In practice, the doctrine turned out to be rife with *damnum absque iniuria:* instances of damage one rightholder could, with immunity or without liability, do to another, and of economic harm resulting from the ordinary practices of economic competition.

Every concept of property rights has encountered the interrelated problem of deploying property rights and interests that economists now call "externalities." Doctrines of competitive injury and of damages against which the victim has no protection or redress (*damnum absque iniuria*) revealed the ineradicable contest among property rights, however such rights might be defined, in the law of a market economy. They marked horizontal conflicts among owners, and required legislative and public policy compromises to resolve them. To prohibit or to make a rightholder pay for all the interrelated exercises of property right that inflict economic harm ("internalizing the externalities") would inhibit productive action and eviscerate the force of the rights. But to allow the rights-invading use of rights and to pick and choose in the imposition of liability for the prejudicial consequences was to recognize the inability of logic alone to allocate rights, and establish unavoidable and interlocking choices. The courts found no way to resolve the conflicts, or to make the selections, by probing more deeply into the system of categories and doctrines. It was necessary to take a stand and to justify it by reference to judgments of purpose, whether avowedly factional or allegedly impersonal.[9]

The courts had to contain ecological hazards, but making people responsible for the consequences of their activities had to be balanced against the need to encourage risk-taking behaviour in production and finance. The courts never found a way to distinguish in rule-bound terms, the "good" risk-bearing activities from the "bad" ones; one of the reasons to prefer land as a commodity ideal-type was the impossibility of making such a distinction. Similarly, the people's willingness to pay a premium for the privilege of running a risk was part of the historical justification of "capitalism," if capitalism is understood not only as a market economy but also as a particular version of that economy rewarding personal success with personal wealth. The result was reliance on the older concept of the proprietarian order and legislation to mediate use of the land by the various rightholders.

---

8   J. Singer, "The Legal Rights Debate in Analytical Jurisprudence from Bentham to Hohfeld" [1982] Wis. L. Rev. 1011.

9   R.M. Unger, *What Should Legal Analysis Become?* (New York: Verso, 1996).

The affirmation of Aboriginal tenure creates greater tensions in a strained and indeterminate property law in Canada. It introduces inherent tenure into a delegated jurisdiction of property rights and interests. The constitutional affirmation of Aboriginal tenure makes the fiction of Crown tenure vulnerable. The vital question, therefore, is how the constitutional order will go about creating a sound and neutral property regime. The courts have the obligation to reform property law in Canada. At present the legal system affords less protection for Aboriginal tenure and rights than it does for the beneficial interest of the provinces in ceded land and for non-Aboriginal grantees.

The courts are now faced with working out the implications of constitutional protection of Aboriginal tenure, without the belief that specific property rules are implicit in a political and economic order. The contemporary courts must choose between competing constitutional purposes and private policy and objectives and attempt to justify their choices. The lack of any rights-based theory to guide the decisions will undermine the sense of objectivity of the courts and the illusion that judicial choices are made by "reified logic."[10]

How the constitutional rights associated with Aboriginal tenure interact with contradictory property regimes of the federal and provincial governments is a central issue. As Justice McLachlin stated in *New Brunswick Broadcasting Co. v. Nova Scotia (Speaker of the House of Assembly)*: "It is a basic rule, not disputed in this case, that one part of the Constitution cannot be abrogated or diminished by another part of the Constitution."[11] Further, the Court concluded elsewhere: "where apparent conflicts between different constitutional principles arise, the proper approach is not to resolve the conflict by subordinating one principle to the other, but rather to attempt to reconcile them."[12]

19. Constitutional Interpretative Principles

Placing Aboriginal and treaty rights in the constitution of Canada allowed Canadian courts to create innovative interpretative principles to give a fair hearing to the constitutional rights of Canadian Aboriginal peoples. In acknowledging Aboriginal tenure and rights and treaty rights as part of the supreme law of Canada and as an integral part of the constitutional supremacy that defines the rule of law, the Supreme Court of Canada paved the way for a pluralistic legal system. In the process, the Court rejected colonial jurisprudence that held Aboriginal tenure and rights were legal anomalies and constructs of policy inconsistent with the constitutional status of *sui generis* tenure and rights.

The Court has noted on several occasions that the constitutional reforms of 1982 transformed the Canadian system of government from a system of parliamentary

---

10   Singer, *supra* note 8 at 1056-59.

11   [1993] 1 S.C.R. 319 at 373 (S.C.C.) [hereinafter *New Brunswick Broadcasting*].

12   *Harvey, supra* note 1.

supremacy to constitutional supremacy.[13] It has declared that the essence of constitutionalism in Canada is embodied in section 52(1) of the *Constitution Act, 1982*:

> [t]he Constitution of Canada is the supreme law of Canada, and any law that is inconsistent with the provisions of the Constitution is, to the extent of the inconsistency, of no force or effect.[14]

This principle requires that all government action comply with the constitution, since it binds all governments, both federal and provincial, including the executive branch.[15] Governments may not transgress its provisions, since their "sole" claim to exercise lawful authority rests in the powers allocated to them under the constitution and "can come from no other source."[16]

The constitutionalism principle bears considerable similarity to the rule of law, although they are not identical. The rule of law principle requires that all government action must comply with the law, including the constitution. The Supreme Court of Canada has affirmed that the principles of constitutionalism and the rule of law are the foundation of the Canadian order. The rule of law, it observed in *Roncarelli v. Duplessis*, is "a fundamental postulate of our constitutional structure";[17] in the *Patriation Reference*, it stated, "[t]he 'rule of law' is a highly textured expression."[18] The Court has stated the rule of law "vouchsafes" to the citizens and residents of the country a stable, predictable, and ordered society in which to conduct their affairs. It provides a shield for individuals from arbitrary state action.[19]

In the *Manitoba Language Rights Reference*, the Court outlined two elements of the rule of law.[20] First, the law is supreme over the acts of both government and

13   *Re Reference by the Governor General in Council Concerning Certain Questions Relating to the Secession of Quebec from Canada*, [1998] 2 S.C.R. 217, 161 D.L.R. (4th) 385 (S.C.C.) [hereinafter *Quebec Secession Reference*]. Professor Hogg has stated that federalism is inconsistent with the idea that "omnicompetent" parliamentary sovereignty prevents judicial review of the wisdom or policy of legislation, *infra* note 232 at 301-307. H.J. Stephen, *Commentaries on the Laws of England*, 21st ed. by L. Crispin Warmington (London: Butterworth, 1950), states that, "no direct authority in the shape of decided cases can be adduced in support of the legislative omnipotence of Parliament," and that: "for almost three centuries it has been universally acknowledged, and no doubt the only reason why during all that period it has never been called into question in a court of law is that no one has ever thought it worth while to dispute it" (iii, 288). In the past, this idea allowed Canadian courts to uphold federal legislation imposing unilateral restriction on Aboriginal and treaty rights. See Canada, *Partners in Confederation: Aboriginal Peoples, Self-Government, and the Constitution* (Ottawa: Canada Communication Group, 1993) at 25-27.

14   *Quebec Secession Reference, ibid.* at para. 72.

15   *Operation Dismantle Inc. v. The Queen*, [1985] 1 S.C.R. 441 at 455 (S.C.C.).

16   *Quebec Secession Reference, supra* note 13 at para. 72.

17   [1959] S.C.R. 121 at 142 (S.C.C.).

18   *Reference Re Resolution to Amend the Constitution*, [1981] 1 S.C.R. 753 at 805-806, 125 D.L.R. (3d) 1 (S.C.C.) (*sub nom. Reference Re Amendment of the Constitution of Canada (Nos. 1, 2 and 3)*) [hereinafter *Patriation Reference*].

19   *Quebec Secession Reference, supra* note 13 at para. 70.

20   *Reference Re Manitoba Language Rights*, [1985] 1 S.C.R. 721 at 747-49 (S.C.C.) [hereinafter *Manitoba Language Rights*].

private persons. Second, "the rule of law requires the creation and maintenance of an actual order of positive laws which preserves and embodies the more general principle of normative order."[21] Additionally, as confirmed in *Provincial Judges Reference*, "the exercise of all public power must find its ultimate source in a legal rule."[22] Thus, law must regulate the relationship between the state and the individual.

Taken together, stated the Court in *Quebec Secession Reference*, these three considerations make up a principle of profound constitutional and political significance.[23] Constitutional supremacy and the rule of law are beyond the reach of simple majority rule and politics. The Court provided three overlapping reasons. First, the Canadian constitution protects fundamental human rights and individual freedoms that might otherwise be susceptible to government interference. Second, the constitution ensures that Aboriginal peoples of Canada and other vulnerable minority groups are endowed with the institutions and rights necessary to maintain and promote their identities against the assimilative pressures of the majority. Third, the constitution provides for a division of political power among different levels of government that would be defeated if one democratically elected level of government could usurp the power of the others by exercising its legislative power to allocate additional political power to itself unilaterally.[24]

In *Quebec Secession Reference*, the Court rejected the "superficially persuasive" argument that the constitution can be legitimately circumvented by resort to a majority vote in a province-wide referendum.[25] While this argument appeals to the principles of democracy and self-government, the Court declared this argument is "unsound," because it misunderstands the meaning of popular sovereignty and the essence of a constitutional democracy:

> Canadians have never accepted that ours is a system of simple majority rule. Our principle of democracy, taken in conjunction with the other constitutional principles discussed here, is richer. Constitutional government is necessarily predicated on the idea that the political representatives of the people of a province have the capacity and the power to commit the province to be bound into the future by the constitutional rules being adopted. These rules are "binding" not in the sense of frustrating the will of a majority of a province, but as defining the majority which must be consulted in order to alter the fundamental balances of political power (including the spheres of autonomy guaranteed by the principle of federalism), individual rights, and minority rights in our society. Of course, those constitutional rules are themselves amenable to amendment, but only through a process of negotiation which ensures that there is an opportunity for the constitutionally defined rights of all the parties to be respected and reconciled.

---

21   *Ibid.* at 749.

22   *Reference Re Remuneration of Judges of the Provincial Court of Prince Edward Island*, [1997] 3 S.C.R. 3 at para. 10 (S.C.C.), additional reasons at, [1998] 1 S.C.R. 3 (S.C.C.).

23   *Quebec Secession Reference, supra* note 13 at para. 71.

24   *Ibid.* at paras. 73-74.

25   *Ibid.* at paras. 75-76.

In this way, our belief in democracy may be harmonized with our belief in constitutionalism. Constitutional amendment often requires some form of substantial consensus precisely because the content of the underlying principles of our Constitution demand it. By requiring broad support in the form of an "enhanced majority" to achieve constitutional change, the Constitution ensures that minority interests must be addressed before proposed changes which would affect them may be enacted.[26]

The Court explained the relationship of constitutional supremacy and democratic government:

> It might be objected, then, that constitutionalism is therefore incompatible with democratic government. This would be an erroneous view. Constitutionalism facilitates—indeed, makes possible—a democratic political system by creating an orderly framework within which people may make political decisions. Viewed correctly, constitutionalism and the rule of law are not in conflict with democracy; rather, they are essential to it. Without that relationship, the political will upon which democratic decisions are taken would itself be undermined.[27]

Consistent with these constitutional principles of constitutional supremacy, rule of law, and a long tradition of respect for minorities, the Court noted that framers of the *Constitution Act, 1982* included explicit protection for existing Aboriginal and treaty rights in section 35. Moreover, section 25 of the *Charter* provided a non-derogation clause in favour of the rights of Aboriginal peoples. The "promise" of section 35, as it was termed in *R. v. Sparrow*,[28] recognized not only the ancient occupation of land by Aboriginal peoples, but also their contribution to the building of Canada, and the special commitments made to them by successive governments. The protection of these rights reflects an important underlying constitutional value.[29]

A unified Supreme Court of Canada in *Sparrow* held that section 35(1) is not a codification of the existing or accumulated case law on Aboriginal or treaty rights.[30] While Aboriginal peoples must prove that Aboriginal rights exist,[31] the Court affirmed that Aboriginal rights cannot be extinguished by federal Acts or regulations. It held that section 35(1) cannot be read so as to incorporate the specific manner in which Aboriginal and treaty rights were regulated before 1982,[32] and stated that federal-provincial statutory or regulatory control of an Aboriginal right does not mean that the right is

---

26   *Ibid.* at paras. 76-77.

27   *Ibid.* at para. 78.

28   *R. v. Sparrow*, [1990] 1 S.C.R. 1075 at 1083, [1990] 3 C.N.L.R. 160 (S.C.C.) [hereinafter *Sparrow* cited to S.C.R.].

29   *Quebec Secession Reference, supra* note 13 at para. 82.

30   *Sparrow, supra* note 28 at 1105-1106.

31   *Ibid.* at 1091-93. The Court refused to equate "existing" with the idea of actual, or exercisable. See *R. v. Eninew* (1984), 10 D.L.R. (4th) 137, 32 Sask. R. 237 (Sask. C.A.) [hereinafter *Eninew* cited to D.L.R.]. This approach answers the problem of how law can persist as order in a world of pervasive change.

32   *Sparrow, ibid.* at 1091 and 1109.

extinguished, even if the control is exercised in "great detail."[33] Finally, the Court stated that the sovereign's intention is controlling and that extinguishing Aboriginal rights could only be proven if the sovereign's written command is clear and plain.[34]

The Court declared that section 35(1) operates as a limitation on the powers of the federal Parliament, government conduct, and as a "strong" check on legislative power[35] as well as provincial legislatures.[36] The Court stressed the necessity of constitutional principles of interpretation regarding existing Aboriginal rights under section 35(1).[37] In a conflict between ordinary provincial legislation and the provisions of the constitution of Canada, the Supreme Court in *R. v. Big M Drug Mart*[38] declared, and affirmed in *Sparrow*,[39] the principle of constitutional supremacy:

> Section 52 sets out the fundamental principle of constitutional law that the Constitution is supreme. The undoubted corollary to be drawn from this principle is that no one can be convicted of an offence under an unconstitutional law.[40]

The Supreme Court held that section 52 embodies the mandate of the judiciary to protect Canada's constitution.[41] Under section 52, the duty of the judiciary is to ensure that constitutional supremacy prevails over federal and provincial law. Additionally, the judiciary's duty is to ensure that legislatures do not transgress the limits of their constitutional mandate and engage in the illegal exercise of power. If either Parliament or a legislative assembly transgresses the limits of the established constitutional mandate, the consequence of such non-compliance is invalidity. The words "of

---

33   *Ibid.* at 1095-1101, 1111-19. In *Denny v. The Queen*, [1990] 2 C.N.L.R. 115 at 127 (N.S. C.A.), the court affirmed the Aboriginal right to fish for food strictly on a constitutional interpretation of the *Constitution Act, 1982*, s. 35(1), and independent of the force and effect of the terms of the Míkmaq treaties; *Constitution Act, 1982*, being Schedule B to the *Canada Act 1982* (U.K.), 1982, c. 11. The Court stated: "based upon the decision in *Isaac*, this [aboriginal] right has not been extinguished through treaty, other agreement or competent legislation. ... Given the conclusion that the appellants possess an aboriginal right to fish for food in the relevant waters, it is not necessary to determine whether the appellants have a right to fish protected by treaty."

34   *Sparrow, ibid.* at 1098-99; *R. v. Alphonse*, [1993] 5 W.W.R. 401, [1993] 4 C.N.L.R. 19 (B.C. C.A.) [hereinafter *Alphonse* cited to C.N.L.R.].

35   *Sparrow, ibid.* at 1110.

36   *Ibid.* at 1115, 1110; *R. v. Howard*, [1994] 2 S.C.R. 299, [1994] 3 C.N.L.R. 146 (S.C.C.), Gonthier J.

37   *Sparrow, ibid.* at 1101-1109. In this case the Court stated that s. 35(1) must be interpreted in a purposive and liberal way so as to entrench existing Aboriginal rights. These rights, the Court continued, must not be viewed in a vacuum. Aboriginal history and traditions need to be examined to determine the purposes of these rights. The s. 35(1) rights are relative to other constitutional rights, found in ss. 91 and 92 of the *Constitution Act, 1867* (U.K.), 30 & 31 Vict., c. 3, reprinted in R.S.C. 1985, App. II, No. 5 [hereinafter *Constitution Act, 1867*]. Aboriginal claimants must first show they are holders of a right. They need to then demonstrate a *prima facie* interference with that right. Any conflicting legislation, to be valid, must be constitutionally justified.

38   [1985] 1. S.C.R. 295 (S.C.C.), Dickson C.J.C. [*hereinafter Big M Drug Mart*].

39   *Sparrow, supra* note 28 at 1106.

40   *Big M Drug Mart, supra* note 38 at 313; *Sparrow, ibid.* at 1106, 1117-18.

41   *Big M Drug Mart, ibid.*; *Manitoba Language Rights, supra* note 20 at 745.

no force or effect" in section 52 mean that a law thus inconsistent with the constitution has no force or effect because it is invalid.[42]

Thus, the other constitutional provisions, federal law, provincial law, common law doctrine, and prior decisions must be consistent with Aboriginal tenure and rights and treaty rights. No constitutional document is supreme over another.[43] Each divided Crown authority is required to act within the constitutional division of powers: each legislative exercise of authority over Aboriginal tenure, rights, and treaty rights is to be consistent with its delegated constitutional authority. In *R. v. Alphonse*,[44] Justice Macfarlane stated that section 35(1) constitutional analysis "stands as a separate and subsequent review, which is properly done after division of powers issues have been resolved."[45] To the extent that provincial legislation is inconsistent with division of powers and the Aboriginal or treaty rights of the Aboriginal peoples, they are each "of no force or effect" by virtue of section 52(1) of the *Constitution Act, 1982*. If no constitutional authority is delegated to a legislative body, then the justification test is not reached. Further, each legislative enactment that infringes upon the Aboriginal or treaty rights must bear the burden of justification.[46]

In *Sparrow*, the Court recalled:

> [W]hile British policy towards the native population was based on respect for their right to occupy their traditional lands, a proposition to which the Royal Proclamation of 1763 bears witness, there was from the outset never any doubt that sovereignty and legislative power, and indeed the underlying title, to such lands vested in the Crown ... .[47]

To characterize constitutional rights of Aboriginal peoples as political rights or policy is to undermine Aboriginal tenure in the constitutional supremacy and rule of law of the Canadian order. Such characterization suggests that Aboriginal tenure is not a part of the supreme law of Canada, but a policy interest.

It is difficult to conceive of prerogative law as policy. Prerogative law is part of the constitutional traditions of the United Kingdom, and distinct from the parliamentary traditions, which are more familiar to the colonizers. The *Royal Proclamation of 1763* was part of the prerogative or imperial law of the United Kingdom and is part of the constitutional order. As part of the imperial order, it was a controlling document in the constitutional law of Canada. Lord Denning in *Secretary of State* stated that the Crown in the 1763 Proclamation, under the Great Seal:

> gave solemn assurances to the Indian peoples of Canada. These assurances have been honoured for the most part ever since. ... The royal proclamation of 1763 had great impact throughout Canada. It was regarded as of high constitutional importance. It was ranked by

---

42   *Manitoba Language Rights, ibid.* at 744.

43   *Harvey, supra* note 1; *New Brunswick Broadcasting, supra* note 11 at 373.

44   *Alphonse, supra* note 34.

45   See K. McNeil, "Aboriginal Title and the Division of Powers: Rethinking Federal and Provincial Jurisdiction" (1998) 61 Sask. L. Rev. 431; B. Slattery, "First Nations and the Constitution: A Question of Trust" (1992) 71 Can. Bar Rev. 261 at 284-86.

46   McNeil, *ibid.*

47   *Sparrow, supra* note 28 at 1103.

the Indian peoples as their Bill of Rights, equivalent to our own Bill of Rights in England 80 years before. ... To my mind the royal proclamation of 1763 was equivalent to an entrenched provision in the constitution of the colonies in North America. It was binding on the Crown 'so long as the sun rises and the river flows'.[48]

Chief Justice Lamer in *Delgamuukw* stated the judicial committee "had originally ... thought that the source of aboriginal title in Canada was the Royal Proclamation, 1763. ... However, it is now clear that although aboriginal title was recognized by the *Proclamation*, it arises from the prior occupation of Canada by aboriginal peoples."[49] Justice La Forest in *Delgamuukw* states, "the treatment of 'aboriginal title' as a compensable right can be traced back to the Royal Proclamation, 1763."[50]

The 1763 Proclamation did not relate to legislative power over Aboriginal nations and lands. It was not addressed to Aboriginal nations and tribes; instead it was a prohibition on the activities of the colonial governors, assemblies, and subjects toward Aboriginal nations and tenure. The Aboriginal nations affirmed the principles as controlling British governments and subjects in the *Treaty of Niagara*, and as protecting their unpurchased Aboriginal tenure.

Chief Justice Dickson in *Guerin* held that reserved, unpurchased land in British Columbia remained part of the larger Aboriginal tenure, regardless of how the Crown recognized the pre-existing rights.[51] He noted that Aboriginal tenure is independent of, and distinct from, English land law concepts.[52]

The unified Court in *Sparrow* affirmed that the principles derived from *Nowegijick, Taylor and Williams,* and *Guerin* should guide the interpretation of the solemn

---

48   *Secretary of State, supra* note 3 at 122, 124.

49   *Delgamuukw, supra* note 2 at para. 114.

50   *Ibid.* at para. 203.

51   *Guerin v. The Queen,* [1984] 2 S.C.R. 335 at 379, [1985] 1 C.N.L.R. 120 (S.C.C.) [hereinafter *Guerin* cited to S.C.R.]. Wilson J. stated that Indian title has an existence altogether apart from s. 18(1) of the *Indian Act.* The Supreme Court, in *Calder v. Attorney-General of British Columbia,* [1973] S.C.R. 313, 34 D.L.R. (3d) 145 (S.C.C.) [hereinafter *Calder* cited to S.C.R.], conceded that Aboriginal title derives from sources independent of the Crown. As a legal right the ultimate source for Aboriginal title derives from historical occupation and use of the land. According to the courts in *Johnson v. M'Intosh,* 21 U.S. (Wheat. 8) 543, 5 L.Ed. 681 (U.S. 1823) [hereinafter *M'Intosh*]; *Worcester v. Georgia,* 31 U.S. (6 Pet.) 515, 8 L.Ed. 483 (U.S. 1832) [hereinafter *Worcester*]; and *Mitchel v. United States,* 34 U.S. (9 Pet.) 464 (U.S. 1835) [hereinafter *Mitchel v. U.S.*], it is independent of treaty, executive orders, or legislative enactments. Dickson C.J.C. restated this position at 382: "...aboriginal understanding of words and corresponding legal concepts in Indian treaties are to be preferred over more legalistic and technical constructions. This concern with aboriginal perspective, albeit in a different context, led a majority of this Court in *Guerin* to speak of the Indian interest in land as *sui generis,* the nature of which cannot totally be captured by a lexicon derived from European legal systems."

52   *Guerin, ibid.* at 379.

commitments that give meaning to section 35(1).[53] Constitutional interpretation is a process of reconciliation. Since all constitutional rights are relative to each other, section 35(1) suggests that while regulation affecting Aboriginal rights are not precluded, such regulation must be enacted according to a valid objective:

> [Section 35(1)] does not mean that any law or regulation affecting aboriginal rights will automatically be of no force or effect by the operation of s. 52 of the *Constitution Act, 1982*. Legislation that affects the exercise of aboriginal rights will nonetheless be valid, if it meets the test for justifying an interference with a right recognized and affirmed under s. 35(1). ... Rights that are recognized and affirmed are not absolute. Federal legislative powers continue, including, of course, the right to legislate with respect to Indians pursuant to s. 91(24) of the *Constitution Act, 1867*. These powers must, however, now be read together with s. 35(1). In other words, federal power must be reconciled with federal duty and the best way to achieve that reconciliation is to demand the justification of any government regulation that infringes upon or denies aboriginal rights. Such scrutiny is in keeping with the liberal interpretive principle enunciated in *Nowegijick, supra*, and the concept of holding the Crown to a high standard of honourable dealing with respect to the aboriginal peoples of Canada as suggested by *Guerin v. The Queen, supra*.[54]

Canadian legal history illustrates that judicial interpretation and justification contain a colonial legacy, and reviewing courts must look beyond "superficially neutral" legislative infringements of Aboriginal rights and of governments' social and economic objectives:

> Our history has shown, unfortunately all too well, that Canada's aboriginal peoples are justified in worrying about government objectives that may be superficially neutral but which constitute *de facto* threats to the existence of aboriginal rights and interests. By giving aboriginal rights constitutional status and priority, Parliament and the provinces have sanctioned challenges to social and economic policy objectives embodied in legislation to the extent that aboriginal rights are affected. Implicit in this constitutional scheme is the obligation of the legislature to satisfy the test of justification. The way in which a legislative objective is to be attained must uphold the honour of the Crown and must be in keeping with the unique contemporary relationship, grounded in history and policy, between the Crown and Canada's aboriginal peoples. The extent of legislative or regulatory impact on an existing aboriginal right may be scrutinized so as to ensure recognition and affirmation.[55]

---

53   *Sparrow, supra* note 28 at 1108; N. Lyon, "An Essay on Constitutional Interpretation" (1988) 26 Osgoode Hall L.J. 95; W. Pentney, "The Rights of the Aboriginal Peoples of Canada in the *Constitution Act, 1982*, Part II, Section 35: The Substantive Guarantee" (1988) 22 U.B.C. L. Rev. 207; B. Schwartz, *First Principles, Second Thoughts: Aboriginal Peoples, Constitutional Reform, and Canadian Statecraft* (Montreal: Institute for Research on Public Policy, 1986) c. 24; B. Slattery, "Understanding Aboriginal Rights" (1987) 66 Can. Bar Rev. 727 [hereinafter Slattery, "Understanding Aboriginal Rights"]; B. Slattery, "The Hidden Constitution: Aboriginal Rights in Canada" (1984) 32 Am. J. Comp. L. 361.

54   *Sparrow, supra* note 28 at 1109.

55   *Ibid.* at 1110.

Given the generality of section 35(1), and in light of the complexities of Aboriginal history, society, and rights, the Court established that the contours of a justificatory standard must be defined in the specific factual context of each case:

> The constitutional recognition afforded by the provision therefore gives a measure of control over government conduct and a strong check on legislative power. While it does not promise immunity from government regulation in a society that, in the twentieth century, is increasingly more complex, interdependent and sophisticated, and where exhaustible resources need protection and management, it does hold the Crown to a substantive promise. The government is required to bear the burden of justifying any legislation that has some negative effect on any aboriginal right protected under s. 35(1).[56]

In providing guidance for the Canadian courts in Aboriginal tenure cases, Chief Justice Lamer in *Delgamuukw* held that Aboriginal tenure transformed from a common law recognition to part of the Constitution of Canada.[57] However, in understanding the purposes of section 35(1), courts should not focus on the reasons for elevating a pre-existing common law doctrine to constitutional status:[58]

> The pre-existence of Aboriginal rights [in the common law] is relevant to the analysis of s. 35(1) because it indicates that Aboriginal rights have a stature and existence prior to the constitutionalization of those rights and sheds light on the reasons for protecting those rights; however, the interests protected by s. 35(1) must be identified through an explanation of the basis for the legal doctrine of Aboriginal rights, not through an explanation of why that legal doctrine now has constitutional status.[59]

The purposes and reasons for recognizing and affirming existing Aboriginal rights in the constitution of Canada are intimately related to providing constitutional equality to the rights of Aboriginal peoples and their perspectives. The affirmation of Aboriginal rights included the constitutional validity of the Aboriginal heritage, culture, and laws,[60] and created the preconditions and vantage points necessary for fair and equitable constitutional reconciliation.

In view of the constitutional reforms, Canadian courts have begun to decolonize and rethink Aboriginal and treaty rights. The Supreme Court has held that once Aboriginal rights are established, they must be interpreted according to the constitutional fiduciary duty of a "generous and liberal" interpretation in favour of Aboriginal people, and in a way that allows Aboriginal rights to develop over time: *sui generis* inter-

---

56   *Ibid.*

57   *Delgamuukw, supra* note 2 at para. 133.

58   *R. v. Van der Peet,* [1996] 2 S.C.R. 507, reversing (1993), 175 C.N.L.R. at para. 29 [hereinafter *Van der Peet* cited to C.N.L.R. unless otherwise stated].

59   *Ibid.*

60   Justice McLachlin concurred on this point in her dissenting opinion in *Van der Peet, ibid.* at para. 268. See Mark Walters, "British Imperial Constitutional Law and Aboriginal Rights: A Comment on *Delgamuukw v. British Columbia*" (1992) 17 Queen's L.J. 350 at 412-13; B. Slattery, "The Legal Basis of Aboriginal Title" in Frank Cassidy, ed., *Aboriginal Title in British Columbia: Delgamuukw v. The Queen* (Lantzville, B.C.: Oolichan Books, 1992) at 121-22.

pretative principles that build on the strength of Aboriginal law, knowledge, and perspectives.[61]

In *Guerin*,[62] a case involved with the Crown's fiduciary duty with respect to federally reserved Aboriginal lands, Justice Dickson held that "[t]he fiduciary relationship between the Crown and the Indians has its roots in the concept of Aboriginal, native or Indian title."[63] The Crown's fiduciary duty arises because "the Indian interest in the land is inalienable except upon surrender to the Crown."[64] The source of the fiduciary obligation to the Indians with respect to the lands was both the *sui generis* nature of Aboriginal tenure and the historic powers and responsibility assumed by the Crown.

In *Sparrow*, the Court declared that the legislative fiduciary duty had transformed into a constitutional duty:

> Section 35(1), ... affords aboriginal peoples constitutional protection against provincial legislative power. We are, of course, aware that this would, in any event, flow from the *Guerin* case, *supra*, but for a proper understanding of the situation, it is essential to remember that the *Guerin* case was decided after the commencement of the *Constitution Act, 1982*. ... In our opinion, *Guerin*, together with *R. v. Taylor and Williams* (1981), 34 O.R. (2d) 360, ground a general guiding principle for s. 35(1). That is, the Government has the responsibility to act in a fiduciary capacity with respect to aboriginal peoples. The relationship between the Government and aboriginals is trust-like, rather than adversarial, and contemporary recognition and affirmation of aboriginal rights must be defined in light of this historic relationship.[65]

The Court declared that the words "recognition and affirmation" incorporate the fiduciary relationship into constitutional supremacy and rule of law, thus placing restraints on the exercise of governmental power:

> There is no explicit language in the provision that authorizes this Court or any court to assess the legitimacy of any government legislation that restricts aboriginal rights. Yet, we find that the words "recognition and affirmation" incorporate the fiduciary relationship referred to earlier and so import some restraint on the exercise of sovereign power.[66]

Constitutional fiduciary obligations refocused the issue of federal legislative powers over Indians and lands reserved to Indians.

Because the Crown has a constitutional fiduciary obligation to Aboriginal peoples, the Court held, all dealings between the government and Aboriginals carry "the honour of the Crown";[67] thus constitutional, statutory, and regulatory provisions protecting the constitutional rights of Aboriginal peoples must be given a "generous and

---

61 *Sparrow, supra* note 28 at 1091-93. See *Eninew, supra* note 31.

62 *Guerin, supra* note 51.

63 *Ibid.* at 376.

64 *Ibid.*

65 *Sparrow, supra* note 28 at 1105-1108.

66 *Ibid.* at 1109.

67 *Ibid.* at 1110, 1114.

liberal" interpretation in favour of Aboriginal people.[68] If a reviewing court has any doubt or ambiguity as to what falls within the scope and definition of section 35(1), the doubt is to be resolved in favour of Aboriginal peoples.[69]

Chief Justice Lamer cautioned reviewing courts to remember that section 35(1) did not create Aboriginal tenure or rights,[70] which are not delegated rights from the Crown, but rather affirmed and recognized the pre-existing rights of Aboriginal peoples. Additionally, Chief Justice Lamer asserted the fiduciary obligations and "generous and liberal" interpretative principles must inform the Court's purposive or interests analysis:[71]

> because constitutions are, by their very nature, documents aimed at a country's future as well as its present; the Constitution must be interpreted in a manner which renders it "capable of growth and development over time to meet new social, political and historical realities often unimagined by its framers."[72]

A "generous and liberal" interpretation of the purposive analysis of Aboriginal and treaty rights ensures that constitutional rights of Aboriginal peoples are relevant to future circumstances, and not viewed as static.

Chief Justice Lamer explained that these interpretative principles ensure that a reviewing court must identify the purpose or "rationale" of an existing Aboriginal or treaty right, and articulate "the reasons underlying" the constitutional protection:[73]

> the Aboriginal rights recognized and affirmed by s. 35(1) are best understood as, first, the means by which the Constitution recognizes the fact that prior to the arrival of Europeans in North America the land was already occupied by distinctive Aboriginal societies, and as, second, the means by which that prior occupation is reconciled with the assertion of Crown sovereignty over Canadian territory. The content of Aboriginal rights must be directed at fulfilling both of these purposes.[74]

Also, a "generous and liberal" interpretation of the constitutional recognition and affirmation of Aboriginal rights ensures that the courts recognize and affirm these rights as part of the supreme law of Canada, rather than policy. Such protective analysis will ensure the focus on these constitutional rights as between the rights of Aboriginal peoples and the Crown and "Canadian society as a whole."[75]

---

68   *Ibid.* at 1106; *Van der Peet, supra* note 58 at paras. 23-25; *R. v. George*, [1966] S.C.R. 267 at 279 (S.C.C.).

69   *Van der Peet, ibid.* at para. 25; *R. v. Sutherland*, [1980] 2 S.C.R. 451 at 464, [1980] 3 C.N.L.R. 71 at 80 (S.C.C.).

70   *Van der Peet, ibid.* at para. 28.

71   *Ibid.* at para. 24.

72   *Ibid.* at para. 21, citing *Hunter v. Southam Inc.*, [1984] 2 S.C.R. 145 at 155 (S.C.C.); and *Big M Drug Mart, supra* note 38 at 344.

73   *Van der Peet, ibid.* at para. 27.

74   *Ibid.* at para. 43.

75   *Ibid.*

The *sui generis* nature of Aboriginal tenure and rights is a judicial remedy for the colonial legacy of failing to accord equal respect for Aboriginal tenure and rights and the British legal traditions, as well as for attempts to assimilate Aboriginal law to British common law and to adapt it to the usual context and constitutional analysis of rights and obligations. The notion of *sui generis* introduces an Aboriginal perspective, while completing Aboriginal tenure's terminological journey from British "uses," to French or civil law "*usufruct*" derived from Roman law, to Latin "self-generated." This strange linguistic journey for the courts had imposed British categories, implicitly and wrongly inferring that Aboriginal peoples had no linguistic conceptions of their land. Recognizing these historical terms as unhelpful analogies, Justice Dickson selected the concept of *sui generis* to avoid colonial categories.[76]

Chief Justice Dickson used the concept of *sui generis* in his search for a fair and just legal language to discuss Aboriginal tenure and rights. Linguistic analysis is a fundamental, and often overlooked, stage in the judicial process: to determine if the legal discourse of investigation is capable of rendering justice to Aboriginal law and thought. This inquiry called into question the unexamined context of British colonization and its discourses that inform constitutional and legal analysis.[77] The *sui generis* category raises awareness of the distinction between the English language and Aboriginal languages, their categories and interpretative discourses. The *sui generis* concept alerts reviewing courts to the dangers of imposing British legal analysis on Aboriginal and treaty rights, and affirms Aboriginal law, its vision and voice as unique forms of constitutional analysis.

By interpreting the strength and scope of section 35(1) in terms of a *sui generis* framework, the Supreme Court of Canada has taken tentative steps toward creating a constitutional interpretative regime that builds on the plurality of Aboriginal law and thought. These judicial efforts decolonize the dominant discourse that has stifled Aboriginal tenure and rights while "masquerading as culturally neutral, comprehensive, or unavoidably ethnocentric."[78]

By creating a critical distance from the conventional interpretative regime of constitutional discourse, the *sui generis* framework avoids the typical impasse of constitutional analysis. British constitutional discourse is "an assemblage of languages" formed in struggles with other cultures and held together by its customary linguistic usage, habitual activity, and public institutions, but its stability lies in its power to exclude and assimilate.[79] Such discourse responds to constitutional recognition by assimilating demands into existing categories or rejecting them as incompatible with existing norms or the integrity of the constitutional association. Thus, only if compat-

---

76   *Guerin, supra* note 51 at 379.

77   J. Tully, *Strange Multiplicity: Constitutional Law in an Age of Diversity* (New York: Cambridge University Press, 1995) at 34-43. Also see the Cambridge historical critiques led by Quentin Skinner and John Dunn. See Quentin Skinner and Nicolas Phillipson, eds., *Political Discourse in Early Modern Britain* (New York: Cambridge University Press, 1993), and John Dunn, *The History of Political Theory and Other Essays* (New York: Cambridge University Press, 1996).

78   Tully, *ibid.* at 35.

79   *Ibid.* at 38-41.

ible with prevailing norms are the demands adjudicated.[80] McGill University professor of philosophy, James Tully, summarized the intellectual challenge facing the courts:

> The language in which claims to cultural recognition are taken up and adjudicated is the language of contemporary constitutionalism. ... This is an extremely complex language. It is a vast network of conventions, of ways of employing these terms over three hundred years. It is far more complicated than anyone who can use these terms imagines. ... A person could easily spend a lifetime trying to describe the use of just one of these terms over a small stretch of time, say, for example, the term: "property". ... The modern features [of the language of constitutionalism] were developed during the age of European imperialism, and served to legitimate it. ...[81]

To understand which parts of the received vocabulary of constitutional analysis thwart the rights of Aboriginal peoples and require revision, the Court has determined that the facts of each case must govern the approach, guided by the constitutional fiduciary relationship and constitutional supremacy. Thus the Court aims to create a just and fair respect for Aboriginal cultural diversities and to accommodate Aboriginal law and knowledge in the Canadian order.

The Court emphasized the importance of contextual analysis and a case-by-case approach to the *sui generis* rights and tenure.[82] The context of the appeal in *Sparrow* was the Aboriginal right to fishing that has always been a basic human right among the Musqueam people and crucial to their world-view, collective traditions and ceremonies:

> Courts must be careful, then, to avoid the application of traditional common law concepts of property as they develop their understanding of what the reasons for judgment in *Guerin, supra*, at p. 382, referred to as the "*sui generis*" nature of aboriginal rights. (See also Little Bear, "A Concept of Native Title," [1982] 5 *Can. Legal Aid Bul.* 99.)

> While it is impossible to give an easy definition of fishing rights, it is possible, and, indeed, crucial, to be sensitive to the aboriginal perspective itself on the meaning of the rights at stake.[83]

As in the constitutional fiduciary interpretative principles of Crown activities, Chief Justice Lamer declared a *sui generis* analysis the correct way of approaching the

---

80   *Ibid.* at 43-44.

81   *Ibid.* at 36-37.

82   *Sparrow, supra* note 28 at 1109, 1119.

83   *Ibid.* at 1112. The Court never defined Aboriginal rights. It was content to stress the importance of the context of Aboriginal rights. The evidence presented was that the fishing spots for salmon were within ancient Musqueam territory. The Musqueam had fished the spots from time immemorial. The evidence also showed that the salmon was always an integral part of Musqueam culture and life. The Privy Council held that the constitutional federal authority to legislate respecting the fisheries under s. 91(12) of the *Constitution Act, 1867, supra* note 37, was regulatory, not proprietary; such constitutional authority does not necessarily empower the federal Government to affect existing proprietary rights or confiscate property. See *Attorney-General Canada v. Attorney-General Ontario*, [1898] A.C. 700 at 712-13 (P.C.) [hereinafter *A.G. Can. v. A.G. Ont.*].

constitutional definition of Aboriginal tenure and rights. Since *sui generis* analysis begins with recognizing distinctive and pre-existing Aboriginal orders and laws as part of constitutional supremacy, reviewing courts must address Aboriginal tenure and rights from an Aboriginal legal perspective. Chief Justice Lamer in *Van der Peet* stressed that reviewing courts must define constitutional rights of Aboriginal peoples "in a manner which recognizes that Aboriginal rights are *rights* but which does so without losing sight of the fact that they are rights held by Aboriginal people because they are *Aboriginal*."[84]

Aboriginal legal traditions are a holistic vision of law in contrast to atomistic British law. Because no single principle or unified Aboriginal perspective exists, courts cannot be expected to comprehend the existing cultural and legal diversity in a singular perspective. Aboriginal orders reflect ecological diversity; Aboriginal tenures and rights arise through different world-views and languages, different interactive legal traditions or customary laws, and diverse ceremonies that create the legal heritages.[85]

As in other societies, Aboriginal orders and laws reveal the innermost secrets of Aboriginal peoples' vital connection to an environment.[86] The differences between Aboriginal law and the British law reflect different ways of ordering human relationships. In *Van der Peet*, Chief Justice Lamer articulated some of these factors:

> In my view, the doctrine of Aboriginal rights exists, and is recognized and affirmed by s. 35(1), because of one simple fact: when Europeans arrived in North America, Aboriginal peoples *were already here*, living in communities on the land, and participating in distinctive cultures, as they had done for centuries. It is this fact, and this fact above all others, which separates Aboriginal peoples from all other minority groups in Canadian society and which mandates their special legal, and now constitutional, status.

> More specifically, what s. 35(1) does is provide the constitutional framework through which the fact that Aboriginals lived on the land in distinctive societies, with their own practices, traditions and cultures, is acknowledged and reconciled with the sovereignty of the Crown. The substantive rights which fall within the provision must be defined in light of this purpose; the Aboriginal rights recognized and affirmed by s. 35(1) must be directed towards the reconciliation of the pre-existence of Aboriginal societies with the sovereignty of the Crown.[87]

Chief Justice Lamer cautioned reviewing judges not to ignore or neglect sources of pre-existing Aboriginal laws and traditions when they focus on the reconciliations

---

84   *Van der Peet, supra* note 58 at para. 20.

85   Slattery, "Understanding Aboriginal Rights," *supra* note 53 at 737, explains that Aboriginal rights concern "the status of native peoples living under the Crown's protection, and the position of their lands, customary laws, and political institutions." Cited in *Van der Peet, ibid.* at para. 42.

86   Unger, *supra* note 9 at 47.

87   *Van der Peet, supra* note 58 at paras. 30-31.

between these distinct legal systems.[88] He affirmed Justice Brennan's characterization of Aboriginal tenure in *Mabo*[89] as persuasive:[90]

> Native title has its origin in and is given its content by the traditional laws acknowledged by and the traditional customs observed by the indigenous inhabitants of a territory. The nature and incidents of native title must be ascertained as a matter of fact by reference to those laws and customs. ... [T]he rights and interests which constitute a native title can be possessed only by the indigenous inhabitants and their descendants ... . The common law can, by reference to the traditional laws and customs of an indigenous people, identify and protect the native rights and interests to which they give rise. ... Australian law can protect the interests of members of an indigenous clan or group, whether communally or individually, only in conformity with the traditional laws and customs of the people to whom the clan or group belongs and only where members of the clan or group acknowledge those laws and observe those customs (so far as it is practicable to do so).[91]

In *Van der Peet*, Chief Justice Lamer stated:

> "[T]raditional laws" and "traditional customs" are those things passed down, and arising, from the pre-existing culture and customs of Aboriginal peoples. The very meaning of the word "tradition"—that which is "handed down [from ancestors] to posterity", *The Concise Oxford Dictionary* (9th ed. 1995),—implies these origins for the customs and laws that the Australian High Court in *Mabo* is asserting to be relevant for the determination of the existence of Aboriginal title. To base Aboriginal title in traditional laws and customs, as was done in *Mabo*, is, therefore, to base that title in the pre-existing societies of Aboriginal peoples. This is the same basis as that asserted here for Aboriginal rights.[92]

Justice L'Heureux-Dubé in *Van der Peet* said directly: "it is fair to say that prior to the first contact with the Europeans, the Native people of North America were independent nations, occupying and controlling their own territories, with a distinctive culture and their own practices, traditions and customs."[93] Also in *Van der Peet*, Justice McLachlin agreed, "[t]he issue of what constitutes an Aboriginal right must, in my view, be answered by looking at what the law has historically accepted as fundamental Aboriginal rights":[94]

> The history of the interface of Europeans and the common law with Aboriginal peoples is a long one. As might be expected of such a long history, the principles by which the inter-

---

88 *Delgamuukw, supra* note 2 at para. 148.

89 *Van der Peet, supra* note 58 at paras. 38-40.

90 *Ibid.* at paras. 38, 40.

91 *Mabo and Others v. State of Queensland [No. 2]* (1992), 107 A.L.R. 1 at 42-43, 175 C.L.R. 1 (Aust. H.C.) [hereinafter *Mabo* cited to A.L.R.].

92 *Van der Peet, supra* note 58 at para. 40.

93 *Ibid.* at para. 106, citing *Worcester, supra* note 51 at 542-43. Marshall C.J.'s general description of Aboriginal societies in North America; *Calder, supra* note 51 at 328, Hall J.; *R. v. Sioui*, [1990] 1 S.C.R. 1025 at 1053, [1990] 3 C.N.L.R. 127 (S.C.C.), Lamer J. (as he then was) [hereinafter *Sioui*].

94 *Van der Peet, supra* note 58 at para. 227.

face has been governed have not always been consistently applied. Yet running through this history, from its earliest beginnings to the present time is a golden thread—the recognition by the common law of the ancestral laws and customs the Aboriginal peoples who occupied the land prior to European settlement.[95]

Professor Kent McNeil commented that the composite judicial vision of Aboriginal tenure that emerges from *Mabo* and *Van der Peet* judgments is of an Indigenous community that has:

> laws and customs governing land rights and interests, that was in exclusive occupation of a territory at the time the Crown acquired sovereignty. Regardless of the nature of the rights and interests stemming from those internal laws and customs, as against the Crown, the community's exclusive occupation of the territory would have given it a proprietary title akin to ownership.[96]

Analogous reasoning provided the basis for asserting Aboriginal tenure in *Delgamuukw*,[97] where Chief Justice Lamer declared pre-existing systems of Aboriginal law were part of the source of Aboriginal tenure.[98] He agreed with the Gitksan nation that Aboriginal tenure may be established, at least in part, by reference to Aboriginal law contained in the oral history, traditions, and ceremonies.[99] He noted that the *adaawk*, a collection of sacred and oral traditions about ancestors, histories, and territories, and *kungax*, a spiritual song, dance, or performance tying the people to the land, were of integral importance in Aboriginal law of each nation.[100] He also noted that the territorial affidavits of hereditary chiefs were important and relevant to the existence and nature of the land tenure system within each nation and, therefore, material to the proof of title.[101]

Chief Justice Lamer declared that the Aboriginal perspective on the occupation of their lands could be partially gleaned from their traditional laws because those laws were elements of the practices, customs, and traditions of Aboriginal peoples.[102] He stated at the time the Crown claimed sovereignty, Aboriginal laws in relation to land would be relevant to establishing the occupation of lands. Specifically, he stated these relevant laws included, but were not limited to, Aboriginal laws governing land use.[103] As well, the Court noted that Aboriginal laws under which permission may be granted to other Aboriginal nations to use or reside even temporarily on land would reinforce the finding of exclusive occupa-

---

95 *Ibid.* at para. 263.

96 K. McNeil, "Aboriginal Title and Aboriginal Rights: What's the Connection" (1997) 36 Alta. L. Rev. 117 at 140, citing *Mabo, supra* note 91 at 51, 75, 217, Brennan J., 207-214, Toohey J.; compare to Deane and Gaudron JJ. at 88-90.

97 *Delgamuukw, supra* note 2 at para. 148.

98 *Ibid.* at paras.114, 126, 147.

99 *Ibid.* at para. 146.

100 *Ibid.* at para. 94.

101 *Ibid.* at para. 106.

102 *Ibid.* at para. 148, citing *Van der Peet, supra* note 58 at para. 41.

103 *Delgamuukw, ibid.* at para. 148.

tion.[104] If such permission were the subject of treaties between the Aboriginal nations in question, those treaties would also form part of the Aboriginal perspective.[105] Presumably, this would also include permission to non-Indians under treaties with the Crown.

20. Constitutional Protection of Aboriginal Tenure

Under constitutional supremacy, the Court has found Aboriginal tenure is inherent in section 35(1); its existence is constitutionally entrenched. All legislatures, Crown officials, and courts have the duty to protect Aboriginal tenure as part of the "supreme law of Canada"; to relieve them of their duty would deny constitutional supremacy and its commitment to the rule of law.[106] In *Delgamuukw*, the Supreme Court established "guidelines" for governments and courts to evaluate and protect Aboriginal tenure; because it found the trial court's factual findings unreliable, it did not decide if the Gitksan or Wet'suwet'en nations have Aboriginal tenure or self-government. Chief Justice Lamer stated the fundamental guideline was that Aboriginal tenure is a real property right in Canadian law: "the right to the land itself" that is distinguishable from Aboriginal rights.[107] Under Aboriginal law, Aboriginal tenure is an "exclusive" right that is capable of being shared with other Aboriginal nations, but it is not controlled by the common law principles of exclusivity.[108] Aboriginal tenure, the equivalent of the Crown's original title or tenure in British law, is the overarching legal system that organizes all Aboriginal occupation and uses of land.

The Court identified three "component rights" of Aboriginal tenure:

> First, aboriginal title encompasses the right to *exclusive* use and occupation of land; second, aboriginal title encompasses *the right to choose* to what uses land can be put, subject to the ultimate limit that those uses cannot destroy the ability of the land to sustain future generations of aboriginal peoples; and third, that lands held pursuant to aboriginal title have an inescapable *economic component*.[109]

---

104 *Ibid.* at para. 157.

105 *Ibid.*

106 *Quebec Secession Reference, supra* note 13 at paras. 71-72, and 53-54; *Manitoba Language Rights, supra* note 20 at 22; *Patriation Reference, supra* note 18 at 876-78.

107 *Delgamuukw, supra* note 2 at para. 138. Canada, *Report of the Royal Commission on Aboriginal Peoples,* vol. 2 (Ottawa: Canada Communication Group, 1996) at 573 stated that Aboriginal tenure is "recognized and affirmed" by s. 35(1) and described it as "a real interest in land that contemplates a range of rights with respect to lands and resources."

108 *Delgamuukw, ibid.* at para. 156. The court warned of the dangers of importing the common law principle of exclusivity into the concept of Aboriginal title.

109 *Ibid.* at para. 166. Compare to Justice L'Heureux-Dubé's characterization in *Van der Peet, supra* note 58 at para. 115: "The traditional and main component of the doctrine of Aboriginal rights relates to Aboriginal title, i.e. the *sui generis* proprietary interest which gives Native people the right to occupy and use the land at their own discretion, subject to the Crown's ultimate title and exclusive right to purchase the land"; citing *St. Catherine's Milling and Lumber Co. v. The Queen* (1888), 14 A.C. 46 at 54 (P.C.) [hereinafter *St. Catherine's*]; *Calder, supra* note 51 at 328, Judson J., and at 383, Hall J; and *Guerin, supra* note 51 at 378 and 382, Dickson J. (as he then was), "Aboriginal title lands are lands which the Natives possess for occupation and use at their own discretion, subject to the Crown's ultimate title." See *Guerin, ibid.* at 382.

As no other property right in Canada has been accorded constitutional protection, Aboriginal tenure and its component rights can prevent others from intruding on their lands.[110] These component rights carry a constitutional fiduciary duty to Canadian governments, and are entitled to equal protection of the law. If these component rights conflict with other constitutional authorities or rights, they may be subject to judicial reconciliation without the necessity of extinguishing Aboriginal rights.

A. Aboriginal tenure as right in the land

In *Delgamuukw*, the Supreme Court affirmed that Aboriginal tenure is a "right in the land itself" that is enforceable by the court against provinces and individuals.[111] It affirmed that Aboriginal tenure was a constitutional "real property tenure" enforceable by the court no less than any British law title or estate holder. Aboriginal law defines this *sui generis* land tenure, since the fragmented categories of British property or civil law's *numerus clausus* and their distinctions between real and personal property are not categories of Aboriginal tenure. British categories and remedies, however, may apply if they are consistent with Aboriginal law.

Aboriginal tenure is the proprietary order that forms the basis of uses and occupation in Aboriginal territory. It is distinct from both the feudal or manorial notion of tenure in British history and law and the civilian concept of property ownership that is derived from Roman law, which is in principle unitary and absolute. Aboriginal tenures are derived from Aboriginal world-views and laws, and each Aboriginal nation determines how to use and occupy the land. They do not share the ideal-type of land as commodity or its view of property as multiple divisions or fragmentation of estates, uses and interests, or a "bundle" of these "rights."

Unlike the fiction of Crown tenure in British law, Aboriginal tenure plays an active role in determining the uses of a territory. Aboriginal tenure encompasses an Aboriginal nation's full range of legitimate uses, including ecological, collective, family, and individual rights. Aboriginal tenure is a shared order, not in "spirit" different from the multiple divisions of interest in the land of British law. Similar to common law, in most Aboriginal law, a person cannot absolutely own a "title" or "estate" in Aboriginal territory, but rather a family or clan may be responsible for a resource over time. However, the British classification of common law "estates" by the characteristics of time in freehold and non-freehold estates, present and future possession, and legal and equitable enjoyment diverges from Aboriginal thought and law.

In the absence of a treaty reconciliation with the Crown, the Supreme Court of Canada has established a judicial test that an Aboriginal nation must meet to prove Aboriginal tenure at the time the Crown asserted sovereignty:

> In order to make out a claim for aboriginal title, the aboriginal group asserting title must satisfy the following criteria: (i) the land must have been occupied prior to sovereignty, (ii) if present occupation is relied on as proof of occupation pre-sovereignty, there must

---

110 *Delgamuukw, supra* note 2 at para. 155.

111 *Ibid.* at para. 138.

be a continuity between present and pre-sovereignty occupation, and (iii) at sovereignty, that occupation must have been exclusive.[112]

The relevant evidence includes Aboriginal laws,[113] oral histories,[114] and evidence of physical occupation of the land at the time[115] and today.[116]

Drawing on the public international law idea of critical date extending sovereignty to a foreign territory,[117] in *Delgamuukw*, the Court found that the British Crown asserted Sovereignty over the territory not by discovery or conquest, but by a treaty cession of the *Oregon Boundary Treaty* (1846):

> ...in the context of aboriginal title, sovereignty is the appropriate time period to consider for several reasons. First, from a theoretical standpoint, aboriginal title arises out of prior occupation of the land by aboriginal peoples and out of the relationship between the common law and pre-existing systems of aboriginal law. Aboriginal title is a burden on the Crown's underlying title. However, the Crown did not gain this title until it asserted sovereignty over the land in question. Because it does not make sense to speak of a burden on the underlying title before that title existed, aboriginal title crystallized at the time sovereignty was asserted. ... Finally, from a practical standpoint, it appears that the date of sovereignty is more certain than the date of first contact. ... For these reasons, I conclude that aboriginals must establish occupation of the land from the date of the assertion of sovereignty in order to sustain a claim for aboriginal title. McEachern C.J. found, at pp. 233-34, and the parties did not dispute on appeal, that British sovereignty over British Columbia was conclusively established by the Oregon Boundary Treaty of 1846. This is not to say that circumstances subsequent to sovereignty may never be relevant to title or compensation; this might be the case, for example, where native bands have been dispossessed of traditional lands after sovereignty.[118]

In agreeing, Justice La Forest stated that the assertion of sovereignty date in certain situations may not be the only relevant time to consider, since continuity may still exist

---

112 *Ibid.* at para. 143, Lamer, C.J.C.

113 *Ibid.* at para. 148: "For instance, there may have been aboriginal settlements in one area of the province but, after the assertion of sovereignty, the aboriginal peoples may have all moved to another area where they remained from the date of sovereignty until the present. This relocation may have been due to natural causes, such as the flooding of villages, or to clashes with European settlers."

114 *Ibid.* at paras. 84, 87, 107.

115 *Ibid.* at para. 149.

116 *Ibid.* at paras. 153-54.

117 Ian Brownlie, *Principles of Public International Law* (New York: Oxford University Press, 1990) at 130. Judge Huber, in the *Las Palmas Case (United States v. The Netherlands)* (1928), 2 R.S.A. 829, had to consider whether Spanish sovereignty over the island subsisted at the critical date in 1898. In doing so he gave a new dimension to the rule under discussion: "As regards the question which of different legal systems prevailing at successive periods is to be applied in a particular case (the so-called intertemporal law), a distinction must be made between the creation of rights and the existence of rights. The same principle which subjects the act creative of a right to the law in force at the time the right arises, demands that the existence of the right, in other words its continued manifestation, shall follow the conditions required by the evolution of law."

118 *Delgamuukw, supra* note 2 at para. 145.

where the present occupation of one area by Aboriginal people is connected to the pre-sovereignty occupation of another area.[119]

In the *Quebec Secession Reference*, the Supreme Court of Canada acknowledged British "sovereignty is a political fact for which no purely legal authority can be constituted."[120] The assertion of "sovereignty" does not extinguish Aboriginal tenure; it only creates an "ultimate" right to purchase it and "fiduciary obligations" of the Crown toward Aboriginal peoples until they consent to such sale. In *Guerin*, the Court acknowledged the fiduciary relationship between the Crown and the Aboriginal nations in British Columbia began when the historic occupiers of North American lands had contact with colonizers as agents of European sovereigns.[121]

Aboriginal tenure and rights do not depend on any recognition by the Sovereign by any treaty, executive order, common law decision, or legislative enactment:[122] In *Sparrow*, the unified Court held that the 1763 Proclamation witnessed the respect of the Crown for the right of an Aboriginal "population" to occupy its traditional lands,[123] even though "there was from the outset never any doubt that sovereignty and legislative power, and indeed the underlying title, to such lands vested in the Crown."[124] In *Van der Peet*, Justice McLachlin noted the assertion of sovereignty was related to the legal acceptance of the existing property and customary law of the territory's inhabitants:

> For centuries, it has been established that upon asserting sovereignty the British Crown accepted the existing property and customary rights of the territory's inhabitants. Illustrations abound. For example, after the conquest of Ireland, it was held in *The Case of Tanistry* (1608), Davis 28, 80 E.R. 516, that the Crown did not take actual possession of the land by reason of conquest and that pre-existing property rights continued. Similarly, Lord Sumner wrote in *In re Southern Rhodesia*, [1919] A.C. 211, at p. 233 that "it is to be presumed, in the absence of express confiscation or of subsequent expropriatory legislation, that the conqueror has respected [pre-existing Aboriginal rights] and forborne to diminish or modify them". Again, Lord Denning affirmed the same rule in *Oyekan v. Adele*, [1957] 2 All E.R. 785, at p. 788:
>
> > In inquiring ... what rights are recognised, there is one guiding principle. It is this: The courts will assume that the British Crown intends that the rights of property of the inhabitants are to be fully respected. Whilst, therefore, the British Crown, as Sovereign, can make laws enabling it compulsorily to acquire land for public purposes, it will see that proper compensation is awarded to every one of the inhabitants who has by native law an interest in it; and *the courts will declare the inhabitants entitled to*

---

119 *Ibid.* at para. 197.

120 *Quebec Secession Reference, supra* note 13 at para. 142, citing H. W. R. Wade, "The Basis of Legal Sovereignty" [1955] Cambridge L.J. 172 at 196.

121 *Guerin, supra* note 51 at 383-84.

122 *Ibid.* at 112, citing *Calder, supra* note 51 at 390, Hall J. Confirmed in *Guerin, supra* note 51, and *Sparrow, supra* note 28; see also the decision of the High Court of Australia in *Mabo, supra* note 91.

123 See the judgment of Justice McLachlin in *Van der Peet, supra* note 58 at para. 263, in which she discussed the "golden thread" of recognition of ancestral laws.

124 *Sparrow, supra* note 28 at 1103.

> *compensation according to their interests, even though those interests are of a kind unknown to English law. ...* [Emphasis added.] [125]

Moreover, Justice McLachlin summarized the existing principle of the assertion of sovereignty's relationship to Aboriginal tenure:

> This much is clear: the Crown, upon discovering and occupying a "new" territory, recognized the law and custom of the Aboriginal societies it found and the rights in the lands they traditionally occupied that these supported. At one time it was suggested that only legal interests consistent with those recognized at common law would be recognized. However, as Brennan J. points out in *Mabo,* at p. 59 [C.L.R.; p. 49 C.N.L.R.], that rigidity has been relaxed since the decision of the Privy Council in *Tijani v. Secretary, Southern Nigeria,* [1921] 2 A.C. 399, "[t]he general principle that the common law will recognize a customary title only if it be consistent with the common law is subject to an exception in favour of traditional native title."

> It may now be affirmed with confidence that the common law accepts all types of Aboriginal interests, "even though those interests are of a kind unknown to English law": *per* Lord Denning in *Oyekan, supra,* at p. 788. What the laws, customs and resultant rights are "must be ascertained as a matter of fact" in each case, *per* Brennan J. in *Mabo,* at p. 58 [C.L.R.; p. 49 C.N.L.R.]. It follows that the Crown in Canada must be taken as having accepted existing Native laws and customs and the interests in the land and waters they gave rise to, even though they found no counterpart in the law of England. In so far as an Aboriginal people under internal law or custom had used the land and its waters in the past, so it must be regarded as having the continuing right to use them, absent extinguishment or treaty.[126]

In *Delgamuukw,* the hereditary chiefs argued for proprietarian governance. They claimed their Aboriginal tenure arose from long-term communal use and ownership of the territory rather than personal use or possession of land.[127] Both the Gitksan and the Wet'suwet'en nations comprise houses and clans: four Gitksan and four Wet'suwet'en clans are subdivided into houses. Each house has one or more hereditary chief as its titular head, selected by the elders of their house, as well as possibly the head chief of the other houses of the clan. Every person is automatically a member of his or her mother's house and clan.

The hereditary chiefs of the houses claimed jurisdiction over land and people in the territory. The trial court characterized such claims as "Aboriginal sovereignty" or a right to "govern the territory free of provincial control in all matters where their aboriginal laws conflict with the general law."[128] Typically, these territories are marked by physical and tangible indicators and by traditions and ceremonies in the feast houses. The hereditary chiefs entered evidence of totem poles carved with the houses' crest or distinctive regalia. In addition, the court noted the Gitksan houses have an *adaawk,*

---

125 *Van der Peet, supra* note 58 at para. 264.

126 *Ibid.* at paras. 268-69.

127 *Delgamuukw, supra* note 2, trial court at 147.

128 *Ibid.* at 128.

sacred oral traditions about histories and territories. The Wet'suwet'en each has a *kungax*, which binds them to their land. Each house makes decisions ceremonially and has a feast hall, where they tell and re-tell their stories, identifying their territories and their sacred connection with their lands.

Canadian courts have described the Aboriginal tenure of the hereditary chiefs as "communal," but have attributed to this word concepts drawn from nineteenth-century British and civil law notions of private property as distinguished from collective property. McEachern C.J. held Aboriginal rights are "communal in nature," consisting of subsistence activities and are not proprietary (private estates). In contrast, Chief Justice Lamer emphasized that Aboriginal tenure is held communally, and constitutes a proprietary interest in the land itself, which can compete on an equal footing with other proprietary interests.[129] Since the Aboriginal tenure is held collectively over persons and territory, individual hereditary chiefs or Aboriginal persons cannot hold or "own" it. The Aboriginal nations hold this collective right to land for all their members. That community also makes decisions with respect to that land. The courts have stated that their communal tenure is distinguishable from "normal" individual property interests in British and Canadian law, and makes it *sui generis*.[130] A more accurate analogy to Aboriginal concepts of communal tenure would be the allodial tenure of the Crown in the United Kingdom.

B. Aboriginal tenure as a proprietarian order

That Aboriginal tenure is a proprietarian order similar to the Crown's proprietarian order in the United Kingdom is demonstrated by its inalienability to British subjects, government, and entities. As part of a public international law and United Kingdom proprietarian order, Aboriginal tenure could only be conveyed to the Crown. The prohibitions on individual purchases of land held under Aboriginal tenure maintained the Aboriginal proprietary order and the British proprietary order as parallel and distinct tenures. Under the public international law and British common law tenurial principles, Aboriginal deeds to private purchasers did not give British purchasers any title or estate in British law, but an interest in Aboriginal tenure or law.

John Locke discussed this conceptual problem in colonial law when he accepted a position as Commissioner of Trades and Plantations (1696-1700), a new Subcommittee of the Privy Council.[131] The Commission of Trades and Plantations was appointed to reform the colonial system during the Restoration.[132] The central weak-

---

129 *Ibid.*, S.C.C. at para. 113.

130 *Ibid.* at para. 115.

131 J. Tully, *An Approach To Political Philosophy: Locke In Contexts* (Cambridge, U.K.: Cambridge University Press, 1993) at 140. Locke had been secretary to Lord Shaftesbury, then secretary of the Lord Proprietors of Carolina (1668-71), and also secretary to the Council of Trade and Plantations (1673-74).

132 *Ibid.* There is no collection of Locke's colonial writing, nor a bibliography of them. Locke applied his theory and policy on colonial affairs in the Fundamental Constitution of Carolina (1669), Carolina's agrarian laws policy (1671-72), and a reform proposal for Virginia (1696).

ness of the British overseas administrative system in America, to Locke and the Sub-committee, was not only its failure to respect Aboriginal tenure but also the English colonizers' purchases from Aboriginal nations by deeds.

Locke agreed with James Harrington's analysis of the relationship between economic and political power in *Oceana*[133] that property rights distribution within any society determined the normative forms of political authority. Harrington had reasoned that if most of the property was held by a king, an absolute monarchy would emerge; if nobility controlled the land, then either an aristocracy or a mixed monarchy would emerge; and if people owned most of the land, a popular form of government would emerge.

Property rights, Locke offered, were a form by which the tacit consensus that establishes society continued to be operationally manifested.[134] If one disliked the form of civil society, one was free to leave it, but if one continued to hold property in society, one was assumed to continue to accept society. This operational consensus also gave political sovereigns the right to redistribute the estates and interests of individuals in society for the public good, as well as the right to regulate property by taxation.[135]

Under his theory of tacit consent or operational consensus, Locke argued that when the British colonizers purchased land from the Aboriginal nations, they eroded His Majesty's jurisdiction over them and their settlements. The colonizers' right to purchase lands from the Aboriginal nations could be seen as freeing them from prerogative jurisdictions and placing them under Aboriginal tenure, not rendering them "absolute owners" or conferring allodial title, as asserted by the colonists. Locke recognized not only that the tenure of the Aboriginal sovereigns[136] could not be diminished by a colonial purchase, but also that the purchaser created a relationship with the Aboriginal nation. As grantor, the Aboriginal nation could retain a present and future interest in the purchased land. This was the conceptual problem with individual and colonial purchases of land title from the Aboriginal nations that arose in the southern colonies of Great Britain, which prerogative legislation sought to prohibit by preventing individual purchases.

The Crown dealt with this conveyance issue in the southern colonies in the *Mohegan Indian* case and in prerogative law, such as the 1763 Proclamation. Chief Jus-

---

133 C. Blitzer, *An Immortal Commonwealth: The Political Thought of James Harrington* (New Haven, Conn.: Yale University Press, 1960); T.W. Dwight, "Harrington and His Influence on American Political Institutions" (1887) 2 Pol. Sci. Q. 1.

134 John Locke, "The Second Treatise of Government" in *Two Treatises on Government*, ed. by Peter Laslett (New York: Cambridge University Press, 1988) at §§ 3, 27.

135 *Ibid.* at §§ 124, 127, 134, 138.

136 Locke characterized Aboriginal governments in America as independent states under "kings" or "rulers," in his "Second Treatise" *ibid.* at §§ 144-5.

tice Marshall in *M'Intosh*[137] established that Aboriginal tenure was a distinct pattern of land tenure, as he had implied in *Fletcher v. Peck*, not derived from the common law, but recognized and respected as a tenure system by federal law until purchased by the federal government. He affirmed that a private purchase by British subjects from an Aboriginal nation created an estate under the Aboriginal tenure system, and such a British estate under Aboriginal law could be abolished in a treaty conveyance between the tribe and the federal government unless reserved in the treaty: [138]

> If an individual might extinguish the Indian title for his own benefit, or, in other words, might purchase it, still he could acquire only that title. Admitting their power to change their laws or usages, so far as to allow an individual to separate a portion of their lands from the common stock, and hold it in severalty, still it is a part of their territory, and is held under them by a title dependent on their laws. The grant derives its efficacy from their will; and, if they choose to resume it, and make a different disposition of the land, the Courts of the United States cannot interpose for the protection of the title.[139]

Thus the Marshall Court conceptualized Aboriginal tenure as separate from the Crown's or federal title. An Aboriginal nation might determine the different estates under its land tenure; such estates are derivative of the Aboriginal law. The "person who purchases lands from the Indians, within their territory," the Court continued:

> incorporates himself with them, so far as respects the property purchased; holds their title under their protection, and subject to their laws. If they annul the grant, we know of no tribunal which can revise and set aside the proceeding. We can perceive no legal principle which will authorize a Court to say, the different consequences are attached to this purchase, because it was made by a stranger. By the treaties concluded between the United States and the Indian nations, whose title the plaintiffs claim, the country comprehending the lands in controversy has been ceded to the United States, without any reservation of their title ... . Their cession of the country, without a reservation of this land, affords a fair presumption, that they considered it as of no validity.[140]

Under the United States Supreme Court's holding, the Aboriginal nations "had an unquestionable right to annul any grant they had made to American citizens,"[141] because as sovereign governments they had a right to convey all the lands by treaty to

---

137 *M'Intosh, supra* note 51. The purchasers of the land under tribal dominion claimed the land under a proper legal conveyance: a deed poll, duly executed and delivered at the British military post, at a public treaty council, in contravention of the 1763 Proclamation. This policy was inaugurated by the Board of Trade after a recommendation to such effect at the Albany Conference in 1754. See Georgina C. Nammack, *Fraud, Politics, and Dispossession Of The Indians: The Iroquois Land Frontier in the Colonial Period* (Norman: University of Oklahoma Press, 1969). See *Worcester, supra* note 51 at 543, 547. The United States Congress prohibited its citizens or states from purchasing Aboriginal lands in § 4 of the *Indian Trade and Intercourse Act* of July 22, 1790, now embodied in 25 U.S.C. §177 (1970). See F. Prucha, *American Indian Policy in the Formative Years: The Indian Trade and Intercourse Acts, 1780-1834* (Cambridge, Mass.: Harvard University Press, 1962) at 144-47.

138 *M'Intosh, ibid.* at 572.

139 *Ibid.* at 593.

140 *Ibid.* at 593-94.

141 *Ibid.*

the United States, without reservation of estates granted under the tribal tenurial system. This theory is consistent with a proprietarian order, as well as the modern American police powers of the state.

In 1825, Justice Thompson in *Jackson v. Porter*, restated the holding:

> A purchaser, from the natives, at all events, could acquire only the Indian title, and must hold under them and according to their laws. The grant must derive its efficacy from their will, and if they choose to resume it and make a different disposition of it, courts cannot protect the right before granted. The purchaser incorporates himself with the Indians, and the purchase is to be considered in the same light as if the grant had been made to an Indian; and might be resumed by the tribe, and granted over again at their pleasure.[142]

The courts have recognized the proprietarian nature of the Aboriginal tenure.[143] In *Cherokee Nation*, Chief Justice Marshall for the majority stated: "the Indians are acknowledged to have an unquestionable, and, heretofore, unquestioned right to the lands they occupy."[144] The two dissent justices explained:

> notwithstanding we do not recognize the right of the Indians to transfer the absolute title of their lands other than to ourselves, ... the principle is universally admitted, that this occupancy belongs to them as a matter of right, and not by mere indulgence. They cannot be disturbed in the enjoyment of it, or deprived of it, without their free consent; or unless a just and necessary war should sanction their dispossession. In this view of their situation, there is as full and complete recognition of their sovereignty, as if they were the absolute owners of the soil.[145]

In *Worcester*, the Court held as a matter of law under the United States constitution: "The Indian nations had always been considered as distinct, independent political communities, retaining their original natural rights, as the undisputed possessors of the soil from time immemorial."[146] Chief Justice Marshall stated that it was "the universal conviction that the Indian nations possessed a full right to the lands they occupied."[147] These descriptions correspond to the concept of allodial tenure of land or *sui generis* Aboriginal tenure.

Lord Watson articulated this view for the judicial committee in *St. Catherine's Milling*:

> The territory in dispute has been in Indian occupation from the date of the [1763] proclamation until 1873. During that interval of time Indian affairs have been administered suc-

---

142   1 Paine 457, 13 Cas. (no. 7143) 1 (N.Y. Cir. 1825).

143   *Calder, supra* note 51 at 151, 193-96. *U.S. v. Santa Fe Pacific Railroad Co.*, 314 U.S. 339 at 347 (U.S. 1941) [hereinafter *Santa Fe*]; *St. Catherine's, supra* note 109; *R. v. Symonds* (1847), [1840-1932] N.Z.P.C. Cas. 387 at 390; *Mitchel v. U.S., supra* note 51 at 745-46, 749, 752 and 758; *Worcester, supra* note 51 at 544-46 and 559-61; *M'Intosh, supra* note 51 at 587-88.

144   *Cherokee Nation v. Georgia*, 30 U.S. (5 Pet.) 1 at 17 (U.S. 1832).

145   *Ibid.* at 55.

146   *Worcester, supra* note 51 at 559-60.

147   *Ibid.* at 560.

cessively by the Crown, by the Provincial Governments, and (since the passing of the British North America Act, 1867), by the Government of the Dominion. The policy of these administrations has been all along the same in this respect, that the Indian inhabitants have been precluded from entering into any transaction with a subject for the sale or transfer of their interest in the land, and have only been permitted to surrender their rights to the Crown by a formal contract, duly ratified in a meeting of their chiefs or head men convened for the purpose.[148]

In *Guerin*, Chief Justice Dickson[149] reached the same conclusion:[150]

It is true that the *sui generis* interest which the Indians have in the land is personal in the sense that it cannot be transferred to a grantee, but it is also true, as will presently appear, that the interest gives rise upon surrender to a distinctive fiduciary obligation on the part of the Crown to deal with land for the benefit of the surrendering Indians. These two aspects of Indian title go together, since the Crown's original purpose in declaring the Indians' interest to be inalienable otherwise than to the Crown was to facilitate the Crown's ability to represent the Indians in dealings with third parties. The nature of the Indians' interest is therefore best characterized [in British law] by its general inalienability, coupled with the fact that the Crown is under an obligation to deal with the land on the Indians' behalf when the interest is surrendered. Any description of Indian title which goes beyond these two features [in British law] is both unnecessary and potentially misleading.[151]

In *Delgamuukw*, Chief Justice Lamer reinforced the point:

The idea that aboriginal title is *sui generis* is the unifying principle underlying the various dimensions of that title. One dimension is its *inalienability*. Lands held pursuant to aboriginal title cannot be transferred, sold or surrendered to anyone other than the Crown and, as a result, [are] inalienable to third parties. This Court has taken pains to clarify that aboriginal title is only "personal" in this sense, and does not mean that aboriginal title is a non-proprietary interest which amounts to no more than a licence to use and occupy the land and cannot compete on an equal footing with other proprietary interests.[152]

---

148 *St. Catherine's, supra* note 109 at 54.

149 *Guerin, supra* note 51 at 376-82, Beetz, Chouinard and Lamer JJ. concurring. Mr. Justice Estey, at 394, found that the Crown acted as the statutory agent of the Indian Band (tribal or community interest) in arranging a lease of their reserved land with a non-Indian. Madam Justice Wilson described the Crown's liability as a breach of a trust. She stated, at 355, that the surrender document created an express trust in the Crown. She noted that the *Indian Act* provisions did not create a fiduciary obligation towards Aboriginals on reserves, but, at 356, the *Indian Act*, "recognized the existence of such an obligation." Her Ladyship saw Indian title as a property or beneficial interest sufficient to constitute a trust *res* or *corpus*.

150 *Ibid.* at 379-80. He discussed *St. Catherine's, supra* note 109, and *Ontario Mining Co. v. Seybold (The Star Chrome Case)*, [1903] A.C. 73 (P.C.), affirming (1901), 32 S.C.R. 1 (S.C.C.); *Amodu Tijani v. Southern Nigeria (Secretary)*, [1921] 2 A.C. 399 at 404 (P.C.); and *Calder, supra* note 51.

151 *Guerin, ibid.* at 382. This characterization does not take one much further than the *Royal Proclamation of 1763*. See B. Slattery, *The Land Rights of Indigenous Canadian People, as Affected by the Crown's Acquisition of their Territories* (Saskatoon, Sk.: Native Law Centre, 1979).

152 *Delgamuukw, supra* note 2 at para. 113.

C. Aboriginal tenure distinguished from Aboriginal rights

Since Aboriginal tenure is a constitutionally protected *sui generis* proprietarian tenure, the Supreme Court of Canada in *Delgamuukw* created a distinctive test for Aboriginal tenure different from Aboriginal rights:

> Aboriginal title is a right in land and, as such, is more than the right to engage in specific activities which may be themselves aboriginal rights. Rather, it confers the right to use land for a variety of activities, not all of which need be aspects of practices, customs and traditions which are integral to the distinctive cultures of aboriginal societies.[153]

In constitutional analysis, the relation of Aboriginal tenure to Aboriginal rights is similar to the judicial distinction between the existence of the power or an exercise of the power.[154]

The Court has said that Aboriginal tenure does not have to conform to the test for Aboriginal rights, but requires a connection to or relationship with specific land, and its ecology. Aboriginal rights are independent "site-specific" activities,[155] which "must be an element of a practice, custom or tradition integral to the distinctive culture of the Aboriginal group claiming the right,"[156] and established before European contact.[157]

In *Adams*,[158] and in the companion decision *Côté*,[159] the Supreme Court considered and rejected the proposition that claims to Aboriginal rights must be grounded in an underlying claim to Aboriginal tenure. The Supreme Court held that Aboriginal rights are activities that can exist independently of proof of Aboriginal tenure:

> ...while claims to Aboriginal title fall within the conceptual framework of Aboriginal rights, Aboriginal rights do not exist solely where a claim to Aboriginal title has been made out. Where an Aboriginal group has shown that a particular activity, custom or tradition taking place on the land was integral to the distinctive culture of that group then, *even if they have not shown that their occupation and use of the land was sufficient to sup-*

---

153 *Ibid.* at para. 111. Compare to L'Heureux-Dubé J.'s characterization in *Van der Peet, supra* note 58 at para. 116: "The concept of Aboriginal title, however, does not capture the entirety of the doctrine of Aboriginal rights. Rather, as its name indicates, the doctrine refers to a broader notion of Aboriginal rights arising out of the historic occupation and use of Native ancestral lands, which relate not only to Aboriginal title, but also to the component elements of this larger right—such as Aboriginal rights to hunt, fish or trap, and their accompanying practices, traditions and customs—as well as to other matters, not related to land, that form part of a distinctive Aboriginal culture," citing W.I.C. Binnie, "The *Sparrow* Doctrine: Beginning of the End or End of the Beginning?" (1990) 15 Queen's L.J. 217; and Douglas Sanders, "The Rights of the Aboriginal Peoples of Canada" (1983) 61 Can. Bar Rev. 314.

154 *New Brunswick Broadcasting, supra* note 11 at 274-75. McLachlin J. stated: "The important question is whether we are here treating the fruit of the legislative tree, or the tree itself ... in this case, the issue is not the fruit of the constitutional tree (the exercise of a power) but the tree itself."

155 *Van der Peet, supra* note 58.

156 *Ibid.* at para. 46, Lamer C.J.C.

157 *Ibid.* at paras. 205-207. Compare L'Heureux-Dubé and McLachlin JJ.'s dissenting opinions at paras. 164-79 and 244-50 respectively.

158 *R. v. Adams*, [1996] 4 C.N.L.R. 1 (S.C.C.) [hereinafter *Adams*].

159 *R. v. Côté*, [1996] 4 C.N.L.R. 26 (S.C.C.) [hereinafter *Côté*].

port a claim of title to the land, they will have demonstrated that they have an Aboriginal right to engage in that practice, custom or tradition. The *Van der Peet* test protects activities which were integral to the distinctive culture of the Aboriginal group claiming the right; it does not require that that group satisfy the further hurdle of demonstrating that their connection with the piece of land on which the activity was taking place was of a central significance to their distinctive culture sufficient to make out a claim to Aboriginal title to the land. *Van der Peet* establishes that s. 35 [of the *Constitution Act, 1982*] recognizes and affirms the rights of those peoples who occupied North America prior to the arrival of the Europeans; that recognition and affirmation is not limited to those circumstances where an Aboriginal group's relationship with the land is of a kind sufficient to establish title to the land.[160]

In *Delgamuukw*, Chief Justice Lamer elaborated a "spectrum" of Aboriginal tenure and rights:

> The picture which emerges from *Adams* is that the aboriginal rights which are recognized and affirmed by s. 35(1) fall along a spectrum with respect to their degree of connection with the land. At the one end, there are those aboriginal rights which are practices, customs and traditions that are integral to the distinctive aboriginal culture of the group claiming the right. However, the "*occupation and use of the land*" where the activity is taking place is not "*sufficient to support a claim of title to the land*" (at para. 26, emphasis in original). Nevertheless, those activities receive constitutional protection. In the middle, there are activities which, out of necessity, take place on land and indeed, might be intimately related to a particular piece of land. Although an aboriginal group may not be able to demonstrate title to the land, it may nevertheless have a site-specific right to engage in a particular activity. I put the point this way in *Adams,* at para. 30:

>> Even where an aboriginal right exists on a tract of land to which the aboriginal people in question do not have title, that right may well be site specific, with the result that it can be exercised only upon that specific tract of land. For example, *if an aboriginal people demonstrates that hunting on a specific tract of land was an integral part of their distinctive culture then, even if the right exists apart from title to that tract of land, the aboriginal right to hunt is nonetheless defined as, and limited to, the right to hunt on the specific tract of land.* [Emphasis added.]

> At the other end of the spectrum, there is aboriginal title itself. As *Adams* makes clear, aboriginal title confers more than the right to engage in site-specific activities which are aspects of the practices, customs and traditions of distinctive aboriginal cultures. Site-specific rights can be made out even if title cannot. What aboriginal title confers is the right to the land itself.[161]

Justice La Forest's concurring opinion stated that the generalized claim of Aboriginal tenure should not be defined as merely a compendium of Aboriginal rights, each of which must meet the test set out in *Van der Peet*.[162] This "spectrum" reveals the pro-

---

160 *Adams, supra* note 158 at para. 26.

161 *Delgamuukw, supra* note 2 at para. 138 [emphasis in original].

162 *Ibid.* at para. 193.

prietarian order of Aboriginal tenure. Chief Justice Lamer noted that these constitutional rights are related and that the judicial tests are similar:

> ...the tests for the identification of aboriginal rights to engage in particular activities and
> for the identification of aboriginal title share broad similarities. The major distinctions are
> first, under the test for aboriginal title, the requirement that the land be integral to the dis-
> tinctive culture of the claimants is subsumed by the requirement of occupancy, and sec-
> ond, whereas the time for the identification of aboriginal rights is the time of first contact,
> the time for the identification of aboriginal title is the time at which the Crown asserted
> sovereignty over the land.[163]

D. Right to exclusive use and occupation of land

Chief Justice Lamer stated that the exclusive right to use and occupy lands in an
Aboriginal peoples means "the exclusion of both non-aboriginals and members of
other aboriginal nations."[164] He declared two propositions regarding the right to exclusive use and occupation under Aboriginal tenure:

> ...first, that aboriginal title encompasses the right to exclusive use and occupation of the
> land held pursuant to that title for a variety of purposes, which need not be aspects of those
> aboriginal practices, customs and traditions which are integral to distinctive aboriginal
> cultures; and second, that those protected uses must not be irreconcilable with the nature
> of the group's attachment to that land.[165]

He explained that Aboriginal law rather than British law defines "exclusive": "[e]xclu-
sivity is a common law principle derived from the notion of fee simple ownership and
should be imported into the concept of aboriginal title with caution."[166] In Aboriginal
law, this can mean shared exclusivity with others, for example, where "two aboriginal
nations lived on a particular piece of land and recognized each other's entitlement to
that land but nobody else's."[167]

Thus, Aboriginal nations can determine the uses and non-uses of their land. Aboriginal laws are the sources and content of Aboriginal tenure; and Aboriginal laws regulate the relationship and the exercises among Aboriginal responsibilities, uses, and
occupations, which determine "rights" among all inhabitants, both Aboriginal and non-
Aboriginal. The national or community decision-making authority, recognized by Aboriginal law and its traditions, must consent to resource uses by others.[168] Since Aboriginal tenure and rights are affirmed in the constitution, and other common law
property rights were not, the nations have the right to prevent others from intruding on
or using their lands.

---

163 *Ibid.* at para. 142.
164 *Ibid.* at para. 185.
165 *Ibid.* at para. 117.
166 *Ibid.* at para. 156.
167 *Ibid.* at para. 158.
168 *Ibid.* at para. 115.

E. Sustainable rights

Most Aboriginal world-views and laws create the inalienability of Aboriginal tenure based on an Aboriginal proprietary ideal and the interests of their ancestors and future generations. Aboriginal tenure is the foundation of their connection with the ecological order, and their spiritual relations with the forces of that ecological order. In *Western Sahara*, International Court Judge Ammoun captured the spiritual notion of ancestral relations as the basis of the ownership of the soil:

> the ancestral tie between the land, or "mother nature", and the man who was born therefrom, remains attached thereto, and must one day return thither to be united with his ancestors. This link is the basis of the ownership of the soil, or better, of sovereignty.[169]

Aboriginal tenure is considered sacred; it can be shared, but never treated as a commodity. This sustainable development component of Aboriginal tenure affirms the tenure as a proprietarian order—an idea that is coming to be recognized as an incident of all land tenures.

In *Delgamuukw*, the Supreme Court declared that as long as Aboriginal nations, tribes, and peoples maintain their relationship to their land, Aboriginal tenure continues.[170] Aboriginal tenure is "perpetual" in the civil law sense of ownership and distinct from the common law division of estates according to time. Aboriginal tenure, in enduring for as long as the connection with the land is honoured and respected by Aboriginal peoples, is distinguished from "normal" property interests.[171]

The sustainable nature of Aboriginal tenure controls the decisions of the hereditary chiefs and members concerning responsibilities for and uses of the land. While the Aboriginal peoples have a constitutional right to choose possible uses of the land, they cannot destroy the ability of the land to sustain future generations of Aboriginal peoples:[172]

> ...[U]ses of the lands that would threaten that future relationship are, by their very nature, excluded from the content of aboriginal title.

> Accordingly, in my view, lands subject to aboriginal title cannot be put to such uses as may be irreconcilable with the nature of the occupation of that land and the relationship that the particular group has had with the land which together have given rise to aboriginal title in the first place.[173]

As in the case of all sustainable rights, Aboriginal law and tenure impose inherent fiduciary duties on decision-makers. This fiduciary limitation on the representatives of the

---

169 *Western Sahara Case (Morocco v. Western Sahara; Mauritania v. Western Sahara)*, Advisory Opinion, [1975] I.C.J. Rep. 16 at 85-86.

170 *Delgamuukw, supra* note 2 at para. 154; see *Mabo, supra* note 91 at 43.

171 *Delgamuukw, ibid.* at para. 115.

172 *Ibid.* at para. 166.

173 *Ibid.* at paras. 127-28.

Aboriginal nations prevents the exercises or uses that are irreconcilable with or destroy their relationship to Aboriginal tenure.[174]

Chief Justice Lamer's "ultimate" or future limitation articulates Aboriginal tenure's divergence from the view of property as commodity in a market economy. He is silent, however, on conflict with the "ultimate" underlying interest of the Crown and the relationship of this limitation to the justified infringement test. The Court has held that the federal or provincial government may regulate activities within Aboriginal tenure, if such infringements can be justified by a valid "legislative objective that is compelling and substantial"[175] and consistent with the special fiduciary relations between the Crown and Aboriginal peoples, and also with the Aboriginal law fiduciary obligations to future generations.[176]

The sustainable development standards govern the "inescapable economic component" of Aboriginal tenure. In *Delgamuukw*, the Supreme Court unanimously ended the distinction between legal treatment of Aboriginal and non-Aboriginal property. In the past, the false distinction between Aboriginal tenure and common law tenures has prevented the Aboriginal peoples from benefiting from their ancient territory and their rights.

21. Extinguishment Theories

The Victorian and the United States common law of colonization asserted that sovereignty over a foreign territory carried the power to create and to extinguish indefeasible private rights and interests within the territory.[177] The courts could review the legality of the exercise of prerogative power, but not its merits.[178] However, the common law did not have any doctrine of expropriation of land since the common law was based on possession, time, and concurrent enjoyment; thus, as the Australian High Court held, the common law was limited by existing Aboriginal tenure, its uses and possession.[179]

Neither the Crown nor governments nor Victorian common law assumptions or categories of private rights and interests can be controlling perspectives on extinguishing Aboriginal tenure as a *sui generis* tenure, since it is not a derivative estate granted by the Crown. In *Delgamuukw*, the Supreme Court asserts the controlling perspectives are the Aboriginal nation's consent and sustainable uses. The common law courts have

---

174   *Ibid.* at paras. 111, 166.

175   *Ibid.* at para. 161.

176   *Ibid.* at para. 162.

177   *Calder, supra* note 51 at 404; *Te Weehi v. Regional Fisheries Officer*, [1986] 1 N.Z.L.R. 680 at 691-92; *Mabo, supra* note 91 at 46-52; *Joint Tribal Council of the Passamaquoddy Tribe v. Morton*, 528 Fed. 2d 370 at 376 (U.S. 1975).

178   *Santa Fe, supra* note 143; *Tee-Hit-Ton Indians v. United States*, 348 U.S. 272 at 281-85 (U.S. 1954).

179   *Mabo, supra* note 91 at 33-42.

uniformly asserted that Aboriginal tenure cannot be extinguished unless the wording of colonial legislative or executive action reveals a clear and plain intention of the sovereign to do so. Moreover, the courts have declared that this requirement flows from the seriousness of the consequences to Aboriginal inhabitants of extinguishing their traditional tenure.[180]

Within written constitutions in British colonies, the legal exercise of governmental authority with respect to Aboriginal tenure is determined by the scope of constitutional authority.[181] Consistent with the proprietarian nature of *sui generis* Aboriginal tenure, the unified Supreme Court in *Van der Peet* and *Delgamuukw* held that under the constitutional supremacy doctrine and section 35(1), Aboriginal tenures and rights cannot be extinguished:

> At common law Aboriginal rights did not, of course, have constitutional status, with the result that Parliament could, at any time, extinguish or regulate those rights ... it is this which distinguishes the Aboriginal rights recognized and affirmed in s. 35(1) from the Aboriginal rights protected by the common law. Subsequent to s. 35(1) Aboriginal rights cannot be extinguished and can only be regulated or infringed consistent with the justificatory test...[182]

In *Delgamuukw*, Chief Justice Lamer restated *Sparrow's* principle that to be recognized and affirmed by section 35(1) Aboriginal tenure or rights must have existed in 1982; rights that were extinguished by the sovereign before that time are not revived by the provision.[183] In the Canadian federal system, he stated, the courts need to determine whether Aboriginal tenure or rights have been extinguished, which raises constitutional division of powers issues concerning which level of government has jurisdiction.

In reviewing the trial judges' decision in *Delgamuukw*, the British Columbia Court of Appeal reversed the trial judge's conclusion that before Confederation in 1871 there had been blanket extinguishment of Aboriginal tenure or rights.[184] The Court of Appeal held that a trial judge would have to make detailed determinations about the location and scope of existing Aboriginal tenure and the sovereign's clear and plain intent and wording to extinguish it.[185] This issue was not appealed to the Supreme Court.

In *Delgamuukw*, the Lamer Court was faced with three specific extinguishment issues: 1) whether the province of British Columbia, from the time it joined Confeder-

---

180 *Sparrow, supra* note 28 at 1094; *Hamlet of Baker Lake v. Minister of Indian Affairs* (1979), 107 D.L.R. (3d) 513 at 552, additional reasons at (1979), [1982] C.N.L.R. 139 (Fed. T.D.) [hereinafter *Baker Lake*]; *Calder, supra* note 51 at 404; *Santa Fe, supra* note 143 at 353-54.

181 *Mabo, supra* note 91 at 46, 49.

182 *Van der Peet, supra* note 58 at para. 28. Justice L'Heureux-Dubé agreed with the dissenting opinion in *R. v. Horseman*, [1990] 3 C.N.L.R. 95 at 117, [1990] 1 S.C.R. 901 (S.C.C.) [hereinafter *Horseman*].

183 *Delgamuukw, supra* note 2 at para. 172.

184 *Ibid.*, B.C. C.A. at 490. Hutcheon J.A. for the minority opinion in the Court of Appeal agreed that there had not been blanket extinguishment of Aboriginal tenure, *ibid.* at 764.

185 *Ibid.*

ation in 1871, until the entrenchment of section 35(1) in 1982, had the jurisdiction to extinguish the tenure or rights of Aboriginal peoples in that province; 2) if the province was without such jurisdiction, whether provincial laws of general application that were not "in pith and substance" aimed at the extinguishment of Aboriginal rights, could be implied to extinguish; and 3) whether a provincial law, which could otherwise not extinguish Aboriginal tenure or rights, could be given that effect through referential incorporation by section 88 of the federal *Indian Act*.[186] The Court declared that the province never had constitutional authority to extinguish *sui generis* Aboriginal tenure, that it had never been extinguished in the past, and that Aboriginal tenure continues as a constitutionally protected tenure in British Columbia that must be respected by courts.[187]

As had the British Columbia Court of Appeals, the Supreme Court rejected federal and provincial Crown arguments that prior to 1982 Aboriginal tenure was extinguished. It denied each of their five extinguishment theories: that the assertion of Crown sovereignty had extinguished Aboriginal tenure; that colonial land legislation before Confederation extinguished the Aboriginal peoples' relations to the land; that the creation of land grants by British Columbia to settlers extinguished Aboriginal tenure because the Aboriginal people were precluded from sustaining their relationship to the land; that the establishment of federal Indian reserves in British Columbia extinguished Aboriginal tenure because the Aboriginal peoples "abandoned" their territory; and that section 88 of the *Indian Act* allowed provincial laws of general application to extinguish Aboriginal rights.

As Justice Hall had said to similar arguments in *Calder*, the Court said these arguments are "self-destructive."[188] Chief Justice Lamer declared that the Crown failed to establish any legal basis to justify the legal dispossession of Aboriginal peoples by provincial authority:

> The vesting of exclusive jurisdiction with the federal government over Indians and Indian lands under s. 91(24), operates to preclude provincial laws in relation to those matters. ... What must be answered, however, is whether the same principle allows provincial laws of general application to extinguish aboriginal rights. I have come to the conclusion that a provincial law of general application could not have this effect, for two reasons. First, a law of general application cannot, by definition, meet the standard which has been set by this Court for the extinguishment of aboriginal rights without being *ultra vires* the province. That standard was laid down in *Sparrow, supra*, at p. 1099, as one of "clear and plain" intent. ... As a result, a provincial law could never, *proprio vigore*, extinguish aboriginal rights, because the intention to do so would take the law outside provincial jurisdiction.
>
> Second, as I mentioned earlier, s. 91(24) protects a core of federal jurisdiction even from provincial laws of general application, through the operation of the doctrine of interjurisdictional immunity. That core has been described as matters touching on "Indianness" or

---

186   *Ibid.* at paras. 173-83.

187   *Ibid.* at paras. 114, 126.

188   *Calder, supra* note 51 at 414.

the "core of Indianness" ... It follows that aboriginal rights are part of the core of Indianness at the heart of s. 91(24). Prior to 1982, as a result, [Aboriginal tenure and rights] could not be extinguished by provincial laws of general application. ... [Section] 88 does not evince the requisite clear and plain intent to extinguish aboriginal rights.[189]

In sum, the unceded and unpurchased Aboriginal tenure in British Columbia involves lands reserved for the Indians under federal and Aboriginal jurisdiction in both sections 91(24) and 35(1). British Columbia does not have any power to legislate in relation to *sui generis* Aboriginal tenure reserved for the Indians because such lands are an "Interest other than that of the Province."

Similarly, the Australian High Court concluded that general provisions in Crown Land Acts should not be construed as being directed to Aboriginal peoples with their lands, but restricted to colonizers who were or are in occupation under a Crown grant or without any colour of right.[190] The New Zealand Court of Appeal in *New Zealand Maori Council v. Attorney-General* affirmed that "no activity of State-Owned Enterprise Act will permit the Crown to act in a manner inconsistent with the principles of the Treaty of Waitangi."[191]

In *Sparrow*, the British Columbia Attorney General argued that the federal *Fisheries Act* and its progressively detailed regulations constituted a "complete code" that extinguished the Musqueam Band's Aboriginal right to fish. Relying on past precedents,[192] the Attorney General argued that extinguishment need not be express, but may take place where the sovereign authority is exercised in a manner "necessarily inconsistent" with the continued enjoyment of Aboriginal rights. He submitted that there was a "fundamental inconsistency" between the communal right to fish embodied in the Aboriginal right, and fishing under a special federal licence or permit issued to individual Indians by the Minister subject to terms and conditions which, if breached, may result in the licence's cancellation. Before the *Constitution Act, 1982*, he argued, consent to extinguishment was not required; the intent of the sovereign could be effected not only by written statute but also by valid regulations that displaced any Aboriginal right.

The Supreme Court of Canada rejected these propositions, declaring that the arguments confused regulation with extinguishment. The Court acknowledged that "the power to legislate in relation to fisheries does necessarily to a certain extent enable the Legislature so empowered to affect proprietary rights";[193] but held that even the detailed regulations controlling the fisheries do not extinguish the Aboriginal rights:

---

189   *Delgamuukw, supra* note 2 at paras. 179-81, 183.

190   *Mabo, supra* note 91 at 49.

191   *New Zealand Maori Council v. Attorney-General*, [1987] 1 N.Z.L.R. 641.

192   *Sparrow, supra* note 28 at 1097. For this proposition, the Attorney General particularly relied on *St. Catherine's, supra* note 109; *Calder, supra* note 51; *Baker Lake, supra* note 180; and *Attorney-General for Ontario v. Bear Island Foundation*, [1991] 2 S.C.R. 570, 3 C.N.L.R. 79, reconsideration refused (1995), 46 R.P.R. (2d) 91 (note) [hereinafter *Bear Island*].

193   *Sparrow, ibid.* at 1098 citing, *A.G. Can. v. A.G. Ont., supra* note 83. There, the Privy Council had to deal with the interrelationship between provincial property under s. 109 of the *Constitution Act, 1867, supra* note 37, and the federal power to legislate respecting fishing thereon under s. 91(12).

> The test of extinguishment to be adopted, in our opinion, is that the Sovereign's intention must be clear and plain if it is to extinguish an aboriginal right.

> There is nothing in the *Fisheries Act* or its detailed regulations that demonstrates a clear and plain intention to extinguish the Indian aboriginal right to fish. The fact that express provision permitting the Indians to fish for food may have applied to all Indians and that for an extended period permits were discretionary and issued on an individual rather than a communal basis in no way shows a clear intention to extinguish. These permits were simply a manner of controlling the fisheries, not defining underlying rights.[194]

The Court concluded that the Crown had failed to discharge its burden of proving extinguishment; confirming that this approach was consistent with ensuring that an Aboriginal right should not be defined by incorporating the ways in which it has been regulated in the past;[195] and declaring "an existing aboriginal right cannot be read so as to incorporate the specific manner in which it was regulated before 1982."[196]

As in *Sparrow*,[197] Justice Brennan in *Mabo* stated that a clear and plain intention to extinguish Aboriginal tenure is not revealed by a law that merely regulates the enjoyment of Aboriginal tenure or that creates a regime of control that is inconsistent with its continued enjoyment.[198] Justice Brennan held that the Crown did not clearly intend to extinguish Native title to the Murray Islands when the Islands were annexed in 1879, or when in 1882 it reserved the Murray Islands from sale in the *Crown Lands Alienation Act* of 1876 (Qld), or in 1912, when a proclamation was made pursuant to section 180 of the *Land Act, 1910* which "permanently reserved and set apart" the Murray Islands "for use of the Aboriginal Inhabitants of the State."[199]

In *Delgamuukw*, Chief Justice Lamer affirmed the distinction between laws that extinguished Aboriginal rights and those which regulated them:

> Although the latter types of laws may have been "necessarily inconsistent" with the continued exercise of aboriginal rights, they could not extinguish those rights. While the requirement of clear and plain intent does not, perhaps, require that the Crown "use language which refers expressly to its extinguishment of aboriginal rights" (*Gladstone, supra*, at para. 34), the standard is still quite high. My concern is that the only laws with the sufficiently clear and plain intention to extinguish aboriginal rights would be laws in relation to Indians and Indian lands.[200]

---

194 *Sparrow. ibid.* at 1099.

195 *Ibid.* at 1101.

196 *Ibid.* at 1091.

197 *Ibid.* at 1097.

198 *Mabo, supra* note 91 at 46-52.

199 *Ibid.* at 47-48. Section 180(1) of the *Land Act, 1910* (S.C.A.), empowered the Governor-in-Council to reserve any Crown land from sale or lease, "which, in the opinion of the Governor in Council, is or may be required for public purposes." Section 4 defined "public purposes" to include "Aboriginal reserves." "Crown land" was defined by s. 4.

200 *Delgamuukw, supra* note 2 at para. 180.

The Supreme Court in *Sparrow* and the High Court in Australia in *Mabo* did not unpack all the implications of Aboriginal tenure separate from British law. They still maintained that the sovereign delegated authority to certain governments to extinguish Aboriginal tenure,[201] as if it were an estate in British land law, but such exercise of extraterritorial power must reveal a clear and plain intention to do so.[202] Under the constitutional supremacy of Canada, these propositions are inconsistent with the constitutional protection of Aboriginal tenure and rights, and the existing fiduciary obligations of the Crown to protect these *sui generis* rights.

In the context of Aboriginal rights, in *Sparrow*,[203] the Court rejected the existing judicial argument that, before 1982, an Aboriginal right was automatically extinguished to the extent that it was inconsistent with a statute. Justice Judson, in *Calder*, asserted that a common law Aboriginal tenure could be extinguished by a series of statutes that evinced a sovereign's "unity of intention" inconsistent with it;[204] similarly Mahoney J. declared in *Baker Lake*:

> Once a statute has been validly enacted, it must be given effect. If its necessary effect is to abridge or entirely abrogate a common law right, then that is the effect that the Courts must give it. That is as true of an aboriginal title as of any other common law right.[205]

The Dickson Court in *Sparrow* affirmed the contrary argument of Justice Hall, in *Calder*, that "the onus of proving that the Sovereign intended to extinguish the Indian title lies on the respondent and that intention must be 'clear and plain'"[206] as the controlling constitutional test.

In Australian law, Justice Brennan declared that the Queensland Parliament retains, subject to the constitution and to restrictions imposed by valid laws of the Commonwealth, a legislative power to extinguish Native title:

> The sovereign powers which might be exercised over the waste lands of the Crown within Queensland were vested in the Colony of Queensland subject to the ultimate legislative power of the Imperial Parliament so long as that Parliament retained that power and, after Federation, subject to the Constitution of the Commonwealth of Australia. The power to reserve and dedicate land to a public purpose and the power to grant interests in land are conferred by statute on the Governor in Council of Queensland and an exercise of these powers is, subject to the *Racial Discrimination Act*, apt to extinguish native title.[207]

Avoiding the implications of Aboriginal tenure as an independent and *sui generis* land tenure separate from the Crown and asserting a unified concept of title, similar to Justice Judson in *Calder*, Justice Brennan suggested that in common law a Crown grant

---

201 *Sparrow, supra* note 28 at 1110-1119.

202 *Mabo, supra* note 91 at 46-47.

203 *Sparrow, supra* note 28 at 1110-1119.

204 *Ibid.* at 1098-99.

205 *Baker Lake, supra* note 180 at 551; See also *Bear Island, supra* note 192 at 439-40.

206 *Calder, supra* note 51 at 404.

207 *Mabo, supra* note 91 at 49.

that vests in the private grantee estates of freehold or of leases inconsistent with the continued right to enjoy an Aboriginal tenure in respect of the same land necessarily extinguishes the Aboriginal tenure recognized by the common law.[208] If Aboriginal tenure to any parcel of the "waste lands of the Crown" is extinguished, the Crown becomes the absolute beneficial owner.[209]

This judicial approach, which equates tenure systems with private estates, is inconsistent with the High Court's rejection of similar arguments of *terra nullius* and settled colony status, and raises the general issue of the legitimacy of colonial authority to grant interests in unpurchased Aboriginal tenure to others:

> Aborigines were dispossessed of their land parcel by parcel, to make way for expanding colonial settlement. Their dispossession underwrote the development of the nation. But, if this be the consequence in law of colonial settlement, is there any occasion now to overturn the cases which held the Crown to have become the absolute beneficial owner of land when British colonists first settled here? Does it make any difference whether native title failed to survive British colonisation or was subsequently extinguished by government action? ... [T]here may be other areas of Australia where native title has not been extinguished and where an Aboriginal people, maintaining their identity and their customs, are entitled to enjoy their native title. Even if there be no such areas, it is appropriate to identify the events which resulted in the dispossession of the indigenous inhabitants of Australia, in order to dispel the misconception that it is the common law rather than the action of governments which made many of the indigenous people of this country trespassers on their own land.[210]

In 1996, the High Court of Australia resolved these issues by declaring in *Wik Peoples* that Crown grants of pastoral leases to private colonizers had not extinguished the Aboriginal tenure of the Wik and Thayorre people;[211] instead, the grants had created a regime of co-existing rights on the range land. Extinguishing Aboriginal tenure required showing the sovereign's clear intent and finding that the competing rights "could not possibly co-exist."[212]

As explained in the *Van der Peet* trilogy by the Supreme Court of Canada, Aboriginal rights are entitled to constitutional recognition and are not controlled by "the historical idiosyncrasies of colonialization":

---

208 *Ibid.* Crown grants of lesser interests (*e.g.*, authorities to prospect for minerals) do not necessarily extinguish Aboriginal tenure.

209 *Ibid.* at 52.

210 *Ibid.* at 50-51:

> Where the Crown has validly and effectively appropriated land to itself and the appropriation is wholly or partially inconsistent with a continuing right to enjoy native title, native title is extinguished to the extent of the inconsistency. Thus native title has been extinguished to parcels of the waste lands of the Crown that have been validly appropriated for use (whether by dedication, setting aside, reservation or other valid means) and used for roads, railways, post offices and other permanent public works which preclude the continuing concurrent enjoyment of native title. Native title continues where the waste lands of the Crown have not been so appropriated or used or where the appropriation and use is consistent with the continuing concurrent enjoyment of Native title over the land (*e.g.*, land set aside as a national park).

211 *Wik Peoples v. Queensland* (1996), 141 A.L.R. 129.

212 *Ibid.* at 184.

The entrenchment of Aboriginal ancestral and treaty rights in s. 35(1) of the *Constitution Act, 1982* has changed the landscape of Aboriginal rights in Canada. As explained in the *Van der Peet* trilogy, the purpose of s. 35(1) was to extend constitutional protection to the practices, customs and traditions central to the distinctive culture of Aboriginal societies prior to contact with Europeans. If such practices, customs and traditions continued following contact in the absence of specific extinguishment, such practices, customs and traditions are entitled to constitutional recognition subject to the infringement and justification tests outlined in *Sparrow, supra* and *Gladstone, supra.*[213]

In *Delgamuukw*, Chief Justice Lamer declared that section 91(24) of the *Constitution Act, 1867* vested the federal government with the "exclusive power" to legislate in relation to "Indians, and Lands reserved for Indians"; encompassing within "Lands reserved for the Indians" the "exclusive power to extinguish Aboriginal rights, including Aboriginal title."[214] He extended this principle to include jurisdiction over any Aboriginal right which relates to land.[215]

Past attempts to extinguish Aboriginal tenure were by treaty reconciliations, which were attempts at consensual reconciliation, rather than unilateral extinguishment. While the courts could conceptualize Aboriginal tenure as distinct from British law, they still assumed sovereign commands could unilaterally extinguish it against Aboriginal consent and sustainable land use for future generations. This vestige of colonial law combined with the modern ideal-type of land as a commodity permits the Crown to act as predator against, rather than protector of, Aboriginal tenure.

The exclusive role assigned to colonial governments by prerogative law was to protect Aboriginal tenure until a consensual purchase. No sovereign act authorized or commanded the federal government or the provinces in Canada to extinguish Aboriginal tenure for their own beneficial interest. Colonial self-interest expressed in colonial legislation, rather than in sovereign acts, created the extinguishment theory and refused to place Aboriginal tenure as the starting point of the land recording system. Prior to *Delgamuukw*, courts refused to restrain non-proprietary governments or the Minister of Indian Affairs and Northern Development from issuing competing permits to companies on the basis of Aboriginal tenure.[216]

Occasionally, the Supreme Court appears to confirm unilateral action by the federal government. For example, in addressing the effects of the federal *Natural Resource*

---

213   *Côté, supra* note 159 at para. 51.

214   *Delgamuukw, supra* note 2 at para. 173.

215   *Ibid.* at para. 176.

216   *Kanatewat et al. v. The James Bay Development Corporation and A.G. Quebec*, [1974] R.P. 38 (Que. S.C.), reversing (1973), 41 D.L.R. (3d) 1 (S.C.C.). The Quebec Court of Appeal suspended this interim injunction a week later (on November 22, 1973) in an unreported decision. The Supreme Court of Canada affirmed the suspension of the interim injunction. A year later the Quebec Court of Appeals overturned the decision on its merit, [1975] C.A. 166. Only after constitutional reforms did the courts begin restraining federal or provincial permits on reserved Aboriginal lands, and then only if sufficient evidence showed the activities would interfere with the exercise of Aboriginal rights or uses. See *MacMillan Bloedel Ltd. v. Mullin et al.*, [1985] 2 W.W.R. 722 (B.C. S.C.), reversed, [1985] 3 W.W.R. 577 (B.C. C.A.); *Hunt v. Halcan Log Services Ltd.* (1986), 34 D.L.R. (4th) 504 (B.C. S.C.).

Transfer Act in 1930 to the prairie provinces on existing treaty rights under the *Indian Act*, Justice Cory in *Horseman*[217] asserted:

> ...although it might well be politically and morally unacceptable in today's climate to take such a step as that set out in the 1930 Agreement without consultation with and concurrence of the Native peoples affected, nonetheless the power of the Federal Government to unilaterally make such a modification is unquestioned and has not been challenged in this case. [218]

While constitutional arguments were not raised in this case, this perspective on past regulations is in conflict with the Supreme Court decision in *Sparrow* not to read federal statutes or regulations into the meaning of Aboriginal or treaty rights in section 35(1).

22. Constitutional Tests and Remedies

Property rights are not self-defining. Because a wide variety of property interests exists, courts make constant choices among competing interests. In the past, courts have not protected Aboriginal tenure from intrusion and interference by legal or equitable principles, creating a property regime that grants protection to the provinces, corporate entities, and private parties over Aboriginal tenure and rights. After *Delgamuukw* the courts must now make the land title system consistent with the constitutional order by applying legal remedies, such as trespass, and equitable remedies where the courts have used legal theory to generate general principles. Because the application of legal or equitable remedies to Aboriginal tenure requires detailed, independent study, this discussion focuses on constitutional remedies.

Constitutional, legal, and equitable remedies for Aboriginal tenure violations are developing. So long as the court guidelines for remedies for Aboriginal rights are unprincipled, judicial interpretation is applied on a case-by-case basis. The typical remedy of the Supreme Court in Aboriginal rights cases has been to order a new trial for possible infringements by federal or provincial governments. Alternatively, it has held that federal or provincial regulation has not infringed Aboriginal rights. Occasionally, it has found that a certain activity is not protected as an Aboriginal right. These remedies may or may not be appropriate for Aboriginal tenure.

At present, a reviewing justice must determine whether the infringing legislation or regulations are consistent with the constitutional division of power and the Aboriginal tenure in accordance with section 52(1) of the *Constitution Act, 1982*. If the infringing legislation is inconsistent with either constitutional provision, the legislation or regulations can be struck down. Even if the relevant legislation or regulations, as ordinary provincial law, are consistent with the existing constitutional division of power, sections may constitute an unjustified infringement of the guaranteed constitu-

---

217 *Horseman, supra* note 182.

218 *Ibid.* at 934.

tional rights of Aboriginal peoples or invoke the broad remedial powers of section 24(1) of the *Charter*. In this situation, the infringing sections are subject to judicial scrutiny to see if the section's objectives can be justified and are consistent with the constitutional fiduciary obligations of the government to Aboriginal peoples.

In *Delgamuukw*, the Lamer Court discussed extinguishment of Aboriginal tenure in relation to division of powers, and affirmed the authority of the federal Parliament under section 91(24) and the Aboriginal peoples under section 35(1), leaving no authority for provincial governments.[219] The Lamer Court stated that division of powers between the federal Parliament and provincial legislatures was a legal response to reconciling the unity of the constitution with the underlying political and cultural diversities.[220] Despite the division of powers, the preamble of the *Constitution Act, 1867* declared the continuity with "a Constitution similar in Principle to that of the United Kingdom."[221] In the division of powers, the imperial Crown explicitly transferred its derivative jurisdiction acquired by existing treaty reconciliations over "Indians and Lands reserved for the Indians" to the federal government in section 91(24) of the 1867 Act, rather than allowing the provinces to continue to exercise jurisdiction. This section created continuing federal obligations regarding lands reserved for the Indians and precluded provincial authority under sections 92 or 109.

Because Aboriginal tenure originates from pre-existing systems of Aboriginal law and existed through the Aboriginal laws' sharing of occupations, activities, and uses among members, *sui generis* Aboriginal tenures are distinct from any delegated federal jurisdiction. The imperial Crown and its governmental agents have the obligation to protect Aboriginal tenures, but Aboriginal tenures were never characterized as "property" that belonged to either the federal government or the provinces. In *St. Catherine's Milling*, Lord Watson explained federal jurisdiction under "Lands reserved for Indians" as administrative, rather than legislative:

> The territory in dispute has been in Indian occupation from the date of the proclamation until 1873. During that interval of time Indian affairs have been administered successively by the Crown, by the Provincial Governments, and (since the passing of the British North America Act, 1867), by the Government of the Dominion. The policy of these administrations has been all along the same in this respect, that the Indian inhabitants have been precluded from entering into any transaction with a subject for the sale or transfer of their interest in the land, and have only been permitted to surrender their rights to the Crown by a formal contract, duly ratified in a meeting of their chiefs or head men convened for the purpose. Whilst there have been changes in the administrative authority, there has been no change since the year 1763 in the character of the interest which its Indian inhabitants had in the lands surrendered by the treaty.[222]

---

219 McNeil, *supra* note 45.

220 *Quebec Secession Reference*, *supra* note 13 at para. 43. See *Secretary of State, supra* note 3 at 125-26, 131-32.

221 *Quebec Secession Reference*, *ibid.* at para. 44; *Constitution Act, 1867, supra* note 37.

222 *St. Catherine's, supra* note 109 at 54.

Lord Watson stated the "natural" meaning of the phrase "Lands reserved for Indians" was:

> ...sufficient to include all lands reserved, upon any terms or conditions, for Indian occupation. It appears to be the plain policy of the Act that, in order to ensure uniformity of administration, all such lands, and Indian affairs generally, shall be under the legislative control of one central authority.[223]

In *Delgamuukw*, the Lamer Court found that federal jurisdiction over "Lands reserved for the Indians" included all Aboriginal tenure and land rights in the province of British Columbia, not only Indian reserves.[224] In the context of whether British Columbia had the power to extinguish Aboriginal title after 1871, the Lamer Court held "that jurisdiction over aboriginal title must vest with the federal government,"[225] implying "the jurisdiction to legislate in relation to Aboriginal title," and "the jurisdiction to extinguish that title."[226] This vested jurisdiction operates to preclude provincial jurisdiction to make laws[227] or extinguish Aboriginal tenure or rights, "because the intention to do so would take the law outside provincial jurisdiction":[228]

> ...s. 91(24) protects a core of federal jurisdiction even from provincial laws of general application, through the operation of the doctrine of interjurisdictional immunity. That core has been described as matters touching on "Indianness" or the "core of Indianness". ... It follows that aboriginal rights are part of the core of Indianness at the heart of s. 91(24).[229]

The division of powers precludes provincial regulation over land reserved for the Indians. As Lamer stated, "[t]he vesting of exclusive jurisdiction with the federal government over Indians and Indian lands under s. 91(24), operates to preclude provincial laws in relation to those matters."[230] This is a federal responsibility shared with the Aboriginal peoples of Canada in accordance with section 35(1).

---

223 *Ibid.* at 59.

224 *Delgamuukw, supra* note 2 at 174.

225 *Ibid.* at para. 181.

226 *Ibid.* at paras. 173ff. Similar reasoning was advanced for Aboriginal rights relating to land. The Court asserted that the federal government had, "the power to legislate in relation to other aboriginal rights in relation to land," which, "encompasses within it the exclusive power to extinguish Aboriginal rights, including Aboriginal title."

227 *Ibid.* at para. 179.

228 *Ibid.* at para. 180.

229 *Ibid.* at para. 181. See generally, for intergovernmental or interjurisdictional immunity, J. Vaissi-Nagy, "Intergovernmental Immunity in Canada" in P. Lordon, *Crown Law* (Vancouver: Butterworths, 1991) c. 5 at 129-69.

230 *Delgamuukw, ibid.* at para. 179. Under the doctrine of paramountcy, where the federal government has a constitutional interest in property, provincial legislation over such interest is not binding, even if it that normally falls within its jurisdiction, and federal legislation may override it and render it inoperative; see *A.G. B.C. v. A.G. Canada (Johnny Walker case)* (1923), [1924] A.C. 222 at 236-261 (P.C.); *Reference re Waters and Water-Powers*, [1929] S.C.R. 200 at 212-13, 223-26 (S.C.C.); *Alberta Government Telephones v. I.B.E.W.*, [1989] 2 S.C.R. 318 (S.C.C.); *R. v. Red Line Ltd.* (1930), 54 C.C.C. 271 (Ont. C.A.); *Re Young*, [1955] 5 D.L.R. 225 (Ont. C.A.); *Re Glibbery* (1962), 36 D.L.R. (2d) 548 (Ont. C.A.); C.H.H. McNairn, "Crown Immunity from Statute—Provincial Governments and Federal Legislation" (1978) 56 Can. Bar Rev. 145; K. Swinton, "Federalism and Provincial Government Immunity" (1979) 29 U.T.L.J. 1.

In 1951, changes to the *Indian Act* permitted provincial laws that would otherwise not apply to Indians to do so by federal law.[231] Section 88 of the *Indian Act* allows incorporating by reference provincial laws of general application as federal law, which constitutionally would not apply as provincial law because they touch on the Indianness at the core of section 91(24).[232] However, section 88 does not evince a clear and plain intent to extinguish Aboriginal tenure or rights prior to constitutional reforms.[233] Under section 35(1) federal laws cannot extinguish constitutional rights, and may at best regulate these rights if consistent with the rights, since the Court suggested section 88 is not authorized to infringe on constitutional rights.[234] Section 88 expressly prohibits any justification for provincial infringement as federal law on treaty rights and federal laws.[235] La Forest J. concurred: "The respondent province had no authority to extinguish Aboriginal rights either under the *Constitution Act, 1867* or by virtue of s. 88 of the *Indian Act*."[236]

The federal government never extinguished any Aboriginal tenure in British Columbia, and the *Delgamuukw* "implication" of federal legislative authority to extinguish in section 91(24) is not convincing. While in 1867 the imperial Crown vested jurisdiction in the federal government over existing "Lands reserved for the Indians" in the confederating colonies, it granted no jurisdiction to the federal government in the western Indian country or the Pacific coast colonies, which remained imperial foreign jurisdictions.

By imperial statute in 1866, the British Columbia colony was created through the union of New Caledonia and Vancouver Island, and was granted a Legislative Council.[237] The *British Columbia Terms of Union* with Canada in 1871 did not delegate exclusive authority to the federal government to legislate or extinguish Aboriginal tenure. Article 13 of the Terms of Union articulates the constitutional obligation and standards:

> The charge of the Indians, and the trusteeship and management of the lands reserved for their use and benefit, shall be assumed by the Dominion Government, and a policy as liberal as that hitherto pursued by the British Columbia Government shall be continued by the Dominion Government after the Union.

> To carry out such policy, tracts of lands of such extent as it has hitherto been the practice of the British Columbia Government to appropriate for that purpose, shall from time to time be conveyed by the Local Government to the Dominion Government; and in cases of disagreement between the two Governments respecting the quantity of such tracts of land

---

231 *Delgamuukw, ibid.* at para. 182.

232 P.W. Hogg, *Constitutional Law of Canada*, 4th ed. (Toronto: Carswell, 1996).

233 *Delgamuukw, supra* note 2 at para. 172.

234 *Ibid.* See also McNeil, *supra* note 45 at 447-48.

235 *Côté, supra* note 159 at 192.

236 *Delgamuukw, supra* note 2 at 206.

237 *Union of Vancouver Island with British Columbia Act*, 1866 (U.K.), 29 & 30 Vict., c. 67.

to be so granted, the matter shall be referred for the decision of the Secretary of State for the colonies.[238]

Delgamuukw states that since 1871, the exclusive power to legislate and extinguish Aboriginal tenure in relation to "Indians, and Lands reserved for the Indians" has been vested with the federal government by virtue of section 91(24).[239] However, the terms explicitly provided for a federal trusteeship and management of "the lands reserved for their use and benefit" and for no one else; the power of legislation was limited to the "liberality" of the existing colonial legislative regime. The imperial Crown retained the authority to regulate disputes over the amount of lands reserved for the Indians transferred to federal jurisdiction, rather than federal or provincial authority. No imperial delegation authorized the federal government in its trusteeship capacity to either regulate or extinguish an independent Aboriginal tenure not expressly transferred by treaty to the imperial Crown.

A treaty purchase or cession by the imperial Crown in the western Indian country could transfer jurisdiction of the territory to the Crown, but courts cannot imply that such transfers allow either the constitutional fiduciary to regulate the land for other peoples' benefit or to extinguish Aboriginal tenure. Lord Watson held that only the imperial Crown could acquire land reserved for Indians by treaties.[240] Even the imperial treaties of cession do not provide clear and plain proof of "purchase" or extinguishment of Aboriginal tenure. Cession creates a shared derivative legal interest in the imperial Crown, dependent on fulfilling treaty obligations, and does not clearly extinguish the Aboriginal tenure.

The Dickson Court held that the federal government's obligation to the imperial Crown was to protect Aboriginal title.[241] Protection does not imply destroying the protected. The 1763 Proclamation reserved the Aboriginal tenure for the Indians in the western Indian country under the Crown's sovereignty and protection, and expressly provided that the colonial governors could purchase Aboriginal tenure for the benefit of the imperial Crown. The benefit of the imperial Crown is a constitutional interest distinct from the federal government. Under section 91(24) the federal government's authority regarding lands reserved for the Indians has been judicially declared as administrative and subject to the 1763 Proclamation;[242] it is not a proprietary interest or ownership.[243] Federal jurisdiction to protect Aboriginal tenure does not imply that the federal government has a beneficial interest or owns the land.[244]

The Crown's fiduciary duty derives from the sovereign protection of unceded Aboriginal tenure by the 1763 Proclamation, affirmed by Article 13 of the *British*

---

238 *Terms of Union of British Columbia with the Dominion of Canada* (Victoria: Queen's Printer, 1893). This is also reprinted in R.S.C. 1985, App. II, No. 10 [hereinafter *British Columbia Terms of Union*].

239 *Delgamuukw, supra* note 2 at para. 173.

240 *St. Catherine's, supra* note 109.

241 *Guerin, supra* note 51 at 383; *Sparrow, supra* note 28 at 1104-1108.

242 *Secretary of State, supra* note 3 at 125.

243 *St. Catherine's, supra* note 109 at 54.

244 See *A.G. Can. v. A.G. Ont., supra* note 83, cited in *Sparrow, supra* note 28 at 1098.

Columbia Terms of Union, and section 35(1) of the *Constitution Act, 1982*. Reading these constitutional rights together, Chief Justice Lamer has ruled that the federal government has a constitutional fiduciary responsibility to "safeguard one of the most central of native interests—their interest in their lands" from provincial interference.[245] The implied federal government authority to legislate or extinguish any protected tenure without the involved Aboriginal peoples' consent is inconsistent with the spirit and purposes of safeguarding the *sui generis* tenure. Safegarding is different from legislation and extinguishment, especially since under the *St. Catherine's* decision, the "sovereign" clear and plain extinguishment of Aboriginal tenure ends federal authority and begins provincial jurisdiction.

Additionally, the Chief Justice's implication in regards to legislative powers and extinguishment continues to confuse jurisdiction with proprietary interest. There is nothing in imperial law or federal law that demonstrates a clear and plain intention to extinguish Aboriginal tenure in British Columbia; even if such legislation existed, Aboriginal tenure cannot be defined by past imperial or federal legislation or regulation.[246] *Sparrow* held Aboriginal rights cannot be extinguished by implied sovereign authority such as legislation "necessarily inconsistent" with the continuing enjoyment of the inherent Aboriginal right or by progressive restrictive federal regulations.[247]

Since 1982, the constitution of Canada is supreme and sovereign authority; the federal government has never been declared the sovereign of Canada. In *Sparrow*, the Court stated imperial policy respected the Aboriginal right to occupy their lands, despite the Crown's claims of sovereignty, legislative power, and ultimate underlying title to Aboriginal lands.[248] Section 35(1) provides Aboriginal peoples with constitutional protection against federal and provincial legislative power:

> [H]istorical policy on the part of the Crown is not only incapable of extinguishing the existing aboriginal right without clear intention, but is also incapable of, in itself, delineating that right. The nature of government regulations cannot be determinative of the content and scope of an existing aboriginal right. Government policy can however regulate the exercise of that right, but such regulation must be in keeping with s. 35(1).[249]

On this basis, since 1982, the constitutional scope of the federal authority over *sui generis* Aboriginal tenure is a shared jurisdiction. Section 35(1) limits the activities of the federal government over Aboriginal tenure as defined by section 91(24). In *Sparrow*, the Court stated:

> Federal legislative powers continue, including, of course, the right to legislate with respect to Indians pursuant to s. 91(24) of the *Constitution Act, 1867*. These powers must, however, now be read together with s. 35(1). In other words, federal power must be reconciled with federal duty and the best way to achieve that reconciliation is to demand the justifi-

---

245 *Delgamuukw, supra* note 2 at para. 176.

246 *Sparrow, supra* note 28 at 1101.

247 *Ibid.* at 1097.

248 *Ibid.* at 1103.

249 *Ibid.* at 1101.

cation of any government regulation that infringes upon or denies aboriginal rights. Such scrutiny is in keeping with the liberal interpretive principle enunciated in *Nowegijick, supra*, and the concept of holding the Crown to a high standard of honourable dealing with respect to the aboriginal peoples of Canada as suggested by *Guerin v. The Queen, supra*.[250]

Since constitutional reform in 1982, the Court declared that the federal government could not unilaterally extinguish Aboriginal rights.[251] The federal government must justify any legislative objectives that interfere with existing Aboriginal tenure, laws, or rights and provide fair compensation for the interference.

In *Delgamuukw*, the Court rejected the provincial Crown argument that the imperial Parliament in s. 109 of the *Constitution Act, 1867* "vested" the province with the underlying title to Aboriginal tenure. Section 109 provides:

> All Lands, Mines, Minerals, and Royalties belonging to the several Provinces of Canada, Nova Scotia, and New Brunswick at the Union, and all Sums then due or payable for such Lands, Mines, Minerals or Royalties, shall belong to the several Provinces of Ontario, Quebec, Nova Scotia, and New Brunswick in which the same are situate or arise, subject to any Trusts existing in respect thereof, and to any Interest other than that of the Provinces in the same.[252]

The Attorney General of British Columbia translated the idea of lands "belonging" to the several provinces to a concept of a "right of ownership" carrying the right to grant fee simples to third parties. These provincial grants extinguished Aboriginal tenure, and so by negative implication excluded Aboriginal tenure from the scope of section 91(24).[253]

The Court rejected the province's submission on grounds that it failed to take account of the qualifying language of the imperial delegation to the provinces in section 109. The "beneficial interest" of the provinces in lands, mines, minerals, and royalties were "subject to any Trusts existing in respect thereof, and to any Interest other than that of the Provinces in the same." Prerogative law and courts have always asserted that unextinguished Aboriginal tenure is an interest other than the provinces, and that it carries a special fiduciary or trust obligation. These principles were confirmed by the use of "trusteeship" of lands reserved for Indian use and benefit in the *British Columbia Terms of Union*. Chief Justice Lamer confirmed these principles in a contemporary context:

> In *St. Catherine's Milling*, the Privy Council held that aboriginal title was such an interest, and rejected the argument that provincial ownership operated as a limit on federal jurisdiction. The net effect of that decision, therefore, was to separate the ownership of lands held pursuant to aboriginal title from jurisdiction over those lands. Thus, although

---

250 *Ibid.* at 1109.

251 *Delgamuukw, supra* note 2 at paras. 174-75; *Van der Peet, supra* note 58 at para. 28.

252 *Constitution Act, 1867, supra* note 37.

253 *Delgamuukw, supra* note 2 at para. 175.

on surrender of aboriginal title the province would take absolute title, jurisdiction to accept surrenders lies with the federal government. The same can be said of extinguishment—although on extinguishment of aboriginal title, the province would take complete title to the land, the jurisdiction to extinguish lies with the federal government.[254]

Additionally, Chief Justice Lamer noted, "even if the point were not settled, I would have come to the same conclusion."[255]

The Court's reasoning in *Delgamuukw* would logically also apply to the *Constitution Act, 1930*[256] and the *Natural Resource Transfer Agreements, 1930*,[257] which extend section 109 to the Western provinces.[258] In imperial law, the *Constitution Act, 1930* was not a statute of United Kingdom Parliament. Rather, it confirmed the existence of the federal-provincial agreements, and pursuant to section 1 made the *Natural Resources Transfer Agreements* binding on the federal government and involved provinces.[259] The Act was silent on its effect on existing Aboriginal treaties. Paragraph 1 of the Agreements provided for the public lands transfer:

> In order that the Province may be in the same position as the original Provinces of Confederation are by virtue of section one hundred and nine of the *Constitution Act, 1867*, the interest of the Crown in all Crown lands, ... within the province ... shall from and after the coming into force of this agreement and subject as therein provided, belong to the Province, subject to any trusts existing in respect thereof, and to any interest other than that of the Crown in the same ...

This continues the Aboriginal limitation of section 109 and limits the scope of provincial management and sale of public lands in section 92(5) and of provincial property and civil rights in section 92(13) of the *Constitution Act, 1867*. It means that a provincial government does not have any jurisdiction over any existing Aboriginal trust or any interest other than that of the Crown; its provincial jurisdiction is limited by any Aboriginal interest in lands not purchased by the Crown, but held by the imperial Crown.[260]

Paragraphs 2 and 10 reinforce this conclusion. Paragraph 2 vests existing treaties and contractual interests, and would require Aboriginal consent to any modifications:

> The Province ... will carry out in accordance with the terms thereof every contract to purchase or lease any Crown lands, mines or interest and every other arrangement whereby any person has become entitled to any interest therein as against the Crown, and further agrees not to affect or alter any term of any such contract to purchase, lease or other arrangements by legislation or otherwise, except either with the consent of all the parties

254 *Ibid.*
255 *Ibid.* at para. 176.
256 (U.K.), 20 & 21 Geo. V, c. 26.
257 *Ibid.* at Schedules R.S.C. 1970, App., No. 25.
258 *Ibid.* at para. 1 of Schedules.
259 *R. v. Badger,* [1996] 1 S.C.R. 771, [1996] 2 C.N.L.R. 77 at para. 47 (S.C.C.) [hereinafter *Badger*].
260 See *St. Catherine's, supra* note 109 at 58-60; *Sioui, supra* note 93; and *Simon v. The Queen,* [1985] 2 S.C.R. 387, [1986] 1 C.N.L.R. 153 (S.C.C.).

thereto other than Canada or in so far as any legislation may apply generally to all similar agreements relating to land, mines or minerals in the Province or to interest therein, irrespective of who may be that parties.[261]

Paragraph 10 affirms and recognizes federal administrative jurisdiction over lands reserved for the Indians within the provinces:

All lands included in Indian reserves within the Province, including those selected and surveyed but not yet confirmed, as well as those confirmed, shall continue to be vested in the Crown and administered by the Government of Canada for the purposes of Canada ... .[262]

No provincial jurisdiction exists on all lands included in Indian reserves under paragraph 10, and this is consistent with section 91(24) of the *Constitution Act, 1867* and the treaties. In the treaty reconciliations, the Aboriginal chiefs and headmen had surrendered land to the Government of the Dominion of Canada, for Her Majesty the Queen and Her successors, and placed the ceded lands under the jurisdiction of the chiefs.

Paragraph 10 creates a constitutional reversionary interest in provincial unoccupied Crown land: that land may revert to the federal administration for the purposes of fulfilling its obligations under the prerogative treaties:

the Province will from time to time, upon request of the Superintendent General of Indian Affairs, set aside, out of the unoccupied Crown lands, hereby transferred to its administration, such further areas as the said Superintendent General may, in agreement with the Minister of Mines and Natural Resources of the Province, select as necessary to enable Canada to fulfill its obligations under the treaties with the Indians of the Province, and such areas shall hereafter be administered by Canada in the same way in all respects as if they had never passed to the Province under the provisions hereof.

This interest is consistent with section 35(3) of the *Constitution Act, 1982*, which provides that treaty rights "includes rights that now exist by way of land claims agreements or may so be acquired."

Section 52(1) of the *Constitution Act, 1982* establishes constitutional supremacy:

The Constitution of Canada is the supreme law of Canada, and any law that is inconsistent with the provisions of the Constitution is, to the extent of the inconsistency, of no force or effect.

---

261 *Constitution Act, 1867, supra* note 37. Although most treaties were signed before contract theory and law was fully developed, the judicial committee and Canadian courts have characterized treaties as analogous to contracts, albeit of a very solemn and special public nature; *St. Catherine's, supra* note 109 at 51 and *Badger, supra* note 259 at 76. Since public contracts are distinct from private contracts, recent case law rejects equating treaties with private contract law; *Pawis v. The Queen* (1979), [1980] 2 F.C. 18, 102 D.L.R. (3d) 602 (Fed. T.D.); *Town of Hay River v. The Queen* (1979), [1980] 1 F.C. 262, 101 D.L.R. (3d) 184 (Fed. T.D.); *R. v. Tennisco,* [1981] 4 C.N.L.R. 138 at 148 (Ont. H.C.).

262 *Constitution Act, 1867, ibid.* In some agreements, this is paragraph 11.

This section is the only explicit constitutional remedy governing Aboriginal tenure and rights in the 1763 Proclamation,[263] section 91 (24) of the *Constitution Act, 1867*, Article 13 of *British Columbia Terms of Union,* and section 35 (1) of the *Constitution Act, 1982*.

The Supreme Court has affirmed in *Sparrow* that the constitutional rights of the Aboriginal peoples will be enforced as any other constitutional rights; in *Van der Peet* the Court affirmed that Aboriginal rights are equal to other constitutional rights. The Dickson Court held that a constitutional right is "unalterable by the normal legislative process and unsuffering of laws inconsistent with it."[264] The judiciary has a duty "to ensure that the constitutional law prevails,"[265] a duty vital to protecting Aboriginal tenure.

In *Sparrow*, the Dickson Court did not directly apply the section 52(1) inconsistency test, but approved of its application by the Nova Scotia Court of Appeals in *Denny, Paul and Syliboy*.[266] In the latter case, Chief Justice Clarke held that to the extent that a federal regulatory scheme fails to provide a section 35 (1) entitlement to fish, it is "inconsistent with the Constitution" as mandated by section 52, and such regulatory scheme is "of no force or effect." Subsequent courts have avoided the application of section 52 in the context of constitutional rights of Aboriginal peoples, even though the questions were usually situated as an inconsistency test. Rather, courts have attempted to reconcile the constitutional rights with the regulations through the judicially created test of justified infringement.

Conflicts with Aboriginal tenure require the application of the section 52 inconsistency test to force legislatures to create constitutionally valid legislative schemes without the judicial interest balancing. Aboriginal tenures must be coordinated with other constitutional provisions, and cannot be abrogated or diminished by judicial interpretation of other parts of the constitution, federal or provincial laws.

The broad remedial powers of section 24(1) of the *Charter* may apply to infringement of Aboriginal peoples' constitutional rights under section 35(1), since they are specifically guaranteed against abrogation by section 25 of the *Charter*:

> The guarantee in this Charter of certain rights and freedoms shall not be construed so as to abrogate or derogate from any aboriginal, treaty or other rights or freedoms that pertain to the aboriginal peoples of Canada including
>
> (a) any rights or freedoms that have been recognized by the Royal Proclamation of October 7, 1763; and
>
> (b) any rights or freedoms that now exist by way of land claims agreements or may be so acquired.

---

263 *Secretary of State, supra* note 3 at 125, 140-141.

264 *Van der Peet, supra* note 58 at paras. 535-36.

265 *Ibid.* at 407.

266 *Sparrow, supra* note 28 at 1116-18.

Section 24(1) provides:

> Anyone whose rights or freedoms, as guaranteed by this Charter, have been infringed or
> denied may apply to a court of competent jurisdiction to obtain such remedy as the court
> considers appropriate and just in the circumstances.

An argument can be made that when protected Aboriginal tenure in section 25 is infringed by individual rights under the *Charter*, section 24(1) may grant appropriate and just remedy. This remedy is stronger than the judicially created justified infringement test for Aboriginal rights.

The justified infringement test is not created out of section 35(1)'s wording but rather from the Court's constitutional interpretation:

> There is no explicit language in the provision that authorizes this Court or any court to
> assess the legitimacy of any government legislation that restricts aboriginal rights. Yet, we
> find that the words "recognition and affirmation" incorporate the fiduciary relationship
> referred to earlier and so import some restraint on the exercise of sovereign power. Rights
> that are recognized and affirmed are not absolute. Federal legislative powers continue,
> including, of course, the right to legislate with respect to Indians pursuant to s. 91(24) of
> the *Constitution Act, 1867*. These powers must, however, now be read together with s.
> 35(1). In other words, federal power must be reconciled with federal duty and the best way
> to achieve that reconciliation is to demand the justification of any government regulation
> that infringes upon or denies aboriginal rights.[267]

This interpretation does not address the inconsistency provision of section 52(1). Conflicting constitutional authorities cannot be judicially resolved by abrogating or diminishing one part of the constitution by another; they all became part of constitutional supremacy in 1982. As each constitutional source may shape the others, conflicting constitutional parts must be judicially read as creating relative constitutional rights, none being absolute except the constitution itself.

Unlike other constitutional conflicts, however, conflicts with the constitutional rights of Aboriginal people and other parts of the constitution are controlled by the constitutional fiduciary obligation, which gives rise to the Court's "test" for justifying infringements of section 35(1). Yet, for unexplained reasons, in the application of the infringement test, the constitutional principles vanish. There is no generous liberal interpretation of section 35(1); doubts in federal regulatory schemes are not interpreted in favour of the Indian; nor its remedial purposes applied in the reconciliations. The constitutional duty of the judiciary to ensure that constitutional law prevails and that the rights of section 35(1) cannot be altered by normal legislative processes of laws inconsistent with section 52(1) are not applied.

In *Delgamuukw*, Chief Justice Lamer's infringement analysis began with the non-binding "precedent" that the constitutional rights of Aboriginal peoples, including Aboriginal tenure, are not absolute, and they may be infringed by federal[268] and

---

267 *Ibid.* at 1109.
268 *Sparrow, supra* note 28 at 1103.

provincial governments[269] that satisfy the justification test. Referring to provincial governments infringing on constitutional rights does not take into account the constitutional division of power principle. As Professor McNeil stated:

> what is interesting—and in my view disturbing— ... is the ease with which the Chief Justice concluded that the justification test applies to provincial infringements of Aboriginal issues ... . What is missing here is any mention of the question of whether the provinces have constitutional authority to infringe Aboriginal and treaty rights, given exclusive federal jurisdiction over "Indians, and Lands reserved for the Indians." This division of powers question logically precedes the issue of the applicability of the *Sparrow* test, as the test obviously is not available to justify infringement by provincial laws that encroach on federal jurisdiction.[270]

The general principles governing the justification test laid down in *Sparrow*, and suggestively elaborated in *Gladstone* and *Delgamuukw*, may operate with respect to federal infringements of Aboriginal tenure. When considering the "test" for *prima facie* interference under section 35(1), the Dickson Court in *Sparrow* suggested the Aboriginal beneficiaries must show that the infringement was "unreasonable," "undue," and "unnecessary" to assert standing. This is a different test from the personal effect of a legislative infringement of personal rights needed to establish standing under the *Charter*;[271] different from private fiduciary law where the beneficiary of a fiduciary obligation (the duty of loyalty) does not need to show any harm.

In *Gladstone*, the Lamer Court turned from unreasonable harm standing to an analysis of the involved Aboriginal right that was harmed. The test in *Gladstone* was whether the Aboriginal right infringed amounted to the "exclusive" use of a resource, determined by whether the right had an internal limit.[272] This is a vague test, because all constitutional rights are not exclusive but relative, and all have limits, both internal and external. In the context of case-by-case adjudication, no case can establish a controlling principle that gives exclusive use to an entire resource to involved parties; it can only determine relative rights between respective parties. To argue that Aboriginal peoples cannot have an exclusive use or remedies under constitutional supremacy is inconsistent with the Court's implicit protection of existing governmental and commercial monopolies of the immigrants. The issue is why the courts should sustain the historical exclusive monopoly of the immigrants faced with constitutional reform and equality of the law.

In *Sparrow*, the Court asserted that Mr. Sparrow's Aboriginal right to fish salmon for food, ceremonial, and social purposes was "internally limited" and declared, after

---

269 *Côté, supra* note 159 at 189. This involves a user fee to maintain roads, and does not infringe the Aboriginal right to fish.

270 McNeil, *supra* note 45 at 449-50.

271 *Canadian Charter of Rights and Freedoms*, Part I of the *Constitution Act, 1982*, being Schedule B to the *Canada Act 1982* (U.K.), 1982, c. 11. The plaintiff only has to show the effect the impugned legislation has on him or her, not whether this effect can somehow be justified in a larger scheme of things.

272 *Delgamuukw, supra* note 2 at 163.

valid conservation measures, the right must be given top priority.[273] In *Gladstone*, by contrast, the Court perceived that the two brothers' attempt to sell herring spawn commercially under their Aboriginal rights was not internally limited, but limited only by supply and demand or the market. Chief Justice Lamer explained:

> Had the test for justification been applied in a strict form in *Gladstone*, the [A]boriginal right would have amounted to an exclusive right to exploit the fishery on a commercial basis. This was not the intention of *Sparrow*...[274]

The Court did not explain why a right to sell herring spawn, to use Aboriginal rights as a commodity right, requires an "indulgent" test. Under *Sparrow*, after conservation measures, the Heiltsuk brothers would have a top priority in exercising their ancient trade. Under the indulgent test of *Gladstone*, the constitutional right of the Heiltsuk amounted to a vague "priority" in the year-to-year allocation of herring spawn in a manner "respectful" to non-Aboriginal users of the resource.

Under the test, upon showing an unreasonable or unnecessary harm to the constitutional rights of the Aboriginal people, the court must search for a compelling and substantial legislative objective. If a valid legislative objective is found, then the objective or action is measured by its consistency with the constitutional fiduciary duty of the Crown, the special trust relationship, and the responsibility of the honour of the Crown, in terms of the allocation of conflicts and priorities.

In the Court's search for a compelling and substantial legislative objective, the Court has read federal and provincial statutes and regulation as constitutional documents, rather than as ordinary legislation conflicting with constitutional rights. Such reasoning does not accord with the Dickson Court's prohibition in *Sparrow* against using these statutes to define Aboriginal rights, although government policy "*can* however regulate the exercise of that right, but such regulation must be in keeping with s. 35(1)."[275]

After *Gladstone*, the case-by-case scope of legislative objectives that can be judicially justified in a commercial setting is unjustly broad. This extended version of substantial and compelling legislative objectives is justified as a "reconciliation" of Aboriginal peoples with the British sovereign interpreting that such reconciliation entails recognizing that "distinctive Aboriginal societies exist within, and are a part of, a broader social, political and economic community."[276] This assumption suggests that community privileges, the immigrant privileges of colonization ideology, should control constitutional interpretation. It was well known in 1982 that Aboriginal peoples existed within these contexts. The Court equates these communities with the British sovereign without clear and plain intent or wording to that effect. Also, the Court confuses political sovereignty with constitutional supremacy.

In *Sparrow*, the Dickson Court warned that "history has shown, unfortunately all too well, that Canada's aboriginal peoples are justified in worrying about government

---

273 *Sparrow, supra* note 28 at 1116.

274 *Delgamuukw, supra* note 2 at para. 164.

275 *Sparrow, supra* note 28 at 1101.

276 *R. v. Gladstone*, [1996] 2 S.C.R. 723 at para. 73 (S.C.C.).

objectives that may be superficially neutral but which constitute *de facto* threats to the existence of aboriginal rights and interests."[277] By recognizing and affirming the constitutional rights of Aboriginal peoples, the constitution has sanctioned Aboriginal peoples' challenges to social and economic policy objectives embodied in legislation. To the extent that Aboriginal rights are negatively affected, the governments must justify the implicit and explicit policy objectives and their impact. Before a court the government should not be able to hide behind the social and economic policy or their rightholders. Section 35(1) gives Aboriginal peoples rights in the face of government policy objectives and conduct, as well as a strong check on legislative power, in an increasingly more "complex, interdependent and sophisticated society, where exhaustible resources need protection and management."[278]

In *Sparrow*, the Dickson Court rejected the British Columbia Court of Appeal's "public interest" as a legislative objective:

> We find the "public interest" justification to be so vague as to provide no meaningful guidance and so broad as to be unworkable as a test for the justification of a limitation on constitutional rights.[279]

The court found the valid legislative objective to be conservation and resource management. It rejected any "presumption" of "the validity of a legislative enactment" in the test for justifying a constitutional right infringement.[280]

In *Gladstone*, Chief Justice Lamer for a divided court found that there was not sufficient evidence to assess the legislative objectives behind the allocation. He found it necessary to go beyond conservation and resource management to "other 'compelling and substantial' objectives" of the "broader social, political and economic community."[281] Lamer suggested that after conservation goals were met, "objectives such as the pursuit of economic and regional fairness" and the recognition of the "non-aboriginal participation in the fishery" might be valid legislative infringements on Aboriginal rights. He inferred that such objectives are "in the interest of all Canadians" and part of a reconciliation.[282] This analysis was disputed by Justice McLachlin's dissent, who regarded the approach as "indeterminate and ultimately more political than legal."[283] Professor McNeil asserted that such a suggestion appears to "look very much like the 'public interest' justification that the Court rejected in *Sparrow*"[284] and appears to be a unilaterally imposed judicial infringement on the constitutional rights of Aboriginal peoples.[285]

---

277 *Sparrow, supra* note 28 at 1110.

278 *Ibid.*

279 *Ibid.* at 1113.

280 *Ibid.* at 1114.

281 *Gladstone, supra* note 276 at paras. 69, 73.

282 *Ibid.* at para. 75.

283 *Van der Peet, supra* note 58 at para. 302.

284 K. McNeil "How can Infringement of the Constitutional Rights of Aboriginal Peoples be Justified?" (1997) 8 Const. Forum 35.

285 *Ibid.* at 36.

The Lamer Court approach fails to recognize that private rights are not constitutionalized as are those of the Aboriginal peoples; private rights and freedom are mediated by reasonable limits prescribed by law, such as the non-abrogation and derogation section 25 of the *Charter*, and governmental authority limited by section 35(1). These sections represent the existing constitutional reconciliation of the various Canadian interests, and reflect the sovereign intent in constitutional interpretation, within which the judicial reconciliation of the multicultural reality of Canada must be carried out.

In *Delgamuukw*, in the context of Aboriginal tenure, Chief Justice Lamer extended his suggestion of valid legislative objectives:

> In my opinion, the development of agriculture, forestry, mining, and hydroelectric power, the general economic development of the interior of British Columbia, protection of the environment or endangered species, the building of infrastructure and the settlement of foreign populations to support those aims, are the kinds of objectives that are consistent with this purpose and, in principle, can justify the infringement of aboriginal title. Whether a particular measure or government act can be explained by reference to one of those objectives, however, is ultimately a question of fact that will have to be examined on a case-by-case basis.[286]

These suggested legislative objectives, however, violate the constitutional division of powers: the Chief Justice has already held that "[t]he vesting of exclusive jurisdiction with the federal government over Indians and Indian lands under s. 91(24), operates to preclude provincial laws in relation to those matters."[287]

The constitutional fiduciary obligation requires that when the government exercises substantial and compelling authority that interferes with a constitutional right of Aboriginal peoples, it must do so in a way that upholds its duty to act in a "trust-like, rather than adversarial" manner; federal power must be reconciled with federal duty.[288]

The Lamer Court has not identified any clear operational principle of constitutional fiduciary obligation, except to state that the obligation is a function of "legal and factual" context. The fiduciary duty has been applied in the idea of a priority. In *Sparrow*, for example, the Musqueam right to fish was given the top priority or first allocation after valid conservation measures. Under *Gladstone*'s indulgent test the federal fiduciary must demonstrate that both the procedural allocation process and the substantive effects of the allocation of the resource "reflect the prior interest of aboriginal rights holders in the fishery,"[289] but the priority is indeterminate. The discretion of the

---

286 *Delgamuukw*, *supra* note 2 at para. 165.

287 *Ibid.* at para. 179.

288 *Sparrow*, *supra* note 28 at 1108.

289 *Ibid.* para. 164; citing *Gladstone*, *supra* note 276 at para. 64. The indulgent test is determined by asking the following questions:

> whether the government has accommodated the exercise of the aboriginal right to participate in the fishery (through reduced licence fees, for example), whether the government's objectives in enacting a particular regulatory scheme reflect the need to take into account the priority of aboriginal rights holders, the extent of the participation in the fishery of aboriginal rights holders relative to their percentage of the population, how the government has accommodated different aboriginal

fiduciary's freedom to share a traditional resource of an Aboriginal beneficiary with the immigrant remains undefined and unregulated by the Court.

In the context of Aboriginal tenure in *Delgamuukw*, Chief Justice Lamer argued that the three component rights of Aboriginal tenure will be relevant to the fiduciary duty and its degree of scrutiny of the infringing measure or action. Because Aboriginal tenure encompasses the right to exclusive use and occupation of land, the Crown's fiduciary duty requires that Aboriginal tenure be given a "high priority." Under the indulgent test of *Gladstone*,[290] the federal government would demonstrate "'both that the process by which it allocated the resource and the actual allocation of the resource which results from that process reflect the prior interest' of the holders of Aboriginal title in the land":[291]

> By analogy with *Gladstone*, this might entail, for example, that governments accommodate the participation of aboriginal peoples in the development of the resources of British Columbia, that the conferral of fee simples for agriculture, and of leases and licences for forestry and mining reflect the prior occupation of aboriginal title lands, that economic barriers to aboriginal uses of their lands (e.g., licensing fees) be somewhat reduced. This list is illustrative and not exhaustive. This is an issue that may involve an assessment of the various interests at stake in the resources in question. No doubt, there will be difficulties in determining the precise value of the aboriginal interest in the land and any grants, leases or licences given for its exploitation. These difficult economic considerations obviously cannot be solved here.[292]

In *Delgamuukw*, Aboriginal tenure encompasses the self-determining right to choose to what uses land can be put and an "inescapable" economic component, which suggests that the fiduciary duty may be articulated and "accommodate[d]" in a manner different than the idea of priority. The Lamer Court has stated that the fiduciary duty analysis of the infringing legislative objectives can be articulated in other ways;[293] depending on the nature of the constitutional right in question, it does not always have to be given priority.[294]

The self-determination component of Aboriginal tenure will create a governmental duty of "good faith" consultation with the Aboriginal holders of the Aboriginal right:[295]

> [These consultations must proceed] with the intention of substantially addressing the concerns of the aboriginal peoples whose lands are at issue. In most cases, it will be signifi-

---

rights in a particular fishery (food versus commercial rights, for example), how important the fishery is to the economic and material well-being of the band in question, and the criteria taken into account by the government in, for example, allocating commercial licences amongst different users.

290 *Delgamuukw, ibid.* at para. 167.

291 *Ibid.*

292 *Ibid.*

293 *Ibid.* at para. 162, citing *Sparrow, supra* note 28 at 1119.

294 *Delgamuukw, ibid.*

295 *Ibid.* at para. 168.

cantly deeper than mere consultation. Some cases may even require the full consent of an aboriginal nation, particularly when provinces enact hunting and fishing regulations in relation to aboriginal lands.[296]

That the nature and scope of the duty will vary according to the context[297] raises questions about the division of powers, and the federal government safeguarding Aboriginal tenure from provincial legislation.

Similarly, the economic aspect of Aboriginal title suggests that compensation is relevant to the question of justified regulation of Aboriginal tenure (as suggested in *Sparrow* and *Gladstone*). In *Delgamuukw*, Chief Justice Lamer stated:

> Indeed, compensation for breaches of fiduciary duty are a well-established part of the landscape of aboriginal rights: *Guerin*. In keeping with the duty of honour and good faith on the Crown, fair compensation will ordinarily be required when aboriginal title is infringed. The amount of compensation payable will vary with the nature of the particular aboriginal title affected and with the nature and severity of the infringement and the extent to which aboriginal interests were accommodated. Since the issue of damages was severed from the principal action, we received no submissions on the appropriate legal principles that would be relevant to determining the appropriate level of compensation of infringements of aboriginal title. In the circumstances, it is best that we leave those difficult questions to another day.[298]

This component of Aboriginal tenure affirms the existing principle of both common law and statute that the Crown may not expropriate a property interest without compensation, and applies the principle to external regulation of Aboriginal tenure. Justice La Forest's concurring opinion articulated that under the fiduciary duty test these legislative objectives are subject to accommodation of the rights of Aboriginal peoples:

> This accommodation must always be in accordance with the honour and good faith of the Crown. Moreover, when dealing with a generalized claim over vast tracts of land, accommodation is not a simple matter of asking whether licences have been fairly allocated in one industry, or whether conservation measures have been properly implemented for a specific resource. Rather, the question of accommodation of "aboriginal title" is much broader than this. Certainly, one aspect of accommodation in this context entails notifying and consulting aboriginal peoples with respect to the development of the affected territory. Another aspect of accommodation is fair compensation. ... In summary, in developing vast tracts of land, the government is expected to consider the economic well being of *all* Canadians. But the aboriginal peoples must not be forgotten in this equation. Their legal right to occupy and possess certain lands, as confirmed by s. 35(1) of the *Constitution Act, 1982*, mandates basic fairness commensurate with the honour and good faith of the Crown.[299]

Fair compensation is a revenue-sharing issue between the Crown and the Aboriginal peoples, rather than an issue between the Aboriginal peoples and the pur-

---

296 *Ibid.*

297 *Ibid.* at para. 168.

298 *Ibid.* at para. 169.

299 *Ibid.* at paras. 203-204 and also para. 168.

chasers from the Crown. The Supreme Court and the Privy Council held in *St. Catherine's* that under section 109 the provinces could acquire a beneficial interest in Aboriginal territories as a source of revenue only when the estate of the Crown is disencumbered of the Indian tenure.[300] Since the Lamer Court held that Aboriginal tenure in British Columbia was not extinguished by provincial or federal legislation and the province had not acquired beneficial interest under section 109, Aboriginal tenure has not been disencumbered. On this basis, neither the provincial nor federal Crown has any "ultimate" interest, since section 35(1) has vested the tenure in the Aboriginal peoples.

Both the Court of Appeal and the Supreme Court in *Delgamuukw* have suggested that compensation is appropriate for past federal and provincial regulation of Aboriginal tenure.[301] Justice Macfarlane for the majority of the British Columbia Court of Appeal held that compensatory damages from the province might be the appropriate remedy for pre-1982 regulatory infringements of Aboriginal tenure.[302] Justice La Forest in the Supreme Court declared that Aboriginal tenure is a compensable right that can be traced back to the 1763 Proclamation:[303]

> Indeed, the treatment of "aboriginal title" as a compensable right can be traced back to the *Royal Proclamation, 1763*. The relevant portions of the *Proclamation* are as follows:
>
> > ...such Parts of Our Dominions and Territories as, *not having been ceded to or purchased by Us, are reserved to them* [aboriginal peoples] or any of them, as their Hunting Grounds. ... We do, with the Advice of our Privy Council strictly enjoin and require, that *no private Person do presume to make any purchase from the said Indians of any Lands* reserved to the said Indians ... but that, *if at any Time any of the Said Indians should be inclined to dispose of the said Lands, the same shall be Purchased only for Us*, in our Name ... . [Emphasis added.]
>
> Clearly, the *Proclamation* contemplated that aboriginal peoples would be compensated for the surrender of their lands; see also Slattery, "Understanding Aboriginal Rights," *supra*, at pp. 751-52.

These issues revolve around past land grants and licences of unpurchased Aboriginal tenure by the Crown to third parties—the oldest issue in North American jurisprudence regarding frauds and abuses.

The Court has not determined how fair compensation for regulatory infringements should be calculated. In *Delgamuukw*, Justice La Forest deliberated that Aboriginal tenure is the equivalent of Crown tenure rather than an individual fee simple estate under Crown tenure:

> More specifically, in a situation of expropriation, one asks whether fair compensation is available to the aboriginal peoples; see *Sparrow, supra*, at p. 1119. ... It must be emphasized,

---

300 *St. Catherine's, supra* note 109 at 46.

301 *Delgamuukw, supra* note 2 at para. 145.

302 *Ibid.* at paras. 38-40; B.C. C.A., *supra* note 2 at 537; [1993] 5 C.N.L.R. at paras. 236-48, 262-79. The minority would have remitted the issue of damages to the trial judge.

303 *Ibid.*, S.C.C. at para. 203.

nonetheless, that fair compensation in the present context is not equated with the price of a fee simple. Rather, compensation must be viewed in terms of the right and in keeping with the honour of the Crown. Thus, generally speaking, compensation may be greater where the expropriation relates to a village area as opposed to a remotely visited area. I add that account must be taken of the interdependence of traditional uses to which the land was put.[304]

The Court of Appeal and the Supreme Court judgment in *Delgamuukw* have resolved the dispute between Justices Judson and Hall in *Calder* in favour of Justice Hall's decision.[305] Justice Judson suggested that since Aboriginal title was not a private property right, the Crown could extinguish Aboriginal title without compensation.[306] Justice Hall suggested that Aboriginal title was a private right and:

[t]he precise nature and value of ... [Aboriginal] right or title would, of course, be most relevant in any litigation that might follow extinguishment in the future because in such an event, according to common law, the expropriation of private rights by the government under the prerogative necessitates the payment of compensation.[307]

In the past, courts have not applied the rules of fair compensation for unilateral apportionment of Aboriginal tenure or ceded lands in a treaty. Failure to require compensation is contrary to the theory of fiduciary obligations and fair compensation articulated by the Supreme Court.

In *Delgamuukw*, the Lamer Court stated its preference for negotiations to reconcile Aboriginal tenure in the constitution of Canada:

By ordering a new trial, I do not necessarily encourage the parties to proceed to litigation and to settle their dispute through the courts. As was said in *Sparrow*, at p. 1105, s. 35(1) "provides a solid constitutional base upon which subsequent negotiations can take place". Those negotiations should also include other aboriginal nations which have a stake in the territory claimed. Moreover, the Crown is under a moral, if not a legal, duty to enter into and conduct those negotiations in good faith. Ultimately, it is through negotiated settlements, with good faith and give and take on all sides, reinforced by the judgments of this Court, that we will achieve what I stated in *Van der Peet*, supra, at para. 31, to be a basic purpose of s. 35(1)—"the reconciliation of the pre-existence of aboriginal societies with the sovereignty of the Crown". Let us face it, we are all here to stay. [308]

Justice La Forest agreed: "I wish to emphasize that the best approach in these types of cases is a process of negotiation and reconciliation that properly considers the complex and competing interests at stake."[309]

The Lamer Court in *Quebec Secession Reference* relied on a constitutional duty

---

304   *Ibid.* at para. 203.

305   *Ibid.* at para. 51.

306   *Calder, supra* note 51 at 343-44.

307   *Ibid.* at 352.

308   *Delgamuukw, supra* note 2.

309   *Ibid.* at para. 207.

to negotiate in the context of Quebec's secession from Canada.[310] It held the federalism principle, in conjunction with the democratic principle, dictates that any clear repudiation of the existing constitutional order would give rise to a reciprocal obligation on all parties to Confederation to negotiate constitutional changes to respond to that desire, with the corollary obligation to come to the negotiating table:

> What is the content of this obligation to negotiate? At this juncture, we confront the difficult inter-relationship between substantive obligations flowing from the Constitution and questions of judicial competence and restraint in supervising or enforcing those obligations. This is mirrored by the distinction between the legality and the legitimacy of actions taken under the Constitution. We propose to focus first on the substantive obligations flowing from this obligation to negotiate; once the nature of those obligations has been described, it is easier to assess the appropriate means of enforcement of those obligations, and to comment on the distinction between legality and legitimacy.[311]

The conduct of the parties in such negotiations, the court said, would be governed by the same constitutional principles that give rise to the duty to negotiate: federalism, democracy, constitutionalism, the rule of law, and the protection of minorities.[312] A "clear" repudiation by the people of Quebec of the existing constitutional order would place an obligation on the other provinces and the federal government to acknowledge and respect that expression of democratic will by entering into negotiations and conducting them in accordance with these underlying constitutional principles,[313] but there would not be a legal obligation to accede to the secession of a province:[314]

> The democracy principle, as we have emphasized, cannot be invoked to trump the principles of federalism and rule of law, the rights of individuals and minorities, or the operation of democracy in the other provinces or in Canada as a whole. No negotiations could be effective if their ultimate outcome, secession, is cast as an absolute legal entitlement based upon an obligation to give effect to that act of secession in the Constitution. Such a foregone conclusion would actually undermine the obligation to negotiate and render it hollow.[315]

The Court also rejected the reverse proposition: that a clear expression of self-determination by the people of Quebec would impose no obligations upon the other provinces or the federal government. It stated that the continued existence and operation of the Canadian constitutional order could not remain indifferent to the clear expression of a majority of Quebecers that they no longer wish to remain in Canada. This would amount to the assertion that other constitutionally recognized principles necessarily trump the clearly expressed democratic will of the people of Quebec, and fail to give sufficient weight to the underlying constitutional principles that must

310 *Quebec Secession Reference, supra* note 13.

311 *Ibid.* at para. 89.

312 *Ibid.* at para. 90.

313 *Ibid.* at para. 88.

314 *Ibid.* at para. 90.

315 *Ibid.* at para. 91.

inform the amendment process, including the principles of democracy and federalism.[316]

The Court sought to reconcile both propositions by declaring that no constitutional right or principle is absolute to the exclusion of the others:[317] no one people's rights "trump" the others. The relativity of constitutional rights and principles suggests that other parties cannot exercise their rights in such a way as to amount to an absolute denial of Quebec's rights, and, similarly, that so long as Quebec exercises its rights while respecting the rights of others, it may propose secession and seek to achieve it through a negotiation process that must be conducted in conformity with the constitutional principles.[318]

The Court declared that it has no supervisory role over the political aspects of constitutional negotiations.[319] The judicial methods appropriate for the search for truth are ill-suited to constitutional negotiations. To the extent that the questions are political in nature, it is not the role of the judiciary to interpose its own views on the different negotiating positions of the parties, even were it invited to do so:[320]

> The reconciliation of the various legitimate constitutional interests outlined above is necessarily committed to the political rather than the judicial realm, precisely because that reconciliation can only be achieved through the give and take of the negotiation process.[321]

The Court held that the initial impetus for negotiation is subject only to political evaluation, and properly so.[322] The Canadian constitution and history require the participants to reconcile the rights, obligations, and legitimate aspirations of all Canadians within a framework that emphasizes constitutional responsibilities as much as it does constitutional rights.[323] A party's refusal to conduct negotiations in a manner consistent with constitutional principles and values would damage the legitimacy of that party's assertion of its rights, and perhaps the negotiation process as a whole:

> Those who quite legitimately insist upon the importance of upholding the rule of law cannot at the same time be oblivious to the need to act in conformity with constitutional principles and values, and so do their part to contribute to the maintenance and promotion of an environment in which the rule of law may flourish.[324]

In *Delgamuukw*, the Court acknowledged that the task of courts is to articulate the parties' legal positions before negotiations. In the British Columbia Court of

---

316 *Ibid.* at para. 92.

317 *Ibid.* at para. 93.

318 *Ibid.* at para. 94.

319 *Ibid.* at para. 100.

320 *Ibid.* at para. 101.

321 *Ibid.* at para. 101.

322 *Ibid.* at para. 100.

323 *Ibid.* at para. 104.

324 *Ibid.* at para. 95.

Appeal, Justice Macfarlane stated, "[w]hile negotiations are to be encouraged, and ultimately may be the preferred way to finally resolve Aboriginal issues, the role of the court is to deal with the issues arising directly from the judgment under appeal."[325] He stated, "[t]he question of the extent, if any, of [Aboriginal] self-regulation which does not conflict with valid federal or provincial legislation is a question which is ripe for negotiation, and is better suited to the reconciliation process which the parties seemed disposed to pursue."[326] However, he added, "[n]o order of this court is required to permit the parties to enter into such negotiations."[327]

In his concurring judgment, Justice Wallace recognized that "many of the issues discussed in the case can and probably should be resolved by negotiation," but argued:

> the role of the Court of Appeal is not one of tailoring its judgment so as to facilitate settlement. This court is restricted to declaring the legal status of the respective rights claimed. These rights must be established by specific trial evidence of the particular aboriginal occupation and use of the specific territories in question.[328]

The joint request to allow the details to be negotiated won more support from the minority Court of Appeal judges in *Delgamuukw*. Justices Hutcheon and Lambert agreed that the issues should be "split" for negotiation, and the unresolved matter brought back for a new trial.[329] Lambert J.A. expressed preference for the exact nature of Aboriginal tenure to be "settled by negotiation, and by political accommodation," while recognizing the obligation of the courts to decide the legal questions should negotiations not succeed.[330]

Professor Roach agreed with this balanced remedial approach, and argued that it was sensitive to the particular context and the judiciary's ultimate obligation to enforce the legal rights of Aboriginal peoples:[331]

> there are strong *de jure* reasons why negotiation is a legitimate component of Aboriginal rights enforcement. Aboriginal rights, like minority language education rights, are group rights and negotiation provides an excellent opportunity for groups to specify their priorities. The uncertainty which surrounds aborigine's rights means that the range of acceptable solutions is wider and hence more amenable to negotiation. Most importantly, negotiation is consistent with the distinct purposes of Aboriginal rights, given the importance of treaties and the government's fiduciary obligations to act in a non-adversarial trust-like capacity. Given its recognition of the need for distinctive remedial approaches in the Aboriginal rights contexts, it can only be hoped the Supreme Court will be more willing to

---

325 *Delgamuukw, supra* note 2, 104 D.L.R. (4th) 470 at 490 (B.C. C.A.).

326 *Ibid.* at 542.

327 *Ibid.* at 543.

328 *Ibid.* at 601.

329 *Ibid.* at 794, Hutcheon J.A., and at 621, Lambert J.A.

330 *Ibid.* at 747.

331 Kent Roach, *Constitutional Remedies in Canada* (Aurora, Ont.: Canada Law Book, 1997) para. 15-685 at 15-31.

consider court-supervised negotiation as a legitimate aspect of remedies for Aboriginal rights.[332]

In his view, the uncertainty surrounding Aboriginal tenure is, if anything, a reason that negotiation may be useful. Remedies that incorporate negotiation attempt to find more comprehensive solutions and present a favourable alternative to continued uncertainty or a piecemeal process of litigating Aboriginal tenure acre by acre, prosecution by prosecution, individual by individual. The judiciary could construct an order that requires the other Crowns to negotiate with Aboriginal people.

As *Quebec Secession Reference* declared, negotiations are appropriate as a way to formulate constitutions. Negotiations are, however, not an appropriate way to implement existing constitutional provisions where great disparities of bargaining power exist among groups. Although negotiation is often represented as "best practice," from an Aboriginal perspective, such practice ignores the complex power, duties, and financial position of the parties. Aboriginal peoples have found it difficult to negotiate with their oppressors. The federal government as a constitutional fiduciary is in a conflict of interest in the negotiations: negotiating for Aboriginal tenure with the beneficiaries while constitutionally safeguarding Aboriginal tenure.

Treaty negotiations make sense only from the colonizer's perspective to eliminate Aboriginal tenure and replace it with the Crown's tenure. The extinguishment could only operate if section 35(1) were suspended because its constitutional purpose is to safeguard the unpurchased Aboriginal tenure. To assert treaty negotiations are the best way to "extinguish" Aboriginal tenure is inconsistent with "recognizing and affirming" Aboriginal tenure. This contradiction affirms that the colonial legacy remains deeply embedded in the judicial consciousness and jeopardizes the court's duty under constitutional supremacy.

Historical records leave little doubt that from the outset of treaty negotiations, the Crown has not kept the its promises or commitments and has left the Aboriginal people feeling resigned, disgusted, hopeless, and indifferent to the promises of the governments. Following the *St. Catherine's* ruling, the federal Parliament by section 94 of the 1867 Act could have made a provision for protecting Aboriginal tenure relative to "property and civil rights," and the courts and the provinces could have adopted such legislation. The *Sparrow* and *Delgamuukw* decisions of the Supreme Court of Canada offered the federal Parliament and the provinces another opportunity to remedy an injustice and assert constitutional supremacy. The long list of court cases initiated by the federal government since *Sparrow*, however, shows a resistance to complying with the constitutional rights of Aboriginal people.

In this context, judicial optimism about negotiation is not a substitute for constitutional integrity. Requiring Aboriginal groups to negotiate constitutional implementation devalues rights in the constitutional order. The duty of courts is to declare constitutional rights and settle cases based on constitutional principles. If Aboriginal peoples choose to negotiate constitutional implementation, they cannot ignore the constitution-

---

332   *Ibid.*, para. 15-687 at 15-32.

al difficulties of inter-delegation of constitutional rights between section 35(1) and sections 91 or 92. They must be aware that only administrative duties can be transferred in their negotiations, since they have no mandate to extinguish Aboriginal tenure for future generations.

No express power of inter-delegation of constitutional powers, responsibilities, or duties between the federal government and the provinces exists in the Canadian constitution. In the *Nova Scotia Inter-delegation* case,[333] the Supreme Court held that various legislative bodies of Canada could not alter the constitutional distribution of power in the absence of explicit authority in the constitution itself; there is no implied authority. The Court suggested that a constitutional amendment would be necessary, and a constitutional amendment was enacted to enable a national pension scheme in 1951.[334] The Court has held that administrative inter-delegation was valid.[335]

Administrative inter-delegation is an important tool of cooperative federalism; however, it does not divest the delegator of constitutional powers. It does not confer a permanent power on the delegatee. The delegator retains a continuing power to legislate on the same topic concurrently if it chooses, and it can withdraw the delegation at any time.[336] Thus, it is questionable if Aboriginal peoples in their negotiations with the federal Crown can delegate either Aboriginal or treaty rights to the federal or provincial jurisdictions without a constitutional amendment. The negotiations can do no more than create administrative inter-delegation, referential legislation, conditional legislation, or some mixture of these devices. If there is any enlargement of legislative authority in the treaty negotiation over Aboriginal tenure or rights, it may be unconstitutional. Further, the concept of negotiation appears inconsistent with the ultimate limitation on collective Aboriginal tenure that the use of the land cannot destroy the ability of the land to sustain future generations.

---

333 *Attorney-General of Nova Scotia v. Attorney-General for Canada* (1950), [1951] S.C.R. 31 (S.C.C.).

334 *British North America Act*, 1951 (U.K.), 14-15 Geo. VI, c. 32, reprinted in R.S.C. 1985, App. II, No. 35.

335 *P.E.I. Potato Marketing Board v. Willis*, [1952] 2 S.C.R. 392 (S.C.C.).

336 Hogg, *supra* note 232 at 355.

VI

SUI GENERIS ABORIGINAL TENURE

The inescapable conclusion from the Court's analysis of Indian title up to this point is that the Indian interest in land is truly *sui generis*. It is more than the right to enjoyment and occupancy although, as Dickson J. pointed out in *Guerin*, it is difficult to describe what more in traditional [English] property law terminology.

La Forest and L'Heureux-Dubé JJ. in *Delgamuukw*[1]

Pure insight, however, is in the first instance without any content; it is rather the sheer disappearance of content; but by its negative attitude towards what it excludes it will make itself real and give itself a context.

Hegel, *Phenomenology of Mind*[2]

23. The Unifying Principle

The Dickson and Lamer Courts have created a new constitutional framework for Aboriginal tenure. They have rejected the idea that Aboriginal tenure is a subdivision of Crown tenure, ending the colonial jurisprudential foundation. They have established that Aboriginal tenure has always been a distinct and unique land tenure system, a *sui generis* tenure to British land law. In rejecting negative perspectives on Aboriginal tenure and respecting traditional laws and knowledge, the judiciary has created a new insight. Based on this insight about what Aboriginal tenure is not, they have established that Aboriginal land tenure is created by Aboriginal law and traditions. This unifying constitutional context affirms imperial treaties and law.

In *Delgamuukw*, Chief Justice Lamer affirmed "the unifying principle" of *sui generis* Aboriginal tenure, one aspect of which is its "inalienability" to third parties:

---

1   *Delgamuukw v. British Columbia*, [1997] 3 S.C.R.1010 at para. 189, [1998] 1 C.N.L.R. 14 (S.C.C.) [hereinafter *Delgamuukw* cited to S.C.R. unless otherwise stated], relying on *Canadian Pacific Ltd. v. Paul*, [1988] 2 S.C.R. 654 at 678 (S.C.C.).

2   G.W.F. Hegel, *The Phenomenology of Mind*, trans. J.B. Bailie, vol. 2 (London: Swan, Sonnenschein, & Co., 1910) at 549.

> This Court has taken pains to clarify that aboriginal title is only "personal" in this sense, and does not mean that aboriginal title is a non-proprietary interest which amounts to no more than a licence to use and occupy the land and cannot compete on an equal footing with other proprietary interests ... .[3]

The *Delgamuukw* decision directs reviewing judges and lawyers to explore and articulate the complex, multidimensional nature and content of this *sui generis* constitutional right. To protect, preserve, and enhance Aboriginal tenure will require an extraordinary procedural and substantive effort on the part of the judiciary and legal profession.

The *sui generis* Aboriginal tenure precludes the application of "traditional real property rules" to explain the content of that title.[4] As Justice La Forest stated in his concurring opinion: "This *sui generis* interest is not equated with fee simple ownership; nor can it be described with reference to traditional property law concepts."[5] This empowers Aboriginal knowledge and law to explain the content of Aboriginal tenure.

Justice Macfarlane for the British Columbia Court of Appeal and Chief Justice Lamer for the Supreme Court of Canada agreed that the starting principles for any constitutional analysis of a *sui generis* Aboriginal tenure arise from operation of Aboriginal law and do not depend on a recognition by, or grant from, the imperial Crown. Aboriginal laws organized the occupation and possession on their lands, and the resulting land tenure has been categorized by the Canadian courts as "communal" land laws in their human-centred way of looking at property.[6]

These starting principles direct lawyers and courts to implement the interpretative principles of constitutional law and *sui generis* law, as well as to use comparative law and conflict of law analysis to understand Aboriginal laws. These principles also direct the courts to confront and overcome the biases and prejudices of the fiction of

---

3   *Delgamuukw, supra* note 1 at para. 113, relying on *Canadian Pacific Ltd. v. Paul,* [1988] 2 S.C.R. 654 at 677 (S.C.C.).

4   *Delgamuukw, ibid.* at para. 130; *St. Mary's Indian Band v. Cranbrook (City),* [1997] 2 S.C.R. 657 at para. 14 (S.C.C.) additional reasons at, [1997] 2 S.C.R. 678 (S.C.C.) [hereinafter *St. Mary's*]. In *Mitchell v. Peguis Indian Band,* [1990] 2 S.C.R. 85, [1990] 3 C.N.L.R. 46 (S.C.C.), Dickson C.J.C. stated at 82 [C.N.L.R.]:

> that aboriginal understanding of words and corresponding legal concepts in Indian treaties are to be preferred over more legalistic and technical constructions. This concern with aboriginal perspective, albeit in a different context, led a majority of this Court in *Guerin,* to speak of the Indian interest in land as a *sui generis* interest, the nature of which cannot be totally captured by a lexicon derived from European legal systems.

5   *Delgamuukw, ibid.* at para. 190. Justices Mcfarlane for the majority, with Wallace concurring and Lambert in dissent in the British Columbia Court of Appeal, recognized that Aboriginal title and Aboriginal rights are *sui generis,* and not easily explicable in terms of ordinary "western" jurisprudential analysis or common law concepts, at paras. 31, 42 and 48.

6   *Delgamuukw, supra* note 1 at para. 31. These principles were derived from *Baker Lake v. Minister of Indian Affairs and Northern Development,* [1979] 3 C.N.L.R. 17 (Fed. T.D.), additional reasons at (1979), [1982] C.N.L.R. 139 (Fed. T.D.); *Calder v. British Columbia,* [1973] S.C.R. 313, [1973] 4 W.W.R. 1 (S.C.C.); *Guerin v. The Queen,* [1984] 2 S.C.R. 335, [1985] 1 C.N.L.R. 120 (S.C.C.); *R. v. Sparrow,* [1990] 1 S.C.R. 1075, [1990] 3 C.N.L.R. 160 (S.C.C.) [hereinafter *Sparrow* cited to S.C.R. unless otherwise stated]; and *Mabo v. Queensland* (1992), 107 A.L.R. 1, 175 C.L.R. 1 (H.C.) [hereinafter *Mabo* cited to A.L.R. unless otherwise stated].

Crown tenure and the common law perspective as the exclusive sources of law, as well as to see the deep structure or "big picture"[7] of Canadian property law that constitutionally respects Aboriginal law and tenure. Only when reviewing courts have understood Aboriginal tenure from an Aboriginal perspective can they begin to determine the relationship of Aboriginal tenure to Crown tenure and the common law perspectives. Against the background of constitutional equality of laws and section 52(1) of the *Constitution Act, 1982*, the common law perspectives must be consistent with Aboriginal law. Such judicial interpretation will effectively replace past attempts to force Aboriginal tenure into the categories of British land law.

The uniqueness of Aboriginal law and tenure will require explanation and evaluation, and such processes will require changes in the judicial rules of procedure, evidence, and land claim processes. In *Van der Peet*, Chief Justice Lamer declared that the constitutional and legal structure must change to accommodate Aboriginal rights, and the rules of evidence should be adapted to take into account the *sui generis* nature of Aboriginal rights.[8] In *Delgamuukw*, he declared the courts must give due weight to the Aboriginal perspective and relationship with the land by coming to terms with oral traditions, customs, and practices, which, for many Aboriginal nations, are the only record of their past:

> Notwithstanding the challenges created by the use of oral histories as proof of historical facts, the laws of evidence must be adapted in order that this type of evidence can be accommodated and placed on an equal footing with the types of historical evidence that courts are familiar with, which largely consists of historical documents.[9]

In 1992, the Australian High Court in *Mabo v. State of Queensland*[10] struggled with the conceptualization of Aboriginal tenure within the British common law traditions, rather than as *sui generis*. It held that Aboriginal tenure was a right "as against the whole world to possession, occupation, use and enjoyment of the lands."[11] The High Court emphasized that the source and nature of Aboriginal tenure was the Aboriginal legal system: "Native title has its origin in and is given its content by the traditional laws acknowledged by and the traditional customs observed by the indigenous inhabitants of a territory."[12] Whatever the past difficulties of British common law con-

---

7   See C. Bell, "Jack Woodward, *Native Law*," book review of *Native Law* by Jack Woodward in [1990] 3 C.N.L.R. at 6-7.

8   *R. v. Van der Peet*, [1996] 2 S.C.R. 507 at para. 49 (S.C.C), reconsideration refused, (January 16, 1997), Doc. 23803 (S.C.C.).

9   *Delgamuukw, supra* note 1 at para. 87.

10 *Mabo, supra* note 6 at 1.

11 *Ibid.* at 55.

12 *Ibid.* at 42, Brennan J. At 83 Deane and Gaudron JJ. stated: "[S]ince the title preserves entitlements to the use and enjoyment under the traditional law or custom of the relevant territory or locality, the contents of the rights and the identity of those entitled to enjoy them must be ascertained by reference to that traditional law or custom." This conclusion was codified in *Native Title Act 1993* (Cth.), No. 110 of 1993, s. 223(1)(a): "the rights and interest [...] possessed under the traditional law acknowledged, and the tradition customs observed, by the Aboriginal peoples ... ."

ceptualizing of Aboriginal tenure, the High Court concluded that it is a proprietary interest derived from Aboriginal law:

> If it be necessary to categorize an interest in land as proprietary in order that it survive a change in sovereignty, the interest possessed by a community that is in exclusive possession of land falls into that category. Whether or not land is owned by individual members of a community, a community which asserts and asserts effectively that none but its members has any right to occupy or use the land has an interest in the land that must be proprietary in nature: there is no other proprietor. ... There may be difficulties of proof of boundaries or of membership of the community or of representatives of the community which was in exclusive possession, but those difficulties afford no reason for denying the existence of a proprietary community title capable of recognition by the common law. That being so, there is no impediment to the recognition of individual non-proprietary rights that are derived from the community's laws and customs and are dependent on the community title. *A fortiori*, there can be no impediment to the recognition of individual proprietary rights.[13]

Aboriginal tenure must be judicially ascertained according to the law and customs of the Aboriginal people connected with the land. Like the Supreme Court of Canada in *Sparrow*, the Australian High Court in *Mabo* stated that the past interferences by colonial law on Aboriginal law and its land tenure system are not relevant: "It is immaterial that the laws and customs have undergone some change since the Crown acquired sovereignty provided the general nature of the connection between the Indigenous people and the land remains."[14] The High Court also noted, "if the clan or group, by ceasing to acknowledge those laws, and (so far as practicable) observe those customs, loses its connection with the land or on the death of the last of the members of the group or clan," Aboriginal tenure ends. However, the Court rejected the suggestion that Aboriginal tenure is limited to ancient uses practiced before exposure to "European civilization."[15]

Understanding and developing the positive insight in *Delgamuukw* into the *sui generis* conception of Aboriginal tenure in the constitution of Canada will require reviewing courts and involved lawyers to understand Aboriginal thought and its constitutional order. The pre-colonization Aboriginal laws that organized Aboriginal uses and responsibilities on the land, the pre-existing Aboriginal legal systems before the assertion of British sovereignty, all inform the *sui generis* nature of Aboriginal tenure.[16] Aboriginal knowledges inform Aboriginal laws, and Aboriginal laws are the context of Aboriginal tenures, not a limitation on their content. In *Delgamuukw*, Chief Justice Lamer concluded that Aboriginal tenure encompasses the Aboriginal law and "the right to exclusive use and occupation of the land" for "a variety of purposes, which need not be

---

13   *Mabo, ibid.* at 36, Brennan J.

14   *Ibid.* at 51, Brennan J. See *R. v. Sparrow, supra* note 6, C.N.L.R. at 176, 182-83, for a similar result in federal fishing regulations being immaterial to Aboriginal rights.

15   *Mabo, ibid.*

16   *Delgamuukw, supra* note 1 at para. 114: see *Mabo, ibid.* at 50-51, Brennan J., and 80-81, 86-87, Deane and Gaudron JJ., and 180-182, Toohey J.

aspects of those Aboriginal practices, customs and traditions which are integral to distinctive Aboriginal cultures"[17] that define Aboriginal rights in section 35(1).

Aboriginal law determines the proprietary titles, rights, and interests of the family or members.[18] Aboriginal laws organizing land tenure systems were matrilineal rather than patrilineal.[19] Although Aboriginal languages did not distinguish between gender categories, most Aboriginal laws of tenure were developed by the "women" as head of an extended family through a consensus process, and implemented by the "men."

To point the way forward to understand the Aboriginal context surrounding Aboriginal tenure, this part of the book will attempt to give a context to the unifying principle of *sui generis* Aboriginal tenure by revealing its source and nature in Aboriginal knowledge, language, heritage, and law. The following sections seek to explain how Aboriginal knowledge and language articulate the legal vision of Aboriginal tenure, the Aboriginal "langscape" of property in North America. To paraphrase Jacques Derrida: to address Aboriginal tenure in the Aboriginal language is the unifying condition of all possible justice in Canadian law.[20]

Aboriginal knowledges, languages, and laws sustain a vision of land and inform a *sui generis* land tenure. Most Aboriginal languages and law do not have the English idea of "tenure" or "property," but instead have a law based on belonging to "an ecology" and being responsible for it. Aboriginal legal systems view and respect land as a cooperative ecological order. To make these abstractions as clear as possible in English, our explanations of the vision of land will focus specifically on a Míkmaq legal and language perspective. We will conclude with how Aboriginal tenure intersects with traditional ecological knowledge in international law.

24. Aboriginal Knowledge and Heritage Enfold *Sui Generis* Aboriginal Law and Tenure

No uniform or universal Aboriginal perspective on Aboriginal knowledge exists in Canada. Yet such diversity is the foundation for understanding Aboriginal laws, tenures, and rights in the Constitution of Canada. These Aboriginal systems of knowledge are the only foundation for knowing a *sui generis* Aboriginal law and its tenure.

---

17   *Delgamuukw, ibid.* at para. 117.

18   *Ibid.* at paras. 140-141.

19   *Ibid.* at para. 12. McEachern C.J. found that the "fundamental foundation of both Gitksan and Wet'-suwet'en society is that they are divided into clans and Houses. Every person born of a Gitksan or Wet'-suwet'en woman is automatically a member of his or her mother's House and clan." See A. Mills, *Eagle Down is Our Law: Witsuwit'en Law, Feasts, and Land Claims* (Vancouver: U.B.C. Press, 1994), especially "Witsuwit'en law" at 141-64. The common expression of Witsuwit'en law is the ways of the people on the surface of the earth (*yinkadinii' ha ba aten*).

20   Jacques Derrida, "Force of Law: The 'Mystical Foundation of Authority'" in Drucilla Cornell, Michel Rosenfeld, and David Gray Carlson, eds., *Deconstruction and the Possibility of Justice* (New York: Routledge, 1992) at 3.

They define the nature of a group's attachment to the land, the uses and the limitations on uses of the land, and the Aboriginal practices, customs, and traditions.

Aboriginal heritage is so intimately based on Aboriginal knowledge that often the terms are interchangeable. Aboriginal knowledge refers to the integrated body of knowledge developed over time through the relations with an ecosystem that covers all aspects of life. It is dynamic and cumulative, representing generations of experiences, careful empirical observation, and various experiments. It is stored in heritage by Aboriginal memories and ceremonies, learned and expressed in the oral and symbolic traditions of the peoples. Shared and transmitted orally and ceremonially, the collective wisdom of the people informs the law.

Indigenous peoples regard all products of the human mind and heart as interrelated within Aboriginal or Indigenous knowledge. They assert that all knowledge flows from the same source: the relationships among a global flux that needs to be renewed, their kinship with the other living creatures that share the land, and their kinship with the spirit world. Since the ultimate source of knowledge and creativity is the changing ecosystem itself, the art and science of some specific people manifest the same underlying relationships and can be considered as manifestations of the people as a whole. Perhaps the unity of various Indigenous knowledges in Canada is best expressed as all the expressions of the vibrant relationship between the people, their ecosystem, and the other living beings and spirits that share the land. These multi-layered relationships, which Tewa Pueblo educator, Gregory Cajete, describes as the "strands of connectedness,"[21] are the basis for maintaining legal, social, economic, and diplomatic relationships—through sharing—with other peoples.

All aspects of this knowledge are interrelated and cannot be separated from the traditional territory of the people concerned. Similarly, there is no need to separate reality into categories of living and non-living, renewable or non-renewable. The people themselves decide what tangibles and intangibles constitute the knowledge of a particular Aboriginal people. Many national and international definitions of Aboriginal or Indigenous knowledge stress the principle of its totality or holism and diverse modes. The *Report of the Royal Commission on Aboriginal Peoples* views Aboriginal knowledge:

> as a cumulative body of knowledge and beliefs, handed down through generations by cultural transmission, about the relationship of living beings (including humans) with one another and their environment.[22]

The Director-General of United Nations Educational, Scientific and Cultural Organisation (UNESCO), Frederico Mayor, has defined Indigenous knowledge:

---

21   G. Cajete, *Science: A Native American perspective* (doctoral dissertation, 1986) [unpublished] at 17.

22   Canada, *Final Report of the Royal Commission on Aboriginal Peoples*, vol. 4 (Ottawa: Minister of Supply and Services, 1995) at 454 [hereinafter RCAP]. See also Inuit Circumpolar Conference, *A Report of Findings: The Participation of Indigenous Peoples and the Application of their Environmental and Ecological Knowledge in the Arctic Environmental Protection Strategy*, vol. 1 (Ottawa: Indian and North Affairs, Canada, 1993) at 27-37.

The indigenous peoples of the world possess an immense knowledge of their environments, based on centuries of living close to nature. Living in and from the richness and variety of complex ecosystems, they have an understanding of the properties of plants and animals, the functions of ecosystems and the techniques for using and managing them that is particular and often detailed. In rural communities in developing countries, locally occurring species are relied on for many—sometimes all—foods, medicines, fuel, building materials and other products. Equally, people's knowledge and perceptions of the environment, and their relationship with it, are often important elements of cultural identity.[23]

The United Nations Special Rapporteur, Dr.-Mrs. Daes, has presented the best operational definition of Indigenous knowledge and heritage with the assistance of many Indigenous organisations and peoples. In her report on protecting the heritage of Indigenous people, she pointed out that Indigenous knowledge and heritage is "a complete knowledge system with its own concepts of epistemology, philosophy, and scientific and logical validity."[24] The Rapporteur further concluded that diverse elements of any Indigenous knowledge system "can only be fully learned or understood by means of the pedagogy traditionally employed by these peoples themselves, including apprenticeship, ceremonies and practices."[25] Moreover, the Rapporteur stressed the role of land or ecology as the Indigenous knowledge system's "central and indispensable classroom" in which the heritage of each Indigenous peoples has traditionally been taught.[26]

She codified these insights in the *Principles and Guidelines for the Protection of the Heritage of Indigenous Peoples* (1995), which merged the concepts of Indigenous knowledge and heritage into a definition of heritage:

11. The heritage of Indigenous peoples is comprised of all objects, sites and knowledge, the nature or use of which has been transmitted from generation to generation, and which is regarded as pertaining to a particular peoples; clan heritage of an Indigenous people also includes objects, knowledge and literary or artistic works which may be created in the future based upon its heritage.

...

13. Every element of an Indigenous peoples' heritage has traditional owners which may be the whole people, a particular family or clan, an association or society, or individuals who have been specially taught or initiated to be its custodians. The traditional owners of

---

23 Mayor, cited in A.R. Emery and Associates, *Guidelines for Environmental Assessment and Traditional Knowledge* (Ottawa: Centre for Traditional Knowledge, 1997) [prototype].

24 Sub-Commission on Prevention of Discrimination and Protection of Minorities, Commission on Human Rights, United Nations Economic and Social Council, *Preliminary Report of the Special Rapporteur, Protection of the Heritage of Indigenous People*, UN ESC, UN Doc. E/CN.4/Sub.2/1994/31 (1994) at para. 8.

25 *Ibid.*

26 *Ibid.* at para. 9.

heritage must be determined in accordance with Indigenous peoples' own customs, laws and practices.[27]

Many non-Indigenous scholars have offered partial definitions of Aboriginal knowledge, each of which has its limitations. Douglas A. West stated the issue:

> Any discussion of indigenous knowledge begins with a statement of qualifications and a qualification of statements. In order to appreciate the depths and meanings of indigenous knowledge, the reader should avoid the revered social science position of an objective "veil of ignorance." We are confused, perplexed and in awe when considering the plurality of differences inherent among indigenous knowledge. We carry the biases of centuries of interpretations and categorisations that fill the pages of academic and popular literature.[28]

Aboriginal knowledge is a systemic and interrelated concept that has few boundaries. Yupiaq scholar Oscar Kawagley has noted the wide variety of Eurocentric terms for Indigenous knowledge: cross-cultural epistemology; traditional technology; Indigenous anthropology; anthropological knowledge; traditional knowledge; traditional ecological knowledge; ways of knowing; wisdom of the elders; Inupiaq rules for living; cultural ecology; spiritual ecology; "Bush" consciousness; Indigenous knowledge systems; and sacred ways of knowing.[29]

Aboriginal elders argue that all elements of Aboriginal knowledge within a language group should be managed and protected as a single, interrelated, and integrated whole. They should not be fragmented into English categories, since that destroys their meaning. Attempting to subdivide Aboriginal knowledge into separate Eurocentric legal categories such as "culture," "art," "intelligence," "law," "science," and "medicine," or into separate elements such as songs, stories, science, or sacred sites is inappropriate since most Aboriginal languages do not have such distinctions. Such foreign imposition on Aboriginal knowledge and language should be avoided.[30]

Clarifying Aboriginal knowledge and tenure in Canada is a different research project from exploring the existing dominant conceptualizations of Aboriginal knowl-

---

27   *United Nations Guidelines for the Protection of the Heritage of Indigenous Peoples,* GA Res. 95-12808(E), UN GAOR, 40th Sess., UN Doc. E/CN.4/Sub. 2/1995/3 (1995) at paras. 12-13 at 6. The heritage of Indigenous peoples is defined in Art. 12 to include:

> all moveable cultural property as defined by the relevant conventions of UNESCO; all kinds of literary and artistic works such as music, dance, song, ceremonies, symbols and designs, narratives and poetry; all kinds of scientific, agricultural, technical and ecological knowledge, including cultigens, medicines and the phenotypes and genotypes of flora and fauna; human remains; immovable cultural property such as sacred sites, sites of historical significance, and burials; and documentation of Indigenous peoples' heritage on film, photographs, videotape, or audiotape.

28   In S. O'Meara and D.A. West, eds., *From Our Eyes: Learning from Indigenous Peoples* (Toronto: Garamond Press, 1996) at 1.

29   A.O. Kawagley, *A Yupiaq World View: A Pathway to Ecology and Spirit* (Prospect Heights, Ill.: Waveland Press, 1995).

30   See generally E. Daes, "Indigenous People and Their Relationship to Land," Preliminary working paper presented to the Sub-Commission on Prevention of Discrimination and Protection of Minorities, UN Doc. E/CN.4/Sub. 2/1997/17 at paras. 5-13.

edge and tenure. To acquire an Aboriginal perspective on knowledge requires extended conversations with elders of each language group in Canada. To sustain Aboriginal knowledge, one must be willing to take on responsibilities associated with that knowing. For example, when an elder says, "I know," it is a temporary reference point or marking. If such knowledge is to be contained or the relationship to be sustained over time, then the Elder must teach others how to renew it.

Conceptualizing Aboriginal knowledge entails research into: locally specific systems of customary jurisprudence with respect to the right of acquiring and sharing knowledge; the classification of types and the meaning of knowledge; the responsibilities that attach to possessing various kinds of knowledge that are embedded uniquely in each culture and language; and the localized content and meaning of Aboriginal knowledge. Thus, any framework for understanding or protecting particular perspectives about Aboriginal knowledge must be contextual, decentralized, and respectful of the linguistic categories, rules, and relationships unique to each knowledge-system.

A. Aboriginal languages enfold Aboriginal law and tenure

Aboriginal knowledge or epistemology is transmitted primarily though Aboriginal languages. Aboriginal languages articulate how to relate respectfully to the lands and form attachments to the land. They provide the best evidence of Aboriginal knowledge, law, and tenure, since they are the repositories of such knowledge. Aboriginal languages provide the deep and lasting cognitive bonds that affect all aspects of Aboriginal life. Through sharing a language, Aboriginal people share belief of how the world works and what constitutes proper action. Sharing these common ideals creates a shared cognitive experience for Aboriginal societies that are understood as Aboriginal knowledge.

Anguished by the historical record of residential schools, missionary invasion in communities, and cognitive imperialistic public schooling, Aboriginal peoples and elders have testified repeatedly to their languages' importance and the need to arrest their erosion.[31] Eli Taylor, an elder from the Sioux Valley First Nations, eloquently explains the importance of maintaining Aboriginal languages:

> Our Native language embodies a value system about how we ought to live and relate to each other ... it gives a name to relations among kin, to roles and responsibilities among

---

31 M.E. Jamieson, *The Aboriginal Language Policy Study, Phase II: Implementation Mechanism, September 1988* (Ottawa: National Indian Brotherhood, Assembly of First Nations, 1988); *Towards Linguistic Justice for First Nations: The Challenge: Report on the Aboriginal Languages and Literacy Conference, January 20-23, 1991* (Ottawa: Assembly of First Nations, 1991); *Towards Rebirth of First Nations Languages* (Ottawa: Assembly of First Nations, First Nations Languages and Literacy Secretariat, 1992); Canada, Standing Committee on Aboriginal Affairs, *You Took My Talk: Aboriginal Literacy and Empowerment: Fourth Report of the Standing Committee on Aboriginal Affairs* (Ottawa: Queen's Printer, 1990); Canada, *Public Hearings: The Royal Commission on Aboriginal Peoples*, CD-ROM: *Royal Commission on Aboriginal Peoples* (Ottawa: Royal Commission on Aboriginal Peoples, 1993).

family members, to ties with the broader clan group ... there are no English words for these relationships ... .[32]

Knowing the ecosystem is a matter of relationships. It is not a knowing derived from curiosity or control, but rather from caring about each other and the world. Fundamental to Aboriginal knowledge is the awareness that beyond the immediate sensible world of perception, memory, imagination, and feelings, there lies another world from which knowledge, ability, or medicine is derived and by which peoples survive and flourish. The complementary modes of knowing and caring about the sensory and the spiritual realms inform the essence of Aboriginal knowledge, and this way of knowing has been continually transmitted in the oral tradition from the spirits to the elders and elders to the youth through their spiritual teachings.[33]

The cognitive transmission process reveals another important aspect of Aboriginal language and knowledge. The transmission is intimate and oral; it is not distant or literate. Any Eurocentric attempt to change the language is a direct attempt to modify or destroy Aboriginal knowledge or consciousness. Suppression of Aboriginal languages and the written translations of Aboriginal language have been part of the colonizer's tools, and like other colonial activities and law should not be used to undermine existing Aboriginal connections with the land.

B. Aboriginal visions of land

Out of the sounds of the life forces in the ecology, the structure of Aboriginal languages and law is centred on the process of being or sustaining a shared world-view, a cognitive solidarity, and a tradition of responsible action. That world-view creates a series of visual descriptions clearly identifiable within the space and with specific boundaries and uses embedded in the original languages. Out of these descriptions comes a specialized cognitive map of their space or "territory" with paths of movement and cycles of existence.

Aboriginal order is based on the law of belonging to an ecological space. It is not a race-based law. It is usually based on kinship ties, specialized access to resources, and a high degree of social equality. Aboriginal people do not speak of living "there"; rather, each family or person "belongs" to the space or territory. Belonging is directly tied linguistically and experientially to a space as well as to shared knowledge. Belonging to a space, more than just living in a place or using its resources is attendant with benefits and obligations. Belonging is a special responsibility. Sharing and mobility discourage the accumulation of inessential resources, while relationships shape law, legal choices, placement, and ultimately life.

While the Aboriginal order is based on an extended family-centred organization, it is not an isolated or stationary organization. Aboriginal peoples live and work in dif-

---

32   *Towards Rebirth of First Nations Languages, ibid.* at 14.

33   M. Battiste, "An Historical Investigation of the Social and Cultural Consequences of Micmac Literacy" (Dissertation archived with University Microfilms International) [unpublished].

ferent places, not travelling randomly, but travelling to the resources to create and harvest bio-diversity and to trade. Mobility among Aboriginal peoples is not recent, nor
was it introduced by modern means of travel; it was a sustainable way of life.

Across countless generations, comforted by the safety of Aboriginal languages,
elders and storytellers have revealed the principles of Aboriginal law. In different languages, at various length and details, these oral teachings give form and context to the
law. These laws tell of a sacred world transforming into a consensual order. Many laws
exist within these teachings or stories, responding to the noblest understandings of
Aboriginal world-views and thoughts on the proper way to live in a dynamic and
changing environment.[34]

Aboriginal consciousness and land laws are reflected in the law of belonging to
a place that acknowledges the ability of the forces and resources in a space to move the
spirit and the mind. Aboriginal consciousness honours processes and relationships
rather than fixed rules, which leads to an understanding and acceptance of the interre-
lationships, expressive energies, and experiences of an ecological place. Awareness of
the generative order is the source of all Aboriginal law. To understand the shared spatial order of any Aboriginal nation is to identify the Aboriginal law and traditions, and
the legal processes of linguistic responsibilities, descriptions, and pathways. To understand the order is to live within it, learn its teachings, and to act in accordance with the
teachings. Every Aboriginal language speaker knows the normative order and how to
maintain, protect, and renew the land. Such knowledge is fundamental to their identity, personality, and humanity. It must be noted again that it is difficult to separate one
Indigenous concept from another when trying to describe Indigenous peoples' relationship to their lands, territories, and resources.

In *Delgamuukw*, Chief Justice Lamer affirmed that these teachings are transmitted and recorded in a *sui generis* method:

> The Aboriginal tradition in the recording of history is neither linear nor steeped in the
> same notions of social progress and evolution [as in the non-Aboriginal tradition]. Nor is
> it usually human-centred in the same way as the western scientific tradition, for it does not
> assume that human beings are anything more than one—and not necessarily the most
> important—element of the natural order of the universe. Moreover, the Aboriginal histor-
> ical tradition is an oral one, involving legends, stories and accounts handed down through
> the generations in oral form. It is less focused on establishing objective truth and assumes
> that the teller of the story is so much a part of the event being described that it would be
> arrogant to presume to classify or categorize the event exactly or for all time.

> In the Aboriginal tradition the purpose of repeating oral accounts from the past is broad-
> er than the role of written history in western societies. It may be to educate the listener, to
> communicate aspects of culture, to socialize people into a cultural tradition, or to validate
> the claims of a particular family to authority and prestige. ...

---

34 See generally RCAP, *supra* note 22, vol. 1 (*Looking Forward, Looking Backward*) at 628-34 and vol.
2 (*Restructuring the Relationship*) at 117-19, 434-62. Daes, *supra* note 30.

> Oral accounts of the past include a good deal of subjective experience. They are not sim-
> ply a detached recounting of factual events but, rather, are "facts enmeshed in the stories
> of a lifetime". They are also likely to be rooted in particular locations, making reference
> to particular families and communities. This contributes to a sense that there are many
> histories, each characterized in part by how a people see themselves, how they define
> their identity in relation to their environment, and how they express their uniqueness as
> a people.[35]

Nor is the established Eurocentric chronology of time the Aboriginal peoples' own version of their past. The Aboriginal peoples' version of time is filled not with bold sweep-
ing trends over long periods, but rather with a specific space filled with experiences and
feelings. Past experiences inform modern discussions about these places.

Through their langscape, the naming of the land, the Aboriginal peoples' experience and wisdom continue. Aboriginal people talk about past experiences motivated by
specific concerns, for example, the "snow blinding moon" or February. Ultimately their
lives revolve around specific places in their sacred space. Objects come and go, but
places in the sacred space continue as essential to explanation and descriptions. The
places are not transitory; they remain the focal point of a past both spatial and oral.
When the Aboriginal past is talked about, the locational components constitute the unifying factor connecting space, time, and motivation. Talking about the past involves
experiences: characters, events, and objects. Actions from the past involve causation
rather than logic. Not everyone knows precisely the same amount of detail or the same
version, but they take certain places as starting points for discussion that is sometimes
narrative, sometimes not.

Often in Aboriginal peoples' discussion of the past, the topics turn to "the first"
or spatial anomalies. An example of a first is the Mi'kmaq district of *Sikniktewaq*
(roughly New Brunswick) describing the low grumbling sounds that the glacier made
as it turned a river into a gulf, splitting Prince Edward Island (*Epekwith*) from the continent. Spatial anomalies provide an explanation about new experiences. Spatial questions provide the impetus for Aboriginal peoples to ask why something is there, and
perhaps to correlate it with a certain time period or to reinforce a narrative *per se*.
Through this endless process, Aboriginal people come to know about their sacred
space, and fill it with culture, knowledge, and values. Most Aboriginal peoples know
which families to ask for detailed knowledge. No singular account explains their collective past, nor does everyone know every specific detail. Often no account deals with
any fixed chronological time; dates for events can only be approximated. Progression
of time is connected to the specific lives of known people; in other words, it is linked
with memory, a matter of culture, not chronological time.

Memory in the oral traditions is measured in terms of generations or winter counts
or ancestors' lives. If the event happened during the lifetime of a certain person, then it
is usually linked to certain events during that lifetime. If the event is not located within
the family history, then the actual date is not important or not remembered. It is part of
daily life. As each generation passes on, past events separate from individual lives and

---

35   *Delgamuukw, supra* note 1 at para. 85, relying on RCAP, *ibid.*, vol. 1 at 33; Daes, *ibid.*

enter the great store of experiences that occurred "before my time." Thus "my time" is current experience; "before my time" is the collective oral traditions held by the families. Time and event are linked in memory or symbolic literacy, not in written literacy.

Discrepancy arises occasionally, but Aboriginal peoples accept inconsistency in the broad understanding of cycles and the living past. Each version provides different perspectives on past values and events. Instead of a concept of a singular "true" history, they have an account of experiences or topistic space; that is, a distinctive mode of apprehending place, responding holistically to the identity and character of a particular location. Validity or justification of historical descriptions rests on family relationships rather than on content, on such claims as "that was the way it was told to us or me."

How Aboriginal languages and law appropriate a space and attach responsibilities to it also reveals their ecological consciousness. Their notion of self does not end with their flesh, but continues with the reach of their senses into the land itself. Their notion of the space is more than vision; it includes the other non-visual senses. Thus, they can speak of the land as their flesh; they are the environments.

Many of these oral teachings have been translated into English, some more accurately than others. Paula Gunn Allen has translated the unifying vision of land in these teachings:

> We are the land. To the best of my understanding, that is the fundamental idea embodied in Native American life and culture ... . More than remembered, the earth is the mind of the people as we are the mind of the earth. The land is not really the place (separate from ourselves) where we act out the drama of our isolate destinies. It is not a means of survival, a setting for our affairs, a resource on which we draw in order to keep our own act functioning. It is not the ever-present "Other" which supplies us with a sense of "I." It is rather a part of our being, dynamic, significant, real. It is ourselves, in as real a sense as such notion as "ego, libido" or social network, in a sense more real than any conceptualization or abstraction about the nature of human being can ever be ... . Nor is this relationship one of mere "affinity" for the Earth. It is not a matter of being "close to nature." The relationship is more one of identity, in the mathematical sense, than of affinity. The Earth is, in a very real sense, the same as ourself (or selves). [36]

Leroy Little Bear of the *Kainaiwa* (Blood Tribe) of the Blackfoot Confederacy has translated a similar principle that the land was considered the mother, the giver of life:

> Tribal territory is important because the Earth is our Mother (and this is not a metaphor: it is real). The Earth cannot be separated from the actual being of Indians. The Earth is where the continuous and/or repetitive process of creation occurs. It is on the Earth and from the Earth that cycles, phrases, patterns, in other words, the constant flux and motion can be observed and experienced. In other words, creation is a continuity, and if creation is to continue, then it must be renewed, and consequently, the renewal ceremonies, the

---

36   "*Iyani*: It Goes This Way" in G. Hobson, ed., *The Remembered Earth: An Anthology of Contemporary American Indian Literature* (Albuquerque: University of New Mexico Press, 1980) at 91. See also Paula Gunn Allen, ed., *Spider Woman's Granddaughters: Traditional Tales and Contemporary Writing by Native American Women* (New York: Fawcett Columbine, 1990).

telling and re-telling of the creation stories, the singing and re-singing of songs, which are the humans' part in maintenance of creation. Hence, the annual sundance, the societal ceremonies, the unbundling of medicine bundles at certain phases of the year. All of these are interrelated aspects of happenings that take place on and within Mother Earth.[37]

Similarly, the Anishinaki poet and writer, Gerald Vizenor, summarizes an Ojibwa principle of the land:

> The land is everything to me. The land is part of my language, part of the way I perceive the world. The water, the trees, the smell of pine, the smell of autumn, the smell of wet leaves in the springs. It is all part of my imagination, part of my dreams.[38]

As the courts have noted, intractable problems of translation arise when the unifying principle of Aboriginal law is forced into the common law categories of British law, and popular notions of "ownership" and "jurisdiction." Yet with the colonial assertion that Aboriginal nations or peoples did not have a system of property rights, to survive and protect themselves from others, Aboriginal people have had to attempt to translate and teach their lawyers to articulate their vision of land law to political institutions and courts in common law vocabulary. Since often the Aboriginal world-view has no expression for abstract noun-ideas, it has been very difficult, if not impossible, to translate between the two encodings and conceptualizations of land tenure. These translations are not integral to *sui generis* analysis. Under the Supreme Court's *sui generis* characterization of Aboriginal law and tenure, Aboriginal lawyers do not have to explain Aboriginal land and law within the confines of British concepts of land law. They have to explain and situate Aboriginal law and tenure within Aboriginal world-view and thought.

Aboriginal world-view requires a coming into a relationship with the ecology; situating Aboriginal law signifies one's discovery of what there is in one's world and self that is sacred and spiritual. Some relationships of a space are produced through ancient agreements and renewal ceremonies with the "keepers" of the forces. These ecological covenants determine the law and customary actions of the people toward the resources. Though these spaces often appear to guests as "natural," to the Aboriginal people they are places created by agreements. Other spaces are ordered by ceremonies and rituals that reflect the teaching of the covenants and are required for renewal of the resources. The entire community's daily existence is based on the spatial concerns of shared resources, and on the equitable allocation of resources. Aboriginal peoples do not conceptualize managing the resources; rather, they manage their space. Their spa-

---

37   L. Little Bear, "Relationship of Aboriginal People to the Land and the Aboriginal Perspective on Aboriginal Title" in CD-ROM: *For Seven Generations: An Information Legacy of the Royal Commission on Aboriginal Peoples* (Ottawa: Minister of Supply & Services, 1996), cited in Royal Commission on Aboriginal Peoples, *Treaty Making in the Spirit of Co-existence. An Alternative to Extinguishment* (Ottawa: Canada Communication Group, 1994) at 10-11.

38   (1993) Spring Issue, Native Peoples at 35. See also the elegant Anishinaki legal consciousness and perspective in J. Borrows, "Living Between Water and Rocks: First Nations, Environmental Planning and Democracy" (1997) 47 U.T.L.J. 417.

tial consciousness, rather than the intentions or will of those families who nourished and protected the resource, shapes cultural and resource utilization and innovation.

A council of elders with consultation of all the extended families equitably divides the prime spaces of an ecology once or twice a year. Aboriginal law allocates use of spaces based on actual participation; the spaces are allocated so that general community livelihood is ensured. The sense of community solidarity is enhanced not only by Aboriginal law, but also by a responsible family acquiring secure "rights" to certain space or resources.

Far from being an ideological construct or a fungible commodity, the Aboriginal vision of land law is a shared and sacred ecological space. It is an ecological proprietarian legal order. Upon being asked to sign a land cession treaty, a Blackfoot chief summarized the ecological proprietarian legal order and rejected the idea of land as a commodity:

> Our land is more valuable than your money. It will last forever. It will not even perish by the flames of fire. As long as the sun shines and the waters flow, this land will be here to give life to man and animals. We cannot sell the lives of men and animals; therefore we cannot sell this land. It was put there for us by the Great Spirit and we cannot sell it because it does not belong to us. You can count your money and burn it within the nod of a buffalo's head, but only the Great Spirit can count the grains of sand and the blades of grass on these plains. As a present to you, we will give you anything we have that you can take with you; but the land, never.[39]

Generally, the Aboriginal law manifests many different visions of land tenure derived from the unifying principle and ecological proprietarian order. These laws can be translated into a linguistic world-view or "langscape" that defines a concept of territory or land, but typically they describe a concept of space, of different realms enfolded into a sacred space. Their mother, the earth, is a series of ecological spaces; each filled with resources, sights and sounds, and memories.

As such principles illustrate, an Aboriginal world-view is a spatial rather than a material consciousness. This spatial consciousness is reflected in the Gitksan chiefs' 1884 petition to the Government of Canada characterizing their territory as similar to an animal, with the villages its heart. The wrongful occupation of a part of their terri-

---

39   T.C. McLuhan, *Touch the Earth* (Toronto: New Press, 1971) at 53. Special Rapporteur José R. Martínez Cobo, *Study of the Problem of Discriminaton Against Indigenous Populations: Conclusions, Proposals, and Recommendations*, vol. 5 (New York: UN, 1987) at paras. 196-97, affirms this view. His study forms the basis of the policy and doctrine adopted by the United Nations in regard to the relationship of Indigenous peoples with their lands, territories, and resources:

> It is essential to know and understand the deeply spiritual special relationship between indigenous peoples and their land as basic to their existence as such and to all their beliefs, customs, traditions and culture. ... For such peoples, the land is not merely a possession and a means of production. The entire relationship between the spiritual life of indigenous peoples and Mother Earth, and their land, has a great many deep-seated implications. Their land is not a commodity which can be acquired, but a material element to be enjoyed freely.

tory was conceptualized as cutting off their foot.[40] Such a vision is reflected in the vision of the territory of the Blackfoot Confederacy as an old man.[41]

Aboriginal space or territory is never at rest: it is assumed eternal, yet remains tolerant to flux. It is a whole ecosystem that must be refined by endless ceremonies of renewal and realignment that unite Aboriginal peoples with its uniqueness or topistic integrity. The forces within a space can be analogized as frequencies from an enfolded realm.

Sharing space links those who belong to the land. In this sense, the law of belonging to the land means maintaining a series of spaces, such as fishing stations, hunting stations, and harvesting stations, renewed again and again by specific kinds of behaviours and ceremonies. These ecological spaces are not self-renewing. Shared knowledge about maintaining a particular space penetrates Aboriginal law and manifests shared values, beliefs, traditions, and customary behaviours. The law and teachings not only determine what is physically available to the families—what they can use—but also regulate their choices about the rate of resource use, and whether to modify their resources to increase the availability of useful resources. Aboriginal law allocates among allied families and friends the responsibility for managing the resources, and creates a customary transnational trading code with other nations and peoples to increase choices and resources.

New resources that facilitate sharing traditional resources are accepted, while objects that strain the communal solidarity have little impact. When new resources find their way into Aboriginal life, they are typically subservient to their awareness of space usage and the enfolded realms, no matter how they might be used in the context of other cultures.

C. *Míkmáki*: the sacred space[42]

The Míkmaw version of their ecology (*nestumou*) and their Living Lodge (*maqmikéwíkam*) will illustrate concretely this broad Aboriginal worldview. This brief sketch, though incomplete, may help others grasp the nature of a particular Algonquian world-view of "property."

"*Míkmáki*" became the concept that the allied people (Míkmaq) called their national territory. Not the usual land description, it is translated as the "space or land of friendship." It stressed the voluntary political confederation of the various Algonquian families into the Holy Assembly or *Santé Mawíomi* and their shared world-

---

40   D. Monet and *Skanu'u* [Ardythe Wilson], *Colonialism on Trial: Indigenous Land Rights and the Gitksan and Wet'suwet'en Sovereignty Case* (Gabriola Island, B.C.: New Society Publishers, 1992) at 1.

41   Little Bear, *supra* note 37.

42   An earlier version appears in J.Y. Henderson, "Míkmaw Tenure in Atlantic Canada" (1995) 18 Dal. L.J. 216 at 225-36. This section is derived from discussion with Kep'ten Steve Augustine, Dr. Marie Anne Battiste, Jikep'tin Alex Denny, Patrick and Eleanor Johnson, John J. and Sharon Paul, Kep'ten Noel Marshall, Professor Joe B. Marshall, and Professor Murdena Marshall and students at Míkmaq Studies of the University College of Cape Breton.

view. Wherever their language was spoken was *sitgamúk*, their ancient space, every part of which was sacred to the allied people. This space extended approximately twenty thousand square miles. In modern terms, Míkmáki as a territorial concept describes the territory now called Newfoundland, St. Pierre de Miquelon, Nova Scotia, New Brunswick, northern Maine, Prince Edward Island, the Magdalene archipelago, and the Gaspé Peninsula of Quebec. It is the beginning or eastern door of Canada.

Although it is possible to view Míkmáki as a territorial concept, in the Míkmaw context or langscape it expresses their sacred order. Their sacred order is not a cosmological order; it is the result of millennia of field observations and direct experience by their ancestors. These experiences are encoded within their language and symbolic literacy, an important part of the implicit order in which they live, as well as practical knowledge.

The sacred order in which the Míkmaq live is expressed as a sustaining relationship. Consistent with their verb-oriented reality, a process of being with the universe, the order was and is a widely shared, coherent, and interrelated world-view connecting all things. For example, the Míkmaq conceptualize animals with a certain *mntu* (or force) and consider them a "separate nation." An important feature of this order is the use of human kinship as a general analogy for ecological relations. The most obvious and widespread manifestation of this reciprocal relationship is the totemic clan system that categorizes social obligations, such as sharing and deference, as well as proper moral and ethical considerations within the ecological relationship. Plants, animals, and humans are related, and each is in an endless cycle as both producer and consumer with respect to the other.

Nestumou, the sound that describes the Míkmaw experiences on a part of the earth, is a sound that validates their identity within an ecosystem and a langscape that creates an appropriate cultural literacy. Literally, the "understood realms," *Nestumou* describes everything for which they have experiences, not everything that could exist. *Nestumou* includes both the visible and the invisible realms, and is discussed in terms of Lodges (*wikwóm*). *Nestumou* expresses their cumulative wisdom about eight interconnected levels of meaning or understandings (*nestunk*) that transform each other. The nestunk are the Deep Earth Lodge (*lamqamuk*), the Root Lodge (*wjipisekek*), the Water Lodge (*lampoqókóm*), the Earth Lodge (*kinuwsitagamino*), the Ghost Lodge (*wskïtekmujuiokóm*), and the Ancestors' Lodge (*skïékmujuawti*).

The centre of the sacred realm is the Living Lodge (*maqmikéwíkam*) composed of three realms: the underwater lodge, the earth lodge, and the ghost lodge. It comprises the spirals of the unfolding realms of daily Míkmaq life and the immanent enfolded realms of intuitive and transcendental experiences. Surrounding these realms are five other realms: the deep earth, root lodges, the sky lodge, the light lodge, and the ancestors' lodge. Interconnecting each of these lodges are the forces (*mntu*), and each of these lodges is associated, regardless of form, with certain keepers of forces.

The Míkmaq relations to the forces of the Living Lodge realm (*maqmikéwíkam*) are direct and extremely complex. This is often simply called nature in English; but it is a very difficult concept in Míkmaw thought, perhaps best expressed as *niskammelkikóim* (creation space) with the power to shape the people's identities. The Living

Lodge is a spiritual realm, a sacred space; a place for reverence and respect that reveals a natural truth and way of life. These understandings are woven throughout Míkmaw consciousness and form their human order.

The Míkmaq understand how limited their knowledge is about this realm. Their space in the Living Lodge is always in a state of flux (*muspekjamkewey*): it has always been a place of forms that dissolve and flow into everything else, a realm characterized by its transformations—the changing of forms and shapes—known through observations. Their environment cannot be known except though their linguistic knowledge of the place where they exist. All aspects of existence in the Living Lodge merge in an ongoing, indivisible process: a realm fragile yet resilient, delicate yet tough, sacred yet changeable. The air, forest, and sea are alive.

In this continual flow, the Living Lodge has always had many ways of creating harmony out of flux. It makes little sense to create any form of fixed world-view in this realm; the known truth is that unending change requires cognitive and physical flexibility. Míkmaw knowledge is not a description of reality; rather it constitutes perceptions about the nature of change, insights about patterns or styles of the flux. Life is not static. To see things as permanent is to be confused about everything; the alternative is to understand the need for creating temporary harmonies through alliances and relationships among all forms and forces.

The Míkmaq are content and comfortable with the Living Lodge's transformations. They understand life and death as non-paradoxical, that consciousness is their greatest gift, and that their role in renewing balance occurs by sharing and communicating with everything. They have a transcendent view of the world that seeks harmony with all things around them. They understand that they have to bring together all those things that are essential for the Living Lodge's regeneration, yet they have no notion of any uniqueness in the realm over the rest of the breathers.

Míkmaq thoughts and language honour the vastness of the creative, mysterious flux rather than the greatness of any Life Giver's power. Awareness of the sacred flux, a source of Míkmaw consciousness in the Living Lodge, can be acquired or lost, and it creates an understanding of what are now called in English the environment and ecology. Understanding the holiness of the Living Lodge is so urgent, so utterly linked with the pulse of feeling in the Aboriginal soul, that it becomes the singular sign of life and knowledge. Even when every other aspect of nature has failed them, they do not reject the sacred processes.

The Living Lodge has all kinds of spiritual controllers, who create a sacred spectrum. Each deserves and receives respect for its abilities. Each spiritual controller or keeper is referred to as a member of one's own immediate family, as a close relative, as an ally of the Míkmaq. Curing human disease is understood as a function of understanding the relationship with the spirits of a particular ecology. A person's willingness to restore his or her identity with the land and its guardian spirits is essential to a particular space or surrendering to the sustaining elegance of the space. The land and its spirits are a living reality that precedes human desires or values. It is the basis for all subsequent understanding of culture and self, which, in turn, renews and humanizes the space. Cultural traditions are an articulation of the awareness of the space and its spirits, which confirm their spatial identity and create a feeling of rightness or certainty in their beliefs.

Regardless of forms, these allies are parabolic: their meaning is discovered by experience rather than by reflection. The heightened experience or awareness of one's allies often increases the power of introspection: by silent dialogue, allies allow one to be aware of what other life forms or forces are thinking, or how they are influencing the seeker. They provide sustained experiences that allow one to see and learn the sacredness of life on earth, to recognize the manifestation of the holy in Living Lodge.

The Living Lodge and all its spiritual controllers find its highest expression in the creative processes of life (for example, babies). Life-generating processes exchange and mingle powers that produce Míkmaw consciousness and verb-based language, which reflect these forces. They hear singing in the wind not as poetry but as spirituality. From the sounds of the Living Lodge around them they create their speech and ideographs. Their consciousness or knowledge is contained as a form of aesthetic literacy—a symbolic literacy and an oral tradition—derived from the flux of the Living Lodge. Most Míkmaq favour subtlety and poetic understatement as modes of expressing the holiness of the Living Lodge. Meaning is derived from the context or relations of things. For the Míkmaq, symbolic literacy and prayer are considered art—an act of expression that makes evident much of the unique sensibility of their soul.

Like other Aboriginal people, the Míkmaq do not regard their environment as "natural." Instead, they view it as created by interactions between their ancestors and the ancestors of other life forms or species. Every tree, every shore, every mist in the woods, and every clearing is holy in their memory and experience, recalling not only their lives but also the lives of their ancestors since the world began. Hence, the entire langscape is a symbolic historical and educational record, testifying to the unique experience and identity of the people. All physiographic features within Míkmáki have ancient names in Míkmaq language (transcribed by explorers and missionaries) that witness their knowledge of its resources and continuous use of the ecosystem.

The Míkmaq are not inclined to make vast philosophical judgments or to create such an elaborate system of thought about the Living Lodge; they do not believe that the world placed some spirits in a superior position to others. Of course they are not perfect, but they have devised a code of behaviours to which they are equal—instead of a morality impossible to realize. This sacred order was never viewed as a commodity that could be sold, only shared.

Organized through extended family structures, the allied people identified with a hunting district (*sakamowti*) certain hunting and fishing stations under the responsibility of certain families, and the settlements (*wigamow*) that belonged to each of them. From each district or *wigamow* or settlement of kinsmen and their dependants, the *Santé Mawíomi* or Grand Council was created. The *Mawíomi* or Council recognizes one or more *kep'ten* ("captains") to show the people the good path, to help them with gifts of knowledge and goods, and to sit with the whole *Mawíomi* as the government of all the Míkmaq. From among themselves the *kep'ten* recognize a *jisagamow* ("grand chief") and a *jikep'ten* ("grand captain"), both to guide them and one to speak for them, and from others of good spirit they choose advisers and speakers, or *putuís*, as well as the leader of the warriors or *smankus*.

Government always has been and remains spiritual, persuasive, and non-coercive. The cruelties of repressive laws and majoritarian oppression were unknown until the recent interventions of European habits and laws. The continuity and authority of the *Mawíomi* exist in Míkmaw culture, in a common bond or vision that transcends temporary interests. This bond arises naturally from the fate of being born into a family (*munijinik*), community (*wikamouw*), territory (*míkmáki*), and people (*kinuk*).

A respectful human could participate in the consciousness and order, but could not possess or own them. The allied people felt spiritual forces of the land held them and established their relationship with the land. Inherent in their world-view is a conviction that the universe contains a limited amount of energy (*mntu*), which is continually running down and hence requires renewal by all participants. This conception of a sacred order as dynamic, finite, and fragile has important consequences for the way Aboriginal peoples manage and participate in the use of the resources.

The relationship between the Míkmaq and the land embodies the essence of the intimate sacred order. As humans, they have and retain an obligation to protect the order and a right to share its uses, but only the future unborn children in the invisible sacred realm of the next seven generations have any ultimate ownership of the land. In the custom of the Míkmaq, the *Santé Mawíomi* was and is the trustee of the sacred order and territory for future generations. Part of its duty is to regulate the natural resources of Míkmáki among the allied people and through the Nikmanen trading customs to increase the bio-diversity. This is more of a management right to ensure discipline in consumption of the resources rather than a symptom of ownership.

Inherent in this sacred order is the conviction that the resources had to be renewed as well as shared. Rather than managing, which implied human domination, the Míkmaq developed rituals for sharing or harmonizing the human and spiritual realms. These renewal rituals and ceremonies brought the people and the land into a fragile equilibrium or balance, thereby achieving basic subsistence and material well-being. These rituals and ceremonies created a harmony that emphasized stability and minimized risk for the harvesting of the resources, rather than growth and wealth accumulation. The quest for harmony also created the need for diversification by trade and modification of habitats, thereby developing surplus capacities and sharing.

Sharing of resources is the equivalent of consensus in creating government structures. Just as the managers of shared resources sustain them, the leaders of communities, districts, and nations are managers of shared authority and spaces. Sharing the harvest is neither random nor universal, but based on patterns, kinship, and correspondence. It is an honour, a duty, and a privilege; those who have a little more to share may gain prestige, influence, and dignity.

Managing a space and sharing are integral to the Míkmaq's ethical development, to the development of family, friendship, and self. Míkmaq see no distinction between collective or individual interests. The goal of creating a sustaining space and a sharing and caring community that everyone can participate in and belong to is the ultimate interest. Everyone must come to this realization; everyone must come to understand the beauty and dignity of maintaining, protecting, and renewing family space and traditions. Through this developmental process, Míkmaq establish a clear understanding of their humanity and their relation to the environment. Through this process, Míkmaq understand the needs of the biological realms and the ethical significance of their desires, freedoms, and responsibilities.

In Míkmaq language, *netukulimk* refers to the responsibility of a Míkmaq user to be mindful that the Life Givers and the keepers have consented to the conditional use of the resources. The prime condition was sharing the harvest among the communities of the place; feasts were an integral part of that sharing. Míkmaw had little understanding of the possessive nature of the Europeans. Moreover, sharing manages demand, and serves to mitigate many of the incentives to consume a resource. These sentiments of sharing are generated by the Míkmaw concept of space as spirals of a relative network of family sites and paths among resources. Within the Míkmaq, words for particular locations are encoded not only for the use of the land but also for its special significance for families. Certain families or peoples had "rights" to use certain animals, plants, materials, and access sites (hunting and fish traps) because of their particular relationship. Their Aboriginal narratives, in songs and stories, and the ceremonies associated with each space link the present and the past.

The Míkmaw view provides a vision of a proper social order. The Aboriginal nations were generous; sharing whatever they possessed with an open-handedness that amazed the immigrants. Greed was always considered a wrong, while private management of the resource, along with a bundle of rights and duties, was the legal norm. Míkmaw "property rights" were usually obtained not through use or purchase, but through kinship as endowments or legacies. Everyone (no matter the gender) has relative claims, through birth and marriage, to the use of a great variety of sites and resources, which can also be claimed by others on the same ground. Often the word for kinship and ownership are the same. It is inconceivable in a Míkmaq world-view, however, that an individual could claim an exclusive use or entitlement to a particular site or that any family could lose its relationship to a site.

Renewal ceremonies also emphasize the relationship between space and claims in the Aboriginal Míkmaw worldview. The places of certain ceremonies are bound to a specific location and cannot be transported. They symbolically reiterated and renewed the ancient relationships between a particular family and people and a particular ecosystem. This grounding in a particular ecosystem is categorized as "geopiety." In the renewal ceremonies, various family claims are continually being asserted and adjusted. While each renegotiation affects family allegiance and identity, this is seen as relatively unimportant; the crucial factor is the periodic equalization of shared rights among the collective families.

This process of resource adjustment created considerable self-serving confusion among the Europeans. They deduced that the Aboriginal Míkmaw tenure systems were essentially collective or communal and that no individual owned the land. Indeed that is the case, but what created the perplexity was that those resources were private family entitlements. The confusion is unravelled when one understands that in an Aboriginal tenure the role of the family or individual is more managerial than proprietary.

What strangers or guests did not understand was that each family or personal claim to a resource or space is based on permissions by local, regional, or national consensus. While these boundaries may be imprecise or shifting to an outsider, they are part of a complex tenure based on sharing rather than on exclusive use. Very few distinctions exist between personal and real property. If these distinctions exist, it is to give dignity and honour to the Míkmaq or family by sharing them, for example, to exhibit their generosity to others.

The sacred order itself is never individualized. The tenure is held for future generations. A family or an "individual" might enjoy wide administrative authority over a resource or space (a legacy), but they had no right to withhold the use of the resources or the products of their use to another insider. The system of kinship relations united everyone in a web of complementary rights and responsibilities. Each person is simultaneously a parent, child, uncle, aunt, or cousin to others. This implicit order is non-hierarchical and reproduces itself without the need to accumulate more people, land, or goods. The continued strength of any claim in the Aboriginal tenure is a function of sound management and generosity. These legacies are "strong" enough to create incentives to conserve, but "weak" enough to create incentives to share. The Míkmaq legacy became vested in a family or person after seven generations of sound management and generosity. A right of succession or inheritance is based on actual services to the elderly managers as well as resource management, rather than on kinship.

Because of their understanding of the surrounding ecology and the value system of the Living Lodge, scarcity of resources was rare among the Míkmaq. Each family and person had a unique role in harvesting the ecology. There were few customary principles that governed access to, and control of, material resources; however, there were clear rituals about sharing the resources. Each family leader and their resources were linked. If one family faltered in the management of their resources, for any reason or in any manner, their extended family or allies in other districts united with the family to resolve the problem. If family management of a resource was a persistent problem creating scarcity or discomforts, the *saya* or *sakamowti* was criticized and if necessary the situation adjusted by the *Mawíomi*.

There are other examples in Míkmaw order that address the root causes of scarcity, thus preventing it from becoming a problem. In the difficult situations where any Míkmaq took food or clothing, the local settlement (*wikamouw*) discussed the reasons something was taken, and if poverty or need was found, then the taker was not punished. In these situations, typically the extended family and settlement were criticized, since they failed to be aware of the poverty and had not taken care to provide for the needs of its members or visitors. If the predicament continued, the district leaders (*sakamowti*) or *Mawíomi* provided the takers with necessary space and responsibilities to harvest food, build shelter, or make a new settlement.

Additionally, any district chief or family leader who was negligent or careless with the resources or did not deal in a generous and fair manner with other Míkmaq was deprived of respect, dignity, and ultimately responsibilities. Similarly, if travellers or visitors within the sacred space had anything taken from them, the district chief and local community was responsible, because of their negligence and lack of watchfulness. These were grand and fundamental maxims of the customary law among the Míkmaq in the land of friendships. Most of these maxims were directly incorporated in the treaties with the imperial Crown and form the context of the treaties.

25. Aboriginal Tenure and Renewing Ecological Orders

In *Delgamuukw*, the Lamer Court established that Aboriginal tenure includes a sustainable right. It encompasses the right to exclusive use and occupation of land and an "inescapable economic component," but the choices available to Aboriginal peoples under Aboriginal tenure are "subject to the ultimate limit that those uses cannot destroy the ability of the land to sustain future generations of Aboriginal peoples."[43] The Court's insights are not new, but have been widely shared in Aboriginal thought and law and converge with the existing international law as expressed in human rights convenants and sustainable development conventions.[44]

While some may view this qualification as a patronizing limitation, especially those who believe land is a commodity, this "ultimate limit" is best conceptualized as an integral part of Aboriginal worldview and law. In most Aboriginal teaching the original law says Aboriginal peoples were placed on our mother (the earth) to be the caretakers— instructed to deal with life, the plants, animals, minerals, and humans, as if they were a part of themselves. Aboriginal peoples cannot differentiate or separate themselves from other life-forms. Because Aboriginal peoples are the caring part of Creation, their interactions and decisions with the life-forms of our mother, are required to be carried out with the seventh generation in mind; each generation has the responsibility to ensure the survival of the seventh generation; they cannot simply think of their own desires and needs.[45]

To sustain Aboriginal tenure as an ecological order rather than as a commodity in their *sui generis* analysis, practicing attorneys and reviewing courts should recognize the unity and consensus of these intersecting principles. These principles are complementary sources of the nature and content of Aboriginal tenure and its components, and typically are conceptualized in international law as "indigenous knowledge" or "traditional ecological knowledge."[46]

---

43 *Delgamuukw, supra* note 1 at para 166.

44 L. Clarkson, V. Morrissette and G. Regallet, *Our Responsibility to the Seventh Generation: Indigenous Peoples and Sustainable Development* (Winnipeg, Man.: International Institute for Sustainable Development, 1992).

45 *Ibid.* See, "Indigenous Perspective and Relations with the Environment."

46 *Ibid.* See generally Daes, *supra* note 30; Environmental Assessment Workshop, 1995, cited in Emery, *supra* note 23 at 4-5; Colorado Journal of International Environmental Law, *Endangered Peoples Indigenous Rights and the Environment* (Niwot: University Press of Colorado, 1994); The Rural Advancement Foundation International, *Conserving Indigenous Knowledge: Integrating two systems of innovation* (New York: UNDP, 1994); United Nations, *Report of the United Nations conference on Environment and Development*, UNEP, UN Doc. A/CONF.151/26/Rev.1 (Vol. I) (1993); R.A. Williams, "Encounters on the frontiers of international human rights law: redefining the terms of indigenous peoples' survival in the world" [1990] Duke L.J. 981.

International law accepts the Aboriginal tenure as a proper vision of human rights and established sustainable relationships with ecosystems.[47] International law is guided by the great human rights principles embodied in the Universal Declaration of Human Rights and the International Covenants on Human Rights, particularly the prohibition of discrimination and the principles of equality and self-determination.[48] In addition, contemporary international law is guided by the fundamental values and interests of the Human Rights Covenants and by the draft United Nations declaration on the rights of Indigenous peoples. The draft declaration applies the Human Rights Covenants in Indigenous contexts. Both promote the preservation and well-being of Indigenous cultures and communities, the elimination of poverty and deprivation among Indigenous peoples, and the great goals of equality and justice for Indigenous peoples.[49]

Article 13 of the Indigenous and Tribal Peoples Convention No. 169 (1989) of the International Labour Organization declares: "...special importance for the cultures and spiritual values of the peoples concerned with their relationship with the lands or territories, or both as applicable, which they occupy or otherwise use, and in particular the collective aspects of this relationship."[50] The distinctive nature of Indigenous peoples' relationship to lands is also captured in the draft United Nations declaration on the rights of Indigenous peoples, in both preambular and operative paragraphs, in particular, Article 25:

> Indigenous peoples have the right to maintain and strengthen their distinctive spiritual and material relationship with the lands territories, waters and coastal seas and other resources which they have traditionally owned or otherwise occupied or used, and to uphold their responsibilities to future generations in this regard.[51]

---

47   The United Nations Conference on Environment and Development also adopted UNCED, *Agenda 21*, UN GAOR, 37th Sess., UN Doc. 151/26/Rev.1 (1992) vol. 1, para. 26.4 (b). It offers a comprehensive statement of policy and plan of action. *Agenda 21* includes a separate chapter of programs for Indigenous peoples, as well as references to Indigenous people in its chapters on biodiversity and biotechnology, deforestation, living marine resources, and freshwater resources. Chapter 26 of this plan is devoted entirely to the "role of Indigenous people," and calls upon States, *inter alia*, to "adopt or strengthen appropriate policies and/or legal instruments that will protect Indigenous intellectual and cultural property and the right to preserve customary and administrative systems and practices."

48   *Charter of the United Nations*, Art. 1 ("respect for the principle of equal rights and self-determination of peoples"); *International Covenant on Economic, Social and Cultural Rights* and *International Covenant on Civil and Political Rights*, both contained in GA Res. 2200 (XXI), 21 UN GAOR, Supp. No. 16, UN Doc. A/6316 (1967), came into force on 3 January 1976 and 23 March 1976 respectively. Canada acceded to these covenants on 19 August 1976. The *Optional Protocol to the Covenant on Civil and Political Rights*, annex to GA Res. 2200A, 21 UN GAOR, Supp. No. 16 59, UN Doc. A/6316 (1967), came into force on 23 March 1976, and was acceded to by Canada on 19 August 1976.

49   Daes, *supra* note 30 at para. 4

50   *Indigenous and Tribal Peoples Convention*, I.L.O Conv. 169, I.L.O., 76th Sess., reprinted in (1989) 28 I.L.M. 1382, replacing *Convention Concerning the Protection and Integration of Indigenous and Other Tribal and Semi-Tribal Populations in Independent Countries* [I.L.O. Conv. 107] 328 UNTS 247. See R.L. Barsh, "An Advocate's Guide to the Convention on Indigenous and Tribal Peoples" (1990) 13 Okla. City U.L. Rev. 209.

51   Daes, *supra* note 30 at para. 11.

Article 26 states that Indigenous peoples have the right to own, develop, control, and use the lands and territories, including the right to the full recognition of their laws, traditions and customs, land-tenure systems, and institutions for resource development and management, and the right to effective measures by states to prevent any interference with, alienation of, or encroachment upon, these rights.[52]

Article 27 declares that Indigenous peoples have the right to the restitution of the lands, territories, and resources that they have traditionally owned or otherwise occupied or used, and which have been confiscated, occupied, used, or damaged without their free and informed consent. Where this is not possible, they have the right to just and fair compensation. Unless otherwise freely agreed upon by the peoples concerned, compensation shall take the form of lands, territories, and resources equal in quality, size and legal status. Article 28 provides that Indigenous peoples have the right to the total environment's conservation, restoration, and protection and the productive capacity of their lands, territories, and resources, as well as to the assistance for this purpose from States and through international cooperation.[53]

The proposed American Declaration on the Rights of Indigenous Peoples, drafted by the Inter-American Commission on Human Rights and now under consideration by the Permanent Council of the Organization of American States, contains the following preambular language:

> [The States,] recognizing the respect for the environment accorded by the cultures of indigenous peoples of the Americas, and considering the special relationship between the indigenous peoples and the environment, lands, resources and territories on which they live and their natural resources. ... Recognizing that in many indigenous cultures, traditional collective systems for control and use of land and territory and resources, including bodies of water and coastal areas, are a necessary condition for their survival, social organization, development and their individual and collective well-being ...[54]

Each of these documents underscores a number of elements unique to Indigenous peoples: a profound relationship between Indigenous peoples and their lands, territories, and resources exists; this relationship has various social, cultural, spiritual, economic, and political dimensions and responsibilities; the collective dimension of this relationship is significant; and the intergenerational aspect of such a relationship is also crucial to Indigenous peoples' identity, survival, and cultural viability.[55]

The existing and merging norms and standards contained in the Rio Declaration, the Biodiversity Convention, the International Labour Organization Convention No. 169,

---

52　*Report of the Working Group on Indigenous Populations on its Eleventh Session*, UN ESCOR, Comm'n on Hum. Rts., Sub-Committee on Prevention of Discrimination and Protection of Minorities, 45th Sess., Agenda Item 14, UN Doc. E/CN.4/Sub.2/1993/29 (1993). This draft is considered a multi-lateral treaty among the Indigenous peoples.

53　*Ibid.*

54　*Ibid.* at para. 12, Proposed American Declaration on the Rights of Indigenous Peoples, approved by the Inter-American Commission on Human Rights on 26 February 1997, at its 1333rd session, 95th regular session.

55　*Ibid.* at para. 13.

the proposed United Nations declaration on the rights of Indigenous peoples, the Organization of American States declaration on the rights of Indigenous peoples have affirmed and acknowledged that Aboriginal or Indigenous peoples have a different conceptual framework that arises from their knowledge, heritage, and laws that inform their distinctive relations to their lands or territories.[56]

The emerging human rights norms related to the right to development, intergenerational rights, the right to peace, and the right to safe and healthy environment are areas in which Indigenous peoples are beginning to influence Eurocentric thinking and to develop standards that are more sensitive, responsive, and useful to Indigenous peoples and humanity generally.[57]

In 1987, the report of the Bruntdland Commission, *Our Common Future*, gave recognition to Indigenous peoples' vision of land tenure and use:

> The starting point for a just and humane policy for such groups is the recognition and protection of their traditional rights to land and other resources that sustain their way of life—rights they may define in terms that do not fit into standard legal systems. These groups' own institutions to regulate rights and obligations are crucial for maintaining harmony with nature and the environmental awareness characteristic of the traditional way of life. Hence the recognition of traditional rights must go hand in hand with measures of protecting the local institutions that enforce responsibility in resource use. And this recognition must also give local communities a decisive voice in the decisions about resource use in their areas.[58]

In 1992, the United Nation's *Rio Declaration on Environment and Development*, which Canada signed, stressed the "vital role" that Indigenous peoples may play in achieving sustainable development "because of their knowledge and traditional practices."[59] It offers a comprehensive statement of policy and plan of action. *Agenda 21* includes a separate chapter of programs for Indigenous peoples, as well as references to Indigenous people in its chapters on biodiversity and biotechnology, deforestation, living marine resources, and freshwater resources. Chapter 26 of this plan is devoted entirely to the "role of Indigenous people," and calls upon States to "adopt or strengthen appropriate policies and/or legal instruments that will protect Indigenous intellectual and cultural property and the right to preserve customary and administrative systems and practices."[60] The conference also called on governments and intergovernmental organizations to enter into "full partnership with Indigenous peoples." The conference urged governments to take legal measures to recognize traditional forms of knowledge and to enhance capacity-building for Indigenous communities based on the adaptation and exchange of traditional knowledge.[61]

---

56   *Ibid.* at paras. 5-13.

57   *Ibid.* at para. 89.

58   *Ibid.* G. Bruntdland, *Our Common Future* (Oxford: Oxford University Press, 1987).

59   UNCED, UN GAOR, 37th Sess., Annex I, UN Doc. A/CONF.151/26/vol. I, principle 22.

60   *Ibid.*

61   *Ibid.*, vol. III at para. 26.3.

Additionally, the United Nation's *Convention on Biological Diversity* (1992), in its preamble, recognized:

> the close and traditional dependence of many Indigenous and local communities embodying traditional lifestyles on biological resources, and the desirability of sharing equitably benefits arising from the use of traditional knowledge, innovations and practices relevant to the conservation of biological diversity and the sustainable use of its components.[62]

The convention identified two of the rights of Indigenous peoples: resource use and traditional knowledge. Paragraphs 8(j) and 10(c) of the Convention addressed these rights. Paragraph 8(j) requires that each state party:

> Subject to its national legislation, respect, preserve and maintain knowledge, innovations and practices of Indigenous and local communities embodying traditional lifestyles relevant for the conservation and sustainable use of biological diversity and promote their wider application with the approval and involvement of the holders of such knowledge, innovations and practices and encourage the equitable sharing of the benefits arising from the utilization of such knowledge, innovations and practices[.][63]

Paragraph 10(c) directs state parties to "[p]rotect and encourage customary use of biological resources in accordance with traditional cultural practices that are compatible with conservation or sustainable use requirements."[64] The convention mentions a right to environmental rehabilitation in paragraph 10(d), which relates logically to the issue of use. It directs state parties to "support local populations to develop and implement remedial action in degraded areas where biological diversity has been reduced."[65]

Canada has ratified the Biological Diversity conventions. In *Quebec Secession Reference*, the Lamer Court stated that ratified international conventions are part of the global system of rules and principles that govern the exercise of constitutional authority in Canada.[66] They help define and interpret the proper exercise of constitutional authority by the federal, provincial, and Aboriginal peoples in Aboriginal lands. Both the international and constitutional analysis are helpful in understanding the Aboriginal law and perspective about proper land tenure use, the importance of respecting Aboriginal relationship with the environment, and creating sustainable communities for current and future generations.

---

62 *Convention on Biological Diversity* (5 June 1992), 31 I.L.M. 818 (entered into force 29 December 1993). Also found as UN Doc. UNEP/Bio. Div./N&-IN [hereinafter *Biodiversity Convention*]. See generally I. Attridge, ed., *Biodiversity Law and Policy in Canada: Review and Recommendation* (Toronto: Canadian Institute for Environmental Law and Policy, 1996), especially R.L. Barsh and J.Y. Henderson, "Biodiversity and Aboriginal Peoples" at 35-59.

63 *Biodiversity Convention, ibid.*

64 *Ibid.* at Art. 10(c).

65 *Ibid.* at Art. 10(d).

66 *Re Reference by the Governor General in Council Concerning Certain Questions Relating to the Secession of Quebec from Canada*, [1998] 2 S.C.R. 217 at para. 32, 161 D.L.R. (4th) 385 (S.C.C.), where the Court stated: "the Constitution of Canada includes the global system of rules and principles which govern the exercise of constitutional authority in the whole and in every part of the Canadian state."

Aboriginal tenure and rights and the traditional ecological knowledge currently involve three related issues: identifying the traditional owners under Aboriginal peoples' own systems of laws; respecting the customary law and procedures required for learning and borrowing the use of traditional ecological knowledge; and compensating the right to learn and use this knowledge.

In both Aboriginal tenure and the practices of traditional ecological knowledge, Aboriginal law asserts five major legal corollaries that affect the interpretation of the sustainability rights of Aboriginal tenure. First, every individual human and non-human in the ecosystem bears reciprocal personal responsibilities for maintaining their relationships. Knowledge of the ecosystem is, to this extent, legal knowledge, and the people who acquire this information bear especially heavy burdens of responsibility for teaching others and for mediating conflicts between humans and other species.

Second, since legal knowledge bears heavy personal responsibilities, as well as the power to interfere with relationships between humans and non-humans, it must ordinarily be transmitted individually, on a personal basis, to an apprentice who has already been morally and spiritually prepared to accept those burdens and to bear the power with humility. Much attention is given to preparing the pupil, both in ritual form and through tests of courage, maturity, and sincerity.

Third, Aboriginal knowledge and law are ordinarily transmitted among kin, because they have to do with the responsibilities to the territory or resources of a particular lineage or clan. In a large society composed of many families and clans, some knowledge may attach to the lineage level, some to the clan level, and some to the entire tribe or nation. This "nesting" of different layers of Aboriginal tenure and traditional ecological knowledge is unique to each people. It may be dangerous for outsiders to obtain information that could be used to meddle with what is conceived as an internal affair of the local human and non-human "family." Furthermore, because Aboriginal knowledge is localized to an environment and its peoples, it is not conceived as having general application to other ecosystems.

Fourth, Aboriginal knowledge and law may sometimes be shared with visitors to the territory, so that they can travel safely and subsist from local resources, but it cannot be alienated permanently outside the territory to which it refers. In effect, knowledge can be lent, for a specific time and purpose, and usually in exchange for reciprocal forms of knowledge possessed by the borrowers. The lenders retain the right to conclude the arrangement if the knowledge is misused, or the responsibilities that attach to its possession are not fulfilled.

Fifth, misuse of Aboriginal knowledge or law can be catastrophic, not only for the individual abuser but also for the people, the territory, and (potentially) the earth. Misuse of knowledge and law is tantamount to an act of war on other species, breaking their covenants and returning the land to a pre-moral and pre-legal vacuum. This conception explains why the overall approach of Aboriginal peoples to the ecosystem is "precautionary" in the extreme. Any human activity that goes beyond the bounds of known relationships and interaction among species is, again, tantamount to war and invites disorder.

These concepts of intergenerational equity are embodied in Aboriginal law and point out the necessity of cooperative planning. They are a precious resource in creating sustainable development on Aboriginal lands. In the past, Aboriginal knowledge and law have allowed Aboriginal peoples to respond to the complexities of changing circumstance of a dispossessing, colonial society whose developmental policies were so inherently unsustainable that they created poverty, marginalization, and alienation among Aboriginal peoples.

Aboriginal teachings and laws have allowed Aboriginal peoples to withstand the destruction of much of their land and incredible adversity, to retain and keep alive their sacred connection with the land. Their beliefs in Aboriginal law and tenure have given them the courage and conviction to bring their "claims" before the Canadian courts and the United Nations. The Supreme Court of Canada has affirmed and recognized Aboriginal law and tenure in Canada's Constitution, and now governments and courts face the challenge of creating a strategy for implementing these constitutional rights that respects Aboriginal knowledge, laws, and heritage. Canada needs to find a cooperative strategy for correcting the past injustices, creating justice, and creating sustainable development of the future generations of Aboriginal peoples and all Canadians. Along with the peoples and member-states of the United Nations, Canada needs to develop a strategy of collaboration, not one of conflict and competition, to heal and restore the earth in this century.

VII

TOWARD RECONCILIATION
FOR THE MILLENNIUM

It is a basic rule, not disputed in this case, that one part of the Constitution cannot be abrogated or diminished by another part of the Constitution.

Justice McLachlin in *New Brunswick Broadcasting*[1]

A nation is built when the communities that comprise it make commitments to it, when they forego choices and opportunities on behalf of a nation, ... when the communities that comprise it make compromises, when they offer each other guarantees, when they make transfers and perhaps most pointedly, when they receive from others the benefits of national solidarity. The threads of a thousand acts of accommodation are the fabric of a nation.

Chief Justice Lamer in *Quebec Secession Reference*[2]

Introduction

Delgamuukw is a decisive moment in Canadian constitutional law development—and a source of highly complex problems and constitutional challenges for the Canadian legal system. Under constitutional supremacy, reviewing courts are faced with judging the constitutional validity of legislation and regulation. In the view of Chief Justice Lamer, Aboriginal tenure and rights and their relationship to the equality provisions of section 15 of the *Charter* "may present the court with its toughest test over the next few years."[3] Only the most enduring and cherished sources of Aboriginal

---

1 *New Brunswick Broadcasting Co. v. Nova Scotia (Speaker of the House of Assembly)*, [1993] 1 S.C.R. 319 at 373 (S.C.C.) [hereinafter *New Brunswick Broadcasting*].

2 *Re Reference by the Governor General in Council Concerning Certain Questions Relating to the Secession of Quebec from Canada*, 161 D.L.R. (4th) 385 at para. 96, [1998] 2 S.C.R. 217 (S.C.C.), citing the submission of the Attorney General of Saskatchewan oral submission to the Court [hereinafter *Quebec Secession Reference* cited to S.C.R.].

3 "Interview with Chief Justice Antonio Lamer" *The Globe and Mail* (6 February 1999) A1, A4.

and British legal traditions will be sufficient to meet these challenges and to create a post-colonial society that respects equally British and Aboriginal tenure, knowledge, and laws.

The challenge is to make the present and future an enabling environment for all peoples, and to promote a fair and just society by respecting the treaty reconciliations and creating new reconciliations where needed. As the Lamer Court said, "we are all here to stay."[4] The courts should not, through narrow interests or neglect, compromise the future. The future is the only heritage that remains uncontaminated by colonial thinking and laws. Because of colonial rational dualisms, Aboriginal peoples have not shared in the Canadian past, nor have Canadians shared the Aboriginal past. When all Canadians start to conceive a way to restore our environment, to cleanse our legislative and judicial systems, and to imagine a pluralistic future of fresh chances and unlimited possibilities, we shall begin to share our future. The crucial question is how do we get there? As the Lamer Court understood, the devil will be in the details.

Vision does not come pre-packaged from the past, cannot be commissioned as a report, and requires an enabling legal environment to build a creative, multicultural society. The Dickson and Lamer Courts have witnessed another vision of Canada, and have struggled to articulate it within Canadian legal traditions. Fulfilling their vision will require Canadian democracy to be inclusive, a true democracy with educated citizens who participate. And there is no participation without freedom of expression, no justice without the flow of different and challenging ideas of a pluralistic society.

Thinking and institutions that internalize and act on these new visions will be our greatest breakthrough. Court decisions will then consistently base decisions on new constitutional understandings of Canadian sovereignty within which Aboriginal tenure and rights are foundational to the constitutional order. Reviewing judges will decolonize legislative authority by incorporating Aboriginal thinking and law, relinquishing belief in the ultimate title of an undivided Crown, and by ending colonial interpretative privileges over constitutional rights of Aboriginal peoples. Rather than imposing coercive universals or technical legal constructions, courts will resolve interpretative difficulties in favour of Aboriginal peoples and in ways consistent with the constitutional fiduciary duty. In the complex area of the terms and implications of treaty surrender and cession, such interpretation is particularly crucial to understanding *sui generis* Aboriginal tenure and rights and ensuring full democratic participation.

26. Conceptualizing Canadian Sovereignty

Canadian constitutional law and judicial analysis have been slowly equalizing authority between the Aboriginal peoples and the colonists. The Supreme Court has rejected the higher authority of the colonizers' birthright, personal rights, or political decisions, as well as the absolutist fiction of Crown sovereignty, the democratic fiction

---

4   *Delgamuukw v. British Columbia.* [1997] 3 S.C.R. 1010 at para. 186, [1998] 1 C.N.L.R. 14 (S.C.C.) [hereinafter *Delgamuukw* cited to S.C.R.].

of the "sovereignty" or unlimited power of the legislative branch, and its immunity from judicial review.[5] Constitutional reforms have limited the power of the federal parliament and provincial legislatures to reduce the civil liberties and rights of Aboriginal peoples.

In *Quebec Secession Reference*, the Lamer Court articulated constitutional supremacy and a new version of Canadian "sovereignty," ending the imperial Crown's and United Kingdom's parliamentary sovereignty over the colonies:

> The Constitution is the expression of the sovereignty of the people of Canada. It lies within the power of the people of Canada, acting through their various governments duly elected and recognized under the Constitution, to effect whatever constitutional arrangements are desired within Canadian territory, including, should it be so desired, the secession of Quebec from Canada. As this Court held in the *Manitoba Language Rights Reference*, *supra*, at p. 745, "[t]he Constitution of a country is a statement of the will of the people to be governed in accordance with certain principles held as fundamental and certain prescriptions restrictive of the powers of the legislature and government".[6]

Aboriginal peoples of Canada are an integral part of the Canadian peoples, of Canadian sovereignty, and are no longer the "other" people subordinate to the will of the elected assemblies. Aboriginal tenure and rights and treaty rights are protected constitutional rights equal to other constitutional rights, ending the colonial institutional and ideological structure of the British Crown as the superior "self." Hence, Aboriginal peoples are no longer "outside" the Canadian constitutional order, their treaty and Aboriginal rights within the "foreign jurisdictions" of the sovereignty of the United Kingdom.

In light of constitutional supremacy, Chief Justice Lamer's characterization of the sovereign in *Delgamuukw* contains a troubling inconsistency:

> Because ... distinctive aboriginal societies exist within, and are a part of, a broader social, political and economic community, over which the Crown is sovereign...[7]

This concept of a floating sovereign above the scrambling colonizers is a "hard residue" of colonial thinking retained in Canadian jurisprudence.[8] In our new constitutional order, sovereignty is not something that is exercised over peoples, but something that comes from the people.[9]

The concept of "sovereign" was rarely used in treaty reconciliations with Aboriginal nations and tribes; the typical term in the written treaties was "His" or "Her

---

5   *Hodge v. The Queen* (1883), 9 App. Cas. 117 (P.C.). G. Marshall, *Parliamentary Sovereignty and the Commonwealth* (Oxford: Clarendon Press, 1975) at 1, which notes that the sovereignty of Parliament is rarely mentioned in British courts of law.

6   *Quebec Secession Reference, supra* note 2 at para. 85.

7   *Delgamuukw, supra* note 4 at para. 161, affirming *R. v. Gladstone*, [1996] 2 S.C.R. 723, [1996] 4 C.N.L.R. 65 (S.C.C.) at para. 73.

8   P.H. Russell, "High Courts and the Rights of Aboriginal Peoples: The Limits of Judicial Independence" (1998) 61 Sask. L. Rev. 247 at 275.

9   *Ibid.* at 276.

Majesty." In *Secretary of State*,[10] their Lordships declared that the imperial Crown was indivisible at the time of Aboriginal treaties in North America in British constitutional law, but by "constitutional usage and practice" the Crown became "separate and divisible according to the particular territory in which it was sovereign" creating autonomous communities within the British Empire, equal in status, and in no way subordinate one to another in any aspect of their domestic or external affairs:[11]

> As a result of this important constitutional change, I am of opinion that those obligations which were previously binding on the Crown simpliciter are now to be treated as divided. They are to be applied to the dominion or province or territory to which they relate: and confined to it. Thus the obligations to which the Crown bound itself in the royal proclamation of 1763 are now to be confined to the territories to which they related and binding only on the Crown in respect of those territories; and the treaties by which the Crown bound itself in 1875 are to be confined to those territories and binding on the Crown only in respect of those territories. None of them is any longer binding on the Crown in respect of the United Kingdom. ... But, now that the Crown is separate and divisible, I think that the obligations under the proclamation and the treaties are obligations of the Crown in respect of Canada. They are not obligations of the Crown in respect of the United Kingdom. It is, therefore, not permissible for the Indian peoples to bring an action in this country to enforce these obligations. Their only recourse is in the courts of Canada.[12]

"As the overseas territories gradually came to be settled and colonised," Lord Kerr conceded, "there may have been an indeterminate stage of constitutional development in many cases, when it was uncertain whether rights and obligations concerning the overseas territory arose in right or respect of the Crown here or of the emerging forms of local administration overseas." In Canada, there was "no express statutory or other transfer."[13]

---

10   *R. v. Secretary of State for Foreign and Commonwealth Affairs, Ex rel. Indian Association of Alberta*, [1981] 4 C.N.L.R. 86, [1982] Q.B. 892, [1982] 2 All E.R. 118 (Eng. C.A.), Lord Denning, M.R., May L.J. and Kerr L.J. [hereinafter *Secretary of State* cited to All E.R.]; see also P.W. Hogg, *Constitutional Law of Canada*, 2d ed. (Toronto: Carswell, 1985) at 215-17.

11   *Secretary of State, ibid.*

12   *Ibid.* at 128-29.

13   Lord Justices Kerr and May relied heavily on *Attorney General v. Great Southern and Western Railway of Ireland*, [1925] A.C. 754, 22 I.L.R. 141 (H.L.), debated by the United Kingdom House of Lords. The railway company had agreed to a war-measures contract, turning over much of its track and rolling stock to the Government of the United Kingdom on terms of compensation. When Parliament subsequently emancipated the Irish Free State, a statutory order expressly devolved all contractual obligations in respect of that territory on the new government. The railway sought the agreed compensation from the United Kingdom nonetheless, challenging the devolution order as *ultra vires* the Transport Ministry. The Law Lords concluded that Parliament intended to create a new and wholly independent government, thus explicitly or implicitly vesting it with full responsibility for outstanding debts. There was no demonstration, significantly, that the obligations owed to the railway company were such that performance by the Irish Free State would be of substantially less value than performance by the United Kingdom. Nor was the obligation transferred an object of public international law such as a sovereign guarantee of protection or military assistance.

The Lordships noted that the divisions of the Crown were independent of the imperial treaty order; they were "internal" to the responsible government of the colonizers. Unlike the treaty acquiescence and novation in India,[14] in Canada the divisions of the Crown were not accomplished with Aboriginal treaty nations' consent. Neither the Aboriginal nor treaty nations, who authorized and permitted the Crown to have British subjects settle in their territories, were given any notice of the proposed division of the Crown affecting their existing rights.

Their Lordships in *Secretary of State* did not explain how Aboriginal treaty nations were to have known with whom they were dealing, or where ultimate liability for treaty commitments would lie, yet this was the issue the treaty nations raised about the *Canada Act 1982*. None of the precedents cited by the British courts involved an attempt to assign treaty obligations, as distinguished from purely private contractual commitments, to a successor state. In any case, there appears to be no direct Commonwealth precedent. The closest authority is the decision of the Swiss Federal Court that treaties pass on secession if the parties acquiesce in their continued force and effect—a matter of "tacit novation."[15] Aboriginal treaty nations could not have acquiesced to the "internal" division of Crown authority because they did not know until 1982 that the United Kingdom considered their treaties to have passed "gradually" and "indeterminately" to Canada. Their Lordships interpreted section 35(1) as the Crown's affirmation that the Aboriginal and treaty rights continue in force and effect in the new constitutional order; however, their Lordships did not address the lack of Aboriginal choice about the constitutional transfer of their rights or their distrust of the new constitutional fiduciaries. Indeed, the colonial or imperial vision of an indivisible Crown has been transformed into constitutional sovereignty, and section 52(1) equally distributes the sovereignty throughout the constitutional framework. It redistributes constitutional rights to Aboriginal peoples, and these rights are an integral part of constitutional supremacy.

Chief Justice Dickson has commented on some remaining questions on the effects of the division of the Crown on Aboriginal peoples:

> From the aboriginal perspective, any federal-provincial divisions that the Crown has imposed on itself are internal to itself and do not alter the basic structure of Sovereign-Indian relations. This is not to suggest that aboriginal peoples are outside the sovereignty of the Crown, nor does it call into question the divisions of jurisdiction in relation to aboriginal peoples in federal Canada.[16]

Such division could affect neither the Aboriginal tenure or rights nor the treaty reconciliations of these powers, as it could not give the governments more power than the Aboriginal nations or tribes had delegated to the imperial Crown in the treaties. In pub-

---

14   I. Copland, "Lord Mountbatten and the Integration of the Indian States: A Reappraisal" (1993) 21 J. Imp'l and Commonwealth Hist. 385.

15   *Bertschinger v. Bertschinger* (1955), 22 I.L.R. 141.

16   *Mitchell v. Peguis Indian Band*, [1990] 2 S.C.R. 85 at 109, [1990] 3 C.N.L.R. 46 (S.C.C.), Dickson C.J.C.

lic international law, treaties of cession create derivative entitlements in the grantee,[17] not original tenures or titles for the imperial Crown.[18] Derivative jurisdiction or authorities of the imperial Crown are acquired by a treaty cession in foreign territories: "if the grantee takes possession in accordance with the treaty, the treaty provides the legal basis of sovereignty."[19] The controlling maxim in public international law and British law—that no man can give another any better title than he himself has (*Nemo dat quad non habet*)[20]—operates in the treaty cession:

> The title alleged by the United States of America as constituting the immediate foundation of its claim is that of cession, brought about by the Treaty of Paris, which cession transferred all rights of sovereignty which Spain may have possessed in the region. ... It is evident that Spain could not transfer more rights than she herself possessed.[21]

The division of the Crown, similar to the division of powers in the 1867 Act, relates to sharing the existing derivative jurisdiction of the imperial Crown acquired by European and Aboriginal treaties among the colonial institutions.[22] Section 35(1) expressly affirms Aboriginal and treaty rights in the constitutional supremacy of Canada. Aboriginal laws did not permit negotiators to grant their ancient sources of constitutional authority to either the sovereign or its delegated governments. In the absence of a treaty of purchase, the Crown assumed protective authority over Aboriginal lands to prevent "frauds and abuses." This was the clear and plain intent and wording of imperial law, as set out in the earliest of the decisions of the Privy Council, the royal instructions, and the 1763 Proclamation. In prerogative laws, the Crown's purpose was only to protect Aboriginal order and tenure until the Aboriginal grantors were willing to sell their land to the imperial Crown. The colonial practices of provincial and federal assemblies are not the intent or voice of the imperial Crown, and their statutes did not always reflect the undivided Crown's intent, purposes, and wording.

The *Constitution Act, 1982* has reconciled Aboriginal peoples with constitution-

---

17   *Western Sahara Case (Morocco v. Western Sahara; Mauretania v. Western Sahara)*, Advisory Opinion, [1975] I.C.J. Rep. 12 at 39 [hereinafter Western Sahara]. The Court stated: "[S]uch agreements with local rulers, whether or not considered as an actual 'cession' of the territory, were regarded as derivative roots of title."

18   *Ibid.* In Aboriginal territory, the English doctrine of tenure does not apply; the radical title that is acquired with the Crown's acquisition of sovereignty cannot itself be taken to confer an absolute beneficial title to the occupied land. See also *Mabo and Others v. Queensland [No. 2]* (1992), 107 A.L.R. 1, 175 C.L.R. 1 (H.C.).

19   *Western Sahara, ibid.*

20   Or "*nemo plus juris transferre potest quam ipse habet.*" See Ian Brownlie, *Principles of Public International Law*, 4th ed. (New York: Oxford University Press, 1990) at 176.

21   *Island of Palmas Case (Netherlands v. United States)* (1938), Reports of International Arbitral Awards, TIAS ii 829 at 842. See also L. McNair, *The Law of Treaties* (Oxford: Clarendon Press, 1961) at 656 and 665.

22   The neo-colonial view of the meaning of the divisibility of the Crown under ss. 91 and 92 of the *Constitution Act, 1867* (U.K.), 30 & 31 Vict., c. 3, reprinted in R.S.C. 1985, App. II, No. 5, has been articulated by Hogg, *supra* note 10 at 216-17. The divisibility of the Crown in Canada does not mean that there are 11 Queens or 11 Sovereigns but, rather, it expresses the notion of, "a single Queen recognized by many separate jurisdictions."

al supremacy, the structural division of the imperial sovereignty. It vests their constitutional rights in the constitution of Canada, which is different from the Lamer Court's interpretation of constitutional rights reconciliation of Aboriginal peoples with the sovereignty of the Crown. While the treaty relationships still remain vested with the imperial Crown, the Aboriginal and treaty rights are now vested in the Aboriginal peoples of Canada. The constitution of Canada replaces the indivisible sovereign. Within the constitution, in Justice McLachlin's words, no part can be "abrogated or diminished"[23] relative to any other parts. As part of the constitution, the Aboriginal and treaty rights are integral parts of constitutional supremacy.

To read Aboriginal peoples in Canada out of the divisible sovereignty of Canada would be inconsistent with the constitutional order of Canada. Under imperial treaties, the Aboriginal peoples have always been the source of sovereignty in Canada. These treaties evidence the Aboriginal nations' and tribes' consent to allow the imperial Crown to continue to be "sovereign" over their immigrant subjects and their assemblies. They also evidence the agreements by which the Aboriginal nations and tribes retained their "sovereignty" over their people and jurisdiction over their reserved and ceded lands, and reflect the terms of their consent to share their territory and resources with settlers. In many treaties, and in the absence of treaties, the Aboriginal peoples retained their pre-existing sovereignty, according to their linguistic conception of the term. To assert sovereignty over Aboriginal peoples or their land, the imperial Crown must show an express Aboriginal delegation of such authority. In the absence of such delegation, Aboriginal peoples retain their pre-existing authority over their lands and resources under the protective authority of the Crown.

Upon division of the Crown, the *Constitution Act, 1982* evidences the transfer ("hereby recognized and affirmed") of imperial authority or presumptions to the Aboriginal peoples of Canada. The Aboriginal peoples and their rights became one part of the divided sovereignty. Section 35(1) protects their sovereignty and rights equal to all other constitutional powers. The full implications of section 35(1) are emerging, displacing colonial law that privileged colonizing peoples' legislative regimes as well as the traditions of parliamentary supremacy in favour of the doctrine of constitutional supremacy. The courts have held that colonial legislation cannot define Aboriginal and treaty rights, and that these regulatory infringements are subject to fair compensation. Yet, most of the judicial decisions have wrongly continued to privilege legislation or regulations that interfere with constitutional rights of Aboriginal peoples by questionable reasoning that benefits the immigrant community interests.

In the United Kingdom, the division of the Crown has granted sovereignty to Aboriginal peoples in many territories.[24] The spirit and intent of section 35(1), then, should be interpreted as "recognizing and affirming" Aboriginal legal orders, laws, and jurisdictions unfolded through Aboriginal and treaty rights. For example, the *Interpre-*

---

23 *New Brunswick Broadcasting, supra* note 1 at 373.

24 R. Barsh and J.Y. Henderson, "International Context of Crown-Aboriginal Treaties in Canada" in CD-ROM: *For Seven Generations: An Information Legacy of the Royal Commission on Aboriginal Peoples* (Ottawa: Canada Communication Group, 1996).

tation Act of Canada and the United Kingdom[25] articulates the colonial version of sovereignty, speaking about the broad scope of the concept of "Her Majesty":

> 'Her Majesty', 'His Majesty', 'the Queen', 'the King' or 'the Crown' means the Sovereign of the United Kingdom, Canada and Her other Realms and Territories, and Head of the Commonwealth. ...[26]

The section is silent on the source of authority of Her Majesty in Canada or her other realms and territories or the meaning of constitutional reforms or the divided Crown in Canada. Giving a liberal construction to the words "Her Majesty" as required by the constitutional fiduciary duty, and resolving any "doubtful expression" in favour of the Aboriginal peoples where more than one reasonable interpretation is available, the interpretation of "Her other Realms and Territory" appears to include Aboriginal nations and their unpurchased tenure as part of the Crown as well as ceded lands by treaties. Hence, Aboriginal and treaty rights can be interpreted as informing the constitutional concept of Her Majesty in right of the Aboriginal Peoples.

Since 1982, the constitutional duty of courts and legislatures is to respect Aboriginal peoples and their laws and decisions as part of the sovereignty of Canada. In order to enact a post-colonial jurisprudence, the divisible Crown should be comprehended in a manner that acknowledges its transformation of Aboriginal peoples' constitutional rights within constitutional supremacy. This is an urgent and remedial step in belated nation building and post-colonial Canadian self-determination. Constitutional sovereignty and rights are distinct from colonial institutions and practices.[27] If courts can connect the principles of constitutional supremacy and decolonization to the contagion of institutional legislative authority; end interpretative monopolies over Aboriginal rights; and recognize the constitutional rights, desires, and sensibilities of Aboriginal peoples, they will generate post-colonial institutions and practices, and allow Aboriginal peoples to cease being victims of a historical context they seek to escape.

27. Ultimate Title of the Crown

The Supreme Court of Canada decisions on the constitutional tenure and rights of Aboriginal people have reflected a continuing obsession with the Crown in Canadian legal traditions and have reflected a continuing belief in the undivided Crown rather than in constitutional supremacy constructed on a plurality of treaties with Aboriginal peoples and imperial acts for the colonists. Such judicial assumptions are based on

---

25   R.S.C. 1970, c. I-23, s. 28; R.S.C. 1985, c. I-21, s. 35(1).

26   *Ibid.*

27   J.B. White, "Law as Rhetoric, Rhetoric as Law: The Arts of Cultural and Communal Life" (1985) 52 Chi.-Kent L. Rev. 684; J.T. Noonan, *Persons and Masks of the Law: Cardozo, Holmes, Jefferson and Wythe as Makers of the Masks* (New York: Farrar, Strauss and Giroux, 1976); M. Edelmann, *Politics as Symbolic Action: Mass Arousal and Quiescence* (Chicago: Markham Publication Co., 1971).

coercive universals that take no account of Aboriginal thoughts, legal orders, practices, and arrangements.[28]

In the past, Aboriginal tenure was seen by the courts as a protected "possessory" right, a burden upon the "ultimate" Crown tenure that could be purchased to perfect that future interest.[29] The justification for this burden was the protective or fiduciary interest of the sovereign toward Aboriginal tenure when sovereignty over the territory was asserted to all other nations.[30] The Crown's "underlying title" appeared as the exclusive justification for reconciling Aboriginal title with Crown sovereignty.[31]

In British land law, the Crown's underlying estate or title or "ultimate interest" was an intangible speculative interest based on hope and expectations that only arose if the Aboriginal nations chose to sell. This is less than future possessory interests in British law called "remainders," "reversions," or "executory interests." In public international law, this "ultimate title" rested upon the imperatives of empire and colonization. Under the division of the imperial Crown and constitutional supremacy of Canada, however, no ultimate or radical title of the Crown in the conventional understanding of these terms remains. This future interest is now expressly vested in Aboriginal peoples of Canada under section 35(1) rather than in either the federal government or the provinces. Such constitutional codification exposes the "living tree" of Canadian constitutional supremacy and federalism as deriving from Aboriginal tenure and governance. As Morris Cohen argued: "[i]t would be as absurd to argue that the distribution of property must never be modified by law as it would be to argue that the distribution of political power must never be changed."[32]

The demise of "ultimate title" is manifested in the terms of Georgian treaties with the Míkmaq who retained and reserved their sacred order for themselves and made no mention of sale of lands to the Crown. No evidence exists that they sold or ceded their Aboriginal tenure to the imperial Crown. The compacts agreed to allow British coastal settlements—that is, English reserves within Míkmaw land tenure, or peaceful sharing of the land,[33] refuges created by consensual treaties within sacred space. By this privilege within Míkmaw tenure, allodial tenure was neither created nor controlled by British law. These reserved tenures were subsequently affirmed by prerogative legislation. Lamer J. stated in *Sioui*:

28   See, J.Y. Henderson, "First Nations Legal Inheritances in Canada: The Míkmaq Model" (1995) 23 Man. L.J. 1.

29   *Delgamuukw, supra* note 4 at para. 144.

30   *Ibid.* at para. 145. The Court stated that pre-existing Aboriginal tenure crystallized in British law when sovereignty was asserted. It does not make sense then to speak of Aboriginal tenure being a burden of the Crown's underlying title until the assertion of sovereignty.

31   *Ibid.* at para. 145. Other times the Court talks of the Crown's sovereignty as the interest of the "broader social, political and economic" interests of the entire Canadian community, *ibid.* at para. 161.

32   Morris Cohen, "Property and Sovereignty" (1927) 13 Cornell L.Q. at 16.

33   On the problem of Locke's theory of tacit consent in property law, see J.Y. Henderson, "The Doctrine of Aboriginal Rights in the Western Legal Tradition" in Boldt, *et al.*, eds., *Quest For Justice: Aboriginal Peoples and Aboriginal Rights* (Toronto: University of Toronto Press, 1985).

The British Crown recognized that the Indians had certain ownership rights over their land
... [and] allowed them autonomy in their internal affairs, intervening in this area as little
as possible.[34]

No purchase of Míkmaw tenure has been found in the colonial records; thus under *Del-gamuukw*, the intangible future interest in the contemplation of the Crown was never
perfected. Under section 35(1), the traditional government of the Míkmaw treaty rights
would recognize and affirm the Míkmaw tenure as vested tenure in the law.

28. Treaty Surrender and Cession

Central to almost all the treaties is a provision for orderly and peaceful land sharing and for relations of peace and even kinship. From treaty nations' perspectives, their
national identities, their sovereignty, and their Aboriginal authority were recognized
and affirmed in making treaties with the Crown. The parties to the treaties became
intertwined and interdependent parts of the constitutional supremacy. On this basis, the
treaties set out the terms under which the treaty nations agreed to align themselves with
the undivided Crown, in ways similar to the terms of union whereby former British
colonies entered Confederation as provinces.[35]

The report of the Royal Commission on Aboriginal peoples quoted the words of
Lord Sankey of the Judicial Committee of the Privy Council, who described the British
North America Act as "a living tree capable of growth and expansion within its natural limits."[36] Just as a country's constitution is organic, shaped and reshaped continually by the evolving circumstances of human society, the treaty principles must also be
interpreted within the evolving relationship. The Commission found no need for extinguishment in modern treaty making.[37] This contention affirms the principles of judicial
interpretation whereby the treaties are interpreted as the Aboriginal nations and tribes
understood them at the time they entered the treaties, and flexibly enough to address
new contexts.

The treaties of explicit purchase in Upper Canada raise the issue of derivative
title in the Crown (or purchasers) and of compliance with all terms of the treaty. When
a foreign Crown or purchaser acquires from an Aboriginal nation or tribe by deed or
treaty, do they acquire the title, estate, or interest under Aboriginal tenure or independent of that tenure? Public international law and British tenurial principles of land law
answer that the Crown or purchaser acquires derivative title. Colonization theory interpreted the treaty purchases as extinguishing Aboriginal tenure and replacing it with

---

34   *R. v. Sioui*, [1990] 1 S.C.R. 1025 at 1055, [1990] 3 C.N.L.R. 127 (S.C.C.).

35   J.Y. Henderson, "Empowering Treaty Federalism" (1994) 58 Sask. L. Rev. 241 [hereinafter Henderson,
     "Empowering"]; Canada, *Report of the Royal Commission on Aboriginal Peoples* (Ottawa: Canadian
     Communication Group, 1996) [hereinafter RCAP, *Final Report*].

36   RCAP, *Final Report, ibid*, vol. 2 at 53; *Edwards v. Canada (A.G.)* (1929), [1930] A.C. 124 at 135.

37   Canada, Royal Commission on Aboriginal Peoples, *Treaty Making in the Spirit of Co-existence: An
     Alternative to Extinguishment* (Ottawa: Canadian Communication Group, 1994).

Crown tenure since the colonists received their grants from the Crown. Yet the Aboriginal sale of parts of their tenurial interests remains the source of the Crown power to grant. This issue needs to be addressed and resolved within the entire context of the treaty or conveyancing documents.

In many treaties or documents, such as the 1819 provisional agreement and the *Robinson Treaty* of 1850 between the Principal Men of the Chippewa nation, the Aboriginal sale or grant of derivative title to the Crown is contingent upon the payment of annual annuities or services rather than a one-time payment. In these situations, the Crown's title remains unperfected, dependent on full compliance with the annuities and obligations. As the annuities are perpetual, the contingency creates a perpetual uncertainty in title. In British law, such clauses raise the problem of the improbability of vesting of the Crown derivative title before 1982. Since the treaties are subject to a condition of fulfillment of the annuities and performance of treaty obligations and respect for the retained Aboriginal tenure and rights, the Crown agreement and interest in British law raised the question of a prohibited remote vesting and contingent future interest under the rule against perpetuities.

The reliability, accuracy, and completeness of treaties and land surrenders have remained in doubt:[38]

> The different cultural views, values and assumptions of both parties conflicted in substantial ways. These contradictions were often not evident, or remained unspoken, in the negotiation and conclusion of solemn treaty agreements. In many cases, it is questionable whether the Indian parties understood the legal and political implications of the land conveyance documents they were asked to sign.[39]

The Thalassa Research report for the Royal Commission on Aboriginal Peoples provides examples of frauds and abuses in the sale of Indian lands.[40] The report demonstrates that much, if not most, of the revenues from "surrenders" were used for purposes other than the benefit of the Aboriginal nations who had surrendered the land. Further, the policy of the colonial administration was to make the Indian department financially self-sufficient through Indian land sales. In other words, the Indians paid for their own benefits but had no control over the expenditures.[41] Revenues from the surrender and sale of Indian lands paid for education, health, housing and other services received by Aboriginal nations, as well as making a substantial contribution to general government revenues. In the words of one author:

---

38 P. Kennedy, "Treaty Texts: When Can We Trust the Written Word?" (1995) 3 Social Sciences and Humanities Aboriginal Research Exchange 1, 8, 20-25.

39 RCAP, *Final Report, supra* note 35, vol. 1 at 173.

40 "Nation to Nation: Indian Nation/Crown Relations in Canada" (1994) [unpublished, research study prepared for the Royal Commission on Aboriginal Peoples].

41 See J.F. Leslie, *Commissions of Inquiry Into Indian Affairs in the Canadas, 1828-1858: Evolving a Corporate Memory for the Indian Department* (Ottawa: Indian Affairs and Northern Development, February 1985) at 145-46. Leslie documents six formal commissions of inquiry launched by British officials in the period between 1828 and 1859. He argues that the search for ways to reduce the cost of Indian administration in Canada was an important motivation in establishing the commissions.

To a significant degree the Mississauga and Chippewa [and the Ojibwa generally] financed the foundation of Upper Canada's prosperity at the expense of their self-sufficiency and economic independence. Government profits in the nineteenth century from the sale of Indian land amounted to the difference between the purchase price and the fair market value ... . If the Mississauga and Chippewa had received market value for their lands, the British treasury would have been obligated to finance the development of Upper Canada while the aboriginal population would have become the financial elite of the New World.[42]

Such research illustrates constitutional fiduciary duty breaches of the administrator of the Crown to the Aboriginal nations and peoples, breaches that may deprive the Crown of derivative and unperfected interests.

In the Manitoulin and Saugeen treaties and the Victorian treaties that surrendered land to the Crown without compensation, the issue of Crown title or interest is also ambiguous. Surrenders or cession are not purchases for the imperial Crown. After the *Treaty of Niagara*, most of the Aboriginal nations had an existing treaty relationship with the Crown that reserved their land for themselves, prevented colonial action on their territories as well as individual purchases, and specified a treaty promise to purchase their lands when they were ready to sell. The Report of the Royal Commission on Aboriginal Peoples found there was substantive agreement that the treaties established an economic partnership from which both parties would benefit:

> Compensation was offered in exchange for the agreement of First Nations to share. The principle of fair exchange and mutual benefit was an integral part of treaty making. First Nations were promised compensation in the form of annual payments or annuities, social and economic benefits, and the continued use of their lands and resources.[43]

Subsequent treaty negotiations were conducted in the context of these treaty promises and in the oral traditions of the Aboriginal nations. Once agreement was reached, the treaty commissioners wrote a text that purported to represent the substance of the agreements. The Royal Commission on Aboriginal Peoples undertook extensive historical and legal research on the treaties on a scale unprecedented in Canadian history, and their report concluded:

> It is also doubtful in many cases that the Aboriginal tribes participating in the Victorian treaties knew that the written texts they signed differed from the oral agreements they concluded. ... The possibility that the party recording the oral agreements and preparing the written text took advantage of the other party's lack of understanding of the legal implications of written texts, or that those implications were not communicated to the party that did not read or write, is disturbing.[44]

---

42   I. Johnson, "British-Tribal Relations in the Colonial Period" (1986) [unpublished, archived at the Union of Ontario Indians].

43   RCAP, *Final Report, supra* note 35, vol. 1 at 174.

44   *Ibid.* at 173.

In particular, arrangements respecting the ceding of Aboriginal lands are contested. On the basis of their world-view, language, and legal traditions, the Aboriginal nations understood the surrender and cessions as sharing the land, not ending their relationship with it. While the surrender clauses of the early land sales in Ontario were included in the later-written Victorian treaties, it is questionable whether the Aboriginal grantors knew their implications. In British law, the language of land conveyance documents is construed against the party who drafted them (*contra proferentem*). Further, constitutional interpretative principles assert that treaty terms are to be construed as the Aboriginal negotiators would have understood them, and reject the plain meaning rule and any technical construction of the terms.[45] It would have been difficult, if not impossible, to translate the English technical legal language into the Aboriginal languages.

The text of the 11 Victorian treaties and the modern land claim agreements read that the tribes of the Aboriginal nations "cede, release, surrender, and yield up to the Government of the Dominion of Canada, for Her Majesty the Queen, and Her successors forever, all their rights, titles and privileges whatsoever, to the lands."[46] The Aboriginal nations' ratification treaties used the words "we transfer, surrender and relinquish" to her Majesty the Queen for the use of the Government of the Dominion. None of the treaty negotiations or treaty texts uses the word "purchase" or gives a purchase price.

The imperial Crown's objective may have been to achieve a "cession" of Aboriginal title and the subjection of treaty nations to the Crown's authority. It may have thought it had dominion over Indian lands, even in the absence of a treaty, but the Supreme Court interpretive principles in *Delgamuukw* show that this is an unjustified assumption. The mutual intent of the treaty parties control treaty interpretation.[47] Aboriginal peoples maintain with virtual unanimity that they did not give up either their relationship to the land or their sovereign jurisdiction over the land by entering into treaties with the Crown. Aboriginal oral traditions and teachings assert that the treaty negotiators regard the act of treaty-making as an affirmation of those fundamental rights, and this belief is reflected in the peace and order clause of the written treaty.

These teachings include the ceded lands in the treaties remaining a vital part of the continuing Aboriginal order. What Aboriginal chiefs and delegates did give up was "exclusive" jurisdiction over their territories by consenting to some form of sharing their territory with the Crown's subjects. In each treaty the Crown expressly affirmed that the chiefs and headmen retained their traditional jurisdiction over the "ceded" or "surrendered" land. The chiefs "promised and engaged" to the Crown that they would "maintain peace and good order" between "themselves and others of Her Majesty's

---

45   J.Y. Henderson, "Interpreting Sui Generis Treaties" (1997) 113 Alta. L. Rev. 81 at 81-94 [hereinafter Henderson, "Interpreting"].

46   *Treaty No. 4 Between the Cree and Saulteaux Tribes of Indians and Qu'Appelle and Fort Elice* (Ottawa: Queen's Printer, 1966).

47   Henderson, "Interpreting," *supra* note 45 at 75-80.

subjects, whether Indians or whites, now inhabiting or hereafter to inhabit any part of the said ceded tracts." Specifically, the chiefs promised they would "not molest the person or property of any inhabitant of such ceded tracts, or the property of Her Majesty the Queen."[48]

These treaty guarantees gave all inhabitants quiet enjoyment under Aboriginal jurisdiction and tenure vested by the Crown in the treaty, not under British laws. Her Majesty had no treaty duty or obligation to protect any property interests and was granted little authority "within the country so ceded." On this basis, it was the chiefs who had regulatory authority over settlement, retaining jurisdiction and enforcement responsibilities for all existing or future property interests in the ceded lands. In this respect, the ceded lands and affirmation of Aboriginal jurisdiction kept the territory as a part of the "lands reserved for the Indians" by the Crown and under vested Aboriginal tenure.

As treaty rights are now part of the constitutional order of Canada, these articles are constitutional authority in North America, just as the original grants of the King's prerogative authority to the courts, the House of Lords, and the House of Commons were constitutional authority in England.[49] Both the treaty articles and the earlier Crown grants of political authority were exercised in different contexts and territories but both had constitutional significance. The treaty article is analogous to the "Peace, Order, and good Government clause" in section 91 of the *Constitution Act, 1867*,[50] which gives residual authority to the federal government. The authority that chiefs and headmen had initially exercised by Aboriginal laws over the protected territory is now exercised by the treaties throughout the ceded land under Crown authority,[51] an inviolable and a vested prerogative right.[52] The chiefs' exercise of jurisdiction in the ceded territory did not require any association with the imperial Crown to retain jurisdiction over their ceded territories, providing peace, law, and good order in the ceded land, protecting their ways of life, and continuing their traditional economies based on hunting, fishing, trapping, and gathering.

---

48 *Treaty No. 6 Between Her Majesty the Queen and the Plain and Wood Cree Indians and Other Tribes of Indians at Fort Carlton, Fort Pitt and Battle River with Adhesions* (Ottawa: Queen's Printer, 1966) [hereinafter *Treaty No. 6*]. The chiefs promised that, in addition, they would maintain peace in *Treaties Nos. 8* and *10*. See *Treaty No. 8 Made June 21, 1899 and Adhesion, Reports Etc.* (Ottawa: Queen's Printer, 1966) and *Treaty No. 10 and Reports of Commissioners* (Ottawa: Queen's Printer, 1966).

49 *Halsbury's Laws of England*, vol. 8, 4th ed. (London: Butterworth's, 1973) at paras. 808-817 [hereinafter *Halsbury's*]. Prerogative authority in return was delegated to the courts, and then to Parliament, and became a limitation on prerogative authority in England. Over the course of many centuries Parliamentary power came strictly to limit the prerogative powers. It introduced a distinction between the sovereign's power when acting in association with Parliament, and that when not acting in association with Parliament.

50 Hogg, *supra* note 10 at 435-39.

51 By the principle of legality in English constitutional law, the existence of a power or duty is a matter of law and not fact, and so must be determined by reference to some prerogative or statutory enactment or reported case. See *Halsbury's*, *supra* note 49, vol. 8 at para. 828.

52 *Campbell v. Hall* (1774), Lofft 655 at 281, [1558-1774] All E.R. 440. See also Joseph Chitty Jr., *A Treatise on the Law* (New York: Garland Publishing, 1978) at 29.

In addition to discrepancies between oral and written texts and between Aboriginal and colonial understandings, ambiguities remain within written texts. The Report of the Royal Commission on Aboriginal Peoples, for example, concluded:

> terms such as cede, surrender, extinguish, yield and forever give up all rights and titles appear in the written text of the treaties, but discussion of the meaning of these concepts is not found anywhere in the records of Treaty negotiations.[53]

Additionally, in neither the central treaty negotiations nor the ratification negotiations were the scope of each chief's territorial boundaries discussed. Yet, mysteriously, the central treaty has a description of the boundaries ceded. The ratification treaties did not enlarge on these "ghost" boundaries. This silence created a formidable obstacle to understanding the meaning of treaty cession from either the Crown or Aboriginal perspective.

Although the extent to which these basic differences and assumptions were communicated effectively and understood depended on the historical circumstances in particular locales, in the treaties the Aboriginal tribes did not agree to the Crown's taking over their lands, nor did they agree to come under the control of the Crown. Under the vague term "settlement," there is no evidence in the treaty negotiation or text that the chiefs authorized the Crown to alienate their land to others, or apply British land law within the ceded territory. On this basis, the Crown had no authority to use the land as a market commodity in the absence of discussing rents and profits from the land settlement.

The Aboriginal understanding of the concept of "settlement" was that they would share their lands and resources under the chiefs' jurisdiction. The treaty relationship would respect their agreement to co-exist as separate nations linked in a partnership with the Crown.[54] The chiefs, with the cooperation of the Crown, would resolve any problems that arose from the settlement in a way to maintain the good order and the treaty terms.

Many obligations are interrelated with sharing the land. The Victorian treaties provided for tracts of land reserved for family farms and to be set apart and protected for the Aboriginal parties. In the Robinson treaties, the reserve lands were retained or reserved from the general surrender of Aboriginal tenure. In the later Victorian treaties, the texts were drafted to indicate that all Aboriginal tenure was "surrendered" to the Crown, and from those tracts the Crown was obliged to set apart "Crown land" for reserves on a population-based formula.

Other aspects of the treaty negotiations were also significant in the context of the jurisdiction of the chiefs in the ceded territories. The Crown promised cash payments upon signing and annually at treaty renewal ceremonies, and agreed to provide agricultural and economic assistance, schools, and teachers, and other goods and benefits depending on the particular negotiations. Ammunition and gunpowder (for hunting), twine (for fishing nets), agricultural implements (ploughs), and livestock (horses and

---

53   RCAP, *Final Report*, note 35, vol. 1 at 175.

54   *Ibid.* at 174.

cattle) were promised, if the Aboriginal delegates wished to take up agriculture as a way of life, although they were not so compelled. *Treaty No. 6* included the explicit promises of assistance in the event of famine and health care in the form of a "medicine chest."[55] Gifts of medals and suits of clothes recognized the authority of the chiefs and headmen. These obligations, in British law, created a restraint of anticipation on the Crown interest in the ceded treaty country; the Crown and its administrative agents were required to perform obligations to the treaty beneficiaries to maintain their future interest.

The Royal Commission on Aboriginal Peoples affirmed that Aboriginal negotiators were assured orally that their way of life would not change unless they wished it to:

> They understood that their governing structures and authorities would continue undisturbed by the treaty relationship. They also assumed, and were assured, that the Crown would respect and honour the treaty agreements in perpetuity and that they would not suffer—but only benefit—from making treaties with the Crown. They were not asked, and they did not agree, to adopt non-Aboriginal ways and laws for themselves. They believed and were assured that their freedom and independence would not be interfered with because of the treaty. They expected to meet periodically with their treaty partner to make the necessary adjustments and accommodations to maintain the treaty relationship.[56]

These treaties of cession were not purchases of Aboriginal tenures by the imperial Crown. If a full sale and purchase of the Aboriginal tenures were intended by the Crown in the Victorian treaties, it is hard to conceive of a more convoluted and sibylline way of stating it.[57] The legal context for the selected words evidence a transfer of Aboriginal tenure to the protection of the Crown consistent with the idea of shared territorial jurisdiction.[58] The transfer is similar to placing the land in an imperial escrow account. International law or a law common to both parties, not British land law alone, established the source and nature of the rights, titles, and privileges to the land transferred to the Crown by these treaties.[59]

In international law and legal history, few nations have freely and voluntarily sold the territories in which they lived to others. Most have placed them under an

---

55   *Treaty No. 6, supra* note 48.

56   RCAP, *Final Report, supra* note 35, vol. 1 at 174.

57   In contrast to the text of the treaties, the *Royal Proclamation of 1763* clearly and plainly commanded that: "if at any Time any of the Said Indians should be inclined to dispose of the said Lands, the same shall be Purchased only for Us, in our Name, at some public Meeting or Assembly of the said Indians."

58   See *Re Paulette and Registrar of Titles (No. 2)* (1973), 42 D.L.R. (3d) 8 (N.W.T. S.C.), reversed (1975), 63 D.L.R. (3d) 1 (N.W.T. C.A.), affirmed (1976), 72 D.L.R. (3d) 161 (S.C.C.).

59   See J.H. Smith, *Appeals to the Privy Council from the American Plantations* (New York: Octagon Books, 1965) at 422-42. See William Blackstone, *Commentaries on the Laws of England*, vol. 1 (New York: Oceana Publications, 1967) at 106: "Plantation or colonies, in distant countries ... that have been gained by conquest or ceded to us by treaties ... are founded upon the law of nature, or at least upon that of nations."

alliance, jurisdiction, or protection of another nation.[60] The Aboriginal nations' relationships with the land have always defined their identity, their spiritual ecology, and their reality. The sale of the land, the sale of the rights of future generations, is beyond the linguistic comprehension of most Aboriginal languages.[61]

These conditions in the treaties lend support to an argument for a continuing Aboriginal tenure over the land and against its sale and purchase. Together these terms manifest a distinction between title and jurisdiction in the ceded land that is incompatible with a purchase. At the time of the Victorian treaties, British jurisprudence distinguished acquisition of territory from acquisition of property:

> The first conception pertains to the dominion of public law, the second to that of private law. Territory is the subject matter of the right of sovereignty or *imperium* while property is the subject matter of the right of ownership or *dominium*. These two rights may or may not co-exist in the Crown in respect of the same area. Land may be held by the Crown as territory but not as property, or as property but not as territory, or in both rights at the same time. As property, though not as territory, land may be held by one state within the dominion of another.[62]

The division of authority in the treaties between government and title reinforces the purpose of cession as a protective, not proprietary, nature. The chiefs and headmen did not transfer all the interests in the land.

From an Aboriginal perspective, the treaties of cession between the Aboriginal nations and the Crown were not substantially different from the Crown's creation of derivative estates out of its original tenure in England. In British law, the King reserved some of the land for his estates while allowing others to use the land in exchange for services and taxes.[63] In the Georgian and Victorian treaties, the Aboriginal nations reserved land for themselves and their guests, and they delegated other lands to the Crown to generate taxes and revenues to finance the Crown's treaty obligations.

---

60 M.F. Lindley, *The Acquisition and Government of Backward Territory in International Law, Being a Treatise on the Law and Practice Relating to Colonial Expansion* (New York: Negro University Press, 1969).

61 See generally Henderson, "Interpreting," *supra* note 45.

62 See J.W. Salmond, *Jurisprudence*, 10th ed. by G. Williams (London: Sweet & Maxwell, 1947) at 520; see also British courts in *Attorney-General v. Nissan*, [1970] A.C. 179 at 210-11 (H.L.). Territory acquisition in international law would not necessarily involve acquisition in the domestic law; see *Lord Advocate v. Balfour*, [1907] S.C. 1360 at 1368. The Court in *Smith v. Trustees of the Port and Harbour of Lerwick*, [1903] 5 S.C. (5th) 680 at 691 noted that a legal distinction exists between sovereignty, title to territory, and land tenure. International law and domestic law are independent domains, and the fictions or operations of domestic law cannot affect the validity or meaning of international obligations. See *Elettronica Sicula S.p.A. (ELSI), (United States of America v. Italy)*, [1989] I.C.J. Rep. 15 at 50-51.

63 B. Ziff, *Principles of Property Law* (Toronto: Carswell, 1993) at 36-43.

29. Constitutional Democratic Reforms

In the Commonwealth, the premise of most post-colonial legal thinking is that legal institutions can assume different forms to reflect their multicultural or pluralistic realities. The existing governing structures in Canada can and should be subject to similar changes to realize possibilities in Aboriginal legal thought. The reinterpretation of the political architecture of the constitution, and a new reconciliation with the Crown's delegated spheres of jurisdiction mean working out the effect of vesting the Crown's unextinguished authority directly in the Aboriginal peoples of Canada.[64]

Such a reinterpretation is consistent with constitutional supremacy. The entire vision of Canada transcends the written text of the constitution;[65] the 1867 text outlines the shared authority of the colonizers' quest for representative government, while the 1982 text ends their arbitrary rule over Aboriginal peoples. The Supreme Court of Canada has confirmed that the principle of federalism is a political and legal response to the underlying cultural and social diversity or "political realities" of Canada:[66] facilitating democratic participation of the people by distributing governmental power while respecting this diversity,[67] and furthering collective goals by distinct cultural and linguistic minorities.[68]

Aboriginal peoples of Canada are distinct from the colonial *Indian Act* regime and its Indian bands. Aboriginal peoples are the constitutional rightholders of Aboriginal order, its tenure, law and rights, and the treaty order. Section 35(2) categorized the Aboriginal peoples as including "the Indian, Inuit and Métis peoples of Canada."[69] Under the constitution, neither federal legislation nor regulation can be read to define these categories or their rights; Aboriginal laws and the treaties define the rightholders. Aboriginal knowledge, heritage, language, and law in turn define how Aboriginal peoples will achieve self-determination and coexist within constitutional democracy.[70]

The Court has stated that the principle of democracy has always "informed" the design of our constitutional structure, and continues to act as an essential interpretative consideration, but the underlying constitutional principles are nowhere explicitly described in our constitutional texts:[71]

---

64   Russell, *supra* note 8 at 247.

65   *Quebec Secession Reference, supra* note 2 at para. 55.

66   *Ibid.* at paras. 57-58.

67   *Ibid.* at para. 58, citing *Re the Initiative and Referendum Act,* [1919] A.C. 935 at 942 (P.C.).

68   *Quebec Secession Reference, ibid.* at para. 59.

69   *Constitution Act, 1982,* being Schedule B to the *Canada Act 1982,* (U.K.), 1982, c. 11.

70   Henderson, "Empowering," *supra* note 35 at 311-29.

71   *OPSEU v. Ontario (Attorney-General),* [1987] 2 S.C.R. 2 at 57, 41 D.L.R. (4th) 1 (S.C.C.); *Switzman v. Elbling,* [1957] S.C.R. 285 (S.C.C.); *Saumur v. City of Quebec,* [1953] 2 S.C.R. 299 (S.C.C.); *Boucher v. The King* (1950), [1951] S.C.R. 265 (S.C.C.); *Reference re Alberta Statutes,* [1938] S.C.R. 100 (S.C.C.), affirmed, [1938] 4 D.L.R. 433 (P.C.).

> ...the democracy principle can best be understood as a sort of baseline against which the framers of our Constitution, and subsequently, our elected representatives under it, have always operated. It is perhaps for this reason that the principle was not explicitly identified in the text of the *Constitution Act, 1867* itself. To have done so might have appeared redundant, even silly, to the framers.[72]

Such an explanation does not describe the "exclusive" legacy of representative government,[73] its uneven steps of "evolutionary democracy" toward universal suffrage and more effective representation,[74] or the uneven idea of majority rule in British law and the colonial law. Nor does it explain how the constitution contemplates that Canada shall become a constitutional democracy.[75]

Since 1867, efforts to extend the electoral franchise to those unjustly excluded from participation in our political system—such as women, minorities, and Aboriginal peoples—have continued, with some success, to the present day. Yet constitutional democracy has not yet been achieved, as Aboriginal peoples of Canada are still excluded from representing their constitutional rights under section 35(1) in legislative assemblies. Canadian governments view Aboriginal organizations as a special interest group or lobby.

The Aboriginal peoples and their constitutional rights are as integral to the new concept of constitutional democracy as were the older ideas of representative and responsible governments. Their constitutional rights are exempt from any derogation or abrogation of the constitutional rights of the citizens and permanent residents under section 3 of the *Charter*, which provides the right of citizens to participate in the political process as voters, and section 4, which obliges the House of Commons and the provincial legislatures to hold regular elections and to permit citizens to elect representatives to their political institutions. The Lamer Court announced that the sovereign will of the people and the democratic principle must be taken in the context of the constitutional provisions:

> The relationship between democracy and federalism means, for example, that in Canada there may be different and equally legitimate majorities in different provinces and territories and at the federal level. No one majority is more or less "legitimate" than the others as an expression of democratic opinion, although, of course, the consequences will vary with the subject matter. A federal system of government enables different provinces to pursue policies responsive to the particular concerns and interests of people in that province. At the same time, Canada as a whole is also a democratic community in which citizens construct and achieve goals on a national scale through federal government acting within the limits of its jurisdiction. The function of federalism is to enable citizens to

---

72   *Quebec Secession Reference, supra* note 2 at para. 62.

73   The Canadian philosopher, Charles Taylor, has used this term.

74   *Reference re Provincial Electoral Boundaries (Sask.),* [1991] 2 S.C.R. 158 at 186 (S.C.C.) [hereinafter *Provincial Electoral Boundaries*].

75   *Ibid.* at para. 100.

participate concurrently in different collectivities and to pursue goals at both a provincial and a federal level.[76]

In the past, the legacy of colonialism has prevented Aboriginal peoples' participation as an "equally legitimate majority" in either federal or provincial assemblies. Currently, federal and provincial law and policies deny them the right to represent and speak for their constitutional rights in federal and provincial assemblies. Only the Inuit peoples in the Arctic territories are exceptions.

In discussing the *Constitution Act, 1982*, the Court concluded that a functioning democracy in Canada depends on discussion, since no one has a monopoly on truth, and the Canadian political system is predicated on the faith that in the marketplace of ideas, the best solutions to public problems will rise to the top.[77] Canadian constitutional democracy is committed to empowering cultural diversity and ending the colonial monopoly in the market place of ideas and in the formation of laws by which all must live. This commitment imposes a corresponding "inherent" duty on all participants to engage in discussions in order to address democratic expressions of a desire for change. The constitutional voice of the Aboriginal peoples cannot be excluded in such discussions.

Constitutional democracy is a prerequisite to the substantive goal of self-government that can accommodate cultural and group identities.[78] In the *Quebec Secession Reference*, the Lamer Court announced, "a sovereign people exercises its right to self-government through the democratic process."[79] It is the law that creates the framework within which the "sovereign will" is to be ascertained and implemented. Legitimate democratic institutions rest, ultimately, on this legal foundation: democratic law allows for the participation of, and accountability to, the people through public institutions created under the constitution. Although part of the constitution, Aboriginal peoples are still excluded from the political institutions; their constitutional and political legitimacy is undermined in the process.

In the *Quebec Secession Reference*, the Lamer Court affirmed that Canada as a whole is a democratic community in which citizens construct and achieve goals on a national scale through a federal government acting within the limits of its jurisdiction.[80] In its view, Canadian government cannot survive through adherence to the law alone; governments must be capable of reflecting the aspirations of the people.[81] "Legitimacy" requires an interaction between the rule of law and democratic principles as well as moral values, many of which are embedded in our constitutional structure. The Lamer Court stressed that to equate legitimacy with the "sovereign will" or major-

---

76   *Quebec Secession Reference, supra* note 2 at para. 66.

77   *Ibid.* at para. 68.

78   *Provincial Electoral Boundaries, supra* note 74 at 188.

79   *Quebec Secession Reference, supra* note 2 at para. 64.

80   *Ibid.* at para. 66.

81   *Ibid.* at para. 67.

ity rule alone would be a grave mistake, as it would the exclude other constitutional principles or values:[82]

> The Court must be guided by the values and principles essential to a free and democratic society which I believe embody, to name but a few, respect for the inherent dignity of the human person, commitment to social justice and equality, accommodation of a wide variety of beliefs, respect for cultural and group identity, and faith in social and political institutions which enhance the participation of individuals and groups in society.[83]

The constitution may not legitimately be circumvented by resort to a majority vote in a referendum or unilateral action.[84] The constitution can be amended, but only through a constitutional process of negotiation, which ensures that there is an opportunity for the constitutionally defined rights of all the parties to be respected and reconciled. The Lamer Court held this duty is "inherent" in the democratic principle that is a fundamental predicate of our system of governance.

Constitutional entrenchment of Aboriginal and treaty rights was intended to ensure that elected representatives, the administrative agencies, and the courts gave due regard and protection to the rights of Aboriginal peoples. It provided a safeguard for their distinct human rights and individual freedoms called "Aboriginal rights" that in the past have been susceptible to arbitrary government interference, and ensured their vulnerable heritages were endowed with constitutional protection necessary to maintain and promote their legal order against the assimilative pressures of the immigrant majority.[85]

Canadian democracy will not be complete until the Aboriginal peoples are represented in Canadian institutions in accord with their constitutional rights. Both the Supreme Court and the First Ministers of Canada have affirmed this principle. The Court has affirmed the constitutional rights of Aboriginal peoples, and they have established special rules of constitutional interpretation of these *sui generis* rights to empower Aboriginal understandings and perspectives.

In the consensus report on the constitution in 1992, the Charlottetown Accord, the First Ministers of Canada interpreted the constitutional agenda raised by section 35(1). Along with representatives of the Aboriginal peoples, the First Ministers declared that section 35(1) establishes Aboriginal peoples as one of the three orders of government in Canada,[86] as well as their inherent right to govern their peoples.[87] The Accord also asserted that section 35(1) requires Aboriginal representation in the Senate[88] and the

---

82   *Ibid.* at para. 67.

83   *R. v. Oakes*, [1986] 1 S.C.R. 103 at 136 (S.C.C.).

84   *Quebec Secession Reference*, *supra* note 2 at para. 75.

85   *Ibid.* at para. 74.

86   K. McRoberts and P. Monahan, eds., *The Charlottetown Accord, the Referendum, and the Future of Canada* (Toronto: University of Toronto Press, 1993) at s. 1(b) (Canada Clause).

87   *Ibid.* at 301, s. 41. See especially M.E. Turpel-Lafond, "The Charlottetown Discord and Aboriginal Peoples' Struggle for Fundamental Political Change" at 177.

88   McRoberts & Monahan, *ibid.* at 290, s. 9.

House of Commons,[89] and a role in the Supreme Court of Canada.[90] The Accord establishes that such Aboriginal participation in constitutional democracy under section 35(1) would not affect the rights of the Aboriginal peoples or their jurisdiction and their government powers or the constitutional division of powers.[91] The First Ministers agreed that constitutional processes are needed to clarify and implement treaty rights.[92] Finally, the Accord reasserts that Aboriginal consent is required in future constitutional amendments that directly refer to Aboriginal peoples.[93]

The consensus report interpreted the meaning of section 35 and the necessary reform to create a constitutional democracy in Canada. These provisions fill out section 35, and exist as constitutional principles or conventions. In the *Quebec Secession Reference*, the Lamer Court noted that while a written constitution provides a foundation for exercising constitutional judicial review, unwritten constitutional principles and conventions invite the courts "to turn those principles into the premises of a constitutional argument that culminates in the filling of gaps in the express terms of the constitutional text."[94] The Court noted "[t]hese supporting principles and rules, which include constitutional conventions and the workings of Parliament, are a necessary part of our Constitution because problems or situations may arise which are not expressly dealt with by the text of the Constitution":[95]

> Underlying constitutional principles may in certain circumstances give rise to substantive legal obligations (have "full legal force", as we described it in the *Patriation Reference, supra*, at p. 845), which constitute substantive limitations upon government action. These principles may give rise to very abstract and general obligations, or they may be more specific and precise in nature. The principles are not merely descriptive, but are also invested with a powerful normative force, and are binding upon both courts and governments. "In other words", as this Court confirmed in the *Manitoba Language Rights Reference, supra*, at p. 752, "in the process of Constitutional adjudication, the Court may have regard to unwritten postulates which form the very foundation of the Constitution of Canada."[96]

In a reconciliation for the millennium, the organization of the Crown, government, courts, and economy require two reforms under section 35. First, Aboriginal peoples must exercise their inherent right to govern their peoples in their lands reserved to

---

89   *Ibid.* at 294, s. 22.

90   *Ibid.* at 293, s. 20.

91   *Ibid.* at 300, s. 40 (the general non-derogation clause). Another issue not resolved but discussed was Aboriginal participation in intergovernmental agreements respecting the division of power, *ibid.* at 308.

92   *Ibid.* at 304, s. 48.

93   *Ibid.* at 308, s. 60. See s. 35(1) of *Constitution Act, 1982, supra* note 69.

94   *Quebec Secession Reference, supra* note 2 at para. 53. See *Reference re Remuneration of Judges of the Provincial Court of Prince Edward Island,* [1997] 3 S.C.R. 3 at para. 104 (S.C.C.), additional reasons at, [1998] 1 S.C.R. 3 (S.C.C.).

95   *Quebec Secession Reference, supra* note 2 at para. 32. "The law of the Constitution ... and other constitutional rules, such as the conventions of the constitution, which carry only political sanctions," define the constitutional scheme, *ibid.* at para. 98.

96   *Ibid.* at para. 54.

them and interpret their laws. Second, these Aboriginal peoples should be represented within the federal Parliament and provincial assemblies based on their constitutional rights, not on their race. Both of these reforms are consistent with the wording of section 35 and the constitutional conventions that seek to create a post-colonial Canada. Each is based on the constitutional right to have an equal legitimate relationship within Canada. These reforms can be achieved by ordinary legislation, and do not require any constitutional amendment. Such reforms would begin to end the legacy of the collective disadvantage of Aboriginal peoples.

These reforms will implement the constitutional order on a basis of equality and mutual respect, and free Aboriginal peoples from the tyranny of colonial hierarchies and social divisions. In all the legislative assembly and administrative systems, Aboriginal peoples must have the capacity as delegates or as members to articulate their traditional concepts of governance and law and to assert their perspectives on their constitutional rights. So empowered, they could prevent negative legislation from compromising or intervening in their rights and open a path for reconciliations that would, in turn, provide a path to healing.[97]

The Supreme Court of Canada has established special rules of constitutional interpretation of these *sui generis* rights to empower Aboriginal understandings and perspectives, but the legislative bodies have not. The Court has suggested the best method to resolve these conflicts is by treaty or political negotiation. A proper conception of the relations of constitutional law to politics requires more than negotiation; it requires institutional changes that reflect the constitutional order. The most sustainable and democratic expression of political negotiation is to include Aboriginal peoples within the political institutions, where the direct practical and passionate issues can be discussed and reconciled.

Participation of Aboriginal peoples with representatives of the Canadian people in the federal parliament and the provincial and legislative assemblies is the best way to reconcile the constitutional and legislative differences. Such legislative reconciliation will require Aboriginal guidance. Such transformed institutions of an empowered democracy will relieve the judiciary of its exemplary difficulty in reconciling Aboriginal and treaty rights with the common law perspectives and legislative powers on a case-by-case method. Such reforms would make political institutions, rather than courts, the primary forum for reconciling any past or future legislative interferences with the constitutional rights of Aboriginal peoples.

Out of these institutional reforms can come an inclusive constitutional democracy and relationship necessary for a fair and just constitutional reconciliation. These reforms can respond to the constitutional commitment to correct past disadvantages, prohibit the government from reinforcing the colonial hierarchies and divisions that generated inequality, and allow Aboriginal peoples to escape their past confinement. The Royal Commission on Aboriginal Peoples has demonstrated the economic disparities, the cost of the status quo, and the need for institutional and constitutional

---

97   O. Mercredi and M.E. Turpel, *In the Rapids: Navigating the Future of the First Nations* (Toronto: Viking, 1993).

reforms.[98] These reforms can make Canadian democracy a culture of tolerance, empathy, and legitimate respect for its diversity, rather than an imposed political system to determine laws and policies. Such a new beginning can create a constitutional democracy in Canada for the millennium. It is a relationship that will end the constitutional solitudes and allow Aboriginal peoples and Canadians to build a shared future—the only realm they have a chance to share.

---

98   RCAP, *Final Report, supra* note 35, vol. 4 at 23-83, 117-40.

INDEX